The Patent–Competition Interface in Developing Countries

The Patent–Competition Interface in Developing Countries

THOMAS K. CHENG

OXFORD
UNIVERSITY PRESS

OXFORD
UNIVERSITY PRESS

Great Clarendon Street, Oxford, OX2 6DP,
United Kingdom

Oxford University Press is a department of the University of Oxford.
It furthers the University's objective of excellence in research, scholarship,
and education by publishing worldwide. Oxford is a registered trade mark of
Oxford University Press in the UK and in certain other countries

First Edition published in 2021

Impression: 1

Published in the United States of America by Oxford University Press
198 Madison Avenue, New York, NY 10016, United States of America

British Library Cataloguing in Publication Data

Data available

Library of Congress Control Number: 2021942610

ISBN 978–0–19–285735–4

DOI: 10.1093/oso/9780192857354.001.0001

Printed and bound by
CPI Group (UK) Ltd, Croydon, CR0 4YY

Contents

Table of Cases

CHINA

EUROPEAN UNION

1. Court of Justice

2. Courts of First Instance/General Court

3. European Commission

INDIA

1. Competition Commission of India

ITALY

1. Italian Competition Authority

SOUTH AFRICA

1. Competition Appeal Court

2. Competition Tribunal

UNITED KINGDOM

1. Court of Appeal

2. High Court (Chancery Division)

3. Competition Appeal Tribunal

4. Competition and Markets Authority

UNITED STATES

1. Supreme Court

2. Courts of Appeals

3. District Courts

OTHERS

1. World Trade Organization

Table of Legislation

Table of Other Legal Instruments

Abbreviations

AIFA	Agenzia Italiana del Farmaco (Italian Medicines Agency)
AML	Anti-Monopoly Law (PRC)
API	Active Pharmaceutical Ingredient
API	Application Programme Interface
ARV	Anti-Retroviral
BI	Boehringer Ingelheim
BRICS	Brazil, Russia, India, China, and South Africa
CAC	Competition Appeal Court (South Africa)
CAT	Competition Appeal Tribunal (UK)
CCI	Competition Commission of India
CD	Currency Derivatives
CJEU	Court of Justice of the European Union
CMA	Competition & Markets Authority (UK)
DG	Director General (of CCI)
DSB	Dispute Settlement Body (of the World Trade Organization)
EPO	European Patent Office
EU	European Union
FDI	Foreign Direct Investment
FRAND	Fair, Reasonable And Non-Discriminatory (royalty)
FTC	Federal Trade Commission (US)
GII	Global Innovation Index
GSK	GlaxoSmithKline
ICA	Italian Competition Authority
IP	Intellectual Property
ISOs	Independent Service Organizations
LDCs	Least Developed Countries
LEC	Local Exchange Carrier
NDRC	National Development and Reform Commission (PRC)
NHS	National Health Service (UK)
NPV	Net Present Value
OECD	Organization of Economic Cooperation and Development
OEM	Original Equipment Manufacturer
OES	Original Equipment Supplier
OFT	Office of Fair Trading (UK)
OSS	Operations Support Systems
PHOSITA	Person Having Ordinary Skill In The Art
PRC	People's Republic of China
R&D	Research and Development
RTA	Regional Trade Agreement

SAMR	State Administration of Market Regulation (PRC)
SEP	Standard-Essential Patent
TAC	Treatment Action Campaign (South Africa)
TFEU	Treaty on the Functioning of the European Union
TPDC	Technology Proficient Developing Countries
TRIPS	Agreement on Trade-Related Aspects of Intellectual Property Rights
TTBER	Technology Transfer Block Exemption Regulation (EU)
UNEs	Unbundled Network Elements
UNESCO	United Nations Educational, Scientific and Cultural Organization
UNIDO	United Nations Industrial Development Organization
USPTO	United States Patent and Trademark Office
WIPO	World Intellectual Property Organization
WTO	World Trade Organization

1
Introduction

The notion of the patent–competition interface in developing countries may be oxymoronic to some. Patents protect innovation and most developing countries do not generate much innovation, at least not in the global sense. If developing countries do not generate much patentable innovation, the conflict between patent policy and competition policy that underlies the patent–competition interface will be a matter of low priority for them. While patents may not play a prominent role in most developing countries, this does not mean that developing countries can ignore dynamic efficiency. Growth economists have consistently demonstrated that productivity growth and innovation are the key drivers of economic growth. For developing countries desperate to improve the livelihood of millions of the poor people in their population, there is nothing more important than attaining year after year of consistent economic growth. Growth alone, however, is not a panacea for developing countries. An increase in national income that is concentrated among the rich or that fails to address the developmental needs of these countries such as access to adequate nutrition, healthcare, education, or sanitation would be meaningless to the majority of the population. Broad-based development is imperative. Economic development and a general improvement in the livelihood of the people, however, is premised on growth. The size of the pie needs to grow before it can be spread more evenly among members of the society. For that, we need productivity growth and innovation.

Innovation, however, needs to be understood differently in the context of developing countries. While many industrialized economies are able consistently to produce genuine innovation along the global technological frontier, which can be called frontier innovation, most developing countries rely on technology transfer from the industrialized economies for technological upgrade and productivity growth. Innovation that takes place in developing countries is unlikely to be global in nature but is more likely to be innovation in the local or domestic sense. Such developing country innovation can be called laggard innovation.

Developing countries can innovate and achieve technological upgrade in a number of ways. First, it can acquire technology from foreign technology owners who transfer their technology voluntarily. Voluntary technology transfer may involve export of technological goods to the country, foreign direct investment (FDI) to set up a local subsidiary or joint venture, or technology licensing to a local licensee. Foreign technology transfer is a principal avenue for technological upgrade for developing countries. Under FDI and licensing, the local subsidiary or licensee

The Patent–Competition Interface in Developing Countries. Thomas K. Cheng, Oxford University Press. © Thomas K. Cheng 2021. DOI: 10.1093/oso/9780192857354.003.0001

will need to adapt the technology locally. When a foreign technology is brought into a country, local firms or engineers need to learn to implement it and adapt it to the local environment. Such adaptation necessitates the acquisition of tacit knowledge. In addition to explicitly codified knowledge in the form of blueprint, implementation of a new technology also requires tacit knowledge, which is implicit, uncodified know-how that is necessary for the deployment of a new technology. The operation of a new machine cannot always be reduced to a blueprint or instruction manual. Tacit knowledge is often difficult to transfer and needs to be generated domestically through research and development (R&D). Therefore, acquisition of tacit knowledge is a necessary step in foreign technology transfer and counts as an important form of innovation in developing countries.

Second, local firms can imitate or reverse engineer foreign technology to the extent permissible under existing intellectual property law. Economists have shown that imitation often requires a substantial amount of time and R&D and is not simple and instantaneous replication of a technology that it is often imagined to be. In fact, imitation sometimes can take even longer than coming up with the original innovation. Imitation, especially of advanced technology, requires significant technological capacity and access to the technology. For a technology incorporated in a physical product, imitation or reverse engineering would require importation of the technological good. Therefore, trade of technological goods can constitute an implicit or involuntary kind of technology transfer. The kind of R&D necessary to replicate or reverse engineer the technology would constitute another kind of laggard innovation.

Lastly, if developing countries were to come up with frontier innovation, it would be much more likely to be of the process kind rather than the product kind. Process innovation is much more likely to be discovered during the production or manufacturing process, in which many more developing countries are engaged instead of genuine R&D. Product innovation requires more dedicated R&D. Process innovation will be the third main kind of laggard innovation. As will be discussed in Chapter 2, few developing countries possess genuine innovation capacity to produce frontier innovation. For most developing countries, the main forms of innovation are the acquisition of tacit knowledge in the process of technology transfer and imitation.

In the industrialized economies, the patent–competition interface requires a balance between the competition policy of safeguarding consumer welfare and the patent policy of incentivizing innovation. Competition policy strives for lower prices and higher quality for consumers by prohibiting anticompetitive concerted practices, abuses of market power, and market power-enhancing mergers. Patent policy in the industrialized countries is about the incentives to generate frontier innovation. The patent system aims to spur R&D activities and innovation by providing a financial reward to innovators. This reward is created by giving the patentee a period of exclusivity during which she has the right to exclude others from implementing and commercializing the patented technology. Patent exclusivity does not necessarily create monopoly power or even market power. But in order for the patentee to recoup her R&D costs, the exclusivity must at least allow her to charge supra-competitive prices for her patented product. Therein ostensibly lies the conflict between patent policy and competition policy. This conflict is in fact more nuanced as competition law is also concerned with dynamic efficiency. Consumer welfare is enhanced by the emergence of innovation and new products. Competition policy in thus also concerned with innovation.

Given that what drives technological upgrade in developing countries are foreign technology transfer and laggard, not frontier, innovation, the policy trade-off underlying the patent–competition interface takes on a different character. There are two reasons for this. First, while consumers in industrialized economies may be better positioned to bear higher prices in the name of spurring innovation, consumers in developing countries, many of whom are mired in abject poverty, can ill-afford supra-competitive prices. This means that while industrialized economies enjoy greater leeway for patent policy and can err on the side of favouring innovation when approaching the patent–competition interface, developing countries need to be much more vigilant about protecting consumer welfare and ensuring that the sacrifice of consumer welfare is strictly necessary to secure additional innovation.

As it turns out, there are reasons to question whether patent protection is strictly necessary to generate innovation, including the tendency of the patent system to overcompensate innovators and the availability of other appropriation mechanisms for innovators to monetize their innovation. The importance of patent protection in spurring innovation has been overstated in many instances and developing countries may attach less weight to patent policy in calibrating their approach to the patent–competition interface. If patent protection turns out to play a smaller role in incentivizing innovation, developing countries will have greater room to emphasize competition policy in the patent–competition interface.

Second, the disparate nature of innovation in developing countries means that the dynamic efficiency aspect of the patent–competition interface is no longer chiefly about encouraging patentable innovation. The kind of innovation implicated by patent policy is patentable frontier innovation which most developing countries, with the exception of a few, are not in a position to produce. If an innovation is not patentable, by definition it does not concern patent policy. The impact of patent–competition rules on the incentives to generate patentable innovation is no longer critical. Dynamic efficiency considerations are no longer about innovation incentives. Dynamic efficiency means technological acquisition and adaptation and the focus is on the incentives of foreign technology owners to transfer technology. What developing countries need to be concerned with is how their competition law rules will affect the incentives of foreign technology owners to transfer technology, which is the main driver of technological upgrade, and the opportunities for involuntary technology transfer in the form of imitation and reverse engineering. Without foreign technology transfer, acquisition of tacit knowledge would not matter. Tacit knowledge alone would not improve the country's technological capacity. Separately, certain patent–competition rules, such as those on the unilateral refusal to license, can greatly affect opportunities for imitation and reverse engineering. Patent policy will also continue to play a role in those developing countries that are capable of producing frontier innovation, more likely to be of the process kind.

The patent–competition interface hence takes on much deeper and more multifaceted complexity in developing countries. It is no longer a simple trade-off between innovation incentives and short-term consumer welfare. Patent–competition rules need to be crafted taking due account of their impact on foreign technology transfer and technological upgrade in developing countries. It is important, however, not to treat developing countries as a monolith. Developing countries differ widely in terms of technological capacity. And their approach to the patent–competition interface will need to be tailored to their technological capacity. What is called for is a development stage-specific approach. There are those countries that are limited to no more than simple production or perhaps rudimentary technology adaptation. For these countries, which will be referred to as production countries, patent policy carries little weight. These countries are only capable of production and implementation of basic technology. They are so far behind the global technological frontier or removed from adaptation of cutting-edge technology that the policy balance can be heavily tilted toward the competition policy of protecting consumer welfare.

Other developing countries possess the capacity to adapt foreign technologies but not necessarily to produce genuine innovation in the global sense. For these countries, which will be known as technology adaptation countries, patent–competition rules need to be mindful of their impact on the incentives to transfer technology, especially through FDI and licensing. These countries are in a position to adapt and implement sophisticated imported technology or perhaps to imitate or reverse engineer such technology. Dynamic efficiency in these countries is not about incentives of domestic firms to innovate, but about incentives of foreign technology owners to transfer technology. To the extent that certain patent–competition rules have particular salience for such incentives, they will need to be approached with care. For example, to simplify slightly, a more permissive approach to patent exploitation practices that enhances the robustness of patent protection tends to increase technology transfer and steer modes of transfer toward FDI and licensing, which tends to redound greater technological benefits for developing countries.

Lastly, there are a handful of developing countries that are capable of generating frontier innovation. For these countries, which will be called proto-innovation countries, the patent–competition rules cannot overlook the interests of innovators. Innovation incentives matter in these countries, at least in industries that possess the requisite capacity to innovate. Technological capacity is likely to vary by industry. These countries may need to tailor their patent–competition rules for different industries. To the extent that there are both imitators and innovators in the same industry, as is likely to be the case, patent–competition rules require a delicate balance of the competing interests of these constituents.

The importance of innovation to economic growth means that the patent–competition interface is arguably the most important facet of competition law in developing countries. It is, however, probably the area of competition law in the developing country context that has received the least scholarly attention. This book looks to fill this gap in the literature by proposing a development stage-specific approach to the patent–competition interface that takes into account the technological capacity of individual developing countries. The approach acknowledges that technological upgrade is critical to the attainment of stable economic growth for developing countries. These countries hence need to pursue opportunities for technological upgrade through technology transfer and laggard innovation while keeping consumer welfare loss in check. The prospects for such upgrade, however, vary in different developing countries and the patent–competition rules need to be attuned to those differing prospects.

The remainder of the book applies the proposed approach to the patent–competition interface to various patent exploitation practices, including unilateral refusal to deal and license, patent tying, excessive pricing of pharmaceuticals, reverse payment settlements, and various restrictive licensing practices. Unilateral refusal to license is important because the imposition of a duty to license is a direct affront to patent policy and has immediate implications for the robustness of patent protection, which was shown in economic studies to play a critical role in incentives to transfer technology. Patent tying is arguably the most prevalent kind of patent exploitation practice and is relevant for all developing countries regardless of their technological capacity. Excessive drug prices deserve our special attention because it has an outsized impact on the access to affordable drugs in developing countries. With access to basic healthcare being one of the fundamental development needs, developing country competition authorities must do their best to make sure that drugs are affordable. The inclusion of reverse payment settlements in a book about developing countries may surprise some in light of the complex policy arguments they raise. Despite their complexity, their potential impact on drug prices is too great for developing countries to ignore. Restrictive licensing practices serve as an illustration of the policy dilemma facing the technology adaptation countries when approaching the patent–competition interface. Licensing is only relevant to countries that are capable of receiving and making use of licensed technology, which means it is largely irrelevant to the production countries. Resolution of the policy dilemma will be demonstrated with the examples of no challenge clauses and package licensing.

There are eleven chapters in this book. Following this introductory chapter, Chapter 2 examines the extent to which developing countries should attach weight to innovation incentives under the patent–competition interface and concludes that little weight should be accorded for innovation incentive considerations. This chapter casts doubt on the importance of patent protection in attracting innovation. Chapter 3 surveys the different modes of technology transfer and assesses how they are related to and affected by competition regulation of patent exploitation practices. Chapter 4 integrates all the insights put forward in the previous two chapters and proposes a development stage-specific approach to the patent–competition interface for developing countries.

Chapter 5 delves into the various theoretical issues raised by competition regulation of unilateral refusal to license and compulsory licensing. In particular, it challenges the conventional wisdom that compulsory licensing undermines innovation incentives. Chapter 6 canvasses the case law in the United States and the European Union on unilateral refusal to license and discusses the doctrinal issues raised by these cases. It concludes by proposing a framework for analysing unilateral refusal to license in developing countries that takes into account their existing technological capacity and the need to preserve incentives for technology transfer. Chapter 7 shifts the attention to patent tying and proposes how developing countries should approach patent tying issues. It rejects the argument that patent tying is justified because it generates more innovation incentives and examines how developing countries should approach patent tying when it is used for the purpose of offensive leveraging, defensive leveraging, and price discrimination.

The next two chapters both focus on the pharmaceutical industry. Chapter 8 delves into the phenomenon of exorbitant drug prices in developing countries and surveys the different means afforded by the TRIPS Agreement (Agreement on Trade-Related Aspects of Intellectual Property Rights) to tackle the problem. It reaches the conclusion that none of the mechanisms provided by the TRIPS Agreement is satisfactory and competition law hence has a limited, but important, role to play in regulating excessive drug prices, especially in instances of a sudden and substantial price hike and of reverse price discrimination under which the same drug is more expensive, often much more so, in developing than in developed countries. Chapter 9 investigates issues surrounding the regulation of reverse payment settlements, which have been shown to inflate drug prices and proposes how developing countries should regulate them. Chapter 10 examines competition law regulation of no challenge clauses, post-expiration royalty, and package licensing as illustrations of how the technology adaptation countries should approach licensing practices keeping in mind its impact on technology transfer. Chapter 11 concludes the book.

2
Innovation Incentives in Developing Countries

A. Introduction

This monograph attempts to propose how developing countries should approach the patent–competition interface in light of their developmental considerations. Before one can do that, one must first gain an understanding of the various policy arguments underlying the interface in the developed country context and how these arguments may play out differently in developing countries, and even among different groups of developing countries. What this and the next chapter seek to do is to determine how developing countries may need to approach the patent–competition interface differently from developed countries in order to promote technological upgrade without unduly sacrificing consumer welfare. In fact, a differentiated approach may be called for even among developing countries in light of their varied technological capacities.

The weight that innovation incentives should carry in the patent–competition interface should vary according to the country's technological capacity. In a country devoid of innovation capacity, innovation incentives matter little and competition policy should be given greater emphasis. In such a country, technological progress is mostly achieved through technology transfer. Dynamic efficiency is no longer concerned about innovation incentives but about incentives to transfer technology. How the stringency of the patent–competition rules may influence the incentives of foreign technology owners to transfer technology becomes a matter of serious concern. Under the guidance of relevant economic literature, this and the next chapter will explore the relationship between the patent–competition rules on the one hand and innovation incentives and the incentives to transfer technology respectively on the other hand, and propose a development stage-specific approach to the patent–competition interface.

B. The Patent–Competition Interface: An Overview

The interface with intellectual property is one of the most complex areas within competition law. One reason for the complexity is that it juxtaposes two areas of law which share potentially conflicting objectives and incongruent views on how

The Patent–Competition Interface in Developing Countries. Thomas K. Cheng, Oxford University Press. © Thomas K. Cheng 2021. DOI: 10.1093/oso/9780192857354.003.0002

to achieve those objectives. Of the three main branches of intellectual property, patent law, which aims to encourage innovation and dissemination of technical knowledge and scientific advances through the grant of exclusivity, potentially shares the most acute conflict with competition law. The patent system is premised on the bargain that in exchange for the creation and disclosure of a genuinely novel and useful innovation, the owner of the technology will be awarded a period of exclusivity, during which she will be the only one permitted to practise and exploit the technology. Although this exclusivity does not always translate into substantial market power, it is intended to give the patent owner a modicum of market power to raise prices above marginal costs. Supra-competitive pricing is the very essence of the patent system. Without this ability to charge prices above marginal costs, the patent owner would fail to recoup her investments. Recoupment of research and development (R&D) investments, which is the fundamental objective of the patent system, requires the ability to charge supra-competitive prices. The strength of this market power varies. When coupled with the right market conditions, a patent can confer substantial market power upon the patent owner. This will be the case when there are no reasonable substitutes for the patented product. For example, when a drug is the only known way to treat a disease or condition and the active pharmaceutical ingredient is subject to patent protection, the patented drug will enjoy substantial market power.

It used to be assumed that the patent system conferred a monopoly upon the patent owner.[1] That view has been abandoned and it is now widely recognized that a patent only grants exclusivity, which may or may not morph into substantial market power. Patents are now understood to confer a legal but not an economic monopoly. Nonetheless, it remains true that the operation of the patent system is premised on supra-competitive pricing, which must be paid by consumers. By preventing rivals from replicating and exploiting the patented technology, the patent system pre-empts competition, at least through reverse engineering or outright copying. Competition is of course the very process that competition law aims to protect. Competition law safeguards the competitive process and protects consumer welfare by prohibiting anticompetitive practices and mergers. Consumer welfare is advanced when the quality-adjusted prices of goods fall. In a nutshell, competition law favours more intense competition and lower prices.

While the two instruments may be viewed as complementary in their ultimate policy objective, the conflict between these two areas of law is thus plain to see. Competition law encourages competition and strives for lower prices and higher quality. Patent law rewards innovators by pre-empting competition and allowing them to charge supra-competitive prices. In economic jargon, competition law promotes static efficiency, which can be further separated into allocative efficiency and

[1] John C Stedman, 'Patents and Antitrust—The Impact of Varying Legal Doctrines' (1973) Utah Law Review 588, 590.

productive efficiency, while patent law prioritizes dynamic efficiency. Competition law, however, is also concerned with dynamic efficiency to the extent that it enhances consumer welfare. Allocative efficiency is attained when resources are allocated to uses that place the highest value on them. Productive efficiency requires more efficient use of resources to satisfy needs of individuals in society. Dynamic efficiency focuses on innovation and is improved when the rate of innovation increases. Under patent law, static efficiency is sacrificed to foster dynamic efficiency.

Louis Kaplow has described the conflict underlying the patent–competition interface as 'even more deep-seated than is generally perceived'.[2] In *International Wood Processors v. Power Dry, Inc.*, the United States Court of Appeals for the Fourth Circuit expresses a similar view that 'there may be conflict between the patent laws on the one hand, which encourage monopoly power by granting patent holders the right to exclude and be free from competition, and the antitrust laws, on the other hand, which generally proscribe monopoly and encourage competition'.[3] Not everyone shares the same pessimistic view about the relationship between these two areas of law. Herbert Hovenkamp argues that the conflict between patent and competition laws 'is readily exaggerated'.[4] The source of the apparent conflict between these two areas of law is the 'deep uncertainty about the optimal amount and scope of IP protection'.[5] The implication of this argument is that if the patent system provided the optimal amount of innovation incentives to potential innovators, there would be no need for competition law to intervene. Competition policy considerations should only be accorded weight in patent–competition cases when the patent system has provided excessive innovation incentives.

Mark Lemley, a prominent intellectual property law scholar in the United States, endorses the view and further notes that the patent system does not always provide optimal incentives. He observes that

> there is good evidence that IP rights do not always promote innovation. Sometimes they interfere with innovation, particularly if the rights are too strong or last too long, so that generation after generation of potential improvers must get permission from one (or, worse, many) existing stakeholders before innovating in a field.[6]

[2] Louis Kaplow, 'The Patent–Antitrust Intersection: A Reappraisal' [1984] Harvard Law Review 1817–18.

[3] 792 F.2d 416, 426 (4th Cir. 1986).

[4] Herbert Hovenkamp, 'United States Antitrust Policy in an Age of IP Expansion' (Social Science Research Network 2004) SSRN Scholarly Paper ID 634224 <https://papers.ssrn.com/abstract=634224> accessed 31 March 2019.

[5] ibid 2.

[6] Mark A Lemley, 'Industry-Specific Antitrust Policy for Innovation' (Social Science Research Network 2010) SSRN Scholarly Paper ID 1670197 3 <https://papers.ssrn.com/abstract=1670197> accessed 29 March 2019.

Competition law can thus be used as a counterweight to patent law. Lemley argues that the extent of competition law intervention into patent exploitation practices should vary in accordance with the strength of patent rights. Competition law enforcement should be strong when patent rights are strong and should be rolled back when patent rights weaken.[7] Policy-makers should aim to achieve a delicate balance between the two. Excessively strong patent rights impede innovation, unnecessarily retard competition, and reduce social welfare.[8] Over-emphasis on competition risks the loss of innovation in the name of static efficiency.[9] Competition may backfire as a tool to spur innovation.[10]

Lemley's argument implies that patent law and competition law seek to achieve the same policy objectives.[11] Dynamic efficiency is indisputably the primary preoccupation of the patent system, which imposes a trade-off of short-term static efficiency loss for longer-term dynamic efficiency gains. It is, however, incorrect to say that competition law is only concerned with static efficiency. Lemley argues that this view is at least 'oversimplified'.[12] Competition law strives for improvement in consumer welfare. Economists have long argued that over the long term, dynamic efficiency is a much more important source of improvement for consumer welfare and economic progress than is static efficiency.[13] In the long run, consumers derive much more benefit from the emergence of new products and new technologies than the production of existing products at lower costs. Therefore, competition law values both static efficiency and dynamic efficiency to the extent that they enhance consumer welfare.[14] While the trade-off between static efficiency and dynamic efficiency underlying the patent system has been largely determined by the legislature, competition law allows the recalibration of this trade-off on a case-by-case basis after taking into account market conditions and other pertinent factors.

This view is echoed by Suzanne Scotchmer, who has asserted that the conflict between patent and competition laws 'is more a short-run tension than a long run tension, since in the long run intellectual property law leads to innovation, which improves the welfare of consumers'. Since consumer welfare is the concern of competition law, there is no fundamental inconsistency.[15] Robert Pitofsky has similarly emphasized the common policy objectives of patent and competition laws, asserting that

[7] Mark Lemley, 'A New Balance Between IP and Antitrust' (2007) 13 Southwestern Journal of Law and Trade in the Americas 237, 254.
[8] ibid.
[9] ibid.
[10] ibid.
[11] ibid 247.
[12] Lemley, 'Industry-Specific Antitrust Policy for Innovation' (n 6) 2.
[13] Donald Turner, 'Basic Principles in Formulating Antitrust and Misuse Constraints on the Exploitation of Intellectual Property Rights' [1984] Antitrust Law Journal 485, 485.
[14] ibid.
[15] Suzanne Scotchmer, *Innovation and Incentives* (MIT Press 2004) 161.

> both antitrust, by protecting competition, and intellectual property, by rewarding innovation, create incentives to introduce new products. In addition, antitrust for the most part has no quarrel with the argument that market power is more acceptable if it is reasonably necessary to achieve efficiencies, including efficiencies connected with innovation. When modest anticompetitive effects of a transaction are significantly outweighed by the positive consumer welfare consequences of innovation, antitrust has historically struck the balance in favor of innovation.[16]

Competition law thus serves as a counterbalance to patent law in pursuit of the common policy objective of improving consumer welfare through encouraging innovation. Competition law can be viewed as a tool to recalibrate the innovation incentives generated by the patent system. This recalibration is necessary because the patent system may sometimes provide excessive protection and unduly suppress competition. The conceptualization of competition law as a counterbalance to patent law implicitly acknowledges that the two areas of law deploy conflicting tools in pursuit of their common policy objective. Patent law creates market power through exclusivity, whereas competition law promotes competition, which keeps market power in check, by prohibiting anticompetitive practices. As the US Court of Appeals for the Second Circuit observed in *SCM Corp. v. Xerox Corp.*,

> The conflict between the antitrust and patent laws arises in the methods they embrace that were designed to achieve reciprocal goals. While the antitrust laws proscribe unreasonable restraints of competition, the patent laws reward the inventor with a temporary monopoly that insulates him from competitive exploitation of his patented art.[17]

A further source of uncertainty for the patent–competition interface is the lack of consensus on the relationship between competition and innovation. In the trade-off between static efficiency and dynamic efficiency, it is clear that increased competition or weaker patent protection lowers prices and raises static efficiency. In contrast, there is much less clarity on how dynamic efficiency is promoted. Even though patent and competition laws are said to pursue the common policy objective of advancing consumer welfare by promoting innovation, the two areas of law share different visions of how this can be achieved and what kind of market structure is most conducive to innovation. Patent law implicitly subscribes to the view that monopoly supports greater innovation while competition law, unsurprisingly, places its faith in competition.

[16] Robert Pitofsky, 'Challenges of the New Economy: Issues at the Intersection of Antitrust and Intellectual Property' (2001) 68 Antitrust Law Journal 913, 917.

[17] 645 F.2d 1195, 1203 (2d Cir. 1981).

This harkens back to the long-running debate between adherents of Joseph Schumpeter and Kenneth Arrow on whether competition or monopoly induces more innovation. Schumpeter famously argues that monopoly is more conducive to innovation because R&D is costly and monopoly profits are necessary in order to fund the research needed to generate innovation.[18] He further observes that markets progress through innovation, whereby firms compete for the market through innovation, displacing an old monopoly with a new one.[19] Kenneth Arrow and others have disputed these claims, arguing that innovation is more abundant in a competitive market.[20] According to Arrow, a monopolist suffers from a major disincentive to innovate because a new product introduced by a monopolist will simply displace its own existing product. Therefore, innovation is a double-edged sword for a monopolist. Meanwhile, a monopolist's competitors do not suffer the same disincentive because they do not bear the costs of the lost revenue from the displaced product. Innovation will merely allow these competitors to capture the market from the monopolist. Arrow calls this 'the replacement effect'. This debate has spawned a large body of theoretical and empirical literature aiming to settle the debate.[21] A definitive resolution remains elusive.

While the academic debate rages on, policy-makers and enforcers nonetheless must take an explicit or implicit view of the matter. Given the fundamental belief in competition law that competition is inherently beneficial to society and propels economic progress, it should come as no surprise that competition law generally subscribes to the Arrowian view. For example, in the US Department of Justice–Federal Trade Commission 1995 Guidelines for the Licensing of Intellectual Property, the two agencies identified as a potential harm of cross-licensing arrangements and patent pools the possibility of a reduction in innovation competition.[22] This theory of harm is premised on 'the economic hypothesis that competition leads to more R&D than cooperation'.[23] In his advocacy for robust competition law enforcement to foster innovation, Jonathan Baker posits that firms innovate in an attempt to escape product market competition.[24] FM Scherer argues that with respect to abuse of dominance cases in the high-technology sectors, the presumption

[18] Joseph A Schumpeter, *Capitalism, Socialism, and Democracy* (3rd edn Harper Perennial Modern Classics 2008) 87–120.

[19] ibid.

[20] Kenneth Arrow, 'Economic Welfare and the Allocation of Resources for Invention' (National Bureau of Economic Research, Inc 1962) NBER Chapters 619–20 <https://econpapers.repec.org/bookchap/nbrnberch/2144.htm> accessed 31 March 2019.

[21] Richard J Gilbert and Steven C Sunshine, 'The Use of Innovation Markets: A Reply to Hay, Rapp, and Hoerner' (1995) 64 Antitrust Law Journal 75.

[22] US Department of Justice and Federal Trade Commission, 'Antitrust Guidelines for the Licensing of Intellectual Property' (2017) 30 <https://www.justice.gov/atr/IPguidelines/download> accessed 29 July 2021.

[23] Scotchmer, *Innovation and Incentives* (n 15) 172.

[24] Jonathan Baker, 'Beyond Schumpeter vs. Arrow: How Antitrust Fosters Innovation' (2007) 74 Antitrust Law Journal 575, 579.

should be 'in favor of keeping structural and behavioral barriers to innovative new entry as low as possible'.[25] In the eyes of competition law enforcers and commentators alike, competition promotes innovation.

In contrast, by relying on the supra-competitive pricing permitted by patent exclusivity to spur innovation, patent law clearly holds the Schumpeterian view and presumes that market power is conducive to innovation. Therefore, while there seems to be common ground between patent and competition laws regarding their policy objectives, the two areas of law rely on different tools to achieve their objectives and hold different views on the structural conditions most conducive to innovation. While it may be an overstatement to say that there is a fundamental conflict between patent and competition laws, it is not entirely accurate to say that the conflict is readily exaggerated. In positing competition law as a counterbalance to patent law, Lemley and others implicitly accept that these two areas of law operate through conflicting means.

It remains to be determined how the balance between the two bodies of law should be struck. Almost twenty years ago, Pitofsky cautioned against tilting the balance in competition law too far towards the preservation of innovative incentives generated by the patent system. He argued that

> [a]n approach that grants broad exceptions to antitrust principles in favor of intellectual property holders distorts the balance too far in the direction of incentives to innovate by sacrificing too much in the way of competition and opportunities for follow-on innovation.[26]

Lemley characterizes the prevailing approach to the patent–competition interface in the United States as one which 'treats IP [intellectual property] rights as having primacy within their established boundaries, and relegates antitrust to the role of policing departures from those boundaries'.[27] He argues for a more nuanced industry-specific approach to the patent–competition interface, asserting that both areas of law play an equally important role in encouraging innovation and promoting dynamic efficiency and should be treated as equals.[28] The nature of the industry and the invention in question determine which tool should be used.[29]

[25] FM Scherer, 'Technological Innovation and Monopolization' (2005) No 05-07 64 <https://www.antitrustinstitute.org/work-product/aai-working-paper-no-05-07-technological-innovation-and-monopolization/> accessed 31 March 2019.

[26] Robert Pitofsky, 'Antitrust and Intellectual Property: Unresolved Issues at the Heart of the New Economy' (2001) 16 Berkeley Technology Law Journal 535, 545.

[27] Lemley, 'A New Balance Between IP and Antitrust' (n 7) 255.

[28] ibid 256.

[29] ibid.

C. Dynamic Efficiency Considerations in Context

1. Overview

Within the patent–competition interface, one may ascribe to competition law the role of an *ex-post* adjustment mechanism for the fundamental trade-off underlying the patent system between static efficiency loss and dynamic efficiency gains. The patent system has struck a general trade-off between these two through setting the length of the patent term and delineating the scope of patent rights. The need for an adjustment mechanism is perhaps unsurprising because the patent system largely operates through rules of general application that do not make fine adjustments in accordance with the product or market at issue. Although some commentators have argued that the patent system, at least as it exists in the United States, does tailor its rules to different industries,[30] rules in the patent system by and large apply across the board. The length of the patent term is the same regardless of the product at issue. The scope of patent rights also does not vary by industry or product. Moreover, the trade-off in the patent system is made *ex ante* before the innovator has made the R&D investment. Competition law by nature operates on an *ex-post* basis and makes case-by-case adjustments. It allows for much more finely tuned adjustments of the trade-off between static efficiency and dynamic efficiency.

The patent system presupposes a causal relationship between the patentee reward generated by supra-competitive pricing and innovation incentives. While this relationship is highly intuitive, it has not gone unchallenged. It is important to examine the relationship between the patent system and the reward it offers on the one hand, and innovation incentives the system purportedly generates on the other hand. While the ensuing discussion may be so misconstrued, it is important to clarify that the purpose of this inquiry is not to undermine or question the fundamental rationale of the patent system. It is fully recognized that competition law must respect the fundamental trade-off underlying the patent system and should only seek to make adjustments at the margin. The purpose of this inquiry is merely to assess the efficacy of the patent system in spurring innovation. If the effectiveness is found to be low, or the relationship between patentee reward and increased innovation seems uncertain, one needs to be more cautious about sacrificing consumer welfare to reward potential innovators. The ensuing inquiry will demonstrate why the patent system is a fairly suboptimal mechanism for generating innovation incentives and attracting innovations. This is particularly pertinent in the context of developing countries, especially the least developed ones, given that their consumers can ill-afford the supra-competitive prices charged by patent owners.

30 Dan L Burk and Mark A Lemley, 'Policy Levers in Patent Law' (2003) 89 Virginia Law Review 1575.

The fundamental argument of this monograph is that the relative weight to be attached to static and dynamic efficiencies varies across countries and depends on a number of factors. Readiness to accept static efficiency loss must reflect the state of the general consumers in the country. The poorer they are, the less they can afford supra-competitive prices. While poor consumers are not confined to developing countries, it remains true that the general body of consumers in developing countries, especially the least developed ones, is much poorer than those in developed economies. There is hence a more pressing need to protect consumers in developing countries from supra-competitive pricing. If the incentive effects of the patent system are uncertain, the potential costs of shifting the balance toward static efficiency will be lower.

The relative importance of dynamic efficiency considerations depends on the country's distance from the global technological frontier and the amount of innovative capacity in the country. The closer a country is to the global technological frontier, the less able it is to grow simply by copying other countries' technologies. Such a country must rely on its own innovative effort to grow. Innovation hence plays a more important role in its growth than in the growth of technological laggards. This country may justifiably decide that it would err on the side of innovation incentives despite the uncertain efficacy of the patent system in encouraging innovation. For technological laggards, a group which includes almost all developing countries, growth is much less likely to come from genuine innovation in the global sense, which can be called frontier innovation, because they are much less capable of generating such innovation. For these countries, growth is often achieved through the acquisition and adaptation of foreign technologies, which shares a more complicated relationship with patent protection. Dynamic efficiency considerations and innovation incentives may carry less weight. These countries should be mindful of the doubtful effectiveness of the patent system in spurring innovation, which may counsel in favour of competition policy in the patent–competition interface.

Distance from the global technological frontier is also related to the amount of innovative capacity. The simple point is that the innovation incentives generated by the patent system will have much more meaningful impact in a country amply populated by potential innovators. In a country bereft of individuals or firms that can produce frontier innovation, reward provided by the patent system is unlikely to generate much innovation and will be largely unclaimed. There is unlikely to be much dynamic efficiency gains regardless of the static efficiency loss incurred by the country. The patentee reward in such a developing country will mostly only accrue to foreign innovators. In a country where patent protection is unlikely to attract much domestic innovation, policymakers may hesitate to err on the side of patent policy.

A note of clarification is in order. Most of the ensuing discussion and economic studies cited are concerned with the impact of increased patent protection on innovation incentives. These studies attempt to determine whether developing countries will enjoy greater innovation by raising the level of patent protection. The apparent discrepancy between the focus of these studies and that of this monograph, however, does not detract from their applicability to the patent–competition interface. This is because both the patent system and the patent–competition rules bear the same relationship with innovation incentives. Both act on the patentee reward by adjusting the scope of patent rights. The patent system adjusts the size of the patentee reward by lengthening or shortening the patent term and varying the scope of protection. The patent–competition rules do the same by shifting the boundary of permissible patent exploitation practices. A patentee will reap greater financial benefits from her innovation if competition law gives her greater scope to exploit her patents by allowing her to impose more restrictions on the sale of her product or the licensing of her technology. As far as patentee reward is concerned, raising the level of patent protection is equivalent to relaxing the patent–competition rules on patent exploitation. If the ensuing discussion shows that increasing patentee reward by raising patent protection does not generate greater amount of innovation for one reason or another, the same would be true for increasing patentee reward by relaxing the patent–competition rules.

2. The Imprecise Nature of the Patent System as an Innovation Incentive Mechanism

There are a number of reasons to be cautious about giving too much deference to patent policy in the patent–competition interface. One of them is that the patent system has an arguable tendency to overcompensate innovators and a minor reduction in patentee reward should not result in significant reduction in innovation incentives. As Hovenkamp observes, the confused state of both the law on and the theoretical discussion of the patent–competition interface is largely due to the uncertainty regarding the optimal amount of patent protection.[31] Patent protection comprises two dimensions: patent length and the scope of patent rights.[32] Variation along either dimension changes the size of the patentee reward, which presumably alters innovation incentives.[33] Competition regulation of patent rights affects the scope of such rights, which is the channel through which competition law influences innovation incentives.

The uncertainty regarding the scope of patent rights stems from the fact that there is a mismatch between what patentee reward currently offers to innovators

[31] Hovenkamp (n 4) 2.

[32] Robert Merges and Richard Nelson, 'On the Complex Economics of Patent Scope' [1990] Columbia Law Review 839, 839–40. Kaplow (n 2) 1823. Scotchmer, *Innovation and Incentives* (n 15) 98.

[33] Kaplow (n 2) 1823.

and what it ought to cover. In order to generate the socially optimal amount of innovation incentives, what the patent system should seek to do is to compensate innovators for their risk-adjusted costs of innovation.[34] When deciding whether to undertake R&D for innovation, a potential innovator undertakes a profitability analysis. An innovator will undertake R&D so long as she expects to make enough from the innovation to cover the actual and opportunity costs of R&D. This would be the cost–benefit analysis undertaken by individual innovators. A systemic perspective would also require patentee reward to take into account the fact that not every R&D project succeeds. Many of them in fact fail.[35] Therefore, the patent system must cover the risk-adjusted costs, and not just the actual R&D costs, of innovation.[36]

The mismatch lies in the fact that the patent system currently makes no attempt to match the patentee reward with costs of innovation, risk-adjusted or otherwise. This is largely because of the prohibitive information costs involved in obtaining information about R&D costs *ex ante*.[37] Instead of innovation costs, patentee reward seems to be calibrated to match the value of innovation.[38] The patent system is currently set up to allow the innovator to capture the value of her innovation, even though this may vastly exceed the innovation costs. Innovators can thus be overcompensated, sometimes grossly so. Recall that patentee reward is derived from a loss of consumer welfare.[39] If the patent system grossly overcompensates innovators, it means that a slight reduction in patentee reward is unlikely to result in a significant loss in innovation. This gives competition law enforcers considerable leeway to shift the balance underlying the patent–competition interface toward competition policy without sacrificing innovation incentives.

There are four relevant parameters in the determination of optimal patent protection: (1) social benefits, (2) private benefits, (3) social costs, and (4) private costs.[40] Social benefits consist of private benefits and external benefits, which are benefits not captured by the innovator. Social costs consist of private costs and external costs, which are costs borne by society as a whole. Private costs and benefits are what guide the innovator's R&D investment decision. If private benefits exceed private costs, the investment will be undertaken. A positive outcome in this private cost–benefit analysis, however, does not necessarily mean that the innovation is beneficial to society. An innovation is only socially beneficial if its social benefits

[34] Richard Gilbert and Carl Shapiro, 'Optimal Patent Length and Breadth' (1990) 21 RAND Journal of Economics 106, 107.

[35] Adam B Jaffe and Josh Lerner, *Innovation and Its Discontents: How Our Broken Patent System Is Endangering Innovation and Progress, and What to Do About It* (Princeton University Press 2004) 41–42.

[36] ibid 41.

[37] Nancy Gallini and Suzanne Scotchmer, 'Intellectual Property: When Is It the Best Incentive System?', in Josh Lerner and Scott Stern (eds), *Innovation Policy and the Economy* (MIT Press 2002) 55; Jaffe and Lerner (n 35) 38.

[38] Scotchmer, *Innovation and Incentives* (n 15) 97.

[39] Kaplow (n 2) 1823–25; Jaffe and Lerner (n 35) 37–41.

[40] ibid.

exceed its social costs, meaning that society is overall better off with the innovation.[41] A further clarification is that the benefits and costs of patent protection may differ from those of innovation. There are instances where it will be useful to highlight their differences.

The external benefits of innovation include the direct and indirect benefits of the innovation to society that are not captured by the innovator. To the extent that patent protection is responsible for attracting the innovation, the external benefits of innovation may coincide with the external benefits of patent protection. To the extent that innovation is spurred by other financial incentives, however, the social benefits of innovation exceed the social benefits of patent protection.[42] For the present purpose, it is assumed that the social benefits of innovation are the same as the social benefits of patent protection. Making such an assumption does not detract from the main argument of this section and simplifies the discussion. The benefits of cumulative innovation and technological spillovers are the same regardless of whether the innovation is motivated by patent protection or other appropriation mechanisms. It will be noted subsequently, however, that the benefits of innovation do often diverge from those of patent protection.

Direct benefits refer to the immediate impact of an innovation on social welfare. For a process innovation such as a cost-reducing technology, its direct social benefit are the costs society saves in the production of an existing product.[43] For a product innovation in the form of a new product, the direct social benefit is the difference in consumers' willingness to pay for the improved product as compared to the original product, or the additional consumer surplus created by the new product.[44] Indirect social benefits generally refer to the beneficial impact of an innovation on the innovative activities taking place in the rest of the industry and economy in general. These can be in the form of the opportunities for cumulative innovation and the spillovers created by the initial innovation. Lemley asserts that 'improvements may in many cases dwarf the original work in terms of their practical significance'.[45] Other commentators have similarly emphasized the importance of cumulative innovation.[46]

Meanwhile, William Baumol has written extensively on the importance of spillovers from innovation. He estimates that innovators are able to capture only 20 per cent of the value created by their innovations; the remaining 80 per cent of

41 Gilbert and Shapiro (n 34) 107.

42 Richard Levin and others, 'Appropriating the Returns from Industrial Research and Development' (1987) 3 Brookings Papers on Economic Activity 783.

43 Suzanne Scotchmer, 'Standing on the Shoulders of Giants: Cumulative Research and the Patent Law' (1991) 5 Journal of Economic Perspectives 29, 31.

44 ibid.

45 Mark A Lemley, 'Economics of Improvement in Intellectual Property Law' (1996) 75 Texas Law Review 989, 997.

46 Scotchmer, 'Standing on the Shoulders of Giants' (n 43); Merges and Nelson (n 32) 843–44, 870; John H Barton, 'Patents and Antitrust: A Rethinking in Light of Patent Breadth and Sequential Innovation' (1997) 65 Antitrust Law Journal 449, 453.

the value is spread across society.[47] He boldly asserts that without these spillovers, a majority of the industrialized world would be condemned to a pre-Industrial Revolution standard of living.[48] Jeffrey Bernstein finds that the social value of innovation is at least twice as high as the private value of innovation in the industries he studied.[49] Timothy Bresnahan concludes that the social benefits of mainframe computers vastly exceed their private benefits.[50]

An innovation may be spurred by patent protection or other financial incentives. To the extent that patent protection is responsible for the innovation, the private benefits of innovation and the private benefits of patent protection coincide. However, if there are other means for the innovators to recoup their investments and monetize their innovation, the private benefits of innovation could far outweigh the private benefits of patent protection. The private benefits of patent protection are the profits for the innovator made possible by the patent system. They are measured against the hypothetical financial reward accrued to the patentee absent patent protection.[51] In other words, the private benefits of patent protection are the additional value patent protection redounds to the innovator. Private benefits of innovation consist of all the revenue earned by the innovator from the exploitation of its innovation, including sale of the final product incorporating the patented technology, licensing of the technology, or even the sale of it in the form of an assignment.[52] The ways in which an innovator can reap financial benefits from her innovation are known as appropriation mechanisms.[53] Patent protection is only one of them. There are many other mechanisms which will be further discussed below. The various financial rewards provided by the different appropriation mechanisms together constitute the private benefits of innovation.

The abundance of appropriation mechanisms means that the private benefits of innovation are likely to far exceed the private benefits of patenting. This has been confirmed by a number of empirical studies.[54] Scotchmer concludes that the average R&D costs are much greater than the average value of patents.[55] Zvi Griliches and co-authors find that the aggregate private value of patents amounts to

[47] William Baumol, *The Free-Market Innovation Machine: Analyzing the Growth Miracle of Capitalism* (Princeton University Press 2004) 121, 134–35.

[48] ibid 125.

[49] Jeffrey Bernstein, 'The Structure of Canadian Inter-Industry R&D Spillovers, and the Rates of Return to R&D' (1989) 37 Journal of Industrial Economics 315, 315–28.

[50] Timothy Bresnahan, 'Measuring the Spillovers from Technical Advance: Mainframe Computers in Financial Services' (1986) 76 The American Economic Review 742, 753.

[51] Erich Kaufer, *The Economics of the Patent System* (Harwood Academic Publishers 1989) 42–43.

[52] James Bessen and Michael Meurer, *Patent Failure: How Judges, Bureaucrats, and Lawyers Put Innovators at Risk* (Princeton University Press 2009) 97.

[53] Alexandra Zaby, *The Decision to Patent* (Springer 2010) 30 <https://www.springer.com/us/book/9783790826111> accessed 4 April 2019.

[54] Zvi Griliches, Ariel Pakes, and Bronwyn H Hall, 'The Value of Patents as Indicators of Inventive Activity' (National Bureau of Economic Research 1986) Working Paper 2083 120 <http://www.nber.org/papers/w2083> accessed 4 April 2019.

[55] Scotchmer, *Innovation and Incentives* (n 15) 275.

roughly only 10 per cent to 15 per cent of the total national expenditures of R&D.[56] James Bessen and Michael Meurer put the figure even lower at 3 per cent.[57] While different studies arrive at varying estimates, they all reach the same conclusion that R&D costs dwarf the private benefits of patent protection. Assuming that R&D is generally profitable, this means that the private benefits of innovation must vastly exceed R&D costs. Even with the more conservative estimates by Griliches and co-authors, the private benefits of innovation exceed the private benefits of patenting by sevenfold to tenfold. This suggests that patent protection is not a very important appropriation mechanism for innovators. All this has led William Landes and Richard Posner to conclude that 'incremental increases in patent protection are unlikely to influence inventive activity significantly and incremental reductions might actually enhance economic welfare'.[58] One way to reduce patent protection incrementally is through the use of competition law.

The costs of innovation and patent protection are different and need to be clearly distinguished. There are direct and indirect external costs of patent protection. The direct external costs are the costs that arise from the administration of a patent system.[59] These include the operating costs for the patent registration office and the legal costs incurred by parties in patent litigation.[60] These costs are no doubt substantial. They are, however, mostly relevant on the systemic level and are unlikely to play an important role in determining the optimal patent protection in individual cases. The indirect external costs of patent protection include the deadweight loss inflicted by the supra-competitive pricing that is made possible by patent protection[61] and the social wastes that arise from the patent race where the loser's R&D investment will come to nought once she loses the race to obtain patent protection.[62] The costs from patent races are not inevitable and could be easily avoided if patent law permits an independent invention defence similar to copyright law.[63]

The indirect external costs of innovation include the costs of creative destruction. These costs are less well-documented but are nonetheless worth mentioning. They refer to the costs imposed by a new innovation on the producers of an existing

56 Griliches, Pakes, and Hall (n 54) 120.

57 Bessen and Meurer (n 52) 113.

58 William Landes and Richard Posner, *The Economic Structure of Intellectual Property Law* (Harvard University Press 2003) 327.

59 'Patent Costs and Impact on Innovation' (European Commission 2014) 17, <https://ec.europa.eu/jrc/communities/sites/jrccties/files/patent_costs_and_impact_on_innovation.pdf> accessed 23 June 2021.

60 ibid 8.

61 Scotchmer, *Innovation and Incentives* (n 15) 99.

62 Partha Dasgupta and Joseph Stiglitz, 'Industrial Structure and the Nature of Innovative Activity' (1980) 90 Economic Journal 266. Jennifer F Reinganum, 'A Dynamic Game of R and D: Patent Protection and Competitive Behavior' (1982) 50 Econometrica 671. Pankaj Tandon, 'Rivalry and the Excessive Allocation of Resources to Research' (1983) 14 Bell Journal of Economics 152.

63 Samson Vermont, 'Independent Invention as a Defense to Patent Infringement' (2006) 105 Michigan Law Review 475.

product.[64] To the extent that the new innovation renders existing products in the market obsolete, the machineries that these firms have installed and the plants that these firms have constructed to produce their now-obsolete products may become redundant.[65] The investments made to produce these existing products will lose their productive value. Innovators do not take into account these costs borne by their rivals when deciding whether to pursue an innovation.[66] From a social perspective, however, these losses could be substantial and may outweigh the benefits of the innovation.[67]

The private costs of innovation and patent protection are again different. The private costs of innovation refer to the direct R&D costs and opportunity costs of innovation. Direct R&D costs are the investments made by the innovator into the R&D that ultimately creates the innovation. Opportunity costs refer to the financial reward the innovator may receive from the best alternative use of her funds. As opposed to R&D, she may decide to boost her production capacity by building a new factory or acquiring more machinery. She may decide to attempt to increase sales by engaging in more marketing or promotion. Or she may seek to improve her firm's operational efficiency by investing in a new IT system. She will choose whichever that gives her the highest rate of return. Her return from the second most profitable alternative would be the opportunity costs of the chosen option.

The private costs of patenting refer to the costs incurred by the innovator to obtain patent protection for her innovation.[68] The two terms, however, seem to be used interchangeably by economists and lawyers alike to refer to R&D costs. When commentators speak of patenting costs what they have in mind often seem to be R&D costs, perhaps together with patenting costs.[69] For most innovations that are not discovered by accident but require significant and continuous inventive effort, R&D costs are likely to far exceed patenting costs.[70] Therefore, for most purposes, it is the private costs of innovation that will be the focus of discussion.

An innovation would be beneficial to society if its total social benefits outweigh its total social costs. An innovation would be worthwhile if it redounded net social benefit to society. A credible argument can be made that the costs of creative destruction should be ignored. Creative destruction is the necessary consequence of every innovation and is the price society pays for technological progress.[71]

[64] Kristiina Huttunen, Jarle Møen, and Kjell G Salvanes, 'How Destructive Is Creative Destruction? The Costs of Worker Displacement' (2006) EconPapers 3–4 <https://econpapers.repec.org/paper/izaizadps/dp2316.htm> accessed 24 June 2021; Baumol (n 47) 137.

[65] Baumol (n 47) 136–37.

[66] ibid 137.

[67] Bessen and Meurer (n 52) 98.

[68] 'Patent Costs and Impact on Innovation' (n 59) 17.

[69] Scotchmer, *Innovation and Incentives* (n 15) 273; Mark Schankerman, 'How Valuable Is Patent Protection? Estimates by Technology Field' (1998) 29 RAND Journal of Economics 77, 94.

[70] Jean O Lanjouw and Mark Schankerman, 'Patent Quality and Research Productivity' (2004) 114 Economic Journal 441; 'Patent Costs and Impact on Innovation' (n 59) 19.

[71] Schumpeter (n 18) 87–120.

Technological advancement would be needlessly retarded if society were to decide against an innovation due to the costs of creative destruction. An important implication of the social cost–benefit analysis for innovation is that it is possible for society to be saddled with excessive innovation.[72] While this may come as a surprise to some, it is merely the natural consequence of the fact that society has limited resources and it cannot invest all its resources into innovation. At some point, society would obtain greater benefits if it invested its resources elsewhere, such as in infrastructure, public health, or education.

A potential misallocation of resources to innovative activities may arise because while an innovation affects the entire society, the decision to invest in an innovation is made by an innovator in light of her private costs and benefits. An innovator will pursue an innovation if she derives a net private benefit from it. An investment in an innovation will be made if the financial reward received by the innovator from the various appropriation mechanisms exceeds the risk-adjusted private costs of innovation, which include both direct R&D costs and the opportunity cost. If the innovation gives her a financial reward that exceeds her returns in her next best investment option plus her R&D costs, she will choose to innovate.

The ideal incentive mechanism for innovation would be one under which all innovations that create net social benefits were pursued, which in turn would require that the private benefits of innovation for an innovator cover her risk-adjusted private costs of innovation. The task of the patent system would then be to ensure that for all socially beneficial innovations, patentee reward supplements whatever shortfalls may exist between the financial reward from other appropriation mechanisms and the innovator's risk-adjusted private costs of innovation. While determining this shortfall may present serious practical complications, the basic principle remains that the patent system seeks to ensure that socially beneficial innovations provide their innovators with net private benefits and are hence created.

The patent system would ideally calibrate the patentee reward such that the total private benefits of innovation just cover the risk-adjusted private costs of innovation.[73] Anything beyond that would constitute a windfall for the innovator and would be socially wasteful.[74] If it was possible for the government to estimate accurately the private costs and the probability of success of innovation, the patent system would be redundant.[75] The patent system is only a second-best option for incentivizing innovation.[76] The information requirements imposed by an ideal reward system mean that the patent system makes no attempt to calibrate

[72] Scotchmer, *Innovation and Incentives* (n 15) 98.
[73] Landes and Posner (n 58) 300.
[74] ibid.
[75] Gallini and Scotchmer (n 37) 55.
[76] Ian Ayres and Paul Klemperer, 'Limiting Patentees' Market Power Without Reducing Innovation Incentives: The Perverse Benefits of Uncertainty and Non-Injunctive Remedies' (1999) 97 Michigan Law Review 985, 1008.

the patentee reward such that the private benefits of innovation just cover the private costs of innovation. Instead, what the patent system seems to do is to allow the innovator to capture much, if not all, of the value of her innovation, which is presumably determined by its social benefits. For example, under US patent law, the pioneer invention doctrine holds that ground-breaking innovations that open up a new field of research or commercial development, which create greater social value, are entitled to broader protection than less significant innovations.[77] As Scotchmer notes, '[g]iven that the length and breadth of patent protection cannot depend on the expected costs of an R&D project, the only way to ensure that firms undertake every research project that is efficient is to let the firms collect as revenue all the social value they create'.[78] Using the social value of an innovation as the benchmark is in fact our third-best option for incentivizing innovation.

The patent system in fact does not even live up to this third-best option. It does not try to match the scope of patent protection with the social value of an innovation. If it did, one would expect the patent term or the scope of patent rights to be adjusted accordingly, which would in turn require the patent system to determine the social value of an innovation. This would entail measurements of its spillover effects and an estimation of the possibility of cumulative innovation, among other things. The patent system makes no attempt to do anything of this sort. The complete absence of any effort by the patent system to ascertain the social value of an innovation and calibrate patentee reward against this value means that patentee reward may even exceed its social value. The scope of a patentee's rights under patent law may allow her to capture the value from spillovers and cumulative innovation beyond that which were made possible by her innovation. For example, the right to exclude may allow the patentee to extract most of the value of a cumulative innovation even though the cumulative innovator may have been responsible for the bulk of the value of her innovation. This would amount to gross overcompensation of innovators and is unjustifiable from a social welfare perspective.

Recall that the first-best innovation reward mechanism should only compensate innovators for their risk-adjusted private costs of innovation. Setting patentee reward against the social value of an innovation already has a tendency to overcompensate innovators. There is in fact the possibility of double overcompensation under the current patent system when the patentee reward exceeds the social value of an innovation. It is of course possible that patentee reward may fall short of this value. There is no *a priori* reason to assume that the patent system will exhibit a systemic bias one way or the other. Such under-compensation would only affect innovation output if the social value and private costs of an innovation are very close in magnitude. In such a case it is possible that allowing a patentee to capture

[77] Burk and Lemley (n 30) 1656; Brian J Love, 'Interring the Pioneer Invention Doctrine' (2011) 90 North Carolina Law Review 379, 382.

[78] Scotchmer, 'Standing on the Shoulders of Giants' (n 43) 31.

the full social value of her innovation would cause the innovation to be produced but under-compensation would result in a loss of the innovation. However, such an innovation is unlikely to be socially beneficial once one takes into account its external costs.[79] The loss of such innovations should not be a matter of grave concern to society.

The foregoing discussion is not meant to pose a challenge to the patent system. While there could be a serious theoretical mismatch between what should be and what is actually offered by the patent system as a reward to secure socially beneficial innovations, there are very strong practical reasons to believe that attempts to correct this mismatch will be futile. The information requirements to correct this mismatch would be overwhelming. As a matter of patent system design, there is little that can be done about overcompensation of innovators. Yet this tendency to overcompensate should not be simply ignored as far as the patent–competition interface is concerned. Given that patentee reward is generated from supra-competitive pricing, the fact that patentee reward tends to exceed what is necessary to secure socially beneficial innovations means that consumer welfare is needlessly sacrificed to generate excessive innovation incentives. There would be room for patent rights to be pared back to lower patentee reward without risking substantial loss of socially beneficial innovations. Static efficiency considerations could be emphasized at the expense of dynamic efficiency without much loss in innovation incentives. One way to achieve this would be through the patent–competition rules, which, by regulating how a patentee may exploit her rights and license her technology, alters the scope of patent rights.

While it may be tempting to argue that many of these issues arise from within the patent system and should be addressed through reforms within the system, as some commentators have argued, there are a few reasons why such reforms are unlikely to be adequate for our purpose. First, there does not seem to be momentum internationally for major reforms of the patent system that will address the concerns raised here. If anything, changes in the global intellectual property system seems to be in the direction of ratcheting up of rights instead of a recalibration of the level of protection. Even if global reform efforts were to materialize, they are likely to be dominated by the industrialized economies such as the United States and the European Union, whose interests are in elevating protection. Developing countries are unlikely to achieve what they want from such global efforts. Second, the overcompensating tendencies of the patent system and other problems that were highlighted earlier are so fundamental to the patent system that it is unlikely that they can be addressed adequately through any reasonably foreseeable reform efforts. Third, the case-by-case nature of competition law adjudication means that it is a superior policy tool to generally applicable patent rules for making fine

[79] FM Scherer, *Industrial Market Structure and Economic Performance* (First, Houghton Mifflin 1980) 448.

adjustments to the balance between static and dynamic efficiencies in individual cases. Even after successful efforts to reform the patent system to address the aforementioned issues, there is always going to be a role for competition law to play in recalibrating the policy balance underlying the patent–competition interface, just as Lemley has convincingly argued.

3. The Availability of Other Forms of Appropriation Mechanism to Recoup R&D Investments

A further reason to believe that dynamic efficiency considerations can be deemphasized without much concomitant loss of innovation incentives is that economists have noted that there are many mechanisms through which an innovator can appropriate the value of her innovation. Patent protection is only one of them. An innovator may choose to keep her innovation secret and rely on trade secrecy to maintain her competitive advantage. This would be particularly effective if the technology cannot be easily reverse engineered, as in the case of a process innovation. Competitors are unlikely to be able to decipher a cost-cutting technology simply from the appearance of the final product. For such an innovation, trade secrecy may more than suffice as an appropriation mechanism. The innovator need not incur the costs to secure a patent.

Apart from trade secrecy, an innovator may resort to what are known as first-mover advantages. The first firm to commercialize a new technology may enjoy a period of lead time over rivals simply due to the time it takes for rivals to replicate the technology. The amount of time that rivals need to replicate the innovator's technology through imitation is called the imitation lag.[80] The longer this imitation lag, the more time the innovator will have to charge supra-competitive prices to recoup her R&D investments before a new entrant emerges. The imitation lag could be so long that the innovator recoups her private costs of innovation without resorting to patent protection. This is likely to be the case for innovations that are not particularly costly to create. Edwin Mansfield establishes the time-consuming and resource-intensive nature of imitation through a number of empirical studies.[81] He finds that imitation costs are usually about 65 per cent of the innovation costs and that it usually takes 70 per cent of the time spent on the original innovation to imitate it. If it took the original innovator five years to create the innovation, it would take the imitating firm three-and-a-half years to reproduce it. In fact, Mansfield finds that in one-seventh of the cases surveyed in his study imitation costs are no

[80] Sidney Winter, 'Appropriating the Gains from Innovation' in George Day and Paul Schoemaker (eds), *Wharton on Managing Emerging Technologies* (Wiley 2000) 242, 250–51.

[81] Edwin Mansfield, Mark Schwartz, and Samuel Wagner, 'Imitation Costs and Patents: An Empirical Study' (1981) 91 The Economic Journal 907; Edwin Mansfield, 'Patents and Innovation: An Empirical Study' (1986) 32 Management Science 173.

smaller than innovation costs. Imitation is not as costless or instantaneous as it is often assumed to be. The significant imitation lag that exists in most cases would give the innovator considerable time to recoup her initial investments.

This first-mover advantage can be enhanced through product differentiation strategies. Marketing and promotion would help the innovator to develop brand loyalty among consumers, which would allow her to hold on to part of her supra-competitive profit even after market entry by competitors. Aside from reinforcing the first-mover advantage, sales and marketing efforts separately constitute a distinct appropriation mechanism.[82] Such efforts would help the innovator to recoup her R&D costs regardless of the magnitude of the first-mover advantage. While brand loyalty can be developed among consumers through marketing and promotion, learning curve advantages allow the innovator to stay ahead of imitating rivals in the production process and maintain an edge in technical skills and know-how.[83] These are advantages that accrue to an innovator by virtue of being the pioneer for the product.

A number of economic studies have found that the degree of reliance on patent protection as an appropriation mechanism varies by the type of innovation and industry at issue. Process innovation is known to be much less reliant on patent protection than product innovation. This is mainly because while it is possible to reverse engineer a product innovation from the physical product, it is very difficult to do the same with process innovation. This may explain the result from one of the most exhaustive studies on appropriation mechanisms for innovators, the so-called Yale survey, in which Richard Levin and co-authors find that patents are the least effective appropriation mechanism for process innovation.[84] Patent protection is rated behind lead time, learning-curve advantages, and trade secrecy as an appropriation mechanism for process innovations.[85] Patent protection is rated ahead of trade secrecy, but rated substantially behind lead time, learning-curve advantages, and sales and marketing as an appropriation mechanism for product innovations.[86] 80 per cent of the sampled businesses give sales and service effort a 5.0 out of a 7-point scale in effectiveness as an appropriation mechanism.[87] Only 20 per cent of the sampled businesses give patents the same rating.[88]

The relative lack of reliance of process innovation on patent protection was further underscored by a study by Silvana Krasteva, in which she shows that R&D incentives for non-drastic process innovation (innovation that does not render existing technology obsolete) are maximized at intermediate levels of protection

82 Klevorick and others (n 42) 795.
83 ibid.
84 ibid 794–95.
85 ibid.
86 ibid 795.
87 ibid 796.
88 ibid.

where some imitation is allowed.[89] The reasoning is that when the innovation is non-drastic, the innovator benefits from imitation by competitors as 'imitation involves an efficiency gain from a competing firm's use of the superior patented technology. For intermediate levels of protection, the innovator and the imitator share in this efficiency gain in a way that makes both of them better off under imitation.[90]

Apart from the type of innovation, studies have also shown that the degree of reliance on patent protection as an appropriation mechanism varies by the industry. The Yale survey classifies the 100 manufacturing industries surveyed in their study into three clusters.[91] The first cluster, consisting of food products and metal products, among others, seems to rely exclusively on sales and marketing as an appropriation mechanism.[92] The second cluster deploys a wider range of appropriation mechanisms, including first-mover advantages, learning curve advantages, and secrecy.[93] The third cluster, which mainly consists of pharmaceuticals and chemicals, is the only group that utilizes patent protection extensively.[94] These results are consistent with Mansfield's findings which show that the pharmaceuticals and chemicals industries rely much more on patent protection as an appropriation mechanism than other industries.[95]

There are reasons why patent protection is more important to the pharmaceuticals and chemicals industries. Both industries are marked by low appropriability, meaning that appropriation of investment returns is difficult absent government intervention. This is because technology in both industries tends to be relatively codifiable and requires relatively little tacit knowledge to implement, hence rendering it susceptible to imitation. This means that both imitation costs and imitation lag are low. However, imitation in both industries is highly profitable. The amount of R&D investment in both industries tends to be very high and the profit potential for products in both industries, especially pharmaceuticals, tends to be significant. The demand for medications tends to be inelastic and the market structure for the industry highly concentrated.[96] High profit potential and low appropriability together lead to a high level of dependence on patent protection. Industries that do not share these characteristics are unlikely to rely on patent protection to the same extent.

These results have been corroborated in a subsequent study, known as the Carnegie Mellon survey, in which Wesley Cohen and co-authors update the results

[89] Silvana Krasteva, 'Imperfect Patent Protection and Innovation' (2014) 62 Journal of Industrial Economics 682.
[90] ibid 683.
[91] Klevorick and others (n 42) 801.
[92] ibid.
[93] ibid 801.
[94] ibid 801–02.
[95] Mansfield, Schwartz, and Wagner (n 81) 174.
[96] FM Scherer, 'A Note on Global Welfare in Pharmaceutical Patenting' (2004) 27 World Economy 1127, 1135.

of the Yale survey and reach largely similar results.[97] They assert that patents 'are unambiguously the least central of the major appropriability mechanisms overall'[98] and that 'in no industry are patents identified as the most effective appropriability mechanism'.[99] Similar to the Yale survey, they observe industry variations in reliance on patents as an appropriation mechanism. Patents are particularly important for a number of industries such as pharmaceuticals, chemicals, medical equipment, and computers.[100] Importantly, firms obtain patent protection for strategic reasons, especially in complex product industries such as information and communication technologies (ICT) as opposed to discrete product industries such as pharmaceuticals and chemicals. Almost 55 per cent of the respondents in complex product industries report that they seek patent protection to gain leverage in negotiations with rivals.[101] Therefore, it cannot be taken for granted that patent protection leads to innovation. Firms patent for a variety of reasons that have nothing to do with protecting their innovation.

The conclusions from the Yale and the Carnegie Mellon surveys have been corroborated by other survey studies undertaken in the United States, the United Kingdom, and Europe. They further cast doubt on the notion that patent protection is necessary to generate and sustain innovation incentives. In a subsequent paper following the Carnegie Mellon survey, Cohen and co-authors again find that patents are the least effective among all the appropriation mechanisms in the United States but are comparatively effective in Japan.[102] They conclude that institutions, policies, cultures, and norms all have a bearing on appropriability conditions, intra-industry R&D information flows, and other R&D spillovers, which shape the incentive to seek patent protection.[103]

A subsequent survey that focuses on start-ups, the Berkeley Patent Survey, also reaches the same result.[104] The survey covered 1,332 start-ups founded between 1998 and 2008.[105] Executives reported that patents offer a 'slight' to 'moderate' incentive to innovate.[106] There are again industry differences in terms of reliance on patents. Patents are the most important appropriation mechanism for biotechnology start-ups and the second most important mechanism after first mover

[97] Wesley M Cohen, Richard Nelson, and John P Walsh, 'Protecting Their Intellectual Assets: Appropriability Conditions and Why U.S. Manufacturing Firms Patent (or Not)' (National Bureau of Economic Research, Inc 2000) NBER Working Paper 7552 <https://econpapers.repec.org/paper/nbrnberwo/7552.htm> accessed 5 April 2019.

[98] ibid 9.

[99] ibid.

[100] ibid.

[101] ibid 19.

[102] Wesley M Cohen and others, 'R&D Spillovers, Patents and the Incentives to Innovate in Japan and the United States' (2002) 31 Research Policy 1349, 1359.

[103] ibid 1364.

[104] Stuart JH Graham and others, 'High Technology Entrepreneurs and the Patent System: Results of the 2008 Berkeley Patent Survey' (2009) 24 Berkeley Technology Law Journal 1255.

[105] ibid 1272.

[106] ibid 1285.

advantages for medical devices and IT hardware.[107] Patents, however, are the least effective appropriation mechanism for software start-ups.[108]

The same conclusion extends to small firms in Europe. Anthony Arundel focuses on a comparison between trade secrets and patents as appropriation mechanisms and finds that European firms of all sizes value trade secrets over patents as an appropriation mechanism.[109] For product innovations, the reliance on trade secrets seems to be greater for smaller firms than for larger firms.[110] Firms of varying sizes seem to value trade secrets similarly as an appropriation mechanism as far as process innovation is concerned.[111] Lastly, R&D intensity has no bearing on a firm's relative reliance on trade secrets and patents.[112]

Small firms in the United Kingdom hold the same attitude toward patents as their European counterparts. In a recent survey, Bronwyn Hall and co-authors find that only 4 per cent of British firms that engage in innovation obtained patent protection.[113] They report that firms do not prefer formal IP over informal IP (which the authors did not expressly define in their paper but it seems to refer to trade secret protection) and that 'general innovation of any kind is negatively associated with a preference for patents over secrecy or formal IP over informal IP'.[114] Unsurprisingly, process innovation is less likely than product innovation to be patented.[115] Although the low percentage of UK firms in the survey that rely on patent protection can be partially explained by the size, earlier studies nonetheless show that close to half of large firms eschew patents.[116]

Commentators have also cited anecdotal evidence to cast doubt on the importance of patents as an appropriation mechanism. Using the smartphone industry as an example, Michele Boldrin and David Levine, long-standing critics of the patent system, argue that in many emerging innovative industries, first-mover advantages provide sufficient returns to innovators even without patent protection.[117] They further contend that the political economy of the patent system is such that it will always be captured by rent-seekers and will never be able to perform the functions that it is meant to perform.[118] Further examples of successful innovations that did

107 ibid 1290.
108 ibid.
109 Anthony Arundel, 'The Relative Effectiveness of Patents and Secrecy for Appropriation' (2001) 30 Research Policy 611, 615.
110 ibid 617.
111 ibid.
112 ibid.
113 Bronwyn H Hall and others, 'The Importance (or Not) of Patents to UK Firms' (2013) Working Paper 19089 <https://www.nber.org/system/files/working_papers/w19089/w19089.pdf> accessed 29 July 2021.
114 ibid 4.
115 ibid.
116 ibid 22.
117 Michele Boldrin and David K Levine, 'The Case Against Patents' (2013) 27 Journal of Economic Perspectives 3, 10–11.
118 ibid 14–18.

not rely on patent protection can be found across eras, from the Cornish Pumping Engine during the Industrial Revolution[119] to financial products such as derivatives launched by investment banks.[120] The latter in particular seems to rely on first-mover advantages, which gave firms such as Goldman Sachs and JP Morgan lasting advantages over competitors in their respective class of financial products, to generate rent for the innovator.[121]

Peter Moser observes that the introduction of plant patents did not lead to increased innovation in food technology and notes that nearly half of the plant patents filed in the United States between 1930 and 1970 were related to roses.[122] Patents historically did not play a very important role in attracting innovation. Data from the world's fairs between 1851 and 1915 indicate that countries without patent laws were as innovative as countries with patent law, although their innovations tended to be concentrated in industries in which trade secrecy was a feasible appropriation mechanism.[123] Their innovations were of comparable quality.[124] To underscore the relative unimportance of patent protection, Moser finds that 89 per cent of the British exhibits exhibited at the world's fairs between 1851 and 1915 were unpatented.[125]

Marcus Holgersson and Martin Wallin move beyond empirical analysis to examine the issue from a theoretical perspective. They put forward a theoretical framework comparing what they call the patent management trichotomy of patenting, publishing (disclosure of technical knowledge), and trade secrecy along the dimensions of appropriation advantage and freedom to operate.[126] Freedom to operate refers to a firm's ability to act in the market free from constraints imposed by other firms such as through patenting.[127] Patenting is not always the superior technological management strategy. Secrecy generates direct appropriation advantages while publishing provides static freedom to operate.[128] They caution that 'patent management is not only about patenting, it is also about considering alternative strategies such as publishing and secrecy'.[129]

[119] Alessandro Nuvolari, 'Collective Invention during the British Industrial Revolution: The Case of the Cornish Pumping Engine', Paper prepared for the DRUID Winter Conference, Copenhagen (18–20 January 2001) <https://silo.tips/download/collective-invention-during-the-british-industrial-revolution-the-case-of-the-co> accessed 29 July 2021 .

[120] Helios Herrera and Enrique Schroth, 'Profitable Innovation Without Patent Protection: The Case of Derivatives' (2003) Discussion Paper 03-02 <https://ftp.itam.mx/pub/academico/inves/herrera/03-02.pdf> accessed 29 July 2021 .

[121] ibid 26.

[122] Petra Moser, 'Patents and Innovation: Evidence from Economic History' (2013) 27 Journal of Economic Perspectives 23, 28–29.

[123] ibid 26–27.

[124] ibid.

[125] Petra Moser, 'Innovation without Patents: Evidence from World's Fairs' (2012) 55 Journal of Law & Economics 43, 54.

[126] Marcus Holgersson and Martin W Wallin, 'The Patent Management Trichotomy: Patenting, Publishing, and Secrecy' (2017) 55 Management Decision 1087, 1093.

[127] ibid 1088.

[128] ibid 1094.

[129] ibid.

To sum up, the foregoing discussion establishes that the patent system has a tendency to overcompensate innovators by failing to match patentee reward with the private costs or even the social value of innovation. This suggests that less deference can be shown to dynamic efficiency considerations within the patent–competition interface. Minor adjustments to the scope of patent rights can be made without significant impact on innovation incentives. This would be especially the case if the particular type of innovation at issue does not heavily rely on patents as an appropriation mechanism. Economic studies have demonstrated that different industries exhibit varying degrees of reliance on the patent system as an appropriation mechanism. There are industry-specific variations in the degree of reliance on the patent system. This suggests that developing countries may need to develop an industry-specific approach to the patent–competition interface to take these variations into account.

4. The Mismatch between Innovation Incentives Generated by the Patent System and the Technological Capacity of Developing Countries

(a) Technological capacity of developing countries

The last reason to be leery of attaching too much weight to dynamic efficiency considerations in the patent–competition interface in developing countries is that a developing country may simply not be in a position to take advantage of the innovation incentives generated by its patent system. Developing countries vary in terms of their domestic technological capacity. As Daniel Benoliel notes, '[e]vidence increasingly shows that developing countries differ not only in their propensity to attract FDI [foreign direct investment], trade, and technology, but also in their ability to innovate'.[130] Many developing countries have relatively low intensity of R&D activity as well as low quality of R&D activity compared to the industrialized economies.[131] It may risk stating the obvious to point out that innovation incentives would only spur innovation if there were potential innovators in the country to take advantage of those incentives.

Countries can be roughly classified into three categories as far as their technological capacity is concerned. The first group consists of countries with the capacity to engage in not much beyond basic production and perhaps implementation of rudimentary technology. These countries do not innovate or adapt foreign technology. Jeffrey Sachs has called these countries 'the marginalized, which include the Andean part of South America, almost all of sub-Saharan Africa, and large

[130] Daniel Benoliel, *Patent Intensity and Economic Growth* (Cambridge University Press 2017) 49–50.
[131] ibid 145.

Table 2.1 Table Showing Classification of Developing Countries by Technological Capacity

Group	The Marginalized	The Technological Diffusers	The Innovators
Type of capacity	Production	Imitation/Technology absorption	Innovation
Countries	South America (Andean part), Sub-Saharan Africa, and large parts of Central and South Asia	China, India, a large part of Latin America, and parts of Eastern Europe and the former Soviet Union	North America, most of western and northern Europe, Japan

parts of Central and South Asia'.[132] These countries are said to possess only a basic production capacity. The second group consists of countries with the capacity to absorb foreign technology either through voluntary technology transfer or imitation, but not the capacity to innovate and produce its own new technology. Sachs calls these the technological diffusers, and includes in this group China, India, a large part of Latin America, and parts of Eastern Europe and the former Soviet Union.[133] These countries are said to possess an imitation or technology adaptation capacity. The third group consists of countries with the capacity to innovate along the global technological frontier. They are the innovators that enjoy endogenous growth, 'in which innovative activity takes place on a significant scale, and patented products and technologies are produced and sold domestically and on world markets'.[134] These countries are said to possess an innovation capacity.

Countries with an innovation capacity clearly would respond to the innovation incentives created by their own patent system. Dynamic efficiency considerations matter in these countries. Countries with only a production capacity are incapable of genuine innovation and are so far from acquiring an innovation capacity that dynamic efficiency considerations can be largely discounted. Countries with an imitation or technology adaptation capacity rely on technology importation for technological progress and will want to facilitate technology transfer as much as possible. Some of these countries may possess innovation capacity in certain industries and may need to pay heed to innovation incentives as well.

The fact that the importance of dynamic efficiency considerations varies in accordance with the country's technological capacity is encapsulated in a U-shape relationship between per capita income and patent protection. Technological

132 Jeffrey Sachs, 'The Global Innovation Divide' in Adam Jaffe, Josh Lerner, and Scott Stern (eds), *Innovation Policy and the Economy*, vol 3 (National Bureau of Economic Research 2003) 131, 133.

133 ibid.

134 ibid 132–33.

capacity is presumed to correlate positively with per capita income, which is by and large true. Prior to the TRIPS Agreement (Agreement on Trade-Related Aspects of Intellectual Property Rights), which mandates a minimum level of patent protection among all signatory countries, economists consistently find that the amount of patent protection offered in a country follows a U-shape relationship with its level of development as measured by per capita income. Keith Maskus and co-authors describe this relationship as follows:

> The poorest countries allocate virtually no resources to invention and innovation and have little intellectual property to protect. As incomes and technical capabilities grow to moderate levels, some inventive capacity emerges, particularly of the adaptive kind, but competition remains based on imitation, and the majority of economic and political interests prefer weak protection. As an economy develops, additional inventive capacity and demands for high-quality products emerge, and more firms lobby for effective protection, a process that is abetted by foreign firms interested in servicing growing markets. Finally, protection shifts up sharply at the highest level of income.[135]

The relatively high levels of patent protection at the lowest levels of income are attributed to past colonial influences. Many poor developing countries inherited intellectual property laws which maintained a fairly high level of protection from their European colonial masters.[136] With no domestic imitators to clamour for laxer intellectual property laws to facilitate imitation, these poorest countries have persisted with the legacy level of protection. As domestic producers begin to acquire technological capacity and seek to replicate foreign technologies, they push for lower levels of protection. The level of protection is shown to reach its nadir at USD2,000 per capita at 1985 prices and to remain at that level until income rises to USD8,000 per capita at 1985 prices, when domestic producers begin to acquire innovation capacity and lobby for stricter patent protection.[137] These results corroborate the notion that dynamic efficiency considerations tend to grow in importance as income rises and the country industrializes. However, with the advent of the TRIPS Agreement, developing countries have ratcheted up their level of patent protection across the board[138] and such a U-shape relationship is no longer observed.[139]

[135] Keith Maskus and others, 'Intellectual Property Rights and Economic Development in China' in Mario Cimoli and others (eds), *Intellectual Property and Development* (Oxford University Press 2005) 298.

[136] Commission on Intellectual Property Rights, 'Integrating Intellectual Property Rights and Development Policy' (2002) 22 <www.iprcommission.org/papers/pdfs/final_report/CIPRfullfinal.pdf> accessed 5 April 2019.

[137] ibid.

[138] Walter Park and Douglas Lippoldt, 'International Licensing and the Strengthening of Intellectual Property Rights in Developing Countries During the 1990s' (2005) 40 OECD Economic Studies 7, 10.

[139] Commission on Intellectual Property Rights (n 136) 22.

History is replete with examples of countries which lowered their level of patent protection to facilitate domestic technology acquisition. The patent system in Japan was designed to facilitate technology transfer until the 1980s, when the country emerged as a technological powerhouse.[140] It was only reformed to focus on protecting innovation once Japan had emerged as a major innovator.[141] Switzerland adopted a similar strategy and did not introduce a patent system until its domestic watchmakers had established themselves as technological leaders and were threatened by imitators.[142] The domestic chemical and textile industries, however, remained reliant on foreign technology and opposed the introduction of a patent system.[143] As a compromise, the Swiss patent system initially only protected mechanical inventions, which would benefit the watchmaking industry, but not chemical inventions, which would have stopped the domestic chemical manufacturers from adopting foreign technology.[144] Switzerland did not extend patent protection to chemical compounds until 1907, after Germany had threatened trade sanctions.[145]

While the production and the innovation countries face fairly clear policy choices with respect to dynamic efficiency considerations, the middle group of countries may confront a dilemma. These countries can be further divided into two groups. The first group consists of countries that only possess the capacity to absorb or imitate foreign technology. These may be called the imitation or technology adaptation countries. Frontier innovation, or genuine innovation along the global technological frontier, is out of their reach. Innovation in the domestic context only encompasses absorption and adaptation of foreign technology. Dynamic efficiency considerations for these countries should not focus on encouraging frontier innovation, but on facilitating technology transfer from developed countries.

The second group consists of countries that may possess some innovation capacity or are on the cusp of developing such capacity in some industries. They may be close enough to acquiring innovation capacity that the extra financial incentives provided by the patent system may propel domestic firms to make the final push toward innovation. Dynamic efficiency considerations for these countries are concerned with encouraging frontier innovation in some industries while facilitating foreign technology transfer in some others. These may be called the

[140] Keith Maskus, *Intellectual Property Rights in the Global Economy* (Institute for International Economics 2000) 143.

[141] ibid.

[142] Ove Granstrand, 'Innovation and Intellectual Property Rights' in Jan Fagerberg, David Mowery, and Richard Nelson (eds), *The Oxford Handbook of Innovation* (Oxford University Press 2006) 270–71.

[143] Petra Moser, 'How Do Patent Laws Influence Innovation? Evidence from Nineteenth-Century World's Fairs' (2005) 95 The American Economic Review 1214, 1220.

[144] Granstrand (n 142) 271.

[145] ibid.

proto-innovation countries. For instance, China, India, and a few other developing countries are said to have world-class capacity in 'space, nuclear energy, computing, biotechnology, pharmaceuticals, software development and aviation'.[146] It would be a mistake to overlook their innovation or proto-innovation capacity and adopt an inappropriate policy stance towards the patent–competition interface. Industry-by-industry analysis may be needed.

(b) Classification according to technological capacities

While determining the technological capacity of a country is fraught with difficulty and every measure of innovative effort and output suffers its own drawbacks, some commentators have attempted to identify the proto-innovation developing countries. Shamnad Basheer and Annalisa Primi rely on two indicators to measure the technological capacity of developing countries.[147] They identify two important dimensions of technological capacity: innovative effort and technological capabilities, and use R&D expenditure as a percentage of gross domestic product (GDP) and the share of medium- or high-technology products in total manufacturing value added respectively to quantify these two dimensions.[148] They call countries that demonstrate sufficient innovative effort and technological capabilities 'technologically proficient developing countries (TPDCs)'.[149] These include Russia, Taiwan, China, India, Brazil, South Africa, Ukraine, Malaysia, Belarus, Argentina, Mexico, Turkey, Chile, and Indonesia.[150]

Another way to measure innovation output is patent count. Patent count is by no means the perfect measurement of genuine innovation. Firms may patent for reasons that have nothing to do with protecting genuine innovations. They may do so for defensive purposes or to fulfil government policy requirements, as alleged to be the case in China. They may also apply for multiple patents for different aspects of the same innovation, which may result in double-counting or even multiple-counting of innovations. Nonetheless, patent counts are the most readily accessible statistic for a country's innovative output. What follows is an attempt to identify proto-innovation countries using patent counts.

The World Intellectual Property Organization (WIPO) publishes an annual report on the number of patent applications by and grants to both domestic and foreign applicants across the world. This report provides a sense of the innovative activity and output of developing countries. WIPO reports that in 2017, China originated the greatest number of patent applications worldwide, filing more than

[146] Shamnad Basheer and Annalisa Primi, 'The WIPO Development Agenda: Factoring in the 'Technologically Proficient Developing Countries' in Jeremy DeBeer (ed), *Implementing WIPO's Development Agenda* (Wilfred Laurier University Press 2008) 100, 104.

[147] ibid 105.

[148] ibid 106.

[149] ibid 102.

[150] ibid 105.

twice as many applications as the United States.[151] China was responsible for more than 1.38 million out of the total number of some 3.17 million patent applications worldwide.[152] This is to be contrasted with the patent applications from low-income and lower middle-income countries. They together only accounted for 4.4 per cent of the patent applications across the globe that year.[153] Discounting the three innovation outliers of China, the United States, and Japan, in general, high-income countries received almost four-and-a-half times as many applications as upper middle-income countries, which in turn received somewhat less than twice as many applications as lower-middle income countries, which in turn received almost eight times as many patent applications as low-income countries.

The number of patent applications received, however, may not provide an accurate indication of domestic innovation capacity. What matters is the number of applications originated domestically. Once China is excluded from the upper middle-income countries, the percentage of resident patent applications for the four income groups, from low to high, were 83.1 per cent, 30 per cent, 42.8 per cent, and 58.6 per cent respectively. The average number of resident patent applications for the four income groups were 437, 739, 1,358, and 15,450 respectively. To the extent that the number of domestic patent applications is a reliable indicator of technological capacity, one can see a considerable gulf in the technological capacity between industrialized economies on the one hand and developing countries on the other.

Statistics from the number of patent grants largely confirm the trends observed in patent applications. In 2017, 1,404,600 patents were granted worldwide, of which 62.3 per cent were granted in high-income countries, 29.9 per cent were granted in China, 5.5 per cent in upper middle-income countries excluding China, 1.7 per cent in lower middle-income countries, and 0.5 per cent in low-income countries. The total percentage of patents granted in low-income and lower middle-income countries was just above 2 per cent of the global total, and the total percentage of patents granted in developing countries excluding China was no more than 8 per cent of the global total. Industrialized economies accounted for 57.3 per cent of patents granted to resident innovators. China accounted for 37.7 per cent. The remaining 5 per cent was shared among all other developing countries. The average number of patents granted to resident innovators and overall can be calculated for each of the four income groups. China again is excluded from the upper middle-income countries to produce a more accurate picture. The average number of patents granted in each of the four income groups, from low to high, were 650, 612, 1707, and 15,096 respectively. The average number of patents granted to resident

[151] World Intellectual Property Organization, 'Filings for Patents, Trademarks, Industrial Designs Reach New Records in 2017' <https://www.wipo.int/pressroom/en/articles/2018/article_0012.html> accessed 6 April 2019.

[152] ibid.

[153] World Intellectual Property Organization, *World Intellectual Property Indicators 2018* (2018) 39.

innovators in each of the four income groups, from low to high, were 345, 136, 721, and 8,421 respectively. These figures show a yawning gap between industrialized economies and developing countries as a whole, excluding China.

Overall, the figures from the WIPO 2017 Report confirm that developing countries, with the notable exception of China, have considerably weaker technological capacity than industrialized economies. Based on the number of patent applications and grants in 2017, developing countries with significant technological capacity, or the proto-innovation countries, can be identified. Using the figure for the lower middle-income developing countries of 739 as the threshold, the following developing countries can be considered technological adaptation countries: Brazil (5,480), India (14,961), Indonesia (2,271), Iran (15,264), Kazakhstan (1,055), Malaysia (1,166), Mexico (1,334), Romania (1,098), Russian Federation (22,777), Saudi Arabia (909), Thailand (979), Turkey (8,175), Ukraine (2,271), and China.[154] Using the average number of resident patent applications from the upper middle-income developing countries of 1,358 as the threshold, only Brazil (5,480), India (14,961), Indonesia (2,271), Iran (15,264), Russian Federation (22,777), Turkey (8,175), Ukraine (2,283), and of course China can be deemed to have significant innovation capacity.[155] These can be deemed as the proto-innovation countries.

The same exercise can be repeated using the number of patent grants to resident innovators. Using the threshold of 136 for lower middle-income countries, the following countries can be said to have technological adaptation capacity: Argentina (176), Belarus (771), Brazil (714), Chile (161), Colombia (166), India (1,712), Iran (3,668), Iraq (323), Kazakhstan (650), Malaysia (437), Mexico (407), Romania (396), Russian Federation (21,037), South Africa (595), Sudan (165), Turkey (1,757), Ukraine (1,224), and China.[156] Using the stricter threshold of the average number of resident patent grants in upper middle-income countries in 2017 of 721, only Belarus (771), India (1,712), Iran (3,668), Russian Federation (21,037), Turkey (1,757), Ukraine (1,516), and China can be said to have significant innovation capacity and constitute proto-innovation countries.[157]

Combining the two lists, Brazil, India, Indonesia,[158] Iran, Kazakhstan, Malaysia, Mexico, Romania, Russian Federation, Turkey, Ukraine, and China can be considered the technological adaptation countries, while only India, Iran, Russian Federation, Turkey, Ukraine, and China can be said to have significant innovation capacity and qualify as the proto-innovation countries. Thus even with the more generous thresholds of the average for lower middle-income countries, only 12 of the 140 developing countries under the World Bank classification can be said to

[154] ibid 85–89.
[155] ibid.
[156] ibid 90–94.
[157] ibid.
[158] Note that the number of resident patent grants in 2017 is not available for Indonesia.

possess the technological capacity for adaptation of foreign technologies. Only six can be considered as genuine innovators or proto-innovation countries.

There is significant overlap between the countries on this list and the ones identified by Basheer and Primi.[159] Combining the two, the list of technological adaptation countries includes: Argentina, Belarus, Brazil, Chile, Indonesia, Kazakhstan, Malaysia, Mexico, Romania, and South Africa. Taiwan is excluded because the World Bank no longer classifies Taiwan as a developing country.[160] And the proto-innovation countries include India, Iran, Russian Federation, Turkey, Ukraine, and China. To the extent that these countries possess varying technological capacity in different industries, an industry-specific approach to the patent–competition interface may be required.

The foregoing classification should only be taken as an illustration. The point here is not to come up with a precise classification of countries; ultimately each country can assess its own technological capacity and self-categorize. The point is to demonstrate that developing countries should adopt approaches to the patent–competition interface tailored to their own technological capacity. For the sake of completeness, two other ways to classify countries based on their technological capacity will be mentioned. These include the classification put forward by Benoliel, which uses a more comprehensive measure of innovation but covers a smaller list of countries,[161] and the WIPO Global Innovation Index.[162]

Benoliel measures the innovative performance of countries within the framework of endogenous growth theory, which forecasts the convergence of country coalitions to 'multiple innovation-based growth equilibria'.[163] He puts forward the concept of patent intensity, which is based on propensity to patent and Gross Domestic Expenditure on R&D (GERD) intensity rates, as a proxy for the extent of domestic innovation.[164] Propensity to patent is defined as 'the percentage of patentable inventions that are in fact patented'.[165] His classification consists of a clustering analysis of seventy-nine countries 'based on yearly data series between 1996 and 2013'.[166] Propensity to patent is measured by 'the rate of issued patents . . . with the United States Patent and Trademark Office (USPTO) and European Patent Office (EPO) patents listed by inventor country search categories'.[167] GERD intensity in turn measures 'the sum and rate of supply of R&D.[168]

159 These include Russia, Taiwan, China, India, Brazil, South Africa, Ukraine, Malaysia, Belarus, Argentina, Mexico, Turkey, Chile, and Indonesia.

160 World Bank, 'World Bank Country and Lending Groups – World Bank Data Help Desk' <https://datahelpdesk.worldbank.org/knowledgebase/articles/906519-world-bank-country-and-lending-groups> accessed 6 April 2019.

161 Benoliel (n 130).

162 Cornell University, INSEAD and World Intellectual Property Organization, 'Global Innovation Index 2020—Who Will Finance Innovation?' (World Intellectual Property Organization 2020).

163 Benoliel (n 130) 46.

164 ibid.

165 ibid 47.

166 ibid 62.

167 ibid.

168 ibid.

He classifies these seventy-nine countries into three categories, which he calls patent clusters: the 'Leaders', the 'Followers', and the 'Marginalized',[169] which roughly equate the innovation countries, the technological adaptation countries, and the production countries respectively. There were 21 countries in the Leaders category, 32 countries in the Followers category, and 26 countries in the Marginalized category.[170] The Leader countries are characterized by high patent count by GERD and high GERD.[171] Examples include the United States, Germany, Japan, and South Korea.[172] The Follower countries are those with a low patent count by GERD but not a low GERD.[173] Examples include China, Russia, and Romania.[174] The Marginalized countries, unsurprisingly, are both low in terms of patent count by GERD and GERD itself.[175] These include Tajikistan, Burkina Faso, and Mongolia.[176]

We have previously identified Argentina, Belarus, Brazil, Chile, Indonesia, Kazakhstan, Malaysia, Mexico, Romania, and South Africa as possessing technological adaptation capacity. There seems to be a significant discrepancy between the foregoing classification and Benoliel's. It turns out that the main reason is that Benoliel's Follower countries are not exclusively developing countries. They include many high-income countries such as Australia, Spain, and Norway. He himself notes that his patent clusters do not correspond closely with the World Bank classification of developing countries.[177] There are twenty-two Follower developing countries. These include Belarus, Bulgaria, Brazil, China, Colombia, Croatia, Cuba, Egypt, India, Kazakhstan, Malaysia, Mexico, Morocco, Pakistan, Romania, Russia, Serbia, South Africa, Thailand, Tunisia, Turkey, and Ukraine.[178] Every country that was previously identified as possessing technological adaptation capacity is on Benoliel's list of Follower countries except for Chile and Indonesia, which are missing from his data set. And every country that was previously identified as either technological adaptation or proto-innovation is on his list except for Argentina and Iran. Despite some minor discrepancies, the overlap is significant.

WIPO publishes the Global Innovation Index (GII). The methodology of the Index is comprehensive and consists of some eighty indicators which fall into three categories in terms of nature of data: 'quantitative/objective/hard data', 'composite indicators/index data', and 'survey/qualitative/subjective/soft data'.[179] The objective hard data are drawn from a variety of public sources such as the United

[169] ibid 65.
[170] ibid.
[171] ibid 66.
[172] ibid.
[173] ibid.
[174] ibid.
[175] ibid.
[176] ibid.
[177] ibid 90.
[178] ibid 70.
[179] Cornell University, INSEAD and World Intellectual Property Organization (n 162) 369.

Nations Educational, Scientific and Cultural Organization (UNESCO), United Nations Industrial Development Organization (UNIDO), WIPO, and the World Bank.[180] The indicators can also be grouped into seven categories in terms of subject matter focus, namely institutions, human capital and research, infrastructure, market sophistication, business sophistication, knowledge & technology outputs, and creative outputs.[181] By way of example, there are indicators on government effectiveness and rule of law under institutions; expenditure on education and GERD as a percentage of GDP under human capital and research; government online service and electricity output under infrastructure; percentage of knowledge-intensive employment and FDI net inflows as a percentage of GDP under business sophistication; patents by origin and intellectual property receipts as a percentage of total trade under knowledge and technology outputs; and finally, trademarks by origin and creative good export as a percentage of total trade under creative outputs.[182]

In the 2020 GII rankings, the top twenty-two developing countries are (in the order of their ranking) China, Malaysia, Bulgaria, Vietnam, Thailand, Ukraine, Romania, Russian Federation, India, Montenegro, the Philippines, Turkey, Mauritius, Serbia, Mexico, Costa Rica, North Macedonia, Mongolia, Moldova, South Africa, Armenia, and Brazil.[183] There is quite a lot of overlap between this list and the Follower countries identified by Benoliel, yet one should not be surprised by the discrepancies between these two lists as the GII encompasses a much wider range of factors and is not solely focused on patent count and GERD. One can probably delve into the methodologies behind these two classifications to analyse and understand the differences in outcome. Again, the point is not to reconcile different classifications and come up with a definitive one; it is to illustrate the possibility of distinguishing and classifying developing countries based on their technological capacity.

The patent–competition interface will need to be handled with utmost care for the proto-innovation countries where both genuine domestic innovators and domestic imitators are present. The interests of the innovators and the imitators are likely to conflict at least in some instances as far as the patent–competition rules are concerned, the most obvious of which is the unilateral refusal to license intellectual property as a competition law violation. While the innovators would loathe compulsory licensing as it undermines the right to exclude bestowed upon them by the patent system, the imitators could benefit tremendously from it. In crafting the patent–competition rules, there needs to be a careful balancing of the interests of the domestic innovators and imitators.

[180] ibid.
[181] ibid 215.
[182] ibid.
[183] ibid xxxii.

(c) Empirical studies on the impact of increased patent protection on innovation

Aside from this small number of proto-innovation countries or TPDCs, as Basheer and Primi call them, patentee reward is unlikely to spur innovation in developing countries. Carlos Correa argues that

> [t]he impact of strengthened IPRs on domestic innovation in developing countries will depend strongly on the available scientific and technological capabilities. With the exception of a few developing countries which have been able to build up a reasonable R&D infrastructure . . . , most developing countries are unlikely to substantially improve their innovative performance just on the basis of an expanded and stronger IPRs regime.[184]

Economic studies, which will be discussed below, have repeatedly shown that when a developing country raises patent protection, which presumably raises patentee reward, the main impact is to increase patenting by foreign innovators. The impact on the domestic innovators has been shown to be negligible, if not negative in some instances. Entry of foreign innovators into the domestic market crowds out domestic potential innovators and causes their innovative activity to drop. These studies have also shown that there is a threshold in terms of per capita income below which increased patent protection does not enhance innovation incentives. To the extent that per capita income serves as a proxy for innovation capacity, this corroborates the earlier point that patentee reward will only create its desired effects when there are domestic innovators to take advantage of the innovation incentives.

Josh Lerner has undertaken a fairly comprehensive study of 177 significant changes in patent protection, both changes that increase and decrease protection, in 60 countries from 1852 to 1998. The changes he studies include extensions of patent duration and expansion of patentable subject matter. The objective of his study is to determine the impact of these changes in patent protection on the amount of innovative activity, as reflected by patent applications by both domestic and foreign innovators in their home jurisdiction and by domestic innovators in the United Kingdom, which serves as a control. The United Kingdom is chosen because of the relative constancy of its patent policy.[185] The event window is chosen to be five years before and after the change in the law.[186] The application data are normalized by the global patenting trends at the time of reform so that changes in patent applications are the result of the changes in the law and not of longer-term trends.[187]

[184] Carlos Correa, *Intellectual Property Rights, the WTO and Developing Countries: The TRIPS Agreement and Policy Options* (Zed Books—Third World Network 2000) 38.

[185] Josh Lerner, 'Patent Protection and Innovation Over 150 Years' (National Bureau of Economic Research 2002) Working Paper 8977 13 <http://www.nber.org/papers/w8977> accessed 6 April 2019.

[186] ibid 15.

[187] ibid 17–18.

Prior to the adjustment, Lerner finds that the number of domestic patent applications increases for both domestic and foreign innovators. There does not seem to be any change in the number of applications in the United Kingdom.[188] What is striking is that after adjustments, he finds that the number of foreign applications rises dramatically, while the number of domestic and British filings by domestic innovators drops.[189] Keith Maskus sums up Lerner's finding as follows:

> in most cases national patent reforms benefited international inventors, far more than domestic inventors, at least in the short term. Indeed, applications by domestic firms seemed to be crowded out, perhaps due to greater commercial competition from abroad.[190]

Patricia Higino Schneider studies the relationship between the level of patent protection, as encapsulated in this index often known as the Ginarte–Park Index compiled by Juan Carlos Ginarte and Walter Park, and innovation rate.[191] Her sample group includes nineteen developed and twenty-eight developing countries.[192] While she finds a moderately positive relationship between patent protection and innovation rate, as measured by the number of patent applications filed by residents of a particular country with US Patent and Trademark Office, the results diverge dramatically after the sample group is split into developed and developing countries.[193] While the relationship becomes strongly positive in developed countries, the relationship turns negative for developing countries.[194]

One of the potential flaws in these studies is reverse causality. These studies are meant to determine whether enhanced patent protection leads to greater propensity to patent. But it is possible that the causation flows in the opposite direction and that a greater propensity to patent causes potential patent owners to push for heightened protection. Some authors have tried to avoid this problem by shifting their study from the macro level to firm level, the assumption being that R&D investments at the firm level are unlikely to affect the level of patent protection nationwide. Brent Allred and Walter Park examine the relationship between the level of patent protection and what the authors call firm innovation investment, which is calculated by dividing R&D expenditures and sales.[195] The sample group consists

188 ibid 17.

189 ibid 19–20.

190 Keith Maskus, *Private Rights and Public Problems: The Global Economics of Intellectual Property in the 21st Century* (Peterson Institute for International Economics 2012) 47.

191 Patricia Higino Schneider, 'International Trade, Economic Growth and Intellectual Property Rights: A Panel Data Study of Developed and Developing Countries' (2005) 78 Journal of Development Economics 529.

192 ibid 534.

193 ibid 536, 538.

194 ibid 540–41.

195 Brent Allred and Walter Park, 'The Influence of Patent Protection on Firm Innovation Investment in Manufacturing Industries' (2007) 13 Journal of International Management 91, 97.

of 706 firms in 29 countries.[196] The Ginarte–Park Index is again used to measure the level of patent protection and changes in the level of protection.[197]

Allred and Park find that 'even after controlling for firm size, industry structure, and other national factors, a country's patent rights and changes in patent rights are positively related to domestic firm innovation investment'.[198] Importantly, the authors test for reverse causality and find that it is absent in the relationship between levels of patent protection and changes in the level of protection on the one hand and firm innovation investment on the other hand.[199] Allred and Park's results replicate the developed-developing country divide found in Lerner's study. It transpires that the positive relationship only holds true for developed countries. They find that the positive relationship remains significant for countries with per capita GDP that exceeded USD10,000 in 1995.[200] The relationship remains positive but becomes only marginally significant for firms located in developing countries.[201] This is consistent with the results from previous studies that patent protection only spurs innovation in countries with meaningful technological capacity.

Allred and Park conduct another study that attempts to determine the relationship between the level of patent protection as measured by the Ginarte–Park Index on the one hand and patent filings by domestic and foreign innovators and firm-level R&D expenditures on the other.[202] The patent filing data cover 100 countries from 1965 to 2000.[203] R&D expenditure data cover a sample of 2,446 firms from 35 countries.[204] Allred and Park find a U-shape relationship between the level of patent protection and domestic patent filings in the overall sample.[205] Once the sample is segregated into developed and developing countries, a generally positive relationship emerges between the level of patent protection and domestic patent filings in developed countries, and a significantly negative relationship for developing countries.[206] This causes the authors to conclude that 'the effects of patent reform depend on the stage of development. Patent rights have a positive effect on domestic patenting after a critical level of protection has been reached'.[207] Contrary to the results of Lerner's study, however, Allred and Park do not find increased patent protection to lead to a rise in patent filings by foreign innovators.[208]

196 ibid.
197 ibid.
198 ibid 101.
199 ibid 102.
200 ibid 103.
201 ibid.
202 Brent B Allred and Walter G Park, 'Patent Rights and Innovative Activity: Evidence from National and Firm-Level Data' (2007) 38 Journal of International Business Studies 878.
203 ibid 885.
204 ibid.
205 ibid 889.
206 ibid.
207 ibid.
208 ibid 892.

As for R&D expenditures, Allred and Park find that the level of patent protection has a U-shaped relationship with firm-level R&D in developed countries and 'no significant linear or nonlinear effect on firm-level R&D in developing countries'.[209] This result is doubly significant because patenting data may not always reflect the underlying innovative effort as not every innovation can be patented under domestic patent law and firms may choose to patent or not patent an innovation for a variety of reasons. This is especially the case in developing countries, where the level of innovation capacity may not reach a level that allows firms to produce patentable innovations. Instead, innovations in developing countries may only warrant protection as utility models. For instance, China, Russia, Ukraine, Turkey, Brazil, and Thailand are among the top ten countries with the highest number of utility model applications.[210] Developing countries together account for almost half of the top twenty countries with the highest number of utility model applications.[211] Domestic R&D expenditures, however, are a direct indication of the amount of innovative effort made by domestic firms. The two studies by Allred and Park together suggest that patent protection does not create the expected incentive effect on domestic innovative effort in developing countries.

Another study by Lee Branstetter and co-authors contradicts Allred and Park's finding and corroborates Lerner's conclusion that increased patent protection leads to a higher level of patenting by foreign innovators. Their study examines how patent reform events that raise patent protection influence the amount of technology transfer and resident and non-resident patenting in sixteen of mostly developing countries (Japan was the only exception).[212] Their study period spans almost two decades from 1982 to 1999 and the reform events hail from 1986 to 1997.[213] They find that technology transfer from developed country firms to developing countries clearly accelerated following the reform events.[214] They also find that the average number of patent filings by residents increased by 29 per cent from 26,239 in 1994 to 33,896 in 1999, and that the average number of non-resident patent filings increased by almost 200 per cent from 13,953 in 1994 to 41,482 in 1999.[215] Further regression analysis confirms that the reform events had no impact on resident patent filings but that at least 52 per cent of the increase in non-resident filings can be attributed to the reform events.[216] It is clear that increased patent

[209] ibid 893–94.
[210] World Intellectual Property Organization (n 153) 70.
[211] ibid.
[212] Lee Branstetter, Raymond Fisman, and C Fritz Foley, 'Do Stronger Intellectual Property Rights Increase International Technology Transfer? Empirical Evidence from U.S. Firm-Level Panel Data' (2006) 121 Quarterly Journal of Economics 321, 333.
[213] ibid 332, 334.
[214] ibid 334–39.
[215] ibid 332.
[216] ibid 342.

protection has a positive and significant impact on non-resident patent filings in developing countries.[217]

Findings of a negative or negligible impact on domestic patenting is not confined to developing countries. Mariko Sakakibara and Lee Branstetter have found the same result even in Japan, one of the most innovative countries in the world.[218] They study the impact of the 1988 reform to Japanese patent law on R&D expenditures and innovative output. The reform in particular consists of two components: (1) switching from allowing only one independent, single claim for each invention to permitting multiple, dependent claims, as is the case under US patent law; and (2) providing restoration of patent term of up to five years for time spent on obtaining drug approvals, including safety and efficacy tests.[219] These amount to fairly significant expansion of the scope of patent rights and should substantially raise patentee reward. In particular, the expansion of patent term for the pharmaceutical industry should lead to an increase in innovative activity, given the reliance of the industry on patent protection.

They conduct regression analysis to determine the impact of these reforms on the real R&D expenditure by 307 publicly traded Japanese manufacturing firms and find that the reforms had no impact on firm R&D spending.[220] They find that Japanese firms began to increase R&D spending in the early 1980s, but they had cut back by the time of the reform.[221] There was in fact a relative decline in R&D spending in 1988 and 1989.[222] They conclude that '[o]ne sees in this picture no evidence of an increase in R&D spending that could plausibly be attributed to patent reform'.[223] They use the number of US patent grants as another proxy of innovative activity because Japanese patent grants do not provide a reliable measure. While the number of Japanese patent applications decreases, the number of claims in each patent increases.[224] Similar to R&D expenditure, Sakakibara and Branstetter find that US patenting began to pick up in the early 1980s and there is no evidence of a reform-induced increase in patenting around the time of the reform. They conclude that '[t]here is no evidence from this of a patent reform-induced increase in innovative output'.[225]

Summarizing the results of these empirical studies, Maskus asserts that:

[217] ibid.

[218] Mariko Sakakibara and Lee Branstetter, 'Do Stronger Patents Induce More Innovation? Evidence from the 1988 Japanese Patent Law Reforms' (2001) 32 The RAND Journal of Economics 77.

[219] ibid 79.

[220] ibid 88.

[221] ibid.

[222] ibid.

[223] ibid.

[224] ibid 93.

[225] ibid 95.

> the medium-term effect of patent revisions is to attract more patent applications from abroad as multinational firms seek to exploit their inventions in more locations. Even in the average lower-income to middle-income countries it seems to take some time for any domestic responsiveness to emerge… legal patent reforms have little, if any, impacts on domestic innovation in poor countries. This lack of response is likely due to a mixture of factors, ranging from weak business and investment environments to poor governance to a virtual absence of IPRs enforcement.[226]

The fundamental premise of the patent system is that short-term static efficiency loss will be more than made up for by long-term dynamic efficiency gains. Once it is established that increased patent protection does not generate greater innovation incentives and produce higher innovative output, it should come as no surprise that the total welfare of these countries should suffer.

This has been corroborated by a number of economic studies for a range of developing countries of different sizes and at different levels of development. Alan Dearborn finds that extending patent protection to a country with little innovation capacity will result in a welfare loss to that country that outweighs the welfare gain to the innovation country.[227] In fact, he argues that extending patent protection across the world will lead to global welfare loss.[228] Arvind Subramanian has similarly found that the welfare of individual countries will be worse off as a result of extension of patent protection because static efficiency loss is not compensated for by dynamic efficiency gains.[229] Just as there is a minimum threshold of economic development and technological capacity above which patent protection will induce meaningful innovative activity, it has been suggested that a similar threshold exists for net welfare gains for raising intellectual property protection.[230]

The pharmaceuticals and chemicals industries particularly rely on patents as an appropriation mechanism. Therefore, one would expect the introduction of patent protection to have especially pronounced effect on the amount of innovative activity in these two industries, which exhibit a very strong tendency to patent their innovations given their susceptibility to imitation and reverse engineering. Increased patent protection should have a strong positive correlation with patenting in these two industries.

[226] Maskus, *Private Rights and Public Problems* (n 190) 63–64.

[227] Alan V Deardorff, 'Welfare Effects of Global Patent Protection' (1992) 59 Economica 35, 46–47.

[228] ibid 48.

[229] Arvind Subramanian, 'Trade-Related Intellectual Property Rights and Asian Developing Countries: An Analytical View' in Arvind Panagariya, Muhammad Ghulam Quibria, and Narhari Rao (eds), *The Global Trading System and Developing Asia* (Cambridge University Press 1997) 305, 328.

[230] Correa (n 184) 26.

Yi Qian sets out to verify this hypothesis in a study of twenty-six countries that introduced patent protection for pharmaceuticals between 1978 and 2002.[231] She uses citation-weighted US patent awards as the measure of innovation output.[232] The US is chosen presumably because the high patenting costs in the United States mean that only valuable innovations will be patented there. Somewhat surprisingly, Qian finds that the introduction of patent protection for pharmaceuticals had no impact on the number of US patents awarded to a particular country, suggesting that increased patent protection had no impact on innovative output.[233] She does, however, find that the introduction of patent protection increased the number of citation-weighted US patents subject to the country's level of development, education attainment, and degree of economic freedom.[234] Qian concludes that

> patents are important for innovation conditional on a country's development level. A more developed country with pharmaceutical patents is likely to have more innovations compared to a similarly developed country without patents, or a less developed country with patents.[235]

She also finds that in countries with higher educational attainment and greater economic freedom, the extension of patent protection to pharmaceuticals exerts a positive and significant impact on US patent awards.[236] Educational attainment is an indirect indicator of the human aspect of innovation capacity, and wealthier countries generally spend more on R&D. Her results together affirm the conclusion that increased patent protection will only lead to greater innovation in countries with the requisite innovation capacity.

In addition to cross-country studies, there have been a number of studies of the effects of the introduction of patent protection for pharmaceutical products on innovative output and overall welfare within individual countries. These are possible because a number of developed and developing countries did not introduce patent protection for pharmaceuticals until the late 1970s in the case of Italy and until after the adoption of TRIPS in the case of some developing countries. Economists are able to study the impact of the introduction of patent protection for pharmaceuticals in these countries.

FM Scherer and Sandy Weisburst study the impact of the introduction of patent protection for pharmaceuticals in Italy.[237] Italy did not introduce patent protection

231 Yi Qian, 'Do National Patent Laws Stimulate Domestic Innovation in a Global Patenting Environment? A Cross-Country Analysis of Pharmaceutical Patent Protection, 1978–2002' (2007) 89 The Review of Economics and Statistics 436.

232 ibid 444.

233 ibid 445.

234 ibid 446–47.

235 ibid 446.

236 ibid 447.

237 FM Scherer and Sandy Weisburst, 'Economic Effects of Strengthening Pharmaceutical Patent Protection in Italy' (1995) 26 International Review of Industrial Property and Copyright 1009.

for pharmaceuticals until the Italian Supreme Court declared in March 1978 that it was unconstitutional for a 1939 legislation to exclude pharmaceuticals from patentable subject matter.[238] Scherer and Weisburst find that (1) the patent reforms in Italy 'had little or no impact on the trend of inflation-adjusted R&D expenditures',[239] (2) there was no increase in the new pharmaceutical products introduced by Italian firms,[240] and (3) Italy suffered from a serious deterioration in the balance of trade for drugs as imports soared due to the surge in the import of patented pharmaceutical products from other European countries.[241] There was much consolidation in the Italian pharmaceutical industry following the introduction of patent protection, with much of it in the form of takeover of Italian firms by foreign pharmaceutical companies.[242] Italy's prominent generic industry began to decline over time and generic production slowly shifted to India, which has since taken over as the hub for generic drug production in the world.

The same sorry state of affairs was predicted for developing countries that introduced pharmaceutical patents following the TRIPS Agreement, which has largely been borne out by subsequent events. Correa concludes based on a number of economic studies of Lebanon, South Korea, and Argentina that pharmaceutical R&D in those countries were not expected to increase after the introduction of patent protection.[243] This is because 'the development of new chemical entities is outside the reach of local companies in any developing country, since there are no firms in such countries big enough (in terms of total sales) to finance the high costs of pharmaceutical R&D'.[244] Maskus shares a similar view, asserting that

> [f]ew, if any, firms in developing countries are likely to find it attractive to engage in fundamental R&D in competition with the major international research-based pharmaceutical companies, which have expertise in research and marketing and benefit from significant economies of scale.[245]

The lack of anticipated dynamic efficiency gains on the part of developing countries following the introduction of pharmaceutical patents means that these countries were expected to suffer overall welfare loss. Scherer concludes that the number of new drugs introduced must increase threefold to compensate developing country consumers for the welfare loss they sustain from the increased prices following the introduction of pharmaceutical patents.[246] He predicts, however, that the actual increase would only be 15.5 per cent.[247]

238 ibid 1009.
239 ibid 1020.
240 ibid 1021–22.
241 ibid 1022.
242 Maskus, *Intellectual Property Rights in the Global Economy* (n 140) 165.
243 ibid.
244 Correa (n 184) 43.
245 Maskus, *Intellectual Property Rights in the Global Economy* (n 140) 220.
246 Scherer, 'A Note on Global Welfare in Pharmaceutical Patenting' (n 96) 1129.
247 ibid.

The foregoing discussion suggests that developing countries should be circumspect about claims of dynamic efficiency gains as a result of elevated patent protection. Numerous economic studies have suggested that raising patent protection in developing countries will not attract greater domestic innovation and will tend to benefit mostly foreign innovators. This means that dynamic efficiency considerations deserve less weight in developing countries. In a developing country bereft of innovation capacity, innovation incentives generated by the patent system do not tend to attract domestic innovation. Where there are no potential innovators in the country, innovation incentives will go to waste and will not spur innovation.

This would be the case for countries that merely possess a production capacity. The focus of the patent–competition interface in these countries should be on minimizing consumer welfare loss. For the technology adaptation countries, technological progress comes in the form of technology absorption and not origination. Dynamic efficiency considerations should not be concerned with innovation incentives but with incentives for technology transfer. The patent–competition interface becomes a balancing of the interests of consumers and technology adopters. Lastly, for countries that possess the capacity to innovate in at least certain industries, which have been called the proto-innovation countries, there are three classes of conflicting interests involved: consumers, technology adopters, and domestic innovators. While the innovators will benefit from the innovation incentives provided by the patent system, the technology adopters would appreciate patent–competition rules that facilitate licensing and other forms of technology transfer. The patent–competition interface takes on the highest degree of complexity for these countries.

5. External Impact of Innovation Incentives Generated by Developing Country Patent Systems

The impact of the innovation incentives generated by the domestic patent system need not be confined within the national borders. A foreign innovator can patent her innovation in the host country and sell the product there. The product may be imported from a foreign location. The patented technology may be transferred to a local affiliate through FDI, or it may be licensed to a local manufacturer. Whatever the means of transfer, patent protection plays a role. The existence of patent protection allows the foreign innovator to reap her financial reward. The fact that a foreign innovator can tap into multiple markets means that she will no longer only consider the innovation incentives provided by her domestic patent system when considering her R&D investment decisions. She will pay attention to a number of patent systems. Innovation incentives thus spill over national boundaries and can have substantial externalities. The question is whether a developing country competition authority should consider these externalities when calibrating its approach to the patent–competition interface.

The answer to this question would depend on a number of factors. The first one is the likelihood that the innovative incentives created by the domestic patent system would be considered by foreign innovators. Economists have provided some guidance on this. The size of domestic market as reflected by population size or other measures has been found to be a key factor in the responsiveness of innovators to the innovation incentives generated by a patent system.[248] Although most of these studies focus on the responsiveness of domestic innovators, the same logic should apply to foreign innovators.

A foreign innovator would not consider the profitability of every market across the globe when deciding whether to invest in a technology. She will focus on the lucrative markets, which should include the developed countries such as the United States, Europe, and Japan and developing countries with a substantial domestic market such as China, India, and Brazil. Multinational firms are unlikely to attach much weight to the domestic market of small developing countries. The fact that most innovations are only patented in a limited number of jurisdictions lends support to this proposition.[249] Belize or Burundi, for example, are unlikely to feature prominently in her decision-making process. Even when aggregated, the profit potential of these countries' markets is unlikely to amount to more than a few percent of the global profit of a multinational corporation.[250] An innovation that would have been abandoned after a slight loss of profit is unlikely to be ground-breaking and a huge boon to global welfare.[251]

The profit potential of a large developing country such as the BRICS (Brazil, Russia, India, China, and South Africa) countries cannot be dismissed so casually. Practically every multinational firm would attach a great deal of importance to the Chinese market. While one may assume that larger patentee reward from a large developing country market would translate into greater innovation incentives for developed country firms, theoretical models by some development economists have shown the contrary. These models repeatedly reach the same conclusion that raising intellectual property protection, which has the same effect as relaxing competition law restrictions on patent exploitation practices, would retard innovation in developed economies. These models make different assumptions about the mode of technology transfer.

[248] Elhanan Helpman, *The Mystery of Economic Growth* (Harvard University Press 2004) 50.

[249] Jeffery Atik and Hans Lidgard, 'Embracing Price Discrimination: TRIPS and the Suppression of Parallel Trade in Pharmaceuticals' (2006) 27 University of Pennsylvania Journal of International Law 1043, 1058.

[250] Jean O Lanjouw, 'A Patent Policy Proposal for Global Diseases' (2001) 7 <https://www.brookings.edu/research/a-patent-policy-proposal-for-global-diseases-2/> accessed 8 April 2019.

[251] Scherer, *Industrial Market Structure and Economic Performance* (n 79) 448.

Assuming imitation to be the only mode of technology transfer, Carmelo Parello constructs a model based on the international product cycle to examine the impact of increased patent protection in developing countries on the rate of innovation in developed countries and the rate of imitation in developing countries.[252] He concludes that increased patent protection reduces the rate of both in the absence of FDI.[253] Edwin Lai incorporates FDI as an alternative means of technology transfer and examines the impact of increased patent protection on both developed and developing countries.[254] Lai reaches the same conclusion as Parello's when imitation is the only means of technology transfer but finds that both the rate of innovation in developed countries and the rate of imitation in developing countries receive a boost when FDI is the mode of transfer.[255] Elhanan Helpman constructs a slightly more complicated model and reaches the same result as Parello's and Lai's under the assumptions of no FDI and low imitation rate.[256] Maskus speculates that innovation in developed countries slows down because innovators expect each innovation to be more profitable as a result of reduced imitation, thereby losing the incentive to engage in R&D.[257]

More recent research by Lee Branstetter and Kamal Saggi produces contradictory results. They find that an increase in patent protection in the global South reduces imitation in these countries, boosts innovation in the global North, and increases the inflow of FDI from developed countries to developing countries, resulting in a substantial relocation of production to the latter.[258] This difference in result can be explained by the perhaps more realistic assumption in Branstetter and Saggi's model that both imitation and FDI are endogenously determined.[259] In the real world, the local imitation rate will obviously be influenced by the level of patent protection prevailing in the country. Branstetter and Saggi's results notwithstanding, the preponderance of the literature firmly takes the view that increased patent protection in developing countries retards innovation in developed countries. This provides a persuasive reason for the competition authority of a large developing country to discount the incentive effect of its domestic patent system for foreign innovators, at least where there is negligible technology transfer through FDI.

[252] Carmelo Pierpaolo Parello, 'A North-South Model of Intellectual Property Rights Protection and Skill Accumulation' (2008) 85 Journal of Development Economics 253.

[253] ibid 135.

[254] Edwin Lai, 'International Intellectual Property Rights Protection and the Rate of Product Innovation' (1998) 55 Journal of Development Economics 133.

[255] ibid 265–66.

[256] Elhanan Helpman, 'Innovation, Imitation, and Intellectual Property Rights' (1993) 61 Econometrica 1247, 1275.

[257] Maskus, *Intellectual Property Rights in the Global Economy* (n 140) 139.

[258] Lee Branstetter and Kamal Saggi, 'Intellectual Property Rights, Foreign Direct Investment and Industrial Development' (2011) 121 The Economic Journal 1161, 1163.

[259] ibid 1162.

Even if one were inclined to question the conclusions of these theoretical models, there remains the question of how much weight a developing country competition authority would want to give to the dynamic efficiency gains of foreign innovators when these gains result from a welfare transfer from downtrodden domestic consumers to wealthy multinational firms. The fact of welfare transfer is the essential consequence of patent exclusivity. It is not up to competition law to revisit this policy trade-off. However, when competition law is asked to delineate the scope of patent rights which may influence the magnitude of this trade-off, a competition authority should be allowed to take into account the fact that the extra innovation incentives that may flow from permitting a patent exploitation practice will cause additional welfare loss on the part of its consumers. The justification is even stronger if the product concerned is a basic necessity consumed by a broad spectrum of consumers, some of whom can ill-afford higher prices.

D. Conclusion

It is didactic to tie back the foregoing discussion about patent protection to the patent–competition rules. As mentioned at the beginning of this section, patent rules and the patent–competition rules interact with innovation incentives in the same way by altering the size of the patentee reward. The causal link is that both sets of rules adjust the scope of patent rights, encompassing both the scope of protection and the freedom the patentee is given to exploit her technology, which generates a financial reward for the patentee, which in turn attracts potential innovators to innovate. In a nutshell, the link goes from legal rules to scope of patent rights to patentee reward to innovation incentives to innovation. If the causal link is broken anywhere along the way, one can no longer be sure that adjusting the legal rules will produce the desired effect on innovation.

The foregoing discussion highlights a number of important gaps along this causal link that cast doubt on the weight that should be accorded to patent policy in the patent–competition interface in developing countries. The existence of multiple appropriation mechanisms and the varying degrees of reliance on patents in different industries mean that the link between patentee reward and innovation incentives is more tenuous than what the conventional wisdom assumes. Potential innovators derive motivations to innovate from many other sources than patents. Increasing patentee reward is not the only way to generate innovation incentives. The converse is also true that reducing patentee reward does not necessarily lower innovation incentives. The fact that the current patent system exhibits a tendency to overcompensate innovators means that it is possible to reduce patentee reward without undermining innovation incentives.

The perhaps obvious observation that innovative incentives will only translate into innovation when accompanied by the requisite technological capacity implies another break in the causal link between innovation incentives and innovation. The two cannot be directly equated with each other. The extent to which a developing country can take advantage of the innovation incentives generated by the domestic patent system is dependent on its technological capacity. In the production countries, innovation incentives will amount to nothing and the sacrifice by consumers to bear the supra-competitive pricing will be in vain. In the technology adaptation countries, dynamic efficiency should not target innovation but technology transfer. Innovation policy should focus on facilitating technology transfer from foreign technology owners rather than on attracting domestic innovation. Lastly, the proto-innovation countries, there needs to be a delicate balance of the interests of domestic innovators, imitators, and consumers. These countries require the most nuanced approach to the patent–competition interface.

Lastly, it was pointed out that innovation incentives need not only generate domestic innovation, they can also benefit foreign innovators. From the perspective of developing countries, however, sacrificing the welfare of downtrodden domestic consumers to subsidize innovation by multinational firms in advanced economies seems ill-advised at best. Consumer welfare deserves a greater weight in the patent–competition interface when domestic dynamic efficiency benefits are in doubt.

3
Technology Transfers in Developing Countries

A. Introduction

For developing countries that are devoid of innovation capacity, which includes a vast majority of them, technological progress can only be achieved and measured in terms of technological absorption and adaptation. If these countries cannot originate cutting-edge technology, the only way for them to acquire it is through learning from others. Only a very small number of countries originate most of the technology in this world.[1] An earlier study found that foreign sources of technology account for over 90 per cent of productivity growth in all but five countries in the world.[2] These five countries are the United States, Japan, Germany, United Kingdom, and France, which served as the main research centres of the world.[3] Innovations from the United States, Japan, and Germany alone drove more than half of the growth in OECD (Organisation of Economic Cooperation and Development) countries.[4] One would expect the percentage to be even higher for developing countries.

The balance of power has since shifted, with China and South Korea emerging as major research centres as reflected in patent grants to domestic innovators. According to the 2018 report by the World Intellectual Property Organization (WIPO), the United States, Japan, South Korea, Germany, and China together account for 85 per cent of patent grants to domestic innovators worldwide.[5] Although the cast of protagonists has changed, it remains the case that a handful of countries originate the vast majority of technology in the world. To the extent that patent grants represent novel productive technology, foreign sources of technology are likely to remain the predominant driver of productivity growth in most countries.

[1] Wolfgang Keller, 'International Technology Diffusion' (2004) 42 Journal of Economic Literature 752, 752.

[2] ibid.

[3] Jonathan Eaton and Samuel Kortum, 'Trade in Ideas Patenting and Productivity in the OECD' (1996) 40 Journal of International Economics 251, 252.

[4] ibid.

[5] World Intellectual Property Organization, 'World Intellectual Property Indicators 2018' (2018) 78–81.

The Patent–Competition Interface in Developing Countries. Thomas K. Cheng, Oxford University Press. © Thomas K. Cheng 2021. DOI: 10.1093/oso/9780192857354.003.0003

As a country gradually approaches the global technological frontier however, the importance of technology absorption declines and domestic innovation plays an increasingly central role to economic growth.[6]

Technology adaptation requires technology transfer from technology-originating countries, most of which are developed countries. There are different forms of technology transfer, some of which are voluntary or intentional in nature and some of which involuntary or unintentional. Voluntary or intentional technology transfer includes international trade, foreign direct investment (FDI), and licensing.[7] International trade refers to the importation of technological goods into a developing country. FDI entails a foreign firm investing to set up operational capacity through an affiliate in a host country. Technology is transferred intra-firm as part of the FDI process. Licensing takes place when a foreign technology owner licenses its technology to a local firm for royalty payments or a license fee. It requires the foreign firm to part with control of the technology.

Involuntary or unintentional technology transfer refers to imitation of the technology. Imitation has been described as the process 'through which a rival firm invests resources to understand the technological or design secrets of another firm's formula or products'.[8] Imitation can be accomplished through outright copying from simple product inspection or reverse engineering, both of which could be curtailed by patent protection.[9] Which mode of imitation is necessary depends on the replicability of the technology. The technology in some industries such as pharmaceuticals and chemicals can be deciphered and replicated fairly easily. In some other industries such as complex machinery and electronics, the technology is deeply embedded in the product and requires sophisticated reverse engineering to be uncovered, if it can be uncovered at all. Both methods of replication will be referred to as imitation as both are unauthorized forms of technology transfer. Both modes of imitation require access to the embodiment of the technology. Importation of the technological good would thus be a prerequisite for imitation.[10] In assessing the impact of increased patent protection on involuntary technology transfer, one must also consider how such an increase affects trade in technological goods.

[6] Jérôme Vandenbussche, Philippe Aghion, and Costas Meghir, 'Growth, Distance to Frontier and Composition of Human Capital' (2006) 11 Journal of Economic Growth 97.

[7] Keith Maskus, *Intellectual Property Rights in the Global Economy* (Institute for International Economics 2000) 136–37.

[8] Keith Maskus, *Private Rights and Public Problems: The Global Economics of Intellectual Property in the 21st Century* (Peterson Institute for International Economics 2012) 69.

[9] Maskus, *Intellectual Property Rights in the Global Economy* (n 7) 136–37.

[10] Maskus, *Private Rights and Public Problems: The Global Economics of Intellectual Property in the 21st Century* (n 8) 66.

B. Technological Capacity and Technology Transfers

The extent to which technology transfer is a relevant consideration for a developing country depends on its technological capacity to absorb and adapt imported technology.[11] For the production countries, technology transfer is largely irrelevant. Unless and until these countries have acquired the capacity to absorb imported technology, it matters little whether the pertinent legal rules are conducive to technology transfer. The institutional environment will make little difference if there is no capacity to learn and acquire the imported technology. As the Commission on Intellectual Property Rights observes:

> The ability of countries to absorb knowledge from elsewhere and then make use and adapt it for their own purposes is also of crucial importance. This is a characteristic that depends on the development of local capacity through education, through R&D, and the development of appropriate institutions without which even technology transfer on the most advantageous terms is unlikely to succeed.[12]

Technology transfer will be of paramount importance to the technology adaptation countries, which possess the capacity to absorb foreign technology but not the capacity to originate technology. The fact that there are only a handful of major research centres in the world means that a vast majority of the countries in the world belong to this category. Technological progress in these countries is mainly achieved through technology transfer from developed countries and not through domestic innovation. Therefore, contrary to the conventional sense of dynamic efficiency which focuses on incentives for domestic innovation, dynamic efficiency in these countries should be concerned with encouraging technology transfer from foreign firms. Whether the pertinent legal rules promote incentives to transfer technology thus matters. When balancing static efficiency against dynamic efficiency considerations under the patent–competition interface, the focus should be on how the patent–competition rules may affect the incentives of foreign technology owners to transfer their technology to developing countries. The same applies to the proto-innovation countries in those industries where the country currently lacks innovation capacity and relies on foreign technology.

[11] Yifei Sun and others, 'Subcontracting and Supplier Innovativeness in a Developing Economy: Evidence from China's Information and Communication Technology Industry' (2013) 47 Regional Studies 1766.

[12] Commission on Intellectual Property Rights, 'Integrating Intellectual Property Rights and Development Policy' (2002) 24–25 <www.iprcommission.org/papers/pdfs/final_report/CIPRfullfinal.pdf> accessed 5 April 2019.

C. The More Nuanced Relationship between the Patent–Competition Rules and Technology Transfers

1. Comparison between Innovation and Technology Transfer

The paramount policy concern is how the patent–competition rules shape the incentives to transfer technology. There is a key difference, however, between innovation incentives on the one hand and incentives to transfer technology on the other. With innovation incentives, there is only one outcome which is of concern: the amount of innovation. The question is whether changes in legal rules boost or undermine innovation. Research and development (R&D) or innovation is the investment decision of interest. The situation with technology transfer is different. A foreign firm does not decide whether to transfer technology to a developing country. The decision is whether and how to enter a foreign market, either as an export market or as a production base for re-export elsewhere.

There are three major methods of market entry: international trade of technological goods, FDI, and licensing. When a foreign firm decides to export to a developing country, it can import the good from an overseas manufacturing facility. If it decides to establish a production base in a developing country, either for the local market or re-export, it can build its own production facility in the host country, either through a subsidiary or by entering into a joint venture with a local partner, or it can license its technology to a local firm. Each of these methods brings about different extents of technology transfer. The existence of the various means of market entry and technology transfer means that it is necessary to consider the impact of the patent–competition rules on the incentives to undertake them separately.

Another important difference between innovation incentives and the incentives for technology transfer is the range of determinants for them. Profitability is what ultimately guides a profit-maximizing firm's decision regarding any investment option, be it to invest in R&D or to enter a market. The firm compares the costs and the benefits of the contemplated course of action. The difference between R&D investments and market entry is that while the profitability of an innovation is largely determined by patentee reward, at least for industries that rely on patents as an appropriation mechanism (in any case, the profitability of other appropriation mechanisms is not directly affected by competition law and is not a focus of our inquiry), the profitability of market entry is shaped by a wide range of economic factors beyond legal rules. The patent system and the patent–competition rules hence do not play a determinative role in the decision-making process regarding market entry and technology transfer. The only exception is perhaps the robustness and effective enforcement of patent protection. One can imagine that if export to the local market exposes the technology owner to a high risk of local imitation, she may abstain from that market altogether. Imitation will inflict a heavy cost of market entry on the technology owner.

The relevant research question is whether changes in the patent–competition rules alter incentives to transfer technology. As in the case of innovation incentives, economic studies on technology transfer focus on patent protection and not the patent–competition rules. These studies attempt to determine whether increased patent protection generates greater incentives for different modes of technology transfer. Therefore, there is the important question of the extent to which the outcome of studies about patent protection are applicable in the context of the patent–competition rules.

When the focus is on innovation incentives, under the somewhat simplifying assumption that the sole determinant of innovation incentives is patentee reward, the question becomes how changes in legal rules, including patent law and the patent–competition rules, alter patentee reward. The fact that changes in patent law and changes in the patent–competition rules both adjust the scope of patent rights in similar ways, which ultimately, together with the patent term, determine the size of the patentee reward means that there is considerable similarity between the causal impact of patent protection and the patent–competition rules on innovation incentives. Raising the level of patent protection has the same effect on patentee reward as relaxing competition regulation of patent-exploitation practices. Therefore, much of the economic literature on patent protection and innovation incentives can be readily applied to the context of the patent–competition rules.

The situation is more complex with the incentives for technology transfer. The economic literature on technology transfer is more varied. Some studies examine the relationship between patent protection and one mode of technology transfer. Other studies look at how changes in the level of patent protection cause foreign firms to shift between different modes of transfer. Moreover, the implications that can be drawn from the relevant economic studies are more subtle and complex because patent protection is not the sole, or even a major, determinant of the incentives for technology transfer. Most of the economic studies discussed below have attempted to isolate the effects of these other economic factors through various statistical techniques. What these authors have mostly focused on are the macro-level factors such as population size and educational level. They have not taken into account individual market characteristics (and they probably could not have) that ultimately determine the profitability of market entry through technology transfer. It is important to bear this in mind when reviewing these studies.

The way the economic evidence is used and interpreted by economists means that it is possible to draw different implications for various patent–competition rules from their studies. In the case of innovation incentives, the patent–competition rules can be treated as a monolith because they are all assumed to affect patentee reward in the same way: by altering the scope of patent rights. In the case of the incentives for technology transfer, however, the economists have emphasized different aspects of patent protection that may have disparate degrees of relevance for various patent–competition rules. Before further exploration of this issue, it is important first to acquire some understanding of how economists have attempted to quantify and measure patent protection.

Most of the economic studies that will be discussed below use the Ginarte–Park Index, or some modification thereof, as a quantitative indicator of patent protection. The index consists of five main components: 'extent of coverage; membership in international patenting agreements; provisions for loss of protection; enforcement mechanisms; and duration of protection'.[13] Membership in international patenting agreements is not directly related to any substantive patent rules. Extent of coverage and duration of protection relate to the scope of patent rights and should affect the profitability of market entry generally. Lengthening patent term would extend the patent owner's period of exclusivity and allow her to reap greater benefit from her technology. Extending the scope of coverage means that more technology becomes patentable. Both raise the benefits of market entry. Owners of these technologies will be able to enter foreign markets more profitably than before. Provisions for the loss of protection and enforcement mechanisms reflect the robustness and the enforceability of patent protection. This determines the patent owner's ability to protect her rights and to forestall competition from imitators in the local market.

It is worth noting that in the context of the relationship between patent protection and technology transfer, what economists often refer to by patent protection are not changes in the scope of patent rights but the existence and strength of patent protection in the first place. The argument is that the conferral and strengthening of patent protection creates an effectively enforceable property right, which facilitates property transfer and forestalls imitation by local firms. The focus is on the technology owner's right to exclude rivals from the market, and not the scope of her other patent rights. Weakness in patent protection may expose foreign firms to risks of imitation and raise the costs of technology transfer, thereby lowering the profitability of market entry for the technology owner. Imitation will be an especially significant consideration for foreign technology owners if there is high local imitation capacity.

2. Classification of the Patent–Competition Rules According to their Relationship with Technology Transfer

The subject of this inquiry is of course not patent law but the patent–competition rules. Therefore, these economic studies would only be of use if they could be analogized to the patent–competition rules. This would require some understanding of the relationship between the patent–competition rules and technology transfer. As

[13] Michael Nicholson, 'The Impact of Industry Characteristics and IPR Policy on Foreign Direct Investment' (2007) 143 Review of World Economics 27, 33–34.

far as their impact on technology transfer is concerned, the patent–competition rules can probably be classified into three categories. The first category are the usual ones that adjust the scope of patent rights. Examples include whether it is legal to tie the sale of patented product with an unpatented product and whether it is legal to implement a resale price maintenance scheme for a patented product.[14] In the case of innovation incentives, any rule that adjusts the size of patentee reward by way of the scope of patent rights is presumed to influence innovation incentives.[15] The situation with technology transfer is more complicated. There is a more remote and tenuous link between the patent–competition rules and incentives to transfer technology. The decision to enter a foreign market and transfer technology is to a large extent determined by market factors. Therefore, only those patent–competition rules that have a significant impact on the profitability of market entry will affect incentives for technology transfer. And only for these rules would the economic studies on patent protection and technology transfer be relevant.

The second category of rules are those that implicate the robustness of patent protection. These arguably include no challenge clauses, which prohibit a licensee from launching a validity challenge against the patent owner,[16] and reverse payments, which allow a patent owner to forestall validity challenges by paying off or otherwise compensating potential challengers.[17] These rules affect a technology owner's ability to exclude an imitating rival from the market by pre-empting validity challenges. The only patent–competition rule that directly implicates the right to exclude and hence the robustness of patent protection is regulation of unilateral refusal to license intellectual property.[18] The imposition of a duty to license would directly override a patent owner's right to exclude and allow imitating rivals to enter the market.[19] To the extent that the patent–competition rules allow the technology owner effectively to exclude rivals from the market, they will help lower the costs of market entry by the technology owner. Economic studies that focus on the robustness of patent protection would be relevant to these patent–competition rules. When economists speak of heightened patent protection in this context it would be equivalent to reduced likelihood that competition law will impose a duty

[14] A famous US case involving such a tie was *International Salt Co. v. United States*, 332 US 392 (1947).

[15] A famous US case involving such an RPM scheme was *United States v. General Electric*, 272 US 476 (1926).

[16] Thomas K Cheng, 'Antitrust Treatment of No Challenge Clause' (2016) 5 New York University Journal of Intellectual Property and Entertainment Law 437, 439.

[17] Einer Elhauge and Alex Krueger, 'Solving the Patent Settlement Puzzle' (2012) 91 Texas Law Review 283, 284.

[18] Herbert J Hovenkamp, Mark D Janis, and Mark A Lemley, 'Unilateral Refusals to License in the U.S.' [2005] Faculty Scholarship 13, 13 <https://scholarship.law.upenn.edu/faculty_scholarship/1920> accessed 29 July 2021.

[19] Howard A Shelanski, 'Unilateral Refusals to Deal in Intellectual and Other Property' (2009) 76 Antitrust Law Journal 369, 370.

to license intellectual property, or greater tolerance on the part of competition of no challenge clauses and reverse payments.

The third category of rules pertains specifically to licensing. Some patent–competition rules focus on vertical agreements and licensing practices in particular. These include the permissibility of grantbacks,[20] the legality of territorial allocation among licensees,[21] and the enforceability of a FRAND (Fair, Reasonable, And Non-Discriminatory) obligation on owners of standard-essential patents (SEPs),[22] among others. These rules do not uniformly affect the profitability of technology transfer but skew the relative attractiveness of the three modes of technology transfer. Although none of the economic studies focuses on licensing rules specifically, some of them do touch on the profitability of licensing vis-à-vis other technology transfer options. These studies tend to focus on how patent rules help to lower the costs of licensing. Even though these studies may not be directly analogous as the patent–competition rules may influence both the costs and benefits of licensing, they nonetheless shed light on how the patent–competition rules may influence the incentives to license. The impact of these licensing rules on the relative attractiveness of the three market entry options would be particularly relevant to the extent that any of these options are more beneficial to developing countries.

3. Some General Observations about the Relationship between Patent Protection and Incentives to Transfer Technology

The relationship between patent protection and the incentive to engage in intentional technology transfer has been characterized as 'at least as complex and ambiguous as the linkages between patents and innovation'.[23] In many ways, it is more complex and ambiguous, no less because patent rules are only one of the myriad considerations for technology transfer. A number of specific observations have been made about this relationship, the first two of which are related to the type of technology transferred. First, it has been noted that patent protection is particularly relevant for the transfer of easily imitable technology.[24] This is a corollary of the fact that easily imitable technologies such as those in the pharmaceutical and chemical industries rely more heavily on patents as an appropriation mechanism. Without robust patent protection, it would be difficult for pharmaceutical

[20] US Department of Justice and Federal Trade Commission, 'Antitrust Guidelines for the Licensing of Intellectual Property' 33.

[21] ibid 5–6.

[22] Tuire Anniina Väisänen, *Enforcement of FRAND Commitments under Article 102 TFEU: The Nature of FRAND Defence in Patent Litigation* (Nomos Verlagsgesellschaft mbH 2011).

[23] Maskus, *Private Rights and Public Problems: The Global Economics of Intellectual Property in the 21st Century* (n 8) 64.

[24] Carlos Correa, *Intellectual Property Rights, the WTO and Developing Countries: The TRIPS Agreement and Policy Options* (Zed Books–Third World Network 2000) 31.

and chemical firms to profit from their innovations, both domestically and abroad. This point, however, is perhaps more relevant to the robustness of protection than the scope of patent rights.

Second, it has also been contended that weaker patent protection will lower the quality of the technology transferred.[25] The idea is that weaker patent protection reduces the technology owner's ability to protect a licensed technology. Technology owners will hence choose to transfer an older technology to safeguard their economic interests. This again seems to pertain more to the effectiveness of enforcement and the robustness of protection rather than the scope of patent rights. If local patent law does not allow foreign technology owners to protect their technologies effectively, they will only choose to transfer an older technology to minimize the potential loss of their competitive advantages. This point ties back to the earlier discussion about imitation risks. The greater the imitation risks, the older is the technology transferred. This means that if the patent–competition rules allow the technology owner greater leeway to forestall imitation, foreign technology owners will be inclined to transfer more up-to-date technology.

Third, it has been argued that increased patent protection has a positive impact on inward voluntary technology transfer by increasing import of technological goods and raising the quality of inward FDI and licensing.[26] This assertion has been qualified by the observation that

> these impacts generally are found only in larger and middle-income countries, where domestic imitation threats are real. There is little evidence of these effects in the poorest and smallest developing economies, where, if anything, patents are not of much relevance for [technology transfer] or domestic industrial development. Similarly, some of these positive impacts seem to be governed by important threshold effects in the levels of income and education.[27]

This corroborates the earlier observation that technology transfer and FDI are unlikely to benefit developing countries with poor technological capacity and small domestic markets. No amount of favourable patent law can overcome a country's weak technical capability and unattractiveness as an investment destination.

With respect to involuntary technology transfer through imitation, its relationship with patent protection is relatively straightforward. The more robust is patent protection, the more difficult it will be to imitate a foreign technology. Therefore, one should expect a negative relationship between patent protection and imitation. This is implied in the observation that patent protection is particularly relevant

[25] Keith Maskus and others, 'Intellectual Property Rights and Economic Development in China' in *Intellectual Property and Development* (Oxford University Press 2005) 314.

[26] Maskus, *Private Rights and Public Problems: The Global Economics of Intellectual Property in the 21st Century* (n 8) 81.

[27] ibid.

for the transfer of easily imitable technology. After all, the essence of patent rights is the right to exclude, or at least the right to try to exclude.[28] Part and parcel of patent protection is the ability to stop others from practising and exploiting one's technology.

D. Different Modes of Technology Transfer

It is argued that increased patent protection is generally conducive to intentional technology transfer. One of the greatest anomalies as far as the relationship between patent protection and intentional technology transfer is concerned is China. Proponents of the view that intellectual property rights (IPRs) are important for technology transfer must confront the case of China, which has been by far the greatest beneficiary of technology transfer over the last three decades despite its lamentable record in intellectual property protection.[29] One obvious explanation for this apparent anomaly is the fact that intellectual property protection is only one of the many considerations facing a multinational firm contemplating technology transfer.[30] When a private firm approaches this decision, its objective is not to transfer technology to the host country. Instead, the firm seeks to optimize the mode of supplying or establishing a production base in the host country.

The decision-making process for the foreign firm is a choice among the three modes of market entry: import, FDI, and licensing. The firm has usually already chosen the host country and is merely considering the best way to enter the market. If the firm has decided to establish a production base, then the choice would be between FDI and licensing. We assume that the firm is planning to enter the host country market in the future and thus all three modes of technology transfer are viable. The patent–competition rules have disparate impact on these three options. Import is probably the least affected by these rules as it only entails the sale and transport of a patented good to an overseas location. Licensing, as mentioned earlier, is often directly regulated by patent–competition rules and should be fairly sensitive to them. FDI probably stands somewhere in between.

John Dunning proposes a framework, the OLI paradigm, for conceptualizing a multinational firm's market entry decision.[31] OLI stands for the advantages of ownership, localization, and internalization.[32] Ownership advantages include

[28] Carl Shapiro, 'Antitrust Limits to Patent Settlements' (2003) 34 RAND Journal of Economics 392, 395.

[29] Maskus, *Private Rights and Public Problems: The Global Economics of Intellectual Property in the 21st Century* (n 8) 64.

[30] European Patent Office, 'Patents, Trade and Foreign Direct Investment in the European Union' (2017) 11 <http://www.iprhelpdesk.eu/news/epo-study-patents-trade-and-foreign-direct-investment-european-union> accessed 9 April 2019.

[31] John H Dunning and Sarianna M Lundan, *Multinational Enterprises and the Global Economy* (2nd edn, Edward Elgar Publishing Ltd 2008) 116–33, 318–27.

[32] ibid 101–02.

'technology and information, managerial, marketing and entrepreneurial skills, organisational systems, incentive structures, and favored access to intermediate or final goods markets'.[33] They identify the competitive advantages of a multinational firm in the global market that will allow it to enter multiple markets.

Localization advantages include 'the costs and quality of particular factor endowments, the size, character, and growth of domestic markets[,] and the policies of host government, for example, taxes and fiscal incentives'.[34] To this list one can further add local demand patterns, transportation costs, proximity to customers, ability to build a supplier-customer network, and natural resources.[35] They determine whether the firm will choose to produce the good in a foreign location and export it to the host country or locate production facilities in that country. In other words, localization or location advantages explain the firm's choice between international trade on the one hand, and FDI or licensing on the other hand.

Internalization advantages are reasons 'why a foreign firm prefers to retain full control over the production process instead of licensing its intangible assets to local firms'.[36] The decision may be due to 'high transaction costs involved in regulating and enforcing licensing contracts'.[37] It may also be attributed to the rest of the legal regime such as rules that regulate licensing. To this one may also add some underlying economic factors such as the existence of suitable local partners. Internalization advantages refer generally to the costs and benefits of licensing and inform the firm's choice between FDI and licensing.

The OLI paradigm suggests that there is a wide range of considerations affecting the attractiveness of the host country for market entry and the relative merits of the different modes of entry. Labour costs, size of the domestic market, and other relevant government policies are probably more important considerations than the patent system or the patent–competition rules when a foreign firm chooses between the three modes of market entry. This is quite different from the situation with innovation incentives, under which patentee reward as partially determined by the patent–competition rules plays a much more direct and important role in the R&D decision. While the patent system or the patent–competition rules may play some role in the choice between trade and localization of production, they are unlikely to override the underlying economic considerations of labour costs and market size. Maskus notes that 'strong IPRs alone are insufficient for generating strong incentives to invest in a country. If that were the case, recent FDI flows to developing

[33] ibid 96.

[34] ibid 324.

[35] Maskus, *Intellectual Property Rights in the Global Economy* (n 7) 121–22.

[36] Beata Smarzynska Javorcik, 'The Composition of Foreign Direct Investment and Protection of Intellectual Property Rights: Evidence from Transition Economies' (2004) 48 European Economic Review 39, 41.

[37] ibid.

countries would have gone largely to Sub-Saharan Africa and Eastern Europe'.[38] If the economic factors are favourable, a foreign firm is likely to adhere to its decision to localize production regardless of the patent–competition rules.

The decision between FDI and licensing, which pertains to internalization advantages, is probably more susceptible to the influence of the patent–competition rules so long as there are suitable local licensing partners. A foreign firm is more likely to resort to licensing if permissible licensing rules allow it to impose restrictions on licensees to protect its economic interests.[39] Permissible licensing rules may also allow the firm to extract more rents from its licensees such that licensing may present a more profitable option than FDI.[40] Therefore, to the extent that licensing is preferable from a developing country's perspective, patent–competition rules can be adjusted to steer foreign firms' decision towards licensing.

If the patent–competition rules may steer a firm to choose one mode of technology transfer over others then it is important to determine whether any mode of transfer is particularly advantageous to developing countries. Various modes of technology transfer contribute to a developing country's technological capacity in different ways. To the extent that a particular mode of transfer makes greater contributions to local technological capacity, developing countries may want to encourage it. Among the three modes of technology transfer, licensing probably results in the greatest enhancement to local technological capacity, followed by FDI, and by importation of technological goods.[41] Importation of technological goods can enhance local technological capacity in two ways. If the good being imported is a final product, it may present an opportunity for local firms to reverse engineer the technology.[42] However, this benefit would only materialize if there is local imitation capacity.[43] For countries that lack this capacity, this benefit could be illusory. If the good being imported is an advanced intermediate good such as a piece of complex machinery, importation would enhance local production capacity, allowing local firms to produce a more advanced product or an existing product at lower cost.[44] However, one can argue that this does not amount to a

[38] Keith E Maskus, 'The Role of Intellectual Property Rights in Encouraging Foreign Direct Investment and Technology Transfer', *Intellectual Property and Development: Lessons from Recent Economic Research* (Oxford University Press 2005) 54.

[39] Maskus, *Private Rights and Public Problems: The Global Economics of Intellectual Property in the 21st Century* (n 8) 68–69.

[40] Ryuhei Wakasugi and Banri Ito, 'The Effects of Stronger Intellectual Property Rights on Technology Transfer: Evidence from Japanese Firm-Level Data' (2009) 34 Journal of Technology Transfer 145, 152.

[41] Vinod Kumar, Uma Kumar, and Aditha Persaud, 'Building Technological Capability Through Importing Technology: The Case of Indonesian Manufacturing Industry' (1999) 24 Journal of Technology Transfer 81, 83.

[42] Maskus, *Private Rights and Public Problems: The Global Economics of Intellectual Property in the 21st Century* (n 8) 53.

[43] Elhanan Helpman, 'Innovation, Imitation, and Intellectual Property Rights' (1993) 61 Econometrica 1247, 1276.

[44] Maskus, *Intellectual Property Rights in the Global Economy* (n 7) 138.

genuine improvement as it only enhances production capacity and does not augment the local capacity to innovate.

FDI and licensing both entail the transfer of a foreign technology to a host country, the only difference being the extent of local control of the technology transferred. Under FDI, the technology remains confined within the multinational firm, even though local employees will be given access to it. This gives rise to the possibility of spillover to local firms through lateral movement of employees between firms. Under licensing, there is true localization of the technology in the sense that locals firms will have full possession of a foreign technology. While some economists have argued that ownership of technology does not matter so long as it is located in the host country,[45] the better view is that ownership of technology and productive resources matter and that the host country receives greater benefit from the technology when it is in local possession.[46] At the very least this avoids the well-documented problem of enclave production where multinational firms set up local subsidiaries equipped with their own production network insulated from the rest of the economy, thereby redounding minimal benefit to the local economy.[47] This will greatly limit the technological spillovers to local firms and reduce the overall beneficial effect of the technology transfer on the local economy. Therefore, if given a choice, developing countries should prefer licensing to FDI to import as a means of technological transfer. To the extent that patent–competition rules may influence the choice among these three modes of market entry, it will have to be taken into account by policy-makers.

1. International Trade in Technological Goods

David Coe and Elhanan Helpman show that the technology embodied in traded goods is an important means of technology transfer.[48] International trade of technological goods contributes to local technological capacity in two ways, depending on the good at issue. If the good is a final product, importation of the good may allow local firms to reverse engineer the good to replicate the technology. This will enhance the technological capacity of local firms regardless of

[45] Christian Gollier and Jullien Bruno, 'National Champions under Credit Rationing' in Oliver Falck, Christian Gollier, and Ludger Woessmann (eds), *Industrial Policy and National Champions* (The MIT Press 2011) 153.

[46] Alice Amsden, *Escape from Empire: The Developing World's Journey through Heaven and Hell* (The MIT Press 2007) 142–47. Michele Di Maio, 'Industrial Policies in Developing Countries: History and Perspectives' in Mario Cimoli, Giovanni Dosi, and Joseph Stiglitz (eds), *Industrial Policy and Development: The Political Economy of Capabilities Accumulation* (Oxford University Press 2009) 107, 129.

[47] Tilman Altenburg and Wilfried Lütkenhorst, *Industrial Policy in Developing Countries: Failing Markets, Weak States* (Edward Elgar Publishing Ltd 2015) 124.

[48] David Coe and Elhanan Helpman, 'International R&D Spillovers' (1995) 39 European Economic Review 859, 871–72.

whether they can produce and sell the product unfettered by patent protection. Knowledge of a more advanced product would enhance their capacity for product development in the future. Access to a large quantity of the product is often not necessary for successful reverse engineering. Usually only a small amount of the foreign product is sufficient. Another prerequisite for reverse engineering is a certain level of local technological capacity. As indicated earlier, imitation itself takes time, effort, and technical knowledge. The mere availability of the foreign product would not suffice if there was no local capacity to reverse engineer the technology. The patent–competition rules would have a bearing on the ease of imitation. If competition law requires the technology owner to share its technology with local firms, it may obviate the need for reverse engineering altogether.

If the good is an intermediate good such as advanced machinery, importation of such a good may enhance local production capacity without the need for local firms to engage in any reverse engineering. For instance, China acquired cutting-edge capacity to produce high-performing solar photovoltaic panels by purchasing machines or turnkey production lines from the United States, Germany, and Japan.[49] For this kind of improvement to local technological capacity to materialize, local firms would need a steady flow of the intermediate good. Local firms are assumed not to have the capacity to reverse engineer such complex machinery. Therefore, it will matter to local firms whether the patent–competition rules will affect the willingness of foreign technology owners to continue to export such goods to the host country.

As in the case of innovation incentives, the economic literature is focused on the patent system and not the patent–competition rules. Therefore, the findings of the economic studies will need to be adapted for our purpose. Economists have studied the relationship between patent protection and the incentive to export a technological good, and their focus seems to lie mainly on the robustness of protection, which presumably only concerns goods that can be reverse engineered. Pamela Smith argues that developing countries can be classified along two dimensions for this purpose: the strength of patent protection and imitation capacity.[50] The impact of patent protection on the import of technological goods depends on the interplay of these two attributes. Increased patent protection exerts two effects on import. First, there is the market power effect. Increased patent protection gives the technology owner more market power, which reduces the elasticity of the demand curve facing her.[51] She can thus boost profit by raising prices and cutting output. Second, there is the market expansion effect, which arises from the fact that heightened patent protection eliminates imitators from the market, thereby

[49] European Patent Office (n 30) 12.

[50] Pamela Smith, 'Are Weak Patent Rights A Barrier to U.S. Exports?' (1999) 48 Journal of International Economics 151, 153.

[51] Maskus, *Intellectual Property Rights in the Global Economy* (n 7) 112.

leaving more room for the technology owner to increase output. This effect shifts the firm's demand curve outward and induces larger sales to the local market.[52]

Keith Maskus and Mohan Penubarti hypothesize that 'the market-expansion effect is likely to dominate in larger countries with highly competitive local imitative firms, while the market-power effect would be stronger in smaller economies with limited ability to imitate. The effects would be expected to vary sector by sector as well'.[53] Whether the market expansion effect will materialize depends on whether there is currently any local imitation capacity. If there is no imitator in the local market to be ousted by heightened patent protection, the market power effect will dominate and there will be a drop in the import of the technological good. This leads Maskus to conclude that for industrializing economies with real imitative threats such as China and Turkey, the market expansion effect should dominate.[54]

This is precisely what Smith finds. She finds that in countries with a weak imitation capacity, the market power effect dominates the market expansion effect after patent protection is enhanced, thereby leading to a reduction in US exports to those countries.[55] In countries with a strong imitation capacity, the market expansion effect dominates the market power effect, thereby raising US exports to those countries.[56] This result has been corroborated by further studies.[57] In particular, Olena Ivus finds that increased patent protection following the Agreement on Trade-Related Aspects of Intellectual Property Rights (TRIPS) added about USD35 billion (2000 dollars) to the value of patent-sensitive exports from developed countries to eighteen developing countries.[58] Kristie Briggs finds that elevating patent protection has no impact on import of technological goods into low-income countries, but has a significant positive impact on import into middle-income countries.[59] To the extent that there is a positive correlation between income level and imitation capacity, Briggs' finding lends further support to the notion that raising patent protection increases inflow of technological goods into countries with high imitation capacity.[60]

52 ibid.

53 ibid.

54 ibid 117.

55 Smith, 'Are Weak Patent Rights A Barrier to U.S. Exports?' (n 50) 164.

56 ibid.

57 Catherine Y Co, 'Do Patent Rights Regimes Matter?' (2004) 12 Review of International Economics 359; Olena Ivus, 'Do Stronger Patent Rights Raise High-Tech Exports to the Developing World?' (2010) 81 Journal of International Economics 38.

58 Ivus (n 57) 45.

59 Kristie Briggs, 'Does Patent Harmonization Impact the Decision and Volume of High Technology Trade?' (2013) 25 International Review of Economics & Finance 35, 38–39.

60 These studies suggest that there is a correlation between imitation capacity and importation of technological goods, which in turn indicates that the threat of reverse engineering has a bearing on foreign technology owners' willingness to export. One can thus infer that local imitators require a fairly significant amount of goods for reverse engineering purposes. Otherwise one should not see a correlation between imitation risk and the volume of import.

Ivus obtains a similar result with respect to industry-level variations in imitation capacity.[61] Industries with the strongest local imitation capacity will see a surge in import following an increase of patent protection, whereas industries with a low local imitation capacity may witness a fall in import.[62] She emphasizes that while the amount of technology diffusion in a single industry may fall as a result of heightened patent protection, the number of industries in which multinational firms export to the country will increase, hence leading to greater amount of technology transfer and also increased scope for imitation.[63] The overall imitation rate and the diffusion of technology to the country will rise.[64]

The foregoing focuses on the impact of elevating patent protection on the existing trade volume of technological goods. A slightly different way to look at the issue is whether patent protection shifts the mode of market entry between trade and localization of production. It has been noted that 'FDI is likely to supplant direct exports of a good where trade and transport costs are high, the fixed costs of building foreign plants are low, local productivity is high relative to wage costs, the size of the host market is large, and the research and development (R&D) and marketing intensity of the product is substantial'.[65] This suggests that this decision is largely informed by economic factors. Nonetheless, some studies have found that more robust patent protection tends to shift the mode of market entry away from trade to FDI and licensing.[66] The implication seems to be that FDI and licensing expose the technology owner to a greater risk of imitation, despite possibly promising a greater financial reward. Technology owners would prefer FDI and licensing if the imitation risk is manageable, which can be achieved through more robust patent protection.

Practically all the studies discussed above focus on imitation risk and the robustness of patent protection. The inference would thus seem to be that only those patent–competition rules that implicate robustness of protection would affect trade volume and technology owners' willingness to export technological goods to a host country. These include no challenge clauses, reverse payments, and the unilateral refusal to license intellectual property. Even then, imitation risk would only be a relevant issue in countries that possess the requisite imitation capacity and in industries where imitation is easy and relatively low-cost. Under these circumstances, a reduced readiness on the part of competition law to compel a technology

[61] Olena Ivus, 'Trade-Related Intellectual Property Rights: Industry Variation and Technology Diffusion' (2011) 44 The Canadian Journal of Economics 201.

[62] ibid 218–19.

[63] ibid 217.

[64] ibid.

[65] Maskus, 'The Role of Intellectual Property Rights in Encouraging Foreign Direct Investment and Technology Transfer' (n 38) 55.

[66] Pamela Smith, 'How Do Foreign Patent Rights Affect U.S. Exports, Affiliate Sales, and Licenses?' (2001) 55 Journal of International Economics 411; Nicholson (n 13); Walter Park and Douglas Lippoldt, 'International Licensing and the Strengthening of Intellectual Property Rights in Developing Countries During the 1990s' (2005) 40 OECD Economic Studies 7.

owner to share her technology would lead to a market expansion effect and an increase in the import of technological goods. This is because if the technology owner is subject to a duty to license, local imitators may be able to acquire the technology and start competing with the owner. The same applies to no challenge clauses, which would have prevented local licensees from challenging the validity of the patent. But all this would only be relevant for a product that is subject to the threat of reverse engineering.

Raising patent protection can also have some unintended negative effects on the prospect for developing countries to improve their technological capacity. Scherer argues that increased

> patent protection may shield product imports from imitative local competition, permitting production to be centralized in some other nation where economies of scale are exploited more fully and wage conditions are more favorable. Lacking such patent protection, MNEs [multinational enterprises] may feel compelled to commence on-shore production in order to neutralize 'made-at-home' advantages enjoyed by indigenous rivals.[67]

Given that localization of production redounds more benefit to the host country than mere importation, raising patent protection could in fact be counterproductive. Again, what Scherer has in mind here seems to be robustness of protection rather than scope of patent rights. His insight would be relevant to those patent–competition rules that implicate robustness of protection.

2. Foreign Direct Investment

Commentators seem to have mixed views on whether increased patent protection will attract more FDI. Maskus describes the relationship between the two as 'subtle and complex. While the weight of the theory seems to lie on the side of a positive impact, overall it is ambiguous.'[68] Correa concurs, characterizing the available evidence on the issue as 'inconclusive. Data on FDI flows to countries with allegedly low levels of IPRs protection show that the perceived inadequacies of intellectual property protection did not hinder FDI inflows in global terms.'[69] The Commission on Intellectual Property Rights goes one step further, asserting that

[67] FM Scherer and Sandy Weisburst, 'Economic Effects of Strengthening Pharmaceutical Patent Protection in Italy' (1995) 26 International Review of Industrial Property and Copyright 1009, 1014.

[68] Maskus, *Intellectual Property Rights in the Global Economy* (n 7) 130.

[69] Correa (n 24) 27.

> [w]hat is clear from the literature is that strong IP rights alone provide neither the necessary nor sufficient incentives for firms to invest in particular countries. If this was the case, then large countries with high growth rates but weak IPR regimes would not have received large foreign investment inflows in the past and even now.[70]

One consensus among commentators is that least developed countries (LDCs) do not receive much FDI, especially technology-related FDI, and this will not change regardless of the amount of patent protection offered. This has been attributed to their extremely low productivity, education and skills, underdeveloped infrastructure, poorly designed government regulation, and prevalence of corruption.[71] Correa issues a damning assessment on the prospect of the least developed countries, asserting that for 'the least developed countries, which have historically received an insignificant amount of FDI[,] [t]here are no reasons to think that higher IPRs standards may by themselves change this situation in any substantial manner'.[72] This is corroborated by recent research by Siew Mei Chan and Tuck Cheong Tang, who find that there is no direct effect of increased intellectual property protection on FDI inflows into low-income countries.[73]

The relationship between intellectual property rights and FDI, at least in more developed countries, seems to be a favourite topic of study among economists, who have produced voluminous literature on the topic. Some studies have suggested that heightened patent protection increases the inflow of FDI, especially to developing countries.[74] After surveying the then-existing literature, Carlos Primo Braga and Carsten Fink find that there is generally a positive link between intellectual property protection and FDI.[75] Lee Branstetter, Raymond Fisman, and C Fritz Foley also find that intra-firm royalty payments by developing country affiliates to multinational firms increased following patent law reforms in sixteen countries between 1982 and 1999, suggesting greater amount of internal technology transfer through FDI.[76] Jeong-Yeon Lee and Edwin Mansfield find that weak patent protection has a significant negative impact on FDI by US firms.[77] Some theoretical work

70 Commission on Intellectual Property Rights (n 12) 23.

71 Maskus, *Intellectual Property Rights in the Global Economy* (n 7) 122.

72 Correa (n 24) 30.

73 Siew Mei Chan and Tuck Cheong Tang, 'Foreign Direct Investment Inflows and Intellectual Property Rights: Empirical Evidence from Different Income Groups' (2017) 46 Global Economic Review 372, 383.

74 Peter Nunnenkamp and Julius Spatz, 'Intellectual Property Rights and Foreign Direct Investment: A Disaggregated Analysis' (2004) 140 Review of World Economics 393.

75 Carlos Primo Braga and Carsten Fink, 'The Relationship Between Intellectual Property Rights and Foreign Direct Investment' (1998) 9 Duke Journal of Comparative & International Law 163, 180.

76 Lee Branstetter, Raymond Fisman, and C Fritz Foley, 'Do Stronger Intellectual Property Rights Increase International Technology Transfer? Empirical Evidence from U.S. Firm-Level Panel Data' (2006) 121 Quarterly Journal of Economics 321.

77 Jeong-Yeon Lee and Edwin Mansfield, 'Intellectual Property Protection and U.S. Foreign Direct Investment' (1996) 78 The Review of Economics and Statistics 181, 184.

also reaches the same conclusion. Hitoshi Tanaka and Tatsuro Iwaisako conclude that increased patent protection promotes FDI and innovation in developed countries.[78] Elias Dinopoulos and Paul Segerstrom reaches the same result, which they attribute to a lower relative wage for R&D personnel in developed countries.[79]

Other studies have indicated an inconclusive relationship. Peter Nunnenkamp and Julius Spatz fail to find any significant relationship between patent protection and US FDI, concluding that 'IPR protection may not provide additional explanatory power to market- and location-related driving forces of FDI'.[80] They only find a significant relationship for patent protection once host-country characteristics and industry-specific factors are taken into account.[81] This is consistent with the earlier observation that the choice of FDI destination is largely determined by economic factors. Chan and Tang also find that in the short run, increased intellectual property protection has no significant impact on FDI inflows for all the countries surveyed, from low-income to high-income.[82]

A few studies have qualified the positive impact of patent protection on FDI by the type of industry and the type of activity at issue. The impact is greater where the industry is reliant on patents as an appropriation mechanism, which in turn depends on the kind of technology in use in the industry. If the technology sought to be transferred is relatively old or the industry is relatively low-tech, such as textiles and apparel or service industries, patent protection is unlikely to be an important consideration.[83] Unsurprisingly, patent protection has been found to be a greater concern in industries where the technology is relatively imitable, including pharmaceuticals, chemicals, food processing, and software.[84] Nunnenkamp and Spatz find that patent protection matters the most to FDI in transport equipment, electrical equipment, and machinery.[85] Somewhat counterintuitively, and contrary to Maskus' finding, they find that FDI in the chemical industry is not sensitive to the level of patent protection.[86] One reason Nunnenkamp and Spatz offer for this slightly anomalous finding is that US FDI in the chemical industry seems to be concentrated in the industrialized countries and that licensing seems to be the preferred mode of technology for US chemical manufacturers.[87] Beata Smarzynska Javorcik finds that patent protection has a significant impact on FDI in six industries which she calls IPR-sensitive industries.[88] These include drugs, cosmetics,

[78] Hitoshi Tanaka and Tatsuro Iwaisako, 'Intellectual Property Rights and Foreign Direct Investment: A Welfare Analysis' (2014) 67 European Economic Review 107.

[79] Elias Dinopoulos and Paul Segerstrom, 'Intellectual Property Rights, Multinational Firms and Economic Growth' (2010) 92 Journal of Development Economics 13, 23.

[80] Nunnenkamp and Spatz (n 74) 402.

[81] ibid.

[82] Chan and Tang (n 73) 383.

[83] Maskus, *Intellectual Property Rights in the Global Economy* (n 7) 125.

[84] ibid.

[85] Nunnenkamp and Spatz (n 74) 408.

[86] ibid 409.

[87] ibid.

[88] Javorcik (n 36) 49–51.

and healthcare products, chemicals, machinery and equipment, and electrical equipment.[89] This is more consistent with Mansfield's finding about the degree of reliance on patents by different industries.

The impact of patent protection is also greater for R&D-related activities as opposed to marketing and distribution. Javorcik finds that FDI tends to shift from distribution to manufacturing in countries with higher levels of patent protection.[90] This effect is observed across all industries regardless of whether it is IPR-sensitive.[91] However, it has also been found that FDI in manufacturing tends to concentrate in countries with larger population.[92] In a survey of ninety-four US firms on their FDI preferences, Mansfield finds that only 20 per cent of the surveyed firms deem intellectual property protection to be important for investments in sales and distribution, 30 per cent of the firms for investments in rudimentary production and assembly facilities, 50–60 per cent of the firms for investments in manufacturing facilities for components and complete products, and 80 per cent of the firms for investments in R&D facilities.[93] Lee and Mansfield also find that among chemical firms, weak patent protection would deter them from investing in relatively sophisticated manufacturing and R&D.[94]

The strength of patent protection also interacts with a range of other factors, including distance from the location of the investor and the educational level in the host country, to influence FDI. Nunnenkamp and Spatz find that impact of patent protection on FDI depends on host-country characteristics. For example, they find that the quality of patent protection is no longer a significant factor for US investors in countries within 3,900 miles of the United States, suggesting that geographical proximity overrides the importance of patent protection.[95] They also find that patent protection fades in importance in countries with low levels of corruption and high regulatory quality.[96] They conjecture that for these countries, foreign investors may be willing to assume that overall excellence in regulatory quality extends to intellectual property enforcement as well. Lastly, they also find that high quality of local human capital together with strong patent protection cause foreign investors to shift away from FDI as the mode of technology transfer.[97]

The relationship between patent protection and FDI thus seems to be contingent and industry- and activity-specific. The positive impact seems to be much more pronounced in countries that are otherwise viable FDI destinations. Perhaps more

[89] ibid 44.
[90] ibid 55.
[91] ibid.
[92] ibid.
[93] Edwin Mansfield, 'Intellectual Property Protection, Foreign Direct Investment, and Technology Transfer' (International Finance Corporation 1994) No 19 1–2.
[94] Lee and Mansfield (n 77) 185.
[95] Nunnenkamp and Spatz (n 74) 405.
[96] ibid.
[97] ibid 406.

worryingly, Biswajit Dhar and Reji Joseph report that FDI does not necessarily result in technology transfer, noting that 'the foreign firm usually exercises its superior bargaining power to refuse technology transfer to the host countries'.[98] The same concern does not exist for international trade and licensing. For international trade, technology transfer happens when the good reaches the destination country. And licensing by definition entails technology transfer to a local partner. The technology transfer benefit through FDI cannot be taken for granted. Successful technology transfer through FDI usually requires the host country government to impose conditions, which both China and India have practised to great effect.[99] This does not augur well for most developing countries, which lack the vast domestic markets of China and India to bargain effectively with multinational firms. If this was indeed true, FDI as a mode of technology transfer may deserve less attention from developing countries from the perspective of calibrating the patent–competition interface.

It remains to be determined what lessons can be drawn from the above studies for the patent–competition rules. This would require an understanding of how improvement in patent protection was measured in these studies. Of the studies surveyed in this section, including Mansfield (1994), Lee and Mansfield (1996), Nunnenkamp and Spatz (2004), Javorcik (2004), and Branstetter, Fisman, and Foley (2006), the former two are based on surveys of business executives on their perception of the patent system in the country at issue. Nunnenkamp and Spatz (2004) rely on the Ginarte–Park Index and a survey by the World Economic Forum, again, on perceptions of business executives.[100] Jovorcik (2004) uses the Ginarte–Park Index and another index that is more focused on copyright and trademark.[101]

As mentioned earlier, the Ginarte–Park Index encompasses patent rules that pertain to both scope of patent rights and robustness of protection. Branstetter, Fisman, and Foley do not rely on a particular index and instead focus on episodes of patent reform in sixteen countries, which cover: (1) scope of patentability, (2) effective scope of protection, (3) length of patent term, (4) effectiveness in enforcement, and (5) administration of the patent system.[102] Given the mixed focus of the measurements of patent protection used in these studies, their findings probably do not have special relevance to any category of patent–competition rules. These studies can be construed as saying that any patent–competition rules that adjust the scope of patent rights in a similar way to the patent rules examined

[98] Biswajit Dhar and Reji Joseph, 'The Rise of the South and New Paths of Development in the 21st Century' (UNCTAD 2012) No 6 18.

[99] ibid.

[100] Nunnenkamp and Spatz (n 74) 397–98.

[101] Javorcik (n 36) 46.

[102] Branstetter, Fisman, and Foley (n 76) 333–34.

in these studies would produce a similar effect on FDI, subject to the industry-specificity and activity-specificity highlighted above.

One final caveat on FDI in developing countries is in order. Most developing countries receive negligible FDI. Asia accounts for three quarters of the FDI to developing countries.[103] All the least developed countries together only received 3 per cent of the developing country FDI in 2019.[104] FDI in most developing countries is rarely in R&D-intensive activities. Only 6 per cent of announced FDI projects in 2019 were R&D related, with the pharmaceutical industry having the highest percentage at merely 17 per cent.[105] Even if FDI goes into R&D, it is usually devoted to adaptation of foreign technology or products to the local market.[106] Therefore, it is probably important to be realistic about the contribution of FDI to technology transfer to developing countries.

3. Licensing

Economists have produced a number of theoretical studies to model the relationship between patent protection and licensing. Guifang Yang and Keith Maskus construct a dynamic general-equilibrium model of the product cycle to study the effects of strong patent protection in the global South on the incentives of firms in the global North to innovate and to license advanced technologies to firms in the global South.[107] They conclude that stronger patent protection in the global South would increase both the rate of innovation in the global North and the extent of licensing to the global South.[108] They assert that:

> [s]tronger IPRs not only would create a better legal framework for the enforcement of licensing contracts, reducing the costs associated with establishing and policing an arm's-length relationship, but also would raise the rent share the licensor receives. Therefore, the degree of IPRs protection not only would determine the size of the pie (the size effect) but also the distribution of the pie between the two licensing parties (the distribution effect). Firms would be encouraged to license technology to the South in order to take advantage of lower labor costs there and earn higher instantaneous economic returns.[109]

[103] United Nations Conference on Trade and Development, 'World Investment Report 2019' (United Nations Conference on Trade and Development 2019) 12 <https://unctad.org/system/files/official-document/wir2019_en.pdf> accessed 29 April 2021.

[104] ibid.

[105] ibid 23.

[106] ibid 24.

[107] Guifang Yang and Keith Maskus, 'Intellectual Property Rights, Licensing, and Innovation in an Endogenous Product-Cycle Model' (2001) 53 Journal of International Economics 169.

[108] ibid 181.

[109] ibid.

Lei Yang and Keith Maskus produce another theoretical model to study the choice between export and licensing for a developed country firm with a superior product technology.[110] They find that strengthening patent protection boosts technology transfer through licensing to the global South and raises export from the South by reducing the Southern firm's marginal cost of production.[111] The amount of know-how transferred increases with the technological absorption capacity of the developing country firm.[112] They are, however, not as confident about the beneficial welfare effect of increased patent protection, concluding that the technological absorption capacity of the developing country will determine the welfare effects of increased protection and that excessive patent protection would hurt both competition and welfare.[113]

Sunil Kanwar finds that increased patent protection tends to raise royalty and license fee payments, from which he infers an increase in technology transfer.[114] Specifically, he finds that reforms implemented by developing countries to comply with the TRIPS Agreement increased the total value of technology transfer by between 2.6 per cent and 3.3 per cent .[115] Kanwar's analysis suggests that most of this increase is due to the increase in the scope of patentability introduced by TRIPS in pharmaceuticals, chemicals, and agricultural products.[116] The validity of his conclusion, however, is open to question. If the same technologies had previously been accessible to developing countries, perhaps through reverse engineering, and the TRIPS Agreement only forced these countries to pay for them, then there would be no increase in the amount of technology transferred. Kanwar is unable to distinguish between the two scenarios. Therefore, the only conclusion one can confidently draw from his study is that royalty payments made by developing countries increased after the TRIPS Agreement was signed, which is exactly what the multinational firms in developed countries had intended.

Usha Nair-Reichert and Roderick Duncan focus on the substitutability between different modes of technology transfer.[117] They made a number of findings. First, increased patent protection renders licensing more attractive vis-à-vis export.[118] Second, when faced with a higher imitation capacity in the host country, technology owners tend to prefer licensing to export.[119] However, if imitation capacity

110 Lei Yang and Keith Maskus, 'Intellectual Property Rights, Technology Transfer and Exports in Developing Countries' (2009) 90 Journal of Development Economics 231.

111 ibid 234.

112 ibid.

113 ibid 235.

114 Sunil Kanwar, 'Intellectual Property Protection and Technology Licensing: The Case of Developing Countries' (2012) 55 The Journal of Law and Economics 539.

115 ibid 557.

116 ibid 561.

117 Usha Nair-Reichert and Roderick Duncan, 'Patent Regimes, Host Country Policies, and the Nature of MNE Activities' (2008) 16 Review of International Economics 783.

118 ibid 795.

119 ibid.

is constrained by a high level of patent protection, there is less licensing and greater reliance on trade.[120] The implication seems to be that licensing is a preferred strategy for managing imitation risks. Interestingly, they find no support in their data for the commonly held hypothesis that raising patent protection in countries with a strong imitation capacity shifts the mode of technology transfer from FDI to licensing.[121] The general belief is that more secure patent protection gives firms greater comfort in parting with their technology and licensing it to third parties.[122] This conclusion is hardly surprising as their results indicate an opposite relationship between patent protection and licensing from the conventional position. They find that licensing increases when patent protection weakens.

Results from Pamela Smith's study contradict those of Nair-Reichert and Duncan's. She finds that increased patent protection generally encourages technology transfer regardless of the mode, especially in countries with strong imitation capacity.[123] The positive effect, however, is greater with FDI and licensing than with exports. She finds that there is a 0.91 per cent larger increase in FDI and licensing than in export for the same amount of increase in patent protection.[124] Therefore, stronger patent protection enhances the location advantage of the host country. She further finds that there is a 1.14 per cent larger increase in licensing vis-à-vis export and FDI for the same amount of increase in patent protection.[125] Stronger patent protection lowers the internalization advantage of keeping production within the firm and renders licensing more attractive. She concludes that imitation risk is the greatest when a technology is transferred outside the technology owner's home country and outside the firm, and that this risk is the greatest when technology transfer takes place in a country with high imitation capacity.[126] FDI seems to be the compromise option for technology owners when there is a substantial risk of imitation.[127]

Lastly, Michael Nicholson examines how variations in industry characteristics affect a technology owner's choice between different modes of transfer. He reports that

> [w]hen a firm in an industry with high capital costs considers entering a country with high IPRs, they are less likely to engage in FDI. If IPRs are weak, firms with similar characteristics are more likely to engage in FDI. This suggests that the

[120] ibid.
[121] ibid.
[122] Guifang Yang and Keith Maskus, 'Intellectual Property Rights and Licensing: An Econometric Investigation' (2001) 137 Review of World Economics 58.
[123] Pamela Smith, 'How Do Foreign Patent Rights Affect U.S. Exports, Affiliate Sales, and Licenses?' (2001) 55 Journal of International Economics 411, 427.
[124] ibid.
[125] ibid.
[126] ibid 434.
[127] ibid 427.

greater the risk to their proprietary asset, the more likely a firm is to internalize overseas production.[128]

When patent protection is high, foreign investors with a high level of knowledge-based assets are more willing to forego internalization and resort to licensing instead of FDI. This harkens back to the same theme that patent protection is more important to industries that are more susceptible to imitation.

Three of the four aforementioned studies use the Ginarte–Park Index, or a modified version of it, as an indicator of the level of patent protection. Kanwar incorporates an extra measurement that focuses on enforcement into the Ginarte–Park Index to add further weight to enforcement. This extra measurement covers 'the legal enforcement of contracts, judicial independence, impartiality of courts, integrity of the legal system, protection of property rights, restrictions on the sale of physical property, and military interference'.[129] Smith uses a slightly different index compiled by Rapp and Rozek that was actually the original basis of the Ginarte–Park Index. The Rapp–Rozek Index focuses on 'coverage of inventions, examination procedures, term of protection, transferability of rights, compulsory licensing, and effective enforcement against infringement'.[130] Therefore, the findings of these studies reflect the importance of patent rules that pertain to both robustness of protection and scope of patent rights, with Kanwar's probably more tilted towards the former given his modification to the Ginarte–Park Index.

The foregoing discussion has a number of implications for the patent–competition rules. With the exception of Nair-Reichert and Duncan, the thrust of these studies seems to be that among the three modes of technology transfer, licensing faces the greatest imitation risk and therefore relies most heavily on patent protection. These studies find that heightened patent protection generally leads to a shift to licensing by technology owners. Nair-Reichert and Duncan's finding seems to suggest that international trade exposes technology owners to the greatest imitation risk and licensing is used as a risk management strategy. Overall, the weight of evidence seems to be against Nair-Reichert and Duncan.[131] Since imitation risk is related to the robustness of patent protection, this should mean that a tightening of the patent–competition rules that enhances the robustness of patent protection should similarly encourage more licensing by technology owners. It was suggested earlier that licensing redounds the greatest technical benefits to a developing country by transferring technology into the hands of local firms. Developing countries therefore should prefer licensing as a mode of technology transfer. This means that the patent–competition rules should be calibrated to minimize imitation risks.

[128] Nicholson (n 13) 41.
[129] Kanwar (n 114) 546.
[130] Smith, 'How Do Foreign Patent Rights Affect U.S. Exports, Affiliate Sales, and Licenses?' (n 123) 421.
[131] Maskus, *Intellectual Property Rights in the Global Economy* (n 7) 123, 129.

This would seem to suggest that no challenge clauses and reverse payments should be permitted and a duty to license intellectual property should only be imposed judiciously.

4. Summing Up

An industry-specific approach to the patent–competition interface may be required. The relationship between patent protection and all three modes of technology transfer has industry-specific variations dictated by the degree of imitability of the technology in the industry, which in turn determines the relative importance of different appropriation mechanisms. For trade in technological goods, the impact of increased patent protection on the volume of trade varies with local imitation capacity. Ivus finds that industries where there is the strongest local imitation capacity will see a surge in import following an increase in patent protection, whereas industries with a low local imitation capacity may witness a fall in import. Even though it was not explicitly spelled out in her study, one can imagine that local imitation capacity will only be an issue where the technology of the industry suffers from high imitability, which varies by industry.

The impact of increased patent protection on FDI also depends on the industry at issue. Industries where the technology is relatively imitable and that rely heavily on patents as an appropriation mechanism see a closer relationship between patent protection and FDI. According to Javorcik, drugs, cosmetics, and healthcare products, chemicals, machinery and equipment, and electrical equipment are examples of such industries. Nicholson also reports industry-specific variations in the likelihood to resort to licensing as a mode of technology transfer which are based on the amount of knowledge-based assets in the industry. Foreign investors with a high level of knowledge-based assets are more willing to forego internalization and resort to licensing as opposed to FDI when the level of patent protection is high.

One further comment on the relationship between the patent–competition rules and licensing is in order. While increased patent protection tends to raise royalty and license fee payments either through the 'market power' effect of allowing the technology owner to charge a higher fee for the same technology transferred or the 'market expansion' effect of increasing the amount of technology transferred, the patent–competition rules may have a different impact on the level of royalty payments. On the one hand, more relaxed patent–competition rules may enhance the technology owner's market power by giving her greater ability to forestall potential rivals. This should allow her to charge higher royalty. On the other hand, it is possible that if patent–competition rules are relaxed to allow the patentee to impose a range of licensing restrictions on the licensee, the patentee may be willing to accept a lower royalty payment. Presumably these restrictions redound other economic benefits to the patentee such that she is willing to accept lower royalty payments.

To the extent that developing countries would like to minimize their royalty and license fee payments to foreign technology owners, they would need to calibrate their patent–competition rules accordingly.

5. Involuntary Transfers

Technology can be transferred voluntarily from technology owners in developed countries through various means such as international trade, FDI, and licensing. It can also be transferred involuntarily. There are two main ways in which this can take place. The first one is through imitation such as outright copying and reverse engineering. The second is through compulsory licensing to local firms. The extent to which imitation is feasible is dependent on the robustness of patent protection. If patent law is vigorously enforced and patent owners can effectively halt imitators, imitation would be largely impractical. If, however, patent law is loosely enforced, imitation as a technology transfer mechanism would become a distinct possibility. Therefore, the feasibility of imitation as a means of technology transfer is largely contingent on patent protection, in particular the enforceability of the patent right to exclude. There is not much of a role for patent–competition rules to play.

In contrast, patent–competition rules can play a determinative role in the possibility of compulsory licensing. Although the patent law of some countries such as China does permit compulsory licensing under some limited circumstances,[132] compulsory licensing is very much the exception rather than the norm in patent law. Competition law, at least as practised in some jurisdictions, does consider a unilateral refusal to license intellectual property as a possible violation. To the extent that patent–competition rules adopt an aggressive attitude toward unilateral refusal to license, they can serve to facilitate involuntary technology transfer.

There are two senses in which compulsory licensing can be ordered under the patent–competition rules. The first is where the technology owner is subject to a duty to actively assist rivals in acquiring the technology. The technology owner will be required to transfer know-how and other forms of tacit knowledge needed to implement the technology. The owner may also need to assist rivals in acquiring the capacity to implement the technology. The second is where rivals have acquired the ability to implement the technology through other means, perhaps reverse engineering or independent research, and the technology owner is only required to consent to rivals' implementation of the technology subject to a royalty payment. In other words, compulsory licensing in this second sense merely amounts to authorization rather than active assistance. Compulsory licensing under the second sense is only feasible in developing countries that are already fairly technologically

[132] Patent Law 2008, art 50 (PRC).

advanced. They must possess imitation capacity in the industry concerned. It will be a much less intrusive obligation to technology owners. This does not mean that developing countries should embrace patent–competition rules as a means to compel technology transfer. The extent to which developing countries should compel technology transfer is highly complex and the discussion will be deferred to subsequent chapters on unilateral refusal to license.

One of the strongest objections to the imposition of a duty to license under competition law is that it will undermine innovation incentives. While it may seem like a highly intuitive argument, there is in fact some evidence to the contrary. In a model incorporating market imperfections such as lack of information asymmetry about product quality, Jiahua Che, Larry Qiu, and Wen Zhou find that multinational firms refrain from entering developing country markets for a variety of reasons, with weak patent protection being only one of them.[133] In such case, local firms may engage in imitation when permitting such imitation is part of the equilibrium for the market. Che, Qiu, and Zhou argue that 'imitation in the shadow of IPR enforcement can be an alternative channel for technology transfer and that strengthening such enforcement may not be in the best interests of either the host country or multinationals'.[134] In particular, they find that where imitation is part of the equilibrium strategy under the assumption of information asymmetry about product quality, heightening patent protection reduces social welfare[135] and deferring increase in protection raises the profits of the multinationals without affecting the overall social surplus.[136] A more detailed discussion of the potentially adverse impact on compulsory licensing on innovation incentives will be deferred to Chapter 4.

Separately, the extent to which overriding patent protection undermines innovation incentives crucially depends on the degree of the industry's reliance on patents as an appropriation mechanism. Patents are only an important appropriation mechanism for a select few industries such as pharmaceuticals and chemicals. For the remaining industries, overriding patent protection may not have significant impact on innovation incentives. This opens the possibility for imposing a duty to license patents that may be less objectionable.

[133] Jiahua Che, Larry Qiu, and Wen Zhou, 'Entry, Reputation and Intellectual Property Rights Enforcement' (2014) 47 The Canadian Journal of Economics 1256.

[134] ibid 1276.

[135] ibid 1272.

[136] ibid 1276.

4

A Proposed Approach to the Patent–Competition Interface

A. A Development Stage-Specific Approach

The relevance of innovation and technology transfer as a means of technological progress varies widely according to the technological capacity of the country at issue. For the production countries, innovation is mostly beyond reach and innovation incentives carry very little weight. Competition authorities in these countries should emphasize consumer welfare in their approach to the patent–competition interface. It is only when these countries have acquired rudimentary technological capacity and developed the requisite human capital that technology transfer will start to become a relevant issue.

For the technology adaptation countries, dynamic efficiency considerations should be about technology transfer rather than innovation because technology transfer is likely to be the main way in which they will achieve technological progress. These countries face a dilemma between voluntary and involuntary technology transfer. As far as the patent–competition rules are concerned, developing countries can facilitate involuntary technology transfer by adopting an aggressive attitude toward unilateral refusal to license intellectual property. However, economic studies have shown that robustness of patent protection is an important consideration for foreign technology owners when contemplating export and licensing as modes of technology transfer. Suppression of imitation, either by raising patent protection or showing reluctance to impose a duty to license, will increase importation of technological goods and licensing to local firms. Adopting an appropriate approach to the unilateral refusal to license intellectual property would hence be of paramount importance.

For the proto-innovation countries, their domestic constituencies comprise innovators, imitators, and consumers. While the imitators would clearly favour an approach to the patent–competition interface that favours technology transfer and protects the technology transferees, the innovators would prefer robust patent protection and permissive patent–competition rules that give them substantial leeway to exploit their patents. Meanwhile, domestic consumers would opt for lower prices and greater access to technological goods. It is probably impossible to fashion an overarching approach to the patent–competition interface across all kinds of practice and all industries for these countries. Each category of

The Patent–Competition Interface in Developing Countries. Thomas K. Cheng, Oxford University Press. © Thomas K. Cheng 2021. DOI: 10.1093/oso/9780192857354.003.0004

patent-exploitation practice presents disparate trade-offs between the interests of these three constituencies which may need to be resolved differently. For example, licensing rules would present particularly tricky issues as these countries contain both licensors and licensees and their conflicting interests may need to be balanced carefully when calibrating the appropriate approach to these rules.

B. An Industry-Specific Approach

Apart from an approach that is sensitive to the stage of development, developing countries require an approach to the patent–competition interface that takes into account the characteristics of specific industries. The foregoing discussion has already provided a number of justifications for an industry-specific approach. Lemley argues that patent and competition laws should be treated as equals in the patent–competition interface and that the nature of the industry and the invention in question dictate which tool should be used. The relationship between patentee reward and innovation incentives turns out to be industry-specific as different industries demonstrate varying degrees of reliance on patents as an appropriation mechanism. The extent to which innovation incentives will translate into concrete innovations depends on the existence of innovation capacity in the country at issue. Although the classification based on technological capacity has been done on a country-by-country basis, variations in innovation capacity are likely to be industry-specific, or perhaps firm-specific. Furthermore, economic studies have shown that the effect of increased patentee reward on FDI varies across industries, with industries that rely more on patents as an appropriation mechanism showing greater sensitivity to changes in patent protection. The impact of the robustness of patent protection on import of technological goods and licensing varies according to local imitation risks, which vary by industry both because of disparate local technological capacity and the ease of imitation inherent in the technology in different industries.

C. Feasibility of the Proposed Approach

1. Enforcement Capacity

One concern about the proposed approach to the patent–competition interface in developing countries is enforcement capacity. This is an especially valid concern for least developed countries, whose competition authorities may simply not have the capacity to apply complex competition rules to patent exploitation practices, which present highly intricate policy trade-offs. There is no question that competition law, especially effects-based rules, could be difficult to apply and place a heavy demand on enforcement capacity. It is therefore important that constraints imposed by limited enforcement capacity be taken into account when devising analytical frameworks for developing countries, especially the least developed ones. For countries with low enforcement capacity, preference should be given to simple '*per se*' rules or presumptive illegality rules. These rules will avoid the all-embracing, full-circumstance analysis that is often required under effects-based rule.

It is no doubt going to be a difficult balancing act to devise rules that are simple enough for developing countries to apply but not so blunt that they may give rise to high error costs, but this difficulty should not be a reason for giving up. Developing countries and their competition authorities owe it to themselves and their consumers to try their best to police against patent exploitation practices that may harm their consumers without creating any significant dynamic efficiency benefits for them. Giving up would leave vulnerable consumers to exploitation by patentees, who are often multinational corporations. One can argue that there are other areas of law, such as intellectual property law, that are also highly complex to administer and could be beyond the enforcement capacity of some developing countries, but that has not stopped industrialized economies from forcing developing countries to adopt them. It would seem duplicitous for industrialized economies to insist that developing countries have the capacity to enforce complex intellectual property law, which tends to benefit the former, but not the capacity to apply competition rules that may be no more complex to protect the interests of their domestic consumers.

2. Concerns under the TRIPS Agreement

Another possible concern with the proposed approach, especially the industry-specificity aspect of it, is that it may be inconsistent with the Agreement on Trade-Related Aspects of Intellectual Property Rights (TRIPS Agreement), in particular with Article 27, which stipulates that patent protection shall be available for all products and processes 'in all fields of technology'[1] and more importantly, that patent rights shall be enjoyable 'without discrimination as to ... the field of technology'.[2] This can be interpreted to limit a developing country's ability to apply an industry-specific approach to the patent–competition interface.

A closer examination of the provisions in the TRIPS Agreement, however, suggests that this concern may be overstated. Article 28 of the TRIPS Agreement delineates the scope of patent rights guaranteed by the agreement. It provides two main rights, the right to exclude and the right to assign, transfer by succession, and

[1] 'Agreement on Trade-Related Aspects of Intellectual Property Rights (Adopted 15 April 1994, Entered into Force 1 January 1995) 1869 UNTS 299 (TRIPS Agreement)' art 27.

[2] ibid.

to conclude licensing agreements. The right to exclude is usually not implicated in the patent–competition rules apart from the unilateral refusal to deal doctrine. Article 31 specifically addresses conditions that need to be met for compulsory licenses to be deemed compatible with the TRIPS Agreement. None of the rights guaranteed by Article 28 are meant to be absolute. They are qualified by Article 30, which allows TRIPS signatories to impose limited exceptions to patent rights so long as they 'do not necessarily conflict with a normal exploitation of the patent'[3] and 'do not unreasonably prejudice the legitimate interests of the patent owner, taking account of the legitimate interests of third parties'.[4] More pertinently, Article 40(1) of the TRIPS Agreement acknowledges that 'some licensing practices or conditions pertaining to intellectual property rights which restrain competition may have adverse effects on trade and may impede the transfer and dissemination of technology'.[5] Article 40(2) further authorizes the World Trade Organization (WTO) member states to adopt 'appropriate measures to prevent or control such practices'.[6] The provision then proceeds to enumerate a number of anticompetitive licensing practices that may be subject to regulation, such as exclusive grantbacks, no challenge clauses, and coercive package licenses.

There is scant WTO jurisprudence on the precise scope of Articles 30 and 40. There has been one case decided on the scope of Article 30 and none on Article 40. The one case that dealt with the scope of Article 30 was the *Canada—Pharmaceutical Patents* case, which was not concerned with the patent–competition rules in general but with an exception provided by Canadian patent law for generics to accelerate the regulatory approval process.[7] Therefore, the case is of limited relevance except for the notion that patent rights are not absolute, which should be uncontroversial, and that any exception to patent rights must meet the cumulative conditions of being limited, consistent with the normal exploitation of patent rights, and not unreasonably prejudicing the legitimate interests of patent owners.

Article 40 is directly concerned with competition regulation of patent exploitation practices. The lack of jurisprudence on Article 40 means that there is no WTO decisional practice on whether an industry-specific approach to the patent–competition interface is consistent with this article. The key to answering this question is the meaning of 'appropriate measures' in Article 40 and whether an industry-specific approach to the interface constitutes discrimination of patent rights by field of technology under Article 27. The possible meaning of appropriate measures is so broad that it is certainly possible to fit an industry-specific approach within it, especially when the approach is derived from sound competition

3 ibid art 30.
4 ibid.
5 ibid art 40(1).
6 ibid art. 40(2).
7 WTO, *Canada—Pharmaceutical Patents* (17 March 2000) WT/DS114/R.

principles with due regard to consumer welfare, the widely acknowledged objective of competition law.

As to whether such an approach constitutes discrimination, the WTO has a very well-developed body of jurisprudence on non-discrimination in one particular context, that is, whether like products are accorded differential treatment under the rubric of the national treatment and most favoured nation obligations of the WTO member states. This body of jurisprudence, however, principally focuses on the existence of distinctions between similar products and is not concerned with disparate treatment across industries. Therefore, it is of limited relevance as well.

While a definitive answer to the question of whether an industry-specific approach to the patent–competition interface violates the non-discrimination obligation awaits adjudication, a good argument can be made that it does not. The nature of competition analysis requires an examination of market, and by extension, industry conditions. By authorizing WTO member states to regulate exercise of patent rights under competition law, Article 40 must have implicitly endorsed such an analytical approach, as indicated by the reference in paragraph 2 to 'an adverse effect on competition in the relevant market'.[8] The proposed industry-specific approach is nothing more than a more formalized version of such analysis. It merely represents a more permanent incorporation of industry conditions in the analysis. In any case, the industry-specific approach only prescribes the analytical approach but not the outcome of cases. Whether a particular patent exploitation practice violates domestic competition law still requires a case-by-case determination of adverse effects in a relevant market, which seems to be what Article 40 requires.

The Doha Ministerial Declaration on the TRIPS Agreement and Public Health subsequently adopted by the WTO member states recognizes that individual countries can use to the fullest extent the flexibilities for competition law provided in the Agreement. Clause 5(b) of the Declaration recognizes that each member 'has the right to grant compulsory licenses and the freedom to determine upon which such licenses are granted'.[9] While this declaration is made in the context of public health and aims to promote access to affordable medicine for all, it does illustrate the degree of flexibility afforded to each member state to craft its own competition policies.

D. Conclusion

The chapter puts forward a development stage-specific approach to the patent–competition interface that was built upon in Chapters 2 and 3 by illustrating that

[8] TRIPS Agreement (n 1) art 40(2).

[9] WTO, *Ministerial Declaration on the TRIPS Agreement and Public Health* (14 November 2001) WT/MIN(01)/DEC/W/2.

developing countries face different policy considerations from developed countries when tackling the patent–competition interface. While developed economies have a tendency to emphasize patent policy and dynamic efficiency considerations, developing countries may not be able to afford to do that, given the level of poverty of the vast majority of their consumers. Developing countries need to be much more cautious about sacrificing consumer welfare for the sake of uncertain dynamic efficiency gains. This is especially in light of the tendency of the patent system to overcompensate innovators, the existence of a variety of appropriation mechanisms for innovators to recoup their investments, and the fact that most developing countries simply do not possess the technological capacity to benefit from the innovation incentives generated by their patent systems. Studies have repeatedly shown that patentee reward tends to benefit foreign innovators rather than domestic innovators in developing countries. A developing country competition authority may rightfully ask whether it would want to sacrifice the welfare of downtrodden domestic consumers to provide often negligible innovation incentives to multinational firms.

The lack of genuine domestic innovation capacity means that most developing countries rely on technology transfer by foreign technology owners to attain the technological progress that is critical to economic growth. This means that dynamic efficiency in the context of these countries is no longer concerned with innovation incentives but instead with the incentives to transfer technology. Developing countries hence need to be mindful of how their patent–competition rules may affect such incentives. Technology transfer can be voluntary and involuntary. Voluntary technology transfer may take place through international trade of technological goods, foreign direct investment (FDI), or licensing. Involuntary technology transfer can be accomplished by imitation or compulsory licensing. Economic studies show that the robustness of patent protection affects incentives to export technological goods and to license technology. They further show that the impact of patent protection on FDI depends on the industry and the type of activity at issue. The impact is greater in industries that tend to rely more heavily on patents as an appropriation mechanism and in activities that are more research-intensive.

Analogizing these results to the patent–competition rules, this means that those rules that have the strongest implications for the robustness of patent protection, such as unilateral refusal to license intellectual property, reverse payments, and no-challenge clauses, will have the most significant impact on the incentives to export technological goods and to license technology. Enforcing these rules in favour of stronger patent protection may attract more import of such goods, at least in countries with significant imitation capacity, and more technology licensing. More permissive competition regulation of licensing may also encourage more licensing activities. Given that licensing tends to redound greater benefits to the host economy than other means of technology transfer, developing countries that rely on technology transfer may want to adjust their patent–competition rules to encourage technology licensing. All this of course only applies to those developing countries with a technology absorption capacity. For those that only possess the capacity to engage in basic production, technology transfer is not a matter of concern and these countries should focus on protecting domestic consumer welfare when approaching the patent–competition interface.

5
Unilateral Refusal to License Patents—A Theoretical Perspective

A. Patent Exploitation Practices in Developing Countries: A Classification

There is a wide variety of patent exploitation practices. As in the rest of competition law, these practices can be categorized into horizontal agreements, vertical agreements, and abuse of dominance or monopolization. Some of these practices, such as traditional price fixing and other forms of cartel conduct, resale price maintenance, and vertical non-price restraints, are common across both patent-related and non-patent-related areas of competition law. The remainder are specific to the patent context. Patent-specific horizontal agreements include cross-licensing, patent pools, conduct arising out of the standard-setting context, research and development (R&D)-related joint ventures, and patent settlements, often involving a payment by a patentee to a patent challenger known as a reverse payment.[1] Patent-specific vertical agreements mostly arise in the licensing context when the licensor attempts to impose licensing restrictions on the licensee.[2] Among these are price- or output-restricted licenses, tying or exclusive dealing obligations, package and blanket licenses, various grantback provisions, royalty-related violations, and restrictions on the licensee's right to challenge the patent's validity, also known as no challenge clauses. Lastly, abuses of dominance encompass unilateral refusal to license patent rights, fraudulent conduct in the patent application process, improper enforcement of patent rights, predatory innovation or product changes, and, perhaps only in the European Union, excessive pricing as applied to technological goods or even to the determination of royalty payments.[3]

These patent exploitation practices are not equally relevant to developing countries. Some only have salience to those countries where there are potential competitors to global technological leaders. Horizontal practices among technology owners such as cross-licensing and patent pools will be of little concern to countries

[1] Although reverse payments can also be classified as vertical agreements because they are between a putative licensor and a licensee. However, the main competitive concern between these agreements is the elimination of potential competition. Classification as horizontal agreements is hence more apt.
[2] Herbert Hovenkamp and others, *IP and Antitrust: An Analysis of Antitrust Principles Applied to Intellectual Property Law* (2nd edn, Aspen Publishers 2011) Part C.
[3] ibid Part B.

The Patent–Competition Interface in Developing Countries. Thomas K. Cheng, Oxford University Press. © Thomas K. Cheng 2021. DOI: 10.1093/oso/9780192857354.003.0005

bereft of potential technology owners. Some, such as licensing restrictions, will only be of enforcement interest to countries where potential licensees are located. For countries that lack the capacity to generate innovative technology that can be cross-licensed to technology owners elsewhere and the capacity to import foreign technology through licensing, that is, innovation capacity and technology adaptation capacity respectively, many of these practices are unlikely to have significant domestic impact. Some practices, however, affect every country that imports and consumes products incorporating patented technology.

All these practices, including those taking place in the upstream market, may ultimately harm end consumers to the extent that upstream anticompetitive conduct raises the final retail price. A patent pool consisting of competing technologies may result in higher royalty payments for downstream manufacturers that may be passed on to end consumers.[4] Yet if the locus of the conduct is in the upstream market, all the parties to the conduct are likely to be located elsewhere.[5] It will be difficult for a developing country competition authority to exercise jurisdiction. There will be significant practical difficulties for developing countries to pursue every conduct that may affect their domestic consumers.

It is thus possible to put forward a classification of some kind for the degree of relevance of a patent exploitation practice to developing countries based on their technological capacities. Such classification is not meant to be iron-clad; it would be imprudent to assert categorical irrelevance of a particular patent exploitation practice for a developing country. It may be possible for a certain case to arise under some unusual set of circumstances, which spawns a case-by-case approach to the issues that may defy neat classification. Nonetheless, some generalization about the relevance of a patent exploitation practice to a country in light of its technological capacity should be feasible. Such generalizations, while not entirely airtight—as generalizations tend not to be—will facilitate the ensuing discussion and allow us to approach the subject matter in a more systematic manner.

For developing countries that lack even basic technology adaptation capacity and confine themselves to straightforward implementation of foreign technologies in domestic production, which have been called production countries, patent exploitation practices that arise in the licensing context and horizontally between competing technology owners are unlikely to be an enforcement priority. These countries should focus on those practices that directly harm their domestic consumers, such as excessive pricing and non-patent-specific conduct in the form of price fixing or resale price maintenance involving a patented product. For the latter category of conduct, the fact that the product is patented only tangentially affects

[4] ibid s 34.3c.

[5] Excluding China, 874,800 of 980,456 patents granted in the world in 2017 were granted in high-income countries. This means over 90 per cent of all the patents worldwide were granted in these countries. World Intellectual Property Organization, 'World Intellectual Property Indicators 2018' (2018) 42, 44.

the analysis. Unilateral refusal to deal may also be of interest to the extent that these countries rely on a patented input in their production. Compulsory licensing of a patented technology under the essential facilities doctrine, however, is unlikely to feature in these countries. They probably need not delve into the most complex patent–competition issues that may require the competition authority to balance competition policy against patent policy.

Even though it may seem like a practice that affects an upstream relationship between potential technological competitors which should be left to more established jurisdictions, reverse payments should be an enforcement concern even for these production countries, which are also likely to be the poorest developing countries with the most rudimentary enforcement capacity. This is because despite being relatively removed from the final consumers, reverse payments can have a significant impact on the retail prices for pharmaceutical products. Reverse payments are widely suspected as being responsible for raising drug prices.[6] As complex as reverse payments may be, they are too important for developing country consumers to be ignored by any competition authority, developing country or otherwise. Enforcement against reverse payments, however, will be fraught with difficulty for developing country competition authorities, no less because the parties involved are likely to be located elsewhere.[7] It may be difficult for these authorities to exercise jurisdiction and impose an effective remedy on the firms involved.

The situation is more complicated for those developing countries that possess the capacity to receive technology transfer from global technological leaders through voluntary means such as foreign direct investment (FDI) or licensing or involuntary means such as outright imitation by way of reverse engineering. These technology adaptation countries will need to pay attention to a much wider range of patent exploitation practices, including licensing restrictions. Unilateral refusal to license will obviously be of interest to these countries where firms with the capacity to replicate foreign technology exist. It may also be invoked by domestic firms that compete with foreign technology owners in the aftermarket or the downstream market. While these firms may not yet be capable of producing genuine

[6] Keith M Drake, Martha A Starr, and Thomas McGuire, 'Do "Reverse Payment" Settlements of Brand-Generic Patent Disputes in Pharmaceutical Industry Constitute an Anticompetitive Pay for Delay?' 2014 National Bureau of Economic Research 20292 6. The authors report that announcement of a reverse payment settlement is followed by 6 per cent increase in the share price of the brand manufacturers.

[7] Almost all the brand manufacturers and a vast majority of the generic manufacturers hail from the industrialized economies. According to Market Research Reports, all of the top ten pharmaceutical companies in the world in 2019 by revenue are based in developed countries. 'World's Top 10 Pharmaceutical Companies by Revenue' (*Market Research Reports*, 7 March 2019) <https://www.marketresearchreports.com/blog/2019/01/30/world%E2%80%99s-top-10-pharmaceutical-companies-revenue> accessed 4 March 2020. With the notable exception of India, all of the top ten generic manufacturers in the world in 2019 are based in industrialized economies. 'The World's Biggest Generic Pharmaceutical Companies in 2018' (*Pharmaceutical Technology*, 3 April 2019) <https://www.pharmaceutical-technology.com/features/biggest-generic-pharmaceutical-companies-2018/> accessed 4 March 2020.

innovation along the global technological frontier, which can be called frontier innovation, they may acquire important technical know-how or product knowledge through their involvement in the aftermarket or the downstream market. Acquisition of such know-how and knowledge may be play a pivotal role in the country's technological upgrade.

Horizontal practices arising between owners of substitute or complementary technologies, such as cross-licensing, patent pools, standards setting-related issues, and R&D joint ventures, are likely to be pertinent only to developing countries that are capable of generating frontier innovation in industries in which these practices are common. The information and communications technology (ICT) industry is one in which standard-setting activities and patent pools feature prominently.[8] Developing countries that possess genuine innovation capacity at least in certain sectors have been previously called proto-innovation countries or technologically proficient developing countries by Shamnad Basheer and Annalisa Primi.[9] Only countries that have nurtured genuine competitors and collaborators in the global technological arena need to be concerned with horizontal patent exploitation practices.

Patent-related abuse of dominance such as fraudulent conduct in the patent application process, improper enforcement of patent rights, and predatory innovation or product changes tend to be brought by firms that are directly affected by the conduct, which may include technological competitors and imitators. A firm whose innovation is blocked by a fraudulently obtained patent will have the incentive to bring what is known in the United States as a Walker Process claim.[10] A firm selling a product that does not infringe the dominant firm's technology may be subject to a vexatious lawsuit by the dominant firm.[11] These firms can be found in both technology adaptation countries and proto-innovation countries. Because even proto-innovation countries are likely to have highly varied innovation capacity in different sectors, competition authorities in these countries will need to adopt a sector-specific enforcement focus.

The foregoing discussion can be summarized in Table 5.1, with the last three columns listing those patent exploitation practices that may be of particular interest to the category of countries at issue, where practices that are relevant to countries with lower technological capacity are presumed to be of interest also to countries with higher technological capacity:

[8] Valerio Torti, *Intellectual Property Rights and Competition in Standard Setting: Objectives and Tensions* (Routledge 2016) 50–51; Claudia Tapia Garcia, 'Realities of Patent Pools in the Telecommunication Sector', in Proceedings of 7th International Conference on Standardization and Innovation in Information Technology, SIIT (IEEE 28–30 September 2011).

[9] Shamnad Basheer and Annalisa Primi, 'The WIPO Development Agenda: Factoring in the "Technologically Proficient" Developing Countries' in Jeremy DeBeer (ed), *Implementing WIPO's Development Agenda* (Wilfred Laurier University Press 2008) 104.

[10] *Walker Process Equipment v. Food Machinery & Chemical Corp.*, 382 US 172 (1965).

[11] *Professional Real Estate Investors v. Columbia Pictures*, 508 US 49 (1993).

Table 5.1 Patent Exploitation Practices of Enforcement Interest to Different Developing Countries based on their Technological Capacity

Type of Country	Technological Capacity	Horizontal Restraints	Vertical Restraints	Abuse of Dominance
Production Countries	Production and technology implementation	• General cartel conduct • Reverse payments	• Resale price maintenance • Vertical non-price restraints	• Excessive pricing • Unilateral refusal to supply
Technology Adaptation Countries	Voluntary and involuntary technology transfer	None	• Licensing restrictions	• Excessive royalty issues • Unilateral refusal to license • Fraud in patent application • Improper patent enforcement • Predatory innovation
Proto-innovation Countries	Frontier innovation in some sectors	• Cross-licensing • Patent pools • Standard-setting related practices • R&D-related joint ventures	• None	• None

B. General Discussion

1. Unilateral Refusal to Supply Patented Technology in the Developing Country Context

There are two ways in which a firm can be accused of refusing to supply a technology. It can either refuse to supply a physical product or input that embodies a patented technology or refuse to license the technology outright, although there are some situations in which firms have required the buyer of a physical product to take out a license as well.[12] Setting aside this hybrid scenario, these two types of refusal can have different ramifications in terms of remedies and significance for developing countries. The obvious remedy for a refusal to supply a patented input is to compel the firm to supply. To the extent that the patented technology

[12] Qualcomm's 'no license no chip' practice was subject to a US Federal Trade Commission enforcement action. Judge Lucy Koh of the United District Court for the Northern District of California held in the FTC's favour but the decision was later overturned by the United States Court of Appeals for the Ninth Circuit. *FTC v. Qualcomm Corp.*, 2019 WL 2206013. (ND Cal 2019).

cannot be easily reverse engineered from the product itself, the product sale need not amount to technology transfer to the buyers.[13] Being found liable for unilateral refusal to license patent rights usually results in the competition authority or the courts imposing a duty to license on the patentee.[14] Compulsory licensing will force the patentee to part with her technology and authorize the plaintiff to use it subject to reasonable compensation.[15] From the perspective of promoting technological upgrade, compulsory licensing is more beneficial so long as the country at issue possesses the capacity to absorb the transferred technology.

Compulsory licensing poses an acute dilemma for many developing countries. On the one hand, it is a powerful tool for developing country competition authorities to provide domestic firms access to foreign technology. On the other hand, liberal use of compulsory licensing may deter foreign technology transfer. Depending on the industry at issue, readiness to impose compulsory licensing affects the robustness of patent protection that has been shown to affect the readiness of foreign technology owners to engage in technology transfer.[16] In developing countries with a substantial technology adaptation capacity, more robust patent protection will create a market expansion effect, leading to an increase in the importation of technological goods.[17] Liberal use of compulsory licensing may retard importation of such goods.

Robustness of patent protection also has a bearing on the preferred mode of technology transfer. More robust patent protection will steer foreign technology owners from trade of technological goods to FDI or licensing, especially to the latter.[18] This is particularly true in countries with a substantial technology adaptation capacity. Licensing exposes the technology owner to the highest degree of imitation risk.[19] Where this risk can be kept in check by minimizing instances of compulsory licensing, foreign technology owners may be more willing to license technology to the country. Licensing redounds the greatest technical benefits to a developing country by transferring technology into the hands of local firms.[20]

[13] Kim Linsu, 'Technology Transfer & Intellectual Property Rights: The Korean Experience' (UNCTAD 2002) Issue Paper No 2 17.

[14] Hovenkamp and others (n 2) s 13.3.

[15] 'Compulsory Licensing of Pharmaceuticals and TRIPS' (*World Trade Organization TRIPS and Health: Frequently Asked Questions*, March 2018) <https://www.wto.org/english/tratop_e/trips_e/public_health_faq_e.htm> accessed 4 March 2020.

[16] Peter Nunnenkamp and Julius Spatz, 'Intellectual Property Rights and Foreign Direct Investment: A Disaggregated Analysis' (2004) 140 Review of World Economics 393, 408; Beata Smarzynska Javorcik, 'The Composition of Foreign Direct Investment and Protection of Intellectual Property Rights: Evidence from Transition Economies' (2004) 48 European Economic Review 39, 49–51; Pamela Smith, 'How Do Foreign Patent Rights Affect U.S. Exports, Affiliate Sales, and Licenses?' (2001) 55 Journal of International Economics 411, 427.

[17] Pamela Smith, 'Are Weak Patent Rights A Barrier to U.S. Exports?' (1999) 48 Journal of International Economics 151, 164. Kristie Briggs, 'Does Patent Harmonization Impact the Decision and Volume of High Technology Trade?' (2013) 25 International Review of Economics & Finance 35, 38–39.

[18] Smith (n 16) 411.

[19] ibid.

[20] Michele Di Maio, 'Industrial Policies in Developing Countries: History and Perspectives' in Mario Cimoli, Giovanni Dosi, and Joseph Stiglitz (eds), *Industrial Policy and Development: The Political*

Therefore, developing countries face conflicting considerations as far as compulsory licensing is concerned. On the one hand, compulsory licensing can be deployed as an outright means of involuntary technology transfer. On the other hand, doing so too readily could deter future technology transfer by foreign technology owners. Applying the same standard to domestic innovation, to the extent there is any, could also deter domestic R&D investment. A delicate balance will need to be struck between these considerations.

2. Competition Policy v. Patent Policy Revisited

The prohibition of the unilateral refusal to supply patented technology, either in the form of a refusal to supply a patented product or a refusal to license a patented technology, is a highly controversial area within the patent–competition interface. The essence of patent rights is the right to exclude,[21] or as Carl Shapiro has famously asserted, to try to exclude others from practising or commercializing an innovation.[22] In particular, compulsory licensing, which is the usual remedy in a unilateral refusal to license case, overrides this right to exclude and is thus a direct affront to patent protection.[23] For this reason, commentators have called for 'special scrutiny' of cases involving unilateral refusal to supply patented technology.[24] When a competition authority or a court imposes a duty to supply or license, it is essentially invoking competition policy to override patent rights. To some commentators, this amounts to a usurpation of the patent system.

Given that unilateral refusal to supply patented technology implicates the essence of patent protection, it should come as no surprise that the controversy surrounding this area of law closely parallels the debate on the appropriate balance between competition and patent policies in the patent–competition interface. There are supporters on either side of the debate. Some US commentators believe that patent law should enjoy primacy over competition law and that a unilateral refusal to supply patented technology claim should rarely, if ever, be upheld. According to Professor Herbert Hovenkamp, Mark D Janis, and Mark A Lemley, '[t]he starting point for understanding the unilateral refusal to license cases is the

Economy of Capabilities Accumulation (Oxford University Press 2009) 129; Alice Amsden, *Escape from Empire: The Developing World's Journey through Heaven and Hell* (The MIT Press 2007) 142–47; Tilman Altenburg and Wilfried Lütkenhorst, *Industrial Policy in Developing Countries: Failing Markets, Weak States* (Edward Elgar Publishing Ltd 2015) 124.

[21] For example, Section 154 of the US Patent Act provides for the right to exclude by a patentee. 35 USC s 154 (2018).

[22] Carl Shapiro, 'Antitrust Limits to Patent Settlements' (2003) 34 RAND Journal of Economics 392, 395.

[23] Herbert J Hovenkamp, Mark D Janis, and Mark A Lemley, 'Unilateral Refusals to License' (2006) 2 Journal of Competition Law & Economics 1, 1.

[24] ibid.

fundamental principle that an intellectual property owner has no obligation to use its right at all'.[25] David McGowan goes one step further and asserts that '[i]n patent cases, the right to engage in pure exclusion is all but absolute'.[26] He defines cases of pure exclusion as 'those in which the owner of a valid intellectual property right, validly obtained, unilaterally refuses to sell or license the technology covered by the right to a party wishing to obtain the technology'.[27] He contrasts pure exclusion with conditional exclusion, where the patentee's willingness to license is premised on the licensee's acceptance of certain terms and conditions.[28]

Section 271(d)(4) of the US Patent Act explicitly provides that a patent owner cannot be found guilty of patent misuse solely for her refusal to license the patent.[29] Although patent misuse is only a defence in a patent infringement suit, some US commentators have argued that the implication of Section 271(d)(4) must be that unilateral refusal to license cannot be an antitrust violation.[30] It would defy common sense if unilateral refusal to license does not constitute a patent misuse, which would only temporarily suspend a patentee's ability to enforce her rights, but could be grounds for an antitrust violation, which can result in trebled damages.[31] The US Department of Justice and the Federal Trade Commission seem to concur, taking the view that unilateral refusal to license patent rights should rarely, if ever, amount to an antitrust violation.[32] It has been argued that even if patent law needs to recalibrate its balance between generating innovation incentives for inventors and ensuring consumers adequate access to patented technology, adjustments should be made within patent law and not by antitrust law.[33] In the slightly different context of platform interoperability, Alan Devlin, Michael Jacobs, and Bruno Peixot argue that if any adjustments need to be made to the innovation incentives provided by intellectual property, it should be done through industry-specific legislation adopted by the legislature.[34]

Not everyone subscribes to the patent primacy view. Simon Genevaz asserts that '[a] careful reading of intellectual property laws shows that immunity runs

[25] ibid 2.

[26] David McGowan, 'Networks and Intention in Antitrust and Intellectual Property' (1999) 24 Journal of Corporation Law 485, 493.

[27] ibid 491.

[28] ibid.

[29] Hovenkamp, Janis, and Lemley (n 23) 3.

[30] Peter M Boyle, Penelope M Lister, and J Clayton Everett Jr, 'Antitrust Law at the Federal Circuit: Red Light or Green Light at the IP-Antitrust Intersection' (2001) 69 Antitrust Law Journal 739, 749.

[31] ibid 749.

[32] US Department of Justice and Federal Trade Commission, 'Antitrust Guidelines for the Licensing of Intellectual Property' 3.

[33] Thomas F Cotter, 'Intellectual Property and the Essential Facilities Doctrine' (1999) 1999 The Antitrust Bulletin 211, 250.

[34] Alan Devlin, Michael Jacobs, and Bruno Peixoto, 'Success, Dominance, and Interoperability' (2009) 84 Indiana Law Journal 1157, 1182.

contrary to congressional intent'.[35] This is echoed by Marina Lao, who observes that a '[c]lose examination of the purposes of the patent and copyright laws suggests that such limited application of antitrust principles [in unilateral refusal to license cases] would not subvert'[36] the policy objectives of the patent system. The patent statute does not clearly delineate the limits of the right to exclude.[37] It is up to antitrust law to do so, applying antitrust principles.

The uncertainty about the proper boundary of patent rights is compounded by the general perception that the US patent system is heavily skewed toward patentees. The patent examination system in the United States strongly favours patent applicants. It has been commented that the US Patent and Trademark Office (USPTO), the agency responsible for reviewing patent applications, is more concerned with helping applicants get patents than scrutinizing patent applications for worthy innovation.[38] The *ex-parte* nature of patent application proceedings means that the examiner only receives information from the applicant during the examination process.[39] Fortunately, this design flaw has been ameliorated somewhat by recent reforms.[40] This is further exacerbated by the highly publicized shortage of staff and resources at the USPTO.[41] It has been reported that patent examiners in the USPTO had less than twenty hours to examine each patent application.[42] The poor quality of patent examination is perhaps reflected in the fact that 46 per cent of patents that are litigated to judgment in the United States are eventually invalidated, despite the presumption of validity under the Patent Act.[43] If patents are of such questionable quality, they should not be entitled to deference from antitrust law.

Advocates of a pro-competition view do not base their argument solely on the flaws of the patent system. Some have argued that even if the patent system worked perfectly, it still suffers from some inherent limitations that render patent law

[35] Simon Genevaz, 'Against Immunity for Unilateral Refusals to Deal in Intellectual Property: Why Antitrust Law Should Not Distinguish between IP and Other Property Rights' (2004) 19 Berkeley Technology Law Journal 742, 753.

[36] Marina Lao, 'Unilateral Refusals to Sell or License Intellectual Property and the Antitrust Duty to Deal' (1999) 9 Cornell Journal of Law and Public Policy 193, 213.

[37] ibid 198.

[38] Adam B Jaffe and Josh Lerner, *Innovation and Its Discontents: How Our Broken Patent System Is Endangering Innovation and Progress, and What to Do About It* (Princeton University Press 2004) 137.

[39] James Langenfeld, 'Intellectual Property and Antitrust: Steps Toward Striking a Balance' (2001) 52 Case Western Reserve Law Review 91, 106.

[40] The 2011 Patent Reform Act provides for *inter partes* review on the grounds of novelty and obviousness. John Villasenor, 'The Comprehensive Patent Reform of 2011: Navigating the Leahy-Smith America Invents Act' (Brookings Institution 2011) Policy Brief No 184 <https://www.brookings.edu/research/the-comprehensive-patent-reform-of-2011-navigating-the-leahy-smith-america-invents-act/>.

[41] Langenfeld (n 39) 106.

[42] Quentin Hardy, 'Search 500,000 Documents, Review 160,000 Pages In 20 Hours, And Then Do It All Over Again' (*Forbes*, 24 June 2002) <https://www.forbes.com/asap/2002/0624/050.html> accessed 4 March 2020.

[43] John R Allison and Mark A Lemley, 'Empirical Evidence on the Validity of Litigated Patents' (1998) 26 American Intellectual Property Law Association Quarterly Journal 185, 205.

unsuitable for the role of fine-tuning the balance between these two policies in individual cases. Béatrice Dumont and Peter Holmes contend that

> [i]t is impossible to design an optimal system in advance. The actual conditions in the innovation market and product market will emerge after a patent has been granted. There has to be a degree of flexibility in any event. Given that competition policy is case law driven and IPR [intellectual property rights] rules tend to be set in stone for many years, it makes sense for the ground rules to be set in IPR legislation and for tweaking to be done by the application of competition policy.[44]

If case-by-case calibration of the policy balance needs to be done in unilateral refusal to license cases, it can only be accomplished through competition law, which 'is the only device available to address the point that the optimal degree of patent protection depend[s] on the market conditions, something which cannot be handled *ex ante* by the patent law'.[45] Some commentators, however, have cautioned against the expansive use of competition law to second-guess the patent system. Mattias Ganslandt notes that competition law can be used by national governments 'to redistribute rents from foreign IPR holders to domestic consumers or competing firms'.[46] Devlin, Jacobs, and Peixot warn that 'there will invariably be "sore losers" eager to seek pecuniary compensation through the competition laws'.[47]

The foregoing discussion highlights a number of important themes that will be explored below. These themes point to some central considerations in the adjudication of cases involving unilateral refusal to supply patented technology. The first is the extent to which the patent system should be accorded deference by competition law, especially in light of its tendency to overcompensate inventors and it not being relied upon as a major appropriation mechanism in many industries. This necessitates an assessment of the impact of competition law intervention on innovation incentives in the concrete setting of the imposition of a duty to supply or license. The second is the extent to which the boundary of a duty to supply or license should be demarcated by patent scope if competition law were to intervene to restrict the patentee's right to exclude. This is a concept that seems to be popular among some courts and commentators. The problem is that no one seems to know exactly how to define patent scope, even though everyone who invokes the concept seems to have some implicit notion in mind. The third is what are the considerations that should inform the adjudication of cases involving unilateral refusal to

[44] Béatrice Dumont and Peter Holmes, 'The Scope of Intellectual Property Rights and Their Interface with Competition Law and Policy: Divergent Paths to the Same Goal?' (2002) 11 Economics of Innovation and New Technology 149, 161.

[45] ibid 161.

[46] Mattias Ganslandt, 'Intellectual Property Rights and Competition Policy' in Keith E. Maskus (ed), *Intellectual Property, Growth and Trade* (Emerald Insight 2015) 243.

[47] Devlin, Jacobs, and Peixoto (n 34) 1185.

supply patented technology, and whether a duty to supply or license should only be imposed under highly exceptional circumstances, and if so, what those circumstances should be. Lastly, implicit in the foregoing discussion seems to be this assumption that competition law can intervene on the simple ground that patent protection results in supra-competitive prices for consumers. There is scant mention of the weighing of competitive harm caused by the refusal to supply or license against the benefits of imposing a duty to do so. Does the rather exceptional nature of the offence of unilateral refusal to supply patented technology mean that the need for a coherent theory of harm can be dispensed with? If not, what should those theories be?

C. Overview of Relevant Legal Doctrines

1. Introduction of the Unilateral Refusal to Deal and the Essential Facilities Doctrines

Before turning to a full discussion of the theoretical and policy arguments pertaining to the unilateral refusal to supply patented technology, it is important to introduce two legal doctrines that are relevant for our purpose: the unilateral refusal to deal doctrine and the essential facilities doctrine. The former can be found on both sides of the Atlantic whereas the latter is largely confined to the United States. These are two closely intertwined yet distinct doctrines that can be applied to scenarios involving unilateral refusal to supply patented technology. The unilateral refusal to deal doctrine holds that under some specific circumstances, it will be illegal for a dominant firm to withhold supply of a product or input to a competitor if the refusal to supply forecloses a competitor in either the primary product market, the downstream market, or an aftermarket. The essential facilities doctrine compels a dominant firm to share an essential facility in its possession with competitors if the facility is critical to the competitors' ability to compete and it is feasible to provide access to the facility.[48] Applied in the patent context, the essential facility[49] will be a patented technology.

The US and the EU courts hold divergent attitudes toward the two doctrines. Despite having been invoked on a number of occasions by the US courts, some US commentators harbour great hostility towards the two doctrines. Notably, Justice Antonin Scalia has imposed significant constraints on the vitality of the unilateral refusal to deal doctrine in *Trinko*.[50] Meanwhile, the European courts have not

[48] Herbert Hovenkamp, *Federal Antitrust Policy: The Law of Competition and Its Practice* (4th edn, West Publishing Co. 2011) s 7.5.

[49] Hovenkamp and others (n 2) s 13.3c.

[50] *Verizon Communications v. Law Offices of Curtis Trinko*, LLP, 540 US 398 (2004).

displayed the same degree of aversion to imposing a duty to share a critical input. Despite having never explicitly endorsed or invoked the essential facilities doctrine, the EU courts have at times decided cases in ways that are reminiscent of the doctrine. On the whole, the European courts have displayed greater willingness to impose a duty to supply or share, especially in recent years, than the US courts. The case law applying these doctrines has been subject to different formulations on both sides of the Atlantic, even though they tend to point to the same underlying policy considerations.

The line between these two doctrines is not always so clear. It is at times difficult to draw a clear distinction between them.[51] One way to distinguish the two doctrines is based on their scope of application. Although the boundary between them has not always been very clear, one can generally deduce that the unilateral refusal to deal doctrine tends to apply to a physical product or input while the essential facilities doctrine is more often invoked in cases involving an infrastructure or an intangible asset. The *Commercial Solvents*[52] case in the European Union and *Aspen Skiing*[53] in the United States, both of which involve a product or a service, are generally understood to be unilateral refusal to deal cases. Meanwhile, the *Associated Press*[54] case in the United States is usually viewed as an essential facilities case, even though it concerned a concerted refusal to deal. Without insisting on a strict categorization of cases, we will generally apply the unilateral refusal to deal doctrine and the essential facilities doctrine to physical input and intangible assets respectively. This categorization is also consistent with the evolution of the EU case law, where one can see a clear line of cases involving physical input and another line implicating critical infrastructure or intellectual property. Where the possibility of compulsory licensing of a patented technology is suggested, it will be done through application of the essential facilities doctrine. The unilateral refusal to deal doctrine will mostly be mentioned in the context of a refusal to supply a patented input.

2. Theories of Harm

Every competition law case requires a theory of harm. This is especially important in unilateral refusal to deal cases where it is usually very easy to demonstrate how competitors are harmed by the refusal to supply. A survey of the leading unilateral refusal to deal and essential facilities cases, however, suggests that the courts have not always been explicit in specifying the theory of harm in the case. In

[51] Cyril Ritter, 'Refusal to Deal and "Essential Facilities": Does Intellectual Property Require Special Deference Compared to Tangible Property?' (2005) 28 World Competition 281, 283–85.

[52] Cases 6 and 7/73, *Istituto Chemioterapico Italiano Spa and Commercial Solvents Corp. v. Commission* [1974] ECR 223.

[53] *Aspen Skiing Co. v. Aspen Highlands Skiing Corp.*, 472 US 585 (1985).

[54] *Associated Press v. United States*, 326 US 1 (1945).

unilateral refusal to deal cases, the emphasis is often on the factual circumstances surrounding and the justifications for the refusal to supply. The courts do not often articulate how the refusal to supply harms competition and consumers. In the essential facilities cases, the focus is instead on the degree of essentiality of the facility, which in turn hinges on the uniqueness of the facility and the extent to which competition will be eliminated by a denial of access. Nonetheless, most of these cases seem to be implicitly based on the premise that denial of access to the facility forecloses downstream competition. Before further exploring the implications of the use of these doctrines to widen access to technology, it is important to acquire a clearer understanding of the various scenarios in which a refusal to supply an essential input or provide access to an essential facility can harm competition.

(a) Unilateral refusal to deal

Commentators such as Richard Gilbert, Carl Shapiro, and Dennis Carlton have articulated a number of scenarios in which a refusal to supply an essential input or provide access to an essential facility (collectively referred to as 'refusal to deal') may harm competition. According to Gilbert and Shapiro, a unilateral refusal to deal may create competitive harm in the following four scenarios: (1) enhancement of entry barriers and creation of the double-entry requirement;[55] (2) facilitation of price discrimination;[56] (3) foreclosure of upstream or downstream competition;[57] and (4) creation of effective exclusivity.[58] They do not clearly specify whether these theories of harm only apply to tangible input or to intellectual property as well. They speak generally of essential input.[59] Nor do they draw a distinction between the unilateral refusal to deal doctrine and the essential facilities doctrine, which makes sense because there is probably no meaningful distinction between the two from an economic perspective.[60] In the ensuing discussion, it will be important to determine the applicability of these theories of harm to intellectual property and hence their relevance to the essential facilities doctrine.

In addition to these four scenarios, commentators have noted that a unilateral refusal to deal may allow the dominant firm to leverage its market power into related markets such as the aftermarkets.[61] Such monopoly-leveraging theories of harm are highly reminiscent of the competitive harm created by tying and bundling. Therefore, to the extent that unilateral refusal to deal is used to achieve results that are tantamount to tying or bundling, as in many of the US refusal to deal cases, the discussion will be deferred to Chapter 6.

[55] Richard J Gilbert and Carl Shapiro, 'An Economic Analysis of Unilateral Refusals to License Intellectual Property' (1996) 93 Proceedings of National Academy of Sciences 12750.
[56] ibid 12751.
[57] ibid.
[58] ibid.
[59] ibid.
[60] ibid 12750–51.
[61] Lao (n 36) 213, 217–18.

(i) Enhancement of entry barriers and creation of the double-entry requirement

A unilateral refusal to deal may raise entry barriers if competitors have to produce a substitute for the input to which they have been denied access.[62] Denial of access by the dominant firm would not create much problem for competitors if there were alternative sources of supply of the sought-after input. But if competitors cannot source the input elsewhere and need to produce the input themselves, the refusal to supply would raise entry barriers. The dominant firm's refusal to supply may be motivated by a desire to forestall entry of a new competitor in either the input market or the final product market.[63] How the denial of access to a critical input would forestall entry into the final product market probably needs no explanation. Such denial can also erect barriers in the input market if, by denying downstream rivals access to the critical input, the dominant firm succeeds in keeping the size of these rivals small enough so that they do not generate sufficient demand for an alternative supplier of the input. Any potential alternative supplier would be denied minimum efficient scale. A potential entrant into either market must enter both at the same time, creating a two-level entry requirement.[64]

The application of this theory of harm to the unilateral refusal to license patented technology presents some difficulty. In characterizing the denial of access to an input and the two-level entry requirement as a competitive harm, the implicit presumption is that a producer of the downstream final product should not be expected to produce the input also. The input and the final product are often produced by different firms. This kind of presumption may have greater applicability to a physical input than to intellectual property. For instance, Boeing is not expected to produce every component in the aircraft it produces.[65] Component producers expect to sell their aircraft components to Boeing. In contrast, there is no expectation that Boeing should be able to license any technology it needs for its aircraft if the technology owner has not made her technology available for licensing.[66] The denial of access to technology may not be deemed to raise entry barriers or create the two-level entry requirement. Therefore, this theory of harm should have more limited application to a refusal to license patented technology, while it readily applies to a refusal to supply an intermediate input that incorporates a patented technology. This means that this theory of harm is more relevant for the unilateral refusal to deal doctrine.

[62] Gilbert and Shapiro (n 55) 12750.

[63] ibid 12751.

[64] ibid 12751.

[65] Boeing outsources up to 65 per cent of the airframe of 787 Dreamliner to outside suppliers, for example. Jeremy Bogaisky, 'Boeing's Vertical Leap: Where Will It Squeeze Suppliers Next?' (*Forbes*, 6 June 2018) <https://www.forbes.com/sites/jeremybogaisky/2018/06/06/boeings-vertical-leap-where-will-it-squeeze-suppliers-next/#5a175a5f248a> accessed 4 March 2020.

[66] Catherine Jewell, 'Giving Innovation Wings: How Boeing Uses Its IP' (*World Intellectual Property Organization*, February 2014) <https://www.wipo.int/wipo_magazine/en/2014/01/article_0004.html> accessed 4 March 2020.

The situation is different if a complementary product market is involved. A patentee can refuse to license her technology to a complementary product supplier not because it wants to leverage its market power from the primary product market into the complementary product market but because she wants to prevent the emergence of a viable supplier of the complementary product, thereby creating a two-level entry requirement for a future entrant into the primary product market.[67] An apt illustration of this strategy would be the slew of unilateral refusal to deal cases in the United States in the late 1990s involving photocopier manufacturers and independent service organizations (ISOs).[68] By making it impossible for customers to obtain repair services from ISOs, the likes of Kodak and Xerox managed to eliminate ISOs from the market, effectively requiring any future entrant into the photocopier market to provide repair services at the same time.

(ii) Facilitation of price discrimination

Whether enabling price discrimination counts as a theory of harm depends on whether price discrimination harms or benefits consumers. It is well known in the economic literature that price discrimination can be either anticompetitive or procompetitive depending on its effect on the output level.[69] Price discrimination can be output-enhancing if it results in an increase in output by allowing the supplier to lower its price to price-sensitive customers.[70] Price discrimination can be output-reducing if the market-wide output level would be higher when the seller charges a uniform price.[71] Therefore, establishing this theory of harm would entail two steps. The first one is to determine whether the unilateral refusal to deal does in fact facilitate price discrimination. The second one is to ascertain whether the price discrimination at issue is output-enhancing or output-reducing.

Assuming that the price discrimination at issue is output-reducing, a unilateral refusal to deal can facilitate price discrimination as follows. Imagine a producer of a raw material which has a low-value use and a high-value use. The producer cannot prevent arbitrage between low-value users and high-value users once the raw material is sold. The producer would ideally prefer to charge the high-value users a higher price and the low-value users a lower price. But the high-value users would simply purchase the raw material from the low-value users if she does that. If the producer can accurately estimate the low-value users' needs, she can control the amount of the raw material sold to these users such that they do not have surplus to

[67] Dennis W Carlton, 'A General Analysis of Exclusionary Conduct and Refusal to Deal: Why Aspen and Kodak Are Misguided' (National Bureau of Economic Research 2001) Working Paper 8105 14; Lao (n 36) 218.

[68] *Image Technical Services v. Eastman Kodak*, 125 F.3d 1195 (9th Cir. 1997); *In re Independent Service Organizations Antitrust Litigation (Xerox)*, 203 F.3d 1322 (Fed. Cir. 2000).

[69] Mark Armstrong and John Vickers, 'Price Discrimination, Competition and Regulation' (1993) 41 Journal of Industrial Economics 335, 336.

[70] ibid.

[71] ibid.

resell to the high-value users. But if the producer cannot do that, the only way for her to extract the full surplus from the downstream users is by forward integrating into the downstream production of the low-value use and continuing to sell the raw material to the high-value users at an elevated price. The producer would need to refuse to supply the raw material to other low-value users.

It is again not entirely clear that this theory of harm has much relevance for patented technology. Downstream integration and unilateral refusal to supply are necessary to accomplish price discrimination in the example because arbitrage is unpreventable. The same is not true of patented technology. The raw material producer, in this case the patentee, can easily prevent arbitrage by including a clause that prohibits sub-licensing and any further transfer of the technology in the licensing agreement. This should suffice unless the patentee is somehow prohibited from charging different levels of royalty to different users. This could be the case if the patentee is subject to a stringent FRAND (Fair, Reasonable, And Non-Discriminatory) licensing obligation imposed by a standard-setting body.[72] Even then, a FRAND obligation appropriately construed should allow a patentee to charge different royalties to licensees that put the technology into different uses.[73] Therefore, this theory of harm is mainly relevant for a refusal to supply a patented input under the unilateral refusal to deal doctrine.

(iii) Foreclosure of upstream or downstream competition

Unilateral refusal to deal may help a firm protect its market power in the downstream market.[74] The owner of an essential input would only supply an input if she can secure adequate compensation for the loss of revenue following market entry.[75] There would be no reason for her to refuse to supply the input if she could extract all the surplus through pricing of the input.[76] She would be indifferent between supplying the input to a downstream competitor and exploiting the downstream market herself by withholding supply. But if she cannot secure adequate compensation, the owner would foreclose downstream competition by withholding the essential input.

Apart from protecting the input owner's downstream market power, Yongmin Chen provides another motive for an input owner to refuse to supply. Refusal to deal can help shield the input owner from future upstream competition. He posits that an essential input owner may refuse to supply 'when there is potential upstream competition in the future, and the downstream dominance achieved through refusal to deal enables the monopolist to maintain monopoly profit via

[72] Joseph Farrell and others, 'Standard Setting, Patents, and Hold-Up' (2007) 74 Antitrust Law Journal 603, 636–38.

[73] ibid 638–41.

[74] Gilbert and Shapiro (n 55) 12751.

[75] ibid.

[76] Carlton (n 67) 10.

vertical control even when the upstream market becomes competitive'.[77] The incentive to refuse to deal would be stronger if supplying an independent downstream firm would render future upstream competition more likely.[78]

There are two ways in which this could be the case. First, the existence of independent downstream firms provides potential customers for future upstream competitors and allows them to reach minimum efficient scales more quickly. Second, if a follow-on innovation on the essential input is possible and likely, the incumbent input supplier may reduce the likelihood of follow-on innovation by foreclosing competitors from the downstream market, thereby making it more difficult for the innovator to recoup her investment. In a slightly different vein, Carlton argues that a refusal to deal strategy will allow the dominant firm to transfer its market power downstream, which will in turn let the dominant firm hang on to its market position despite changes and innovation in the upstream market.[79] In this case, upstream innovation will continue, but the innovator will receive few benefits as she would still be subject to the dominant firm's market power.

The classic version of this theory of harm, which entails simple foreclosure of downstream competition, is readily applicable to unilateral refusal to license patented technology under the essential facilities doctrine as well as general unilateral refusal to deal. In fact, foreclosure of downstream competition is the quintessential theory of harm under the essential facilities doctrine. Chen's and Carlton's variations of the theory, which emphasize the use of downstream foreclosure to protect the dominant firm's upstream market position, are likely to be less relevant to the essential facilities doctrine. An essential facility owner should have an iron-clad position in the upstream market and need not use downstream foreclosure to protect it.

(iv) Creation of effective exclusivity

One final theory of harm was articulated by Dennis Carlton and is largely based on the facts of the famous *Aspen Skiing* case. *Aspen Skiing* has been generally interpreted as standing for the proposition that it is illegal monopolization when a dominant firm sacrifices an existing profit-maximizing course of conduct with the intent to harm a rival.[80] According to Carlton, Ski Co., the dominant ski mountain operator in the case, could have attained exclusivity in the operation of ski slopes in Aspen by refusing to deal with customers and other intermediaries that deal with Highlands.[81] This would clearly amount to exclusive dealing. Direct imposition of exclusivity in this manner, however, was not feasible in that case. Instead,

[77] Yongmin Chen, 'Refusal to Deal, Intellectual Property Rights, and Antitrust' (2013) 30 Journal of Law, Economics & Organization 533, 553.
[78] ibid.
[79] Carlton (n 67) 16.
[80] Trinko, 540 US at 408–09.
[81] Carlton (n 67) 24.

what Ski Co. did was to use a non-linear pricing schedule to impose exclusivity, which was facilitated by the termination of the six-day, four-mountain ski pass and the refusal to sell ski slope day passes to Highlands at retail prices.[82] Consumers' vacation habit in Aspen was such that most skiers skipped Highlands' facilities, effectively resulting in exclusivity. This would prevent Highlands from becoming an effective competitor if there were significant scale economies in the maintenance of ski slopes.[83] Carlton stops short of arguing that this constellation of facts would always establish a viable theory of harm but suggests that it is at least worth investigating under a Rule of Reason analysis.[84]

A case which provides a more direct illustration of the use of unilateral refusal to deal to achieve exclusivity is the US *Lorain Journal* case. In that case, the incumbent newspaper met the emerging threat of a radio station by refusing to accept advertisements from any firms that also advertised with the radio station.[85] The exclusivity desired by the newspaper was accomplished by its refusal to deal with any customers that advertised with the rival radio station.[86] The US Supreme Court found that the newspaper's actions were designed to destroy its competitor given that it was an indispensable medium of advertising in the town.[87] Where unilateral refusal to deal is used to accomplish exclusivity, the theory of harm is well-established and should not present much difficulty.

A slight variation of the aforementioned theory of harm involves complementary products. It applies when the forestalling of effective rivals in the complementary product market harms other consumers who only consume the complementary product and not the primary product. It is possible to imagine a situation in which the complementary product can be independently consumed, and these consumers will be harmed if suppliers of the complementary product are prevented from attaining efficient scales by the dominant firm's refusal to deal.[88]

Carlton illustrates this with the example of a monopoly resort hotel on an island and restaurants.[89] The hotel is the primary product and restaurants are the complementary product.[90] The hotel guests are already subject to the market power of the resort.[91] By requiring all the guests to eat in the hotel and refusing to let those who prefer to eat out stay in the hotel (or at least by incorporating the meal costs into the room rate so that guests will have no incentive to eat out), the resort hotel can deny scale economies to independent restaurants that serve both the hotel guests

[82] ibid.
[83] ibid.
[84] ibid.
[85] *Lorain Journal v. United States*, 342 US 143, 150–51 (1951).
[86] 342 US 152–53.
[87] 342 US at 152.
[88] Carlton (n 67) 12.
[89] ibid.
[90] ibid.
[91] ibid.

and the locals.[92] The locals have no need for the hotel service and only care for good restaurants.[93] By forcing all the hotel guests to eat at the in-house restaurants, the resort hotel manages to harm the downtown restaurants and their customers.[94] This is another example of the use of unilateral refusal to deal to achieve exclusivity. The competitive harm of the conduct arises not from the refusal to deal but from the coerced exclusivity.

On its face, this theory of harm can apply to both the unilateral refusal to deal doctrine and the essential facilities doctrine. In fact, this theory of harm shares many similarities with the foreclosure of downstream competition. The one main difference is that under this theory of harm, exclusivity is usually attained in the primary product market itself. In *Aspen Skiing* it was ski slope operations in Aspen, and in *Lorain Journal* media advertising in Lorain. There was no downstream market involved. Given that the facility in essential facilities cases usually does not constitute its own market, the use of unilateral refusal to deal to attain exclusivity in that market is unlikely to be a salient concern.

Overall, while all four aforementioned theories of harm may apply to unilateral refusal to supply a patented input, the foreclosure of downstream competition will be chiefly relevant to unilateral refusal to license patented technology in essential facilities cases. The theory of harm involving complementary products is likely to be less relevant for the essential facilities doctrine. The case law shows that essential facilities cases rarely involve a complementary product.

(b) The essential facilities doctrine

Theories of harm in essential facilities cases and the corresponding European cases (collectively referred to as essential facilities cases) share some ostensible similarities with those under the unilateral refusal to deal doctrine. Almost by definition the focus of an essential facilities case cannot be the market in which the facility is situated, if it is theoretically sound to define such a relevant market.[95] This is because by virtue of being essential, which is most often understood as being critical to a rival's ability to compete and being incapable of economically practical replication by rivals, the facility owner has monopolized that market. The facility owner cannot acquire further power in that market. If the facility is truly essential, it is not necessary for the facility owner to undertake any action to defend her market position. The main competitive concern under the essential facilities doctrine is foreclosure of vertically related markets.

The facility owner may leverage her position in the facility market into vertically related markets.[96] The market most often at issue is the downstream market. In

[92] ibid.
[93] ibid.
[94] ibid.
[95] Gregory J Werden, 'The Law and Economics of the Essential Facility Doctrine' (1987) 32 St. Louis University Law Journal 433, 459.
[96] ibid.

most cases, the essential facility serves as a critical input in downstream production and the facility owner is accused of using the essential facility to exclude rivals in the downstream market.[97] Some have argued that foreclosure of downstream competition is the only acceptable theory of harm under the doctrine.[98] Douglas Melamed defends the use of the doctrine to police foreclosure of downstream competition, asserting that such use of the doctrine is consistent 'with the fundamental antitrust notion that a monopolist is entitled to the fruits of its "skill, foresight and industry"'[99] but not more.

In the intellectual property context, Genevaz insists that the essential facilities doctrine should only apply when downstream competition is impaired because competition law

> should not impose duties to share when the refusal is proper exercise of exclusionary IP-related privileges. On the other hand, imposing duties to share on downstream markets does not 'rip-off' the owner of the facility because the innovator's legal reward is not altered in the primary market for the product embodying its intellectual property.[100]

The implicit assumption in this argument is that the rightful reward to an innovator under the patent system is the primary product within the scope of her invention and not products or markets that are derived from, or related to, the original invention. Patent protection does not empower the innovator to collect rent in the downstream market. This is reminiscent of the scope of patent test mentioned earlier.

Tying the boundary of the doctrine to the patent scope test immediately invites a number of problems, not least of which is the fact that patent scope is not self-defining and is instead determined by relevant legal rules. It smacks of circular logic to argue that the boundary of a legal doctrine is determined by a legal test which itself is defined by legal rules. There needs to be a principled basis to determine what those rules are. A further problem with Genevaz's logic is that if the intellectual property itself does not constitute a relevant product and cannot only be put to commercial use by being deployed in the production of a downstream product, it is not clear whether the patentee's control should be limited to the technology market or also extends to the downstream product market. How far do the so-called exclusionary intellectual property-related privileges extend? What

[97] A Douglas Melamed and Ali M Stoeppelwerth, 'The CSU Case: Facts, Formalism and the Intersection of Antitrust and Intellectual Property Law' (2002) 10 George Mason Law Review 407, 422; Robert Pitofsky, Donna Patterson, and Jonathan Hooks, 'The Essential Facilities Doctrine Under United States Antitrust Law' (2002) 70 Antitrust Law Journal 443, 452.

[98] Hovenkamp, Janis, and Lemley (n 23) 11.

[99] Melamed and Stoeppelwerth (n 97) 422. (internal quotations in the original)

[100] Genevaz (n 35) 761.

if the technology itself is practically worthless unless it is used to produce a downstream product, which is the only commercial use of the technology? Does it make a difference if the technology has many downstream uses? Ultimately, there is only one principled benchmark for determining the permissible scope of patent rights, which is the amount that is necessary to allow the innovator to recoup her R&D investments. Patent rights should allow an innovator to do no more and no less.

It is worth noting that much of the EU case law on unilateral refusal to license intellectual property has concerned weaker rights such as copyright on TV programming information and database rights. The implication of this on the applicability of the EU case law on unilateral refusal to license patent rights in the developing country context will be explored in Chapter 6.

(c) Applicability to developing countries

The aforementioned theories of harm have varying applicability to developing countries in the patent context. Developing countries could be seeking to gain access to the patented technology directly or to a physical product embodying the patented technology. The physical product could be either an intermediate input or a final product sold directly to consumers. While it is in theory possible for a dominant firm to refuse to sell a final product to consumers, it is highly unlikely in reality. So long as consumers are willing to pay the profit-maximizing price and the firm has sufficient supply, there should be no reason why the firm would refuse to sell. A quick look at the US and the EU unilateral refusal to deal and essential facilities cases suggests that an overwhelming majority of the cases involves an intermediate input, either in the form of a physical input or an asset or infrastructure. Therefore, we can tentatively narrow down the possible scope of application to a patented physical input or a patented technology as an essential facility. Refusal to supply a patented intermediate input will be analysed as general unilateral refusal to deal while refusal to license a patented technology will fall under the rubric of the essential facilities doctrine and its corresponding EU cases.

The extent of applicability of the various theories of harm—enhancement of entry barriers, facilitation of price discrimination, foreclosure of vertically related markets, and creation of effective exclusivity—to developing countries would depend on the level of the country's technological capacity. This is because these theories of harm pertain to competitors in different markets, some in the primary market itself, some in the vertically related upstream or downstream market, and some in the complementary product market. To be a competitor in these various markets with a global technological leader requires different levels of technological capacity.

A competitor in the primary market competes head-on with the global technological leader and therefore should require the highest level of technological sophistication. The competitor itself must be able to generate genuine novel, patentable innovation along the global technological frontier. Such a firm is unlikely to be found in any developing country with the possible exception of proto-innovation developing countries. Of the four theories of harm, creation of effective exclusivity is most directly pertinent to competitors in the primary product market. The competitive animus is targeted at a direct primary competitor in both *Aspen Skiing* and *Lorain Journal*. Therefore, creation of effective exclusivity is chiefly only applicable to proto-innovation countries, although it could also be relevant to technology adaptation countries where imitation allows their firms to compete in the primary product market with a global technological leader.

The remaining three theories of harm all implicate vertically related markets to varying extents. Focusing on the downstream market, a competitor that purchases a patented intermediate input can be simply an assembler or a manufacturer with no independent innovation capacity of its own. It could be an iPhone assembler who imports all the components and whose only responsibility is to assemble the product. Product assembly does not require an ability to innovate and can be found in all sorts of developing countries, from production to technological adaptation to proto-innovation.[101] Therefore, all theories of harm that can arise in this scenario will have universal applicability to developing countries. These include enhancement of entry barriers, facilitation of price discrimination, and foreclosure of vertically related markets.

A competitor that licenses a patented technology will need to have the capacity to absorb and utilize a licensed technology. In order words, it must have the capacity for technology adaptation. A firm that has nothing more than rudimentary technical capabilities will not be able to make use of a sophisticated technology licensed from a global technological leader. Such a licensee will not be found in a production country. Therefore, a theory of harm that is predicated on technology licensing, namely foreclosure of downstream competition under the essential facilities doctrine, will only be applicable to technology adaptation countries and proto-innovation countries. As mentioned earlier, the other three theories of harm have limited application in the licensing context. Facilitation of price discrimination only applies to physical input. Creation of effective exclusivity only applies to the primary product market, to which the essential facilities doctrine by definition does not apply. Enhancement of entry barriers may have some residual relevance to technology licensing.

Lastly, a competitor in a complementary product market is probably harder to generalize in terms of technological capacity. While a complementary product generally should require less sophistication than the primary product, it could nonetheless be somewhat technologically advanced. If the complementary product is paper used in a printer, then the technological capacity required to produce it is low. But if the complementary product is the flat-screen monitor for a computer,

[101] Jeffrey Sachs, 'The Global Innovation Divide' in Adam Jaffe, Josh Lerner, and Scott Stern (eds), *Innovation Policy and the Economy*, vol 3 (National Bureau of Economic Research 2003) 133.

Table 5.2 Relevant Theory of Harm for Different Developing Countries based on their Technological Capacity

Theory of Harm	Scope of Application	Directly Affected Markets	Relevant Developing Countries
Enhancement of entry barriers	Physical input	Primary product; Downstream (two-level entry requirement); Complementary product	All
	Technology Licensing	Downstream; Complementary product	All (depending on product or technology)
Facilitation of price discrimination	Physical input	Downstream	All
Foreclosure of vertically related markets	Physical input	Downstream	All
	Technology licensing	Downstream	Technology adaptation; Proto-innovation
Creation of effective exclusivity	Physical input	Primary product	Technology adaptation (only if imitation allows firms to compete with global technological leader); Proto-innovation
		Complementary product	All (depending on product)

then some technological capacity is definitely needed. Therefore, a theory of harm that implicates competitors in a complementary product market could, depending on the complementary product at issue, have relevance for all three types of developing countries. This includes both enhancement of entry barriers and creation of effective exclusivity.

D. Critique of the Doctrines

The unilateral refusal to deal doctrine and the essential facilities doctrine have been subject to a number of criticisms, some of which focus on the substance of the doctrines and some of which focus on implementation. The most common and important one is that compelled sharing of an input or an asset would lower the incumbent's incentive to invest in developing the input or the asset. Another common criticism of both doctrines is that compelled sharing of an input or asset would require the competition authority or the courts to determine the terms of dealing, which in turn would require the authority or the courts to engage in on-going supervision, or worse still, to become a rate-setting regulatory authority. It was said that the US government litigation against AT&T that culminated in a consent decree mandating the break-up of the company effectively turned the presiding judge, Judge Harold Greene, into a 'one man Federal Telephony Commission'.[102]

One reason for the overwhelming aversion to compulsory licensing is the property right-centric view on intellectual property. Patents and intellectual property are generally viewed as a form of property.[103] Given that owners of physical property are usually given an almost absolute right to exclude unwanted physical entry into their properties, the analogy to physical property imbues defenders of intellectual property with an equally broad right to exclude.[104] This probably explains why the general refusal to deal doctrine and the essential facilities doctrine elicit such visceral reaction from some American commentators, who tend to hold private property in much higher regard.[105] Not everyone, however, shares this view of intellectual property. As Bruce Abramson points out, post-Chicagoans tend to view intellectual property as a regulatory device. Under this post-Chicagoan view,

> [i]f patents create great opportunities for exploitation, antitrust law should scrutinize patentees closely, examine the data, and identify abuses. If the abuses are systematic, the policymakers in Congress should consider rewriting the patent laws to frustrate their recurrence. If such a rewrite results in a weakening of patent rights, so be it; the entire purpose of a liberal regulatory mechanism is to serve the public by filling an economic gap that the free market is unable to fill on its own. In the patent context, that means rewarding innovation to generate innovation. At the patent/antitrust interface, it means curtailing those rewards before they harm the competitive markets that we want them to bolster.[106]

Post-Chicagoans are less afraid to tinker with the policy balance underlying the patent system. They are mindful that '[t]he nature of the IP system, as a general framework that essentially grants the same legal rights irrespective of the value and

[102] Brett Frischmann and Spencer Weber Waller, 'Revitalizing Essential Facilities' (2008) 75 Antitrust Law Journal 1, 41.

[103] Stephen L Carter, 'Does It Matter Whether Intellectual Property Is Property' (1992) 68 Chicago-Kent Law Review 715, 715.

[104] Mark A Lemley, 'Property, Intellectual Property, and Free Riding' (2005) 83 Texas Law Review 1031, 1031–32.

[105] Gerald Friedman, 'The Sanctity of Property Rights in American History' (University of Massachusetts Amherst 2001) No. 14 <https://scholarworks.umass.edu/cgi/viewcontent.cgi?article=1008&context=peri_workingpapers> accessed 29 July 2021 .

[106] Bruce Abramson, 'Intellectual Property and the Alleged Collapsing of Aftermarkets' (2007) 38 Rutgers Law Journal 399, 466.

cost of innovation, implies, almost by necessity, that some innovations are excessively rewarded'.[107] There is much greater room for intervention by competition law when the innovation incentives generated by the patent system are excessive.

1. Detrimental Impact on Innovation Incentives

One of the most powerful, and to many, fatal criticisms of compelled sharing of an input or asset is that it undermines innovation incentives, both on the part of the incumbent and the competitors.[108] This is a particularly salient criticism in the context of patents because the main policy justification for a patent system is to generate innovation incentives. Undermining innovation incentives would disrupt if not usurp the patent system. If compulsory licensing has such a devastating effect on innovation incentives, it would constitute a sufficient reason to counsel against it.

That compulsory licensing undermines innovation incentives is a mainstream, but by no means consensual, view in the field. Many have argued that the incentive dampening effect of compulsory licensing is overstated. Recall the conclusions in Chapter 2 that the patent system has a tendency to overcompensate innovators and that the degree of dependence on patents as an appropriation mechanism varies widely by industry. The incentive-dampening effect is thus only a serious concern in the industries that rely heavily on patents as an appropriation mechanism, namely chemicals and pharmaceuticals.[109] In other situations, the industry may not be one where patents play an important role for appropriation. The innovator may not rely on the market to recoup investments as the market in question may be secondary to the firm's primary profit-making activity.[110] Competitive pressure may already be sufficient to drive the firm to innovate.[111] The innovation may have been developed with limited investment.[112] In these situations, it should be possible to pare back patentee reward somewhat without a significant loss in innovation incentives. This suggests that reduction in innovation incentives is not the silver bullet against compulsory licensing as is often suggested.

(a) Incumbent's innovation incentives

Analysis of the impact of compulsory licensing on innovation incentives can be approached from three perspectives: the incumbent innovator, the competitor

[107] Ganslandt (n 46) 242.

[108] Devlin, Jacobs, and Peixoto (n 34) 1162.

[109] Richard Levin and others, 'Appropriating the Returns from Industrial Research and Development' (1987) 1987 Brookings Papers on Economic Activity 801–802.

[110] *Purple Parking Ltd. & Anor v. Heathrow Airport Ltd.* [2011] EWHC 987 (Ch).

[111] Case T-201/04, *Microsoft v. Commission* [2007] ECR II-3601.

[112] Case C-418/01, *IMS Health GmbH & Co OHG v. NDC Health GmbH & Co KG* [2004] ECR I-5039.

innovator, and the cumulative innovator. These are the three main groups of stakeholders whose innovation incentives can be affected by compulsory licensing. While much of the discussion about the incentive-dampening effect of compulsory licensing has focused on the incumbent, the impact on the latter two groups should not be overlooked. As the EU General Court noted in the *Microsoft* case, incentives effects have to be assessed from an industry-wide perspective.[113] It is possible that the boost to competitors' innovation incentives more than outweighs the loss of incentives on the part of the incumbent. Cumulative innovation also should not be overlooked. It plays a critical role in the technological progress in society. If compulsory licensing facilitates cumulative innovation, it could tilt the argument in favour of it.

The mainstream view is that patent protection is needed to generate innovation incentives for the incumbent and that any rolling back of such incentives will reduce innovation. Devlin, Jacobs, and Peixot label as 'myopic'[114] attempts to use compulsory licensing to reduce consumer harm, asserting that 'it will rarely be true that depriving an intellectual property holder of its right to exclude will not affect *ex ante* investment incentives'.[115] McGowan launches an even more powerful attack, suggesting that the over-compensating tendency of the patent system should not be construed to support intervention. He cautions against the illusion of precision in judicial making, noting that

> [w]hile we may presume that the goal of intellectual property laws is (or should be) to allow exclusion to the point where the marginal gain in innovation or creation equals the marginal social cost of excluding access to the work, courts deciding concrete cases will find it difficult to make such decisions.[116]

This difficulty is compounded by the fact that adverse decisions affect not only the incentives of the original innovator, but also those of future innovators, which are very difficult to ascertain.[117]

Many commentators have disputed this view. Howard Shelanski questions many of the fundamental assumptions of this view:

> Development of IP does not always require more capital or risk than, for example, construction of specialized manufacturing facilities, natural resource exploration, or real estate development. Moreover, not all IP investment improves social

[113] Case T-201/04, *Microsoft v. Commission* [2007] ECR II-3601, para. 706.
[114] Devlin, Jacobs, and Peixoto (n 34) 1159.
[115] ibid 1162.
[116] McGowan (n 26) 495.
[117] Jeffrey K Mackie-Mason, 'What to Do about Unilateral Refusals to License?' Testimony for the Federal Trade Commission and Department of Justice Hearing on Competition and Intellectual Property Law and Policy in the Knowledge-Based Economy (1 May 2002) 11.

> welfare. Many patents lack economic value and are never practiced or enforced. Other IP may be developed for purely defensive purposes of protecting markets and blocking competition, although such cases may be hard to distinguish from bona fide innovation efforts. On the other side, much valuable innovation is never patented, and scholars have cast doubt on the link between innovation incentives and IP protections.[118]

Shelanski thus believes that R&D investments should not be entitled to special protection and that patents do not always represent socially valuable innovation. Echoing the views mentioned earlier about the flaws in the patent system, Shelanski argues that

> [t]he more invalid patents there are, the greater the likelihood that the balance between costs and benefits of mandatory dealing in IP weighs in favor of a legal standard more likely to result in liability. Imprecision in the patenting process is another reason not to have a conclusive presumption that an assertion of IP rights constitutes a valid business justification for otherwise anticompetitive conduct.[119]

Genevaz also highlights the erroneous assumptions of the mainstream view that 'the acquisition of monopoly power is the only way to appropriate revenues deriving from inventions'[120] and that 'antitrust liability would necessarily have overall adverse effects on incentives to innovate'.[121] In a nutshell, Shelanski and Genevaz believe that patents are not necessary to secure innovation.

Lao questions the primacy of patent protection as a source of innovation incentives by implicitly taking Arrow's side in the famous Schumpeter–Arrow debate and arguing that competition may spur more innovation than monopoly. She challenges the idea that exclusivity or monopoly power is needed to attract innovation, arguing that if competition is more effective in attracting innovation, increasing intellectual property protection may in fact be counterproductive.[122] Other commentators seem willing to concede that patentee reward incentivizes innovation, but caution that it is possible for the patent system to provide excessive incentives. Concurring with Shelanski that R&D investment need not improve social welfare, Thomas Cotter notes that R&D is subject to the law of diminishing returns and that beyond a certain point, greater protection does not necessarily lead to more innovation.[123] Concurring with Cotter, Joe Bauer observes that 'it does not follow

[118] Howard A Shelanski, 'Unilateral Refusals to Deal in Intellectual and Other Property' (2009) 76 Antitrust Law Journal 369, 386.
[119] ibid 387.
[120] Genevaz (n 35) 745.
[121] ibid.
[122] Lao (n 36) 216.
[123] Cotter (n 33) 218.

that every increase in the duration or scope of protection for intellectual property will maximize consumer welfare. Indeed, there is substantial evidence that affording too much protection will actually lessen incentives for innovation.'[124] James Langenfeld believes that in addition to failing to generate more innovation, excessive patent protection also reduces overall welfare by allowing the innovator to appropriate all the social benefits from an innovation and leaving nothing behind for society.[125]

The efficacy of the patent system has been said to be 'indeterminate and highly situation-specific'.[126] Even then, those who defend the patent system argue that despite its tendency to overcompensate innovators, the high degree of information asymmetry between the system's administrators and innovators means that attaining the optimal level of protection will be elusive.[127] Even assuming that this is true, it is unclear why this indeterminacy should be resolved in favour of innovators. This is especially questionable in light of the system's proven tendency to overcompensate. The best argument commentators have offered is that the high risk and uncertainty of R&D investments mean that innovators should be given every benefit of the doubt.[128] This is hardly a satisfactory argument. If the efficacy of the patent system is case-specific, there are strong reasons for competition law to intervene. The case-by-case analysis under competition law would counterbalance the systemic and sweeping tendencies of the patent system.

The imprecise nature and the overcompensating tendencies of the patent system means that there is room for competition law intervention without significant loss in innovation incentives. Applying the envelope theorem, Ian Ayres and Paul Klemperer have offered a theoretical proof for this proposition. They argue that reducing the monopolist's market power and supra-competitive pricing at the margin will substantially reduce deadweight loss while causing little loss to the monopolist.[129] The basic geometry of the demand curve means that the last bit of monopolist pricing contributes only small profit to the incumbent while inflicting heavy deadweight loss on society.[130] Patentee reward thus can be reduced at the margin without substantial loss of innovation incentives. Although the focus in their article is on limited patent infringement, their insight has equal application to compulsory licensing. Their model provides that the infringer pays full damages

124 Joseph P Bauer, 'Refusals to Deal with Competitors by Owners of Patents and Copyrights: Reflections on the Image Technical and Xerox Decisions' (2006) 55 DePaul Law Review 1211, 1224.

125 Langenfeld (n 39) 96–97.

126 Frischmann and Waller (n 102) 34.

127 Devlin, Jacobs, and Peixoto (n 410) 1181.

128 Ian Ayres and Paul Klemperer, 'Limiting Patentees' Market Power Without Reducing Innovation Incentives: The Perverse Benefits of Uncertainty and Non-Injunctive Remedies' (1999) 97 Michigan Law Review 985, 994.

129 ibid.

130 Genevaz (n 35) 751–52.

for the infringement.[131] When transposed to the setting of compulsory licensing, their model would imply that the putative compulsory licensee pays the monopolist royalty rate. Ayres and Klemperer ascribe great importance in their model to the infringer (compulsory licensee), calling her the 'perfect agent[] of society—restraining the excesses of monopoly pricing without personal profit'.[132]

Ayres and Klemperer's argument has two premises. First, there is uncertainty and delay in the adjudication of infringement.[133] This should not pose a serious obstacle, as uncertainty and delay are inherent in every legal proceeding, patent infringement or competition. Second, there needs to be sufficiently high price elasticity of demand in the market.[134] When price elasticity is low, a small drop in monopolist price has negligible impact on deadweight loss but significantly reduces innovation incentives. Genevaz thus concludes that 'the validity of Ayres and Klemperer's conclusion varies from industry to industry'.[135] This condition raises some concern. Every case in which unilateral refusal to license could be in dispute is by definition a monopolization or abuse of dominance case, which means the defendant's product is unlikely to face an elastic demand.[136] This may limit the applicability of Ayres and Klemperer's insight.

Going beyond Ayres and Klemperer's theoretical insights, some commentators believe that selective compulsory licensing should have negligible impact on innovation incentives. Genevaz encapsulates the issue succinctly when he states that

> the question is not whether monopoly power fosters incentives to innovate, but rather is whether incentives to innovate in the industry at issue are sufficiently sensitive that liabilities for unilateral refusals to deal would induce a significant decrease of incentives to invest in R&D.[137]

Ritter is convinced that innovation incentives have low sensitivity to compulsory licensing, questioning if one

> compare[s] the number of compulsory licenses ordered by antitrust enforcers with the total amount of IP produced in any given timeframe[, i]s it reasonable to believe that firms will scale back their R&D investment because they observe, say, Microsoft having to grant a compulsory license and being deprived of some revenue?[138]

131 Ayres and Klemperer (n 128) 994.
132 ibid.
133 ibid 999.
134 Genevaz (n 35) 752.
135 ibid.
136 ibid.
137 ibid 751.
138 Ritter (n 51) 296.

Ritter's instinct is confirmed by FM Scherer, who has produced case studies showing that compulsory licensing has not lowered the innovation incentives of US corporations historically.[139]

The incentive dampening effect of compulsory licensing will be further ameliorated by royalty payments. Compulsory licensing does not mean free licensing.[140] The licensee still needs to offer the patentee adequate compensation. The financial impact of compulsory licensing can be effectively managed. McGowan describes the patent system as a 'rate of return structure',[141] under which innovators are provided a rate of return through 'the right to preclude others from using the creator's work. This "property" right to exclude forces those who wish to use an innovation to bargain with the owner and to pay him or her for the use.' [142] Conceptualizing the patent system as a rate of return structure implies that there is no unqualified right to exclude and that it is possible to fully compensate a patentee with monetary payments. The only question is the appropriate royalty rate. The royalty can be set between the monopoly profit that the incumbent would earn if she were allowed to monopolize the innovation and the duopoly profit that would result once a new entrant is introduced to the market so that the incumbent would not be made completely worse off by compulsory licensing.[143] In fact, it is possible to set the royalty at such a level that, in theory, the patentee should be indifferent as to whether compulsory licensing is imposed or not.

One issue that has long bedevilled commentators in this area of law is to what extent a patentee should be allowed to leverage its market position from the primary product market into complementary product markets or aftermarkets. Some have attempted to apply standard monopoly leveraging analysis.[144] Some have tried to answer the question with reference to the scope of the patent, which has been discussed earlier.[145] Others retort that patent scope was always meant to be a technical specification and was never intended to demarcate the permissible scope of recovery for the patentee.[146] A more detailed treatment of this will be deferred to the discussion of the scope of patent test in Chapter 6. Suffice it to note for now that ultimately whether a patentee should be allowed to recover from adjacent markets comes down to adequacy of innovation incentives. It seems very difficult to try to resolve this dispute over patent scope through logic or doctrinal arguments.

139 FM Scherer, 'Antitrust, Efficiency, and Progress' (1987) 62 New York University Law Review 998, 1018.

140 Daniel A Crane, 'Intellectual Liability' (2009) 88 Texas Law Review 253, 257.

141 McGowan (n 26) 493.

142 ibid.

143 John T Wenders, 'Entry and Monopoly Pricing' (1967) 75 Journal of Political Economy 755.

144 Genevaz (n 35) 762–63.

145 Lao (n 36) 198.

146 Herbert J Hovenkamp, 'IP and Antitrust Policy: A Brief Historical Overview' (University of Iowa 2005) No 05-31 37.

If one accepts that the patent system exists to provide innovation incentives, the strongest argument for allowing the patentee to extend its exclusivity into adjacent markets would be to ensure adequate compensation for the patentee's R&D investments. Recall that most commentators who have expressed a view on the issue concur that a patentee should not be allowed to make up for a shortfall in patentee reward from related markets.[147] Brett Frischmann and Spencer Waller note that the primary product market should generate sufficient innovation incentives and opening the secondary markets to competitors should have little impact.[148] Langenfeld asserts that even an absolute property right for an innovation does not extend the patent monopoly to products or services beyond the scope of the patent.[149] Lao characterizes claims that prohibiting a patentee from leveraging into complementary product markets would undermine innovation incentives as 'unfounded or, at least, exaggerated'.[150] If the protection of innovation incentives in the primary market is an insufficient reason to preclude all unilateral refusal to license claims, it is only logical that it fails to justify giving the patentee carte blanche to leverage into related markets.

(b) Competitor's innovation incentives

Compulsory licensing does not only affect the incumbent's innovation incentives but it may also influence competitors' willingness to invest in innovation. Being granted access to the incumbent's technology means that competitors will no longer have to develop their own technology. Using a stylized model, Gilbert and Shapiro argue that in a competitive R&D race scenario, imposing compulsory licensing will reduce the innovation incentives of both the winner and the loser.[151] The winner's pay-off is reduced because she needs to share the fruit of her success with the loser through compulsory licensing.[152] The loser's pay-off from losing the race is augmented by compulsory licensing, which means that the loser is less afraid of losing and tries less hard to win the race.[153]

Whether there is a loss in social welfare in this scenario depends on the degree of similarity between the competitor's and the incumbent's technologies. If the competitor's innovation is largely duplicative and redundant from a social perspective, a reduction in the competitor's innovation incentives may have little impact. Economists have concluded that in a patent race, where two firms vie to be the first to come up with an invention, the addition of one firm to hasten the arrival of an invention is often highly lucrative for the first inventor but redounds little

147 Lao (n 36) 213.
148 Frischmann and Waller (n 102) 33.
149 Langenfeld (n 39) 99.
150 Lao (n 36) 218.
151 Gilbert and Shapiro (n 55) 12753.
152 ibid.
153 ibid.

extra value to society.[154] In Gilbert and Shapiro's competitive R&D race scenario, the kind of R&D engaged by the winner and the loser could in fact be duplicative. Having the loser try less hard may not be so detrimental after all. In contrast, if a competitor's innovation would create a different path for follow-on innovation, society would gain from the competitor's R&D effort and the loss of the competitor's innovation incentives would be a real cost for society.

The case for a loss of competitor's innovation incentives due to compulsory licensing is more nuanced than is generally assumed. The fact that a competitor has been granted access to the incumbent's technology does not necessarily mean that there will be only one path for follow-on innovation. Competitors may build on the incumbent's technology, improve it, and develop new complementary products for it. Having two innovators work on the same product may augment the long-run level of innovation.[155] By opening the door for the competitor to pursue further improvements, compulsory licensing may augment a competitor's innovation incentives. It is exactly in light of this kind of situation that the European Commission declared in the *Microsoft* case that Microsoft's reduced innovation incentives may be more than offset by competitors' enhanced willingness to invest in R&D such that the industry benefits overall.[156]

(c) Cumulative innovator's innovation incentives

Cumulative innovation would not be an issue at all if the initial innovation were a dead-end technology that could not be further improved upon. In reality, not many technologies belong to this category. Even paper clips have been improved by plastic casing.[157] Numerous scholars have noted the importance of cumulative innovation for technological progress.[158] They have also asserted that overly

[154] Paul A David, 'Intellectual Property Institutions and the Panda's Thumb: Patents, Copyrights, and Trade Secrets in Economic Theory and History' in Mitchel B Wallerstein, Mary E Mogee, and Robin A Schoen (eds), *Global Dimensions of Intellectual Property Rights in Science and Technology* (National Academic Press 1992) 33.

[155] Shelanski (n 118) 383.

[156] COMP/37792, *Microsoft* [2004] OJ L32/23, para 783.

[157] Henry Petroski, *Invention by Design; How Engineers Get from Thought to Thing* (Harvard University Press 1996) 8–43.

[158] Michele Boldrin and David K Levine, *Against Intellectual Monopoly* (Cambridge University Press 2008) 147; Edmund Kitch, 'The Nature and Function of the Patent System' (1977) 20 Journal of Law & Economics 265; Joel Mokyr, 'The Industrial Revolution and the New Economic History' in Joel Mokyr (ed), *The Economics of the Industrial Revolution* (Routledge 2012) 1 ; William Baumol, *The Free-Market Innovation Machine: Analyzing the Growth Miracle of Capitalism* (Princeton University Press 2004) 12, 51; Jaffe and Lerner (n 38) 18. William Landes and Richard Posner, *The Economic Structure of Intellectual Property Law* (Harvard University Press 2003) 318; Mark A Lemley, 'Economics of Improvement in Intellectual Property Law' (1996) 75 Texas Law Review 989, 997; Robert Merges and Richard Nelson, 'On the Complex Economics of Patent Scope' [1990] Columbia Law Review 839, 870; Suzanne Scotchmer, 'Standing on the Shoulders of Giants: Cumulative Research and the Patent Law' (1991) 5 Journal of Economic Perspectives 29, 29.

expansive patent protection retards cumulative innovation.[159] Imposition of compulsory licensing may facilitate cumulative innovation.

Suppression of cumulative innovators' innovation incentives would be of little concern if the initial innovator is always better positioned to improve on her initial invention than are other innovators or is at least better able to spot potential improvers and enter into licensing arrangements with them. This would not be the case if the sources of improvement are often unexpected and unpredictable, defying coordination by the initial innovator and if unrelated third parties are equally good, if not better, at producing improvements. Compulsory licensing may be called for if a subsequent innovator comes up with an improvement but is refused a license to use the initial technology for one reason or another.[160]

Keen believers in market efficiency would argue that if the improvement creates substantial value beyond the initial invention, the initial innovator and the improver would always be able to enter into a mutually advantageous licensing agreement that splits the surplus created by the improvement between them.[161] Such an agreement would be especially likely if the improvement would not put the cumulative innovator in direct competition with the initial innovator. This would indicate a limited role for compulsory licensing. Competition law should abstain if intervention would not increase cumulative innovation but would merely alter the split of surplus between the initial and the cumulative innovators. The reality, however, is often more complicated than that. The incumbent's sole concern may not simply be the monetization of her innovation. Yongmin Chen notes that there could be anticompetitive motivations for the incumbent's refusal to supply a possible downstream follow-on innovator:

> By not supplying the downstream rival now, the monopolist may either reduce this possibility or maintain monopoly profit through downstream dominance even when the upstream market becomes competitive. This strategic, or 'anti-competitive' motive, may outweigh the short-term benefits of surplus extraction from supplying the downstream competitors.[162]

One can go further and question whether competition law should be agnostic about allocation of surplus between the initial and cumulative innovators, for this allocation can have implications for the innovation incentives of the respective innovators. John Vickers notes that

[159] Lemley (n 158) 998. John Vickers, 'Competition Policy and Property Rights' (2010) 120 The Economic Journal 375, 383–84; Jaffe and Lerner (n 38) 48–49.

[160] Suzanne Scotchmer, *Innovation and Incentives* (MIT Press 2004) 138.

[161] ibid 137–142.

[162] Chen (n 77) 535.

> [s]tronger IP rights would favour division of joint profit that favoured the original incumbent, so higher rather than lower [lump sum license fee]. But Segal and Whinston show that the innovation incentives of the challenger are greater when the incumbent has a lower profit share in the duopoly phase... So laissez-faire towards the incumbent, even though that maximises the value of incumbency, does not necessarily maximise innovation incentives.[163]

A larger share of surplus will obviously allow the cumulative innovator to invest more in R&D. The question is how these enhanced incentives should be balanced against the initial innovator's innovation incentives.

Vickers provides another reason for why compulsory licensing, which may foster technical parity between the initial and the cumulative innovators, may benefit innovation competition. He attributes this to the neck-and-neck effect, which holds that firms often compete harder in innovation when they are neck-and-neck with each other.[164] Therefore, while allowing the incumbent innovator to keep most of her innovation reward would give her greater incentives to strive to win the innovation competition, it would also reduce the neck-and-neck effect when the incumbent innovator has a substantial technological lead over rivals.[165] Vickers thus concludes that

> in a sequential setting, bolstering the prize for innovating [by refusing compulsory licensing] need not boost innovation. There is a composition effect—if firms compete hardest to innovate when neck-and-neck, then reducing the prize for innovating may nevertheless promote innovation if it increases the proportion of neck-and-neck competition.[166]

The conflicting interests of the initial and cumulative innovators create an acute dilemma for competition authorities. On the one hand, refusal to impose compulsory licensing has the unequivocal effect of increasing the initial innovator's patentee reward, which may increase her innovation incentives.[167] On the other hand, such reluctance reduces the opportunities for cumulative innovators to pursue follow-on innovation,[168] which requires access to the original invention.[169] These countervailing effects make it difficult to strike an appropriate balance

[163] Vickers (n 159) 384.

[164] ibid 385.

[165] ibid.

[166] ibid.

[167] Howard F Chang, 'Patent Scope, Antitrust Policy and Cumulative Innovation' (1995) 26 The RAND Journal of Economics 34, 48. Carmen Matutes, Pierre Regibeau, and Katharine Rockett, 'Optimal Patent Design and Diffusion of Innovations' [1996] 27 The RAND Journal of Economics 60, 80.

[168] Lao (n 36) 216–17.

[169] Dumont and Holmes (n 44) 151–52.

between the interests of the initial and the cumulative innovators.[170] In a theoretical model, Chen shows that whether prohibiting unilateral refusal to license advances consumer welfare or not crucially depends on the likelihood of follow-on innovation.[171] Consumer welfare will be harmed by compulsory licensing if such innovation is sufficiently unlikely, but should otherwise be improved by a prohibition of unilateral refusal to license.[172] Empirical evidence on this issue, however, is largely inconclusive.[173] This balance of interests will depend on market characteristics and will vary by industry and country as well.[174] Suzanne Scotchmer, a leading scholar on cumulative innovation, suggests that the nature of the product and innovation markets are relevant considerations.[175]

Setting aside these more variable factors, a number of considerations affect whether compulsory licensing is favourable to cumulative innovation. Competition law intervention may be particularly appropriate against 'overly broad and too all-encompassing patents' that foreclose cumulative innovation and inflict costs on consumers.[176] Moreover, the case for competition law intervention would be the strongest if the initial innovator is not the best positioned to pursue or coordinate follow-on innovation, and there are systemic failures for the initial and cumulative innovators to reach an agreement. While it is impossible to predict the likelihood of difficulties in bargaining on a systemic level, as it probably varies according to the idiosyncrasies of individual parties, there has been much theorization about models of cumulative innovation and their implications for whether the initial or cumulative innovator should be tasked with coordination.

There seems to be two views on the relative efficiency of the initial and cumulative innovators in pursuing and coordinating further improvements. Under Edmund Kitch's prospect theory, the initial innovator is assumed to be best positioned either to come up with further improvements or to identify innovators able to do so. Kitch postulates that the main purpose of the patent system is not to generate innovation incentives but to encourage the commercialization of existing ideas and the exploration of improvements.[177] This is achieved by granting prospective property rights over these as yet undiscovered ideas.[178] The initial innovator is entrusted with the responsibility to coordinate the commercialization of existing innovations and the search for further improvements, with a view to

[170] Gilbert and Shapiro (n 55) 12749.
[171] Chen (n 77) 536.
[172] ibid.
[173] Dumont and Holmes (n 44)154.
[174] ibid 152.
[175] Suzanne Scotchmer, 'Incentives to Innovate' in Peter Newman (ed), *New Palgrave Dictionary of Economics and the Law* (MacMillan 1998) 273, 275–76.
[176] Dumont and Holmes (n 44) 153.
[177] Kitch (n 158) 275–80.
[178] ibid.

avoiding duplicative investments.[179] This theory leaves very little role for the unilateral refusal to license doctrine to play in facilitating cumulative innovation.

Other commentators have disputed Kitch's rosy view of the initial innovator's efficiency, if not omniscience and good faith. First, they have questioned Kitch's assumption that the initial innovator is better positioned than her rivals to identify and pursue improvements. Given that the initial innovator is outnumbered by possible improvers, the initial innovator would have to possess vastly superior capability to pursue potential improvements or identify possible improvers.[180] There is no reason to believe that the initial innovator would possess such a capability. The evolutionary model of innovation presumes that innovation is

> best understood as a quasi-Darwinian process—a process almost of trial and error in which the market selects from among diverse approaches whose relative promise cannot be assessed in advance. This approach implies that a multiplicity of sources of inventive activity is superior to a centralized process directed by the patentee.[181]

This model of innovation implies that new ideas will emanate from unexpected sources and successful coordination by the initial innovator would be well-nigh impossible. Adherence to the prospect theory will lead to a suboptimal level of improvements as 'a single rightholder [will] *under*develop—or even ignore totally—many of the potential improvements encompassed by their broad property rights'.[182]

Second, even assuming perfect information on the part of the initial innovator, the transaction costs involved in reaching agreements with potential improvers would be significant, if not prohibitive.[183] It can be enormously time-consuming and costly for the incumbent innovator to negotiate licensing agreements with these improvers.[184] Uncertainty in R&D further adds to the transaction costs. The potential improver faces an acute dilemma. The improver could alleviate the uncertainty if she began the negotiation *ex post* after developing the improvement.[185] Yet that would expose the improver to potential holdup by the initial innovator.[186] To avoid strategic behaviour on the part of the initial innovator, negotiations must take place *ex ante*.[187] Conducting negotiations *ex ante* would require both parties

[179] ibid.
[180] Scotchmer, *Innovation and Incentives* (n 160) 146–47.
[181] Landes and Posner (n 158) 318.
[182] Merges and Nelson (n 158) 873–84.
[183] Lemley (n 158) 1053, 1055.
[184] Lemley (n 104) 1056.
[185] Lemley (n 158) 1051.
[186] Scotchmer, *Innovation and Incentives* (n 160) 138.
[187] ibid 146–47; Daniel G Swanson and William J Baumol, 'Reasonable and Nondiscriminatory (RAND) Royalties, Standards Selection, and Control of Market Power' (2005) 73 Antitrust Law Journal 1, 7–10.

to predict the prospect and the value of the follow-on innovation, which could be a highly speculative exercise.[188] If the cumulative innovator generally has difficulty persuading the initial innovator of her likelihood of success, or there is a systemic imbalance in bargaining power between the initial and the cumulative innovators, there could be systemic under-compensation of follow-on innovators.

Third, the behavioural assumption of the prospect theory that the initial innovator will behave rationally has also been challenged. The initial innovator may irrationally eschew licensing for non-economic reasons,[189] such as a bitterly fierce rivalry between two competing firms, distrust of a rival's good faith to abide by the licensing agreement, or rational or irrational fear that the licensed technology will somehow assist rivals in ways that are unforeseen by the initial innovator.[190] The personal animosity between Guglielmo Marconi, the patent holder for the diode technology—a crucial component of the early radio—and Lee de Forest, the inventor of the triode, which was a significant improvement over the diode,[191] means that the world was denied the benefits of this significant improvement for years.[192] In light of these three arguments, the prospect theory should be roundly rejected.

Whether the initial innovator or potential improvers are best positioned to generate improvements is ultimately an empirical question. It is possible that despite all these theoretical objections to the prospect theory, initial innovators are nonetheless better positioned than potential improvers to pursue improvements. Yet absent overwhelming evidence to the contrary, competition law should favour competition over market power. Kitch himself admits that the prospect theory condones substantial market power and supra-competitive pricing[193] and yet offers no solution for it.[194] A repudiation of the prospect theory means that it is critical to ensure that potential improvers have adequate access to the initial innovation. There is hence a role for compulsory licensing to play to facilitate cumulative innovation.

Cumulative innovation arises under different circumstances. Economists distinguish three scenarios of cumulative innovation: first, where an initial innovation spawns numerous follow-on innovations; second, where many initial innovations, mostly in the form of research tools, are needed to create a single second-generation innovation; and third, where the subsequent innovation represents an improvement of the initial one and yet the two compete with each other.[195] The second and the third scenarios have been called the 'anticommons' and the 'quality ladder' models of cumulative innovation.[196] This author will call the first

[188] Lemley (n 104) 1068.
[189] Lemley (n 158) 1055–58.
[190] Lemley (n 104) 1055, 57–58, 61.
[191] Jaffe and Lerner (n 38) 51.
[192] ibid.
[193] Kitch (n 158) 274.
[194] Lemley (n 158) 1047.
[195] Scotchmer, *Innovation and Incentives* (n 160) 132–33.
[196] ibid 146.

scenario the 'trunk–branch' model for lack of a better name in the literature. The three scenarios present disparate challenges for competition law interventions.

The need for intervention is the lowest under the quality ladder model for a number of reasons. First, in most quality ladder scenarios, improved versions of the innovation directly compete with, and replace, the initial innovation in the primary product market.[197] Such direct competition may prevent the initial innovator from recouping her initial R&D investment. Second, the loss of cumulative innovation in this case would be less costly for society as it would not deprive society of a product altogether. Society will simply be left with an unimproved version of it. This is in stark contrast with the other two scenarios, where obstacles to the cumulative innovator may preclude the emergence of a new product altogether.

In contrast, there are significant social benefits for the widespread deployment of the 'trunk' technology under the 'trunk–branch' model. The trunk technology can be the basis for many subsequent improvements or new product development.[198] So long as the initial innovator is compensated for her R&D costs, technology diffusion should be the overriding consideration. From a social welfare perspective, the Ramsey intuition dictates that society would be better off if the initial innovator distributed its cost recovery among a wide range of uses, while minimizing the distorting effect within each use.[199] Society would be better off if the trunk technology was deployed as widely as possible. Where the trunk technology can be licensed for multiple uses, there is a persuasive case for competition law intervention as it would be possible to guarantee the initial innovator's recovery without causing much deadweight loss in the market for each use.

The term 'anticommons' was originally coined by Michael Heller and Rebecca Eisenberg in 1998.[200] It describes a situation where a variety of inputs are required for a follow-on innovation. Anticommons presents a particularly tricky situation from a competition law perspective because of the significant possibility of holdup by the owner of any one of the inputs.[201] It would seem to suggest a possible role for competition law intervention to play. As suggested by Scotchmer, the best solution to an anticommons scenario may be joint ownership of the various research tools through consolidation.[202] She notes that the joint price for complementary inputs would be lower than if they were sold separately.[203] It is, however, beyond the remit of a competition authority to compel joint ownership. It would certainly require the authority to go beyond mere compulsory licensing. Therefore, there is a limit to what competition law can do to alleviate an anticommons situation. In

[197] ibid.
[198] ibid 132.
[199] Ayres and Klemperer (n 128) 992.
[200] Michael A Heller and Rebecca S Eisenberg, 'Can Patents Deter Innovation? The Anticommons in Biomedical Research' (1998) 280 Science 698, 698–99.
[201] Scotchmer, *Innovation and Incentives* (n 160) 142–43.
[202] ibid 143–44.
[203] ibid.

sum, the case for competition law intervention is the strongest under the 'trunk–branch' model, followed by the anticommons model, which is in turn followed by the quality ladder model. The relevance of these three models of cumulative innovation for developing countries will be addressed subsequently.

The foregoing discussion analyses the impact on competitor and cumulative innovators' innovation incentives under the assumption that they themselves directly demand access to technology from the incumbent. That need not be the case. These innovators' innovation incentives could be affected even if they were not the parties requesting access. This will be apparent when one combines the various theories of harm with the analysis of innovation incentives. To the extent that the party suffering from competitive harm under these theories, such as the firm that is being subject to the two-level entry requirement, could have entered the market with a substitute technology or a follow-on innovation, the fact that it has now been excluded from the market means that there is a loss of innovation. Under enhancement of entry barriers and foreclosure of downstream competition, if the firm that would have entered the downstream market would have done so with either a substitute technology or cumulative innovation, the unilateral refusal to deal would have cost society potentially important innovation. The same is true of the upstream competitor subject to the two-level entry requirement that would have entered the market if it had not been compelled to enter the downstream market as well and instead could have sold its input to other downstream firms. Recall also Yongmin Chen's postulation that foreclosing downstream rivals can help forestall follow-on innovation in the upstream market by making it more difficult for the innovator to recoup her investment. Cumulative innovation would be retarded in this scenario. Creation of effective exclusivity could also cause a loss of innovation if the firm which would have entered the primary product market but for the exclusivity would have done so with competing or cumulative innovation.

The variations of enhancement of entry barriers and creation of effective exclusivity that are premised on a complementary product are more likely to implicate cumulative innovation than competing innovation. Complementary products are more likely to build on the incumbent's technology in the primary product than to feature a completely novel technology. Therefore, to the extent that unilateral refusal to deal results in exclusion in the complementary product market, the exclusion could additionally inflict a cost in terms of cumulative innovation. Meanwhile, it is unlikely that facilitation of price discrimination will result in a loss of innovation as price discrimination does not entail exclusion of competitors, upstream, downstream, or in a complementary product market.

(d) Implications for developing countries

The central argument of this monograph is that developing countries need to adopt a different and a contextualized approach to the patent–competition interface in light of their domestic technological capacity and their differing needs to attract foreign technology export. The underlying policy dilemma of the patent–competition interface is a balance between static efficiency and dynamic efficiency considerations. Dynamic efficiency considerations may carry different weight and play out differently in different countries depending on the domestic capacity to innovate. This in turn affects how the balance should be struck between static and dynamic efficiencies. In addition, the enforcement capacities of the domestic competition authorities and the courts will need to be taken into account. Complex rules that may reduce error costs and help achieve accurate outcomes could be beyond the capability of a developing country authority or court. Developing countries may need to tailor the applicable rules to their domestic enforcement capacity. In light of their vastly different technological capacities, developing countries cannot blindly follow the approach to the patent–competition interface prevailing in the industrialized economies and will need to fashion an approach that suits their domestic circumstances.

The implications of the foregoing discussion for developing countries can be separated into three perspectives: incumbent innovators, competitor innovators, and cumulative innovators. Despite the highly intuitive argument that compulsory licensing will dampen the incumbent innovator's innovation incentives, many commentators have questioned this view on various grounds. Shelanski points to the many flaws in the patent system and argues that the more flawed is the patent system, the stronger is the justification for compulsory licensing under competition law. Lao challenges the notion that market power is needed to incentivize innovation. While Cotter, Bauer, and Langenfeld acknowledge the incentive effects of the patent system, they observe that it is possible, and in fact not uncommon, for the incentives to be excessive. Lastly, invoking the envelope theorem, Ayres and Klemperer argue that reducing monopolist pricing somewhat will have negligible impact on patentee reward.

Other commentators such as Genevaz and Ritter go beyond the patent system in general and focus specifically on the impact of compulsory licensing. They argue that given the small number of compulsory licensing cases, it is unlikely that judicial intervention will have substantial impact on innovation incentives. While their observation may be valid for the current level of compulsory licensing, which is admittedly quite restrained on both sides of the Atlantic, one cannot be sure that further expansion of compulsory licensing will not reduce innovation incentives. The point will come when increased incidence of compulsory licensing will catch potential innovators' attention. Fortunately, the negative incentive effect of compulsory licensing can be kept in check by imposing an appropriate level of royalty.

If one agrees with these commentators that compulsory licensing will have negligible impact on the incumbent innovator's innovation incentives or that the negative impact can be effectively managed, then competition authorities in developing countries will have a freer rein in imposing compulsory licensing. If one believes that compulsory licensing will dampen the incumbent innovator's innovation incentives, then the question becomes the extent to which developing country competition authorities should take these innovators' interests into account. The appropriate response varies in accordance with the technological capacity of the country at issue. For a production country with negligible innovation capacity, a more liberal stance on compulsory licensing will have little impact on domestic firms, which are unlikely to undertake any meaningful innovation anyway. For a technology adaptation country, there is still negligible domestic innovation and thus compulsory licensing will have minimal effect on domestic firms as incumbent innovators. The impact on domestic competitor innovators, or rather technology adaptors, is more complex and will be examined subsequently. For a proto-innovation country where there are some domestic firms capable of genuine innovations, compulsory licensing may reduce domestic innovation. This could be a matter of serious concern as the innovation capacity in these countries is likely to be relatively nascent and fragile and compulsory licensing may fatally undermine such capacity.

Lastly, compulsory licensing may also deter innovation by foreign incumbent innovators. With respect to these innovators, it was argued in Chapter 2 that multinational corporations are unlikely to take into account the patentee reward provided by every country in which they operate. They are likely to focus on industrialized economies and relatively wealthy developing countries with a substantial domestic market. This means that most developing countries can place little weight on the incentive effects generated by their domestic patent system for foreign innovators. As for the relatively large and wealthy developing countries, even if they subscribe to the more realistic model produced by Branstetter and Saggi and conclude that the incidence of compulsory licensing imposed domestically will affect innovation in industrialized economies and the FDI inflow into developing countries, there remains the question of how that should be traded off against harm to domestic consumer welfare.

In terms of competitor innovators' innovation incentives, the foregoing discussion in the context of industrialized economies will need to be modified to suit the context of developing countries. First of all, competitor innovators' innovation incentives are unlikely to be a relevant issue for production countries that possess little genuine technological capacity. These incentives, however, deserve the attention of competition authorities in technology adaptation and proto-innovation countries, except that in the technology adaptation countries, competitors of foreign incumbent innovators are technology adaptors rather than innovators. In the context of the industrialized economies, the main concern is whether competitor innovation will merely be duplicative of the incumbent's or whether it is likely to lead to alternative paths for future innovation. In the context of developing countries, there is no question that innovation by domestic firms will be duplicative.

Most developing country firms do not produce genuine frontier innovations. Domestic innovation is mostly likely an adaptation of the foreign technology—which is one type of laggard innovation—innovation by developing country standard. Or in the parlance of a classification scheme of innovation based on novelty proposed by the Organisation for Economic Co-operation and Development (OECD), most developing country innovation would be 'new to the market', which is the middle tier of novelty between the lowest level of 'new to the firm' and the highest level of 'new to the world'.[204] An innovation is 'new to the market' 'when the firm is the first to introduce an innovation on its market'[205] while 'new to the firm' represents the minimum level of novelty, and 'new to the world' refers to when the firm is the first to introduce an innovation across all markets and industries.[206] However, this does not mean that the resources invested into such innovation will go to waste. The innovation is only duplicative in the global sense, but not in the local sense. The innovation still enhances domestic innovation capacity.

This can be illustrated by an adapted version of Gilbert and Shapiro's competitive R&D race. A competitive R&D race in the developing country context is likely to feature a developing country firm catching up with the global technology leader through technology adaptation. The race will not be between two equally technologically competent firms trying to produce a genuine innovation along the global technological frontier. If an R&D race were to exist at all, it would take the form of a developing country firm trying to imitate a global technological leader's technology while the latter firm rushes to commercialize the technology and bring it to the market before the imitation succeeds.

Gilbert and Shapiro pessimistically predict that in the typical competitive R&D race, the loser will lose the incentive to invest in R&D when she knows that she can share the fruits of the winner's efforts through a compulsory license. The dynamics are different in a developing country competitive R&D race. The two firms do not begin from the same starting point. Instead, the developing country firm is likely to possess significantly inferior technological capacity. The prospect of a compulsory license at the end of the race may not dampen its incentive to invest in R&D. The domestic firm may still need to improve its technological capacity so that it is in a position to make use of the new technology transferred under a compulsory license. Compulsory licensing may help to promote technological upgrade in developing countries. And if compulsory licensing merely amounts to authorization to use a technology which the licensee acquires independently, which will be discussed in Chapter 6, the incentive effect will be even stronger. The developing country firm will be highly motivated to reverse engineer foreign technology

[204] OECD, 'Oslo Manual: Guidelines for Collecting and Interpreting Innovation Data' (2005) 57 <https://www.oecd-ilibrary.org /docserver /9789264013100-en.pdf? expires=1619714349&id=id&accname= guest&checksum= 8CF7080707935F70C826812901A98516> accessed 29 April 2021.

[205] ibid 58.

[206] ibid 57–58.

which it will be allowed to commercialize under a compulsory license. A compulsory license would be of no use to the firm unless it could acquire the technology independently.

The discussion about competitor innovators in developing countries or competing technology adaptors as they may be more appropriately called, cannot only focus on compulsory licensing and how that affects these adaptors' innovation incentives. For technology adaptors in developing countries, compulsory licensing and other forms of involuntary technology transfer are likely to be a minor source of foreign technology. The bulk of the foreign technology will be likely to be imported through voluntary means such as import of technological goods, foreign direct investment (FDI), and licensing.[207] Recall that Chapter 3 shows that robustness of patent protection affects the amount and the mode of technology transfer. More robust patent protection generally increases the flow of technology transfer and also helps to steer technology transfer to modes that redound greater benefit to the host country, such as FDI and licensing, especially the latter.

Incidence of compulsory licensing obviously has a bearing on the robustness of patent protection. Foreign technology owners may be less willing to engage in FDI or licensing if they know that doing so would expose them to the risk of compulsory licensing and hence of losing their future royalty payment stream. Robustness of patent protection particularly matters for those developing countries with a significant technology adaptation capacity where foreign technology is exposed to an elevated risk of imitation. Therefore, while compulsory licensing may help technology adaptors obtain foreign technology directly through judicial coercion, it may cost these adaptors access to voluntary sources of foreign technology. Given that instances of voluntary technology transfer are likely to outnumber that of compulsory licensing by orders of magnitude, the overall effect of compulsory licensing on competitor innovators/technology adaptors in developing countries may be negative.

As for cumulative innovator's innovation incentives, the first observation that can be made in the developing country context is that Kitch's prospect theory carries even less credibility. It is difficult enough to coordinate cumulative innovation among many possible sources when all the potential innovators are confined to one country or at least to the industrialized economies. The task would be well nigh impossible if potential innovators are spread all over the globe. On a global scale, it is clear that a centralized, coordinated approach to cumulative innovation

[207] UNCTAD, 'Transfer of Technology and Knowledge Sharing for Development: Science, Technology and Innovation Issues for Developing Countries' (UNCTAD 2014) No 8 15–20 <https://unctad.org/system/files/official-document/dtlstict2013d8_en.pdf> accessed 4 March 2020; Bernard M Hoekman, Keith E Maskus, and Kamal Saggi, 'Transfer of Technology to Developing Countries: Unilateral and Multilateral Policy Options' (World Bank 2004) No 3332 6–9 <http://documents.worldbank.org/curated/en/737591468762912473/pdf/wps3332.pdf> accessed 4 March 2020.

is impractical. Potential innovators must be given adequate access to initial technologies for cumulative innovation to materialize.

One can safely assume that the incentive effect on cumulative innovators deserves little attention in production countries. For the remainder of developing countries, the extent to which this effect deserves the competition authority's attention depends on the existence of possible cumulative innovators in the country at issue. Here the previous classification of developing countries into technology adaptation and proto-innovation countries may be less useful. There are reasons to believe that improving an existing technology requires lower technological capacity than coming up with a brand new technology *de novo*. Tinkering with or improving one part of a machine or an aspect of a technology should require less technological capacity than inventing the machine or creating the technology itself. Developing an application for a basic technology may also be technically less demanding than coming up with the basic technology itself in the first place. Therefore, a country that is bereft of genuine initial innovators may nonetheless possess some possible cumulative innovation capacity. The incentive effects on cumulative innovators may hence deserve attention from more developing countries as compared to the effects on incumbent innovators.

Effects on cumulative innovators may deserve special attention from developing countries because cumulative innovation could play an important role in the development of a developing country's technological capacity. It allows the innovator to focus on one aspect of the technology while acquiring some understanding of the rest of the technology. By making improvements to different aspects of the technology over time, eventually the cumulative innovator may acquire the capacity to produce and innovate on the entire technology. The possibility of cumulative innovation allows a technological laggard to acquire innovation capacity on a piecemeal basis.

It was suggested in the context of industrialized economies that the quality ladder model presents the thorniest case for competition law intervention because imposing compulsory licensing where cumulative innovation follows the quality ladder model could severely undercut the initial innovator's recoupment of R&D investment and may not result in the emergence of a brand new product. In the developing country context, this reason for caution has to be balanced against the potential contribution of cumulative innovation to the acquisition of technological capacity. There may be a stronger reason for competition law intervention under a quality ladder model of cumulative innovation in developing countries. The kind of technological learning and upgrade mentioned in the previous paragraph is especially relevant for the quality ladder model. The quality ladder model of cumulative innovation presents the likeliest scenario for technological upgrade through cumulative innovation. It was mentioned that competition law will only have a limited role to play in the context of the anticommons model of cumulative innovation. Joint ownership is often the superior solution and that usually cannot be achieved through competition law intervention. Developing country competition authorities can overlook the anticommons model of innovation.

Lastly, with regards to the 'trunk–branch' model of cumulative innovation, it was argued that compulsory licensing could yield significant social benefits. If the trunk technology has widespread applications, compelled sharing of the technology could make possible many new uses that may redound benefits to consumers. In the context of developing countries, allowing a domestic firm to develop applications for a trunk technology may also have the salutary effect of giving that firm the opportunity to develop its technological capacity. In the process of developing an application for a basic technology, the firm may come to acquire a better understanding of the underlying technology, which may allow it to innovate better in related fields.

The alignment of interests of the various groups of innovators is different in developing countries as compared to industrialized economies. In an industrialized economy, compulsory licensing pits an incumbent innovator's interests against the interests of competitor innovators and cumulative innovators. The three groups of innovators could be found in the same country and there would be a need to balance the countervailing interests of the three groups of innovators when contemplating whether to impose compulsory licensing. The situation is different in developing countries. Incumbent innovators are likely to be absent in most developing countries with the exception of the proto-innovation countries. Developing countries hence predominantly only need to focus on the competitor and cumulative innovators. Cumulative innovators, especially those under the quality ladder and 'trunk–branch' models, benefit from compulsory licensing. Competitor innovators or technology adaptors, however, may lose out if increased incidence of compulsory licensing deters voluntary technology transfer through FDI and licensing.

2. Implementation Difficulties

Another major line of critique of the unilateral refusal to deal doctrine and the essential facilities doctrine centres on implementation difficulties. The argument is that if the competition authority or the courts were to impose compulsory licensing under either doctrine, they would also have to stipulate the terms of dealing or the royalty rate. This is especially true because it has been emphasized that compulsory licensing is not free licensing and adequate compensation must be offered. Absent judicial intervention, the patentee would charge an exorbitant royalty unaffordable to the putative licensee.[208] The compulsory licensing order will not have improved matters and the putative licensee is still denied access to the patentee's technology.

208 Hovenkamp, Janis, and Lemley (n 23) 8.

Therefore, for a compulsory licensing order to make a meaningful difference, the licensing terms must be stipulated or regulated.[209] This would require the authority or the courts to come up with a royalty rate for the license, which can be notoriously difficult.

The authority's or the courts' obligation does not end here. They may have to engage in ongoing supervision to ensure compliance with the order.[210] Given the contentious nature of a compulsory license, there are bound to be disputes between the patentee and the putative licensee. The patentee will understandably drag her feet or offer incomplete access to her technology to minimize the competitive advantage the licensee can obtain from the license. The authority or the courts will have to get involved to settle these disputes for as long as the license is in effect, which could be years after the original dispute. As mentioned earlier, Judge Harold Greene continued his supervision in the original AT&T break-up for years after the consent decree was reached.

The authority and the courts are not completely at sea when trying to determine the appropriate royalty. In the United States, the famous *Georgia-Pacific* case provides what is essentially a bucket list of factors to consider when setting royalty.[211] The inquiry under *Georgia-Pacific*, however, is so open-ended that it is unclear how much guidance is actually given by the case.[212] The difficulty goes beyond coming up with the correct determination once all the relevant data are presented to the authority or the courts. Obtaining accurate data for royalty determination could be fraught with difficulty as the authority and the courts suffer from significant information asymmetry.[213] Most of the relevant information is likely to be in the hands of the dominant firm, which faces strong incentives to supply misleading or outright false information to obtain a favourable outcome.[214] An erroneously set royalty can have serious welfare consequences.[215]

Some commentators, however, believe that the difficulty in royalty setting is often overstated. Ritter asserts that the difficulty in setting the appropriate royalty is exaggerated and that it is no greater than setting the correct access terms for a physical facility.[216] Waller concurs with Ritter. Commenting specifically on the United States, where remedies in refusal to deal cases are set by the courts, he concludes that there is no reason to suspect that the US federal courts would not be up

[209] ibid 16.

[210] ibid.

[211] Makan Delrahim, 'Forcing Firms to Share the Sandbox: Compulsory Licensing of Intellectual Property Rights and Antitrust' (2004) 2004 European Business Law Review 1059, 1967.

[212] *Georgia-Pacific Corp. v. United States Plywood Corp.*, 318 F. Supp. 1116 (SDNY 1970).

[213] Thomas F Cotter, 'Four Principles for Calculating Reasonable Royalties in Patent Infringement Litigation' (2011) 27 Santa Clara Computer & High Technology Law Journal 725, 730.

[214] Gilbert and Shapiro (n 55) 12753.

[215] Werden (n 95) 472.

[216] Ritter (n 51) 295.

to the task.[217] He characterizes the objection to the essential facilities doctrine on institutional capacity grounds as a straw man, noting that

> Areeda and most of the subsequent critics raising the issue of remedy have argued at a high level of abstraction and provide few examples of where the courts have gone wrong. It is simply not clear in which cases the critics believe the courts have embroiled themselves in an endless regulatory process beyond their institutional capabilities.[218]

Focusing on damages and injunctive relief, Waller observes that the US courts have been more than capable of calculating damages awards and crafting and enforcing injunctive relief.[219] He notes a shift from injunctive relief to damages awards in recent essential facilities cases in the United States.[220] Calculation of damages is well within judicial expertise. Even if the courts are asked to craft an injunctive relief, most of the cases have involved the incumbent discriminating against one particular user in the provision of access and the injunction would be a simple order to provide non-discriminatory access.[221] The US courts have done a good job at it.[222] In cases where rate setting is needed, Waller endorses Professor Phillip Areeda's proposal to involve an appropriate regulatory agency.[223] Waller thus concludes that

> [w]hen considering the combination of those few successful essential facilities doctrine cases, those that concern damage awards only, those injunctive cases where there is a preexisting course of dealing, those injunctive cases where the parties can bargain out their differences or resolve them through other dispute resolution procedures, those injunctive cases where a regulatory body can assist the court, and the existence of some degree of judicial common sense, it is hard to see how often Areeda's legitimate concerns will counsel in favor of doing nothing to remedy an actual violation of the law.[224]

Waller's solution is likely to be of relatively limited use in patent compulsory licensing cases. In most of these cases, what the plaintiff wants is access to the defendant's technology. Damages awards may help, but injunctive relief is what the plaintiff is truly after. Royalty setting is hence an inevitable part of the case. In the

[217] Frischmann and Waller (n 102) 379–80.
[218] Spencer Weber Waller, 'Areeda, Epithets, and Essential Facilities' (2008) 2008 Wisconsin Law Review 359, 380.
[219] ibid 379; Frischmann and Waller (n 102) 43.
[220] Waller (n 218) 379.
[221] Frischmann and Waller (n 102) 43.
[222] ibid 42.
[223] Waller (n 218) 381.
[224] ibid 381–82.

context of patent royalty setting, there is no regulatory agency to which the US courts can turn for assistance.[225]

Waller's discussion focuses on the courts because in the United States only the courts can impose remedies. The same is obviously not true in the European Union, where first instance decisions are made by the European Commission, which are then appealed to the European courts. Assessment of damages awards is left to the national courts;[226] the European Commission would only be concerned with the issuance of injunctive relief and setting of an appropriate royalty rate, usually after negotiations with the party involved.[227] While the difficulty in crafting injunctive relief should not be insurmountable, as Waller has argued, the challenge in setting the appropriate royalty would be significant for both the US courts and the European Commission. The Directorate for Competition of the European Commission focuses on competition law matters and does not possess special expertise in rate setting, and certainly not in royalty determination.[228] The only thing that could be of assistance to the US courts and the European Commission would be if there are existing licenses under the patent, which could provide some benchmark for the royalty rate. If royalty setting is difficult for the US courts and the European Commission, it would be even more challenging for a developing country authority.

Given the inevitability of some royalty setting in a compulsory licensing case, it will be helpful to have some guidance, which Gilbert and Shapiro have provided. To the extent that a fixed license fee can be used in lieu of a per-unit royalty rate, a fixed license fee is to be preferred.[229] The only consequence of a flat license fee is a wealth transfer between the licensor and the licensee; it has no impact on overall welfare.[230] A royalty that is proportional to the licensee's total sales has similar welfare effects as a fixed license fee so long as the royalty rate is low.[231]

When still a private practitioner, Makan Delrahim, the former Assistant Attorney General for Antitrust in the United States, raised two further implementation issues with compulsory licensing. First, a compulsory license need not be limited to existing patents. A court can theoretically apply the license to future patents in the pipeline.[232] The *General Electric* case in 1953 was one such example.[233] Extending the license to future patents, however, poses an acute dilemma:

[225] Stanley M Besen, 'Why Royalties for Standard Essential Patents Should Not Be Set by the Courts' (2015) 15 Chicago-Kent Journal of Intellectual Property 19.

[226] Alison Jones and Brenda Sufrin, *EU Competition Law: Text, Cases, and Materials* (5th edn, Oxford University Press 2014) 105–107.

[227] Nicholas Economides, Ioannis Lianos, and Luca Rubini, 'The Quest for Appropriate Remedies in the EC Microsoft Cases: A Comparative Appraisal' in Luca Rubini (ed), *Microsoft on Trial: Legal and Economic Analysis of a Transatlantic Antitrust Case* (Edward Elgar 2010) 393, 420–23.

[228] Jones and Sufrin (n 226) 102–04.

[229] Gilbert and Shapiro (n 55) 12753.

[230] ibid.

[231] ibid.

[232] Delrahim (n 211) 1067.

[233] *United States v. General Electric Co.*, 115 F. Supp. 835 (D.N.J. 1953).

> On the one hand, [extending the license to future patents] makes sense because the value of a compulsory license would evaporate if a monopolist could come out the very next day with a new blocking patent. But on the other hand, the license could potentially harm innovation by taking away or at least reducing the incentives to invest in future research and development in that field.[234]

Second, a compulsory license may extend beyond codifiable knowledge to cover tacit knowledge or technical know-how. Economists have distinguished between codifiable knowledge, which can be written down in blueprints, and tacit knowledge, which refers to know-how that is often difficult to capture in writing.[235] Deployment of a new technology requires both codified technical information spelled out in the patent and blueprint and uncodified know-how.[236] The question is whether a compulsory license should cover know-how as well as codified information.[237] This goes to the fundamental question of the nature of the assistance expected from the patentee. If the patent meets the disclosure requirement and contains sufficient information to allow 'a person having ordinary skill in the art' (PHOSITA) to practise the claimed invention, in theory the patentee needs to do no more than merely authorizing the putative licensee to use the technology under a compulsory license.[238] The licensee should be able to recreate the technology based on the patent itself.

If the compulsory license imposes no obligation on the patentee to assist in the licensee's deployment of the technology and the licensee is merely expected to rely on the technical information contained in the patent, the compulsory license will be quite different from a conventional license and effectively amounts to a covenant not to sue. It is a license merely to authorize the licensee to use the technology, which can be called a mere authorization license. If the patentee is expected to impart know-how to the licensee as well, the obligation to assist becomes considerably more expansive. The patentee may be expected to ensure the licensee's successful deployment of the technology. A compulsory license that covers technical know-how as well as codified information, which can be called an active assistance license, will require more active supervision by the authority or the courts.[239] Given the intangible nature of tacit knowledge, disputes are bound to arise as to the sufficiency of assistance rendered by the licensor.[240] These disputes will need to be settled by the authority or the courts.

[234] Delrahim (n 211) 1067.

[235] Bernard Ancori, Antoine Bureth, and Patrick Cohendet, 'The Economics of Knowledge: The Debate about Codification and Tacit Knowledge' (2000) 9 Industrial and Corporate Change 255, 257–58.

[236] Pranab Bardhan and Christopher Udry, *Development Microeconomics* (Oxford University Press 1999) 153.

[237] Delrahim (n 211) 1067.

[238] Jeanne C Fromer, 'Patent Disclosure' (2008) 94 Iowa Law Review 539, 544–47.

[239] Delrahim (n 211) 1068.

[240] ibid.

In light of the numerous pitfalls for crafting an effective compulsory license, Delrahim issues a list of guidelines for the issuance of compulsory licenses. He urges a 'less is more' approach to compulsory licensing, arguing that 'an overriding goal should be to use the simplest, minimum necessary combination of transfer of rights and government oversight'.[241] The license should rely on objective, verifiable criteria as benchmarks for compliance to avoid needless litigation.[242] The scope of the patent should be narrowly and clearly construed as to field of use, products, or geography.[243] Transfer of know-how should be avoided to the extent possible.[244] The license should be time-limited and should be as clear about the royalty as possible.[245] The scope of potential licensees should also be as clear as possible.[246] Lastly, he argues that compulsory licensing should only be possible when there is 'an extraordinary level of market dominance and a demonstrated history of monopolization and resistance to reform'.[247]

Returning to the implementation of compulsory licensing in the developing country context, while it is important to be honest about the implementation difficulties, there is no need to throw the baby out with the bath water and abandon the enterprise completely. Few things are easy in competition law, especially in the area of the patent–competition interface, which is always fraught with complicated theoretical issues. Even if there is no fully satisfactory solution to some of these implementation issues, one must guard against the tendency to let the best be the enemy of the good. The choice should not be conceived as one between a perfectly crafted and executed compulsory license and none at all.

It is true that an erroneously set royalty rate will distort resource allocation. The resource allocation function of royalty rates, however, should not be overstated. One should try to understand the true nature of the royalty setting process in a usual commercial setting. Unlike the determination of a market-clearing price of a widely traded commodity, which is set by the interplay between market supply and demand, royalty is usually set through private negotiations between the patentee and the putative licensee.[248] In a general commodity market, the market price serves to allocate the product among consumers according to the strength of their demand and their willingness to pay and to signal to producers how much to produce.[249] It performs a resource allocation function on both sides of the market.[250]

[241] ibid.
[242] ibid.
[243] ibid.
[244] ibid.
[245] ibid.
[246] ibid.
[247] ibid 1069.
[248] Mark A Lemley and Carl Shapiro, 'Patent Holdup and Royalty Stacking' (2007) 85 Texas Law Review 1991, 1995–98.
[249] Hal R Varian, *Intermediate Microeconomics with Calculus: A Modern Approach* (W W Norton & Company 2014) 5–6.
[250] ibid.

In the patent licensing context, royalty rates are but a mere reflection of the relative bargaining power of the two parties and only determine how the surplus is split between them.[251] Nor does the royalty give a decisive signal to the patentee as to how much to invest in R&D. Recall that patent protection is only one of the numerous appropriation mechanisms for a technology developer. Her willingness to make R&D investment will not be solely determined by her royalty income. Moreover, the bespoke nature of every transaction means that it is unlikely that the innovator will rely on individual royalty negotiations for her future investment decisions. Therefore, while one should endeavour to set royalty accurately, some deviation from the hypothetical 'efficient' rate will not significantly distort allocation.

The implementation difficulties for a unilateral refusal to deal or an essential facilities claim should be manageable when the remedy sought is confined to damages or injunctive relief, especially when there is a course of prior dealing between the patentee and the putative licensee or when there are other current licensees. The implementation difficulties will be more significant when it comes to royalty setting, which it was argued will be inevitable in many compulsory licensing cases. A competition authority, however, is not entirely at sea when attempting to set royalty. The case law sheds some light on how it should be done. Delrahim, Gilbert, and Shapiro have provided some useful guidance, such as a preference for a flat fee and a royalty based on a low percentage of total sales. The compulsory licensing obligation should be extended to future patents. Delrahim contends that the licensing obligation should not extend to tacit know-how. Whether active assistance by the patentee should be required as part of the compulsory license depends on the nature of the licensing obligation. It will be discussed in Chapter 6.

3. Critiques Specific to the Essential Facilities Doctrine

Apart from the aforementioned critiques that are applicable to both the unilateral refusal to deal doctrine and the essential facilities doctrine, some commentators have offered criticisms that are specific to the essential facilities doctrine. Cotter has observed three weaknesses of the essential facilities doctrine. First, he argues that the essential facilities doctrine is largely superfluous because most of the cases involve unlawful attempts to create or extend monopoly power, which is well covered by the main body of the monopolization or abuse of dominance law.[252] Second, application of the doctrine reduces incentives to invest to create the facility in the first place.[253] Third, the doctrine facilitates collusion by requiring firms to share a facility.[254]

[251] Lemley and Shapiro (n 248) 1995–98.
[252] Cotter (n 33) 233.
[253] ibid 233–34.
[254] ibid 234.

Whether the first critique is valid depends on how it is understood. With the exception of exploitative abuses under EU law, virtually every abuse of dominance or monopolization claim involves the creation or protection or leveraging of monopoly power through some exclusionary conduct.[255] In the case of the essential facilities doctrine, the exclusionary conduct is denial of access to an essential facility. If what Cotter meant is that every essential facilities case entails the creation or protection or leveraging of monopoly power, that is a rather unremarkable observation. If what he meant is that every abuse of dominance claim premised on the essential facilities doctrine can be reformulated by substituting other exclusionary acts for the denial of access to facility, a quick review of the case law and the aforementioned theories of harm shows that this is clearly not the case.

But if what he meant is that those essential facilities doctrine cases that cannot be so reformulated should be excised from the doctrine, which he seems to suggest, then his critique is highly problematic.[256] If it is true that most of the essential facilities cases entail creation or leveraging monopoly power, then they are rightly within the purview of monopolization or abuse of dominance law. And if some of these cases cannot be reformulated by substituting other exclusionary conduct for the refusal to deal, then it means that abolishing the doctrine and relying on other areas of monopolization law will leave some instances of creation or leveraging of market power unaddressed. Cotter has not made a convincing case for why instances of creation or leveraging of monopoly power that are the result of refusal to deal deserve less protection under the law.

Cotter's second critique has already been addressed and the arguments will not be repeated here. Finally, the potential of compelled sharing to facilitate collusion is overstated. First, if the incumbent is so keen on collusion and if collusion is profitable, which it most probably is, she would not have to be judicially compelled to provide access.[257] She would have done so voluntarily. Second, the potential for facilitation of collusion should be manageable given that the sharing is publicly known and subject to some level of regulatory control or judicial oversight.[258] Furthermore, the collusion facilitation potential of mandated sharing carries much less weight in the patent context. In the context of a physical facility single-handedly developed by one firm, sharing of the facility is admittedly not the ordinary state of affairs and compelled sharing of the facility may create more opportunities for competitors to communicate with each other. In the case of a patented innovation, sharing of the technology happens on a regular basis through licensing.[259] Unless the patentee decides to exploit the technology all by herself,

[255] Hovenkamp (n 48) s 6.4.
[256] Cotter (n 33) 233.
[257] Frischmann and Waller (n 102) 39.
[258] ibid.
[259] Carl Shapiro, 'Patent Licensing and R&D Rivalry' (1985) 75 The American Economic Review 25, 25–26.

some amount of licensing must take place.[260] The potential for a licensor and a licensee to collude is always there and compelled sharing under the essential facilities doctrine does not significantly increase the risk.

The essential facilities doctrine has also been criticized for its inability to improve consumer welfare. Abbott Lipsky and Gregory Sidak observe that '[a]dmission of a new entrant to an undersized facility (even one charging rates that are no higher than necessary to cover all costs of operation) cannot improve the downstream equilibrium without capacity expansion.'[261] So long as courts refrain from requiring the facility owner to expand the facility's capacity, compelled sharing under the essential facilities doctrine will simply result in more users sharing the existing limited capacity, which will not improve consumer welfare.

Ignoring for now whether their observation is accurate in the context of physical facilities—and it is certainly possible to imagine scenarios in which that need not be the case, such as if the firm being granted access is a lower-cost producer of the downstream product than existing competitors, or, as Frischmann and Waller argue, even non-discriminatory access at monopoly price is beneficial[262]—it is clear that their observation has no application to patented technology, which as a public good is by definition non-rivalrous in use.[263] Innovation in the form of knowledge does not suffer from limited physical capacity as in the case of physical facilities. Consumer welfare will definitely be improved if a patented technology is shared with a lower-cost producer or implementer. Even if the new firm being given access only has the same cost structure as existing competitors, the increase in market supply following entry by the new firm will drive down the market price, thereby improving consumer welfare. Some commentators,[264] including Lipsky and Sidak themselves,[265] have argued that the essential facilities doctrine is particularly unsuitable for intellectual property. From the perspective of consumer welfare, it seems that the converse is true and compulsory licensing of intellectual property has a greater potential to improve consumer welfare than does mandated sharing of a physical facility.

Gregory Werden has offered not so much a criticism as a significant narrowing of the scope of the essential facilities doctrine. He argues that the doctrine should only be invoked in regulated industries, observing that

> [s]ince there appear to be no situations in which a refusal to deal would be the optimal strategy absent regulation, and since regulation is necessary for relief,

260 ibid.

261 Abbott B Lipsky Jr and J Gregory Sidak, 'Essential Facilities' (1999) 51 Stanford Law Review 1187, 1222.

262 Frischmann and Waller (n 102) 29.

263 Peter Drahos, 'The Regulation of Public Goods' (2004) 7 Journal of International Economic Law 321, 321.

264 Werden (n 95) 479.

265 Lipsky Jr and Sidak (n 261) 1193–94.

> liability should be imposed only if the essential facility is subject to pre-existing price regulation... The conclusion that the essential facility doctrine should be invoked only if the facility is subject to pre-existing price regulation reasonably leads to the proposal that the doctrine be entirely abandoned in favor of regulation.[266]

He further argues that invocation of the doctrine would not address a competition problem in cases involving 'an arbitrary refusal to deal, a refusal to buy, vertical integration into the distribution of one's own product, upstream integration from an unregulated market, or competition for a monopoly franchise'.[267] He asserts without much justification or elaboration that compelled access to intellectual property is harmful.[268] The only scenario in which compelled sharing of a facility would be beneficial is '[i]f the essential facility is a bottleneck that prevents the delivery of the relevant product to certain customers',[269] but only in the presence of regulatory oversight over the price and other terms of access. Despite their different views on the desirable scope of the doctrine, Frischmann and Waller concur with Werden that regulated industries present particularly well suited targets for the application of the doctrine.[270] Frischmann and Waller argue that Justice Scalia got it exactly backwards in *Trinko* when he argued that sectors subject to regulation have less need for antitrust intervention to mandate access to an essential facility.[271]

The argument that the essential facilities doctrine should only apply in regulated industries implies that the essential facilities doctrine has no application to patented technology. In contrast, Frischmann and Waller believe that the doctrine should be readily available for intellectual property. Because Werden does not spell out any independent reasons for excluding intellectual property from the scope of the doctrine, one can only surmise from his general view that it is because intellectual property is not subject to a regulatory regime and therefore the terms of access cannot be readily determined. This harkens back to the aforementioned implementation difficulties of the doctrine. Werden's objection carries less weight to the extent that a satisfactory solution to the challenges of royalty setting is found.

Werden is not the only commentator who has argued that the essential facilities doctrine should not apply to intellectual property. Hovenkamp, Janis, and Lemley have made a similar argument on the grounds that there seems to be no US case law that has so applied the doctrine and that if the barriers to competition are the result of an intellectual property right, the market control conferred by those barriers are 'part and parcel of the incentives conferred by the intellectual property laws themselves'.[272] They advocate a *per se* legality rule for refusal to license intellectual

[266] Werden (n 95) 478.
[267] ibid 479.
[268] ibid.
[269] ibid.
[270] Frischmann and Waller (n 102) 24.
[271] ibid.
[272] Hovenkamp, Janis, and Lemley (n 23) 15.

property, subject to the caveat that the intellectual property is valid and is the very facility to which access is sought instead of being merely incidental to the control of the facility itself.[273] Therefore, while Werden's objection seems to be principally motivated by difficulty in determining the terms of access, Hovenkamp, Janis, and Lemley take the more traditional view that the right to exclude is the essence of intellectual property and should not be overridden. This *per se* legality approach to a unilateral refusal to license intellectual property will be addressed and rejected in Chapter 6.

Other commentators take a slightly different view. Concurring with Frischmann and Waller, Robert Pitofsky, Donna Patterson, and Jonathan Hooks contest that there are no *a priori* reasons why the essential facilities doctrine should not apply to intangible assets such as intellectual property.[274] Reading the US case law slightly differently, Pitofsky, Patterson, and Hooks believe that the US case law poses no barriers to applying the doctrine to intellectual property.[275] Citing cases such as *Data General Corp. v. Grumman Systems Support Corp.*,[276] they observe that '[n]umerous US courts have squarely held or otherwise indicated that the essential facilities doctrine applies to intellectual property and other intangibles'.[277] There is no reason why the doctrine should not apply to intellectual property as the effect of the denial of access is the same regardless.[278]

Going beyond asserting the equivalence of physical facility and intellectual property, Shelanski proposes a benchmark for determining how intellectual property should be treated under the doctrine. He asserts that while there are times when intellectual property should be treated deferentially by antitrust law, such deference is not tantamount to an outright exemption from antitrust law altogether.[279] Instead, how intellectual property should be treated under antitrust law in general and the unilateral refusal to deal doctrine in particular should be determined with reference to impact on incentives to innovate and invest, which is precisely what has been advocated thus far.[280] If one accepts the proposition that compulsory licensing does not significantly dampen innovation incentives, there are no strong arguments for giving intellectual property in general and patents in particular special treatment under the essential facilities doctrine. Even if one does not completely accept this proposition, the foregoing discussion should illustrate that there is room for competition law to intervene without significant impairment of innovation incentives.

[273] ibid 19.
[274] Pitofsky, Patterson, and Hooks (n 97) 453.
[275] ibid.
[276] 36 F.3d 1147 (1st Cir. 1994).
[277] Pitofsky, Patterson, and Hooks (n 97) 452–53.
[278] ibid 453.
[279] Shelanski (n 118) 370.
[280] ibid.

E. Conclusion

This chapter examines the various theoretical issues presented by the application of the unilateral refusal to deal doctrine and the essential facilities doctrine to patented technology. It first clarifies that the unilateral refusal to deal doctrine is usually applied to patented input or product while the essentially facilities doctrine has greater salience in the context of technology licensing. It surveys the various theories of harm for the two doctrines, including enhancement of entry barriers, facilitation of price discrimination, foreclosure of downstream competition, and creation of effective exclusivity. All four are potentially relevant to the unilateral refusal to supply a patented input or product while foreclosure of downstream competition is likely to be the main concern in essential facilities cases. The extent of relevance of these theories of harm to developing countries varies in accordance with their technological capacity. Theories of harm that are premised on harm to a primary product competitor, such as some variation of enhancement of entry barriers and creation of effective exclusivity, will have limited applicability to the production countries. Theories of harm that implicate the downstream market or the complementary product market should be of concern to all developing countries.

The chapter also addresses the various critiques that have been launched against both doctrines. It argues that compulsory licensing is unlikely to dampen the incumbent innovator's innovation incentives in light of a variety of reasons, such as flaws in the patent system, the lack of correspondence between patents and genuine innovation, the greater incentive effect of competition as compared to market power for innovation, and the tendency of the patent system to generate excessive incentives. If having an additional innovator to work on the initial innovation will create more paths to follow-on innovation, then compulsory licensing may spur further innovation by competitor innovators. By opening the door for the competitor to pursue further improvements, compulsory licensing may augment a competitor's innovation incentives. As for cumulative innovators' innovation incentives, it rejects Kitch's prospect theory and argues that a coordinated approach to cumulative innovation is inferior to a decentralized approach and therefore compulsory licensing could be useful where negotiations fail between the initial innovator and improvers. The case for competition law intervention varies in accordance with the model of cumulative innovation. The case is the strongest under the 'trunk–branch' model, followed by the anticommons model, and then the quality ladder model.

The chapter further acknowledges the practical difficulties with royalty setting but argues that these difficulties are manageable and that in any case, compulsory licensing should not be abandoned simply because of these difficulties. Lastly, the chapter examines some of the critiques directed specifically at the essential facilities doctrine and rejects the argument that the doctrine should be inapplicable to intellectual property. Having addressed all the theoretical issues pertaining to the application of the unilateral refusal to deal doctrine and the essential facilities doctrine to patented technology, Chapter 6 will attempt to fashion a suitable approach for developing countries with different technological capacity after surveying various theoretical approaches found in the case law and the literature and the doctrinal considerations raised by the case law. The suggested approach will take into account developing country-specific considerations and enforcement capacity concerns.

6

Unilateral Refusal to License Patents—A Proposed Framework

A. Theoretical Approaches

Having examined the circumstances under which a refusal to supply a patented intermediate input and a refusal to license an essential patented technology can pose competitive harm and evaluated some common critique of the two doctrines, it remains to be seen what is the appropriate analytical framework for determining the legality of these two practices. It turns out that commentators and the courts have proposed a variety of approaches. These approaches run the gamut, ranging from *per se* legality to tests that focus on the permissible scope of patent rights to tests that hinge on pretexts or business justifications or extenuating circumstances. Interestingly, none of these approaches require an express articulation of concrete harm to consumers. The monopoly leveraging test probably comes closest to it. The remainder of the approaches seem to focus on the justifiability of the refusal with reference to some objective benchmarks such as the scope of patent rights or the existence of a valid business justification.

It is perhaps because of this focus on justifications in these tests that has caused the two doctrines to be so controversial. It represents a somewhat inexplicable departure from the usual practice in competition law, where it is necessary first to articulate ways in which a particular business practice can harm competition before entertaining possible justifications.[1] Another source of controversy is that these two doctrines seem to be premised on the default position that a firm or a facility owner is free to refuse to supply an essential input or to provide access to an essential facility absent exceptional circumstances. This effectively frames the entire debate on property right terms instead of focusing on competitive effects.

One may retort that unilateral refusal to deal is unique among the business practices scrutinized by competition law in how it directly implicates property rights. Therefore, it is natural that the analytical approach should focus on property rights. While this argument may have some superficial credibility, it falls apart upon careful consideration. As long ago as 1911 in the *Dr. Miles* case, the

[1] Herbert Hovenkamp, *Federal Antitrust Policy: The Law of Competition and Its Practice* (4th edn, West Publishing Co 2011) s 6.4.

The Patent–Competition Interface in Developing Countries. Thomas K. Cheng, Oxford University Press. © Thomas K. Cheng 2021. DOI: 10.1093/oso/9780192857354.003.0006

US Supreme Court was confronted with the argument that resale price maintenance should be legal because the owner of some proprietary medicine should, by virtue of her property rights, be free to decide whether and how she sells her product, including the terms of the sale.[2] Resale price maintenance can be characterized as a conditional refusal to sell the product unless the resale price stipulation is acceded to. The Supreme Court resoundingly rejected the argument.[3] In fact, all vertical restraints and patent licensing practices can be reconceptualized in the same way. Any vertical restraint is but an owner's refusal to sell her product unless the buyer accepts the distribution condition. Any patent licensing restriction amounts to a refusal to license the patented technology unless the licensee acquiesces to the licensing terms.[4] The difference between unilateral refusal to deal and these other business practices is only one of degree. The former amounts to pure refusal or exclusion whereas the latter constitutes conditional refusal or exclusion.[5] There is no meaningful distinction between the two from a property right perspective.

Therefore, a better approach to determining the legality of a unilateral refusal to deal should be to focus on consumer harm. A coherent theory of harm should be formulated in every case. This is especially true because the property right justifications in the patent context—arguments based on innovation incentives—have been dismissed. A unilateral refusal to deal should not be viewed from the lens of patent property rights but instead should be analysed in light of its competitive harm.

1. *Per Se* Legality

The first legal standard that has been proposed by commentators is *per se* legality, under which a patent owner should have an absolute and unqualified right to refuse to sell a patented intermediate input or to license a patented technology. A refusal to supply or license should be completely beyond the scrutiny of competition law.[6] Hovenkamp, Janis, and Lemley endorse this view, arguing that

> [a]ntitrust law does not itself impose an obligation to use or license intellectual property rights, such that a refusal to use or license the right would violate the antitrust laws. Further, such an obligation would-unlike the vast majority of the

[2] *Dr. Miles Medical Co. v. John D. Park & Sons Co.*, 220 US 373, 382 (1911).

[3] 220 US at 383.

[4] David McGowan, 'Networks and Intention in Antitrust and Intellectual Property' (1999) 24 Journal of Corporation Law 485, 491.

[5] ibid 491–92.

[6] Makan Delrahim, 'The "New Madison" Approach to Antitrust and Intellectual Property Law' (University of Pennsylvania Law School, Philadelphia, 16 March 2018) 2 <https://www.justice.gov/opa/speech/file/1044316/download> accessed 29 July 2021.

antitrust rules we discuss in this text-conflict directly with the rights granted to an intellectual property owner by the intellectual property laws.[7]

Taking a decision-theoretic perspective, Yannis Katsoulacos argues that when the presumption of legality is strong, as in the case of unilateral refusals to deal, a 'low false acquittals' rule such as *per se* legality is superior to alternative rules on welfare grounds.[8]

The justifications for this *per se* legality approach are apparent. A right unilaterally to refuse to supply or license is the corollary of the quintessential patent right to exclude.[9] The right to exclude, however, does not necessarily justify a *per se* legality approach. While it is true that the right to exclude is a fundamental patent right, it is important not to contemplate this right in a vacuum. It should be viewed in light of the policy rationale for the patent system, that is, to generate innovation incentives by providing innovators a financial reward. This right to exclude cannot and should not be an absolute right. It should only be upheld to the extent necessary to generate innovation incentives. It is thus not surprising that the *per se* legality approach has been challenged. Genevaz asserts that *per se* legality for unilateral refusal to deal directly contradicts the policy objectives of the patent system and is indefensible.[10] *Per se* legality is doubly unjustifiable in light of the previously discussed theories of harm, which clearly posit scenarios in which unilateral refusal to supply or license can harm consumers. If property rights did not save resale price maintenance from condemnation in *Dr. Miles*, there are no reasons why these rights should justify *per se* legality for unilateral refusals to deal.

2. Scope of Patent Test

A very popular test in this area of law is the scope of patent test. It is largely only relevant for the unilateral refusal to deal cases and not the essential facilities cases. The essence of the scope of patent test is that a patent owner violates competition law if she 'attempt[s] to broaden the physical or temporal scope of the patent monopoly'.[11] The test is supported by a long line of US Supreme Court cases on tying.[12] It has also been endorsed by commentators.

[7] Herbert J Hovenkamp, Mark D Janis, and Mark A Lemley, 'Unilateral Refusals to License' (2006) 2 Journal of Competition Law & Economics 1, 4–5.

[8] Yannis S Katsoulacos, 'Optimal Legal Standards for Refusals to License Intellectual Property: A Welfare-Based Analysis' (2009) 5 Journal of Competition Law & Economics 269, 291.

[9] 35 USC § 154 (2018).

[10] Simon Genevaz, 'Against Immunity for Unilateral Refusals to Deal in Intellectual Property: Why Antitrust Law Should Not Distinguish between IP and Other Property Rights' (2004) 19 Berkeley Technology Law Journal 742, 746.

[11] John E Lopatka and William H Page, 'Monopolization, Innovation, and Consumer Welfare' (2001) 69 George Washington University Law Review 368, 392.

[12] Marina Lao, 'Unilateral Refusals to Sell or License Intellectual Property and the Antitrust Duty to Deal' (1999) 9 Cornell Journal of Law and Public Policy 193, 198.

It is a test that is very often invoked but whose content and precise boundary remain shrouded in mystery. While most commentators seem to agree that it should be unlawful for a patentee to use unilateral refusal to deal to attempt to monopolize a market beyond that of the primary product covered by the patented technology, the consensus largely ends there.[13] Joseph Bauer contends that it has been an accepted position for nearly a century that a patentee cannot extend her market power to compel customers to purchase unpatented staple supplies from her.[14] There is, however, very little agreement on what the scope of patent means beyond standing for a simple rule against monopoly leveraging. Lao observes that it is unclear under the patent scope test

> whether a firm's refusal to license a patent may be considered an antitrust violation if the practice does not merely bar competitors from the particular area of the invention, but also excludes them from a related antitrust market in which the firm would otherwise have faced competition.[15]

This is partly due to the fact that the case law often neglects to delineate the patent scope and instead seems to evince a belief that the boundary of patent scope is self-evident.[16] The concept lacks any economic rationale or underpinning. Jackie Mackie-Mason asserts that there is no theoretical support for the position that 'the correct amount of expected rent is provided if the property right is unlimited only within the "scope" of the grant, but is limited outside the scope'.[17]

Some have attempted to associate patent scope with the concept of the relevant market under competition law.[18] Such attempts, however, reflect the widely held misconception in competition law that there is a direct correspondence between a patent and a product. It has been noted that 'patents describe inventions, not markets, and that an intellectual property right typically does not create a monopoly or market power'.[19] An antitrust market corresponds with a relevant product and its reasonable substitutes, while a patent may only cover a component of a product or a small part of the overall technology.[20] It is often erroneously assumed that one

13 Lao (n 12); Genevaz (n 10).

14 Joseph P Bauer, 'Refusals to Deal with Competitors by Owners of Patents and Copyrights: Reflections on the Image Technical and Xerox Decisions' (2006) 55 DePaul Law Review 1211, 1242.

15 Lao (n 12) 198.

16 Rita Coco, 'Antitrust Liability for Refusal to License Intellectual Property: A Comparative Analysis and the International Setting' (2008) 12 Marquette Intellectual Property Law Review 1, 36–37.

17 Jeffrey K Mackie-Mason, 'What to Do about Unilateral Refusals to License?' Testimony for the Federal Trade Commission and Department of Justice Hearing on Competition and Intellectual Property Law and Policy in the Knowledge-Based Economy (1 May 2002) 9.

18 Bauer (n 14) 1225, 1234.

19 Herbert J Hovenkamp, 'IP and Antitrust Policy: A Brief Historical Overview' (University of Iowa 2005) No 05-31 37.

20 A Douglas Melamed and Ali M Stoeppelwerth, 'The CSU Case: Facts, Formalism and the Intersection of Antitrust and Intellectual Property Law' (2002) 10 George Mason Law Review 407, 425–26.

relevant product embodies one patented technology.[21] Once that is no longer true, any attempt to link patent scope to relevant market becomes untenable. When a product incorporates multiple technologies, the question arises as to whether the patent scope covers only the patented technology, which may have no independent value, or the entire product, which will inevitably lead to overlapping claims and possible over-compensation.

Allowing the patentee to extend her control over the entire product could give rise to abuse. Peter Boyle and co-authors note that

> precluding antitrust scrutiny [of the extension of monopoly power from a component to the entire product], as a matter of law, would enable an IP owner to contrive antitrust immunity merely by adding to a competitively significant product an insignificant feature that just happens to be subject to patent or copyright protection.[22]

The reverse of this situation is if the same technology can be used in multiple products. Does the scope of patent test mean that the patent owner should be allowed to monopolize each of these multiple markets even though it may amount to gross over-compensation of the owner? Some commentators seem to think so.[23] The justification for this position, however, is far from clear. A further complication with this test arises because monetization of a patent may require sales in an ancillary market.[24] In fact, such sales could be the only way for the patentee to recoup her investments. The scope of patent test, however, should exclude an ancillary market from the patent scope as it lies beyond what should be the primary product. This highlights a problematic fundamental assumption of the scope of patent test that innovators will be adequately rewarded so long as they have exclusive right to profit within the scope of its innovation. This need not be the case.

If competition law does not provide a satisfactory answer, the alternative could be economics. Unfortunately, economics is again of not much help either. Mackie-Mason notes that 'no coherent economic analysis ... gives precise operational meaning to the concept of scope'.[25] One notable attempt to do so is by Paul Klemperer, who defines patent scope as 'the distance from the preferred point to that point beyond which competitors are allowed to produce'.[26] This understanding

[21] Dan L Burk and Mark A Lemley, 'Policy Levers in Patent Law' (2003) 89 Virginia Law Review 1575, 162.

[22] Peter M Boyle, Penelope M Lister, and J Clayton Everett Jr., 'Antitrust Law at the Federal Circuit: Red Light or Green Light at the IP-Antitrust Intersection' (2001) 69 Antitrust Law Journal 739, 760.

[23] ibid 754.

[24] Lopatka and Page (n 11) 397.

[25] Mackie-Mason (n 17) 8.

[26] Paul Klemperer, 'How Broad Should the Scope of Patent Protection Be?' (1990) 21 RAND Journal of Economics 113, 114.

of patent scope, however, is different from what is relevant in the context of unilateral refusal to deal. Klemperer's notion measures 'the degree of protection against imitations',[27] not the breadth of a patentee's rights over a well-defined innovation. His notion of patent scope only sets out the scope of the innovation, not the scope of one's rights over it.

The lack of an economic basis for the concept of patent scope should come as no surprise. Louis Kaplow has noted long ago the indeterminacy of patent scope as a concept.[28] Apart from serving as a simple rule against tying with unpatented staple supplies or complementary products, patent scope does not shed much light on the boundary of the unilateral refusal to deal doctrine.

3. Monopoly Leveraging Test

Another legal test that is very closely related to the scope of patent test is monopoly leveraging, which 'refers to a company with power in a relevant market using, or leveraging, that power to monopolize or gain an unmerited competitive advantage in another related, or complementary, market'.[29] One difference between monopoly leveraging and patent scope is that the former explicitly refers to the patentee's monopoly power in one relevant product market while patent scope, as noted earlier, is not predicated on the concepts of relevant market and market power. Because monopoly leveraging most often arises in the context of tying or bundling, or conduct that effectively accomplishes a tie, it will be discussed in Chapter 7.

4. Intent/Pretext Test

The previous three tests are meant to be benchmarks for assessing the competitive harm of unilateral refusal to deal. The following two tests focus on whether the refusal to deal is justified. The first one directs the attention to the intent of the dominant firm and inquires whether the firm can only offer a pretextual justification for the refusal to deal. The test, which is chiefly associated with the unilateral refusal to deal doctrine, is primarily concerned with the firm's subjective intent. The second one examines the existence or absence of a legitimate business justification. Under this 'no business justification' rule propounded by Jonathan Baker based

27 Béatrice Dumont and Peter Holmes, 'The Scope of Intellectual Property Rights and Their Interface with Competition Law and Policy: Divergent Paths to the Same Goal?' (2002) 11 Economics of Innovation and New Technology 149, 152;

28 Louis Kaplow, 'The Patent-Antitrust Intersection: A Reappraisal' [1984] Harvard Law Review 1848–49.

29 Lao (n 12) 195.

on the US Supreme Court cases of *Aspen Skiing* and *Kodak*, a unilateral refusal to deal under certain market conditions will be condemned if it lacks a valid business justification.

The subjective intent/pretext test is clearly inspired by the *Image Technical Services v. Eastman Kodak* decision by the US Court of Appeals for the Ninth Circuit.[30] In that case, the Ninth Circuit ruled that Kodak's refusal to supply spare parts was unlawful refusal to deal because the justification it offered—that it was trying to protect its intellectual property rights—was pretextual.[31] Kodak's manager testified in trial that intellectual property rights had never crossed his mind.[32] The Court concluded that a refusal to supply intellectual property will be presumed lawful unless the justification for refusal is pretextual.

It is no exaggeration to say that the subjective intent/pretext test has been roundly criticized. Hewitt Pate criticizes the test for turning competition law analysis from a focus on objective effects into an inquiry into subjective intentions.[33] He also characterizes the subjective intent/pretext test as 'impractical and unworkable'.[34] The test entails an inquiry into the subjective intention of a corporate body that 'is likely to confuse jurors and complicate litigation'.[35] Identification of corporate intentions is fraught with difficulty due to a lack of a single controlling mind. What constitutes a corporation's subjective intention crucially depends on which employee or officer is deemed to represent or act on behalf of the corporation.[36] A subjective intent test will also be susceptible to circumvention. Corporate counsel would merely have to stamp every internal document or corporate strategy with an intention to exercise and protect intellectual property to escape liability.[37] While ease of circumvention is a genuine concern, the difficulty in determining corporate intentions should not be overstated. Determination of corporate intentions is regularly done in other legal contexts and the difficulty should not be insurmountable.[38]

A more fundamental critique[39] is that the subjective intent/pretext test 'would seem to stand intellectual property law on its head'.[40] The crux of the argument is

[30] 125 F.3d 1195 (9th Cir. 1997)
[31] 125 US at 1219–20.
[32] 125 US at 1219.
[33] R Hewitt Pate, 'Refusals to Deal and Intellectual Property Rights' (2002) 10 George Mason Law Review 429, 438.
[34] ibid 439.
[35] ibid.
[36] Mihailis E Diamantis, 'Corporate Criminal Minds' (2016) 91 Notre Dame Law Review 2049; Ellis Ferran, 'Corporate Attribution and the Directing Mind and Will' (2011) 127 Law Quarterly Review 239; Ernest Lim, 'A Critique of Corporate Attribution: "Directing Mind and Will" and Corporate Objectives' (2013) Journal of Business Law 333.
[37] McGowan (n 4) 514–15.
[38] See footnote 689.
[39] Jill Boylston Herndon, 'Intellectual Property, Antitrust, and the Economics of Aftermarkets' (2002) Summer-Fall The Antitrust Bulletin 309, 324–25; McGowan (n 4) 514; Pate (n 33) 440.
[40] Herndon (n 39) 324–25.

that the right to exclude is a fundamental right under patent law and exclusion is the essence of patent protection.[41] A patentee should be free to refuse to sell or license her patented product or technology for any and no reason. All acts of exclusion should be within the scope of patent rights and there should be no inquiry into her intent. The logical conclusion of this argument is that unilateral refusal to sell a patented input or license a patented technology should be *per se* legal, which has already been rejected. Even if one dismisses the premise that a patentee should have an unqualified right to exclude, it remains true that the application of the subjective intent/pretext test diverts attention from objective effects. It can also be very complicated to apply in a jury trial. Yet it is important to point out that while this may be a valid concern in the United States, not every jurisdiction uses juries in competition law cases. This may not be a serious consideration for most countries.

One way to render the subjective intent/pretext test more defensible is to conceptualize it from an innovation incentive perspective. The purpose of the patent system is to generate innovation incentives. In the first-best scenario, it should reward patentees up to the point of the risk-adjusted costs of their research and development (R&D) investments, including the opportunity costs of such investments, which should render the patentee indifferent between R&D and alternative investments. That would require perfect information on the part of the patent system administrator and would not be feasible in reality. But when the justification of intellectual property protection is judged to be pretextual, as in the case of *Kodak*, it reveals that the innovator did not deem the practice as essential to the recovery of her R&D investments. It is not always easy to determine what the patentee expressly relies on to recoup her R&D investments. This is one of those instances where we can confidently exclude certain practices from her calculus. If she does not consider the practice essential, permitting it would amount to a windfall and would be counterproductive from an innovation incentive perspective. In this sense, the subjective intent/pretext test produces sensible results.

Ultimately, the most relevant criticism of the subjective intent/pretext test is likely its limited applicability. While the court was able to reach the conclusion of pretext under the particular facts of the *Kodak* case, it is difficult to imagine other circumstances in which the same conclusion can be confidently drawn. This would be especially true if McGowan's prediction came true and corporations habitually rubber-stamped every document with an intention to protect intellectual property in order to circumvent the subjective intent/pretext test. In-house counsel of corporations will also ensure that incriminating evidence of predatory intent will be removed from internal communications.

[41] McGowan (n 4) 514.

5. Jonathan Baker's No Business Justification Rule

Another test that is focused on the justifiability of the unilateral refusal to deal is Baker's no business justification rule. This rule is based on *Aspen Skiing* and *Kodak* and is specifically designed for refusal to license intellectual property.[42] He sums up the rule as requiring the examination of 'two readily observable factors—exclusion that exploits a complementary or collaborative relationship and the absence of a satisfactory business justification—without taking on the task of evaluating harm to competition'.[43] The rule only applies to markets characterized by 'winner-take-all innovation competition', which takes place 'when intellectual property protections and network externalities are both strong and buyers have a low demand for variety'.[44]

The existence of a complementary or collaborative relationship is important because it provides the defendant a leverage with which to harm the plaintiff.[45] Baker argues that there is ample support in the case law for condemning a unilateral refusal to deal without an inquiry into harm to competition or consumers,[46] and justifies doing away with this inquiry on the ground that '[h]arm to competition is probably more difficult to evaluate than the adequacy of the business justification, even in prospect, and particularly in the dominant firm setting, where the fringe is already weak'.[47]

Baker does not specify what constitute valid business justifications. Other commentators have offered some suggestions. Yongmin Chen believes that it would be efficient for a monopolist to refuse to supply '[w]hen the variable profits under monopoly pricing are not high enough to cover such costs [additional fixed (setup or transaction) cost to supply the downstream rival]'.[48] Douglas Melamed and Ali Stoeppelwerth suggest that a monopolist may justifiably refuse to trade with a counterparty if the latter is 'an opportunist, untrustworthy with trade secrets, or an unreliable shepherd of the former's goodwill'.[49] Under Baker's rule, even if the defendant offers a valid business justification, the plaintiff can still prevail by showing that the competitive harm from exclusion outweighs the pro-competitive benefits.[50]

42 Jonathan Baker, 'Promoting Innovation Competition through the Aspen/Kodak Rule' (1999) 7 George Mason Law Review 495, 496–97.
43 Baker (n 42).
44 ibid 496.
45 ibid 502.
46 ibid 503, 506.
47 ibid 518.
48 Yongmin Chen, 'Refusal to Deal, Intellectual Property Rights, and Antitrust' (2013) 30 Journal of Law, Economics & Organization 533, 535.
49 Melamed and Stoeppelwerth (n 20) 420.
50 Genevaz (n 10) 772.

John Lopatka and William Page have criticized Baker's rule on two main grounds. First, they argue that it is premised on harm to innovation that is by nature highly speculative, noting that

> [a] finding of harm to innovation requires, first, a counterfactual inference that innovators would have invented new products but for the predatory conduct and, second, that those products would have been better or cheaper than others in the market. There is reason to be skeptical of the claim of harm to innovation.[51]

Second, they rightly insist that proof of consumer harm, which is obviated in Baker's rule, should be required in every monopolization case.[52] In Baker's defence, he seems to intend to use harm to innovation as a proxy for consumer harm. While it is no doubt true that harm to innovation can be speculative, that seems to be an inevitable part of every case involving innovation unless one adopts simple default rules such as *per se* legality.

The biggest drawback of Baker's rule is not that it is poorly conceived but that it again has limited applicability. It only applies to cases where the plaintiff and the defendant share a collaborative or a complementary relationship and are engaged in winner-take-all innovation competition. This rule is unlikely to have much salience for the majority of developing countries that are bereft of firms capable of engaging in innovation competition with firms from the industrialized economies.

All five benchmarks explored here have their drawbacks. The *per se* legality approach is clearly too permissive and fails to recognize instances in which unilateral refusal to deal can inflict consumer harm. The scope of the patent test suffers from fatal indeterminacy. The concept of patent scope is not self-defining and an accurate determination of the appropriate amount of patentee reward would impose such high information costs that is beyond the capability of any competition authority or courts. The monopoly leveraging test is only relevant when the patentee attempts to extend its market power from the patented product to adjacent markets. The intent test is too easy to circumvent, especially once corporate in-house counsel has adjusted to the rule and learned to insert a reference to a desire to protect intellectual property in every instance of refusal to license or supply. Baker's no business justification rule also suffers from limited applicability as it only applies to cases where the plaintiff and the defendant share a collaborative or a complementary relationship and are engaged in winner-take-all innovation competition.

51 Lopatka and Page (n 11) 371.
52 ibid 388.

B. Case Law on Unilateral Refusal to License

Having surveyed various theoretical approaches to determining the legality of the unilateral refusal to deal doctrine and the essential facilities doctrine, it would be didactic to explore the case law in the United States and the European Union and the doctrinal issues raised in these cases. While developing countries should not slavishly follow the approaches from the advanced jurisdictions, these approaches will serve as a useful basis upon which a contextualized approach to these doctrines for developing countries can be crafted. Developing countries can decide which elements of these approaches to accept and reject in light of their specific policy considerations.

1. The United States

(a) Case law on unilateral refusal to deal

There have been three leading unilateral refusal to deal cases in the context of intellectual property in the US: *In re Independent Service Organizations Antitrust Litigation (Xerox), Data General Corp. v. Grumman Systems Support Corp.*, and *Kodak*. All were decided in the 1990s. All concerned the aftermarket of maintenance in which the defendant denied the plaintiff access to a critical input which the plaintiff needed to provide maintenance services. The primary product was photocopying machines in *Xerox* and *Kodak* and mini-computers in *Data General*, and the input sought by the plaintiff were spare parts in *Xerox* and *Kodak* and diagnostic software in *Data* General. In none of the cases did the plaintiff ask for a direct transfer of the technology in the primary product.

Kodak has already been discussed and will not be repeated here. *Xerox* is of particular importance because it is the leading case on the unilateral refusal to supply intellectual property decided by the US Court of Appeals for the Federal Circuit, the appellate court that hears appeals of all patent-related cases. In *Xerox*, the Federal Circuit held that a patentee's refusal to deal will not be questioned absent fraud on the US Patent and Trademark Office, sham litigation, or illegal tying.[53] In *Data General Corp. v. Grumman Systems Support Corp.*, the US Court of Appeals for the First Circuit did not go as far as the Federal Circuit, but nonetheless proclaimed that 'while exclusionary conduct can include a monopolist's unilateral refusal to license a copyright, an author's desire to exclude others from use of its copyrighted work is a presumptively valid business justification for any immediate harm to consumers'.[54] Even in *Kodak*, the Ninth Circuit only imposed a duty to deal because the Court found that the defendant's intellectual property justification for

[53] 203 F.3d 1322, 1327 (Fed. Cir. 2000).
[54] 36 F.3d 1147, 1187 (1st Cir. 1994).

refusing to deal was pretextual.[55] There is some tension between *Data General* and *Kodak* in terms of their willingness to scrutinize the authenticity of the intellectual property holder's desire to exercise her right to exclude. The *Data General* court's approach is tantamount to *per se* legality because every IP owner can assert a desire to exclude others in a unilateral refusal to deal case. If such a desire is always taken to be a presumptively valid business justification, unilateral refusal to supply intellectual property is always justified. The Ninth Circuit is at least willing to inquire whether the justification is genuine.

These cases thus do not provide useful guidance for our purpose. It was suggested that the Ninth Circuit's subjective intent/pretext test can only apply under narrow circumstances. The *de facto per se* legality approach espoused by *Data General* has already been dismissed as unjustifiably permissive. The *Xerox* court's approach overlooks situations in which unilateral refusal to supply or license intellectual property can inflict competitive harm beyond the three highly circumscribed scenarios specified by the court. The monopoly leveraging test could have applied in these cases, especially *Kodak* and *Xerox*, where the defendant was clearly trying to extend its market dominance into the aftermarkets. In fact, before its remand from the US Supreme Court, *Kodak* was mainly a tying case.

The two leading cases on unilateral refusal to deal in the United States outside the intellectual property context are *Aspen Skiing Co. v. Aspen Highlands Skiing Corp.* and *Verizon Telecommunications v. Trinko*. These cases probably provide more useful lessons for us than the previous three cases. *Aspen Skiing* involved two ski slope operators in Aspen, Colorado, a major ski resort town in the United States. One of them, Ski Co. was the dominant firm and operated three out of the four mountains in Aspen.[56] The rival operator, Highlands, owned the remaining mountain.[57] The two operators had been collaborating to offer a six-day, four-mountain pass, which allowed skiers to use any of the four mountains on any given day during a six-day period.[58] Revenue from the pass was split between the two operators based on actual usage.[59] For the 1977–78 ski season, Ski Co. offered a lower percentage of revenue share than was customary to Highlands.[60] For the next season, Ski Co. offered an even lower percentage that effectively forced Highlands to walk away from the negotiation.[61] The six-day, four-mountain pass was thus terminated.[62] After that, Highlands attempted to revive the pass through other means, such as by offering vouchers which could be used to redeem ski lift tickets at Ski Co's mountains.[63] Highlands also attempted to purchase the ski lift tickets directly

55 125 F.3d 1195, 1219–20 (9th Cir. 1997).
56 472 US at 587.
57 472 US at 588.
58 472 US at 589.
59 472 US at 589.
60 472 US at 592.
61 472 US at 593.
62 472 US at 593.
63 472 US at 594.

from Ski Co. at retail prices but was rebuffed.[64] Highlands' business continued to suffer as skiers shunned its facilities.[65]

The US Supreme Court held that Ski Co.'s refusal to continue to offer the six-day, four-mountain pass with Highlands constituted unlawful unilateral refusal to deal. In reaching this conclusion, the Court emphasized a number of facts. Ski Co. terminated an existing arrangement with Highlands instead of refusing to deal with Highlands *de novo*.[66] Ski Co.'s refusal to deal evinced a predatory intent as it turned down opportunities to sell ski lift tickets at profit-maximizing retail prices.[67] There was demonstrable consumer demand for the six-day, four-mountain pass.[68] And Ski Co. failed to offer any valid business justification for the refusal.[69]

The more recent unilateral refusal to deal case decided by the US Supreme Court is *Trinko*.[70] The case concerned a constructive refusal to deal by Verizon, the incumbent Local Exchange Carrier (LEC), which served the state of New York. The US Congress passed the Telecommunications Act in 1996 to liberalize the fixed-line telephony market by compelling the incumbent LECs to open access to their networks to competitive LECs.[71] The incumbent LECs were required to provide access to individual network elements on an unbundled basis.[72] This allowed competitive LECs to provide fixed-line telephony services by combining individual network elements from the incumbent with its own network elements. AT&T was a competitive LEC, which had signed an agreement to obtain access to Verizon's unbundled network elements (UNEs), in particular, the Operations Support Systems (OSS).[73] The OSS allowed Verizon to provide services to customers and to ensure quality.[74] In late 1999, competitive LECs, including AT&T, complained to the telecom regulators that Verizon provided discriminatory access to its UNEs; some of their orders for access to the OSS were unfulfilled.[75] Mr Trinko, an attorney, brought suit on behalf of similarly situated customers of fixed-line telephony service alleging that Verizon's failure to provide AT&T adequate access to the unbundled network elements constituted unlawful refusal to deal under Section 2 of the Sherman Act.

The US Supreme Court held for Verizon and refused to impose a duty to deal. The Court established the general principle that a dominant firm had no obligation to deal with rivals under US antitrust laws.[76] This principle was supported

[64] 472 US at 593.
[65] 472 US at 594–95.
[66] 472 US at 603–04.
[67] 472 US at 593.
[68] 472 US at 606–07.
[69] 472 US at 608–09.
[70] 540 US 398 (2004).
[71] 540 US at 402.
[72] 540 US at 402.
[73] 540 US at 403.
[74] 540 US at 403.
[75] 540 US at 403.
[76] 540 US at 408.

by a number of reasons. First, compelling the dominant firm to provide access would impair incentives by both the incumbent and the competitors to invest in the acquisition of facilities.[77] Second, compelled sharing would require the antitrust courts to act as central planners and to identify the proper terms for dealing.[78] Third, compelled sharing might encourage collusion among competitors.[79] The Court concluded that this case did not fall within the exception to this general principle established in *Aspen Skiing*.[80] There was no course of prior dealing between AT&T and Verizon.[81] There was also no profit sacrifice by Verizon as Verizon never voluntarily made the unbundled network elements available to customers.[82] Furthermore, the Court suggested that the facts of the case did not warrant the creation of a new exception to the general principle.[83] The Court emphasized that the existence of sectoral regulation under the Telecommunications Act governing access obviated the need for antitrust intervention.[84]

(b) Case law on the essential facilities doctrine

The discussion about the essential facilities doctrine in the United States will be relatively brief as the courts there have reportedly never applied the doctrine to intellectual property, even though such application has never been explicitly ruled out by any US court. As is well known, the essential facilities doctrine originated from the US case of *United States v. Terminal Railroad Association of St. Louis* in the early twentieth century.[85] Even though the US Supreme Court did not invoke the doctrine by name, the case has been interpreted as having applied the doctrine in substance. What followed is a string of cases over the next century, including *United States v. Associated Press*,[86] *Otter Tail Power Co. v. United States*,[87] *Gamco Inc. v. Providence Fruit & Produce Building, Inc.*,[88] *Hecht v. Pro-Football, Inc.*,[89] and *Fishman v. Estate of Wirtz*,[90] that have applied the doctrine in substance or in name. *Hecht* was the first case to invoke the term the 'essential facilities doctrine'.[91] All of these cases except for *Associated Press*, which concerned copyrighted news, involved physical facilities.[92] *Associated Press* could thus count as a case where a

77 540 US at 408.
78 540 US at 408.
79 540 US at 408.
80 540 US at 409.
81 540 US at 409.
82 540 US at 410.
83 540 US at 411.
84 540 US at 412.
85 224 US 383 (1912).
86 326 US 1 (1945).
87 410 US 366 (1973).
88 194 F.2d 484 (1st Cir.), *cert denied*, 344 US 817 (1952).
89 570 F.2d 982 (D.C. Cir. 1977), *cert denied*, 436 US 956 (1978).
90 807 F.2d 520 (7th Cir. 1986).
91 Gregory J Werden, 'The Law and Economics of the Essential Facility Doctrine' (1987) 32 St Louis University Law Journal 433, 443–44.
92 ibid 436, 441–47.

US court has applied the essential facilities doctrine to an intellectual property, albeit only in substance. One US case that unequivocally held that intellectual property could constitute an essential facility is *BellSouth Advertising v. Donnelley Information*.[93] The district court in that case, however, only held that there is no reason why the doctrine cannot apply to intellectual property and did not reach the merit of the essential facilities claim.[94]

The authoritative formulation of the essential facilities doctrine in the US can be found in the *MCI v. AT&T* case. In that case, the US Court of Appeals for the Seventh Circuit spelled out the elements for the essential facilities doctrine as follows: '(1) control of the essential facility by a monopolist; (2) a competitor's inability practically or reasonably to duplicate the essential facility; (3) the denial of the use of the facility to a competitor; and (4) the feasibility of providing the facility'.[95] Unlike the equivalent EU cases, there is no mention of any requirement of a new product or technical improvements that may tailor the doctrine to the specific context of intellectual property. The criterion of the feasibility of providing the facility seems to suggest that the doctrine was formulated with physical facilities in mind as intellectual property does not suffer from capacity constraints. The most recent pronouncement by the US Supreme Court on the doctrine has cast doubt on its remaining vitality. In *Trinko*, Justice Scalia asserted that the Supreme Court has never affirmed or disavowed the doctrine.[96] While the Court stopped short of repudiating doctrine, Justice Scalia's dictum was hardly a ringing endorsement.

2. The European Union

(a) General refusal to deal cases

As Europe has never embraced the essential facilities doctrine, the corresponding dichotomy in the case law in Europe is general refusal to deal cases and refusal to license intellectual property cases. The *Sealink/Holyhead*[97] decision by the Commission and *Oscar Bronner* are highly reminiscent of an essential facilities case, while *Magill*, *IMS Health*, and *Microsoft* concern refusal to license intellectual property.[98] Meanwhile, a number of cases, including *Commercial Solvents*, *Télémarketing*, and *United Brands*, can be classified as general unilateral refusal to deal cases.

93 719 F. Supp. 1551 (S.D. Fla. 1988), *rev'd on other grounds*, 999 F.2d 1436 (11th Cir. 1993).
94 Hovenkamp, Janis, and Lemley (n 7) 14.
95 708 F.2d 1081, 1132-33 (7th Cir. 1983).
96 *Trinko*, 540 US at 410-11.
97 *Sealink/B&I Holyhead: Interim Measures* [1992] CMLR 255.
98 Cyril Ritter, 'Refusal to Deal and "Essential Facilities": Does Intellectual Property Require Special Deference Compared to Tangible Property?' (2005) 28 World Competition 281, 283.

Commercial Solvents involved the upstream supplier of a chemical ingredient for an anti-tuberculosis drug.[99] The supplier terminated supply of the ingredient to a downstream producer of the drug when its Italian subsidiary decided to enter the downstream market.[100] The Court of Justice of the European Union (CJEU) held that

> an undertaking which has a dominant position in the market in raw materials, refuses to supply a customer, which is itself a manufacturer of these derivatives, and therefore risks eliminating all competition on the part of this customer, is abusing its dominant position within the meaning of Article [102].[101]

The Court emphasized it was no excuse that the dominant firm had plans to enter the downstream market and that the plaintiff had itself cancelled its order first.[102] It is particularly noteworthy that the refusal to supply need not result in the exclusion of all competition, as stated in *Magill*, or even the elimination of all effective competition, as stipulated in *Microsoft*. It suffices when the refusal to supply precludes the downstream rival from competing in the market.[103] The implication seems to be that it will not make a difference if there are other downstream suppliers of the anti-tuberculosis drug. The existence of a course of prior dealing clearly seems to have weighed in favour of the party seeking access.

United Brands is a slightly different case which concerns a dominant undertaking's right to use refusal to deal to defend its commercial interests. In that case, United Brands stopped the supply of its Chiquita brand of bananas to its Danish ripener and distributor when the distributor started selling competing bananas under the Dole brand and devoting less effort to selling Chiquita bananas.[104] The Court asserted that

> an undertaking in a dominant position for the purpose of marketing a product—which cashes in on the reputation of a brand name known to and valued by the consumers—cannot stop supplying a long standing customer who abides by regular commercial practice, if the orders placed by that customer are in no way out of the ordinary.[105]

Again, the presence of an existing commercial relationship between the dominant firm and the party seeking supply carried significant weight in the Court's

[99] Cases 6 and 7/73, *Istituto Chemioterapico Italiano Spa and Commercial Solvents Corp. v. Commission* [1974] ECR 223, para 23.
[100] ibid para 23.
[101] ibid para 25.
[102] ibid para 25.
[103] ibid para 25.
[104] Case 27/76, *United Brands v. Commission* [1978] ECR 207, para 175.
[105] ibid para 182.

analysis.[106] The Court emphasized that 'the refusal to sell would limit markets to the prejudice of consumers and would amount to discrimination which might in the end eliminate a trading party from the relevant market'.[107] As in *Commercial Solvents*, the Court paid no heed to the fact that there might be, and in fact there were, other suppliers of banana in Denmark. Consumers were in no way deprived of banana.

In response to United Brands' argument that a dominant firm must be allowed to take action to defend its commercial interests, the CJEU suggested that the firm's counter-measures 'must still be proportionate to the threat taking into account the economic strength of the undertakings confronting each other'.[108] The Court proceeded to conclude that a termination of supply was disproportionate in light of the Danish distributor's conduct.[109] Cessation of supply would deter other distributors from promoting other brands of banana, effectively turning the distribution relationships into exclusive ones, which would serve to strengthen United Brands' dominant position.[110] The cessation of supply also undermines the independence of small- and medium-sized firms, which should be given the freedom to favour competing products over the dominant firm's products.[111] This case again involves a course of prior dealing between the dominant firm and the party seeking access.

In *Télémarketing*, the dominant television station would only sell advertising to advertisers if they also used the firm's own advertising agent.[112] In other words, if an advertiser wanted to advertise with the television station, it must also use the station's affiliated advertising agent to host the telephone number which TV viewers could call in response to the advertisement. The Court held that the conduct at issue constituted refusal to supply services and was governed by the *Commercial Solvents* case.[113] It further added that

> [i]f, further, that refusal is not justified by technical or commercial requirements relating to the nature of the television, but is intended to reserve to the agent any telemarketing operation broadcast by the said station, with the possibility of eliminating all competition from another undertaking, such conduct amounts to an abuse prohibited by Article [102].[114]

[106] ibid para 182.
[107] ibid para 183.
[108] ibid para 190.
[109] ibid para 191.
[110] ibid para 192.
[111] ibid para 193.
[112] Case 311/84, *Centre Belge d'Etudes du Marché-Télémarketing v. Compagnie Luxembourgeoisie de Télédiffusion SA and Information Publicité Benelux SA* [1985] ECR 3261, para 2.
[113] ibid para 25.
[114] ibid para 26.

The Court again took the view that elimination of one competitor in the related market of telemarketing services would suffice. This case differs from *Commercial Solvents* and *United Brands* in that it is not predicated on a course of prior dealing. As Professors Alison Jones and Brenda Sufrin have noted, the facts of the case are highly suggestive of a tying arrangement.[115] It was a conditional refusal to supply premised on the acceptance of a tie.

Overall, the EU cases seem to suggest that a course of prior dealing is a relevant consideration in a unilateral refusal to deal case and that there is no need for all competition or even all effective competition to be eliminated by the refusal to deal. It suffices that a competitor is foreclosed from the relevant market, which condition is almost always met. The EU cases therefore seem to apply a lower bar on imposing a duty to deal than do the US cases. A closer examination of *Commercial Solvents* and *United Brands* suggests that other dispositive factors are at play in the two cases. In *Commercial Solvents*, the Court's main concern seemed to be that the dominant firm refused to supply to facilitate its own downstream market entry. In *United Brands*, the Court viewed the refusal to supply as a means to enforce exclusive distribution. *United Brands* probably constituted a conditional exclusion as opposed to pure exclusion and may be more appropriately analysed as an exclusive dealing case. Only *Commercial Solvents* stands for a pure exclusion case.

(b) Refusal to license intellectual property cases

The European Union has not formally adopted the essential facilities doctrine. It has been noted that the CJEU has never made any references to the doctrine in its judgments.[116] *Oscar Bronner*[117] arguably comes closest to an essential facilities case in the European Union. Instead, there has been a string of cases involving unilateral refusal to license intellectual property rights. These include *Magill*,[118] *IMS Health*,[119] and *Microsoft*.[120] None of them involves patent rights and, with the exception of *Microsoft*, have concerned what is generally perceived to be weaker intellectual property rights. This, however, should not detract from their relevance for our discussion. The European courts have so far not suggested that patent rights will be treated differently as far as unilateral refusal to license is concerned. Even though *Microsoft* concerns copyright protection for software, the explicit recognition in that case of the potential impact of competition law intervention on innovation incentives renders that case particularly relevant to patent rights.

[115] Alison Jones and Brenda Sufrin, *EU Competition Law: Text, Cases, and Materials* (5th edn, Oxford University Press 2014) 510.

[116] Estelle Derclaye, 'Abuses of Dominant Position and Intellectual Property Rights: A Suggestion to Reconcile Community Courts Case Law' (2003) 26 World Competition 685, 702.

[117] Case C-7/97, *Oscar Bronner GmbH & Co KG v. Mediaprint* [1998] ECR I-7791.

[118] Case C-241-242/91 P, *RTE & ITP v. Commission (Magill)* [1995] ECR I-743.

[119] Case C-418/01, *IMS Health GmbH & Co OHG v. NDC Health GmbH & Co KG* [2004] ECR I-5039.

[120] Case T-201/04, *Microsoft v. Commission* [2007] ECR II-3601.

Magill originated what is known as the exceptional circumstances test, which has been modified and expanded in subsequent cases. In that case, which concerned copyrighted TV listing information, the CJEU held that a refusal by a dominant firm to license its intellectual property does not in itself constitute an abuse under Article 102 of the Treaty on the Functioning of the European Union (TFEU) unless exceptional circumstances are found.[121] The CJEU determined that exceptional circumstances were present in that case, namely (1) there was no actual or substitute for the product that would have been created, for which there was a specific, constant and regular potential demand on the part of consumers;[122] (2) the refusal concerned an indispensable raw material for the new product that would have been created;[123] (3) the refusal prevented the appearance of a new product for which there was a potential consumer demand;[124] (4) there was no justification for the refusal; and (5) the refusal allows the dominant undertaking to exclude all competition in the secondary market.[125]

It has been said that the judgment 'sent shockwaves among IP and antitrust lawyers'[126] in Europe, although Ritter argues that the threat of the judgment to intellectual property was 'grossly exaggerated'.[127] The general view is that the Court's stance was largely informed by the weak nature of the intellectual property in the case; Ireland was unusual within the Union in providing copyright protection to TV listing information.[128] Devlin and co-authors hypothesize that '[h]ad Magill sought mandatory licensing of the copyright over the television companies' prime-time shows, no one could seriously posit that the outcome would have been the same'.[129] The implication seems to be that the exceptional circumstances test would not have been available against more robust intellectual property rights such as copyright and patent. The CJEU is yet to apply this test to compel sharing of a patented technology.

Oscar Bronner did not involve intellectual property; what was at issue in the case was a newspaper distribution system in Austria.[130] The discussion of the case will hence be brief as some of the elements of the exceptional circumstances test that are relevant in intellectual property cases are absent. But it is nonetheless relevant for our purpose as it constitutes an instance of the application of the exceptional

[121] *Magill*, para 50.
[122] ibid para 52.
[123] ibid para 53.
[124] ibid para 54.
[125] ibid para 56.
[126] Ritter (n 98) 285.
[127] ibid.
[128] ibid 286. Makan Delrahim, 'Forcing Firms to Share the Sandbox: Compulsory Licensing of Intellectual Property Rights and Antitrust' (2004) 2004 European Business Law Review 1059, 1064; Alan Devlin, Michael Jacobs, and Bruno Peixoto, 'Success, Dominance, and Interoperability' (2009) 84 Indiana Law Journal 1157, 1168.
[129] Devlin, Jacobs, and Peixoto (n 128) 1168.
[130] *Oscar Bronner*, para 7.

circumstances test. The CJEU held that the dominant firm did not commit an abuse by refusing to share its distribution network. There would be only be an abuse if the dominant firm (1) refused to grant access to its facility for which there was no actual or potential substitute; (2) the facility was indispensable to the business of the party requesting access; (3) the refusal was likely to eliminate the party requesting access from the relevant market; and (4) such refusal could not be objectively justified.[131] The Court held that the refusal was not abusive because other distribution methods for newspapers were available and hence the dominant firm's distribution network was not indispensable to competition.[132]

The key significance of this case was in illustrating a clearer application of the *Magill* criteria. The Court made clear that it was relying on *Magill* and that refusal to supply could be abusive regardless of the type of property at issue.[133] Some adaptations of the analytical framework to physical property, however, were necessary. What is missing in the Court's analytical framework in *Oscar Bronner* as compared to that in *Magill* was the new product requirement and the reference to a secondary market, which would make more sense in the context of intellectual property as it is almost always used as an input to produce another product in the downstream market. Estelle Derclaye notes that the omission of the new product requirement could make a substantial difference; compelled sharing would be more likely under the *Oscar Bronner* standard.[134] She further comments that despite the Court's suggestions to the contrary, it is clear from the case that unilateral refusal to deal is treated differently depending on whether physical or intellectual property is at issue.[135]

The third EU case that has tackled the issue of refusal to license intellectual property is *IMS Health*. The intellectual property at issue is what is known as a brick structure, under which Germany is divided into 1,860 geographical units for the purpose of collecting and marketing pharmaceutical sales information.[136] IMS was the incumbent in the relevant market. A new firm called NDC was trying to enter the market but soon encountered difficulty because IMS's brick structure had become the *de facto* industry standard.[137] It would be very difficult for NDC to compete without access to the structure.[138] The main issue in the case was whether IMS could be compelled to share its brick structure with NDC. The CJEU, upon a reference for a preliminary ruling from a German national court, clarified that three cumulative conditions have to be met in order for the refusal to supply to be deemed abusive. These include 'that refusal is preventing the emergence of a

131 ibid para 7.
132 *Oscar Bronner*, para 41.
133 ibid paras 43–47.
134 Derclaye (n 116) 693–94.
135 ibid 695.
136 *IMS Health*, para 4.
137 ibid para 12.
138 ibid para 12.

new product for which there is a potential consumer demand, that it is unjustified and such as to exclude any competition on a secondary market'.[139] The Court emphasized that the conditions were cumulative, which settled a long-running debate since *Magill* as to whether the four conditions set out in *Magill* were cumulative.[140]

IMS Health is widely seen as having significantly diluted the four-part test laid down in *Magill*. It has been argued that despite the Court's protestations to the contrary, the Court did not apply the new market requirement in any meaningful manner. Matthias Lamping argues that '[b]y applying the "two market requirement" developed in the leveraging cases of the 1970s to ordinary essential facility situations, the ECJ had no choice but to consider the essential facility a market in itself, even though it falls short of the economic definition of a market' and that defining an upstream market for the brick structure was entirely artificial.[141] Other commentators have echoed his view.[142]

The significance of the dilution of the new product requirement is that a dominant firm can be ordered to share its intellectual property even if doing so will give rise to a product directly competing with its own.[143] This is a notable departure from *Magill*, in which the CJEU seemed to have placed some emphasis on the fact none of the firms at issue was supplying the product that would have been created, a composite weekly TV guide.[144] The requirement of potential consumer demand for the second product has also been effectively dispensed with because in *IMS Health*, the consumers, the pharmaceutical companies, had no need for another sales database.[145] *IMS Health* is significant for our purpose because it imbues the EU approach to refusal to license intellectual property with important flexibility. If competition law would intervene only where the party seeking access must come up with a new product, the potential use of competition law intervention would be much more limited, as not every developing country possesses the technological capacity to create a new product from an advanced technology.

The last notable case that featured compelled sharing of intellectual property is *Microsoft*. The facts of the case are too well known to be repeated here. The General Court held that Microsoft's refusal to share interoperability information with

[139] ibid para 38.

[140] Derclaye (n 116) 694–95.

[141] Matthias Lamping, 'Refusal to Licence as an Abuse of Market Dominance: From Commercial Solvents to Microsoft' in Reto M Hilty and KC Liu (eds), *Compulsory Licensing: Practical Experiences and Way Forward* (Springer-Verlag 2015) 133.

[142] Haris Apostolopoulos, 'Refusal-to-Deal Cases of IP Rights in the Aftermarket of US and EU Law: Convergence of Both Law Systems through Speaking the Same Language of Law and Economics' (2007) 5 DePaul Business and Commercial Law Journal 237, 259.

[143] Frédéric Marty and Julien Pillot, 'Intellectual Property Rights, Interoperability and Compulsory Licensing: Merits and Limits of the European Approach' (2012) 2012 Journal of Innovation Economics and Management 35, 46.

[144] ibid.

[145] Derclaye (n 116) 696.

competitors infringed Article 102 of the TFEU. The Court explained that for a refusal to share intellectual property to be abusive, these conditions must be met:

> (a) the refusal relates to a product or service indispensable to the exercise of a particular activity on a neighbouring market; (b) the refusal is of such a kind as to exclude any effective competition on that neighbouring market; and (c) the refusal prevents the appearance of a new product for which there is potential consumer demand.[146]

This case has been accused of further watering down the second and third requirements for compulsory licensing set out in the earlier cases.[147] It is no longer necessary that all competition in the second market would be eliminated as a result of the refusal to share. Mere elimination of effective competition would suffice.[148] In that case competitors have remained viable despite Microsoft's refusal to supply interoperability information.

The new product requirement has also been pared back to a showing of retardation of technical development resulting from a loss of innovation incentives on the part of competitors.[149] The General Court placed much emphasis on the fact that Microsoft's competitors had lost their innovation incentives. The Court reasoned that denial of a new product cannot be the only relevant harm to consumers under Article 102 of the TFEU.[150] Retardation of technical developments must count as well. A crucial factor in the Court's consideration was that 'Microsoft's competitors would likely offer different products, providing innovative features that were considered important by consumers in terms of safety, reliability, ease of use and speed performance'.[151] There is, however, no requirement that these technical improvements are incorporated in a clearly identifiable new product.[152] Alan Devlin and Michael Jacobs sum it up when they assert that

> [t]he *Microsoft* ruling significantly expanded the set of so-called exceptional circumstances to include relatively prosaic situations in which smaller rivals demonstrate that they need access to the relevant intellectual property in order to compete 'effectively' with the dominant firm in a neighboring or secondary market, in which access to the intellectual property would enable them either

146 *Microsoft*, para 332.

147 Katsoulacos (n 8) 288.

148 Alan Devlin and Michael Jacobs, 'Antitrust Divergence and the Limits of Economics' (2010) 104 Northwestern University Law Review 253, 280.

149 *Microsoft*, para 647.

150 Mauro Squitieri, 'Refusals to License Under European Union Competition Law After Microsoft' (2014) 11 Journal of International Business and Law 65, 75.

151 ibid 82.

152 Katsoulacos (n 8) 288.

to develop a 'new' product or to make 'technical developments' to their existing ones.[153]

The *Microsoft* court also attached some importance to the fact that in withholding the interoperability information, Microsoft was ending an established course of dealing.[154] Microsoft was willing to supply interoperability information when it was not active in the market. It gradually restricted supply as its market share grew. Frédéric Marty and Julien Pillot argue that the Court considered 'this kind of behaviour [a]s a form of predation which creates a risk of elimination of competition on the work-group server market'.[155] In this respect the CJEU's approach is similar to the US Supreme Court's stance in *Aspen Skiing*.

As compared to the essential facilities doctrine in the United States, the EU approach to refusal to license is more readily applicable to intellectual property. The string of cases from *Magill* and *Microsoft* explicitly or implicitly wrestle with the question of what adaptations to the intellectual property to which access is sought are required of the putative licensee, which should be a crucial question for any court considering mandatory sharing of intellectual property. If no adaptations are required whatsoever, imposition of a duty to license can risk undermining the entire body of intellectual property law. Meanwhile, an overly stringent new product requirement would render the doctrine largely irrelevant for developing countries. Separately, one may question the applicability of the EU case law to patents. None of the EU cases examined in this chapter have implicated patents. In two of the three cases the intellectual property at issue could be regarded as weak ones.

Even though the US and the EU case law may not be directly applicable to developing countries, it nonetheless provides a good starting point for developing countries in trying to derive their own contextualized approach to unilateral refusal to supply patented products or license a patented technology. Regardless of the country at issue, the interface presents certain policy trade-offs which every country must confront. Developing countries can draw lessons from how the United States and the European Union have tackled these policy dilemmas and adjusted their approaches to suit their own circumstances.

3. Developing Countries

There have been a few cases concerning unilateral refusal to deal involving intellectual property rights in India. In both cases, the Competition Commission of India

[153] Devlin and Jacobs (n 148) 273.
[154] Marty and Pillot (n 143) 47.
[155] ibid.

(CCI) ordered the dominant firm to share its intellectual property with rivals. In one of them the intellectual property at issue was deemed to be an essential facility.

In *MCX Stock Exchange v. National Stock Exchange*, at issue was the NSE's refusal to share its currency derivative (CD) segment Application Programme Interface (API) Code with a software provider called Financial Technologies India Limited, which produced the ODIN software.[156] ODIN allowed traders to trade in multiple markets through the same terminal.[157] This refusal made it impossible for ODIN users to access the NSE Currency Derivative segment trading platform through their preferred mode.[158] Traders would need access to an alternative terminal for that. At the time one of NSE's subsidiaries was developing an alternative software called 'NOW' to compete with ODIN.[159] The denial of access meant that most traders would 'confine to one terminal which connects to the dominant player only i.e. to use the "NOW" terminal (free of cost)'.[160] MCX also alleged that NSE engaged in predatory pricing.[161]

The CCI held that there is no general duty on the part of the intellectual property owner to license intellectual property to third parties. In exceptional circumstances, however, intellectual property may constitute an essential facility, to which CCI may order the facility owner to provide access to rivals to promote competition and innovation. The CCI deemed NSE's API code an essential facility and ordered NSE to provide access to it. The CCI argued that 'trading on stock exchanges is being done extensively on internet through electronic applications such as ODIN and NOW. In that sense, these software applications whether backend or frontend are essential facilities.'[162] The CCI also rejected as pretextual NSE's justification for denial of access on the grounds that ODIN had quality issues.[163] The CCI directed the NSE to put in place a system which allowed users a free choice between ODIN, NOW, and other software for trading on the currency segment.[164]

In *Shamsher Kataria v. Honda Siel Cars India Ltd.*, otherwise known as the *Auto Parts* case, the CCI concluded that the car manufacturers' (OEMs) refusal to supply genuine spare parts in the open market constituted an abuse of dominance.[165] The car manufacturers directed their parts suppliers, which are known as the original equipment suppliers (OESs), not to supply their spare parts and components in the open market.[166] They further instructed their dealers not to sell spare parts

[156] Case No 13 of 2009, *MCX Stock Exchange Ltd. v. National Stock Exchange of India Ltd.* CCI Order 23 June 2011, para 2.7.
[157] ibid para 2.8.
[158] ibid para 2.7.
[159] ibid para 2.6.
[160] ibid para 2.8.
[161] ibid para 2.13.
[162] ibid para 10.65.
[163] ibid para 10.63.
[164] ibid para 33.1(d).
[165] Case No 03 of 2011, *Shri Shamsher Kataria v. Honda Siel Cars India Ltd.* CCI Order 25 August 2015.
[166] ibid para 1.5.

over the counter and only sourced spare parts from the OEMs themselves or from authorized vendors.[167] Independent repair workshops were thus unable to obtain spare parts, diagnostic tools, and technical information required to provide maintenance and repair services to car owners.[168] This was done to divert customers to authorized service centres which charged significantly higher prices than independent workshops.[169]

The CCI found that the car manufacturers' agreements with the OESs and the authorized dealers constituted unlawful refusal to deal. The CCI rejected the car manufacturers' argument that their intellectual property rights were compromised by allowing the OESs to sell spare parts in the open market, asserting that 'the mere selling of spare parts and diagnostic tools in the aftermarket by the OESs does not violate the intellectual property rights in such spare parts. Additionally, the OEMs can through its contractual agreements with the OESs ensure that its intellectual property rights are not compromised and are protected.'[170] It also dismissed their concerns about safety and quality control by pointing out that there were less competition restrictive means for addressing those concerns.[171] It further rejected the car manufacturers' invocation of the exception under Section 3(5)(i) of the Indian Competition Act, which exempted the imposition of reasonable conditions that may be necessary for the protection of intellectual property rights from the purview of the Act.[172] The CCI found that the manufacturers did not have valid rights granted under Indian intellectual property law for their spare parts.[173] Even if they had had such rights, the CCI was satisfied that the selling of spare parts would not necessarily compromise those rights.[174]

The CCI rejected the car manufacturers' justifications for limiting their spare parts only to the authorized dealers. These include the need to protect car owners from spurious or counterfeit spare parts and the need to ensure that car owners only obtain repair services from qualified personnel with specialized skills and regular training, which were only available at the authorized dealers.[175] The manufacturers argued that safety concerns would arise if spare parts were fitted by unqualified personnel.[176] The CCI asserted that '[t]he presence of spurious parts/health hazards should not be used as an argument to deny consumer choice. Every car owner (consumer) should have a choice to make a rational decision after taking into account the costs and benefits'.[177] The choice of repairer 'should not be taken

[167] ibid para 1.2.
[168] ibid.
[169] ibid para 1.4.
[170] ibid para 20.6.13.
[171] ibid.
[172] ibid para 20.6.23.
[173] ibid paras 20.6.16–17.
[174] ibid para 20.6.21.
[175] ibid para 20.6.27.
[176] ibid.
[177] ibid para 20.6.28.

away in the guise of consumer protectionism [sic]'.[178] The CCI further rejected the assertion that quality repair services could only be obtained from the authorized dealers.[179] There were several multi-brand repairers that possessed the same scale of operations as the authorized dealers and they should be able to provide repair services of comparable quality. Finally, the CCI noted that the manufacturers' refusal to provide access to spare parts to independent repairers and the high markups they charged on spare parts had the precise effect of driving car owners to use spurious parts.[180]

After surveying the jurisprudence of a number of jurisdictions on the supply of car spare parts, the CCI ultimately concluded that

> both in the mature and the developing competition law regimes of the world, refusal to [provide] access [to] branded or alternate spare parts and technical manuals/repair tools, necessary to repair sophisticated consumer durable products, such as automobiles, is frowned upon, since such practices restricts consumer choice besides foreclosing the market for repairs/maintenance contracts by independent repairers.[181]

The CCI ordered the car manufacturers to put in place an efficient distribution system for their spare parts and to allow OESs to sell spare parts in the open market without restrictions.[182] The CCI's decision was later affirmed by the since-dissolved Competition Appellate Tribunal.[183]

These two cases suggest that the CCI is generally quite open to the possibility of imposing a duty to deal on a dominant firm despite claims of intellectual property protection, perhaps more so than the United States and the European Union.

4. Doctrinal Considerations Raised in the Case Law

Before we can formulate a coherent approach to the two doctrines for developing countries, it is important to acquire a deeper understanding of some doctrinal issues that have been raised in the case law. As it turns out, some of them have special salience for developing countries for reasons that are unrelated to why the US and the EU courts paid attention to them in the first place.

[178] ibid.
[179] ibid.
[180] ibid para 20.6.29.
[181] ibid para 20.6.42.
[182] ibid para 22.3.
[183] Appeal No 60-62 of 2014, *Toyota Kirloskar Motor Private Ltd v. CCI* CAT Order 9 Dec. 2016.

(a) The competitive relationship between the parties and preservation of innovation incentives

The unilateral refusal to deal doctrine and the essential facilities doctrine differ in terms of the nature of the competitive relationship implicated by them. The case law suggests that there are three capacities in which the party seeking access can share a competitive relationship with the dominant firm in a refusal to deal or essential facilities case: in the primary product market,[184] the downstream market,[185] and an aftermarket.[186]

Many unilateral refusal to deal cases in the United States have involved aftermarket competitors. The defendant is usually the producer of the primary product, in a few cases a photocopier, and is trying to foreclose the repair service market by denying plaintiff competing service providers access to spare parts.[187] The US courts have never declared that unilateral refusal to deal claims are confined to aftermarkets and will not be entertained if brought by a primary market competitor, such as a competing photocopier manufacturer. Yet the recurring factual scenario in these cases has spurred some commentators to advocate the use of the scope of patent test for adjudicating unilateral refusal to deal claims.[188] The lack of a clear definition of patent scope notwithstanding, there at least seems to be a consensus that it would cover the primary product. The implication of this test would be that a primary product market competitor, or a horizontal competitor, will have no judicial recourse under the unilateral refusal to deal doctrine. Some have even contended that the ban should apply to vertical competitors as well.[189] Meanwhile in the European Union, the unilateral refusal to deal doctrine may be available to competitors in the primary product market, as evidenced by the *IMS Health* case.

It has been suggested that patent scope should be delineated by the relevant market under competition law.[190] Although no good reasons have been offered for equating these two concepts, the underlying premise for this position seems to be that a patentee should be allowed to exclude in at least one relevant market to recoup her R&D expenses. To put it slightly differently, the permissible scope of a unilateral refusal to deal claim should be demarcated with reference to its impact on innovation incentives. Patent scope is used as a tacit way to balance the competing imperatives of protecting consumer welfare and safeguarding innovation incentives. Tying patent scope to the concept of the relevant market does not seem to change the outcome of the analysis. Under either formulation, the patent scope

[184] Case C-418/01, *IMS Health GmbH & Co OHG v. NDC Health GmbH & Co KG* [2004] ECR I-5039.
[185] Case C-241-242/91 P, *RTE & ITP v. Commission* [1995] ECR I-743.
[186] Case 53/87, *CICCRA v. Renault* [1988] ECR 6039; Case 238/87, *AB Volvo v. Erik Veng* [1988] ECR 6211.
[187] *Image Technical Services v. Eastman Kodak*, 125 F.3d 1195 (9th Cir. 1997); *In re Independent Service Organizations Antitrust Litigation (Xerox)*, 203 F.3d 1322 (Fed. Cir. 2000).
[188] Lao (n 12); Bauer (n 14); Lopatka and Page (n 11).
[189] Devlin, Jacobs, and Peixoto (n 128) 1189.
[190] Bauer (n 14) 1225, 1234.

test would exclude a primary product competitor from the unilateral refusal to deal doctrine. However, it has the benefit of giving the test a sounder theoretical basis.

The US essential facilities and the EU refusal to license cases introduce another wrinkle to the question of the nature of the competitive relationship between the party seeking access and the dominant firm. These cases rarely, if ever, feature an aftermarket. Instead, the typical factual scenario involves the owner of an upstream physical facility or intellectual property that is crucial to a downstream competitor's ability to compete denying that competitor access to the facility or intellectual property.[191] This means that the plaintiff and the defendant compete in the downstream market. The market of interest in an essential facilities case is not the market for the facility and its reasonable substitutes but the one downstream to it.[192] This explains why the widely accepted formulation of the doctrine from the *MCI v. AT&T* case[193] requires the plaintiff to be the facility owner's competitor.[194] What motivates this requirement is the need to ensure that 'a denial of access may in fact result in monopolization; would-be competitors in the vertically related market are excluded, thereby preserving or creating a monopoly'.[195] Hovenkamp, Janis, and Lemley emphasize the importance of a direct competitive relationship between the plaintiff and the defendant, observing that '[a]n antitrust violation is even less likely where the intellectual property owner does not compete directly with the disfavored licensee; in the absence of some showing of monopoly leveraging, it is not clear what incentive the intellectual property owner would have to try to eliminate competition in the downstream market'.[196]

The relevance of a competitive relationship thus seems to go both ways. While the existence of a competitive relationship in the primary product market would raise serious hurdles for a unilateral refusal to deal claim, the lack of any competitive relationship would be similarly problematic in an essential facilities or refusal to license claim. While this makes eminent sense from a competition law perspective—after all, the incidence of competitive harm is a prerequisite for competition law intervention—it also leads to the question of how this relates to the need to preserve innovation incentives. The rationale for disallowing a primary product competitor from bringing a unilateral refusal to deal claim is that the main market in which the patentee competes should be preserved for the patentee to recoup her R&D investment. The same logic should mean that the main market in which the essential facility owner competes should be protected from judicial encroachment as well.

[191] *MCI Communications v. AT&T*, 708 F.2d 1081 (7th Cir.), *cert denied*, 464 US 891 (1983); *Hecht v. Pro-Football, Inc.*, 570 F.2d 982 (D.C. Cir. 1977), *cert denied*, 436 US 956 (1978); *Gamco Inc. v. Providence Fruit & Produce Building, Inc.*, 194 F.2d 484 (1st Cir.), *cert denied*, 344 US 817 (1952).

[192] Werden (n 91) 459.

[193] MCI, 708 F.2d at 1132.

[194] Werden (n 91) 459.

[195] ibid.

[196] Hovenkamp, Janis and Lemley (n 7) 5.

One way to reconcile these conflicting positions is to say that the essential facilities and the EU refusal to license cases only require the parties to share a vertical competitive relationship between the upstream and the downstream markets, and not a horizontal one as direct competitors in the facility or primary product market. In fact, the plaintiff in an essential facilities case by definition cannot be an effective competitor in the facility market or she would not need access to the defendant's facility to compete. If the plaintiff owned a comparable facility which makes her a horizontal competitor, there would be no need for an essential facilities claim.

A close examination of many essential facilities cases, however, suggests that the vertically related, and most often downstream, market in which the plaintiff and the defendant compete is the one in which the facility is put to its most profitable, or even only possible, use. The railroad bridge and switching yards in St Louis in the *Terminal Railroad* case could only be used by railroad companies.[197] AT&T's local telephone network, at least at the time of the case, had only one commercial use: provision of fixed-line telephony service.[198] The football stadium in *Hecht v. Pro-Football, Inc.*, was used to play football.[199] Among the EU refusal to license cases, the brick structure in *IMS Health* could only be used to supply pharmaceutical sales data.[200] The interoperability information in *Microsoft* was only of interest to competing workgroup server providers, who sought to improve on Microsoft's product.[201] Restricting availability of the essential facilities doctrine or the EU refusal to license doctrine to a competitor in the vertically related market which constitutes the most profitable use of the facility or the intellectual property seems to undermine the imperative of incentive preservation.

Defenders of the vertical competitive relationship requirement may argue that the seeming contradiction between the unilateral refusal to deal cases and the essential facilities cases can be explained by the fact that the latter is not meant to apply to intellectual property. Commentators have noted that there is no reported case in the United States in which the doctrine has been applied to intellectual property to impose a duty to license.[202] But this would require a robust justification for why intellectual property should be treated more deferentially than tangible property as far as the essential facilities doctrine is concerned. Physical facilities such as railroad bridges, football stadia, and power transmission networks also require substantial investment.[203] There is no reason to believe that a football stadium is

[197] Robert Pitofsky, Donna Patterson, and Jonathan Hooks, 'The Essential Facilities Doctrine Under United States Antitrust Law' (2002) 70 Antitrust Law Journal 443, 446.
[198] MCI, 708 F.2d at 1094–95.
[199] Hecht, 570 F.2d 982.
[200] *IMS Health*, para 4.
[201] *Microsoft*, para 367.
[202] Devlin and Jacobs (n 148) 277.
[203] Howard A Shelanski, 'Unilateral Refusals to Deal in Intellectual and Other Property' (2009) 76 Antitrust Law Journal 369, 382.

less costly to build than a patentable innovation. It is an untenable proposition that preservation of investment incentives is a less critical concern in physical facilities cases as opposed to intellectual property ones.

From the perspective of incentive preservation, it seems that the current essential facilities doctrine has got it exactly the other way round. The doctrine should only be invocable by firms that do not compete with the facility owner at all, or at least not in the owner's principal market, and this includes firms that compete both upstream and downstream with the facility owner. One explanation for this seemingly counterintuitive position is that the essential facilities cases have mostly featured physical facilities. It would be difficult in most cases to imagine how a physical facility can be used to compete in a completely unrelated market. After all, there is a limited number of purposes to which a football stadium can be put to use. Mandating a lack of a material competitive relationship between the plaintiff and the defendant in an essential facilities case could amount to an evisceration of the doctrine.

The situation in the EU refusal to license cases is slightly different. The EU courts seem to have dealt with the paramount issue of incentive preservation not by limiting availability of relief to a certain class of plaintiffs but by imposing an additional requirement that the plaintiff use the intellectual property obtained to develop a new product. The new product requirement originated from the *Magill* case,[204] and seems to have been watered down in subsequent cases, most prominently in the *IMS Health* case,[205] and subsequently morphed into a requirement of product improvement in *Microsoft*.[206] The original intention behind the requirement in the *Magill* case seems to be to ensure that the claimant is not simply seeking to replicate the dominant firm's product, which would put the claimant in direct competition with the dominant firm. In that case, the undertaking seeking access to TV programming information wanted to publish a weekly TV guide that was not being produced in the market at all.[207] Access to the dominant firm's copyrighted materials would not allow the claimant to frustrate the dominant firm's effort to recoup their investment. In fact, it is not clear that the TV stations invested specifically to produce TV programming information. Such information was merely incidental to the stations' programme production.[208] Although the CJEU did not explicitly emphasize this point, it is fair to assume that the Court paid some attention to the need to preserve investment incentives when compelling sharing of programming information. The Court's decision in *Magill* probably did not have a severe impact on investment incentives.

[204] *Magill*, para 52.
[205] *IMS Health*, paras 48–49.
[206] *Microsoft*, paras 647–65.
[207] *Magill*, paras 10, 52.
[208] ibid paras 10, 53.

The narrative changed quite dramatically in the *IMS Health* case, in which the Court bent over backwards to fit the facts of the case under the new product requirement.[209] The brick structure that was at issue in the case was critical to the dominant firm's main line of business, the sale of pharmaceutical sales data.[210] Although the court seems to have characterized the brick structure as belonging to the upstream market, the dominant firm was not in the business of developing and selling organizational structure for sales data.[211] It was in the business of selling pharmaceutical sales data.[212] Setting aside the issue of whether the Court's distinction of an upstream and a downstream market in that case made sense, it is clear that compelled sharing of the brick structure would have had a direct and immediate impact on the dominant firm's main business and hence should have serious implications for investment incentives.

Broadly construed, *IMS Health* may stand for the proposition that incentive preservation carries little weight when the European courts approach cases involving compelled sharing of intellectual property. Some would argue that the General Court's decision in the *Microsoft* case lends further support to that proposition. The Court did consider innovation incentives but concluded that such incentives would not be impaired by a duty to supply.[213] The Court also argued that Microsoft's refusal to license would impair rivals' incentive to innovation.[214] To the extent that the European courts accord less weight to incentive preservation considerations in these refusal to license intellectual property cases, it would be consistent with the US essential facilities cases where incentive preservation seems to be deemphasized. Between the two, the EU approach provides greater clarity by focusing directly on incentive preservation and the extent of the technical contribution required by the party seeking access. The EU approach may be a more promising route for those developing countries seeking to obtain foreign technology through the essential facilities or a refusal to license doctrine.

(b) A history of prior dealing

One issue that has repeatedly surfaced in the unilateral refusal to deal cases is whether the law should make a distinction between cases in which there is an existing course of dealing between the dominant firm and the party seeking access and cases in which there is none. Cases such as *Aspen Skiing* in the United States and the EU *Microsoft* case have tackled the issue and concluded that the existence of a course of prior dealing should favour the party seeking access. The weight of the scholarly opinion, however, seems to be firmly against this view. No less an

[209] *IMS Health*, paras 48–49.
[210] ibid para 12.
[211] *IMS Health*, paras 43–47.
[212] ibid para 4.
[213] *Microsoft*, paras 698–701.
[214] ibid paras 653–54.

authority than Professor Hovenkamp has argued that favouring existing licensees could be highly problematic. He offers two reasons for it. First, he argues that technology markets often change rapidly and it would be particularly detrimental and counterproductive to lock companies in these markets in an existing business relationship.[215] Second, he observes that intellectual property licenses are often exclusive and thus locking patentees in existing licensing relationships may foreclose future licensees.[216] Both Ritter and Carlton make the obvious argument that attaching extra weight to a course of prior dealing in the analysis would deter intellectual property owners from entering into licensing arrangements in the first place, which could result in great inefficiencies for the economy.[217]

Despite these criticisms, there are good reasons why a course of prior dealing should tilt the case in favour of the party seeking access. In a patent licensing context, the licensee may have made extensive relationship-specific investments to adapt the technology for production purposes.[218] To the extent that these investments or assets cannot be effectively deployed elsewhere, they represent sunk costs that will be lost forever once the licensing relationship is terminated.[219] Such a waste of resources could be particularly costly for developing countries, which suffer from a lack of investments in the first place.[220] Developing countries should guard against such waste of resources. This constitutes a strong argument for developing countries to offer special protection to existing licensees.

It is also true that developing countries are in great need of technology transfers. A legal rule that may deter licensing activities in the first place could be hugely costly for them. This potentially puts developing countries in a dilemma. These two considerations, however, need not deserve equal weight. While allowing a licensor to terminate an existing licensing arrangement will bring about a definite loss of relationship-specific investments, the deterrent effect of the alternative rule on investments is much less certain. Many factors go into a licensing decision, most of which are business considerations.[221] The legal regime is but one of many factors. A somewhat unfavourable rule in the event of a distant possibility is unlikely to

[215] Hovenkamp, Janis, and Lemley (n 7) 30.

[216] ibid.

[217] Ritter (n 98) 284–85. Dennis W Carlton, 'A General Analysis of Exclusionary Conduct and Refusal to Deal: Why Aspen and Kodak Are Misguided' (National Bureau of Economic Research 2001) Working Paper 8105 23–24.

[218] Lori Pressman and others, 'Pre-Production Investment and Jobs Induced by MIT Exclusive Patent Licenses: A Preliminary Model to Measure the Economic Impact of University Licensing' (1995) 7 Journal of the Association of University Technology Managers 28.

[219] Richard Schmalensee, 'Sunk Costs and Antitrust Barriers to Entry' (2004) 94 The American Economic Review 471, 471.

[220] Tildane Kinda, 'Investment Climate and FDI in Developing Countries: Firm-Level Evidence' (2010) 38 World Development 498.

[221] John H Dunning and Sarianna M Lundan, *Multinational Enterprises and the Global Economy* (2nd edn, Edward Elgar Publishing Ltd 2008) 116–44, 318–27.

change a patentee's decision, especially when a course of prior dealing is not a dispositive factor in these cases. It is only one of the relevant considerations.

Further reflection will reveal that the arguments made by Hovenkamp and other commentators do not only counsel against attaching greater weight to a course of prior dealing. Carried to their logical conclusion, they would argue against imposing any duty to deal at all where there is an existing licensing arrangement. That would be a radical position to take. Overall, the weight of the arguments suggests that developing countries adopt the existing position of US and EU case law and emphasize a course of prior dealing in the analysis. The more interesting question perhaps is whether developing country authorities should only pursue unilateral refusal to deal cases where there is a course of prior dealing.

(c) Predatory intent

Intent has featured in some cases where there is suspicion that the justification for the refusal to deal was pretextual. It has also arisen in some other cases where the question is whether the refusal to deal is motivated by a predatory intent to eliminate rivals.[222] The presence of a predatory intent is sometimes helpful to the courts because a unilateral refusal to deal is usually considered such innocuous and competitively neutral conduct that courts are reluctant to condemn it absent evidence of a desire to harm rivals. Almost all cases in which a predatory intent was found have involved a course of prior dealing.[223] When a competitor has been receiving supply of an input to take part in a downstream market, a sudden cessation of that supply can be aptly interpreted as part of an attempt to drive out the competitor. Courts generally believe that taking a competitor's business away by cutting off her supply of a crucial input goes beyond competition on the merits.

Courts have relied on other facts to infer a predatory intent. The obvious one is the defendant's intention to enter the downstream market which the plaintiff has been squeezed out of following the termination of supply. A cessation of supply of a critical input and subsequent entry into the downstream market completes the predation story. This is arguably what the CJEU had in mind when it condemned the refusal to supply in *Commercial Solvents*.[224] Even *Microsoft* partly follows this fact pattern. It was alleged that Microsoft only started to withhold interoperability information when it had plans to enter the workgroup server market.[225]

In *Aspen Skiing*, the US Supreme Court emphasized the fact that the defendant sacrificed profits—it had allegedly refused to sell ski tickets to the rival ski slope operator even at retail prices, which is presumably profit maximizing—to infer an

[222] Cases 6 and 7/73, *Istituto Chemioterapico Italiano Spa and Commercial Solvents Corp. v. Commission* [1974] ECR 223.

[223] *Aspen Skiing Co. v. Aspen Highlands Skiing Corp.*, 472 US 585 (1985); Cases 6 and 7/73, *Istituto Chemioterapico Italiano Spa and Commercial Solvents Corp. v. Commission* [1974] ECR 223.

[224] *Commercial Solvents*, para 25.

[225] Marty and Pillot (n 143) 47.

intent to harm rivals.[226] The essence of the Court's reasoning is that a unilateral refusal to deal motivated by a predatory intent, as evinced by a willingness to sever a profitable course of dealing and sacrifice of profits, that clearly harms consumers and is not justified by pro-competitive justifications should be condemned under Section 2 of the Sherman Act.[227] Given that *Aspen Skiing* has been described as being at or near the outer boundary of the unilateral refusal to deal doctrine under the Sherman Act,[228] a predatory intent can be considered a necessary element in a successful unilateral refusal to deal claim under US antitrust law.

Developing country authorities need to take predatory intent seriously. Because predatory intent is almost always only found where there is a course of prior dealing, the discussion here necessarily overlaps somewhat with that of prior course of dealing. It was argued that developing countries need to attach significant weight to the existence of a course of prior dealing because such dealing suggests the existence of relationship-specific investments, which need to be protected. The rationale for developing countries to take predatory intent seriously is similar in that if the unilateral refusal to deal is driven by a desire to harm or even eliminate a domestic firm that has licensed a technology, it could be particularly costly to the country's technological capacity. The firm being eliminated has the capacity to utilize a foreign technology to engage in downstream production. Developing country authorities should be particularly vigilant against conduct that could further reduce their domestic technological capacity given the dearth of such capacity in these countries in the first place. Technological capacity could be lost once the firm is driven out of the market.[229] Standing up to predatory unilateral refusal to deal may help to protect domestic technological capacity. While it is often said that competition law protects competition, and not competitors,[230] when the competitor is one of the few domestic firms that possess the technological capacity to adapt foreign technologies, it deserves special solicitude from a developing country competition authority.

(d) New product or secondary market

The requirement of a new product or a secondary market is only found in the EU refusal to license cases. The CJEU declared in *IMS Health* that

> the refusal by an undertaking in a dominant position to allow access to a product protected by an intellectual property right, where that product is indispensable for operating on a secondary market, may be regarded as abusive only where the

[226] *Aspen Skiing*, 472 US at 593.
[227] *Trinko*, 540 US at 409–11.
[228] 540 US at 409.
[229] Annetta Fortune and Wil Mitchell, 'Unpacking Firm Exit at the Firm and Industry Levels: The Adaptation and Selection of Firm Capabilities' (2012) 33 Strategic Management Journal 794, 802.
[230] *Brown Shoe Co. v. United States*, 380 US 294, 320 (1962).

> undertaking which requested the license does not intend to limit itself essentially to duplicating the goods or services already offered on the secondary market by the owner of the intellectual property right, but intends to produce new goods or services not offered by the owner of the right and for which there is a potential consumer demand.[231]

The US essential facilities cases do not speak of a new product or a secondary market, mostly because none of them, with the possible exception of *Associated Press*, have involved intellectual property. The secondary market can sometimes be a downstream market or a complementary product market. Complementary product markets raise issues about monopoly leveraging that falls under the rubric of tying and bundling and will be discussed in the next chapter. The ensuing discussion will thus focus on downstream markets and new primary products. The new product requirement originated from *Magill*, but was subsequently watered down in *IMS Health* where there was arguably only one relevant market of the pharmaceutical sales database, even though the Court did seem to rely on some notion of a hypothetical upstream market. The requirement was further diluted in *Microsoft*, where the Court held that it was sufficient to show that the refusal to deal prevented competitors from making technical improvements to the product.

It has been argued that the new product or second market requirement is largely superfluous and is only the legacy of the earlier refusal to deal cases such as *Commercial Solvents* and *Telemarketing*, upon which, according to Lamping, the CJEU 'has erroneously based its subsequent case law involving intellectual property rights'.[232] An alternative interpretation is that the CJEU had a clear objective behind imposing the requirement in intellectual property cases. It has been said that the European courts have adopted a more stringent standard in cases involving intellectual property than those that feature physical property.[233] In requiring the party seeking access to an intellectual property to create a new product or at least make substantial technical improvements to it, the Courts may be trying to prevent the plaintiff from merely replicating the dominant firm's product.[234] This may be motivated by a desire to accord greater respect and protection for intellectual property rights. The Courts believe that they should override such rights only when society will obtain significant benefits in the form of a new or a substantially improved product.

In doing so, the European courts have implicitly made a value judgment that only consumer welfare gains in the form of new product innovations would justify a judicial order of compulsory licensing; mere lower prices for an existing product

[231] *IMS Health*, para 49.
[232] Lamping (n 141) 132–33.
[233] Ritter (n 98) 288.
[234] *IMS Health*, para 49.

do not suffice. When a plaintiff only replicates the dominant firm's product after obtaining access to that firm's intellectual property, the likely consequence is lower prices for consumers.[235] If the dominant firm previously had a monopoly over the product, prices will drop from a monopolistic level to a duopolistic level. The European courts will not trade the integrity of intellectual property for lower prices. Innovation incentives will only be sacrificed in the name of further innovation.

Another more practical reason for the European courts to impose a new product requirement in intellectual property but not tangible property cases is perhaps that it is often not possible to come up with a new product with a physical property. What kind of new product can one come up with after being granted access to a critical port facility or a newspaper distribution network after all? The scope for innovation with a physical property is usually smaller. An insistence on a new product would effectively foreclose the application of the unilateral refusal to deal doctrine to physical property. Having said that, it is important to recall that the requirement has been significantly watered down in *IMS Health* and *Microsoft*. It is not clear how stringent this requirement is anymore under the current case law.

The new product requirement has important implications for developing countries. Regardless of whether a new product or mere technical improvements to an existing product are required, what is clear is that under EU case law, a competitor cannot seek access to the dominant firm's intellectual property merely to replicate its product, *IMS Health* notwithstanding. Either the competitor has to create a new derivative product, as in *Magill*, or improve an existing product, as in *Microsoft*. In an industrialized economy, where the capacity to innovate is abundant, such a stance can be a reasonable compromise. This requirement, however, would greatly limit the utility of the doctrine to developing countries. It means that only firms that possess the technological capacity to innovate or improve on the technology of a global technological leader can avail themselves of the doctrine. A more promising approach for developing countries would be *IMS Health*, which seems to sanction compelled sharing of intellectual property when the result is the creation of a highly comparable product. There was no mention in the case that NDC would produce a technically superior product. The only likely consumer benefit was going to be lower prices for pharmaceutical companies. Alternatively, the technical improvement requirement under *Microsoft* can be interpreted loosely such that any non-negligible technical improvement suffices.

(e) Definition of essentiality or indispensability

The essentiality requirement is the lynchpin of the essential facilities doctrine. The requirement is all the more important because, as it is usually formulated and applied in the United States, the doctrine does not have a separate requirement of

[235] Walter Elberfeld and Elmar Wolfstetter, 'A Dynamic Model of Bertrand Competition with Entry' (1999) 17 International Journal of Industrial Organization 513, 515.

a showing of consumer harm. The essential facilities doctrine is probably unique under US antitrust law in that a monopolization claim can be sustained absent a showing of consumer harm. The most that can be said is that the doctrine presumes that compelled access will increase supply of the downstream product, which will lower prices. Therefore, consumers suffer harm from the denial of access by being forced to pay higher prices. This is different from the kind of harm to competition that is usually required to substantiate a monopolization claim. Although one can argue that the denial of access constitutes one form of exclusion, most commentators would concur that excluding a competitor by refusing to share a private property amounts to competition on the merits and should not be deemed a cognizable harm to competition.[236] In some way compelled sharing of an essential facility is similar to prohibition of excessive pricing, which aims to rectify a consumer harm unaccompanied by any harm to competition. This may help to explain the widespread discomfort with the doctrine in the United States.

The discomfort with the doctrine is further aggravated by the perception that the doctrine suffers from a significant lack of clarity. Brett Frischmann and Spencer Waller observe that '"[e]ssentiality" in the existing test appears to be a rather inarticulate and unrefined demand-side consideration... Many have critiqued the essential facilities doctrine on the grounds that it is too open-ended and insufficiently defined.'[237] Commentators have raised two important questions regarding the meaning of essentiality. The first is what is the requisite degree of difficulty of replicating the facility. The second is the relationship between the defendant's market power and the uniqueness of the facility.

It has been said that the *Terminal Railroad* case, from which the doctrine emanated, may have implied that physical impossibility of duplicating the facility is needed to demonstrate essentiality.[238] Recent cases, however, seem to have lowered the bar from impossibility to impracticability.[239] In *Hecht*, the Court held that '[t]o be "essential" a facility need not be indispensable; it is enough that duplication of the facility would be economically infeasible and if denial of its use inflicts a severe handicap on potential market entrants'.[240]

According to Gregory Werden, the authoritative formulation of the essential facilities doctrine in the *MCI* case still left three questions unanswered, one of which is 'what quantum of effect on the competitor from denial of the facility is necessary'.[241] While *Hecht* only requires a severe handicap, Werden believes that complete exclusion of a competitor is necessary.[242] Abbott Lipsky and Gregory Sidak

[236] Devlin, Jacobs, and Peixoto (n 128) 1170–71.
[237] Brett Frischmann and Spencer Weber Waller, 'Revitalizing Essential Facilities' (2008) 75 Antitrust Law Journal 1, 10.
[238] Abbott B Lipsky Jr and J Gregory Sidak, 'Essential Facilities' (1999) 51 Stanford Law Review 1187, 1212.
[239] ibid.
[240] Hecht, 570 F.3d at 992.
[241] Werden (n 91) 453–54.
[242] ibid 454.

recognize the difficulty in drawing a clear line between a severe competitive advantage and complete exclusion.[243] They ultimately conclude that '[t]he present case law recognizes this distinction, and permits application of the doctrine where the competitive disadvantage is severe, rather than fatal'.[244] Bounded in the concept of essentiality is the notion of uniqueness, which suggests that no feasible alternative is presently available for the facility and that the facility cannot be replicated.[245] The more unique a facility is, the more difficult it is to find a reasonable substitute for it, and hence the more essential it is for the competitor. Even though uniqueness and essentiality are analytically distinct concepts, their application is often collapsed into one.

Richard Gilbert and Carl Shapiro have attempted to formulate a definition of essentiality in economic terms. They propose that 'an input is essential only if an equally efficient firm cannot compete when the input is not available, or equivalently, when its price is infinite',[246] which means 'an equally efficient firm cannot profitably produce any level of output even if the output is sold at the integrated firm's monopoly price'.[247] Essentiality must be assessed with reference to the price of the input and the price of the final product incorporating the input. Gilbert and Shapiro argue that the *MCI* case implicitly uses market prices as the reference point.[248] They further argue that judicial intervention would only be justified when it is impossible for the facility owner and the party seeking access to reach a mutually acceptable agreement, which would only happen when total industry profit absent sharing is higher than that in the presence of sharing.[249]

A related yet distinct issue is the relationship between the dominant firm's market power and the essentiality of the facility. To put it slightly differently, the question is to what extent the defendant's market power can be attributed to the essential facility. Werden notes that this question is still largely shrouded in uncertainty.[250] Lipsky and Sidak argue that the inquiry into essentiality and the assessment of market power should be one and the same.[251] The corollary of this argument is that the inquiry into essentiality should be equally stringent as the legal tests for monopoly power under Section 2, which means that market conditions that preclude a finding of monopoly power would equally negate the application of the doctrine.[252] Werden suggests that the relevant legal test seems to

[243] Lipsky Jr and Sidak (n 238) 1212–13.
[244] ibid.
[245] ibid 1211.
[246] Richard J Gilbert and Carl Shapiro, 'An Economic Analysis of Unilateral Refusals to License Intellectual Property' (1996) Proceedings of National Academy of Sciences 12751–52.
[247] ibid.
[248] ibid.
[249] ibid.
[250] Werden (n 91) 453–54.
[251] Lipsky Jr and Sidak (n 238) 1212–13.
[252] ibid 1214–15.

be 'the existence of monopoly power arising from control over a facility'.[253] He, however, observes that separating the inquiry into essentiality from the assessment of market power ultimately may not be practical because 'it is difficult for a monopolist to possess substantial market power by virtue of control over a facility, and yet have the denial of access not exclude competitors completely'.[254]

One issue that has not been explicitly articulated in this discussion is power in which market. If the relevant market is defined as that for the supply of the relevant input or facility, then the facility owner must possess monopoly power by virtue of her ownership of an essential facility. If the relevant market is defined as that for the downstream product for which the essential facility is a critical input, then the equivalence of the two concepts is no longer certain. Even if downstream production is impossible without the essential input or facility, it is possible for the facility owner to face competition in the downstream market. This could be the case if the facility owner has licensed a critical technology to a number of downstream producers. It is then highly relevant whether the essential facilities doctrine should remain applicable in such a market.

The equivalent concept of essentiality under EU law is indispensability. In *Magill*, the CJEU held that the refusal to supply programming information was abusive because the information was indispensable for the publication of a weekly TV guide.[255] In *Oscar Bronner*, the Court reiterated the requirement of indispensability, but proceeded to conclude that the newspaper distribution network was not indispensable to rival publication because other distribution channels were available.[256] An input is only indispensable when there is no actual or potential alternative for it and that was not true for the distribution network.[257] Rita Coco notes that although the indispensability condition was not met in the case, the decision extended the application of the concept of indispensability to tangible property.[258] In *IMS Health*, the CJEU emphasized the indispensability requirement, noting that a refusal to supply may constitute an abuse if 'the products or services are indispensable in order to carry on a particular business and where there is an actual demand for them on the part of undertakings which seek to carry on the business for which they are indispensable'.[259] In *Microsoft*, the Court again applied the requirement, noting that 'the refusal relates to a product or service indispensable to the exercise of a particular activity on a neighbouring market'.[260] The Court proceeded to endorse the Commission's conclusion that interoperability with the Windows

[253] Werden (n 91) 454.
[254] ibid.
[255] *Magill*, para 53.
[256] Coco (n 16) 18.
[257] ibid.
[258] ibid.
[259] *IMS Health*, para 44.
[260] *Microsoft*, para 332.

operating system is essential to the ability of competing workgroup server operating systems to compete.[261]

The condition of essentiality or indispensability needs to be defined judiciously to suit the circumstances of developing countries. For the essential facilities doctrine to apply to intellectual property, essentiality or indispensability cannot be defined as physical impossibility. It should be understood as impracticability. It would hardly ever be physically impossible to replicate a patented technology unless the requirement expressly takes into account the firm's and the country's current technological capacity. Moreover, there cannot be an insistence on complete exclusion. A severe competitive disadvantage should suffice. Short of standard-essential patents and software that has become a de facto standard by virtue of network effects, it is highly unlikely that denial of access to a technology will result in outright exclusion. Therefore, essentiality and indispensability should refer to a technology that is economically unfeasible and impractical to replicate, the denial of access to which will puts a competitor at a severe competitive disadvantage.

Impracticality of replication also needs to take full account of the existing technological capacity of the firm and the country at issue. It would be rather pointless to insist that a technologically advanced firm in an industrialized economy could replicate the technology when the technology is completely beyond the reach of a developing country firm. Lastly, in terms of the implicit market prices underlying the definition of essentiality, it must take full account of the price reductions after market entry. Even though Gilbert and Shapiro do not clearly specify this point, they must have intended it. It only makes sense to use the post-entry market prices to assess a potential entrant's efficiency.

To sum up, all the doctrinal considerations raised in the US and EU jurisprudence require special attention from developing country authorities. A course of prior dealing often indicates the existence of relationship-specific investments by the licensee. It is important for developing countries to protect investments that are made for technology deployment and adaptation. Predatory intent against a developing country firm, especially one with the technological capacity to utilize an advanced technology, also requires vigilance. The new product requirement imposed under the EU jurisprudence needs to be adjusted according to the technological capacity of the developing country at issue. For a production country, insistence of a genuinely new product would be tantamount to a repeal of the essential facilities doctrine. Production countries are highly unlikely to be able to come up with a genuinely novel product with a frontier technology. The arguments are similar for a technology adaptation country. For sectors in which a proto-innovation country possesses innovation capacity, a heightened new product requirement such as under *Microsoft* or even *Magill* may make sense. Finally, under the essentiality

[261] ibid para 428.

requirement, the standard should be impracticality rather than physical impossibility. Impracticality should be adjudged in light of the technological capacity of the country at issue. A severe competitive disadvantage rather than complete exclusion should suffice.

C. A Proposed Framework for Developing Countries

Developing countries need to fashion their own approach to the patent–competition interface. Despite calls for convergence in global competition law in recent years, developing countries need to be cognisant of the limitations of legal transplant.[262] Transplanting legal rules from foreign jurisdictions that do not fit the local circumstances will only lead to confusion and rejection. The global mainstream approach to competition law is largely informed by the experiences of industrialized economies of continental scale such as the United States and the European Union. What has worked for them need not work for developing countries. In fact, in light of the disparate technological capacity of developing countries and the varying enforcement capacity of their competition authorities, there are good reasons to believe that developing countries need to develop an approach to the patent–competition interface that is sensitive to their domestic circumstances. One size does not fit all even among developing countries.

1. A Proposed Framework

Having examined how the United States and the European Union have approached the two doctrines and the various doctrinal considerations raised in the case law, we are in a position to canvass the previous discussions about theoretical issues, theories of harm, and doctrinal considerations to propose an analytical framework for developing countries to apply them. What follows, however, is merely intended as a suggestion. The foregoing discussion should provide enough ideas for a developing country authority from which to draw to fashion its own approach. For unilateral refusal to supply a physical input, a competition authority may deem refusal by a dominant firm to supply unlawful if (1) it entails the termination of an existing course of dealing between the plaintiff and the defendant, (2) the refusal evinces a predatory intent as shown by a variety of evidence such as the intent to enter the market from which the plaintiff will be displaced or a willingness to sacrifice profit

[262] Larry A DiMatteo, 'Terminology Matters: Dangers of Superficial Transplantation' (2019) 37 Boston University International Law Journal 35. John W Cairns, 'Watson, Walton, and the History of Legal Transplants' (2013) 41 Georgia Journal of International and Comparative Law 637; Emilian Ciongaru, 'Negative Effects of Incorrect Legal Transplantation of European Union Legislation' (2013) 92 Procedia—Social and Behavioral Sciences 186.

opportunities, (3) the refusal inflicts competitive harm, which can be illustrated through one of the four proffered theories of harm, among others, and (4) the refusal is not excused by a valid business justification.

Meanwhile, a unilateral refusal to license patented technology will be deemed unlawful if (1) the refusal pertains to a technology that is essential or indispensable for the plaintiff's operations, with essentiality and indispensability understood as impracticality rather than physical impossibility, (2) the refusal prevents the emergence of a new product which satisfies an unmet consumer demand, where the new product requirement is interpreted flexibly in accordance with the technological capacity of the country at issue, (3) the refusal is not excused by a valid business justification, and (4) the refusal will foreclose the party seeking access from the downstream or other relevant markets, leading to a significant loss of competition in that market.

2. A Summary of Prior Discussions Relevant for Application of Framework

It will be helpful to summarize the foregoing discussion. First and foremost, it is important to reiterate that compulsory licensing under the unilateral refusal to deal doctrine and the essential facilities doctrine is unlikely to have a significant adverse effect on innovation incentives. The impact on the innovation incentives of the incumbent innovator, the competitor innovator, and the cumulative innovator is likely to be benign or neutral. Even if there was any detrimental effect, it is likely to be insubstantial. This is of paramount importance because one of the strongest objections to applying the two doctrines to patented technology is that doing so would undermine innovation incentives. A host of other implementation difficulties have also been addressed. It is also important, however, to recall that liberal use of compulsory licensing may deter voluntary technology transfer by foreign technology owners and may cause them to resort to means of transfer that redound fewer technological benefits to developing countries.

Although it is not meant to be taken as a rigid classification, in general, the unilateral refusal to deal doctrine is more readily applicable to physical input while the essential facilities doctrine is more suitable for technology licensing. The EU refusal to license case law is obviously mostly applicable to technology licensing as well. This is partly because of the way the doctrines are crafted. It also seems to make sense from the perspective of reconciling the conflict between competition policy and patent policy. The essential facilities doctrine imposes the more stringent requirements of essentiality and infliction of a severe competitor disadvantage. Compulsory licensing is more burdensome on patent rights than the compelled supply of a patented input and hence should be used more sparingly. The European courts seem to have made a less explicit distinction between these two doctrines. They have never even mentioned the essential facilities doctrine by name. In substance, however, one can clearly distinguish the *Commercial Solvents* line of cases, which were crafted with physical input in mind, from *Magill* and its progeny, which were intended for intellectual property. For ease of reference we will refer to the *Commercial Solvents* line of cases as the EU unilateral refusal to deal cases.

The two doctrines take divergent analytical approaches. The emphasis under the essential facilities doctrine or its EU equivalent is essentiality or indispensability. The new product or a second market requirement seems to have replaced theories of harm as an indication of consumer harm. Recall, however, that foreclosure of downstream competition is a pertinent theory of harm and should be required in essential facilities cases. Developing countries face a dilemma with respect to the new product requirement. On the one hand, the requirement helps to ensure consumer harm, at least in the form of denial of innovation. On the other hand, insisting on a demanding new product requirement could erect significant hurdles for developing countries to invoke the doctrine. Most developing countries do not possess the technological capacity to utilize an advanced technology to create a new product. The stringent approach to the requirement under *Magill* is probably unrealistic for most of them as it would effectively put the doctrine beyond their reach.

Depending on their technological capacity, developing countries may prefer to emulate the approach to the new product requirement in *IMS Health* and *Microsoft* instead. Those with nothing more than a technology adaptation capacity will probably fail the new product requirement. A more flexible approach to the requirement under *IMS Health* may be advisable. This is further justified by the fact that even under this approach, denial of access to a critical facility would result in higher prices for consumers. As argued earlier, applying the essential facilities doctrine or its EU equivalent in this manner effectively turns it into regulation of excessive pricing. While some advanced jurisdictions such as the US vehemently object to applying competition law to police excessive pricing, such application is more justified in poorer developing countries. Consumers in these countries can ill-afford higher prices and would expect their competition authorities to tackle excessive prices. Those with a higher technological capacity—the proto-innovation countries—are better positioned to improve on the technology to deliver a better product. The *Microsoft* approach would be suitable.

Meanwhile, commentators have stressed the importance of formulating a coherent theory of harm for these cases, which include enhancement of entry barriers, facilitation price discrimination, foreclosure of vertically related markets, and creation of effective exclusivity for the unilateral refusal to deal cases and foreclosure of downstream competition in the essential facilities cases. Given the lack of an essentiality or indispensability requirement, it becomes particularly important for the application of the unilateral refusal to deal doctrine to be guided by a coherent theory of harm. This is especially so because none of the legal tests for the doctrine that have been examined earlier, such as the scope of patent test, the subjective intent/pretext test, and Baker's no business justification rule, seem to provide a principled way in which the doctrine can be broadly applied. If none of these tests can capture most of the circumstances in which a unilateral refusal to deal can inflict consumer harm, it becomes important to articulate a coherent theory of harm.

Other doctrinal considerations that have been previously discussed include a course of prior dealing and predatory intent. It was argued earlier that developing countries need to take cases involving a course of prior dealing and predatory intent seriously. Cases involving prior dealing would most probably feature a plaintiff that has made significant relationship-specific investments. Given the low level of investments in developing countries, investments related to technology implementation deserve special protection. Cases involving predatory intent also call for attention because they involve attempts to drive a developing country firm with technological capacity out of the market. Given the dearth of technological capacity in developing countries, such conduct should not be facilely condoned.

With regard to the competitive relationship between the plaintiff and the defendant, there seems to be a consensus in the United States that they not be competitors in the primary product market as far as the unilateral refusal to deal doctrine is concerned. This is motivated by a desire to preserve the primary product market for the patentee to recoup her R&D investments. The consequence is that most of the cases have involved aftermarkets. In the essential facilities cases, the US courts seem to have adopted contrary logic. As opposed to barring competitors in the downstream market from bringing these cases—and the downstream market in most cases is the market from which investments are recovered—commentators believe that the party seeking access needs to be a downstream competitor. In the EU refusal to license cases, the European courts do not seem to share the same apprehension about letting a primary product competitor seek access to an intellectual property, as evidenced by *IMS Health* and *Microsoft*. In *IMS Health*, the intellectual property was developed with input from the industry.[263] In *Microsoft*, the market from which rivals were allegedly excluded was the work group server operating systems market, which was considered in the case as a secondary market.[264] *Commercial Solvents* does not involve a primary product market; at issue is a downstream market for the chemical ingredient. Still the Court did not seem intent on cordoning off the primary product market from the party seeking access.

To the extent that the US approach is motivated by the need to preserve innovation incentives, these concerns no longer deserve much weight. Therefore, the EU approach, which allows cases involving a primary product competitor to proceed,

263 *IMS Health*, para 5.
264 *Microsoft*, para 454.

is advisable. The requirement of a downstream competitor under the essential facilities doctrine or its EU equivalent serves a useful purpose. In reality, however, it is highly unlikely that a firm which shares no competitive relationship with the facility owner whatsoever will seek access to the facility. And if the facility owner and the party seeking access do compete, they most often do in the downstream market.

3. Nature of Compulsory License and Technological Capacity

One of the issues that has been left unaddressed thus far is the nature of compulsory licensing. Compulsory licensing can be imposed in two senses. The first is where the putative licensee already possess the technology, either through reverse engineering or other means, and is prevented from implementation by the patentee's rights. If a compulsory license is imposed in this situation, it merely requires the patentee to authorize the putative license to use the technology subject to reasonable compensation. It does not entail actual technology transfer. A putative licensee cannot use the compulsory license to obtain technical capability that it does not already possess. This has been called a mere authorization license. A mere authorization license is tantamount to an 'independent invention defense', which exists in US copyright law but not patent law, whereby the infringer will escape infringement if she can prove that she came up with the creation independently.[265]

The second sense in which a compulsory license can be imposed is the conventional understanding that the patentee is required to transfer an actual technology to the licensee. The patentee most probably will also need to transfer the technical know-how necessary for the implementation of the transferred technology. Such kind of compulsory license permits genuine technology transfer. This was previously called an active assistance license. It will redound greater benefits to developing countries, but also invites stronger objection from technology owners.

These two kinds of compulsory license have different degrees of usefulness for developing countries. Different levels of technological capacity are required by the two kinds of license. Mere authorization licenses require the domestic firm to come up with the technology independently through its own imitative effort. The level of technological capacity required may not be much lower than that needed for the original innovation. Recall it was noted in Chapter 2 that the time and effort it takes to imitate a technology is often not much less than that required to create it in the first place. Even active assistance licenses pose technological requirements on the licensee. The licensee must possess sufficient technological capacity to acquire and adapt foreign technology.

[265] Samson Vermont, 'Independent Invention as a Defense to Patent Infringement' (2006) 105 Michigan Law Review 475.

The very important question for developing countries is what type of compulsory license should be imposed even if a unilateral refusal to deal or essential facilities claim is established. Liberal use of compulsory licensing would of course improve the country's access to technology. It would, however, be a meaningless exercise if firms in the country do not possess the capacity to utilize the technology. Therefore, the first prerequisite for the imposition of compulsory license is that firms in the country must possess the requisite technological capacity to absorb and implement the transferred technology. For countries that possess technology adaptation and innovation capacity, they are most likely capable of imitating a foreign technology if given the incentives and the opportunity to. For these countries, the prospect of a mere authorization license may help to spur these domestic firms to invest in R&D to reverse engineer an overseas technology.

Recall the competitive R&D race posited by Gilbert and Shapiro. They argue that the prospect of compulsory licensing would remove the incentives of the competitor to invest to win the race. If, however, the license is an authorization one, the prospect of compulsory licensing may have salutary effects on domestic innovation incentives in the context of an R&D race between a developing country technology follower and a developed country technology leader. The developing country firm will still have full incentives to catch up as it will need to reverse engineer the technology first before it can avail itself of the compulsory license. Therefore, for technology adaptation and proto-innovation countries, compulsory licensing should be confined to mere authorization licenses.

Only production countries should be entitled to active assistance licenses. Because of their poor technology capacity, these countries are unlikely to be beneficiaries of compulsory licenses of technology, especially relatively advanced ones, under the essential facilities doctrine. They are most likely to make use of the unilateral refusal to deal doctrine to obtain essential patented input. To the extent that the supply of such input requires technical assistance such as transfer of know-how, foreign technology owners should be required to provide it. Doing so would allow production countries to make meaningful use of the doctrines to gain access to technology. This approach is also justified from a doctrinal perspective. Under the various theories of harm under the unilateral refusal to deal doctrine, the competitive or consumer harm goes beyond the simple denial of access to a technology and concomitant supra-competitive prices charged by the incumbent. There is independent consumer harm that needs to be remedied. It may hence be more justified to require the patentee to provide active assistance to the licensee to ensure that the patented input can be successfully deployed.

In contrast, even with the theory of harm of foreclosure of downstream competition, the competitive or consumer harm in most essential facilities cases stems from the denial of access to technology. The main theory of harm is that the plaintiff needs access to the defendant's patented technology to compete with the defendant. Where the competitive harm is more confined, it may be appropriate to limit the defendant's obligation to mere authorization and require the plaintiff to bear the responsibility of independently developing the technology.

4. Developing Country-Specific Considerations

(a) Using compulsory licensing to facilitate technology transfer

One of the most conflicting policy questions facing developing countries is to what extent compulsory licensing should be used to facilitate technology transfer. On the one hand, compulsory licensing provides the most effective means for developing countries to secure technology transfer. Despite admonitions about the need to have a coherent theory of harm, the fact is that foreclosure of downstream competition is often not difficult to prove once it has been proven that the technology is essential and denial of access would inflict a severe competitive disadvantage on rivals. More liberal interpretations of the various elements in the essential facilities doctrine or its EU equivalent could open the door to an aggressive use of the doctrine to import foreign technology coercively. An active assistance license directly transfers technology to the licensee. Even a mere authorization license would be highly beneficial to those developing countries that possess the technological capacity to reverse engineer advanced technologies from industrialized economies. These countries do not yet have the capacity to innovate, but they have the ability to imitate. Compulsory licensing would remove the most critical barrier to the commercialization of a reverse engineered technology.

On the other hand, using competition law to facilitate technology transfer raises many difficult issues. First, as mentioned earlier, aggressive use of compulsory licensing may undermine the robustness of patent protection, causing foreign technology owners to abstain from technology transfer or to shift to modes of transfer that redound fewer technology benefits to the country. This is especially pertinent as most of the countries that stand to benefit from a mere authorization license are heavily reliant on foreign technology transfer. Second, the Agreement on Trade-Related Aspects of Intellectual Property Rights (TRIPS Agreement) restricts what developing countries can do in terms of compulsory licensing. Third, even if developing countries manage to stay on the right side of TRIPS, they would incur the opprobrium if not the wrath of industrialized economies, especially the United States which in recent years has taken a more much confrontational approach in trade matters and a more aggressive stance in protecting its intellectual property rights.[266] The industrialized economies would most certainly retaliate against

266 Jerome H Reichman, 'Compulsory Licensing of Patented Pharmaceutical Inventions: Evaluating the Options' (2009) 37 Journal of Law, Medicine & Ethics 247, 258–59; Donald Harris, 'TRIPs after Fifteen Years: Success or Failure, as Measured by Compulsory Licensing' (2011) 18 Journal of Intellectual Property Law 367, 392–93.

developing countries. The political reality of the situation is such that the freedom of action for developing countries may be much more limited than suggested by purely legal analysis. These are the risks that need to be taken into account in formulating a policy regarding the use of compulsory licensing.

The TRIPS Agreement imposes restrictions on the scope of action for developing countries in terms of competition law regulation of patent licensing practices and compulsory licensing. Article 40 of the TRIPS Agreement expressly authorizes developing countries to apply competition law to police abusive patent exploitation practices.[267] Article 31 of the TRIPS Agreement imposes a host of conditions which must be met before a compulsory license can be granted.[268] A compulsory license imposed under competition law, however, is exempted from most of these conditions. Only two conditions continue to apply, which are that the determination shall be made on an individual basis and that adequate compensation shall be offered to the patentee.[269] Any unilateral refusal to supply claim would be individually adjudicated, as is true of every competition law case. Adequate compensation does not mean fully commercial terms. Article 31(k) explicitly provides that 'the need to correct anti-competitive practices may be taken into account in determining the amount of remuneration in such cases'.[270] Therefore, while some compensation must be offered to the patentee for the compulsory license, the royalty need not reflect the full commercial value of the licensed technology. In any case, it has been insisted throughout the foregoing discussion that compulsory licensing is not free licensing and that the patentee must be offered adequate compensation. Both conditions will be fully met under the framework proposed in this chapter.

The TRIPS Agreement does not set out any limitations on how competition law can regulate patent exploitation practices. Article 40(1) acknowledges that 'some licensing practices or conditions pertaining to intellectual property rights which restrain competition may have adverse effects on trade and may impede the transfer and dissemination of technology'.[271] Article 40(2) further authorizes the World Trade Organization (WTO) member states to adopt 'appropriate measures to prevent or control such practices'.[272] The provision then proceeds to enumerate a number of anticompetitive licensing practices that may be subject to regulation, such as exclusive grantbacks, no-challenge clauses, and coercive package licenses.

There is some uncertainty as to whether unilateral refusal to license intellectual property falls within the scope of conduct that can be subject to competition law regulation under the TRIPS Agreement. On the one hand, one can argue that

[267] General Agreement on Trade-Related Aspects of Intellectual Property (hereinafter "TRIPS Agreement"), 1869 UNTS 299, 33 ILM 1197 (1994), art 40.
[268] ibid art 31.
[269] ibid art 31.
[270] ibid.
[271] ibid art 40(1).
[272] ibid art 40(2).

Article 40(1) only refers to licensing practices or conditions. It would be a stretch to argue that licensing practices also encompass a unilateral refusal to license, which clearly contemplates the absence of a license. It is thus arguably not within the intended scope of Article 40(1) for signatories of the TRIPS Agreement to regulate unilateral refusal to license. On the other hand, unilateral refusal to supply intellectual property is well within the ambit of EU competition law. Given that the European Union is one of the two leading competition law jurisdictions in the world, it would be plausible to argue that Article 40, in authorizing TRIPS signatories to apply competition law to regulate patent exploitation practices, permits these signatories to pursue conduct that is regulated under EU competition law. There is, however, the further complication that EU competition law has never prohibited the unilateral refusal to license patent rights. One could hence argue that patents are beyond the scope of the unilateral refusal to deal doctrine under EU competition law. Given the sparse language in the relevant provisions in the TRIPS Agreement and the lack of WTO jurisprudence on these provisions, a definitive answer to this question may be elusive at this point. For our purpose, we will assume that it is permissible to regulate unilateral refusal to license patent rights under the TRIPS Agreement.

The greatest practical difficulty for developing countries to use compulsory licensing to facilitate technology transfer is probably the reaction of the industrialized economies. Aggressive use of competition law to override intellectual property rights, no matter how well justified doctrinally and policy-wise, would probably invite fierce backlash from the industrialized economies. Developing countries, especially the smaller ones with less political clout internationally, would need to tread carefully. This is despite the fact it was established previously that even extensive use of compulsory licensing may not undermine innovation incentives in most instances. Therefore, the imperative to obtain a foreign technology on its own should not support a duty to license. The invocation of both doctrines should be substantiated by a coherent theory of harm. Under the essential facilities doctrine or its EU equivalent, there should be careful consideration of the requirement of essentiality or indispensability. Denial of access should clearly result in foreclosure in the downstream market. And compulsory licenses should be limited to mere authorization licenses in technology adaptation and proto-innovation countries. The patentee should only be required to provide active assistance to the counterparty when a production country compels the patentee to supply patented products under the unilateral refusal to deal doctrine.

(b) Using compulsory licensing to satisfy development needs

Developing countries often suffer severe shortage of basic necessities such as foodstuffs, healthcare, education, energy, and basic sanitation. Poor nutrition, healthcare, and education do not only affect the current well-being of citizens in developing countries, they also undermine their future development potential.

Poor nutrition, especially during childhood, retards growth and cognitive development.[273] Lack of access to timely and adequate healthcare could leave behind lifelong disabilities and prevent citizens of developing countries from reaching their full potential as productive members of society.[274] This is probably an especially timely concern. The same is also true of limited educational opportunities.[275] Therefore, facilitating access to basic necessities is of the utmost importance to developing countries. The United Nations has incorporating access to these necessities as part of the Millennium Development Goals.[276] If the compulsory licensing of a patented technology or the compelled supply of a patented product can make an immediate and substantial contribution to the satisfaction of these basic needs, the two doctrines should be called into service. The archetypal case is if access to a patented drug at affordable prices could significantly improve the public health situation of the country, for example by bringing an epidemic under control.[277]

Compulsory licensing, however, cannot be imposed when access to the technology will only make indirect or insignificant contribution to the development needs of the country. For instance, access to a technology that significantly improves the yield of a cash crop does not meet the immediate and substantial standard. Access to the technology would raise farmers' income. Although there is no doubt that the well-being of many abjectly poor farmers in developing countries would be dramatically improved if the yield of a cash crop was boosted, permitting compulsory licensing in such a situation would risk an excessive erosion of the intellectual property regime. If compulsory licensing can be justified because it merely raises income, it would be very difficult to draw a principled limit on the scope of the doctrine. The argument would be different for a staple crop that serves as the main food source for the citizens of a developing country. Boosting the yield of such a crop would help to secure adequate food supply for the citizens of the country, hence fulfilling one of their basic needs.

[273] Susan P Walker and others, 'Child Development: Risk Factors for Adverse Outcomes in Developing Countries' (2007) 369 The Lancet 145.

[274] World Health Organization, 'Economic Costs of Malaria' <https://www.malariaconsortium.org/userfiles/file/Malaria%20resources/RBM%20Economic%20costs%20of%20malaria.pdf> accessed 4 March 2020.

[275] Pedro Nicolaci da Costa, 'A Lack of Education Can Literally Be Deadly' (*World Economic Forum*, 13 February 2018) <https://www.weforum.org/agenda/2018/02/this-startling-imf-chart-shows-how-poverty-and-lack-of-access-to-education-are-literally-deadly> accessed 4 March 2020.

[276] United Nations, 'Sustainable Development Goals Kick off with Start of New Year' <https://www.un.org/sustainabledevelopment/blog/2015/12/sustainable-development-goals-kick-off-with-start-of-new-year/> accessed 4 March 2020.

[277] Reichman (n 266); Reed Beall and Randall Kuhn, 'Trends in Compulsory Licensing of Pharmaceuticals Since the Doha Declaration: A Database Analysis' [2012] PloS Medicine <https://journals.plos.org/plosmedicine/article%3Fid%3D10.1371/journal.pmed.1001154> accessed 4 March 2020.

5. Country-Specific Recommendations

(a) Production countries

The production countries lack the technological capacity to absorb advanced technology from industrialized economies. They will be unlikely to benefit from compelled technology transfer under the essential facilities doctrine or its EU equivalent. And if the doctrine could somehow be invoked in a production country, perhaps when applied to a more basic technology, the new product requirement should be kept to a minimum. These countries stand to benefit from low prices even if no new or improved product is created. The unilateral refusal to deal doctrine, which mostly applies to patented product, will be of greater interest to these countries. Insisting on a coherent theory of harm will be important when applying the unilateral refusal to deal doctrine. Creation of effective exclusivity is unlikely to be a relevant theory of harm for them given their lack of technological capacity to be a primary product competitor with a global technological leader. Production countries should focus on the other theories of harm, namely enhancement of entry barriers, facilitation of price discrimination, and foreclosure of vertically related markets. Prior dealing and predatory intent will be particularly important considerations for these countries because of the dearth of domestic investments and technological capacity. For these countries, the patentee could only be required to provide active assistance to the counterparty when the patentee is compelled to supply patented products under the unilateral refusal to deal doctrine. Lastly, these countries, being the poorest of developing countries, are the most likely to be in a position to deploy these doctrines to help satisfy development needs.

(b) Technology adaptation countries

The technology adaptation countries will have the capacity at least to absorb imported technology and reverse engineer foreign technology. Therefore, both the unilateral refusal to deal doctrine and the essential facilities doctrine or its EU equivalent will be of relevance. Obtaining a critical physical input may allow these firms to compete with a technologically advanced firm in its primary product market as well as the aftermarket. Therefore, all four theories of harm under the unilateral refusal to deal doctrine will be of interest. Protecting relationship-specific investments and firms with technological capacity from predatory conduct are still important for these countries. When applying the essential facilities doctrine or its EU equivalent, these countries would be wise to follow the approach of *IMS Health* to the new product requirement. These countries are unlikely to possess the technological capacity to make significant improvements to a technologically advanced product. Applying a more stringent new product requirement would effectively eviscerate the essential facilities doctrine in these countries.

Compulsory licenses issued under the essential facilities doctrine should be mere authorization licenses only.

These countries, however, also need to balance the imperative to impose compulsory licensing with the need to attract foreign technology transfer. More robust patent protection generally attracts more technology transfer and helps to steer the mode of transfer to foreign direct investment (FDI) and licensing, which redound greater benefit to developing countries. Overseas technology firms will be less likely to engage in technology transfer through FDI and licensing if they know that doing so will improve the technological capacity of local firms to such an extent that these firms will be in a position to reverse engineer other related technologies, which will render them more likely to invoke the essential facilities doctrine to overcome patent protection.

(c) Proto-innovation countries

The proto-innovation countries possess innovation capacity in at least some industries. In some of them their technological capacity may even rival that of industrialized economies. These countries will need to adjust their approach according to the industry at issue. First of all, both the unilateral refusal to deal doctrine and the essential facilities doctrine will be pertinent to these countries. In those industries in which they do not possess innovation capacity, the analysis largely follows that of the technology adaptation countries. In those industries in which these countries possess innovation capacity, the essential facilities doctrine will need to be applied judiciously. The argument for using compulsory licensing to facilitate technology transfer is even weaker when the country itself possesses the capacity to innovate in the industry at issue. In such an industry, the new product requirement will need to be elevated to provide a meaningful hurdle for the application of the doctrine. The *Microsoft* approach, which requires a technically improved product, should be considered. Among the various theories of harm under the unilateral refusal to deal doctrine, creation of effective exclusivity will be particularly applicable to these countries as they are more likely to possess firms that are primary product market competitors with a global technological leader.

6. Enforcement Capacity Issues

One needs to be mindful of the constraints on the enforcement capacity of developing country authorities when offering suggestions on how they should approach certain competition law issues. Analytical approaches that take into account all the relevant factors, make use of the most advanced theoretical insights, and require the most sophisticated statistical analysis may work well for industrialized economies but be ill-suited for developing countries. Developing country authorities may lack the expertise or resources to employ such advanced analytical approaches.[278] This is especially true for those from the poorest developing countries, whose authorities may be most inadequately funded and most lacking in expertise. Analytical approaches that require a comprehensive account of market conditions and competitive effects may be beyond their reach.

While it is impossible to quantify precisely the institutional capacity of a competition authority (nor would such an exercise be entirely useful), it may be possible to come up with some rough classification and offer suggestions accordingly. For our purpose, we will categorize the institutional capacity of a developing country authority into low, medium, and high. A low-capacity authority would be one that possesses little in-house legal and economic expertise, lacks the resources to undertake large-scale and complex investigations, and is capable of not much more than simple cartel cases and the most straightforward merger review cases, such as a merger to monopoly. Abuse of dominance and complex vertical agreement cases are beyond their reach.

A high-capacity authority would be one that is almost on par with the authorities in advanced jurisdictions in terms of personnel, resources, level of sophistication, and experience. CADE in Brazil, COFECE in Mexico, and the South African Competition Commission come to mind. A high-capacity authority has the capability to handle all sorts of difficult conduct cases and undertake sophisticated economic analysis of the most complicated mergers.

A medium-capacity authority falls somewhere in between. It possesses some modicum of legal and economic expertise and is capable of handling somewhat complex conduct and merger cases. Highly sophisticated economic analysis of mergers such as merger simulation, however, is probably beyond its reach. While external assessment of an authority's institutional capacity may be more impartial and objective, ultimately an authority itself knows best what it is capable of and has no reason to misrepresent its capacity or manipulate the assessment exercise when the purpose of the assessment is to determine an appropriate analytical approach for particular conduct.

Thankfully, most of the elements required under the two doctrines, such as a course of prior dealing and predatory intent under the unilateral refusal to deal doctrine and essentiality or indispensability under the essential facilities doctrine, are generally factual issues that do not require extensive use of economic theory or evidence. Determination of these requirements should entail relatively straightforward fact-finding, at least as compared to a full competitive effects analysis. Authorities at all levels of capacity should be able to handle the analysis under these elements. Analysis under the various theories of harm, however, may require more expertise and may present more difficulties for low-capacity authorities.

[278] Michal Gal, 'The Ecology of Antitrust Preconditions for Competition Law Enforcement in Developing Countries', in Philippe Brusick, Ana Maria Alvarez, Lucian Cernat, and Peter Holmes (eds), *Competition, Competitiveness and Development* (UNCTAD 2004) 28–30.

Authorities that are unable to muster the technical expertise and resources to handle the analysis may need to forego these doctrines. While this may represent a significant loss of enforcement opportunity for these authorities, the risk of erroneous decisions may be too great if no coherent theory of harm is presented in the case. Analysis under these theories of harm is unlikely to present difficulties for the medium-capacity and high-capacity authorities.

It was also mentioned in Chapter 5 that the extent to which level of patent protection affects technology transfer differs by industry, which suggests that an industry-specific approach may be called for. It was also suggested that such an approach may require a relatively high level of enforcement capacity. For authorities with relatively low level of enforcement capacity, it may not be practical to implement an industry-specific approach and these authorities may need to arrive at an assessment of the overall relationship between compulsory licensing and voluntary and involuntary technology transfer. If it is concluded that the negative effect on voluntary technology transfer could be significant, these authorities may need to be particularly cautious about imposing compulsory licensing. This is especially true if the country at issue possesses substantial imitation capacity. It may be somewhat ironic that having established that compulsory licensing need not dampen innovation incentives, developing countries are told to eschew compulsory licensing because of the effects on technology transfer. This, however, seems inevitable if the country at issue relies heavily on FDI or licensing as sources of foreign technology. For countries with a higher level of enforcement capacity, a more discriminating industry-specific approach may help the authority arrive at more precise decisions.

It was mentioned in Chapter 5 that royalty setting will be inevitable in most compulsory licensing cases. In light of the lower institutional capacity of the competition authorities and the courts in developing countries, implementation will present even greater challenges to developing countries as compared to developed ones. If royalty setting is difficult even for developed country decision-makers, it may present insurmountable obstacles to developing country authorities. How a developing country authority or court should handle royalty setting will depend on its institutional capacity. A low-capacity authority is unlikely to encounter the need to set royalty because instances of compulsory licensing imposed under the essential facilities doctrine are likely to be extremely rare in production countries. For a medium-capacity authority, the best that it can do may be to set a range for the royalty and let the parties bargain between them. While proposing a precise number for the royalty without the capacity to digest a large volume of highly technical information and to undertake complex analysis may amount to guesswork, it should be easier to arrive at a relatively broad range of acceptable royalty.

The breadth of the range depends on a number of considerations. First, an authority with a relatively high level of expertise will have the confidence and the ability to arrive at a narrower range. Regardless of the authority's capacity, the authority should compel the parties to negotiate under the threat of direct intervention by the authority. The authority will step in to set the royalty if the parties fail to reach an agreement. Here it is important for the authority to appear impartial. If the authority is known for a pro-licensee tendency, for example, the putative licensee will have greater incentives to hold out, knowing that it is likely to obtain a favourable outcome from the authority should the negotiation fail.[279] Second, the authority may adjust the range in light of policy reasons to achieve a desired outcome. If the authority believes that there are policy reasons for a relatively higher (or lower) royalty, the authority can adjust the maximum (or the minimum) accordingly to push for a desired level of royalty. For a high-capacity authority, royalty can be set in accordance with the prevailing approaches in the advanced jurisdictions, such as application of the *Georgia-Pacific* factors, while cognisant of the difficulties attendant in the exercise.

D. Conclusion

The present chapter and Chapter 5 have tried to illustrate how the unilateral refusal to deal doctrine and the essential facilities doctrine or its EU equivalent can be applied by developing countries to improve their access to technology. Overall, it cannot be said that there is a strong case for these countries to enforce these doctrines against patented technologies aggressively. While there are no strong valid objections to the measured and case-by-case application of these doctrines with respect to patented technology, as dampening of innovation incentives has been shown not to be a persuasive argument against the doctrines when applied on a case-by-case basis, practical considerations and the political reality are such that there is a need for caution. Compulsory licensing may deter technology transfer and cause such transfer to shift to modes that redound fewer technological benefits to developing countries. Moreover, aggressive use of compulsory licensing may invite retaliation from the industrialized economies to the great peril of developing countries, especially the poorer ones with smaller economies. While this does not mean that developing countries should repudiate these doctrines altogether, they will need to apply them in a principled manner, grounded by a valid and coherent theory of harm and taking full account of the myriad policy considerations. This admittedly will not be an easy task for many developing countries. But the reward in terms of alleviation of consumer harm and gains in technological capacity could render the effort worthwhile.

[279] Richard A Epstein and Kayvan B Noroozi, 'Why Incentives for "Patent Holdout" Threaten to Dismantle FRAND. and Why It Matters' (2017) 32 Berkeley Technology Law Journal 1381; Bowman Heiden and Nicolas Petit, 'Patent "Trespass" and the Royalty Gap: Exploring the Nature and Impact of Patent Holdout' (2017) 34 Santa Clara High Technology Law Journal 179; Colleen V Chien, 'Holding Up and Holding Out' (2014) 21 Michigan Telecommunications & Technology Law Review 1.

7
Patent Tying

A. Introduction

After unilateral refusal to license, tying involving a patented tying product ('patent tying') is probably the patent exploitation practice with the greatest salience for developing countries. Unlike some patent exploitation practices such as licensing restrictions or abuses related to standard essential patents (SEPs), which would only be relevant to developing countries with technological adaptation and innovation capacities, patent tying can affect every developing country. Patent tying can extract surplus from consumers and foreclose rivals in the tying and the tied product markets, which can affect every developing country regardless of its technological capacity. This is especially true of surplus extraction. Therefore, developing country authorities should devote attention to patent tying practices.

Compared to unilateral refusal to license, tying probably poses a less acute dilemma in terms of the policy conflict underlying the patent–competition interface. After all, it does not seek directly to override patent protection. The main policy challenges presented by patent tying is whether it can be justified in the name of generating additional innovation incentives and the impact of foreclosure on the acquisition of technological capacity. By imposing a tie, a patentee can implement price discrimination, which would allow the patentee to extract more consumer surplus and hence boost her financial reward from the patent system. It is often argued that increasing patentee reward will boost innovation incentives. If this argument is indeed valid developing countries will have an additional consideration to pay heed to in the regulation of patent tying. If it is shown, however, that patent tying does not boost patentee reward or innovation incentives, the case for caution in regulating patent tying would be much weaker. The potential dynamic efficiency implications of surplus extraction can be set aside. The ensuing discussion will illustrate that in a vast majority of cases, price-discriminating ties will pose direct and unmitigated harm to consumers.

Once the innovation incentive argument in the context of surplus extraction is properly disposed of, attention can be turned to other anticompetitive effects of tying. Another main competitive harm of tying is foreclosure of rivals in the tying and the tied product markets. To the extent that rivals need to acquire technological capacity to compete with the incumbents, foreclosure can retard technological upgrade and render it more difficult for rivals to acquire the requisite technological capacity. The extent to which foreclosure should concern developing

The Patent–Competition Interface in Developing Countries. Thomas K. Cheng, Oxford University Press. © Thomas K. Cheng 2021. DOI: 10.1093/oso/9780192857354.003.0007

countries would vary in accordance with their technological capacity. Economists have come up with a variety of models on the foreclosure effects of tying. Some of them are technology-agnostic while some are premised on a certain degree of technological capacity on the part of the rivals. Some even depict research and development (R&D) competition between the incumbent and rivals. Therefore, while the technology-agnostic ones would be valid for all developing countries, the technology-intensive ones would be more relevant for the technological adaptation countries and the proto-innovation countries. Developing countries in general should also pay greater heed to foreclosure in the tied product market as the tied products are generally technologically less demanding and serve as a stepping-stone for developing country firms to master the tying product technology.

This chapter will begin with a discussion of the price discrimination potential of tying in general. It will examine the different categories of price discrimination and how tying can be used to facilitate price discrimination. Importantly, it will demonstrate that most instances of price discrimination facilitated by tying harm consumers and should constitute grounds for condemning tying unless it can be shown to redound other benefits.

The chapter will next move to an examination of one of the most frequently invoked arguments in defence of patent tying, that it helps to generate additional innovation incentives. It will be suggested that this argument should be rejected on a number of grounds. First, there is no evidence that the current patent system generates insufficient innovation incentives and needs supplementation. Second, even if it is decided that extra innovation incentives are needed, there is no assurance that the additional financial reward provided by patent tying will necessarily be invested in future R&D. Third, allowing the patentee to appropriate all surplus from her innovation through tying will be counterproductive and highly detrimental to social welfare as it precludes technological spillovers, which are a key driver of technological progress. Fourth, relying on patent tying to augment innovation incentives will skew R&D investments toward technologies that give rise to opportunities for tying. Lastly, it has been shown that patent tying actually reduces innovation incentives, especially in the tied product market.

The focus will next shift to foreclosure and the leverage theory. Economists have proposed numerous models of offensive leveraging, which is used to acquire or protect market power in the tied product market, and defensive leveraging, which helps the incumbent protect its position in the tying product market. Some of these models will be examined in relative detail and light will be shed on the implications of these models for developing countries, especially as it pertains to their technological upgrade.

What follows will be a brief discussion of the static welfare effects of patent tying, including the deadweight loss emanating from the exclusion of consumers and the rent-seeking behaviour induced by monopoly power. Any discussion of tying will be incomplete without some attention to the various pro-competitive justifications of tying. These include the ubiquity of tying, elimination of double marginalization, savings of production and distribution costs, savings of consumer search costs, and quality assurance. It will be concluded that most of these justifications are unconvincing. Some of them, such as elimination of double marginalization, are the most beneficial in market conditions when foreclosure is the least probable. Some of them, such as savings in distribution and consumer search costs, are unlikely to be substantial enough to offset significant foreclosure harm. Some of them, such as quality assurance, can often be attained through less competition-restricting means.

The chapter concludes with a proposal for a doctrinal framework for tying in developing countries. Separate proposals are made for developing countries depending on the enforcement capacity of their competition authorities. A simpler qualified *per se* rule is propounded for countries with lower enforcement capacity. Patent tying will be prohibited once a number of conditions are met. Apart from the constituent elements of a tie, including the existence of separate products and the presence of consumer coercion as a result of market power in the tying product market, these include the prerequisites for surplus extraction such as that the tying and the tied products are used in variable proportions and do not share a perfect complementary relationship, and the absence of a price reduction for the tying product prior to the tie and output increase for the tied product following the tie.

For countries with an authority with a higher enforcement capacity, a more sophisticated two-stage framework will be offered. The first stage focuses on surplus extraction. Once the prerequisites for harm are established, the burden shifts to the defendant to show that its tie is justified by some pro-competitive justifications or that the tie does not in fact extract consumer surplus. If the defendant manages to rebut the presumption of surplus extraction, the analysis moves on to the second stage in which the authority or the plaintiff must demonstrate foreclosure effects and that these effects outweigh the pro-competitive benefits offered by the defendant in the previous stage. The plaintiff prevails if it succeeds in doing so.

B. Tying and Price Discrimination

Ever since Ward Bowman's suggestion of metred sales as a justification for tying[1] and George Stigler's explication of block-booking as a price discrimination device,[2] tying has been inextricably linked to price discrimination. Defenders of tying have repeatedly argued that tying should be upheld as a means to implement price discrimination. It allows the incumbent to extract surplus from consumers without

[1] Ward S Bowman, Jr, 'Tying Arrangements and the Leverage Problem' (1957) 67 Yale Law Journal 19.

[2] George J Stigler, 'United States v. Loew's Inc.: A Note on Block-Booking' (1963) 1963 The Supreme Court Review 152.

aggravating deadweight loss and creating other inefficiencies. Critics of tying contend that price discrimination results in a wealth transfer from consumers to the incumbent. Setting aside potentially complicated income distribution implications, there are no reasons to allow a monopolist to extract surplus from consumers with impunity. Einer Elhauge, who has called the various forms of surplus extraction power effects, insists that surplus extraction clearly harms consumer welfare and has long provided the grounds upon which tying is condemned.[3] If tying is viewed as a means to implement price discrimination, one's stance on tying will be informed by one's assessment of the welfare effects of price discrimination. And if one accepts that price discrimination often has an ambiguous impact on total welfare but unequivocally harms consumers, the schism between the critics and the defenders of tying evolves into a debate about the proper welfare standard for competition law.

In the context of patent tying, price discrimination takes on added significance because shift of surplus from consumers to the producer represents more than pure wealth transfer. The increase in surplus may boost patentee reward and hence innovation incentives. Price discrimination can be used to augment patentee reward. This means that price discrimination may have direct dynamic efficiency implications, which deserves special attention from a developing country perspective. This discussion will be deferred to the next section.

1. Different Types of Price Discrimination

Even since Arthur Cecil Pigou, price discrimination has been classified based on degree. Under this textbook classification, first-degree or perfect price discrimination refers to a situation in which a seller is able to charge each consumer the highest price she is willing to pay.[4] First-degree price discrimination is said to be economically efficient because it allows output to reach the competitive level.[5] With perfect price discrimination, the marginal revenue curve coincides with the demand curve, and output is at where the marginal cost curve intersects with the demand curve, which produces a competitive output level.[6] Economists therefore tend to view first-degree price discrimination favourably, which, however, is very difficult to execute in real life.[7]

[3] Einer Elhauge, 'Tying, Bundled Discounts, and the Death of the Single Monopoly Profit Theory' (2009) 123 Harvard Law Review 397, 434–35.

[4] Erik Hovenkamp and Herbert J Hovenkamp, 'Tying Arrangements and Antitrust Harm' (2010) 52 Arizona Law Review 925, 932.

[5] ibid.

[6] Douglas McTaggart, Christopher Findlay, and Michael Parkin, *Economics* (7th edn, Pearson Australia 2015) 226.

[7] Hovenkamp and Hovenkamp (n 4) 933.

With second-degree price discrimination, the seller offers consumers a uniform price schedule under which prices vary depending on the quantity or product variety.[8] A prime example is airfare. Airfare changes over time, rising the closer it is to the date of departure. The idea is that leisure travellers, who are more price-sensitive, tend to plan their travels farther in advance and will hence purchase their tickets ahead of time. In contrast, business travellers, who often have to travel at the last minute and are funded by the company budget, have less flexibility with time and are much less price-sensitive. They are able and willing to pay higher fares for the privilege to travel on short notice. How far ahead one purchases the plane ticket effectively serves as a proxy for price sensitivity. An alternative consumer attribute serves as a proxy for consumers' willingness to pay and allows the seller to vary its prices based on that attribute. Second-degree price discrimination approaches perfect price discrimination as the number of classifications in the price discrimination scheme increases.[9] The continuous as opposed to discrete nature of temporal classifications means that airfare could potentially approximate perfect price discrimination. In theory there could be infinite classifications based on time.

Third-degree price discrimination requires the seller to have the ability to identify and separate consumers in advance based on their willingness to pay. Once consumers are segregated, the seller charges each group a different price. Third-degree price discrimination is only feasible if the seller can readily verify customers' identity and effectively prevent arbitrage between them. Otherwise the whole scheme would unravel. The informational requirement for third-degree price discrimination is higher than that for second-degree price discrimination because the former only works if the seller is able to identify consumers' valuation of the product *ex ante*,[10] while the latter only requires the seller to know 'something about demand generally but could not identify the specific buyers at the time of the sale'.[11]

Instances of third-degree price discrimination include various kinds of discount schemes for different age or customer groups. Take student discount as an example. Students usually have a more limited ability to pay and their identity can be easily verified by requiring the production of a student identity card. They would be promising candidates for third-degree price discrimination. Such discrimination would be more feasible if the product at issue was not easily transferable between customers. One example would be railroad service. Many European countries offer student discounts for railroad service which, once purchased under one traveller's name, cannot be transferred to another traveller. Another example of such a discount scheme is the Japan Rail pass which railroad companies in Japan

8 ibid 934.
9 ibid 935.
10 ibid 936.
11 ibid.

offer to foreign tourists to make railroad travel in the country more affordable.[12] Registration of the pass requires the production of a foreign passport and the pass can only be used by the pass holder, who herself must be a foreign traveller.

The Hovenkamps argue that second-degree price discrimination is more likely to be welfare-enhancing because it does not exhibit 'discontinuities in marginal substitution that are characteristic of third-degree discrimination'.[13] Under second-degree price discrimination, the same price schedule is offered to all consumers. A consumer can shift between different classes of the product at different prices as her valuation changes over time. Consumers self-assign to different product classes.[14] This is not possible under third-degree price discrimination, under which each segregated consumer is only offered a single price. The consumer is excluded from the market if she refuses to accept the price. Such a mismatch would be of no concern if the seller could segregate consumers perfectly based on their willingness to pay. In reality, perfect discrimination is not feasible because whatever attribute the seller can use to distinguish consumers is unlikely to be perfectly correlated with their willingness to pay. Some consumers are bound to be unnecessarily excluded. Regarding second-degree price discrimination, the Hovenkamps assert that:

> the economic consensus is that most instances of it are probably welfare increasing, particularly in the presence of fixed costs. As we show below, variable proportion ties are a form of second-degree price discrimination. Further, they only harm consumer welfare in the most flagrant situations, and they often increase welfare even if output falls. Equally important is the fact that third-degree price discrimination transfers output from higher-value to lower-value customers, thus reducing welfare even if output remains constant. Second-degree price discrimination does not have this effect.[15]

They defend tying on the grounds that variable proportion ties, which are the most common type of tie used to price discriminate, constitute second-degree price discrimination which they argue does not generally harm consumers.

In contrast, as suggested by the Hovenkamps, the welfare effects of third-degree price discrimination are more ambiguous and harder to generalize. Determination of its welfare effects entails a comparison with the but-for world where price discrimination is absent. In the but-for world, the seller would probably charge a price in between the high and low prices offered to the two groups of customers.[16] Third-degree price discrimination thus allows those who will be assigned to the

[12] 'Japan Rail Pass (JR Pass)' <https://www.japan-guide.com/e/e2361.html> accessed 8 May 2020.
[13] Hovenkamp and Hovenkamp (n 4) 934–35.
[14] ibid 936.
[15] ibid 928–29.
[16] ibid 933–34.

low-price group but cannot afford the uniform monopolist price to purchase the product while preventing those who would purchase at the uniform price but are unwilling to do so at the price offered to the high-price group under price discrimination from purchasing the product.[17] In other words, third-degree price discrimination shifts output from high-valuation customers who would have been willing to pay the uniform monopolist price to low-valuation customers who shun that price.[18] This would result in a loss of consumer surplus. Consumer welfare would be harmed under third-degree price discrimination unless it results in an increase in output level,[19] which would happen if the low-valuation group outnumbers the high-valuation group.

2. How Tying Facilitates Price Discrimination

The most common way in which tying is said to facilitate price discrimination is what Bowman calls a metering or counting device[20] or what is more generally known as a variable-proportions tie. It turns out tying can facilitate price discrimination in other ways. Nicholas Economides enumerates three types of price discrimination implemented through tying based on the existing literature:[21] intra-product price discrimination,[22] intra-consumer price discrimination,[23] and inter-product price discrimination.[24]

Intra-product price discrimination is the familiar story of tying as a metering device. The quintessential example is probably printers as the tying product and replacement ink cartridges as the tied product.[25] The basic idea is that different consumers value their printers differently.[26] Some, such as those who home-office, print a lot while some only use their printers sparingly. A high-volume user places a high valuation on her printer whereas a low-volume user has a low valuation for it. In a world of perfect information and no arbitrage, the printer manufacturer would charge high-volume users a high price and low-volume users a low price for the printer. There is, however, probably little that the manufacturer can do at the point of sale to differentiate consumers based on their intensity of use. There is

[17] ibid 934.
[18] ibid.
[19] ibid 928.
[20] Bowman, Jr (n 1) 23–24.
[21] Nicholas Economides, 'Tying, Bundling, and Loyalty/Requirement Rebates' in Einer Elhauge (ed), *Research Handbook of the Economics of Antitrust Law* (Edward Elgar Publishing Ltd 2012) 121, 125, 127, 129.
[22] Bowman, Jr (n 1).
[23] Meyer L Burstein, 'The Economics of Tie–In Sales' (1960) 42 Review of Economics and Statistics 68.
[24] Stigler (n 2).
[25] Elhauge (n 3) 404.
[26] Economides (n 21) 125.

even less that the manufacturer can do to prevent arbitrage. Direct price discrimination is therefore unfeasible.[27]

What the manufacturer can do instead is to tie the sale of printers to the sale of replacement ink cartridges by allowing only its own cartridges to be used with its printers. Replacement cartridges are a suitable metering device because the more one prints, the more often one replaces the ink cartridge.[28] What the incumbent manufacturer sometimes does is to charge a competitive or perhaps even sub-competitive price for the printer, leaving consumers, especially the high-volume users, with substantial surplus. The manufacturer will attempt to appropriate some of this surplus by charging a supra-competitive price for the replacement ink cartridges. The more cartridges one uses, the more one's surplus from the printer will be transferred to the manufacturer. The manufacturer will hence be able to extract more consumer surplus with a tie than without one.[29] Moreover, apart from extracting consumer surplus, a metering tie could foreclose rivals in the tied product market.[30]

As the above example illustrates, tying as a metering device would only work if the tying and the tied products are used in variable proportions. If the two products are used in fixed proportions, usage of the tied product will not vary according to the consumer's intensity of use of the tying product and the manufacturer will not be able to extract more surplus from high-volume users through the sale of the tied product. Raising the price on the tied product would be the same as charging more for the tying product.[31] There is only one fixed price for the bundle. Because the same price schedule is offered to different consumers, who then self-select into different classes, a variable-proportions tie represents second-degree price discrimination.

Intra-consumer price discrimination, which Elhauge simply calls extraction of consumer surplus, can be said to be the mirror image of intra-product price discrimination. Consumers purchase one tying product and multiple units of the tied product under the latter whereas consumers purchase multiple units of the tying product but only one tied product under the former.[32] The two situations share the similarity that there is some leftover surplus associated with the tying product that can only be extracted with the sale of a tied product at supra-competitive prices, but they differ in how the surplus comes about. Under intra-product price discrimination, the surplus arises from the consumers' different valuations of the tying product. When the incumbent charges a uniform price for the tying product, some consumers are left with a large surplus and some with a small surplus, which

[27] ibid.
[28] ibid 125–26.
[29] ibid 125.
[30] ibid 126.
[31] ibid.
[32] ibid 127.

the incumbent can extract through the tie. Under intra-consumer price discrimination, the surplus arises from a single consumer's disparate valuations of the various units of the tying product that she purchases.[33] Because consumers value the various units differently but pay a uniform price for all of them, they are left with some surplus, which the incumbent can appropriate by selling a tied product at supra-competitive prices. Intra-consumer price discrimination only requires an individual consumer to have different valuations across units of the tying product. It is not premised on consumers displaying disparate valuations.[34] In fact, it would work even if all consumers have the exact same valuation patterns for the tying product.[35]

Under a tie, the incumbent charges supra-competitive prices for the tied product, which transfers part of the consumer surplus to the seller. Consumers are clearly harmed by a loss of surplus. Whether consumers will accept the tie comes down to a weighing of whatever surplus is left for consumers from the tying product after the tie against their surplus from purchasing the tied product at competitive prices.[36] If the latter exceeds the former, consumers will lose more than they gain by accepting the tie and will shun it. Conversely, if the former outweighs the latter, it will be worth the consumers' while to accept the tie. Consumers are more likely to accept the tie if they value the tying product more than the tied product so that they stand to lose more surplus by rejecting the tie. If consumers demand a different number of units of and thus enjoy different amounts of surplus from the tying product, as is likely to be the case, the bundle price will be set at a level where some consumers will necessarily turn down the tie.

The last way in which tying can facilitate price discrimination is through what has been called inter-product price discrimination. George Stigler pioneered the analysis of this type of price discrimination with his commentary on the block-booking case of *Loew's* decided by the US Supreme Court.[37] Under the previous two types of price discrimination, the incumbent uses tying to extract consumer surplus associated with the tying product, over which the incumbent has market power. The tied product is necessary because the incumbent cannot extract the surplus through single product sale. And the tied product market is often competitive.

The mechanics under inter-product price discrimination are slightly different. Under this type of price discrimination, the incumbent may wield market power in both markets.[38] To go back to the original example of block-booking discussed by Stigler, it is not always clear which film was the tying product and which the tied product. This probably varies by consumers. Stigler's analysis originally stipulated

[33] ibid.
[34] ibid 128.
[35] ibid.
[36] ibid.
[37] Stigler (n 2).
[38] Nicholas Economides, 'Bundling and Tying' (NYU Stern School of Business 2014) #14-22 5.

that the two products must have negatively correlated demand.[39] It was shown by subsequent commentators that Stigler's logic still works so long as demand of the two products is not very strongly positively correlated.[40] Inter-product price discrimination would not work with perfect complements where the tying and the tied products have no independent use without each other but is feasible even when the tying and the tied products are used in fixed proportions.[41]

Stigler's analysis is often illustrated with a numerical example, which will not be reproduced here.[42] The logic of the example is that when consumers' valuations of two products are not very strongly positively correlated, the seller can increase overall sales of and its profits from the two products while extracting consumer surplus by tying the sale of the two products together.[43] Tying allows the seller to avoid the dilemma of either setting the price of the product at the valuation of the low-valuation consumer and foregoing surplus that accrues to the high-valuation consumer or setting the price at the valuation of the high-valuation consumer, thereby extracting more of her surplus but losing sales to the low-valuation consumer.[44] With a tie, the seller can sell the bundle at the lowest valuation between the two consumers for the entire bundle and sell both products to both of them without leaving too much surplus on the table.[45]

With intra-product price discrimination and intra-consumer price discrimination, tying facilitates price discrimination by allowing the incumbent to charge an inflated price for the tied product. The surplus may be due to different consumers having different valuations of the tying product or the same consumer having disparate valuations of the multiple units of the tying product she consumes herself. In either case, surplus extraction relies on a second product. Intra-product price discrimination will only be an effective surplus extraction tool if consumers' valuation of the tying product is correlated with their demand for the tied product. This would obviate the seller's need to acquire information about consumers' valuation of the tying product.[46] In contrast, intra-consumer price discrimination does not allow precise calibration of surplus extraction against consumers' willingness to pay as each consumer is expected to purchase the same amount of the tied product at the same price. It is a blunter tool of price discrimination but nonetheless helps to extract surplus from consumers. Both types of price discrimination require the

39 Stigler (n 2) 153.

40 Dennis W Carlton and Michael Waldman, 'Robert Bork's Contributions to Antitrust Perspectives on Tying Behavior' (2014) 57 Journal of Law & Economics S121, 135.

41 Economides (n 21) 129.

42 Stigler (n 2) 153.

43 ibid.

44 ibid.

45 ibid.

46 Alan Devlin, 'A Neo-Chicago Perspective on the Law of Product Tying' (2007) 44 American Business Law Journal 521, 544.

tying and the tied products to be used in variable proportions.[47] They have no application to fixed-proportions ties.

With inter-product price discrimination, tying allows the seller to aggregate consumers' valuations across products, which will attract more consumers to buy both products without leaving too much surplus to the high-valuation consumer. It obviates the trade-off between setting a low price to attract the low-valuation consumer and foregoing surplus from the high-valuation consumer. Inter-product price discrimination fails with perfect complements but still works with goods that are consumed in fixed proportions, unlike the other two types of price discrimination.

All three types of price discrimination result in a loss of consumer surplus. Intra-product price discrimination may also foreclose rivals in the tied product market. Inter-product price discrimination tends to increase output level. Intra-product price discrimination could increase adoption of the tying product if the incumbent charges a competitive or even a sub-competitive price for the tying product. Some, however, have argued that this distorts resource allocation between the tying and the tied products and leads to overuse of the tying product and underuse of the tied product.[48]

3. Price Discrimination as a Justification for Tying

Whether facilitation of price discrimination should be accepted as a justification for tying depends on the impact of the various forms of price discrimination on consumer welfare. If a particular form of price discrimination raises consumer welfare, tying should be welcomed as far as it is used to pursue that kind of price discrimination. In contrast, if a particular form of price discrimination harms consumers, tying should be prohibited if it is used to implement that kind of price discrimination.

Intra-consumer price discrimination constitutes pure surplus extraction. That may explain why Elhauge simply calls it extraction of consumer surplus. It may be a misnomer to call it price discrimination because it does not necessarily entail discriminatory treatment of similarly situated consumers. It still works even when consumers do not display differing preferences for the tying product.[49] It does not affect output level or other parameters of competition. It only results in wealth transfer from consumers to the seller and will harm consumer welfare 'whenever the tied [product] buyers' purchases or valuations of the tying product

[47] Elhauge (n 3) 443.

[48] Severin Borenstein, Jeffrey K Mackie-Mason, and Janet S Netz, 'Antitrust Policy in Aftermarkets' (1995) 63 Antitrust Law Journal 455, 470.

[49] Elhauge (n 3) 435.

are significantly larger than for the tied product, which is typically true in actual tying cases'.[50] If competition law takes protection of consumer welfare seriously, intra-consumer price discrimination is the most indefensible of the three. Inter-product price discrimination simultaneously leads to output expansion and surplus extraction. In fact, one cannot be attained without the other. Foreclosure is also a less important concern with ties that bring about this type of price discrimination because the incumbent may already wield market power in both markets. Nonetheless, commentators have argued that inter-product price discrimination harms consumer welfare.[51]

The case for a variable-proportions tie is probably the most complex. At the most basic level, the characterization of the variable-proportions tie as a surplus extraction tool suggests that it results in wealth transfer from consumers to the seller, which is obviously detrimental to consumer welfare. This, however, is not the full picture. Dennis Carlton and Michael Waldman argue that variable-proportions ties are pro-competitive because they avoid inefficient substitution from the monopolized tying product to the competitively priced tied product.[52] By raising the price of the tied product to a supra-competitive level, a variable-proportions tie renders the tying and the tied products equally overpriced in the eyes of the consumers who will no longer shift their purchase from the monopolized product to the competitive product.

There are a number of problems with their argument. First, it would only be valid for tying and tied products that are to some extent substitutable for each other. They cite the example of durable goods such as a photocopying machine and maintenance services.[53] The two are partially substitutable because if the machine is expensive, users can spend more on repair and maintenance to prolong the life of the machine. Their argument about inefficient substitution, however, would have no application if the tying and the tied goods were not substitutes at all, such as printers and ink cartridges or airfare and hotel accommodation. Consumers cannot purchase more ink cartridges to reduce their need for printers or book an extra night of hotel in lieu of their plane ticket. Casual observation suggests that the kind of partially substitutable relationship between the tying and the tied products which Carlton and Waldman have in mind are the exception rather than the rule.

Second, and more importantly, while paying a higher price for the tied product to avoid inefficient substitution may be laudable from the perspective of allocative efficiency, it indisputably aggravates consumer welfare. From the consumers' point of view, if market power in the tying product market is unavoidable, paying

[50] ibid.

[51] ibid 434.

[52] Dennis W Carlton and Michael Waldman, 'How Economics Can Improve Antitrust Doctrine towards Tie-In Sales: Comment on Jean Tirole's "The Analysis of Tying Cases: A Primer"' (2005) 1 Competition Policy International 27, 36.

[53] ibid 34.

less for the tied product is no doubt preferable. What Carlton and Waldman have in mind when insisting that avoidance of inefficient substitution improves welfare is total welfare and not consumer welfare. If one accepts that the ultimate goal of competition law is protection of consumer welfare, avoidance of inefficient substitution hardly counts as a competitive benefit. Carlton and Waldman also note that variable-proportions ties can augment the incumbent's market power and lead to deadweight loss, which is clearly detrimental to consumers. Their claims overall do not detract from the conclusion that variable-proportions ties harm consumer welfare.

The Hovenkamps put forward a more nuanced and sophisticated defence of variable-proportions ties. They clarify that most variable-proportions ties offer the same nominal price to all consumers and hence should be considered as second-degree price discrimination, which is generally less harmful to consumer welfare than third-degree price discrimination.[54] They illustrate this argument with the example of printers and ink cartridges and observe that a tie of these goods discriminates based on a customer's intensity of use and not by the customer's inherent trait. Everyone who prints the same number of pages will pay the same amount per page of printing.[55] They suggest that the correct way to look at the costs of printing to consumers is on the basis of per printed page, which consists of a fixed cost component from the printer purchase and the variable costs of ink cartridges.[56] They further explain that tying has a tendency to shift costs from the fixed costs of the printer to the variable costs of the ink cartridge.[57] The more the overall costs of printing are shifted to the variable costs, which are the same for every consumer, the less price discrimination there is.[58] Therefore, the more successful the tie, the less it discriminates consumers.

While they are no doubt correct to observe that the relevant cost to consumers is the per-page cost of printing rather than the direct costs of the tying and the tied products, it is unclear how the degree of discrimination sheds light on the extent of consumer harm inflicted by the tie. The degree of discrimination may be relevant to the question of the fairness of the price discrimination scheme. Those fairness-minded critics of price discrimination may argue that price discrimination is unfair because like consumers are being treated differently. However, the main source of consumer harm for a variable-proportions tie is not the discriminatory prices but the surplus extraction. A variable-proportions tie still harms consumers even if it extracts the same amount of surplus from different consumers that would have been impossible to extract without the tie. A direct welfare analysis is needed to determine the effects of a variable-proportions tie.

[54] Hovenkamp and Hovenkamp (n 4) 935–36.
[55] ibid 936.
[56] ibid 933.
[57] ibid 941.
[58] ibid.

Analysis of the welfare effects of a variable-proportions tie entails a comparison with the but-for scenario. The Hovenkamps propose dividing consumers into three groups for the purpose of the analysis. The first group consists of low-valuation consumers who previously shunned the tying or the tied product but have been enticed to enter the market by the price reduction on the tying product.[59] They believe that such a price reduction frequently accompanies a variable-proportions tie, with the incumbent trying to shift the monopoly overcharge from the tying product to the tied product.[60] This group of consumers incontrovertibly benefit from the tie. They go from enjoying no surplus to at least some surplus from the two products.[61]

Among the existing users of the tying product, the Hovenkamps divide them into the medium-intensity and the high-intensity groups.[62] Tying lowers the costs of the tying product but raises the costs of the tied product. Whether the tie benefits existing consumers depends on their intensity of use of the tied product. At some point along the spectrum of use intensity, consumers consume the tied product in a sufficiently large quantity that their savings from the cheaper tying product no longer cover the increased costs of the tied product. Those whose intensity of use falls below this threshold would benefit from the tie while those who use the tying product more intensively and hence purchase more tied product will see their welfare suffer.[63]

The Hovenkamps conclude that the relationship between consumer welfare and the output level of the tied product is uncertain. They argue that overall consumer welfare can even increase despite a fall in output level, so long as there is a sufficiently large number of medium-intensity consumers.[64] Curiously, they also argue that an increase in output should be highly suggestive of a rise in consumer welfare 'unless there is reason to believe that the injuries to high-intensity buyers outweigh the improvements obtained by low- and medium-intensity buyers'.[65] It is worth spending some time to dissect these arguments. Despite the Hovenkamps' argument, it would seem that what matters for welfare improvement is not the number of consumers but the surplus they derive from each unit of the tied product.

This can be illustrated with a numerical example. Assume that the high-intensity users forego 5,500 units of the tied product while the medium-intensity users increase their consumption by 5,000. Whether surplus increases or not should not depend on the number of consumers in each category. Unless every consumer derives the same amount of surplus from each unit of the tied product, it should make

59 ibid 944.
60 ibid 942.
61 ibid 944.
62 ibid.
63 ibid.
64 ibid.
65 ibid.

no difference whether five consumers as opposed to 500 users are involved. What matters is how much surplus is created by each unit of the tied product. Their qualification to the assertion that higher output should mean enhanced welfare—'unless … the injuries to high-intensity buyers outweigh the improvements obtained by low- and medium-intensity buyers', which suggests that different consumers may have different valuations of the tied product—confirms this.

In order for the surplus generated by the additional 5,000 units consumed to more than make up for the loss of surplus from the 5,500 units foregone, the Hovenkamps must be implicitly arguing that medium-intensity users tend to derive greater surplus than do high-intensity consumers from each unit of the tied product consumed. If this is what they in fact believe, they have not provided any reason for this counter-intuitive assertion. One would expect high-intensity users to value the bundle more highly than do other users and hence their higher intensity of use. A reverse assumption would be more sensible, which would imply that a fall in output would surely signify a decline in consumer welfare while an increase in output could still be accompanied by a welfare loss if high-intensity users suffer disproportionate loss compared to medium-intensity users.

More importantly, the Hovenkamps' welfare analysis is premised on a price reduction for the tying product. Absent such a price reduction, the welfare effects of a variable-proportions tie would be unequivocally negative. There would be no low-intensity users entering the market *de novo* while all the existing users of the tying product would suffer harm due to the inflated prices for the tied product. The validity of their assumption of the prevalence of a price reduction for the tying product is ultimately an empirical question that cannot be answered by this author here. A casual survey of some of the leading tying cases seems to cast doubt on it. Nothing in the record in the famous US tying case of *Kodak* suggests that Kodak lowered its prices on the photocopying machines when it instituted its policy of refusing to supply spare parts to the independent service organizations.[66] There is similarly no evidence that Hilti reduced the price of its nail guns when it began to require users to purchase replacement nails from it.[67]

Upon reflection, the idea that the incumbent would lower the prices of the tying product when imposing a variable-proportions tie seems somewhat counterintuitive. Nothing about a variable-proportions tie requires the incumbent to do so. Surplus extraction is not premised on a reduced price for the tying product. It would seem that the only reason for the incumbent to do so is if it believes that a price reduction would boost sales of the tying product to low-intensity users who are shunning the tying product at the pre-tying monopolist price to whom the seller would make considerable sales of the tied product later. This strategy costs the seller revenue from its sale of the tying product to medium- and high-intensity

[66] *Eastman Kodak Co. v. Image Technical Services, Inc.*, 504 US 451, 472 (1992).
[67] Case T-30/89, *Hilti v. Commission* [1991] ECR II-1439, para. 18.

users. It is possible that the benefits of such a strategy may outweigh its costs. The fact that some incumbents do lower the price of their tying product when implementing a variable-proportions tie suggests that this can happen. There is, however, no basis to assert the universality of this scenario and build a general welfare analysis of variable-proportions ties based on this assumption.

Variable-proportions ties may benefit consumers only when three conditions are met. First, the incumbent has reduced, preferably by a fairly significant amount, the price of the tying product prior to introducing the tie. Second, output for the tied product increases following the tie. And third, high-intensity users do not place a significantly higher valuation on the two products than medium-intensity users. In the absence of a price reduction for the tying product and an output increase for the tied product, there is a very high chance that consumer welfare will be harmed.

Defenders of tying have raised a number of arguments to justify their position. First, they argue that the welfare effects of tying are generally ambiguous, and that because perfect price discrimination is efficient, the closer tying approximates perfect price discrimination, the more tying should be permitted.[68] Second, they argue that even though economic models that examine tying have tended to assume a monopoly position in the tying product market, most ties we see in the real world tend to be found in oligopolistic markets or perhaps even highly competitive ones in the case of franchise ties.[69] Third, tying that facilitates price discrimination does not result in any extension or leveraging of market power.[70] Fourth, which is more of a legal than an economic argument, is that if price discrimination is generally permitted by law, price-discriminating ties should be lawful as well.[71] Finally, Jerry Hausman and Jeffrey MacKie-Mason propose that price discrimination promotes market entry. This last argument is made in the specific context of patented products and will be addressed in the next section on the relationship between patent tying and innovation incentives.

None of these arguments withstands scrutiny. While many commentators have argued that conduct that approximates perfect price discrimination should be encouraged, they are also quick to acknowledge that price-discriminating ties do not come close to approximating perfect price discrimination.[72] Trying to justify price-discriminating ties based on the alleged allocative efficiency benefits of perfect price discrimination is pointless at best and disingenuous at worst. It is also important to distinguish between total and consumer welfare when one evaluates the

[68] Carlton and Waldman, 'How Economics Can Improve Antitrust Doctrine towards Tie-In Sales: Comment on Jean Tirole's "The Analysis of Tying Cases: A Primer"' (n 52) 35.

[69] Hovenkamp and Hovenkamp (n 4) 930.

[70] Carlton and Waldman, 'Robert Bork's Contributions to Antitrust Perspectives on Tying Behavior' (n 40) 136.

[71] ibid.

[72] Devlin (n 46) 544; Economides (n 38) 3; Hovenkamp and Hovenkamp (n 4) 933.

welfare effects of perfect price discrimination. Perfect price discrimination allows output to approximate that of perfect competition while extracting all consumer surplus. This means that ties that approximate perfect price discrimination may boost total welfare but harm consumer welfare.[73] This has been corroborated by Carlton and Waldman.[74] Allocative efficiency should not be conflated with consumer welfare. Some have further argued that even if a tie improves total welfare overall, that should not be the end of the inquiry. Arguing in the specific context of patent tying, Christopher Leslie believes that competition law should not be entirely agnostic as to the source of the welfare loss:

> Chicago School adherents may argue that if tying gets the patentee more money, it is a transfer of wealth. We must ask, however, from whom the wealth is being transferred and whether such a transfer is appropriate. It may be that the transfer of wealth from consumers of the tied bundle to the patentee is justifiable because the consumers presumably benefit from the patented invention and from their consumption of the bundle. But part of the transfer comes from excluded sellers of the unpatented tied product, who are making fewer sales and perhaps being driven from that product market altogether. These sellers should not be subsidizing the patent holder because they are neither infringing the patent nor benefitting from it.[75]

The implicit argument is that competition law should not be satisfied with a Kaldor–Hicks notion of total welfare. The fact that society comes out on top overall does not mean that welfare loss by some group in society deserves no attention from competition law authorities.

Furthermore, the ambiguity of the welfare effects of price discrimination should not be overstated. It was established that both intra-consumer and inter-product price discrimination harms consumer welfare. Intra-product price discrimination would benefit consumers only under narrow circumstances. It requires the incumbent to reduce the price of the tying product prior to the tie and the output level of the tied product to increase following the tie. The welfare effects of tying are even worse if the buyers are not end consumers but are intermediate buyers who resell to final consumers.[76] Price-discriminating ties are much more likely than not to be detrimental to consumer welfare.

It is true that many of the economic models that examine the competitive effects of tying tend to attribute monopoly power to the incumbent in the tying

[73] Elhauge (n 3) 435.

[74] Carlton and Waldman, 'Robert Bork's Contributions to Antitrust Perspectives on Tying Behavior' (n 40) 135.

[75] Christopher R Leslie, 'Patent Tying, Price Discrimination, and Innovation' (2011) 88 Antitrust Law Journal 811, 851.

[76] Elhauge (n 3) 434.

product market. These models will be discussed in section D.2. The competitive effects under investigation in those models, however, are foreclosure effects. None of them is concerned with price discrimination. None of the foregoing economic analyses of price discrimination presumes or requires monopoly power in the tying product market. All it takes is sufficient market power to permit supra-competitive pricing under which consumer surplus may arise. Such market power exists in oligopolistic markets in which market power is often the result of product differentiation. Admittedly, franchise ties are frequently found where the primary product market, often that of fast food, is highly competitive. Franchise ties, however, can involve information asymmetry and hold-ups that present an altogether different set of theoretical issues and should be assessed separately.

The argument that price-discriminating ties should not be condemned because they do not extend or leverage existing market power in the tying product market can be tackled on two levels. First, it is factually inaccurate. As Economides points out, ties that facilitate intra-product price discrimination could result in foreclosure in the tied product market.[77] Conditions that facilitate intra-product price discrimination could also give rise to foreclosure in the tied product market. The two are not mutually exclusive. Second, foreclosure effects should not be a prerequisite for condemning price-discriminating ties. Such ties have been shown to harm consumers independent of any foreclosure effects. Elhauge has forcefully argued that price-discriminating ties are worthy of antitrust condemnation in their own right.[78]

To argue that price-discriminating ties should be lawful if price discrimination itself is generally tolerated under competition law is tantamount to the contention that a lawful end justifies any means to accomplish that end. This contention has never been accepted by competition law. Competition law regularly attaches legal significance to the means used to achieve the end. In fact, the entire body of law under monopolization or abuse of dominance is premised on the idea that market power acquired through superior product or business acumen is perfectly acceptable while such power attained or defended through exclusionary conduct is not. Merger control also draws a distinction between market power achieved through organic growth as opposed to that attained by mergers or acquisitions. The former is beyond the purview of merger control laws while the latter is subject to full regulatory scrutiny. Therefore, it is untenable to argue that because price discrimination is lawful, price-discriminating ties should automatically be exempted from scrutiny. As Leslie observes, '[t]he ability to price discriminate in some forms does not translate into an affirmative right to price discriminate in all forms, particularly in the form of metered tying that injures competition in the tied product market'.[79]

77 Leslie (n 75) 852.
78 Elhauge (n 3) 432–35.
79 Leslie (n 75) 852.

Overall, there is a persuasive case for a strict stance on price-discriminating ties. Intra-consumer price discrimination and inter-product price discrimination have both been shown to harm consumers. Variable-proportions ties are also likely to be detrimental to consumers except under fairly narrow circumstances. Unless the incumbent has reduced the price of the tying product prior to the tie and the output level of the tied product increases after the tie, a variable-proportions tie should also be deemed illegal.

4. Implications for Developing Countries

The wealth transfer resulting from price discrimination can affect developing countries in two ways. First, it may harm consumers in developing countries as a whole. This would be the case if the price discrimination does not draw an explicit distinction between different groups of consumers and applies equally to all of them, such as under first- or second-degree price discrimination. Second, to the extent that the price discrimination scheme targets particular groups of customers, price discrimination may aggravate income inequality and disproportionately harm the welfare of poor consumers. How price discrimination affects consumers as a whole has already been examined. The ensuing discussion will focus on the relationship between price discrimination and income distribution.

Tying can result in three types of price discrimination: intra-product price discrimination, intra-consumer price discrimination, and inter-product price discrimination. Intra-product price discrimination permits the seller to extract more surplus from consumers of the tying product by effectively varying its price based on the intensity of use. Intra-consumer price discrimination represents pure extraction of consumer surplus. Even though inter-product price discrimination may result in higher output, extraction of consumer surplus is also a necessary consequence. All three of them result in wealth transfer from consumers to producers. Extraction of consumer surplus is the raison d'être of price-discriminating ties.

While it is possible that some consumers are ultra-wealthy and a wealth transfer from them to the producers may improve income equality, the vast majority of consumers in developing countries are likely to be poorer than the firm owners. This is especially the case when the product involved is patented and imported from industrialized economies. Condoning patent tying in a developing country amounts to giving multinational corporations free rein to extract wealth from poor developing country consumers for the benefit of their first-world shareholders. Regardless of other allocative consequences of price discrimination, this fact alone constitutes a sufficient reason for developing countries to take price-discriminating ties seriously.

To the extent that price discrimination draws explicit distinctions between different groups of customers, and these customers exhibit a consistent socio-economic profile, price-discriminating ties could have disparate impact on income distribution. Some types of price discrimination may benefit lower-income groups. Third-degree price discrimination is said to aggravate allocative inefficiency by transferring output from high-valuation customers to low-valuation customers. It is, however, precisely this effect that allows low-income consumers to benefit. Third-degree price discrimination allows the seller to charge a lower price to low-valuation customers who would have shunned the product at the but-for uniform monopolist price.[80] This led Alan Devlin to conclude that 'price discrimination may serve an equitable, as well as an efficiency-oriented, goal'.[81]

The income redistributive effect of price-discriminating ties, however, should not be overstated. First, low-valuation customers are not necessarily low-income. A customer may place a low valuation on a product not because she is poor but because she does not care much for the product. While it is true that there is a limit to a low-income customer's willingness to pay for an expensive product, for many products there is no reason to assume that willingness to pay is correlated with income level. Second, and more importantly, price-discriminating ties tend to result in second-, and not third-degree price discrimination. Price-discriminating ties such as variable-proportion ties do not explicitly offer disparate consumers different prices. Consumers self-assign to different categories based on their own attributes. Intra-consumer and inter-product price discrimination also does not entail discriminatory treatment of different consumers. In fact, the modus operandi of inter-product price discrimination is to aggregate consumers' willingness to pay for different products so that the seller can offer them the same price for a bundle of products. Therefore, price-discriminating ties cannot be said to have a general tendency to improve income distribution.

If we assume that there is some correlation between product valuation and income level, it may be possible to proffer some generalizations about the relationship between price-discriminating ties and income distribution. Intra-consumer and inter-product price discrimination are unlikely to benefit low-income consumers. Neither of them entails low-income customers being offered a lower price. Quite the contrary, both of them require the seller to raise prices on the tied product to increase extraction of consumer surplus. Under intra-consumer price discrimination, the bundle price only goes up by the tied product price to extract surplus. Under inter-product price discrimination, the price is lowered in the sense that the bundle price may consist of the price the low-valuation customer is willing to pay for the bundle. Yet the tie also means that consumers are no longer allowed to purchase individual products separately. Some low-income customers could be priced out of the market if they are unwilling or unable to afford both products at the same time. They may end up losing out on the product they could afford without the tie.

80 Devlin (n 46) 543.
81 ibid.

Variable-proportions ties could conceivably improve the welfare of low-income consumers if the tie is preceded by a price cut for the tying product. With a price cut, the tie could render the bundle affordable to consumers who had previously stayed out of the market. It was noted earlier that the overall welfare effects of a variable-proportions tie come down to a balance of how the tie affects low-, medium-, and high-intensity users. While the overall impact may be uncertain, low-intensity users are likely to benefit from a variable-proportions tie preceded by a price cut for the tying product. To the extent that valuation correlates with income level, such a tie may improve income inequality.

C. Tying and Innovation Incentives

If the tying product is patented—and patent tying is the ultimate focus of this chapter—then extraction of consumer surplus takes on additional significance. It is no longer simply a wealth transfer. The extra surplus may be funnelled into R&D and spur further innovation. In short, patent tying may have implications for innovation incentives. Defenders of patent tying have argued that the practice should be permitted because it will boost the financial reward to the patentee, which in turn will spur innovation incentives. Whatever the short-run effects of patent tying, the increased innovation it will spur in the long term will outweigh the static efficiency loss. The difficulty in quantifying dynamic efficiency gains means that it is well-nigh impossible to verify and rebut this argument. Dynamic efficiency benefits effectively become a trump card and immunize patent tying from competition law scrutiny. Acceptance of this argument would be tantamount to adopting *per se* legality for patent tying, which is what some commentators have advocated.[82] Therefore, this argument needs to be properly analysed and disposed of before we can determine how developing countries should approach patent tying.

1. Tying Enhances Patentee Reward and Hence Innovation Incentives

In a way, patent tying is the quintessential kind of tying conduct. Many of the earliest tying cases in the United States involved patented products. This fact to some extent tainted the US Supreme Court's initial views of tying and was partly responsible for the Court's hostile attitude toward the practice. The Court viewed

[82] Christian Ahlborn, David S Evans, and A Jorge Padilla, 'The Antitrust Economics of Tying: A Farewell to Per Se Illegality' (2004) 49 Antitrust Bulletin 287, 337–38. Mark A Hurwitz, 'Bundling Patented Drugs and Medical Services: An Antitrust Analysis' (1991) 91 Columbia Law Review 1188, 1208.

patent tying as an unlawful attempt to leverage the market power that comes with patent protection into unpatented product markets. Even though the Court's stance on tying has gradually softened over time, the historical legacy of patent tying partly explains the current anomalous treatment of tying as the only non-horizontal restraint that is still subject to the *per se* rule, albeit of a qualified or modified kind, under US antitrust law. It was not until 2006 when the US Supreme Court finally abandoned the presumption that patent protection creates a presumption of market power in tying cases.[83]

As is true of most business practices involving patented products or technology, it is frequently argued that allowing a patentee to practice tying will raise her patentee reward, which in turn will boost her innovation incentives. There are diverse views on whether this constitutes a valid justification for patent tying. Defenders of patent tying argue that it is needed to raise patentee reward. Patent tying is a particularly desirable means to do so because it can boost patentee reward without causing static efficiency loss. Patent tying would be a magic bullet as it would avoid the long-standing trade-off between dynamic efficiency gains and static efficiency losses that underpins patent protection. This could be achieved through price discrimination, which manages to transfer consumer surplus to the patentee without creating deadweight loss. Critics assert that it is not necessary to enhance patentee reward with patent tying. Some resort to the familiar patent scope argument and contend that patent tying allows the patentee to extend her reward beyond the scope of patent grant. Some sidestep patentee reward and directly address innovation incentives, suggesting that tying does not enhance or even suppresses innovation incentives. Tying is alleged to retard innovation in the tied product market. Tying has also been shown to exert a strategic effect on rivals to reduce their incentives to invest in R&D in both the tying and the tied product markets.

Ward Bowman is generally credited with originating the idea that tying as a metering device is justified to the extent that price discrimination boosts patentee reward and hence innovation incentives.[84] He distinguishes between revenue-maximizing and monopoly-creating types of patent exploitation practices and contends that practices that merely allow the patentee to maximize her profit or extract surplus from consumers should be permitted.[85] Aaron Director and Edward Levi, two of the founders of the Chicago School, believe that price discrimination is a mere instance of utilization of the inherent market power granted by patent protection rather than an unlawful extension of it.[86] To these three commentators, tying should be permitted as a profit-maximizing type of patent exploitation.

[83] *Illinois Tool Works v. Independent Ink*, 547 US 28 (2006).
[84] Bowman, Jr (n 1) 26–27.
[85] ibid 19–20.
[86] Leslie (n 75) 822.

It is argued that tying merely allows the patentee to attain or at least approach the full appropriation of the social value of her invention, which is desirable because anything less than full appropriation will lead to under-investment in R&D. In that vein, tying is socially efficient to the extent that it achieves or approximates perfect price discrimination.[87] The more complete is the appropriation of surplus, the closer innovation incentives approach the optimal level. Unlike what was previously argued, consumers are not irreparably harmed by the extraction of consumer surplus facilitated by tying. They are compensated by the resultant boost to innovation. It is postulated that 'tying sellers will devote the additional funds they secure through price discrimination to research product improvements, as well as to other activities, such as broadening their range of products and their number of retail outlets'.[88]

The Hovenkamps extend their defence of patent tying further and argue that patent tying can boost patentee reward without aggravating the extraction of consumer surplus. Tying can augment 'the innovator's returns even as consumer surplus is increased as well, and for reasons additional to the economies of joint provision that most tying arrangements create'.[89] They identify three mechanisms by which this can happen. First, tying can boost the output level for both the tying and the tied products.[90] Second, by raising output level, tying can help to lower the per unit costs of production.[91] If fixed costs are significant, which is likely to be the case for a patented product which requires substantial R&D, an increased level of output means that fixed costs are spread over an expanded output base, which results in lower fixed costs on a per unit basis.[92] They argue that '[t]he larger upfront innovation costs are in relation to production (variable) costs, the more sensitive the final product's price will be to the output rate'.[93] A prohibition of tying will hence significantly reduce the innovator's return by artificially restricting her output level.[94] Third, tying can boost the innovator's revenue by raising prices without a concomitant loss of output.[95] If a revenue increase augments the incumbent's innovation incentives, however, the same logic should imply that tying will lessen the innovation incentives of the incumbent's competitors in the tied product market. If a tie is successful, it will reduce rivals' revenue from the sales of their tied product. The overall innovation performance of the market will depend on the relative impact on the incumbent's and its competitors' innovation incentives. This theme will be picked up later.

[87] ibid 826.
[88] ibid 821.
[89] Hovenkamp and Hovenkamp (n 4) 953.
[90] ibid.
[91] ibid 954.
[92] ibid 955.
[93] ibid.
[94] ibid.
[95] ibid 954.

The Hovenkamps believe that none of these three mechanisms entails a loss of consumer surplus. This belief is doubtful upon closer scrutiny. One of the Hovenkamps' gravest oversights is their exclusive focus on the incumbent to the neglect of its competitors. Many of their conclusions may be true as far as the incumbent is concerned but will no longer hold when considered on a market-wide basis. Regarding the first mechanism of increased output level of the tying and the tied products, a tie in fact need not increase the output level for the incumbent's tying product.[96] While the output level for the incumbent's tied product is likely to increase, this increase is most definitely accompanied by a drop in the incumbent's competitors output.[97] Consumer welfare will be harmed if the overall output for the tied product market falls. And this is likely to be the case if the incumbent's competitors have to raise their prices because their reduced output causes them to lose economies of scale, driving up their per unit costs of production.

Regarding the second mechanism, it should be clear that it is merely derivative of the first. Per unit production costs drop solely due to an increase in output level. A tie need not increase the output level of the incumbent's tying product, while it most probably will raise the output level of the tied product. This leads to the question of whether the fixed costs of the tying product's R&D should be imputed to the tied product. If the tied product's technology is derived from the technology of the tying product, the argument for imputation would be strong. But if the tied product is only a staple product such as salt tablets used in a canning machine or nails in a nail gun, it is not immediately apparent why imputation would make sense. There may be difficulty in demarcating a principled boundary between cases in which imputation is justified and cases in which it is not. Yet there are clear cases in which imputation is indefensible. Tying will not lower the per unit production costs in these cases.

Regarding the third mechanism of higher prices for the tied product, the Hovenkamps observe that consumer welfare is unharmed because there is no concomitant output reduction. They argue that 'tied product output may actually increase, given that consumers who were not in the market at all until the tie took hold have entered'.[98] Again, market-wide output level for the tied product need not increase, especially if there is a significant number of consumers who stop purchasing the tied product following the tie or if rivals are forced to raise prices after losing economies of scale. Even if the focus is confined to the incumbent, consumers of the incumbent's tied product could be harmed by the higher tied product prices. Assuming that we could offset the welfare gains and losses of different consumers, the overall welfare calculus for the incumbent's tied product

[96] Michael D Whinston, 'Tying, Foreclosure, and Exclusion' (1990) 80 The American Economic Review 837, 845.

[97] ibid 844. Barry Nalebuff, 'Bundling as an Entry Barrier' (2004) 119 The Quarterly Journal of Economics 159, 182.

[98] Hovenkamp and Hovenkamp 954.

customers depends on the proportion of new customers who enter the market after the tie is imposed and existing customers who either have always purchased from the incumbent or have been forced to switch to the incumbent's product by the tie. If the tie results in higher tied product prices for all existing customers, which is likely to be the case, overall consumer welfare is unlikely to have been improved. Existing customers will in all likelihood outnumber new customers and thus the consumer welfare loss will outweigh the gain. Even if we exclude the incumbent's long-term customers, there is still no reason to assume that the welfare gains to the new customers will necessarily outweigh the welfare losses to those who have been forced to switch to the incumbent's tied product.

Tying is not the magic bullet that the Hovenkamps suggest. The possibility for tying to boost patentee reward without extracting additional consumer surplus is likely to be much more limited in reality. Jerry Hausman and Jeffrey MacKie-Mason are more realistic when they observe that 'price discrimination misallocates resources among purchasers and thus causes a decrease in social welfare. Customers facing different prices will have different marginal valuations for the patented good, so that some loss in consumer welfare—relative to a first-best world—is inevitable.'[99]

Hausman and MacKie-Mason advance a somewhat different argument in defence of patent tying. They assert that to the extent that it relies on price discrimination, tying does not entail a trade-off between static welfare and dynamic efficiency.[100] Price discrimination boosts producer welfare by creating substantial static efficiency gains. This may at first glance sound similar to the Hovenkamps' argument. Yet there is a subtle difference between the two. Both arguments suggest that price-discriminating ties boost producer welfare. The Hovenkamps, however, focus on how tying can raise patentee reward and hence innovation incentives without inflicting additional consumer welfare loss while Hausman and MacKie-Mason are concerned with how price discrimination can boost production efficiency. They observe that short-term welfare gains 'occur because price discrimination allows patent holders to open new markets and to achieve economies of scale or learning. Further, even in cases where discrimination incurs static welfare losses, it may be efficient relative to other mechanisms, such as length of patent life, for rewarding innovators with profits.'[101] They go so far as asserting that price discrimination involving a patented product 'can be Pareto-improving under some circumstances',[102] meaning that short-term welfare gains and increased innovation incentives can be simultaneously attained.

[99] Jerry A Hausman and Jeffrey K Mackie-Mason, 'Price Discrimination and Patent Policy' (1988) 19 RAND Journal of Economics 253, 253–54.
[100] ibid 254.
[101] ibid 253.
[102] ibid 254.

According to Hausman and MacKie-Mason, there are two main sources of production efficiency gains from patent tying. The first is scale economies, which could be especially pronounced for a patented product because 'initial production facilities may be built well below minimum efficient scale owing to uncertainty about commercial success'.[103] The second is the learning-curve effect, under which unit costs are 'a decreasing function of cumulative output over time'.[104] They argue that these two sources of efficiency gains are important for a variety of reasons. With scale economies, Pareto improvement is no longer predicated on entry into new markets.[105] Moreover, price discrimination accompanied by scale economies may facilitate market entry 'when the marginal cost associated with uniform-pricing output exceeds the reservation price in potential new markets'.[106] They describe the process as follows:

> Suppose there are two markets: one is relatively inelastic and profitable under discriminatory pricing, the other is relatively elastic and not very profitable. It is intuitively clear that the optimal uniform price will be set near the monopoly price for the first, inelastic market; this sacrifices the small profits in the second market for the greater profits in the first. At that relatively high uniform price, demand in the elastic, second market is relatively low, so that total output is low and marginal cost is high. Now let the firm discriminate. The price to the elastic market is dropped substantially, and as a result it elicits a big increase in output. With scale economies marginal cost falls. To a first-order approximation the uniform price was already profit-maximizing for the inelastic market, so that with all else equal the discriminatory price will not be much higher. But the elastic market has a flywheel effect: it drives marginal cost down through a large output increase.[107]

Despite their focus on static efficiency gains, Hausman and MacKie-Mason ultimately relate their discussion back to innovation incentives. They postulate that a patentee maximizes her profit if she is allowed to pursue unconstrained third-degree price discrimination.[108] If price discrimination can generate the same amount of patentee reward at a smaller static efficiency loss, it may be wise from an optimal patent policy perspective to allow price discrimination while shortening the patent term.[109] It should be obvious to the astute observer that Hausman and MacKie-Mason's pro-competitive story ultimately comes down to the rather unremarkable assertion that price-discriminating ties may increase output. The Hovenkamps

[103] ibid 257.
[104] ibid.
[105] ibid.
[106] ibid.
[107] ibid 260.
[108] ibid 263.
[109] ibid 254.

focus on the demand side and examine how the output increase benefits consumers. Hausman and MacKie-Mason direct their attention to the supply-side productive efficiency gains from such an increase. Their pro-competitive story is heavily reliant on market entry, which requires a potential market for the patentee to enter. Absent such a market, what is left are productive efficiency gains from scale economies and learning-curve effect. Moreover, while Hausman and MacKie-Mason rely on third-degree price discrimination in their discussion, patent tying does not result in third-degree price discrimination. This further undermines the persuasiveness of their arguments.

2. Tying Undermines Innovation Incentives

Many arguments have been made against patent tying. Some of them focus on the impact of tying on patentee reward, arguing that it is not necessary to resort to tying to enhance patentee reward or that tying generates excessive reward to the patentee. Some directly tackle the relationship between tying and innovation incentives and assert that tying does not enhance or even reduces innovation incentives. It is argued that the incentive-reducing effect is particularly pronounced in the tied product market. Joseph Farrell and Michael Katz have proposed a model that illustrates this effect. Furthermore, it has been suggested that tying has the strategic effect of reducing rivals' incentives to invest in R&D in general.

The argument that tying is beneficial because it enhances patentee reward is premised on the two alternative notions: either that the patent system currently generates insufficient reward for patentees or that more is always better as far as patentee reward is concerned. The latter notion has already been dismissed in Chapter 2, where it was argued that innovation can be excessive. Given resource scarcity, at some point society would be better off investing additional resources elsewhere. The former notion implies that innovations that redound net social benefits are currently being shunned because the patent system, together with other appropriation mechanisms, provides insufficient returns to innovators to cover their R&D costs. There is no persuasive evidence that the current patent system generates insufficient innovation incentives to attain the socially optimal level of R&D.[110] Given the prohibitive information costs that an optimal patent system, which can perfectly calibrate patentee reward to match innovation costs, entails, it is unlikely that definitive evidence in support of this argument can be furnished.

Patent tying has been harshly treated by both US patent law and antitrust law for most of the last century. Yet there is no indication that the innovation performance

[110] Leslie (n 75) 825.

of the United States has suffered.[111] The burden of persuasion is thus upon those who advocate a change in the status quo. Absent convincing evidence to the contrary, there are no grounds for arguing that the current treatment of patent tying should be relaxed to boost innovation incentives. Moreover, even if the current patent system needs augmentation, it cannot be presumed that permitting patent tying is the best way to achieve it. If one applies the ratio test propounded by Louis Kaplow, we need to compare the ratio between patentee reward and static efficiency loss for each alternative means to determine the best way to generate additional innovation incentives.[112] We need to compare Kaplow's ratio for tying versus other means of augmenting patentee reward such as lengthening the patent term to decide the optimal way to do so.

A related argument is that allowing a patentee to secure her reward through tying extends her rights beyond the scope of the patent grant. This relates back to the scope of the patent test examined in Chapter 6. Nicholas Economides and William Hebert argue that

> it would not be appropriate for the patent system to reward company A (the patent holder for product A) with a monopoly in market B and let company A reap monopoly profits from product B, thereby reducing consumer surplus of product B. In neither case is it appropriate for antitrust immunity to award additional profits in product B to the patent holder for product A.[113]

Defenders of patent rights invoke the patent scope argument and contend that a patentee should be permitted to capture the full social value of her innovation, which includes the surplus that consumers may derive from the innovation, by whatever lawful means. This is well within the scope of her patent grant. If price discrimination is needed for such surplus extraction, then the patentee should be allowed to resort to price-discriminating ties. Recall the argument in Chapter 6 that patent scope is not a self-defining concept and that its meaning is informed by a calculus of the net social benefits of an innovation. The impracticality of ascertaining the net social benefits of every innovation means that patent scope remains an elusive concept and cannot be relied upon to provide meaningful support for the patentee's unrestricted right to engage in price discrimination.

Setting aside the issue of whether patent tying is an appropriate means for surplus extraction, the notion that a patentee should be allowed to capture the full social value of her innovation and anything less than that would amount to undercompensation is also highly questionable. Any value that is unclaimed by the initial

[111] ibid.

[112] Louis Kaplow, 'The Patent-Antitrust Intersection: A Reappraisal' (1984) 97 Harvard Law Review 1813, 1831.

[113] Nicholas Economides and William N Hebert, 'Patents and Antitrust: Application to Adjacent Markets' (2008) 6 Journal of Telecommunications and High Technology Law 455, 465.

innovator will serve as either surplus to consumers or spillovers to other industry participants. Many commentators seem to believe that there is nothing wrong with the innovator's full appropriation of consumer surplus. They view this as purely a wealth transfer about which competition law should be entirely agnostic. From a static efficiency perspective, competition law should not concern itself with wealth transfer and should refrain from intervening absent clear evidence of deadweight loss. This argument would be valid if the goal of competition law was solely to pursue economic efficiency. But if one genuinely regards protection of consumer welfare as one of the most important goals, if not the only goal, of competition law enforcement, such agnosticism would be indefensible.[114] Consumer welfare loss is all the same regardless of the form it takes, wealth transfer or deadweight loss.[115] It was amply demonstrated in the previous section that extraction of consumer surplus constitutes a sufficient reason for outlawing tying. The same applies here to patent tying.

No less important is the issue of whether the innovator should be allowed to appropriate all the technological spillovers. There is considerable intuitive appeal to the idea that an innovator should be allowed to keep the full benefits of her innovation to the exclusion of other firms. After all, the value is created by the innovator. Yet there are a number of problems with this proposition. First, it was established in Chapter 2 any patentee reward beyond the risk-adjusted private costs of innovation would amount to a windfall for the innovator. While we may not always be able to calibrate the patentee reward to match exactly the private costs of innovation, if it is clear that the patentee can cover her R&D costs without resorting to tying, it would be undoubtedly excessive and unnecessary to allow her to tie.

Second, numerous economists such as William Baumol have noted the importance of technological spillovers to economic progress. Baumol postulates that we would have been condemned to a pre-Industrial Revolution standard of living if technological spillovers had been completely precluded.[116] Spillovers have also been an important element in the theoretical account of economic growth. For example, they feature prominently in the growth models proposed by Nobel Laureate Paul Romer in the late 1980s and early 1990s.[117] Under these models, allowing full appropriation of technological spillovers would severely retard economic growth.

Third, providing excessive returns to innovation would spur a patent race.[118] There is a whole body of economic literature that has demonstrated that these patent

[114] Russell Pittman, 'Consumer Surplus as the Appropriate Standard for Antitrust Enforcement' (2007) 3 Competition Policy International 210.

[115] David C Hjelmfelt and Channing D Strother, Jr, 'Antitrust Damages for Consumer Welfare Loss' (1991) 39 Cleveland State Law Review 505, 507–08.

[116] William Baumol, *The Free-Market Innovation Machine: Analyzing the Growth Miracle of Capitalism* (Princeton University Press 2004) 125.

[117] Paul M Romer, 'Increasing Returns and Long-Run Growth' (1986) 94 Journal of Political Economy 1002; Paul M Romer, 'Endogenous Technological Change' (1990) 98 Journal of Political Economy S71.

[118] Elhauge (n 3) 440.

races are often socially wasteful.[119] The reward to winning these races is substantial from a private perspective, but the investment made by the second innovator to try to win the race is often duplicative and redounds few additional benefits to society. If two innovators pursue the same technology, one of whom will be precluded from implementing the technology once she loses the patent race and her R&D investment in the technology will become redundant and wasted. Therefore, despite its intuitive appeal, the notion that the innovator should be allowed to appropriate the entire surplus created by her innovation should be rejected.

Leslie offers an alternative, more defensible position regarding a patentee's right to engage in price discrimination. He notes that 'even if patentees enjoyed an affirmative right to price discriminate, that does not translate into a right to use metered tying to effectuate such price discrimination. Patents confer the right to exclude infringers, not the right to engage without interference in any particular pricing structure'.[120] Therefore, at most, patent rights only authorize the patentee to engage in price discrimination through the sale of the patented product. The patentee crosses the line when it enlists the help of an unpatented product to implement price discrimination.

Some critics of patent tying have shifted their attention away from patentee reward and directly attacked the causal link between permitting tying and generation of innovation incentives. They have made various arguments as to why increased innovation incentives cannot justify patent tying. It has been argued that the fact that proceeds from possibly unlawful conduct could be used for a pro-competitive purpose cannot excuse the conduct.[121] Competition law has never entertained defences of anticompetitive conduct on the grounds that proceeds generated by the conduct will be put to procompetitive uses. As Leslie noted, 'such a defense has no limiting principle'.[122] This defence could even be applied to justify cartel conduct, the cardinal sin of competition law. Such application would be unthinkable, yet there does not seem to be any logical basis upon which to delimit this defence.

One further complication is that there can be no guarantee that the proceeds from tying will indeed be used for further R&D. If increased R&D investment is the grounds upon which tying is upheld, the defendant should somehow be held to account for her commitment to increase investment. A competition authority or the courts would be loath to compel the defendant to dedicate a certain amount of profits to R&D. The imposition of such an obligation would require ongoing close scrutiny of the defendant's operations, which most authorities and courts would

119 Partha Dasgupta and Joseph Stiglitz, 'Industrial Structure and the Nature of Innovative Activity' (1980) 90 Economic Journal 266; Jennifer F Reinganum, 'A Dynamic Game of R and D: Patent Protection and Competitive Behavior' (1982) 50 Econometrica 671; Pankaj Tandon, 'Rivalry and the Excessive Allocation of Resources to Research' (1983) 14 Bell Journal of Economics 152.

120 Leslie (n 75) 833.

121 ibid 830.

122 ibid.

shy away from. Absent an effective enforcement mechanism, it would have to be true that firms that practice tying have a greater propensity to invest their proceeds into R&D than firms that obtain their patentee reward through other means. There is simply no empirical evidence for such a tendency.[123] There are no reasons why these firms would not seek out more efficient uses of their resources if such uses exist. If firms that are allowed to tie do not plough back their extra proceeds from tying into R&D, the proceeds will simply amount to a windfall. Even if such evidence existed, there would still be the question of whether there are superior, less competition-distorting, means to incentivize innovation, which takes us back to an analysis under Kaplow's ratio test.

Moreover, not every technological product gives rise to the opportunity for tying. The likelihood and effectiveness of tying tends to be greater between complementary products.[124] Yet not every technological product is consumed with a complementary product. Permitting tying in the hope of incentivizing innovation would distort R&D investments toward technology and products that are consumed with complementary products. Returns to R&D that generate products susceptible to tying would be artificially inflated. Unless there are reasons to believe that such technology is more socially beneficial than other kinds of technology, relying on tying as an innovation incentive generation mechanism would result in considerable distortion of resource allocation.[125]

Beyond the uncertain effects of increased returns from patent tying on innovation incentives, some critics have gone further and argued that tying positively undermines innovation incentives, especially in the tied product market.[126] This argument would have no application if the tied product was a staple product such as salt tablets or nails, which have limited room for technical improvement.[127] It would also have little relevance for aftermarket products such as spare parts whose technology is derivative of the primary product and for which there is little need for independent R&D. But it would be a pertinent consideration if the tied product incorporates a technology that is distinct and independent from the technology in the tying product, such as a web browser and an operating system.

Tying is said to reduce the innovation incentives of both the incumbent and its rivals in the tied product market. Tying reduces the incumbent's innovation incentives because its offering in the tied product market no longer competes on its merit. Consumers who need the incumbent's tying product or whose surplus from the tying product more than offsets their negative surplus from choosing the incumbent's tied product will opt for the bundle. What attracts consumers to the tied product is no longer the quality of the tied product but that of the tying

[123] ibid.
[124] Devlin (n 46) 540.
[125] Elhauge (n 3) 440.
[126] Leslie (n 75) 834.
[127] ibid 841.

product. If investing in R&D for the tying product boosts the sales of both products, it would be perfectly rational for the incumbent to focus on such investment.[128] Meanwhile, tying reduces the incumbent's rivals' innovation incentives because it shrinks the size of the market from which they can recover their R&D investments. If the market that is left to a rival after a successful tie is insufficient to cover its fixed R&D costs, the rival will refrain from investing in R&D or will exit the market altogether. This is especially likely to be the case if the tying and the tied products are perfect complements.[129]

This is an application of the insight developed by Michael Whinston that under certain market conditions, a monopolist tying product supplier can make use of tying to prevent a rival in the tied product market from recovering its fixed costs of entry, thereby foreclosing the rival from the market.[130] R&D costs are fixed costs that the rival will need to recoup in order to survive in the tied product market. Moreover, foreclosing rivals in the tied product market by undermining their innovation incentives may serve important strategic purposes for the incumbent. For instance, tying can help the incumbent protect its position in the tying product market.[131] Often the most likely challengers to the incumbent's position in the tying product market are rivals in the tied product market. If the incumbent is so successful in its foreclosure strategy that it has created a double-level entry requirement—where an entrant will be required to enter both the tying and the tied product markets at the same time—being required to invest in the R&D for both products means that the entrant will be able to devote fewer resources to the tied product as compared to where the entrant can limit itself to single market entry.[132] The discussion here implicates different theories of foreclosure that will be examined in detail in the next section.

Apart from denying rivals market share from which to recover R&D costs, there are other ways in which the incumbent can undermine its rival's innovation incentives. Joseph Farrell and Michael Katz develop a model in which a monopolist seller of the tying product weakens or perhaps even destroys the innovation incentives of rivals through a number of strategies which they label as price squeeze, exclusionary squeeze, and investment squeeze respectively.[133] Under price squeeze, the incumbent intentionally lowers the price of its tied product below what an independent tied product supplier would charge in order to exert competitive pressure on rivals.[134] Under exclusionary squeeze, the incumbent uses interface or

[128] ibid 843.

[129] Alessandro Avenali, Anna D'Annunzio, and Pierfrancesco Reverberi, 'Bundling, Competition and Quality Investment: A Welfare Analysis' (2013) 43 Review of Industrial Organization 221, 225.

[130] Whinston (n 96) 844.

[131] Dennis W Carlton and Michael Waldman, 'The Strategic Use of Tying to Preserve and Create Market Power in Evolving Industries' (2002) 33 RAND Journal of Economics 194.

[132] Leslie 844.

[133] Joseph Farrell and Michael L Katz, 'Innovation, Rent Extraction, and Integration in Systems Markets' (2000) 48 The Journal of Industrial Economics 413, 415.

[134] ibid.

product incompatibility to squeeze rivals or 'demands a low price for an independently supplied [tied product] as a quid pro quo for granting access'.[135] Lastly, under investment squeeze, the incumbent 'has strategic incentives to invest in improving its variant of [the tied product] in order to drive the leading independent supplier of [the tied product] to price its (still better) product lower than it otherwise would'.[136] By forcing its rivals in the tied product market to lower their prices, the incumbent extracts surplus from that market through sales in the tying product market, thereby weakening rivals' incentives to invest in R&D in the tied product market. It is possible that in the short run, the incumbent's increased R&D more than makes up for the reduced R&D by rivals. In the long run, however, once rivals' products deteriorate to a point where they are no longer competitive against the incumbent's product, the incumbent will lose incentives to keep up with R&D for the tied product. Innovation in the tied product market as a whole suffers.

Jay Pil Choi outlines in another theoretical model the circumstance under which tying can harm rivals' innovation incentives in the tied product market.[137] In his model, Choi demonstrates that foreclosure of rivals from the tied product market itself is not a profitable strategy and is not the source of competitive harm of tying. In fact, he argues that the profitability of tying to the incumbent does not hinge on exit of rivals from the tied product market.[138] The incumbent's increased market share in the tied product market at rivals' expense itself has no independent competitive significance. What matters is that increased market share reduces rivals' innovation incentives. Choi postulates that a firm's innovation incentives are directly proportional to its market share.[139] Increased market share allows the incumbent to spread its R&D costs over a larger number of units.[140] Innovation also becomes more profitable because any cost reduction will benefit a larger output.[141] Meanwhile, tying reduces rivals' market share in the tied product market, thereby reducing their innovation incentives.[142] Therefore, it can be said that 'market foreclosure in the product market translates into foreclosure in the R&D markets'.[143] A tying arrangement gives the incumbent greater incentives to price aggressively, which inevitably will increase the incumbent's market share. An increased market share will help lower the per unit cost and the overall profitability of innovation. By pursuing a tie, the incumbent is effectively making a strategic commitment to more aggressive R&D.[144]

135 ibid.
136 ibid.
137 Jay Pil Choi, 'Tying and Innovation: A Dynamic Analysis of Tying Arrangements' (2004) 114 The Economic Journal 83, 86.
138 ibid.
139 ibid 92.
140 ibid 86.
141 ibid 93.
142 ibid.
143 ibid 94.
144 ibid 93.

Choi argues that tying is not a profitable strategy only on account of its effect on price competition. The costs of increased price competition outweigh the benefits of increased market share. Choi believes that this 'confirms the Chicago school's central contention that tying cannot be used for the purpose of leveraging monopoly power ... and highlights the importance of considering the innovation game in the analysis of tying'.[145] But once one considers the dynamic rents that can be created through R&D, 'bundling may be a profitable strategy. The change in R&D incentives through bundling enables the tying firm to capture a larger share of dynamic rents'.[146] Whether tying is ultimately profitable to the incumbent entails a balance between the harm from increased price competition and the benefits of capturing a larger share of dynamic rents.[147]

Choi concludes that 'bundling is always social welfare reducing even if it can be privately optimal'.[148] There are two main sources of reduction of social welfare. First, tying distorts the innovation incentives of both the incumbent and its rivals in the tied product market.[149] The incumbent is investing too much while rivals are investing too little. The distorted R&D results in asymmetric production costs between the incumbent and its rivals, which create allocative inefficiency.[150] Second, some consumers will be forced by the tie to forego consumption of the tying product, which will cause a loss of consumer welfare.[151] Choi, however, cautions that his conclusions regarding social welfare are sensitive to the R&D specifications in his model.[152] Under alternative specifications, it may be more efficient for the incumbent to undertake all the R&D.[153] Competition in R&D can promote diversity of research approaches, which is particularly important if success in research is highly uncertain, but it can also result in duplication of research efforts.[154] Ultimately the desirability of R&D competition requires a weighing of these two conflicting considerations.

The arguments on balance refute the proposition that generation of innovation incentives provides additional justification for patent tying. There is a dearth of evidence that the current patent system provides insufficient innovation incentives and needs to be supplemented by patent tying. Even if such evidence existed, it has not been proven that tying is the best way to achieve this purpose. Relying on tying to boost innovation incentives will distort R&D investments and cause potential

145 ibid 85.
146 ibid 94.
147 ibid.
148 ibid 96.
149 ibid 97.
150 ibid.
151 ibid.
152 ibid.
153 ibid.
154 ibid.

innovators to focus on technologies that lend themselves to tying, regardless of the relative net social benefits of such innovation.

Allowing a patentee to reap patentee reward may also allow her to extend her rights beyond the scope of her patent grant. If Leslie's interpretation of the patent scope argument is correct, a patentee should only be allowed to practice price discrimination on the patented product. She should not be allowed to commandeer a related product to achieve a result that she could not attain solely with the patented product. There is also little support for the argument that a patentee should be allowed to appropriate the entire surplus created by her innovation. This has been shown to be highly detrimental to social welfare and economic progress. Lastly, theoretical insights suggest that tying retards innovation in the tied product market. Models by Whinston, Farrell and Katz, and Choi all espouse this view. As far as tying is concerned, innovation incentive arguments do not deserve special weight. Patent tying should not be subject to preferential treatment vis-à-vis other kinds of tying arrangements.

3. Implications for Developing Countries

The relationship between patent tying and innovation incentives could have significant implications for technological upgrade by developing countries. There are two main ways in which developing countries could attain technological upgrade: domestic innovation and technological adaptation from foreign sources. A developing country could improve its domestic technological capacity either by native innovation or importing technologies from other countries. The foregoing discussion focuses on innovation incentives generated by the domestic patent system and therefore should have little relevance for technological adaptation. In any case, competition rules on patent tying are unlikely to have a significant impact on the incentives of foreign technology owners to export technology. Discussion in Chapter 3 suggests that the legal rules that feature most prominently in the decision-making process of foreign technology owners are those that implicate the robustness of patent protection and those that affect the relative profitability of the various avenues for technology transfer. Rules on patent tying do not fall within either category. The extent to which patent tying is permitted by competition law, however, helps to determine the financial reward accruing to the patentee, which in turn may influence her incentives to invest further in R&D.

Innovation incentives will only be relevant to developing countries to the extent that there is domestic innovation capacity. This means that the foregoing discussion will probably have little salience to the production countries. For the technological adaptation and the proto-innovation countries, there would be a need to balance other welfare consequences of patent tying against any potential dynamic efficiency benefits if patent tying is found to promote innovation. Fortunately for our purposes, a trade-off is largely avoided because patent tying was not found to be conducive to innovation. The incentive effects of patent tying on innovation were found to be ambiguous at best. In fact, there is evidence that patent tying forecloses innovation in the tied product market, which is where a developing country firm is likely to gain a foothold on the ladder of technological advancement and innovation. If anything, innovation incentive considerations further bolster the argument for developing country authorities to take patent tying seriously. There is no need for these authorities to treat patent tying more leniently in order to spur innovation.

D. Tying and Leveraging and Foreclosure

The quintessential theory of harm for tying is foreclosure. Foreclosure is premised on the idea that the incumbent leverages its market power in the tying product market and extends it to the tied product market. Foreclosure can be said to describe the consequence of leveraging on the incumbent's rivals. Concerns about monopoly leveraging that were raised in Chapter 6 will be addressed here. Often the tied product is a complementary product that must be used together with the tying product. Cartons for aseptic packaging machines and spare parts and repair services for photocopying machines come to mind. Therefore, the ensuing discussion is applicable to scenarios involving complementary products that were alluded to in Chapter 6.

Foreclosure is the competitive harm of tying that has attracted the most attention from the courts and the commentators. In fact, the Hovenkamps argue that foreclosure should be the only competitive concern for tying.[155] The attention has been particularly focused on foreclosure in the tied product market.[156] The majority in the US *Kodak* case characterizes elimination of competitors in the tied product market as 'facially anticompetitive and exactly the harm that antitrust laws aim to prevent'.[157] The then-Court of First Instance also concentrates on foreclosure effects in the tied product market in the *EU Microsoft* case. In addition, academic commentary on the competitive harm of tying has been heavily tilted toward this issue.[158]

155 Hovenkamp and Hovenkamp (n 4) 967.
156 ibid 927.
157 Kodak, 504 US at 478.
158 Bruce H Kobayashi, 'Does Economics Provide a Reliable Guide to Regulating Commodity Bundling by Firms? A Survey of the Economic Literature' (2005) 1 Journal of Competition Law & Economics 707, 727–37; Dennis W Carlton and Michael Waldman, 'Tying, Upgrades, and Switching Costs in Durable Goods Market' (2005) <http://economics.mit.edu/files/4057> accessed 29 July 2021; Jay Pil Cho1i and Christodoulos Stefanadis, 'Tying, Investment, and the Dynamic Leverage Theory' (2001) 32 RAND Journal of Economics 52.

Leveraging can be used both offensively and defensively. Although both kinds of leveraging may involve foreclosure in the tied product market, the ultimate objective is different. The objective of offensive leveraging is to extend market power from the tying product market into the tied product market. The aim is offensive in nature. In contrast, the objective of defensive leveraging is to thwart possible attempts to enter the tying product market by denying a potential entrant access to the tied product. It may still entail the foreclosure and exclusion of rivals in the tied product market. Such exclusion is not the end goal, however. The end goal instead is the protection of the incumbent's position in the tying product market.

1. The Leverage Theory and Foreclosure

The leverage theory is probably the theory of harm for tying with the longest pedigree. It held sway over judicial thinking about tying in the United States for a better part of the last century until the Chicago School adherents came along and sought to debunk it with the single monopoly profit theorem. Beginning in the 1990s, the post-Chicago School commentators started to deconstruct and dismantle the single monopoly profit theorem and illustrate that foreclosure in the tied product market is eminently possible and that tying deserves a closer look from the enforcement authorities and the courts. Given the significant implications of this debate between the original proponents, the Chicago School critics, and the subsequent post-Chicago rehabilitators of the leverage theory on the appropriate legal standard for tying, an examination and possible resolution of the debate will help developing countries to formulate a correct enforcement approach for patent tying.

The leverage theory was first articulated by Justice White of the US Supreme Court more than a century ago.[159] Even Bowman, who is no fan of the leverage theory, acknowledges that 'in a very real sense the conception of the whole Clayton Act depends upon the leverage notion'.[160] Under the leverage theory,

> a monopoly over one good (tying good) could monopolize another (tied good) by selling them only in conjunction with each other. If it did so, a firm seeking to compete in the market for the tied good would be foreclosed from selling to all those who received the tied good in conjunction with their purchase of the tying good.[161]

[159] *Henry v. A.B. Dick Co.*, 224 US 1 (1912).

[160] Bowman, Jr (n 1) 30.

[161] Keith N Hylton and Michael Salinger, 'Tying Law and Policy: A Decision-Theoretic Approach' (2001) 69 Antitrust Law Journal 469, 484–85.

In essence, an incumbent leverages its market power in the tying product market to foreclose rivals in the tied product market, with the ultimate end goal of acquiring a second monopoly.[162] Bowman uses the term 'leverage' to describe 'the establishment of a new or second monopoly'.[163] The Hovenkamps have confusingly associated the leverage theory with the extraction of consumer surplus in contradistinction with foreclosure.[164] The correct dichotomy, however, should be leveraging and foreclosure on the one hand and price discrimination and surplus extraction on the other hand.

Despite its pedigree, the leverage theory has not been without detractors. Not every commentator is ready to accept that monopoly leveraging and the related problem of foreclosure are worthy concerns for competition law. The Hovenkamps observe that '[m]any antitrust theories prior to the 1980s were based on exaggerated views of the anticompetitive possibilities of leverage'.[165] They note that 'leverage was never a significant component in Harvard School antitrust analysis' and has been roundly rejected by the Chicago School since Bowman's article in 1957.[166] Chicago School scholars have long argued that monopoly leveraging and foreclosure are unrealistic. They have focused their attention on a number of limitations of the theory. First, no second monopoly can be created in the tied product market when the tying product is essential for all uses of the tied product.[167] In other words, the leverage theory does not hold when the tied product has no independent uses without the tying product. Carlton and Waldman note that 'in one-period settings, if the monopolist's primary good is essential for all uses of the complementary good, then there is no return for the monopolist to tie because selling individual products and pricing optimally guarantees the monopolist profits at least as high as with tying'.[168] The analysis, however, changes completely in a dynamic setting, where the limitation of essentiality breaks down and tying can be used to hurt competition.[169]

Second, the theory is more applicable to complementary products and less so to non-complementary ones. Despite his ferocious critique of the leverage theory, Bowman concedes the possibility of monopoly leveraging with complementary products. He notes that when complementary products are involved, 'the higher price charged for product B is not a substituted means of charging for product A'.[170]

162 Hovenkamp and Hovenkamp (n 4) 931.
163 Bowman, Jr (n 1) 20.
164 Hovenkamp and Hovenkamp (n 4) 926.
165 ibid 931.
166 ibid.
167 Dennis W Carlton and Michael Waldman, 'Theories of Tying and Implications for Antitrust' (Cornell University The Johnson School 2005) #24-06 17 <https://papers.ssrn.com/sol3/papers.cfm?abstract_id=809304> accessed 29 July 2021.
168 ibid.
169 Carlton and Waldman, 'How Economics Can Improve Antitrust Doctrine towards Tie-In Sales: Comment on Jean Tirole's "The Analysis of Tying Cases: A Primer" ' (n 52) 33.
170 Bowman, Jr (n 1) 25.

Instead, tying of two complementary products 'create the equivalent of another monopoly, a monopoly over product B for use with product A'.[171] He explains that 'in the complementarity case, control over B is essential to securing revenue which could not be realized from A alone; and the tie-in creates the equivalent of a new monopoly of B in addition to the monopoly of the complementary product A'.[172] Critics of the leverage theory have hence limited its scope of application to cases involving complementary products where the tied product has independent uses without the tying product.

This leads us to what was once the powerful critique of the leverage theory: the single monopoly profit theorem. The essence of this theorem is that when the tying and the tied products are used in fixed proportions, as in the case of nuts and bolts and left shoe and right shoe:

> no revenue can be derived from setting a higher price for the tied product which could not have been made by setting the optimum price for the tying product. The imposition of a tie-in under these circumstances determines the identity of the seller, but the amount of the tied product actually sold will not differ at all from that which could be sold if the optimum price for the tying product were set.[173]

If the monopolist wants to increase its profit from the tied product, it will be forced to charge less for the tying product.[174] There is a fixed amount of profit to be made by the monopolist from the market power it wields in the tying product market. It can choose to make all of the profit in either of the tying product or the tied product market, or split it between the two. Tying only affects the allocation of profit between the two markets.

This leads Bowman to conclude that through tying, '[t]he seller has only established a new method of exercising his already existing monopoly in the regulated product. Leverage, therefore, does not exist when the proportions of the two products are fixed'.[175] In fixed-proportions complementary product cases, the demand for the two products is dependent on their total price.[176] A cheaper tied product will in fact boost demand for the tying product. This means that when faced with a more efficient tied good rival, it would be in the monopolist's interest to retreat from the tied product market, let the more efficient rival take over, and raise the price of the tying product.[177]

[171] ibid.
[172] ibid 27.
[173] ibid 22.
[174] ibid 21.
[175] ibid 22.
[176] Hylton and Salinger (n 161) 486.
[177] Ahlborn, Evans and Padilla (n 82) 324.

After dominating economic thinking about tying for decades, the single monopoly profit theorem has since been largely discredited.[178] The stranglehold of the theorem on antitrust thinking, however, means that the leverage theory is yet to achieve full rehabilitation. The leverage theory is more widely accepted in the European Union, which has been largely spared from the Chicago School's onslaught, than in the United States.[179] Keith Hylton and Michael Salinger characterize it as 'a relatively weak part of the Chicago attack'.[180] Elhauge calls single monopoly profits the exception rather than the rule.[181] He has identified five restrictive assumptions of the theorem: '(1) Buyers do not use varying amounts of the tied product with the tying product. (2) Buyer demand for the two products has a strong positive correlation. (3) Buyers do not use varying amounts of the tying product. (4) The competitiveness of the tied market is fixed. (5) The competitiveness of the tying market is fixed'.[182] (1) and (3) pertain to the fixed-proportions stipulation of the theorem, which falls apart as soon the stipulation is relaxed. Elhauge sagaciously observes that

> [t]he single monopoly profit theory does not hold with or without a fixed ratio, with or without a strong positive demand correlation, and with or without substantial tied foreclosure. It takes a combination of a fixed ratio, a strong positive demand correlation, and a lack of substantial tied foreclosure for the single monopoly profit theory to hold.[183]

Apart from the fixed-proportions limitation, one of the main flaws of the theorem is its stipulation of a perfectly competitive tied product market, which Elhauge refers to under (4).[184] This stipulation is premised on a number of critical oversimplifying sub-assumptions about the tied product market, including no entry or fixed costs for tied market rivals, constant marginal costs for the tied product, which in turn requires the absence of scale economies in production, sufficient competition in the tied product market to drive prices to the marginal cost, and the existence of rivals' capacity to supply the entire market on short notice.[185] These assumptions are understandable because the theorem is focused on surplus extraction under static market conditions. Its central tenet is to demonstrate the impossibility for a monopolist to increase her monopoly profits through tying. It, however, overlooks the dynamic aspect of the leverage theory, which is concerned

[178] Hylton and Salinger (n 161) 487.
[179] Nicholas Economides and Ioannis Lianos, 'Elusive Antitrust Standard on Bundling in Europe and in the United States in the Aftermath of the Microsoft Case' (2009) 76 Antitrust Law Journal 483, 553.
[180] Hylton and Salinger (n 161) 487.
[181] Elhauge (n 3) 400.
[182] ibid.
[183] ibid 400–01.
[184] Ahlborn, Evans, and Padilla (n 82) 325.
[185] Elhauge (n 3) 413.

with foreclosure in the tied product market. It does so by flatly stipulating that it is impossible to acquire market power in the tied product market.[186]

It is perhaps the theorem's focus on surplus extraction that misled the Hovenkamps into equating the leverage theory with surplus extraction. The critique of the theory is about surplus extraction, but the theory itself is not. The critique has thus misdirected the commentators' attention. Under the single monopoly profit theorem, the possible dynamic competitive harm of tying is simply assumed away. The theorem's assumptions are highly improbable and are unlikely to hold in many real-world markets. Most of the markets in which tying is likely to be a concern are oligopolistic ones, where foreclosure is much more probable and feasible.[187] Yet these are the markets that have been deliberately omitted from the theorem.

Once these assumptions are relaxed and the tied product market is no longer presumed to be perfectly competitive, the theorem falls apart and foreclosure of rivals in the tied product market becomes a distinct possibility.[188] Tying can result in exit of rivals from the tied product market. It can also 'reduce rival competitiveness by impairing rival efficiency, entry, existence, aggressiveness, or expandability'.[189] Nobel Laureate Jean Tirole notes that the impact of tying on the tied product market 'ranges from little impact on the rivals' ability to compete to total exclusion of competitors'.[190] Two factors may help to determine the extent of impact, including the marginal cost of producing the tied product and the rival's ability to differentiate its product from the tied product.[191] Recall the other qualifications of the leverage theory. Foreclosure of rivals in the tied product market is impossible if the tying and the tied products are used in fixed proportions and if the tied product has no independent use without the tying product.[192]

Tirole further suggests that tying can be analysed through the lens of predation.[193] Elhauge, however, disagrees and clarifies that tying can cause foreclosure effects absent sacrifice of short-term profits or commitment to engage in unprofitable conduct.[194] This is corroborated by Barry Nalebuff's and Richard Schmalensee's models,[195] under which exclusion is achieved without pricing below costs or a sacrifice of profits.[196] These minor disagreements notwithstanding,

186 ibid 413–17.

187 Hylton and Salinger (n 161) 488; Warren Grimes, 'The Antitrust Tying Law Schism: A Critique of Microsoft III and a Response to Hylton and Salinger' (2002) 70 Antitrust Law Journal 199, 200.

188 Ahlborn, Evans, and Padilla (n 82) 325.

189 Elhauge (n 3) 413.

190 Jean Tirole, 'The Analysis of Tying Cases: A Primer' (2005) 1 Competition Policy International 1, 25.

191 ibid.

192 Elhauge (n 3) 416.

193 Tirole (n 190) 20–23.

194 Elhauge (n 3) 404.

195 Richard Schmalensee, 'Commodity Bundling by Single Product Monopolies' (1982) 25 Journal of Law & Economics 67.

196 Kobayashi (n 158) 730.

foreclosure in the tied product market is indisputably one of the chief competitive concerns for tying and should play a decisive role in shaping the enforcement approach to patent tying in developing countries.

2. Offensive Leveraging and Foreclosure in the Tied Product Market

Foreclosure effects are defined as exclusion of rivals either for the purpose of the acquisition of a second monopoly position or the defence of an existing market position. These effects need not necessarily entail the extension of market power. For the purpose of this chapter, offensive leveraging refers to when the locus of the intended effects is in the tied product market, while defensive leveraging is used to defend the incumbent's position in the tying product market.

There is a wealth of literature on the foreclosure effects of tying in the tied product market. This body of literature is too voluminous for an exhaustive survey to be undertaken here. What will be offered instead is a selective overview. Just as the single monopoly profit theorem is based on some critical assumptions, the same is true of offensive leveraging. Tying is most effective as an offensive leveraging weapon when the demand for the two goods is positively correlated and it loses its effectiveness completely when the tying and tied goods have perfectly negatively correlated valuations.[197] This means that offensive leveraging and inter-product price discrimination may not necessarily co-exist. Recall that inter-product price discrimination would be impossible if the demand for the two products shares a very strong positive correlation, which is when offensive leveraging is the most effective.

(a) Whinston (1990)

The leading article on how tying facilitates foreclosure in the tied product market is probably Whinston's 1990 seminal article in the American Economic Review.[198] This article can be said to be the first post-Chicago challenge to the Chicago School's stranglehold on the theoretical thinking on tying.[199] He identifies a notable flaw in the Chicago School-inspired scholarship, which tends to overlook 'the central concern inherent in the leverage theory, namely, that tying may be an effective (and profitable) means for a monopolist to affect the market structure of the tied good market (i.e., "monopolize" it) by making continued operation unprofitable for tied good rivals'.[200] This oversight can be attributed to 'the literature's

[197] Nalebuff (n 97) 160.
[198] Ahlborn, Evans and Padilla (n 82) 325.
[199] Nalebuff (n 97) 162–63.
[200] Whinston (n 96) 838.

pervasive (and sometimes implicit) assumption that the tied good market has a competitive, constant returns-to-scale structure'.[201] Whinston affirms the impossibility of leveraging and foreclosure in light of the Chicago School's assumptions about the tied product market.[202]

Another critical assumption of the Chicago School's defence of tying is that the tied product has no independent use without the tying product. Whinston's analysis confirms that under this assumption, the incumbent will have no incentives to tie to impair competition in the tied product market.[203] Once independent uses of the tied product are allowed, however, tying can be used to hurt rivals in the tied product market.[204] One further assumption is that the tie is irreversible, meaning that consumers cannot defeat the tie by replacing the incumbent's tied good with another complementary product.[205]

One of the critical changes made by Whinston to these assumptions is that scale economies exist in the production process for the tied good, which implies an oligopolistic structure for the tied product market.[206] Foreclosure becomes possible under imperfect competition in the presence of economies of scale.[207] The way tying accomplishes foreclosure is by reducing 'the sales of its tied good market competitor, thereby lowering his profits below the level that would justify continued operation'.[208] Knowing this, potential rivals would refrain from entering the market and existing competitors would exit.[209] Tying would not be profitable to the incumbent on static terms but would be so in a dynamic sense 'when the exclusion of rivals through predation is possible'.[210] Although tying would hurt both the incumbent's and the rival's profits, the rival would suffer more.[211] Whinston concludes that 'tying can lead to a monopolization of the tied good market'.[212]

Whinston also relaxes the assumption of no independent use for the tied product and demonstrates that tying can thus hurt rivals in the tied product market. In the absence of independent uses for the tied product, the incumbent benefits from the increased competitiveness in the tied product market through sales of the tying product.[213] But when there are independent uses for the tied product, some of the surplus generated by a competitive tied product market will elude the incumbent.

201 ibid.
202 ibid.
203 ibid 840.
204 ibid.
205 Carlton and Waldman, 'Theories of Tying and Implications for Antitrust' (n 167) 11.
206 Whinston (n 96) 839.
207 Carlton and Waldman, 'The Strategic Use of Tying to Preserve and Create Market Power in Evolving Industries' (n 131) 195.
208 Whinston (n 96) 839.
209 Ahlborn, Evans, and Padilla (n 82) 326.
210 Whinston (n 96) 840.
211 Ahlborn, Evans, and Padilla (n 82) 326.
212 Whinston (n 96) 839.
213 ibid 854.

This will give the incumbent the incentive to tie to harm rivals. By imposing a tie, the incumbent excludes rivals from the joint use part of the tied product market.[214] Once the two products are tied, the incumbent must sell both products together to realize profits on the tying product.[215] To increase sales of the tying product, the incumbent must cut the price of the bundle, which in turn forces the incumbent to lower the implicit price for the tied product.[216] This may push rivals' sales to an unprofitable level and render their continual operation in the tied product market non-viable.[217] Potential entrants will also be deterred from entering the market.[218] Rivals are thus foreclosed from the tied product market.

Whinston's model is predicated on the incumbent's ability to make a credible pre-commitment to tie prior to market entry.[219] The significance of tying is that it 'represents a commitment to foreclose sales in the tied good market'.[220] In other words, tying commits the incumbent to be aggressive in the tied product market.[221] Whinston characterizes the exclusionary effect of tying as 'strategic foreclosure', which requires the incumbent to make a credible pre-commitment to tie.[222] The credibility of the commitment is important because once entry has occurred, the rational strategy for the incumbent is to accommodate the entrant by lowering output and abstaining from tying.[223] When the incumbent ties, it foregoes profits from lost sales in the tying product market and the lower prices it must offer in the tied product market to match rivals' prices.[224] Therefore, the incumbent would never commit to tie unless it knew it could force the rival out of the tied product market, which would raise the incumbent's profits unless a sufficient number of consumers have negative valuation of the tied product such that they would opt to abandon the tying product instead of accepting the tie.[225] Once the incumbent has committed to tie, however, it can only continue to enjoy monopoly profits from the tying product if it also makes substantial sales of the tied product, which requires the incumbent to cut prices and take significant market share from rivals.[226] A pre-commitment to tie could be made through product design or adjustments to the production process, both of which entail significant sunk costs.[227]

[214] ibid. Carlton and Waldman, 'How Economics Can Improve Antitrust Doctrine towards Tie-In Sales: Comment on Jean Tirole's "The Analysis of Tying Cases: A Primer"' (n 52) 37.
[215] Carlton and Waldman, 'Theories of Tying and Implications for Antitrust' (n 167) 14.
[216] Carlton and Waldman, 'Robert Bork's Contributions to Antitrust Perspectives on Tying Behavior' (n 40) 132.
[217] Whinston (n 96) 854.
[218] Carlton and Waldman, 'Theories of Tying and Implications for Antitrust' (n 167) 14.
[219] Whinston (n 96) 839.
[220] ibid 840.
[221] Nalebuff (n 97) 163.
[222] Whinston (n 96) 840.
[223] ibid.
[224] ibid 844.
[225] ibid 844–45.
[226] ibid 840.
[227] ibid 839.

Whinston notes that tying has an ambiguous impact on consumer welfare. He lists a litany of consumer harm from tying, such as higher prices and loss of variety as a result of rival exit from the tied product market. He contends that 'tying that leads to the exit of the monopolist's tied market rival frequently leads to increases in all prices, making consumers uniformly worse off'.[228] Some consumers, however, may benefit from tying due to the mixed effects of price discrimination on welfare.[229] These mixed effects, however, should not be overstated. It has been demonstrated that price discrimination implemented through tying generally harms consumers. In any case, price discrimination will only benefit a subset of consumers while higher prices and loss of variety affect the entire market. Loss of variety will be a particularly serious concern if the tied product incorporates its own technology. In that case, rival exit will result in the disappearance of a technological path that may give rise to future innovations. When the source of future innovations is uncertain, preservation of research diversity is critical from a dynamic efficiency perspective.[230]

Overall, tying harms consumers under Whinston's analysis. Having said that, Whinston cautions against drawing conclusions from his analysis for policy recommendations. The reasons he gives are that his analysis overlooks other motivations for tying and that there is considerable difficulty in distinguishing between foreclosing and pro-competitive uses of tying.[231]

(b) Nalebuff (1990)

Barry Nalebuff has proposed another influential model on foreclosure. Although his model shares some similarities with Whinston's, one crucial difference between them is that Nalebuff's model does not require a credible pre-commitment to tie.[232] Credibility of commitment is not an issue under Nalebuff's model because tying would still be a rational strategy for the incumbent after successful market entry. Regardless of the success of the foreclosure strategy, the incumbent's profits are higher with a tie than without.[233] The incumbent makes more profit selling the tying and the tied products as a bundle than as separate products.[234] Tying is a superior pricing tool even if it fails to deter entry.[235] Christian Ahlborn and coauthors observe that 'in Nalebuff's model tying becomes a way for the competing firms to differentiate their products and thus relax price competition'.[236] In his numerical example, the incumbent's profits are 50 per cent higher if the products are

228 ibid.
229 ibid.
230 Choi (n 137) 97.
231 Whinston (n 96) 855–56.
232 Ahlborn, Evans, and Padilla (n 82) 327.
233 Nalebuff (n 97) 159.
234 ibid.
235 ibid.
236 Ahlborn, Evans, and Padilla (n 82) 327.

tied even if entry deterrence fails.[237] Profits would more than double if entry deterrence was successful.[238] Therefore, the incumbent would have the incentive to maintain the tie post-entry.[239] In fact, Nalebuff describes the option of unbundling as the 'nuclear bomb'[240] because it is too powerful to be a credible response.[241] The entrant's post-entry profits would be even lower if the incumbent could commit not to bundle following entry.[242]

In his model, there is an incumbent that produces both the tying and the tied products, and a possible new entrant that can enter either market but not both.[243] The incumbent has market power in both markets.[244] Nalebuff calls such a firm a 'multigood monopolist'.[245] Tying is valuable because it 'allows an incumbent to credibly defend both products without having to price low in each'.[246] Tying is not used to leverage market power from one market into another.[247] Instead, it is used to allow the incumbent to pool together its market power in the two markets to protect its positions in both.[248] Tying achieves this by softening the blow of a one-product rival by limiting the number of customers that such a rival can attract, which allows the incumbent to keep its competitive response of price reduction to a minimum.[249] The main function of tying is hence to help the incumbent preserve its market power in both markets.

Tying deters market entry through two effects, which Nalebuff calls 'the pure bundling effect' and the 'bundled discount effect'.[250] The former refers to how 'the incumbent and challenger simply translate their independent pricing strategy into the bundled case without reoptimizing'.[251] The latter arises when the bundle offers a discount from the original à-la-carte prices, which makes entry even less profitable.[252] Nalebuff summarizes the essence of the tying strategy as follows:

> A firm that has only some components of a bundle will find it hard to enter against an incumbent who sells a package solution at a discount. This will be especially true when the consumers have positively correlated values for the components of the package or when the components are complements. Bundling also softens the

[237] Nalebuff (n 97) 183.
[238] ibid.
[239] ibid 173.
[240] ibid 166.
[241] ibid.
[242] ibid 174.
[243] ibid 159.
[244] ibid.
[245] ibid 183.
[246] ibid 159.
[247] ibid 183.
[248] ibid.
[249] ibid.
[250] ibid 168.
[251] ibid.
[252] ibid.

harm done by a one-product (or limited line) competitor. The rival takes fewer customers away, and prices do not fall as far.[253]

The crux of the foreclosure effect is that the price reduction from the bundled discounts hurts the new entrant's profitability but not the incumbent's.[254] The entrant's profits are kept low because it has difficulty capturing market share.[255] Tying leaves a smaller residual demand for either the tying or the tied product sold separately.[256] The tie leaves the entrant only with consumers who have a low valuation for the tying product and hence are willing to forego it.[257] Tying thus results in foreclosure, leaving entrants with insufficient scale to make entry viable.[258] Ahlborn and co-authors contrast Nalebuff's model with Whinston's, noting that '[i]n contrast to Whinston's model, tying makes entry more difficult, not because the monopolist is committed to a price war, but because it deprives the entrant of an adequate scale'.[259] Tying therefore gives the incumbent a relatively low-cost but powerful weapon to deter entry.

Tying will be a more effective strategy when the two products are complements, or more generally, when consumer valuations of the two products are positively correlated,[260] even though according to Nalebuff, complementarity is distinct from positive correlation.[261] Under positive correlation, entry is even less profitable to the rival because the rival will be forced to enter the market at very low prices.[262] In fact, the entrant's profit falls to zero when there is perfect positive correlation.[263] But if entry does occur, positive correlation will hurt the incumbent's profitability more due to the entrant's low prices, which the incumbent will be forced to match.[264] The effectiveness of tying is reduced, although it does not disappear completely, when the two products are substitutes or when consumer valuations are negatively correlated.[265] Under negative correlation, entry is easier for the rival but will be less painful to the incumbent should it occur.[266]

253 ibid 183.
254 ibid 169–70.
255 ibid 165.
256 Kobayashi (n 158) 735.
257 Ahlborn, Evans, and Padilla (n 82) 327.
258 Carlton and Waldman, 'Theories of Tying and Implications for Antitrust' (n 167) 14.
259 Ahlborn, Evans, and Padilla (n 82) 327.
260 Nalebuff (n 97) 174.
261 ibid 178.
262 ibid 177.
263 ibid 178.
264 ibid 177.
265 ibid 174.
266 ibid 177.

(c) Choi and Stefanadis (2001)

Jay Pil Choi and Christodoulos Stefanadis present another model of foreclosure which they characterize as 'a dynamic version of the old leverage doctrine'.[267] The dynamic nature of the model is due to 'the presence of a risky upfront R&D investment',[268] which serves as a prerequisite for market entry. They note that their model is particularly suitable for 'risky and dynamic industries where the primary mode of entry is via innovation with substantial investment costs'.[269] The model's focus on R&D investments renders it particularly relevant for patent tying.

The model consists of an incumbent that possesses market power in both the tying and the tied product markets. The two products are assumed to be perfect complements[270] and are used in fixed proportions.[271] Unlike in other models, in which the entrant, at least initially, can only enter the tied product market, there is potential for entry into both markets in their model.[272] When the incumbent ties, the entrant can no longer rely on the incumbent's complementary product. Once that happens, successful entry into one market will depend on successful entry into the other market.[273] Tying 'makes the prospects of a potential entrant's investment completely contingent on the other firm's success, lowering the probability that the entrant will eventually earn a profit'.[274] Tying thus increases the risks of R&D investment, which reduces a potential entrant's and a second entrant's innovation incentives.[275] This in turn further accentuates the risks of R&D investments, thereby forestalling the possibility of successful simultaneous entries.[276] Their model initially assumes that only the entrants can engage in R&D. The incumbent's technology is already fixed when the game begins.[277] This assumption is subsequently relaxed.

There are three main features that distinguish Choi and Stefanadis' model from the single economic profit theorem. First, in their model, the incumbent is not a pure monopolist but faces potential entry in both markets.[278] Second, whereas under the single monopoly profit theorem the incumbent tries to leverage its market power in a monopolized tying product market into a competitive tied product market, the incumbent has market power in both markets under their model.[279] Third, whereas the focus under the single monopoly profit theorem is

[267] Choi and Stefanadis (n 158) 52.
[268] ibid.
[269] ibid 53.
[270] ibid 52.
[271] ibid 56.
[272] ibid 70.
[273] ibid 52–53.
[274] ibid 60.
[275] ibid 53.
[276] Carlton and Waldman, 'Theories of Tying and Implications for Antitrust' (n 167) 22–23.
[277] Choi and Stefanadis (n 158) 56.
[278] ibid 55.
[279] ibid.

profit extraction, their model is principally concerned with foreclosure of R&D investments.[280]

In their model, potential entrants can only enter the market if their risky R&D investments are successful, which would give rise to an innovative product that is superior to the incumbent's current product. Entrants are presumed to have access to a superior technology to the incumbent's.[281] The incumbent faces a trade-off. If only one entrant succeeds in entering the market with an innovative product, the incumbent would benefit from a superior tied product and could extract the surplus created by this superior product through a 'price squeeze'.[282] But if both entrants succeed with their innovation, the incumbent will be displaced from both markets.[283] It would hence be rational for the incumbent to tie 'when the incumbent's risk of being supplanted by low-cost entry in both components dominates the benefits of entry in a single component'.[284] When the incumbent ties, 'it gives up the prospective benefit of innovation in a single component, but this may be outweighed by the reduced risk of being supplanted by low-cost entry into both components'.[285]

This trade-off presents a dilemma to the incumbent. The incumbent would have overwhelming incentives to unwind the tie when only one of the entrants succeeds.[286] Knowing that the incumbent would unwind its tying decision, potential entrants will be less deterred by the tie, which reduces uncertainty for their R&D investments.[287] In fact, where the pre-commitment to tie is not credible, potential entrants' innovation incentives are not affected at all.[288] Therefore, for the tie to work, the incumbent must be able to make a credible pre-commitment to tie or its tying decision must be irreversible.[289] Similar to Whinston's model, a credible pre-commitment is a critical element in their model of foreclosure.

Choi and Stefanadis extend their model to entry by an integrated entrant that produces both complementary products. This complicates the analysis but does not fundamentally change their conclusion. Bringing the R&D investment for both products under the same roof does not eliminate the uncertainty posed by tying completely. Instead, tying creates two effects for the integrated entrant, which Choi and Stefanadis call the 'own effect' and the 'cross effect'.[290] Own effect refers to the fact that tying reduces R&D investment because market entry requires successful R&D in both markets.[291] Meanwhile, cross effect refers to the internalized

280 ibid.
281 ibid 56.
282 ibid 53.
283 ibid.
284 ibid.
285 ibid 60.
286 ibid 53.
287 ibid.
288 ibid 61.
289 ibid 53.
290 ibid 63.
291 ibid.

externalities created by successful R&D for one product, which benefits both the product itself and the complementary product.[292] Absent integration, the first entrant does not internalize the benefit created by its own R&D to the other entrant. In contrast, an integrated entrant will have enhanced incentives to invest in the R&D for the tying product because it also captures the boost from such R&D to its tied product.[293] The balance between the own effect and the cross effect depends on the probability of success of R&D absent tying. Choi and Stefanadis find that when the probability is less than one-half, 'the own effect dominates the cross effect because it is more likely that innovation in the complementary component will fail, whereas uncertainty limits the positive benefits of additional investment to the complementary component'.[294]

Choi and Stefanadis further relax the assumption that only the entrants can invest in R&D to study the impact of tying on the incumbent's R&D incentives. This allows us to examine technological competition and assess the impact of tying on market-wide innovation incentives. Their conclusions are largely unchanged.[295] They conclude that tying increases the incumbent's innovation incentives because under tying, the incumbent can no longer partake in the surplus created by the entrant's successful innovation, which would require the incumbent to untie.[296] The incumbent can only benefit from its own innovation, which gives it greater incentives to invest in its own R&D.[297] The impact of tying on the entrant's innovation incentives again depends on its probability of success absent tying. If the probability is low (less than one-half in their calculation), the entrant will be likely to forego R&D because the own effect again dominates the cross effect.[298] Tying therefore achieves two benefits for the incumbent. It both protects its position in the market for the two products and gives it an edge in technological competition.

Despite some equivocations, Choi and Stefanadis ultimately conclude that tying harms consumer welfare. Consumer surplus would only increase if both entrants succeed in their R&D, the probability of which is suppressed by tying.[299] The impact on social welfare or market-wide innovation incentives depends on the trade-off between the costs of duplication of research and the benefits of diversity of research pathways, which has been alluded to earlier. The greater the uncertainty of research outcome, the more valuable is a multiplicity of approaches. Absent a very strong case of wasteful duplicated research, this author believes that diversity of research pathways should be favoured. In that case, tying has a clear detrimental impact on general innovation incentives.

[292] ibid.
[293] ibid.
[294] ibid 64.
[295] ibid.
[296] ibid 66.
[297] ibid.
[298] ibid 68.
[299] ibid 62.

(d) Choi (1996)

In an earlier article, Jay Pil Choi gives a dynamic reinterpretation of the meaning of monopoly leveraging. He does this by proposing a model in which the incumbent can make use of tying to pool together its monopoly slack,[300] which can be loosely equated as market power, from two markets to relieve the competitive pressure to which it is subject to pursue pre-emptive R&D. Tying is profitable to the incumbent because it reduces the rent dissipated by the incumbent's investment in pre-emptive R&D,[301] but it is clearly harmful to society as it reduces innovation incentives. Tying is said to permit the incumbent 'to control the rules of the game across the industry's constituent markets, thereby, regulating the rate, direction, timing, and source of commercially viable innovation in the markets'.[302]

The fundamental idea underlying his model is that firms are subject to a constraint to pursue pre-emptive R&D the closer their technological position is to that of their rivals'. The greater is the asymmetry in their initial technological positions, the weaker is the pressure on the technological leader to pursue pre-emptive R&D.[303] The technological leader can undertake R&D at its own pace.[304] Conversely, the more symmetrical their initial technological positions, the tighter is the constraint on the technological leader to pursue pre-emptive R&D, which will dissipate rent.[305] If an incumbent faces a non-binding constraint in one market and a binding constraint in another, the incumbent may shift 'an unused monopoly slack'[306] from the former to relieve pressure in the latter. Choi calls this shift of monopoly slack across markets 'the "leverage" of market power'.[307] Tying allows the incumbent to accomplish exactly that. He describes the role of tying in equalizing the competitive pressure or constraint for pre-emptive R&D in the two markets as follows. It:

> creates an interdependence between constituent markets. This interdependence in the output market effectively turns the two separate R&D games over components into a single one over the system, which allows the firm to utilize the unused monopoly slack in one market to bolster the strategic position in the other market. As a result, this pooling of strategic strengths in two markets can lead to the leverage of monopoly power from one market to another and can be successfully used to exclude rival firms from markets, which otherwise would have been profitable.[308]

300 Jay Pil Choi, 'Preemptive R&D, Rent Dissipation, and the "Leverage Theory"' (1996) 111 Quarterly Journal of Economics 1153, 1153.

301 ibid 1154.

302 ibid.

303 ibid.

304 ibid 1154–55.

305 ibid 1154.

306 ibid 1155.

307 ibid 1169.

308 ibid 1155.

He further contends that tying 'enables the integrated monopoly to deprive the rival firms of a fair shot at competing on a level playing field and, thus, to control the means by which others can be prevented from winning'.[309]

Choi demonstrates that absent R&D competition, tying intensifies price competition and can only reduce the incumbent's profitability. This is because even though tying diverts rival's customers to the incumbent, it also forces the incumbent to sell at the rival's total marginal cost.[310] He concludes that tying is both unprofitable to the incumbent and detrimental to social welfare in the static sense.[311] Tying, however, can be profitable to the incumbent in a dynamic setting once one takes into account the reduced rent dissipation made possible by equalizing the constraints on pre-emptive R&D in the two markets.[312] He shows that where there is technological parity between the incumbent and the rival across the two markets, there will be an excessive incentive for the incumbent to tie due to a 'discrepancy between the consumer surplus effect and the business stealing effect'.[313]

He demonstrates this in a three-stage model.[314] The two firms decide whether to make their products compatible in the first stage. They undertake R&D activities to reduce production costs in the second stage. In the final stage, they compete on price based on the cost structure determined by the R&D they undertook in the previous stage. Tying allows the incumbent to pool together its monopoly slack in different markets because with tying, 'the deciding factor for market dominance is the overall production cost of the bundled products; the distributions of the production costs across components are irrelevant'.[315] This causes the incumbent to determine its R&D strategy from an integrated perspective. The monopoly slack is usually found in the tying product market while the incumbent should be subject to a binding constraint for pre-emptive R&D in the tied product market.[316] It will try to achieve maximum cost savings by optimizing allocation of R&D investments between the two products.[317] R&D competition is now undertaken on a bundle level as opposed to the individual product level.[318] Tying allows the incumbent to increase its overall rent at no cost. With tying, the incumbent is able to increase its rent in the market in which it is subject to a binding constraint for pre-emptive R&D without losing rent in the market in which the constraint is non-binding.[319]

309 ibid.
310 ibid 1156.
311 ibid.
312 ibid.
313 ibid 1173.
314 ibid 1159.
315 ibid 1165.
316 ibid 1168.
317 ibid 1165.
318 ibid 1167.
319 ibid 1168.

The result is that where neither the incumbent nor the rival has a distinct technological advantage in both markets, tying reduces the incumbent's innovation incentives,[320] lowers rival's profits, and harms consumer welfare.[321] In contrast, tying is efficient if one firm is the clear winner in the R&D race in both markets.[322] Tying does not reduce the rival's profits or consumer surplus. The rival will make no profit with or without tying if it is technologically inferior in both markets.[323]

3. Defensive Leveraging and the Enhancement of Market Power in the Tying Product Market

Even though discussion about the anticompetitive effects of tying tends to focus on foreclosure in the tied product market, tying can also be deployed to protect the incumbent's market power in the tying product market. Defensive leveraging is engaged 'to deter or delay later entry into the tying market, thus maintaining [the incumbent's] tying market power for longer or at a higher degree than it would have without tying'.[324] Tirole acknowledges the possibility of defensive leveraging.[325] Even Robert Bork, the great defender of tying, concedes that defensive leveraging is a plausible theory of harm for tying.[326]

According to Elhauge, there are three ways in which this can be accomplished, which include '(1) foreclosing enough of the tied [product] market to deter or delay later entry into the tying [product] market, (2) raising the costs of a partial substitute that constrains tying market power, or (3) transferring market power from a waning technology to the next-generation technology'.[327] These theories tend to work best when the tying and the tied products are complements.[328] Alarmingly, some of these theories do not require the rival in the tied product market to be less efficient than the incumbent. They are still valid even if the rival is more efficient.[329] Despite the conclusions from these models, however, Carlton and Waldman caution against undue reliance on them for policy recommendations. They assert that

> tying is typically driven by efficiency and courts have difficulty judging the extent to which the tie has an efficiency justification, so anything but a high hurdle [for

[320] ibid 1169.

[321] ibid 1172.

[322] ibid 1171.

[323] ibid 1170.

[324] Elhauge (n 3) 417.

[325] Tirole (n 190) 18–19.

[326] Carlton and Waldman, 'Robert Bork's Contributions to Antitrust Perspectives on Tying Behavior' (n 40) 140.

[327] Elhauge (n 3) 417.

[328] Carlton and Waldman, 'The Strategic Use of Tying to Preserve and Create Market Power in Evolving Industries' (n 131) 197.

[329] ibid 195.

finding an antitrust violation] will likely hurt welfare because many of the cases ruled to be antitrust violations will actually be driven by efficiency.[330]

(a) Foreclosure of tied product market to delay entry into tying product market

There are a number of alternative formulations of the first theory. Under the first formulation, as Whinston postulates, the incumbent forecloses sufficient market share in the tied product market such that rivals cannot cover their fixed costs of entry.[331] This may lead to a dearth of competitive suppliers of the tied product, which would require future entrants into the tying product market to enter the tied product market as well. This would create what is known in the literature as the double-level entry requirement.[332] To the extent that it is more difficult for a new entrant to enter two markets at the same time, perhaps due to a lack of available funding, constrained management capability to manage simultaneous entry into two markets, or, to the extent the two markets require different technology, limited R&D capability, successful foreclosure of the tied product market will raise effective entry barriers for the tying product market and help protect the incumbent's market position.

The second formulation of this theory is based on situations in which future entrants into the tying product market are likely to evolve from a tied product producer.[333] This formulation was inspired by the *US Microsoft* case in which the US Department of Justice argued that Microsoft was trying to exclude Netscape in the browser market to prevent it from emerging as a successful middleware. Netscape's success as a middleware would threaten Windows' position in the operating system market by helping other rival operating system developers surmount the applications barrier to entry.[334] By keeping new entrants in the tied product market at bay, tying can help the incumbent to forestall potential challengers in the tying product market.

The third formulation is based on a model developed by Carlton and Waldman.[335] Theirs is a two-period model featuring two firms, one of which is monopolist in the tying product that also sells the tied product.[336] The tie is irreversible in the sense that consumers cannot replace the incumbent's tied product with a tied product from an alternative supplier.[337] The tying and the tied products

[330] Carlton and Waldman, 'Robert Bork's Contributions to Antitrust Perspectives on Tying Behavior' (n 40) 140.

[331] Whinston (n 96) 840.

[332] Bowman, Jr (n 1) 34. Devlin (n 46) 553–54.

[333] Elhauge (n 3) 417.

[334] *United States v. Microsoft Corp.*, 253 F.3d 34, 55 (D.C. Cir. 2001).

[335] Carlton and Waldman, 'The Strategic Use of Tying to Preserve and Create Market Power in Evolving Industries' (n 131).

[336] ibid 195.

[337] ibid 199.

are essential to each other in that they have no independent uses without the other.[338] The second firm can enter the tied product market at some cost in either the first or the second period.[339] It can also enter the tying product market in the second period, but only after it has already entered the tied product market. The significance of the irreversibility of the tie is that the second firm will not be able to sell any tied product if it does not produce the tying product once the incumbent has imposed a tie.[340] Therefore, the second firm will not enter the tied product market at all if it does not also plan to enter the tying product market eventually once a tie is in place.[341]

The two firms are assumed to produce tying products of equal quality but the second firm is assumed to produce a superior tied product if it does enter the market.[342] This superiority assumption is crucial because otherwise there would be no entry by the second firm into the tied product market.[343] In fact, Carlton and Waldman show that the results from their analysis would still apply if the second firm's tying product is superior in quality.[344] Tying is thus so powerful that it can forestall the entry of a rival which produces superior products in both markets. This obviously inflicts greater harm on consumers than when only a superior tied product is withheld from consumers.

If the incumbent does not tie, the second firm will be likely to enter the tied product market in the first period and the tying product market in the second period. Entry into the tying product market is essential to the rival because it allows the rival to capture some of the surplus from its superior tied product.[345] Carlton and Waldman show that the incumbent would only have the incentive to tie if there was a threat of entry into the tying product market in the second period.[346] This is because if the rival cannot enter the tying product market, the incumbent would be better off with rival selling its superior tied product. The incumbent's profit from the tying product increases when the second firm sells its superior tied product.

But if entry into the tying product market is possible, the incumbent will opt to tie, which will help the incumbent fend off entry through the following two mechanisms. The first is Whinston's standard foreclosure story that tying prevents the rival from recovering its fixed costs of entry into the tied product market.[347] The rival will hence abstain from the tied product market in both periods.[348]

338 Ahlborn, Evans, and Padilla (n 82) 335.

339 Carlton and Waldman, 'The Strategic Use of Tying to Preserve and Create Market Power in Evolving Industries' (n 131) 195.

340 ibid 199.

341 ibid.

342 ibid 195.

343 ibid 198.

344 ibid 203.

345 Carlton and Waldman, 'Theories of Tying and Implications for Antitrust' (n 167) 18.

346 Carlton and Waldman, 'The Strategic Use of Tying to Preserve and Create Market Power in Evolving Industries' (n 131) 195.

347 ibid 196.

348 Carlton and Waldman, 'Theories of Tying and Implications for Antitrust' (n 167) 19.

The second is that tying eliminates the rival's incentive to enter the tying product market. Carlton and Waldman explain that 'since in our model the return to the alternative producer of entering the primary market is capturing more of the surplus associated with its superior complementary product, when tying stops the alternative producer from entering the complementary market, it also stops the rival from entering the primary market'.[349]

Carlton and Waldman contend that this theory of harm is particularly relevant for innovative industries with have short product lifecycles but long imitation lags.[350] They conclude that it would be welfare-enhancing to prohibit tying under these circumstances because heterogeneous consumers prefer the variety of choices that comes with competition.[351] It should be noted that this model has been criticized for its restrictive assumptions of the lack of independent use of the tying product without the tied product and high entry costs for the tied product market, which precludes simultaneous entry into both markets.[352]

(b) Raising the costs of a partial substitute

The second theory is based on a scenario described by Whinston in his seminal article on tying. The idea is that the incumbent faces competition from a competitively supplied inferior substitute in the tying product market. The incumbent sells both the tying product and the tied product, which are complements,[353] while the rival only offers the tying product.[354] If the incumbent sells both products separately, its pricing in the tying product market will be constrained by the inferior substitute.[355] Prices will not be brought down to a competitive level because the substitute is an imperfect one, but the incumbent will be prevented from charging the full monopolist price. In that case, it would be beneficial for the incumbent to resort to tying to try to get rid of rivals in the tied product market by denying them minimum efficient scale.[356] Upon exit of these rivals, the inferior tying product supplier will be denied access to the tied product and will be forced to leave the market as well. This removes the constraint on the incumbent's pricing in the tying product market. Tying 'can be viewed as raising (to infinity) the cost of the rival to produce a desirable package for the consumer'.[357]

349 Carlton and Waldman, 'The Strategic Use of Tying to Preserve and Create Market Power in Evolving Industries' (n 131) 196.
350 ibid 196, 205.
351 ibid 204.
352 Ahlborn, Evans, and Padilla (n 82) 328.
353 Whinston (n 96) 852.
354 ibid 850.
355 ibid 852.
356 ibid 853.
357 Carlton and Waldman, 'Theories of Tying and Implications for Antitrust' (n 167) 18.

(c) Transferring market power to an emerging technology

The third theory was developed by Carlton and Waldman. They develop a variant of a two-period network externalities model in which there is a monopolized tying product and a complementary tied product that is characterized by network externalities in the first period and a new product emerging in the second period that serves as a superior substitute for the tying product.[358] The new products produced by the incumbent and the potential new entrant are of the same quality.[359] Carlton and Waldman show that the tying product monopolist can acquire a monopoly position in the market for the emerging product in the second period by pursuing a tie.[360] Ahlborn and co-authors argue that 'tying the complementary good to the monopoly product gives the monopolist a head start in the race to become the standard in the market for the complementary good market'.[361]

Tying plays a pivotal role here through its interaction with the costs for entering the tied product market. A tie instituted by the incumbent will reduce the potential entrant's return from operating in both the emerging product market and the complementary product market in the second period.[362] In particular, a tie 'lowers the profitability of a rival entering the newly emerging market in much the same way it lowered the profitability of a rival entering the primary market'[363] as described in Whinston's model. This will deter the new entrant from entering either market.[364] By depriving the new entrant of a complementary product to be used with its emerging new product, the tie deters the new entrant from entering the new product market.[365] The monopolist retains its monopoly profits even after its original tying product has been rendered obsolete.

Carlton and Waldman characterize the tie as allowing the monopolist to 'swing' or transfer its initial monopoly in the tying product to the market for the newly emerging product.[366] Prohibition of tying would definitely enhance social welfare if the emerging product is of superior quality to the existing tied production combination.[367]

[358] Carlton and Waldman, 'The Strategic Use of Tying to Preserve and Create Market Power in Evolving Industries' (n 131) 197.
[359] ibid 212.
[360] ibid 197.
[361] Ahlborn, Evans, and Padilla (n 82) 328.
[362] Carlton and Waldman, 'The Strategic Use of Tying to Preserve and Create Market Power in Evolving Industries' (n 131) 213.
[363] ibid 196–97.
[364] ibid 213.
[365] Carlton and Waldman, 'Theories of Tying and Implications for Antitrust' (n 167) 19.
[366] Carlton and Waldman, 'The Strategic Use of Tying to Preserve and Create Market Power in Evolving Industries' (n 131) 196.
[367] ibid 215.

4. Implications for Developing Countries

The foregoing theories have varying degrees of applicability to developing countries depending on their technological capacity. The extent to which foreclosing entry into the tying product market protected by patent protection should be of concern to a developing country depends on the likelihood that the country at issue will produce such an entrant.

The first thing we can say is that the impact of patent tying on the incentives of technology transfer is likely to be negligible. Recall that competition rules on patent exploitation practices are most relevant to technology transfer when they implicate the robustness of patent protection and when they regulate licensing, which may affect the choice of means of technology transfer. Competition rules on tying have no impact on the strength of patent protection. Nor does it have any bearing on the ease of involuntary technology transfer such as imitation or reverse engineering. These rules also do not affect the choice among trade of technological goods, foreign direct investment, and licensing. Whether tying is permitted or not should have little impact on the relative profitability of the three means of technology transfer. Therefore, tying overall is unlikely to be of great relevance as far as technology transfer is concerned.

As for the development of domestic technological capacity, tying would be of enforcement interest if it prevents a domestic firm from entering the tying product market and challenging the incumbent's market position by acquiring a comparable innovation. If it were possible to enter the tying product market with a low-tech substitute, the foreclosure effect from tying need not retard technological upgrade. While there may still be static welfare consequences, they are not of particular concern for our purposes. The ensuing discussion assumes that entry into the tying product market requires comparable technological capacity as the incumbent's. Foreclosure of the tying product market will be of little pertinence to the production countries. They are unable to innovate to produce the required technology regardless of the competition rules on tying. As for the technological adaptation countries, to the extent that their technological capacity limits them to the imitation or replication of inferior technology, Whinston's account of a competitively supplied inferior substitute in the tying product market will be especially relevant. A firm in a technological adaptation country will be likely to compete with a global technological leader with a technologically inferior offering. As for the proto-innovation countries, to the extent that they can produce technologies that are directly competitive with the incumbent firm's technology, all of the foregoing theoretical accounts will be of interest.

To the extent that the production of a tied product is less technologically intensive than that for the tying product, foreclosure of the tied product market will be a more serious concern to developing countries than foreclosure in the tying product market. This is likely to be the case in many instances. For example, an ink cartridge is likely to be much simpler to produce than a laser printer and a web browser easier to design and create than a full-fledged operating system. Oftentimes a tied product may allow the new entrant to acquire familiarity with part of the technology as a stepping-stone for mastering the more technologically sophisticated tying product. Foreclosure of the tied product market could mean the loss of a precious opportunity for technological upgrade. This means that aside from all the static welfare effects from the foreclosure of the tied product market, about which Whinston and Nalebuff seem to be ambivalent,[368] there are good reasons for developing countries to focus on foreclosure of the tied product market and take a particularly vigilant attitude toward patent tying.

Offensive leveraging is thus likely to be a more relevant concern than defensive leveraging for developing countries. Defensive leveraging will only matter to those developing countries where a domestic firm is likely to pose a threat to the incumbent's position in the tying product market. Given that the tying product is patented, unless it is possible to compete in that market with a low-tech substitute, the country at issue must possess sufficient technological capacity to produce a likely entrant into the tying product market. Defensive leveraging is unlikely to be an important consideration for the production countries. Its relevance increases with the country's technological capacity. Defensive leveraging will be pertinent for the technological adaptation countries to the extent that it is possible to enter the tying product market with a reverse-engineered or imitated product. Otherwise, entry into the patented tying product market would require genuine innovation capacity and defensive leveraging would only be of interest to the proto-innovation countries.

Models of defensive leveraging that are derived from Whinston's article are of wider applicability than the others. Foreclosure of rivals from the tying product market by depriving them access to a viable tied product may apply to lower-tech firms if it is possible to enter the tying product market with a low-tech substitute. A competitively supplied inferior tying product is also more likely to emanate from a developing country. To the extent that entry by a low-tech substitute is possible or that the inferior substitute is within the capability of a production country, this model will be of interest to all kinds of developing countries. The two models proposed by Carlton and Waldman have greater salience for developing countries with higher technological capacity. Both of them require the challenger to be able to produce a tying product that is of equal quality as the incumbent's. In one of them, the challenger is even expected to produce a superior tied product. Given that the tying product is patented, it is probably of sufficient technological sophistication to be beyond the capability of most production countries. If it is possible to replicate or reverse engineer the technology without falling afoul of the incumbent's patent

[368] Whinston (n 96) 845; Nalebuff (n 97) 181.

protection, then the technological adaptation countries may find these two models to be of interest as well. Otherwise, it will be mostly the proto-innovation countries that will need to pay heed to these two models. The same technological requirements probably apply to the model in which the tying product entrant is evolved from a tied product producer.

Offensive leveraging is concerned with foreclosure in the tied product market, although some of the models implicate both the tying and the tied product markets. To the extent one can generalize that the tying product is technologically more intensive than the tied product, which is likely to be true when the tied product is an aftermarket product or complementary staple product, models focusing on the tied product market will have greater relevance for a wider spectrum of developing countries. Models that envisage R&D competition with the incumbent will have more limited applicability as it requires the developing country at issue to have the capacity to engage in that kind of competition.

Among the four models introduced earlier, Whinston's model, which focuses on the tied product market, does not require R&D on the part of the challenger, and relies on the denial of scale of operation to foreclose rivals, deserves attention from all developing countries which produce tied products that are used with a patented tying product. No particular aspect of the model requires substantial technological capacity. Nalebuff's model allows challenges in either the tying or the tied product market. To the extent that the new competitive threat is expected to emerge in the tying product market, the technological requirement will be greater. Nonetheless, neither the rival's means of challenging the incumbent nor the incumbent's means of foreclosure involves R&D. The incumbent forecloses rivals by denying them market share. Therefore, the kind of foreclosure strategy examined by both models should be of interest to all developing countries that are capable of producing the tying or the tied product.

Both Choi and Stefanadis' and Choi's own models expressly incorporate R&D competition between the incumbent and rivals and would thus only be applicable to countries with substantial technological capacity. Choi and Stefanadis' model stipulates that the entrant have access to a superior technology to the incumbent's existing technology, which rules out entry by imitation. It therefore should only be relevant to proto-innovation countries. To the extent that potential entrants to both the tying and the tied product markets are limited to domestic firms, application of the model could be even more tenuous as it requires the country at issue to be capable of generating innovation in both markets. Choi's own model also presumes substantial technological capacity on the part of rivals. It focuses on the technological distance between the incumbent and rivals in the two markets and discusses how the incumbent can make use of tying to transfer monopoly slack across markets to engage in pre-emptive R&D. The constraint on the incumbent to engage in pre-emptive R&D would be completely non-binding if rivals were far behind in their technological capacity. For Choi's model to be of relevance, the technological distance between the incumbent and the rival must be of sufficient proximity in one of the markets, which requires substantial technological capacity on the part of the developing country.

E. Tying and Static Welfare

1. Static Welfare Harm

Apart from dynamic foreclosure effects, tying can also lead to static welfare loss. First and foremost, as mentioned by Choi, so long as tying results in the exclusion of certain consumers, it will lead to deadweight loss. Consumers will cease to consume the tying or the tied product if they do not desire both products together at the price being offered. The form of exclusion will depend on how the tie is implemented. If a tie is in place, meaning that the tying product will not be sold without the tied product, consumers could still purchase the tied product independently. Only those consumers who desire the tying product but not the tied product will be excluded. The incumbent will raise the bundle price above the stand-alone or à-la-carte price of the tying product. There will be a price increment. If a consumer's valuation of the tied product is smaller than this price increment, or in the more extreme case, the consumer has a negative valuation of the tied product, she will reject the tied product and be excluded from the market. If bundling is in place, which means that the two products are only sold together, then those consumers who only want the tied product will also be excluded. Obviously, this is only relevant if the tied product has independent uses apart from uses with the tying product. If the valuation of the tying product by consumers of the tied product is smaller than the price increment due to the bundle, these consumers will forego the tied product and exit the market. The exclusion of these consumers will obviously result in welfare loss.

Patent tying can also lead to rent-seeking behaviour. It is well-known in economic theory that increased monopoly profits will induce greater effort to strive for the monopoly position. Such rent-seeking investment is socially wasteful and would artificially inflate the private costs of innovation. Alan Sykes has noted that 'monopolists may invest resources in obtaining monopoly, thereby dissipating monopoly profits ex ante and causing further deadweight losses'.[369] Such rent-seeking behaviour is exacerbated in the patent context in particular. The exclusive character of patent protection means that firms will invest significant resources to be the first to patent a new technology. The wasteful character of patent races has

[369] Alan O Sykes, 'TRIPS, Pharmaceuticals, Developing Countries, and the Doha "Solution"' (2002) 3 Chicago Journal of International Law 47, 63.

already been discussed. The waste would be even greater if firms are induced to direct their R&D toward technology that lends itself to tying opportunities.

Such rent-seeking behaviour may be particularly costly from the perspective of a developing country, where resources are scarce. Precious resources that are wasted in the pursuit of a monopoly position will no longer be available for more productive purposes. Patent races, however, will probably be less relevant for developing countries without innovation capacity. Only firms that are capable of patentable innovation can take part in these races. Production and technological adaptation countries are unlikely to feature many firms with that capability. The social waste from patent races will probably only be of concern to the proto-innovation countries.

2. Pro-competitive Benefits

No account of the competitive effects analysis of tying would be complete without addressing its pro-competitive benefits. Those who call for *per se* legality or at least a Rule of Reason approach to tying have mostly based their arguments on the myriad pro-competitive benefits of tying. A detailed examination of each of these pro-competitive justifications is beyond the scope of this chapter. Suffice it to say that in light of all the equally prevalent competitive harm of tying, there are no strong justifications for espousing *per se* legality. Even a pro-competitive presumption for tying would be going too far. As in the rest of competition law, the burden should remain on the defendant to furnish evidence of pro-competitive benefits. The pro-competitive benefits that will be discussed below must be proven and not presumed.

(a) Ubiquity of tying

One of the frequently invoked, perhaps to the point of being hackneyed, arguments made in defence of tying is its ubiquity. This is not so much a pro-competitive benefit itself as the consequence of the alleged benefits of tying. Robert Bork has famously argued that '[e]very person who sells anything imposes a tying arrangement. This is true because every product or service could be broken down into smaller components capable of being sold separately, and every seller refuses at some point to break the product down any further.'[370] Hylton and Salinger are probably two of the more vocal proponents of this argument in recent times. Their argument is essentially that since left shoes are constantly sold together with right shoes and that such ties are clearly welcomed by consumers and ubiquitous in the

370 Robert H Bork, *The Antitrust Paradox: A Policy at War with Itself* (The Free Press 1978) 378.

economy, tying must be overwhelmingly pro-competitive and should be *per se* legal.[371]

There are two problems with this line of argumentation. First, tying law only applies in situations where the tying firm has market power in the tying product market. That is certainly true in the United States after *Jefferson Parish*.[372] Under EU law, tying has always been regulated under abuse of dominance, which requires a dominant position.[373] The chance of tying law being applied willy-nilly to a random shoe manufacturer who sells shoes in pair, as Hylton and Salinger alleges could happen under the qualified *per se* rule, is close to nil. Consumers are in no danger of being forced to shop for left and right shoes separately. This is a straw-man argument that should be summarily rejected. Even Hylton and Salinger themselves concede that the actual legal standard for tying in the United States is not nearly as stringent as that implied by the qualified *per se* rule.[374]

Second, the joint sale of left and right shoes is clearly not within the intended regulatory ambit of tying law. As Warren Grimes points out, such joint sales are referred to as bundled sales and 'the Supreme Court (albeit inconsistently) and many theorists have distinguished between bundled or packaged sales of products, which are almost always pro-competitive or benign, and tied sales, which are a narrower subset of bundled sales far more likely to be anticompetitive'.[375] One way to distinguish between bundled sales and tying, over which legal scrutiny may be justified, is when 'there is substantial demand for the sale of the bundled products as separate items and [] the seller is able to force the bundled sale on an unwilling buyer'.[376] Even Bruce Kobayashi, who is no supporter of the qualified *per se* rule for tying, has noted that tying

> is the sale of two or more separate products in a package. Separate products are defined as those where consumer demand exists for the stand-alone products outside of the bundle. This requirement allows us to rule out trivial cases of perfect complements, such the sale of left shoes and right shoes.[377]

To give due credit to Hylton and Salinger's argument, the line between competitively neutral bundled sales and ties that deserve legal scrutiny is probably not as self-evident as Grimes seems to suggest. Hylton and Salinger provide a number of

[371] Hylton and Salinger (n 161) 500.

[372] Herbert Hovenkamp, *Federal Antitrust Policy: The Law of Competition and Its Practice* (4th edn, West Publishing Co 2011) s 10.3.

[373] Alison Jones and Brenda Sufrin, *EU Competition Law: Text, Cases, and Materials* (5th edn, Oxford University Press 2014) 489.

[374] Hylton and Salinger (n 161) 502.

[375] Grimes (n 187) 215–16.

[376] ibid 216.

[377] Kobayashi (n 158) 710.

examples which do present some difficulty for the boundary drawing exercise.[378] Ultimately, the strongest argument against Hylton and Salinger is that even under what they characterize as an unduly harsh rule from *Jefferson Parish*, we have not witnessed a deluge of frivolous tying cases against bundled sales which are clearly beyond reproach. The apprehension that the qualified *per se* rule may invite a massive number of false positive cases is simply a false alarm.

Ambiguities will always exist in the definition of competitive conduct that triggers the application of a legal rule. Even the definition of price fixing, a cardinal sin under competition law about which there should be the least ambiguity, is by no means airtight when the existence of an agreement is not substantiated by direct evidence and must be inferred from circumstantial evidence. No-one as far as this author is aware, however, has ever argued that the rule for price fixing should be relaxed because of possible disputes about the existence of an agreement. Hylton and Salinger would probably argue that this analogy is inapt because pro-competitive bundled sales are much more commonplace than circumstantial price fixing cases. This is no doubt true. The point remains that in both cases, the ambiguities in definition have not undermined the application of the substantive legal rule. There are hence no persuasive reasons for altering the substantive legal rule for tying to make allowance for imprecisions in definition.

(b) Elimination of double marginalization

It was demonstrated by Augustin Cournot in 1838 that it is better for two monopolized complementary products to be sold by one seller than by two independent sellers.[379] The logic is similar to the elimination of double marginalization in the context of vertical integration.[380] The idea is that when the two complementary products are sold separately, their sellers will set a profit-maximizing price independently without taking into account the impact of a price increase on the sale of the complementary product.[381] They will thus set their prices too high for the purpose of joint profit maximization. Once the two products are brought under one roof and sold as a tie, the seller will internalize the impact of the pricing of one product on the other and set the bundle price in such a way to maximize joint profits. Allowing the monopolist to tie will hence eliminate double marginalization.

Double marginalization can be generalized to a more general setting where complementary products are sold in less than perfectly competitive markets and the two sellers do not coordinate their pricing decisions to maximize joint profits.[382] The Hovenkamps assert that elimination of double marginalization is

[378] Keith N Hylton and Michael Salinger, 'Reply to Grimes: Illusory Distinctions and Schisms in Tying Law' (2002) 70 Antitrust Law Journal 231, 237.
[379] Ahlborn, Evans, and Padilla (n 82) 322.
[380] ibid.
[381] Kobayashi (n 158) 714.
[382] Hovenkamp and Hovenkamp (n 4) 958.

'reasonably likely whenever both the tying and tied markets are subject to pricing above the competitive level and sufficient coordination between producers of complements is unlikely ... The markets need not be monopolized.'[383] Double marginalization can occur when the complementary products are used in fixed or variable proportions.[384]

The parallel between tying and vertical integration for the purpose of elimination of double marginalization has led some commentators to justify tying on the grounds that vertical integration is unobjectionable.[385] Roger Blair and David Kaserman note that there is 'a previously unrecognized symmetry between the economic effects of tying and vertical integration, which in turn raises serious questions regarding the divergent treatment afforded these alternative strategies under existing antitrust laws'.[386] While the Hovenkamps are generally positive about the welfare effects of elimination of double marginalization, Blair and Kaserman argue that for 'an input monopolist facing variable proportions at the downstream stage',[387] the welfare effects of both tying and vertical integration are ambiguous. Specifically, they argue that tying would result in the restriction of output to the monopoly level.[388]

The logic of the elimination of double marginalization is difficult to assail. The logic is at its most persuasive when both markets are monopolized but becomes much more attenuated when the markets fall just short of perfect competition. Where the conditions for elimination of double marginalization exist, it would be a persuasive pro-competitive justification for tying. The Hovenkamps insist that the logic applies whenever the two markets are less than perfectly competitive. But that does not mean that the logic is equally compelling so long as the markets are less than fully competitive. The likely scenario in which this justification will be invoked is when the tie may result in foreclosure, perhaps in the tied product market, but is also justified for eliminating double marginalization. As it turns out, market conditions that are most conducive to foreclosure are also where elimination of double marginalization is least relevant. Foreclosure can inflict the greatest competitive harm when markets are currently competitive. A great deal more competition will be lost if foreclosure succeeds. Meanwhile, double marginalization would be most damaging when both markets are monopolized or highly uncompetitive. The extent of supra-competitive pricing is lower when both markets are more competitive. Therefore, elimination of double marginalization will be at its

[383] ibid 960.
[384] ibid 958–59.
[385] Devlin (n 46) 536.
[386] Roger D Blair and David L Kaserman, 'Vertical Integration, Tying, and Antitrust Policy' (1978) 68 The American Economic Review 397, 397.
[387] ibid 401.
[388] ibid.

most persuasive as a justification when competitive harm from tying is least likely. The justification is most readily available when it is least needed.

(c) Savings in production and distribution costs

Tying is often said to bring about savings in production and distribution costs. It is cheaper to produce and distribute an integrated product as opposed to two separate products. Offering significant product variety may result in diseconomies of scope.[389] Manufacturers can achieve costs savings by reducing the options available on their products. The more a manufacturer restricts the options available on its products, the more likely that the components in the remaining options will be deemed to be a tie. A drug manufacturer may prefer to produce a pill that combines the functions of providing relief for both nasal congestion and cough instead of two separate pills for the symptoms, which tend to come hand in hand.[390] Purchasers of cars may have a wide range of preferences in terms of the stereo equipment in the car. Yet it would not be efficient for Toyota to produce cars of the same model with hundreds of different types of stereo equipment installed. It would be more cost-effective to provide only a few options.[391]

Too much product variety could be socially inefficient. David Evans summarizes the decision that faces a firm when choosing to produce an integrated as opposed to separate products as follows:

> Firms have to weigh the demand for a particular product offering against the costs of making it available as a stand-alone product or as part of another product. Many products are not offered at all because there is not enough demand to warrant businesses incurring the costs of producing and distributing them.[392]

Integrated products also save distribution costs. Separate products need to be packaged and transported separately, which entails higher costs.[393] Integrated products can obviate the need for separate packaging and transportation.

Savings in production and distribution costs are no doubt real but are by no means universal. Substantial savings in production costs are much more likely to materialize when the tying and the tied products are integrated into one product. There is probably not much production cost savings in manufacturing an iPhone and an iPhone case together, for instance. Savings in distribution costs can be attained without physical integration of products, even though the savings could be

[389] David S Evans, 'Tying: The Poster Child for Antitrust Modernization' in Robert W Hahn (ed), *Antitrust Policy and Vertical Restraints* (Brookings Institution 2006) 69.
[390] ibid 70.
[391] Carlton and Waldman, 'Theories of Tying and Implications for Antitrust' (n 167) 4.
[392] Evans (n 389) 70.
[393] ibid 69.

higher when there is actual integration. But such savings are unlikely to be substantial enough to outweigh any significant consumer harm.

(d) Savings in transaction costs and consumer search costs

Tying is said to save transaction costs and consumer search costs. The idea is that for a complex product, most consumers may not have strong preferences with respect to individual components and are only concerned about the functionality of the product as a whole.[394] When that is the case, and when most consumers do not possess the knowledge to make an informed choice about individual components, consumers may prefer the seller to assemble the final product for them.[395] It could often take a lot of time and effort to educate oneself about the different components of a complex product. Compatibility of components is a further complication, which could be beyond the technical capability of most consumers.

The archetypal example is cars. The average consumer wants a car for the locomotion and is relatively indifferent to the performance of individual components. She does not want to spend the time to learn about them and does not possess the technical knowledge to appreciate how different components work together. She would be completely lost if presented with a menu of 10,000 components from which to choose to assemble a car. It would probably be more of a nuisance to her than anything else to be asked to assemble one. The car manufacturer can do the assembling much more quickly than the average consumer. Having the manufacturer do it would also avoid the duplication of search costs incurred by each consumer. Nonetheless, there are bound to be sophisticated consumers who would like to pick at least some of the individual components. To these consumers, a fully assembled car with no options may constitute a tie, even though the assembled car saves significant search costs for a vast majority of consumers.

There are two possible reactions to this pro-competitive benefit. First, it can be effectively dealt with at the product definition stage. Two products or two components of a product that can be integrated with substantial savings in search costs could be deemed one product on cost efficiency grounds.[396] The separate product requirement under the qualified *per se* rule in the United States to some extent already performs this function.[397] Product combinations that generate substantial search cost savings should not fall within the ambit of tying law. Second, outside of cases involving technological integration, toward which many US courts have already shown a flexible attitude,[398] this justification is unlikely to be of great

[394] Ahlborn, Evans, and Padilla (n 82) 320.
[395] Carlton and Waldman, 'Robert Bork's Contributions to Antitrust Perspectives on Tying Behavior' (n 40) 125–26.
[396] Economides and Lianos (n 179) 519; Grimes (n 187) 207.
[397] Economides and Lianos (n 179) 519–20.
[398] Ahlborn, Evans, and Padilla (n 82) 296. Hylton and Salinger (n 161) 472–73.

relevance. The scope for search cost savings in a great many tying cases that do not involve technological integration is likely to be limited.

(e) Protection of goodwill/quality assurance

From the very early cases, defendants have attempted to justify tying with quality assurance arguments. It is often argued that the defendant's tied product needs to be used in order to ensure the performance of the defendant's tying product. The defendant's tying product may deteriorate in quality when used with inferior tied products produced by other suppliers. In the *International Salt* case in the United States, the defendant argued that its machines must be used with its salt tablets to ensure that the salt used is of sufficient purity.[399] This argument was also invoked by the defendant in the EU *Hilti* and *Tetra Pak* cases.[400]

The quality assurance argument is as often invoked as it is rejected. Courts are prone to reject the argument on the grounds that tying is not the least restrictive means for protecting the brand's goodwill. Quality assurance can be accomplished through minimum quality specifications. This was the basis upon which the court rejected the argument in *International Salt*.[401] In *Hilti*, the then-Court of First Instance rejected Hilti's argument on the grounds that there are national laws that ensure product safety and it is not for Hilti to usurp the responsibility for enforcing product safety.[402] The court in *Tetra Pak* rejected the quality assurance argument on similar grounds.[403] Quality assurance is thus not regarded as a persuasive justification for tying on both sides of the Atlantic.

F. Case Law on Tying

1. The United States

Tying is one area of vertical restraint law in which the US courts have displayed a relatively consistent stance over time. With a number of notable exceptions such as *Jerrold Electronics*[404] and *Fortner II*,[405] the US courts have regularly condemned tying arrangements where there is sufficient market power in the tying product market ever since the *Motion Picture Patents* case in 1917.[406] As suggested earlier,

[399] *International Salt Co. v. United States*, 332 US 392, 397 (1947).

[400] Case T-83/91, *Tetra Pak v. Commission (Tetra Pak II CFI)* [1994] ECR II-755, para 79; *Hilti*, para 105.

[401] International Salt Co., 332 US at 397–98.

[402] *Hilti*, para 118.

[403] *Tetra Pak II CFI*, para 83.

[404] *United States v. Jerrold Electronics Corp.*, 187 F. Supp. 545 (E.D. Pa. 1960), *aff'd per curiam*, 365 US 567 (1961).

[405] *United States Steel Corp. v. Fortner Enterprises*, 429 US 610 (1977).

[406] *Motion Picture Patents Co. v. Universal Film Manufacturing. Co.*, 243 US 502, 516 (1917).

judicial attitude toward tying, which often involved patented products in the early cases, was somewhat influenced by the perception that the patentee was attempting unlawfully to extend her market power from the patented product into an unpatented product market. In the *International Salt* case, the US Supreme Court declared that 'it is unreasonable, *per se*, to foreclose competitors from any substantial market'.[407] This rule was reaffirmed in the *Northern Pacific Railway* case, in which the Court compared tying to price fixing, market allocation, and group boycotts and reiterated that tying is subject to the *per se* rule.[408] In *Fortner I*, the Court reiterated its animosity toward tying, asserting that tying arrangements 'generally serve no legitimate business purpose that cannot be achieved in some less restrictive way'.[409]

With the Chicago School's growing influence on US antitrust law, some began to question the suitability of the *per se* rule for tying. Advocacy for reconsideration of the *per se* rule culminated in Justice O'Connor's concurrence in *Jefferson Parish*, in which she contended that '[t]he time has therefore come to abandon the "*per se*" label and refocus the inquiry on the adverse economic effects, and the potential economic benefits, that the tie may have'.[410] She proceeded to call for the abandonment of the *per se* rule in favour of the Rule of Reason for tying arrangements. Justice O'Connor failed to carry the day. Her call for the abandonment of the *per se* rule was met by Justice Stevens' pronouncement that '[i]t is far too late in the history of our antitrust jurisprudence to question the proposition that certain tying arrangements pose an unacceptable risk of stifling competition and therefore are unreasonable "per se"'.[411] *Jefferson Parish* reaffirmed the qualified *per se* rule from earlier cases, under which, to prevail in a tying claim, the plaintiff is required to prove that: (1) there must be separate tying and tied products; (2) there must be evidence of coercion on the part of the seller to force buyers to accept the tie; (3) the seller must possess sufficient market power to coerce buyers to accept the tie; (4) there must be foreclosure of a not insubstantial amount of commerce in the tied product market.[412]

The majority in that case, however, did make a concession to Justice O'Connor. It held that the *per se* rule should only apply when the defendant's market power passes a sufficient threshold such that it can effectively coerce customers to accept the tie. This continues the trend that had begun in *Fortner II* in which the Court insisted on serious proof of market power before condemning a tie.[413] Prior to that, the Court had been quick to assume market power on the part of the defendant.

[407] *International Salt*, 332 US at 395.
[408] *Northern Pacific Railway Co. v. United States*, 356 US 1, 5 (1958).
[409] *Fortner Enterprises*, 394 US at 503 (1969).
[410] *Jefferson Parish Hospital District No. 2 v. Hyde*, 466 US 2, 35 (1984).
[411] *Jefferson Parish*, 446 US at 9.
[412] Hovenkamp (n 372) s 10.1.
[413] *Fortner Enterprises*, 429 US at 620–22.

In *International Salt*, the Court inferred market power from the fact that the defendant's machines were patented.[414] In *Northern Pacific*, the Court based its finding of market power on the considerable size and strategic location of the defendant's land holding.[415] *Jefferson Parish* heightened the standard for market power. It has been understood to stand for the notion that the defendant must possess at least a 30 per cent market share in the tying product market to benefit from the qualified *per se* rule.[416] Hylton and Salinger believe that the Court's tightening of the requirement of market power reflected the Chicago School's influence, even though there was no formal alteration in the doctrine.[417] The federal district courts in the United States dismissed significantly more tying cases in the two decades following *Jefferson Parish* than in the preceding two decades.[418] Justice O'Connor might have lost the battle, but probably won the war in the end.

Although the US Supreme Court has not definitively settled the issue, lower courts seem inclined to apply a more lenient rule for technological tying or integration as opposed to the more typical contractual tying. In contrast with the qualified *per se* rule in contractual tying cases, 'in the technological tying case law we have a rule that puts such a high proof burden on plaintiffs that it seems to presume legality'.[419] The US Court of Appeals for the District of Columbia laid down a narrowly circumscribed exception from the qualified *per se* rule in the *Microsoft* case, in which the Court refused to apply the *per se* rule to a tie between a personal computer operating system and a web browser.[420] The Court began by noting that 'the sort of tying arrangement attacked here is unlike any the Supreme Court has considered'.[421] The Court proceeded to remark on the uniqueness of the tying arrangement at issue:

> In none of these cases was the tied good physically and technologically integrated with the tying good. Nor did the defendants ever argue that their tie improved the value of the tying product to users *and* to makers of complementary goods. In those cases where the defendant claimed that use of the tied good made the tying good more valuable to users, the Court ruled that the same result could be achieved via quality standards for substitutes of the tied good.[422]

The Court noted that some unique efficiencies arise in the context of software integration and applying the qualified *per se* rule would have forced the Court to ignore

[414] *International Salt*, 332 US at 395.
[415] *Northern Pacific*, 356 US at 7-8.
[416] Hovenkamp (n 372) s 10.3a.
[417] Hylton and Salinger (n 161) 476.
[418] Evans (n 389) 85.
[419] Hylton and Salinger (n 161) 479.
[420] *United States v. Microsoft Corp. (Microsoft III)*, 253 F.3d 34 (D.C. Cir. 2001).
[421] *Microsoft III*, 253 F.3d at 90.
[422] *Microsoft III*, 253 F.3d at 90.

them.[423] The Court, however, was careful to confine its holding to the specific factual context of the case.[424]

As it turns out, other circuits have adopted an even more lenient rule than the DC Circuit's toward technological ties. While the DC Circuit applied the Rule of Reason to Microsoft's tying of Internet Explorer to the Windows operating system, under which there is the possibility of balancing anticompetitive effects and pro-competitive benefits, most other circuits have chosen a more permissive rule, upholding technological integration unless their main purpose is to hamper competition rather than to attain some technological benefits.[425] One formulation of this approach is found in *Response of Carolina, Inc. v. Leasco Response, Inc.*, in which the Court declared that condemnation of a technological tie

> must be limited to those instances where the technological factor tying the hardware to the software has been designed for the purpose of tying the products, rather than to achieve some technologically beneficial result. Any other conclusion would enmesh the courts in a technical inquiry into the justifiability of product innovations.[426]

Under *Leasco*, a technological tie will be upheld if it exhibits a substantial technological benefit, while the Rule of Reason under *Microsoft* at least requires the court to balance the harm and benefits of technological integration.[427]

Apart from the substantive legal standard, there are also disparate views on the defendant's burden of proof in a technological tying case. In *Caldera, Inc. v. Microsoft Corp.*, the Court held that the defendant must show that 'the technological improvements must have demonstrated efficiencies' in order to prevail.[428] The *Caldera* court was careful to distinguish this 'demonstrated efficiencies' standard from the lower standard of a plausible claim of some advantage laid down by the DC Circuit in an earlier *Microsoft* case.[429] The differing standards reveal divergent views on the level of scrutiny that courts should apply in evaluating claims of technological benefits. The DC Circuit opined that '[a] court's evaluation of a claim of integration must be narrow and deferential',[430] while the *Caldera* court defended its choice of standard by asserting that '[a]ny other standard would have the potential to allow illegal tying arrangement to deter, or even eliminate, effective competition, which in turn could hurt consumers not just because of higher prices, but because of a lack of technologically improved products'.[431] A combination of

423 *Microsoft III*, 253 F.3d at 92–94.
424 *Microsoft III*, 253 F.3d at 95.
425 Hylton and Salinger (n 161) 472.
426 *Response of Carolina, Inc. v. Leasco Response, Inc.*, 537 F.2d 1307, 1330 (5th Cir. 1976).
427 Hylton and Salinger (n 161) 518.
428 *Caldera, Inc. v. Microsoft Corp.*, 72 F. Supp.2d 1295, 1325 (D. Utah 1999).
429 *United States v. Microsoft Corp. (Microsoft II)*, 147 F.3d 935, 950 (D.C. Cir. 1998).
430 *Microsoft II*, 147 US at 949–50.
431 *Caldera*, 72 F. Supp.2d at 1326.

the permissive substantive standard under *Leasco* with the plausible claim standard of proof from *Microsoft II* would be tantamount to *per se* legality for technological integration cases.

2. The European Union

While tying is mostly addressed as a restrictive agreement under Section 1 of the Sherman Act and Section 3 of the Clayton Act, bundling, as it is called in the European Union, belongs to the province of abuse of dominance under Article 102 of the Treaty on the Functioning of the European Union (TFEU).[432] This largely reflects the fact that the market power requirement under Article 102 TFEU is lower than that under Section 2 of the Sherman Act. The amount of market power sufficient to trigger concerns for tying in the United States roughly corresponds with that connoted by a dominant position under EU law.[433] Yet the reliance of different legal provisions cannot obscure the considerable similarity in the substantive legal standards across the Atlantic. Given the general tendency of the EU competition law to take a stricter approach, it perhaps should come as no surprise that it has adopted a standard akin to the qualified *per se* rule under US antitrust law for bundling. The anomaly here is probably the strict approach in the United States Just like US law, EU law has demonstrated greater flexibility for technical bundling than contractual tying, as can be seen in the EU *Microsoft* case, in which the then-Court of First Instance was more demanding in terms of evidence for foreclosure effects than in past bundling cases.

EU stance on contractual tying is largely informed by two cases, *Hilti* and *Tetra Pak II*. Hilti concerned nail guns used in the construction industry. At the time of the case, Hilti was the largest manufacturer of nail guns in the European Union, with a slightly over 50 per cent market share.[434] Nail guns were used with cartridge strips and nails, which were all subject to patent protection.[435] Hilti's competitors produced compatible nails which could be used on Hilti's nail guns. Hilti then resorted to business practices and legal measures to prevent customers from using competitor-manufactured nails on its nail guns. These included tied sale of nails and cartridge strips to end customers,[436] the refusal to honour guarantees if a customer uses competitor-manufactured nails on Hilti nail guns,[437] and refusal to supply cartridges which might be for resale.[438] These practices gave rise to the tying claim.

432 Ahlborn, Evans, and Padilla (n 82) 306.
433 ibid.
434 *Eurofix-Bauco v. Hilti (Hilti (Commission))* [1988] OJ L65/19, para. 14.
435 *Hilti (Commission)*, para 12.
436 *Hilti (Commission)*, paras 30–31.
437 *Hilti (Commission)*, para 44.
438 *Hilti (Commission)*, para 41.

The European Commission condemned Hilti's practices on the grounds that 'independent producers of Hilti-compatible nails have been severely restricted in their penetration of the market' and that 'customers have been obliged to rely on Hilti for both cartridges and nails for their Hilti nail guns'.[439] Although the European Commission did not formally adopt the analytical structure of the qualified *per se* rule, elements of the rule were clearly present in its reasoning. There were separate tying and tied products of nail guns and cartridges on the one hand and nails on the other hand. There was examination of Hilti's market power in the market for the tying products of nail guns and Hilti-compatible cartridge strips.[440] The reference to customers being obliged to rely on Hilti's cartridge and nails indicated coercion. Lastly, the Commission probably went further than what was required under the qualified *per se* rule in *Jefferson Parish* to refer to the foreclosure of independent producers in the market for Hilti-compatible nails.

Nonetheless, the Commission's condemnation of Hilti's business practices on the grounds that they 'leave the consumer with no choice over the source of his nail and as such abusively exploit him'[441] suggests that the Commission did not rely on foreclosure effects to find tying practices abusive. If deprivation of consumer choice suffices to prohibit a tie, the rule is probably tantamount to *per se* illegality.[442] The only way out for the defendant would be to offer justifications. On appeal, the then-Court of First Instance rejected Hilti's argument that there was no tie because the nail gun, the cartridge strip, and the nails constituted one product system and that its tying practices were justified by safety concerns.[443]

Tetra Pak II was another leading case in which Tetra Pak, the world leading manufacturer of liquid packaging machines, was accused of tying the supply of non-aseptic packing machines to the sale of non-aseptic cartons, purchase of maintenance services, and the supply of spare parts. Tetra Pak produced both aseptic and non-aseptic packaging machines and the cartons that were used with them. Tetra Pak defended the tie on the grounds that the machines and the cartons formed integrated packaging systems and that the tie was objectively justified based on technical reasons, product liability concerns, public health, and the protection of goodwill.[444] These arguments were rejected by the Commission, the then-Court of First Instance, and Court of Justice. The Court of First Instance also rejected Tetra Pak's objective justifications,[445] which was affirmed by the Court of Justice[446].

439 *Hilti (Commission)*, para 74.
440 *Hilti (Commission)*, para 74.
441 *Hilti (Commission)*, para 75.
442 Ahlborn, Evans, and Padilla (n 82) 314.
443 *Hilti (Commission)*, paras 66, 118.
444 *Tetra Pak II CFI*, para 79.
445 *Tetra Pak II CFI*, para 138.
446 Case C-333/94 P, *Tetra Pak International SA v. Commission (Tetra Pak II ECJ)* [1996] ECR I-5951, para 36.

There was much discussion as to whether the machines and the cartons could be treated as an integrated system based on a natural or commercial link between them. Although the discussion was phrased in the specific language of Article 102(d), it is clear what was being argued was whether the machines and the cartons should be treated as two separate products. The Court of First Instance and the Court of Justice both rejected the argument that machines and cartons constitute an integrated packaging system on the grounds that there were independent producers specializing in the production of non-aseptic cartons to be used with third-party machines.[447]

Yet in an observation that suggests that there is still some difference between the inquiry into commercial usage and natural link under Article 102 and the determination of separate products under US law, the Court of Justice noted that the list under Article 102 is not exhaustive and that a tie between two products can still be deemed abusive even if the 'tied sales of the two products are in accordance with commercial usage or there is a natural link between the two products in question'.[448] If two products cannot be deemed distinct in light of commercial usage or the natural link between them, a tie would be impossible as there are no two separate products to tie in a sale.

This shows that the Court of Justice sees the inquiry into commercial usage or natural link more in terms of justifications for the tie than product definition. The lack of discussion of foreclosure effects in the relevant markets and the focus on objective justifications, commercial usage, and natural links in the Court's analysis evinces a presumptive illegality approach under which the only way for the defendant to exonerate itself is to offer possible justifications. This is a continuation of the *Hilti* approach to tying under which the emphasis is on justifications rather than competitive effects.

In the EU *Microsoft* case, the Court of First Instance was confronted with Microsoft's tying of the Windows operating system with Windows Media Player. Moving beyond its rather stringent approach to tying from the previous cases, the Court did not presume the existence of foreclosure effects or overlook the issue completely.[449] Instead, the Court spent much effort in ascertaining how the foreclosure of competitors harmed consumers.[450] The determination of the legality of a technical tie required the Court to consider both anticompetitive effects from the tie and possible objective justifications for it. The *Microsoft* court seemed to require the following four elements to establish a successful technical tying claim:

[447] *Tetra Pak II CFI*, para 82; *Tetra Pak II ECJ*, para. 36.
[448] *Tetra Pak II ECJ*, para 37.
[449] Case T-201/04, *Microsoft v. Commission (EU Microsoft)* [2007] ECR II-3601, para. 857.
[450] *EU Microsoft*, paras 1054–58, 1088.

> the existence of a dominant position in a distinct product market that can be tied, the practice of forcing an undertaking to buy two products at the same time, the existence of the limited competition in the market for the tied good and the lack of objective justification for the tying practice by the dominant partner.[451]

This reorientation of the approach led Ioannis Lianos and Nicholas Economides to assert that the Court 'implicitly injects a structured rule of reason approach into the analysis of technological tying'.[452] The rule adopted, however, was very much an asymmetric Rule of Reason in that the standard of proof for the anticompetitive effects was low while the bar for establishing an objective justification for an abusive tie, as is true of most areas of abuse of dominance law, was very high.[453] To prove anticompetitive foreclosure, there is no need to show actual or direct consumer harm.[454] Instead, most of the consumer harm the then-Court of First Instance relied on 'were indirect and emanated from the fact that Microsoft-as compared with its media player rivals-benefited from an "unparalleled advantage with respect to the distribution of its product" that "inevitably had significant consequences for the structure of competition" on the streaming media player market'.[455] Therefore, the differences in the EU standards for contractual and technological tying should not be exaggerated. While *Microsoft* portends a more lenient rule for technological tying, it does not go anywhere near as far as the highly permissive, and possibly *per se* legality, approach under US law.

G. A Proposed Framework for Developing Countries

Devising an appropriate framework for patent tying in developing countries requires a balancing of the competitive harm and pro-competitive benefits of tying involving a patented tying product, which in turn requires an examination of the impact of tying on innovation incentives and technological upgrades viewed from a developmental perspective. The two main competitive detriments of tying are extraction of consumer surplus and foreclosure in the tying and the tied product markets in the form of offensive leveraging and defensive leveraging.

Extraction of consumer surplus takes on added significance in the context of patent tying in developing countries. On the one hand, the developing country context means that one must pay special attention to how the extraction affects income inequality and the welfare of the poorest members of society. On the other hand,

[451] Aleksander Maziarz, 'Tying and Bundling: Applying EU Competition Rules for Best Practices' (2013) 3 International Journal of Public Law and Policy 263, 268.
[452] Economides and Lianos (n 179) 550.
[453] ibid 551.
[454] ibid.
[455] ibid 556.

appropriated consumer surplus could represent more than simple wealth transfer to innovators. The additional profits could be used to fund further R&D. Extraction of consumer surplus may no longer be purely negative in consumer welfare terms and may redound dynamic benefits to consumers down the road. Foreclosure of rivals in the tying and the tied product markets may no longer be relevant only in static terms and may have implications on the country's opportunity for technological upgrade. Tackling patent tying from a dynamic and developmental perspective hence leads to a more complicated and context-specific analysis.

Extraction of consumer surplus is unequivocally harmful from a consumer welfare perspective if the additional surplus does not create other benefits. It was argued in Chapter 2 that the surplus does not redound any dynamic efficiency benefits if there are no innovators in the country to take advantage of the extra innovation incentives. This means that innovation incentive considerations carry little weight for the production countries. But they may be salient for technological adaptation and especially the proto-innovation countries if patent tying is proven to generate additional innovation incentives. It was demonstrated in section C that patent tying has at best uncertain effects on innovation incentives. There is no guarantee that the extra surplus generated by tying will indeed be invested in R&D. Tying may indeed hamper innovation in the tied product market, which, because of its generally lower technological requirements, is where developing countries are more likely to succeed in innovating. Allowing patent tying will also skew innovation toward technologies that may give rise to tying opportunities.

Overall, the dynamic efficiency benefits of patent tying can be largely discounted and extraction of consumer surplus can be considered as an unmitigated harm from a consumer welfare perspective so long as certain conditions are met. First, consumer welfare loss from a price-discriminating tie is much more likely if the tie is a variable-proportions tie and does not involve perfect complements. Second, under a variable-proportions tie, the tie must be preceded by a price cut for the tying product and followed by an increase in the output level for the tied product in order not to inflict consumer harm.

The extent to which foreclosure is a relevant consideration for a developing country will depend on its technological capacity. In general, offensive leveraging is more relevant than defensive leveraging as developing countries are less likely to host a firm that is in a position to challenge the technological dominance of a complex tying product produced in an industrialized economy. Of all the foreclosure models proposed by commentators, Whinston's is likely to be most widely applicable. Its most essential assumptions are that the industry demonstrates economies of scale and that the incumbent can credibly pre-commit to tie, which binds the incumbent to a low-price strategy, which in turn denies the rival the requisite scale of operations to attain minimum efficient scale. Most manufacturing, regardless of the level of technological sophistication, displays economies of scale. The opportunity for credible pre-commitment is also not technology-sensitive. His foreclosure theories, which can result in both offensive and defensive leveraging, should be relevant for all developing countries. Nalebuff's foreclosure model is also not technology-sensitive, especially when applied to the tied product market.

Other models of foreclosure, such as the offensive leveraging models proposed by Choi and Stefanadis and Choi respectively, and the two defensive leveraging models propounded by Carlton and Waldman, are more applicable to developing countries with substantial technological capacity. It is probably impossible to come up with a doctrinal framework that can encapsulate all these different foreclosure models. Given that Whinston's and Nalebuff's models are the most widely applicable, they should form the basis of the proposed doctrinal framework. Technological adaptation countries and proto-innovation countries may need to add extra layers to this framework to account for other scenarios of foreclosure.

It is important to recall that Whinston cautions against placing too much reliance on his analysis to draw policy conclusions. In particular, he observes that

> [w]hile the analysis vindicates the leverage hypothesis on a positive level, its normative implications are less clear. Even in the simple models considered here, which ignore a number of other possible motivations for the practice, the impact of this exclusion on welfare is uncertain. This fact, combined with the difficulty of sorting out the leverage-based instances of tying from other cases, makes the specification of a practical legal standard extremely difficult.[456]

To these concerns Kobayashi has added the caveat, which applies to both Whinston's and Nalebuff's models, that 'there exist substitutes to bundling as an entry deterrent strategy that would generally not raise antitrust concerns, such as long-term contracts, or quantity discounts'.[457] The apparent implications of their models notwithstanding, Whinston and Nalebuff stop short of advocating for a strict approach to tying.

While their reasons for caution are understandable, they have probably overstated their case. Whinston suggests that the welfare effects of tying are uncertain. Much of this uncertainty, however, comes from the mixed effects of price discrimination. While it is true that under third-degree price discrimination, the consumers who are offered lower prices clearly benefit from it, price-discriminating ties tend to result in second-degree price discrimination. Under the three modes of price discrimination discussed earlier, only intra-product price discrimination may have ambiguous effects on consumer welfare when preceded by a price cut on the tying product and followed by an output increase for the tied product. The ambiguous welfare effects of price discrimination are exaggerated. Once these effects

[456] Whinston (n 96) 855–56.
[457] Kobayashi (n 158) 736.

are set aside, Whinston's conclusions firmly point to tying being detrimental to consumer welfare.

Whinston suggests that there are other motivations for tying which need to be taken into account. Under the modern effects-based approach to competition law analysis, motivations should not be a primary consideration. What matters is not whether there are pro-competitive motivations behind the tie, but whether the tie is justified by pro-competitive benefits. This can be adequately taken into account in an appropriately designed doctrinal framework, which must take into account the various pro-competitive benefits of tying.

Whinston further argues that there is considerable difficulty in sorting out leverage-based from other instances of tying. This seems to be another way for him to voice his concern that tying can serve both anticompetitive and pro-competitive purposes which are difficult to distinguish. The fact is that the two are not mutually exclusive. In reality, many ties may foreclose rivals and extract consumer surplus while serving some beneficial purpose. The defendant should be given the opportunity to prove with convincing evidence that its tie generates pro-competitive benefits. If such evidence is not forthcoming, the focus of the analysis should shift to the anticompetitive effects. Given that virtually every tie extracts consumer surplus and only limited instances of them benefit consumers, a presumption of illegality should apply once possible pro-competitive justifications have been ruled out or rejected. This is consistent with Elhauge's defence of the qualified *per se* rule from *Jefferson Parish* in light of what he calls the power effects and the foreclosure share effects.[458]

A suitable framework for patent tying for a developing country must also take into account the enforcement capacity of the authority or the courts at issue. It would be difficult for an authority or court with rudimentary enforcement capacity to apply a highly sophisticated and context-specific rule. A choice must be made between administrability and context specificity and hence accuracy of the rule. It may be wise to adopt a rule that is relatively easy to apply even if it may come with higher error costs. An authority with a higher enforcement capacity may adopt more sophisticated and precise rules to try to minimize instances of error.

To continue with the previous classification, developing country authorities can be roughly grouped into low-capacity, medium-capacity, and high-capacity ones. A different doctrinal framework may be suitable for each group in light of their enforcement capacity. Although the correlation is by no means perfect, there are good reasons to believe that developing countries with a higher income level and a higher innovation capacity tend to have authorities with a higher enforcement capacity. For instance, proto-innovation countries such as Brazil, China, India, Mexico, South Africa, and Turkey tend to have authorities

[458] Elhauge (n 3) 442–43.

with higher enforcement capacity. To the extent that this correlation holds, countries with lower technological capacity, which are confronted fewer policy considerations, can benefit from simpler rules which are within their authorities' capacity to administer. Countries with higher technological capacity, which may face more complicated policy trade-offs, may apply more complex and context-specific rules.

A low-capacity and a medium-capacity authority would do well with a relatively simple rule that is easy to apply. Given that such an authority is more likely to be found in a country devoid of significant innovation capacity, it will have fewer occasions to be concerned with foreclosure in the context of R&D competition and foreclosure in the tying product market. The range of foreclosure scenarios to which it needs to pay attention will be limited to the less technologically intensive ones described by Whinston and Nalebuff. Extraction of consumer surplus will be of paramount concern given that most of the consumers in the country are likely to be low-income and can ill-afford further loss of surplus. Given that a vast majority of variable-proportions ties extract consumer surplus, a relatively stringent approach to tying may be justified. It may be justified for such an authority to adopt a qualified *per se* rule under which a tie that involves a tying product over which the incumbent holds significant market power will be condemned so long as a number of additional conditions are met. A tie of course would require separate products and coercion. Beyond these basic requirements, additional conditions include the tying and the tied products are not perfect complements, and the tie is not preceded by a price reduction on the tying product and followed by an output increase of the tied product. The requirement of no price reduction for the tying product also ensures that a tie that may improve income distribution and benefit poor consumers will be shielded from scrutiny.

There are also scant reasons for such an authority or court to follow the more permissive approach to technological integration adopted by the US courts. The main rationale for such an approach is to avoid judicial interference which may deter innovation. Given the relative lack of genuine innovation in these countries, deterrence of innovation probably deserves less weight. A low- or medium-capacity authority should devote more attention to protecting its consumers from the static and dynamic harms of technological ties.

A higher-capacity authority may be able to adopt a rule that can take into account a wide range of circumstances. As opposed to a straightforward qualified *per se* rule, a more structured approach may be required. There are two stages in the analysis. The first stage focuses on extraction of consumer surplus as the relevant consumer harm. This is because this harm is more prevalent, widely applicable, and easier to establish. It is only after extraction harm has been ruled out that the focus shifts to foreclosure, which may be more circumstance-specific and may require more precise conditions.

Given the tendency of tying to extract consumer surplus, there should be a presumption of illegality when certain conditions are met. The first step would require that the plaintiff or the authority establish that there is a putative tie, which requires a proof of separate products, existence of coercion, and significant market power in the tying product market. In addition, the plaintiff would be able to establish a presumption of extraction harm by showing that the tie is a variable-proportions tie, that the two products are not perfect complements, and that the tie is not accompanied by an *ex-ante* price reduction for the tying product and an *ex-post* output increase for the tied product. Again, the requirement that the tie not be accompanied by an *ex ante* price reduction for the tying product helps to ensure that ties that may benefit poor consumers are not condemned. Once a putative tie is established, the defendant is given the opportunity to adduce convincing evidence for pro-competitive justifications. The defendant will also be given the opportunity to rebut the presumption that the tie extracts consumer surplus. The proto-innovation countries probably cannot afford to ignore the potential benefits of technological integration completely. Nonetheless, adopting an altogether different rule for technological ties, as some of the US courts have done, is probably a step too far. Instead, the legal rule should give the defendant ample opportunities to argue that its technological integration produces technological benefits.

In the event that the defendant succeeds in rebutting the presumption of surplus extraction, the burden shifts back to the plaintiff to show that one of the foreclosure scenarios applies. If the country at issue has higher technological capacity, the foreclosure scenarios involving R&D competition and the technological capability to enter a patented tying product market will need to be considered as well as the less technologically demanding ones. If foreclosure is established, it is then necessary to balance the competitive harm with the previously proffered pro-competitive justification. The plaintiff will need to show that the harm outweighs the benefit or that there are less restrictive means to achieve the pro-competitive benefit.

Given that the harm and the benefit may be of a different nature, a direct comparison of their magnitude may not be feasible. The overriding importance of technological upgrade in developing countries necessitates giving dynamic harm greater emphasis. Foreclosure that may hamper acquisition of technological capacity should trump a static efficiency benefit. A genuine balancing should only be called for when both the harm and benefit are dynamic in nature. Even though this framework may sound complicated, given that a vast majority of variable-proportions ties extract consumer surplus, the analysis is likely to end at the first stage. Analysis of foreclosure effects and genuine balancing of competitive harm and benefits are unlikely to be frequently needed.

H. Conclusion

On account of the uncertain welfare effects of theoretical models which have demonstrated the competitive harm of tying,[459] the apparent ubiquity of tying,[460] and the many pro-competitive justifications for the practice,[461] some commentators have advocated permissive treatment for tying, going so far as to argue for *per se* legality. They may argue that the case is even stronger for patent tying because of the boost to innovation incentives from a more lenient treatment of patent tying. This chapter rejects all these arguments. Patent tying does not boost innovation incentives, especially in the tied product market. There are additionally a number of other reasons that it would be counter-productive to rely on patent tying to generate innovation incentives. Innovation incentive considerations do not call for a more lenient treatment of patent tying. If anything, the balance of the argument seems to point in the opposite direction.

Stripped of its disproved dynamic efficiency benefits, surplus extraction alone constitutes a sufficient reason to prohibit tying in most instances. Meanwhile, patent tying may retard technological upgrade by developing countries. This is amply illustrated by the various economic models of foreclosure in the tying and the tied product markets. Although the extent of relevance of these models varies with the technological capacity of the developing country at issue, developing countries need to take the technological retardation effects of foreclosure seriously. Developing countries would do well to take a vigilant approach toward patent tying.

[459] Kobayashi (n 158) 736.
[460] Hylton and Salinger (n 161) 500–02.
[461] Tirole (n 190) 14–17.

8

Excessive Pricing for Pharmaceuticals

A. Introduction

Excessive drug prices are one of the most pressing issues facing developing countries. Each year, hundreds of thousands, if not millions, of people die due to a lack of access to essential medicines. It is thus an issue that transcends the patent–competition interface or even competition law in general. A problem this complex and consequential requires a multi-faceted solution. International non-governmental organizations (NGOs) and pharmaceutical companies have tried to alleviate the need for essential drugs through donations. Some developing country governments have taken a proactive role and made use of compulsory licenses and other flexibilities that are permitted under the TRIPS Agreement (Agreement on Trade-Related Aspects of Intellectual Property Rights), such as Article 30 and Article 31. While some of these efforts have been met with success, the TRIPS flexibilities and exemptions suffer from some inherent deficiencies that limit their effectiveness.

This chapter thus proposes that developing countries resort to excessive pricing enforcement to tackle the most egregious instances of excessive drug prices. The proposal is surely not the widespread use of excessive pricing regulation as a general price control tool. It is important to be mindful of the limitations of excessive pricing enforcement and not to overuse or abuse it. This chapter, however, argues that there are, in particular, two instances where such enforcement is justified. The first is sudden and massive price hikes and the second is what this chapter calls reverse price discrimination, which refers to when a certain drug is more expensive, often much more so, in developing countries than in industrialized economies. This counterintuitive phenomenon is more common than is generally realized and justifies enforcement action by developing country competition authorities.

This chapter addresses some of the strongest objections to excessive pricing enforcement in general and in the context of excessive drug prices in developing countries in particular. These include (1) high prices are needed to attract investments and innovation, especially in the pharmaceutical industry where research and development (R&D) is costly; (2) high prices are self-correcting and using excessive price enforcement to correct them will result in unacceptable distortions of the free market; (3) excessive pricing enforcement should be used as a last resort and solutions internal to the intellectual property (IP) laws for an IP-related problem should be preferred; and (4) excessive pricing enforcement faces

The Patent–Competition Interface in Developing Countries. Thomas K. Cheng, Oxford University Press. © Thomas K. Cheng 2021. DOI: 10.1093/oso/9780192857354.003.0008

insurmountable implementation obstacles in the form of a workable definition of excessiveness and design of appropriate remedies. It will be argued that while these are realistic concerns that require careful attention, they do not justify abandoning the welfare of poor patients in developing countries. Excessive pricing enforcement can be made to work in a limited way to help developing countries confront the issue of excessive drug prices.

Such enforcement admittedly will not provide a complete solution. The intricacy and widespread implications of this problem are such that a comprehensive solution is unlikely to be found in competition law alone. Given the number of lives at stake, however, any contribution to addressing the needs for essential medicines in developing countries will be highly valuable and is to be welcome.

B. Drug Prices in Developing Countries

Any analysis about the impact of the patent–competition interface on developing countries would be incomplete without a discussion of the implications of the interface on drug prices. The branded drugs produced by multinational pharmaceutical manufacturers are beyond the reach of most but the wealthiest consumers in many developing countries. This is exacerbated by the fact that many branded pharmaceutical manufacturers adopt the pricing strategy of focusing on the wealthiest consumers in these countries, which means that they do not attempt to price at a level affordable to the general public and that certain drugs are often more expensive in developing countries than in the industrialized economies. The shortage of HIV/AIDS drugs in the early to mid-2000s was probably the most notorious illustration of the drug unaffordability crisis in developing countries. This crisis is not only a matter of concern for the patent–competition interface, it constitutes an international humanitarian crisis and has serious public health implications.

Much of the discussion of a possible solution to this most intractable problem has centred on Articles 30 and 31 of the TRIPS Agreement. Article 30 authorizes the World trade Organization (WTO) members to grant limited exceptions to patent rights under certain conditions while Article 31 sets out the grounds upon which and the procedures for which compulsory licensing can be ordered by a WTO member government.[1] The TRIPS Agreement can be said to provide solutions internal to intellectual property law to excessive drug prices in developing countries. It has often been said that internal solutions to problems arising under intellectual property law are to be preferred to solutions emanating from external sources. As the ensuing discussion will show, however, there are numerous inadequacies in these two articles. Competition law enforcement hence provides a

[1] 'Agreement on Trade-Related Aspects of Intellectual Property Rights (Adopted 15 April 1994, Entered into Force 1 January 1995) 1869 UNTS 299 (TRIPS Agreement)' arts. 30-31.

complement to these internal solutions. Competition law is a particularly promising policy tool because it is exempted from certain general requirements imposed by Article 31 on compulsory licensing, should that be chosen as a remedy.

Competition law enforcement is external to intellectual property law in the sense that competition law is outside of domestic intellectual property law. But its application to intellectual property issues must nonetheless operate within the confines of international intellectual property law embodied in the TRIPS Agreement. Unaffordable drug prices can be regulated under the rubric of excessive pricing, which could be a competition law violation at least under EU law. High drug prices could also be the result of reverse payments or pay-for-delay settlements between branded and generic manufacturers, which are regulated on both sides of the Atlantic. This chapter will examine competition law regulation of excessive pricing. Attention will be turned to reverse payments in Chapter 9.

1. Unaffordable Drug Prices in Developing Countries

(a) Overview of the unaffordability crisis

The problem of unaffordable drugs for developing country consumers is well documented. This problem is exacerbated in developing countries because these countries tend to spend a disproportionate share of their healthcare budget on medicine. The OECD (Organisation for Economic Co-operation and Development) countries on average spend 18 per cent while low- and middle-income countries spend up to 80 per cent of their healthcare budget on medicine.[2] An average North American spends some 6 per cent while an average Asian spends 50 per cent of her healthcare budget on drugs.[3] Drug prices have a more direct impact on patients in developing countries because they tend to pay for them out of pocket. In Vietnam, for example, only a quarter of total healthcare expenditure is covered by the government; the remaining three-quarters comes directly from the patients.[4] Moreover, fewer patients in developing countries are covered by health insurance.[5] 50–90 per cent of the population in low- and middle-income countries pay for medicine out of pocket.[6] Medicines are the second biggest item of

[2] Zaheer-Ud-Din Babar and others, 'The Availability, Pricing and Affordability of Three Essential Asthma Medicines in 52 Low- and Middle-Income Countries' (2013) 31 PhamacoEconomics 1063, 1064.

[3] Mahesh Patel, 'Drug Costs in Developing Countries and Policies to Reduce Them' (1983) 11 World Development 195, 200.

[4] Anh Tuan Nguyen and others, 'Medicine Prices, Availability, and Affordability in Vietnam' (2009) 2 Southern Med Review 2, 2.

[5] Laurens M Niens and others, 'Quantifying the Impoverishing Effects of Purchasing Medicines: A Cross-Country Comparison of the Affordability of Medicines in the Developing World' (2010) 7 PLoS Medicine 1, 2.

[6] Mendis Shanti and others, 'The Availability and Affordability of Selected Essential Medicines for Chronic Diseases in Six Low- and Middle-Income Countries' (2007) 85 Bulletin of the World Health Organization 279, 279.

expenditure after food in developing countries.[7] If medicines are too expensive for most of the population, they either have to forego treatment or go into debt to pay for them.[8]

The unaffordability crisis that has attracted the most global attention concerned HIV/AIDS drugs. In recent years, the focus has shifted beyond HIV/AIDS to chronic diseases that are endemic in the industrialized economies such as cancer and cardiovascular diseases. As developing countries become wealthier and their citizens enjoy greater longevity, chronic diseases that are closely associated with unhealthy lifestyles have become more prevalent. The demand for drugs that treat these diseases has thus risen and the affordability of these drugs has emerged as a public health issue as well.

The prices of HIV/AIDS drugs have dropped significantly in developing countries since the mid-2000s due to the threatened or actual issuance of compulsory licenses, the increased availability of generics, and voluntary price reductions by the branded manufacturers. At the height of the HIV/AIDS crisis in the early 2000s, however, HIV/AIDS drugs were beyond the reach of most but the wealthiest consumers in developing countries. The annual costs of a popular anti-retroviral (ARV) in the United States in the early 2000s was USD7,215 and that of a more recently introduced ARV called Fuzeon was USD20,000.[9] To put these numbers in context, the annual per capita healthcare expenditure in Sub-Saharan Africa was USD29.30, ranging from USD12 in Malawi to USD253 in South Africa.[10] Unsurprisingly, the existence of patent protection makes a huge difference to drug prices. A dose of 150 mg of fluconazole cost USD55 in India, where there was no patent protection for the drug, while the same drug cost USD697 in Malaysia, USD703 in Indonesia, and USD817 in the Philippines, where the drug was patented. Kenya could reduce its annual costs of treatment of fluconazole from over USD3,000 to USD104 by importing generics from Thailand.[11]

Given the prevalence of HIV in Sub-Saharan Africa—it was reported that 15 per cent of the adult population in South Africa were infected[12]—and the unaffordability of ARV treatment, the HIV/AIDS epidemic was expected to decimate the population of these countries. The life expectancy in Zimbabwe was expected to plummet from 71.4 years prior to the advent of HIV/AIDS to 34.6 years

[7] Alexandra Cameron and others, 'Medicine Prices, Availability, and Affordability in 36 Developing and Middle-Income Countries: A Secondary Analysis' (2009) 373 Lancet 240, 240.

[8] Niens and others (n 5) 2.

[9] Kevin Outterson, 'Pharmaceutical Arbitrage: Balancing Access and Innovation in International Prescription Drug Markets' (2005) 5 Yale Journal of Health Policy, Law & Ethics 193, 251.

[10] Justice C Nwobike, 'Pharmaceutical Corporations and Access to Drugs in Developing Countries: The Way Forward' (2006) 4 International Journal on Human Rights 127, 251–52.

[11] ibid 130.

[12] Sara M Allinder and Janet Fleischman, 'The World's Largest HIV Epidemic in Crisis: HIV in South Africa' *Center for Strategic & International Studies* (2 April 2019) <https://www.csis.org/analysis/worlds-largest-hiv-epidemic-crisis-hiv-south-africa> accessed 21 September 2020.

in 2010.[13] HIV/AIDS tends to strike those in their most productive years and hence has a disproportionate impact on the livelihood of the citizens of these countries. A study found that the HIV/AIDS epidemic would reverse the progress in poverty reduction in Burkina Faso, Rwanda, and Uganda and would increase the percentage of those living in extreme poverty from 45 per cent in 2000 to 51 per cent in 2015.[14]

In the last decade or so, more attention is paid to the affordability of drugs used for treating chronic illnesses. Due to the rising incidence of these diseases, the Thai government imposed a compulsory license on Plavix,[15] which is used to treat heart disease, and threatened to do the same for imatinib, which is used to treat leukaemia and other cancers until Novartis reportedly agreed to donate the drug for free to a public health program in Thailand.[16] India also granted a compulsory license for sorafenib, which is sold under the brand name Nexavar and is used to treat kidney and other cancers.[17] The issuance of the license led to a 97 per cent decrease in price from USD15,400 to less than USD300.[18] There are significant price differences even for something as mundane as opioid painkillers. The median costs of opioid medication in developing countries are twice as high as in industrialized economies, at USD112 and USD53 per month respectively.[19] This means that someone earning the median income in developing countries will need to spend more than one-third of her monthly income on such medication.[20]

Beyond such anecdotal evidence, there have been a number of academic studies on drug prices in developing countries and their affordability for the local population. These studies cover a wide range of drugs that are used to treat other conditions beyond HIV/AIDS. Affordability is usually benchmarked in these studies against the daily wage of the lowest paid unskilled government worker.[21] A single asthma (beclometasone 100 Lg) inhaler costs half a day's wages in Afghanistan but almost two weeks' wages in Madagascar.[22] Another type of asthma (budesonide) inhaler costs half a day's wages in Jordan but 48 days' wages in Burkina Faso,

[13] James Thuo Gathii, 'How Necessity May Preclude State Responsibility for Compulsory Licensing under the TRIPS Agreement' (2006) 31 North Carolina Journal of International Law and Commercial Regulation 943, 958.

[14] ibid 959.

[15] Dina Halajian, 'Inadequacy of TRIPS & the Compulsory License: Why Broad Compulsory Licensing Is Not a Viable Solution to the Access Medicine Problem' (2013) 38 Brooklyn Journal of International Law 1191, 1218.

[16] Jatinder Maan and Dinesh Kumar, 'Product Patent in Pharmaceuticals and Compulsory Licensing' in Jatinder Maan and Dinesh Kumar (eds), *Product Patent in Pharmaceuticals and Compulsory Licensing* (IGI Global 2019) 118.

[17] Sudip Chaudhuri, 'Are Medicine Prices High and Unaffordable after TRIPS? Evidence from Pharmaceutical Industry in India' (Centre for Development Studies 2019) 24.

[18] ibid.

[19] Liliana de Lima and others, 'Potent Analgesics Are More Expensive for Patients in Developing Countries' (2009) 18 Journal of Pain & Palliative Care Pharmacotherapy 59, 63.

[20] ibid.

[21] Babar and others (n 2) 1064.

[22] ibid 1072.

51 days' wages in Mozambique, and 107 days' wages in Guinea.[23] A third type of asthma (salbutamol) inhaler is relatively more affordable. In all the countries surveyed a salbutamol inhaler costs four days' wages or less.[24] Since eight such inhalers are needed in one year, an asthma patient can be expected to spend more than one month's wages on a salbutamol inhaler. The availability of generics alleviates the burden on patients in some, but not all, instances. A generic budesonide inhaler can still cost more than fifty days' wages in Mozambique.[25]

A study on the affordability of medical treatment for chronic conditions such as cardiovascular diseases and diabetes finds that for patients who require multiple medications, the monthly treatment costs could be up to a few days' wages of the lowest paid unskilled government worker.[26] For instance, the combined treatment of aspirin, a statin, and an ACE inhibitor for a coronary heart disease patient for a one-month duration costs 1.5 days' wages in Sri Lanka, more than 5 days' wages in Brazil, Nepal, and Pakistan, and more than 18 days' wages in Malawi.[27] This result is corroborated by another study, which finds that one month's treatment with one cardiovascular medication costs 8.3 days' wages when the branded drug is purchased and two days' wages when the generic is purchased.[28] Meanwhile, one month's treatment of intermediate-acting insulin preparations costs more than a few days' wages.[29] One month's treatment of one hypertension medication costs almost two days' wages.[30] For a lowest paid unskilled government worker who requires more than one anti-hypertensives, the treatment would be unaffordable.[31]

One month's course of generic ranitidine to treat stomach ulcer costs more than three days' wages in Africa and eastern Mediterranean[32] and more than twenty-one days' wages in Vietnam.[33] Ghanaian ulcer patients face an even more daunting financial burden as they need to work for sixty-five days to afford a course of treatment with ranitidine.[34] Meanwhile, a week's course of branded ceftriaxone, an antibiotic, costs almost ninety-nine days' wages in Vietnam.[35] Even the generic version costs almost sixteen days' wages.[36]

[23] ibid.
[24] ibid 1078.
[25] ibid 1072.
[26] Mendis Shanti and others (n 6) 284.
[27] ibid 282.
[28] Maaike SM van Mourik and others, 'Availability, Price and Affordability of Cardiovascular Medicines: A Comparison Across 36 Countries Using WHO/HAI Data' (2010) 10 BMC Cardiovascular Disorders 1, 5.
[29] Mendis Shanti and others (n 6) 282.
[30] van Mourik and others (n 28) 7.
[31] ibid.
[32] Cameron and others (n 7) 245.
[33] Nguyen and others (n 4) 5.
[34] Aida Caldera and Ziga Zarnic, 'Affordability of Pharmaceutical Drugs in Developing Countries' (Kiel Institute for World Economics 2015) No. 419 14.
[35] Nguyen and others (n 4) 5.
[36] ibid.

A separate study employs a slightly different metric to measure the affordability of drugs. As opposed to the number of days of wages of the lowest paid unskilled government worker, this study uses the benchmark of the percentage of population that will be pushed into poverty if required to pay for a certain medication.[37] This approach essentially compares the daily per capita income before and after a medicine is purchased.[38] A medicine is deemed unaffordable if its consumption will push a typical household below the poverty line.[39] They find that in Yemen (the study was conducted before the civil war there had begun), an additional 22 per cent of the population would be pushed into poverty if forced to purchase branded glibenclamide, which is used to treat diabetes, in the private sector.[40] In Nigeria, an additional 23 per cent and 12 per cent of the population would be impoverished if forced to purchase branded and generic amoxicillin, an antibiotic, respectively in the private sector.[41]

Unaffordable drug prices have the predictable effect of curtailing access to essential drugs in developing countries. Even though developing countries account for 80 per cent of the global population, they consume only 20 per cent of the global pharmaceutical production.[42] One-third of the global population,[43] or 2 billion people in the developing world,[44] lack regular access to essential medicines. The situation is worse in the poorer parts of the developing world. More than 50 per cent of the population in Africa lack access to affordable drugs.[45] Somewhat surprisingly, despite its vibrant generic industry which has helped to keep drug prices low, only 30 per cent of the Indian population have regular access to essential drugs.[46] The consequence is an unnecessarily enormous toll on human life. For example, 1.7 million people died in 1999 from tuberculosis because they could not afford the required medical treatment.[47] Before the Thai government adopted its

[37] Niens and others (n 5) 2.

[38] ibid.

[39] ibid 3, 5.

[40] ibid 5.

[41] ibid.

[42] Ashley E Sperbeck, 'A Mathematical Solution to the Sine of Madness That Is Pharmaceutical Compulsory Licensing Under the TRIPS Agreement and the Doha Declaration' (2019) 23 Marquette Intellectual Property Law Review 21, 23.

[43] World Health Organization, 'WHO Medicines Strategy: Framework for Action in Essential Drugs and Medicines Policy 2000–2003' (World Health Organization 2000) 9 <https://apps.who.int/iris/bitstream/handle/10665/66503/WHO_EDM_2000.1.pdf;jsessionid=BF71C740AA4CB0FB07832BDA2F3CDF50?sequence=1> accessed 20 September 2020.

[44] Kumariah Balasubramaniam, 'Equitable Pricing, Affordability and Access to Essential Drugs in Developing Countries: Consumers Perspective', Paper delivered at WHO/WTO Secretariat Workshop on Differential Pricing and Financing of Essential Drugs (8–11 April 2001) 3.

[45] World Health Organization (n 43) 9.

[46] Carlos Correa, *Intellectual Property Rights, the WTO and Developing Countries: The TRIPS Agreement and Policy Options* (Zed Books-Third World Network 2000) 35.

[47] Keith E Maskus, 'Parallel Imports in Pharmaceuticals: Implications for Competition and Prices in Developing Countries' (World Intellectual Property Organization 2001) Annex A. 7 <https://www.wipo.int/export/sites/www/about-ip/en/studies/pdf/ssa_maskus_pi.pdf> accessed 20 September 2020.

aggressive compulsory licensing policy, only about 5 per cent of HIV carriers in the country could afford ARVs.[48]

(b) Causes for high drug prices

Developing countries have a serious problem with unaffordable drugs. In order to determine the appropriate policy responses, we must determine, to the extent possible, the causes for high drug prices. If it is, as some have contended, due to patent protection, then the solution may focus on tackling excessive patent protection. If the cause for high drug prices lies elsewhere, other policy measures may be needed. If high drug prices are due to some market imperfections or anticompetitive behaviour, then market reforms or competition law enforcement may be needed. If such prices are the result of market power that cannot be clearly attributed to some remediable features in the market, it may be necessary for developing country authorities to intervene directly against excessive drug prices.

The most obvious explanation for high drug prices in developing countries is patent protection. It was widely predicted that the introduction of patent protection for pharmaceuticals in developing countries would increase drug prices substantially.[49] A number of commentators, however, have disputed this contention. In a study published in 2004, Amir Attaran finds that only seventeen out of 319 medicines on the WHO's Thirteenth Model List of Essential Medicines were patented in developing countries at the time of the study.[50] Most of these were HIV/AIDS drugs that were of more recent vintage in 2004.[51] Attaran offers two explanations for this somewhat surprising state of affairs. First, many of the medicines on the list were old and no longer patentable.[52] Second, multinational pharmaceutical manufacturers often choose not to obtain patent protection in developing countries even when they are entitled to it.[53] He finds that out of the 969 cases in which the drug was patentable, patent protection was only secured in 300 cases, or 31 per cent of the time.[54] The small size of the domestic market in many developing countries, especially those in Sub-Saharan Africa, means that it is not worth the while of these manufacturers to apply for patent protection.[55] In contrast, patenting for pharmaceuticals is more common in populous middle-income countries such as China, Mexico, and South Africa.[56] He asserts that '[p]atents cannot cause essential

48 Alan O Sykes, 'TRIPS, Pharmaceuticals, Developing Countries, and the Doha "Solution"' (2002) 3 Chicago Journal of International Law 47, 47.

49 Thomas K Cheng, 'A Developmental Approach to the Patent-Antitrust Interface' (2012) 33 Northwestern Journal of International Law & Business 1, 59.

50 Amir Attaran, 'How Do Patents And Economic Policies Affect Access To Essential Medicines In Developing Countries?' (2004) 23 Health Affairs 155, 157.

51 ibid.

52 ibid 159.

53 ibid.

54 ibid.

55 ibid.

56 ibid.

medicines to be inaccessible in "many" developing countries because they do not exist 98.6 percent of the time; similarly, patents cannot be a "global" necessity of pharmaceutical business because companies forgo them 69 percent of the time'.[57] According to him, the ultimate cause for lack of access to affordable medicine in developing countries is poverty.[58]

Richard Rozek and Ruth Berkowitz put forward another study in which they show that the introduction of patent protection for pharmaceuticals in nine middle-income developing countries, including South Korea, Taiwan, Hungary, Mexico, Argentina, Brazil, Egypt, Jordan, and Turkey, did not result in higher drug prices.[59] The focus of the study is the mid-1980s to mid-1990s, when South Korea and Taiwan arguably still qualified as developing countries. These are countries of a sufficient population size such that their domestic markets should attract the attention of multinational pharmaceutical manufacturers. They find that except for Hungary, Jordan, and Turkey, prices for branded drugs rose at a rate that was lower than the rate of inflation and that in all nine countries, the real prices of existing branded drugs decreased by 17 per cent after patent protection was introduced for pharmaceuticals.[60] They conclude that 'IPP [intellectual property protection] seems unrelated to prices. Prices across countries are largely dependent on launch dates since inflation and regulation, not IPP, often affect prices and price changes'.[61]

Defenders of pharmaceutical patents have argued that as opposed to higher prices, the main consequence of the introduction of such patents is higher market share for the branded manufacturers.[62] Robert Sherwood argues that in most therapeutic categories competition is ferocious and that such competition should be sufficient to keep prices down.[63] He concludes that some price increases are to be expected from the introduction of pharmaceutical patents but they should be modest.[64] To evaluate his argument, it is worth considering how the introduction of patent protection will affect competition in the drugs market and whether increase in market share without a concomitant increase in price is plausible.

The introduction of pharmaceutical patents should help branded drugs eliminate or at least minimize competition from generic competitors. Without patent protection, generic competitors could replicate a branded drug and compete solely on price. That is no longer possible in the presence of patent protection. If the increase in market share for branded manufacturers mostly comes from the

[57] ibid.

[58] ibid 163.

[59] Richard P Rozek and Ruth Berkowitz, 'The Effects of Patent Protection on the Prices of Pharmaceutical Products: Is Intellectual Property Protection Raising the Drug Bill in Developing Countries' (1998) 1 Journal of World Intellectual Property 179, 181.

[60] ibid 202, 204.

[61] ibid 213.

[62] Robert M Sherwood, 'A Larger Context for Considering Pharmaceutical Patents in Developing Countries' (1999) 1999 World Bulletin 76, 80.

[63] ibid.

[64] ibid 81.

elimination of low-cost generic competitors, the pricing pressure on the branded manufacturers must have lessened and the increase in market share should be accompanied by a price increase, which is what Sudip Chaudhuri finds in India. His results are consistent with Maskus' observation that the pre-TRIPS market structure for drugs in India 'is competitive because of extensive imitation. Thus, the introduction of patents could place marked upward pressure on protected drug prices'.[65]

One criticism of these studies is that they were undertaken too soon after the TRIPS Agreement came into effect. In fact, many of the developing countries were still in the midst of the transition period and had not introduced patent protection for pharmaceuticals. Chaudhuri undertakes a much more recent study of drug prices in India and finds that drug prices in certain therapeutic categories, especially anti-cancer drugs, were very high and that the market for certain therapeutic categories became more concentrated. India is a particularly important country to study because prior to the TRIPS Agreement, it had a highly competitive domestic pharmaceutical market due to the presence of generic manufacturers. The impact of the introduction of pharmaceutical patents on the drug prices should be most acute and observable there. Chaudhuri observes that the proportion of very high prices in the overall market for pharmaceuticals is small, and hence the impact of TRIPS on drug prices may appear insignificant.[66] However, for a patient who needs a particular drug for her cancer, the fact that most other drugs have remained affordable would be cold comfort. In any case, the number of high-priced drugs is increasing.[67]

Chaudhuri finds that a range of anti-cancer drugs are beyond the reach of most Indian consumers. He suggests that the situation is even worse than with the HIV/AIDS drugs in the early 2000s.[68] The annual treatment costs for twenty out of thirty anti-cancer drugs studied exceed USD10,000.[69] In fact, the annual treatment costs for four of them exceed USD50,000 and that for another eight are between USD20,000 and USD50,000.[70] On the basis of purchasing power parity, twenty-five out of thirty of them have annual treatment costs exceeding USD10,000.[71] In addition to drug prices, the introduction of pharmaceutical patents has a substantial impact on market concentration. In the therapeutic category of anti-neoplastics, the four-firm concentration ratio went from 21.4 per cent in 2010 to 2012 to 70.9 per cent in 2016 to 2018.[72] These prices are expectedly unaffordable to the average

[65] Keith E Maskus, 'Intellectual Property Challenges for Developing Countries: An Economic Perspective' (2001) 2001 University of Illinois Law Review 457, 469.

[66] Chaudhuri (n 17) 30.

[67] ibid.

[68] ibid 4.

[69] ibid 15.

[70] ibid.

[71] ibid.

[72] ibid 20.

Indian consumer. Out of the thirty surveyed anti-cancer drugs, the lowest paid, unskilled government employee will need to work for more than ten years to afford one year's supply for seven of them, between five to ten years for one year's supply of six of them, and between one and five years for one year's supply of eleven of them.[73] These figures leave little doubt that these drugs are unaffordable to the average Indian.

The impact of patent protection on drug prices is vividly illustrated by two incidents. In March 2016, the priciest medicine in India was Cabazitaxel, which costs USD18,000 per injection.[74] After the first generic entry in June 2016, the price for the drug dropped by 90 per cent.[75] Following the entry of a few more generic competitors, the price of the drug dropped by a further 4 per cent, bringing the price down to one-sixteenth of the original price.[76] Before the compulsory license for Sorafenib was issued, Bayer was charging USD15,400 for one month's treatment.[77] The compulsory license precipitated a price reduction of 97 per cent, bringing the price down to one-thirtieth of the original price.[78]

Chaudhuri's study confirms that while the TRIPS Agreement may have had minimal impact on the prices for existing drugs, it had enormous consequences for the prices of drugs that were introduced to the market afterwards.[79] Given that existing drugs cannot be granted retroactive patent protection under TRIPS, most of the drugs in the market when Attaran and Rozek and Berkowitz undertook their studies would be highly unlikely to have benefited from TRIPS and to have experienced price increases due to patent protection. It is worth noting that some other studies have reached contrary results to those produced by Chaudhuri's. Duggan and co-authors find that the introduction of pharmaceutical patents will only lead to price increases of 5 per cent and conclude that concerns about the adverse impact of the TRIPS Agreement on drug prices are overblown.[80]

One has to wonder if patent protection causes drug prices to fall, as alleged by Rozek and Berkowitz, why did the US pharmaceutical companies so doggedly pursue patent protection under the TRIPS Agreement? Pharmaceutical companies are profit-maximizing. Their motivation for pursuing patent protection was surely higher, and not lower, profits. Given that their profits must ultimately come from

[73] ibid 18.
[74] ibid 23–24.
[75] ibid 24.
[76] ibid.
[77] ibid.
[78] ibid.
[79] Naomi A Bass, 'Implications of the TRIPS Agreement for Developing Countries: Pharmaceutical Patent Laws in Brazil and South Africa in the 21st Century' (2002) 34 George Washington University International Law Review 191, 206.
[80] Mark Duggan, Craig Garthwaite, and Aparajita Goyal, 'The Market Impacts of Pharmaceutical Product Patents in Developing Countries: Evidence from India' (2016) 106 The American Economic Review 99, 102.

consumers, if patent protection increases their profitability, it must mean that consumers pay more.

The raison d'être of patent protection is to allow the patentee to charge supra-competitive prices to recoup her investment. It is simply counterintuitive that the introduction of patent protection resulted in lower prices. If patent protection reduced the profitability of these companies in the long term, one would expect them to advocate for a repeal of patent protection or at least encourage the use of compulsory licensing to override their patents. We have witnessed none of this. Instead, the pharmaceutical companies have regularly threatened retaliation whenever a developing country proposes to issue a compulsory license.[81] The only logical explanation is that patent protection earns pharmaceutical companies higher profits, which must mean higher prices for consumers.

2. Differential Pricing for Drugs in Developing Countries

To add insult to injury, there is evidence that drug prices in developing countries, at least some of them, are in fact higher than in many industrialized economies. This phenomenon, which will be called reverse price discrimination, will be examined subsequently. To the extent that reverse price discrimination against developing countries exists, it justifiably adds to the outrage of public health advocates against the multinational pharmaceutical manufacturers. It defies common sense for these manufacturers to charge developing country consumers higher prices when they have much lower ability to pay for expensive medicines. Under standard economic theory, third-degree price discrimination requires the seller to charge the consumers according to their willingness to pay.[82] If developing country consumers have less willingness and ability to pay, the seller should charge them lower, not higher, prices.

To the extent that reverse price discrimination exists in developing countries, it could be used as a basis for intervention against excessive pricing. One of the methods which the European courts have used to ascertain the excessiveness of prices is by benchmarking the domestic price against prices in comparable countries.[83] The fact that the price in a developing country is significantly and consistently higher than the prices in the industrialized countries can be used as evidence to substantiate a finding of excessiveness. Cross-country comparisons can also apply between middle-income developing countries and the least developed countries (LDCs). There is similarly no sound economic rationale for pharmaceutical

[81] Halajian (n 15) 1214.

[82] Erik Hovenkamp and Herbert J Hovenkamp, 'Tying Arrangements and Antitrust Harm' (2010) 52 Arizona Law Review 925, 936.

[83] Case C-177/16, *Biedrība 'Autortiesību un komunicēšanās konsultāciju aģentūra - Latvijas Autoru apvienība' Konkurences padome (AKKA/LAA)* EU:C:2017:689, para. 41.

manufacturers to charge a lower price in middle-income countries than in the LDCs. A substantial difference in price between middle-income countries and an LDC can likewise form the basis of a finding of excessiveness.

(a) Reverse price discrimination in developing countries

There is plenty of anecdotal evidence of developing countries being charged higher prices for branded drugs than are the industrialized economies. The Center for Global Development reports that developing countries pay twenty to thirty times more than the international reference prices for omeprazole, which is used to treat heartburn, and acetaminophen, a common painkiller.[84] The retail price for 100 tablets of 150 mg ranitidine was higher in Vietnam than in Australia and New Zealand.[85] The price of 10 mg nifedipine, a medication for hypertension, costs twice as much in Ghana as in the United Kingdom.[86] The price of four weekly doses of bevacizumab, a cancer drug, is USD4,291 in India, which is twice as high as they are in the United Kingdom.[87] On a purchasing power parity basis, the drug costs seven times as much in India as in the United Kingdom.[88] Willem Pretorius notes that prices for the thirty most prescribed patented drugs are 98 per cent more expensive in South Africa than the best price available in the European Union.[89]

Reverse price discrimination also exists between middle-income countries and low-income ones. A study by Médécin sans Frontières in 2002 reported that a year's supply of the HIV/AIDS anti-retroviral Viracept costs USD2,336 in Brazil and USD8,358 in Guatemala, when the per capita income of Guatemala was one-third that of Brazil.[90] Metformin, which treats Type 2 diabetes, is four and a half times more expensive in Armenia and three and a half times more expensive in Tanzania as in the United Arab Emirates.[91] On a purchasing power parity basis, the price differential becomes 37,000 times and 108,000 times respectively.[92]

[84] Center for Global Development, 'New Study Finds Some Poor Countries Paying 20 to 30 Times More for Basic Medicines Than Others' (17 June 2019) <https://www.cgdev.org/article/new-study-finds-some-poor-countries-paying-20-30-times-more-basic-medicines-others> accessed 20 September 2020.

[85] Nguyen and others (n 4) 3.

[86] Kalipso Chalkidou, 'More Health for the Money through Better Purchasing Decisions: The Case of Ghana' (21 November 2017) <https://www.cgdev.org/blog/more-health-money-through-better-purchasing-decisions-case-ghana> accessed 20 September 2020.

[87] Daniel A Goldstein and others, 'A Global Comparison of the Cost of Patented Cancer Drugs in Relation to Global Differences in Wealth' (2017) 8 Oncotarget 71548.

[88] ibid.

[89] Willem Pretorius, 'TRIPS and Developing Countries: How Level Is the Playing Field?' in Peter Drahos and Ruth Mayne (eds), *Global Intellectual Property Rights: Knowledge, Access and Development* (2002) 183, 189.

[90] Nick Gallus, 'The Mystery of Pharmaceutical Parallel Trade and Developing Countries' (2004) 7 Journal of World Intellectual Property 169, 174.

[91] Zaheer-Ud-Din Babar and others, 'The Availability, Pricing, and Affordability of Essential Diabetes Medicines in 17 Low-, Middle-, and High-Income Countries' (2019) 10 Frontiers in Pharmacology 1375.

[92] ibid.

There have been a number of academic studies on the issue, a preponderance of which find that drug prices are not directly correlated with per capita income and that lower-income countries often have higher drug prices than do the industrialized economies. FM Scherer and Jayashree Watal find a weak positive correlation between the prices of fifteen HIV/AIDS ARVs and the per capita income in eighteen low- and middle-income countries. The overall correlation they find is 0.127, which is not what one would expect in the presence of effective differential pricing.[93]

Chantal Morel and co-authors compare the average drug prices in fourteen middle-income countries (Algeria, Brazil, Egypt, India, Indonesia, Malaysia, Mexico, Morocco, the Philippines, Poland, South Africa, Thailand, Tunisia, and Turkey) with those in three high-income countries (France, the United Kingdom, and the United States) and a low-income region in West Africa between 1999 and 2008. Again, their results show that there is not a strong correlation between national income and domestic drug prices and that poorer countries sometimes pay more for the same drug than wealthier countries.[94] They find that drug prices in Mexico were at least similar to, if not higher than, those in the United States.[95] Once manufacturers' discounts are incorporated, Mexican prices are higher than US prices in every year surveyed in the study.[96] In 1999, drug prices in the Philippines exceeded US prices by 15 per cent.[97] They further find that drug prices in several middle-income countries are higher than those in the United Kingdom and those in Morocco are higher than those in France in some years surveyed in the study.[98]

The anomalous pattern is not confined to high-income and middle-income countries. The authors find that drug prices are lower in some middle-income countries, such as India and Egypt, than those in French West Africa, which is considerably poorer.[99] These results lead the authors to conclude that '[t]here is no statistically significant relationship between pharmaceutical prices in middle-income countries and their gross domestic products... [and that p]harmaceutical prices are much more closely associated with the cost of health care, such as the cost per hospital bed day, than with income'.[100] They see no evidence that multinational pharmaceutical manufacturers calibrate their prices in accordance with the income level in the countries.[101]

93 FM Scherer and Jayashree Watal, 'Post-TRIPS Options for Access to Patented Medicines in Developing Nations' (2002) 5 Journal of International Economic Law 913, 932.

94 Chantal M Morel, Alistair McGuire, and Elias Mossialos, 'The Level of Income Appears to Have No Consistent Bearing on Pharmaceutical Prices Across Countries' (2011) 30 Global Pharmaceutical Pricing 1545, 1545.

95 ibid 1548.

96 ibid.

97 ibid.

98 ibid 1549.

99 ibid.

100 ibid.

101 ibid 1550.

Keith Maskus examines the correlation between the prices of twenty drugs and national income across fourteen countries in 1994 and 1998 and finds mixed results.[102] He finds a negative correlation between prices and national income for three drugs, a mildly positive correlation of between 0 and 0.5 for nine drugs, a stronger positive correlation of between 0.5 and 1 for six drugs, and a close to perfectly positive correlation for two drugs.[103] Price control or other peculiarities in the local market may have caused the prices to deviate from the positive correlation that one would have expected to observe.[104] Regardless of the cause for deviation, Maskus' results show that multinational pharmaceutical manufacturers have not been effective in implementing differential pricing.

There is some contrary evidence on the existence of reverse price discrimination. Aida Caldera and Ziga Zarnic examine whether pricing data for HIV/AIDS drugs conform to the Ramsey pricing hypothesis. They find that branded drugs are significantly cheaper in developing countries while the prices of generic drugs do not display the same pattern.[105] The significance of this finding, however, should not be overstated. First, the authors themselves concede that the relationship they find is weak.[106] Second, HIV/AIDS drugs is the one category of drugs in which multinational pharmaceutical manufacturers have been subject to the most intense pressure to reduce prices for developing countries, both from the advocacy work of international NGOs and the aggressive deployment of compulsory licensing by developing countries such as Brazil and South Africa. If there is one category of drug where one would expect prices to be lower in developing countries, it would be HIV/AIDS.

While the foregoing studies may not definitively confirm the existence of reverse price discrimination in developing countries, they indicate that the cross-country pricing patterns do not conform to what standard economic theory would have predicted for effective third-degree price discrimination. Developing country consumers are charged higher prices than their industrialized economy counterparts at least in some instances. It is worth investigating the motivation for such seemingly counterintuitive behaviour. Caldera and Zarnic attribute this peculiar pricing behaviour to misjudgment.

> Due to income skewness, particularly in South Africa, pharmaceutical companies may misjudge some countries as higher-income markets. The small minority of a wealthy elite, which usually has greater access to drugs and is willing

[102] Maskus, 'Parallel Imports in Pharmaceuticals: Implications for Competition and Prices in Developing Countries' (n 47) 30.

[103] ibid.

[104] Nancy E Pirt, 'Regulation of the Export of Pharmaceuticals to Developing Countries' (1987) 25 Duquesne Law Review 255, 275.

[105] Caldera and Zarnic (n 34) 24.

[106] ibid 16.

> to pay for better quality innovator brand drugs, may misleadingly represent the purchasing power of the whole population. This part of the population typically enjoys a comprehensive health insurance that covers among others prescription drug purchases.[107]

This explanation is hardly convincing. Given the extent of the reverse price discrimination practised by the multinational pharmaceutical manufacturers, it is unlikely that they would have repeated the same mistake across such a wide range of developing countries.

Citing a study by Aidan Hollis, Jerome Reichman offers the following explanation for the pricing behaviour of the multinational pharmaceutical manufacturers instead:

> Hollis shows that, in very poor countries characterized by great disparities of income, the rational-acting originator company seeking to maximize profits will logically charge high prices to the affluent sector of the society, because it will earn much greater profits than if it had distributed the same drug to poverty stricken masses at prices they could afford. Calling this the problem of 'highly convex demand curves' for essential goods in countries with large disparities of income, Hollis shows, for example, that the rational-acting firm operating in South Africa would maximize profits 'by selling at the price that only the top 10% can afford.' In effect, 'the firm will maximize its profits by setting a price unaffordable for at least 90% of ... [the] people.' That finding translates to a deadweight loss of 90 percent[.][108]

Hollis contrasts the situation in South Africa with that in Norway, where there is a much higher degree of income equality. Convex demand does not apply in Norway and a pharmaceutical company would have the incentive to offer its drug to a much wider customer base at more affordable prices.[109]

Some have argued that the high drug prices in developing countries and the wide price differential between developed and developing countries are due to other reasons such as a lack of competition in the distribution of drugs in the domestic market or tariffs and local taxes. Kumariah Balasubramaniam disagrees, asserting that whatever market and regulatory distortions cannot explain the significant price differential between developed and developing countries.[110] He cites a paper prepared by the WTO secretariat that states that distribution margins and taxes can increase the retail price of drugs from the manufacturer's selling price by

[107] ibid 17.

[108] Jerome H Reichman, 'Compulsory Licensing of Patented Pharmaceutical Inventions: Evaluating the Options' (2009) 37 Journal of Law, Medicine & Ethics 247, 254–55.

[109] ibid 255.

[110] Balasubramaniam (n 44) 12.

four times.[111] Another paper prepared by the World Health Organization (WHO) puts this effect at 200 per cent.[112] This falls far short of a multiple of fifty-eight that he finds between the manufacturer's selling price and the retail price in some developing countries.[113] He concludes that distribution margins, tariffs, and taxes cannot adequately account for the wide price differentials between countries and these differentials must be the result of a deliberate policy by the multinational pharmaceutical manufacturers.[114]

(b) Parallel trade

One issue that is closely related to differential pricing across countries is parallel trade, which refers to trade of a product across countries unauthorized by the original seller to take advantage of the price differences between them. For third-degree price discrimination to succeed, the seller must be able to identify customers with different willingness to pay and maintain separate prices for each group of customers. The seller must be able to prevent arbitrage. Where arbitrage is possible, the customers who are offered a lower price will resell their products to those who are charged a higher price.[115] The former only needs to charge a price between the prices offered to the two groups of customers to make a profit and the price discrimination scheme will unravel.

Parallel trade is arbitrage on a cross-country scale generated by international price differences.[116] How developing countries should respond to parallel trade would depend on how they are affected by differential pricing. If a particular developing country is being charged a higher price than comparable countries, parallel trade should bring prices down and should be welcome. If, on the contrary, a developing country is charged a lower price than the industrialized economies, condoning parallel trade would undermine the differential pricing scheme put in place by multinational pharmaceutical manufacturers that allows them to recoup their R&D investments from the industrialized economy markets while offering relatively affordable prices to developing country consumers. Disrupting such a differential pricing scheme will in all likelihood force the seller to switch to a uniform price across countries, which will inevitably mean higher prices for developing country consumers.

From a purely national perspective, it would seem that the best strategy for a developing country is to allow parallel import but to ban parallel export. Parallel traders would only have the incentive to import into a particular country if the price there is higher. Therefore, parallel import will almost always benefit domestic

[111] ibid.
[112] ibid.
[113] ibid.
[114] ibid.
[115] Outterson (n 9) 206.
[116] Gallus (n 90) 169.

consumers by bringing prices down. Parallel traders would only export domestic products if the products command a higher price abroad. This means that differential pricing currently favours domestic consumers and permitting parallel export could jeopardize such an advantage. For developing countries collectively, it would be in their interest to prohibit parallel export to the industrialized economies as such trade would likely lead to higher prices in developing countries eventually.

3. Do High Drug Prices in Developing Countries Require Policy Intervention?

If developing countries suffer from high drug prices and reverse price discrimination by the multinational pharmaceutical manufacturers, are there valid grounds for policy intervention? Should developing countries intervene against high drug prices and reverse price discrimination?

(a) The case for policy interventions against reverse price discrimination

The arguments regarding reverse price discrimination are probably easier to refute. Even the most fervent defenders of the pricing practices of the multinational pharmaceutical manufacturers stop short of defending reverse price discrimination.[117] They justify conventional third-degree price discrimination under which developing countries would be charged less for drugs on the grounds that it is the most efficient way for the pharmaceutical manufacturers to recover their R&D costs.[118] Cross-country price discrimination is efficient because it allows these manufacturers to fully exploit the consumers' willingness to pay in the industrialized economies and recover more of their R&D costs from consumers who can afford to pay higher prices. These commentators shy away from defending reverse price discrimination. Instead, they contend that such practice does not exist.[119] Unless one believes that pharmaceutical manufacturers have no obligation to take into account the plight of developing country patients and should be given a free rein to maximize their profits, reverse price discrimination would be indefensible.

The only tenable justification for this practice would be that reverse price discrimination is necessary to allow multinational pharmaceutical manufacturers to recover their R&D costs and that socially beneficial R&D would be abandoned without reverse price discrimination. This would require either reverse price discrimination to provide a significant revenue boost to the pharmaceutical manufacturers or for socially beneficial R&D to be barely profitable for these manufacturers, or both. Apart from drugs that treat tropical diseases endemic in developing

[117] ibid 171.

[118] Caldera and Zarnic (n 34) 3.

[119] Gallus (n 90) 172.

countries such as malaria and African sleeping sickness, it is unlikely that the profitability of a drug will hinge on its sales in developing countries, especially poor LDCs with small domestic markets.[120] For drugs that treat global diseases such as cancer, diabetes, cardiovascular diseases, etc., the bulk of the recoupment of R&D costs will take place in the industrialized economies.[121] A prohibition of reverse price discrimination in developing countries is unlikely to make a significant dent in the profitability of these drugs. As for drugs that treat tropical diseases, they are by and large not sold in the industrialized economies and reverse price discrimination should not be an issue for them. Overall, reverse price discrimination should not be needed to allow the pharmaceutical manufacturers to recover their R&D costs and policy intervention against reverse price discrimination would not undermine the incentives to invest in these drugs.

While it is by no means a universal phenomenon, there is sufficient evidence that reverse price discrimination in drug prices is not an isolated incident and is prevalent enough to warrant a policy response. There are international and domestic dimensions to such a response. In terms of parallel trade, reverse price discrimination means that developing countries often pay more than the industrialized economies for the same drug and would benefit from cheaper parallel imports. Developing countries which suffer from reverse price discrimination should permit parallel imports. Some commentators have argued that developing countries tend to lose out from parallel trade because such trade will inevitably result in the diversion of cheaper drugs sold in their domestic markets to developed country markets.[122] The foregoing discussion, however, suggests that developing countries are not invariably the beneficiaries of international differential pricing and reverse price discrimination does happen. Parallel trade of pharmaceuticals is not always contrary to their interests. By permitting parallel import from the industrialized economies, developing countries can help bring down domestic drug prices without undermining the recovery of R&D costs for the pharmaceutical manufacturers. Most of that cost recovery will continue to take place in the industrialized economies.

Domestically, developing countries can respond to reverse price discrimination in two ways. Multinational pharmaceutical manufacturers are forced to charge such high prices for their products because they are unable to implement effective price discrimination within the domestic market. To the extent that government policies facilitating price discrimination can entice these manufacturers to lower their prices to the general population, developing country governments should adopt such policies. Brand differentiation may render it feasible to price

[120] Sperbeck (n 42) 103.

[121] Colleen V Chien, 'Cheap Drugs at What Price to Innovation: Does the Compulsory Licensing of Pharmaceuticals Hurt Innovation' (2003) 18 Berkeley Technology Law Journal 853, 894.

[122] Gallus (n 90) 172.

discriminate between wealthy patients and the general population. These manufacturers can be encouraged to offer their own authorized generic products to the general population, especially for products that are off-patent already.

The public sector can carry the generic version while the private sector can stock the branded product. Since most wealthy patients in developing countries use private healthcare, this can effectively achieve customer segmentation. Effective customer segmentation may provide the pharmaceutical manufacturers the incentives to offer their products at cheaper prices to the general population. It is also possible, however, that the general population in developing countries is so poor that there is no profitable price at which these manufacturers can sell their products, in which case there may be a limit to what the government can do to facilitate domestic price discrimination.[123]

If such facilitative efforts fail and parallel imports are not forthcoming, developing countries may consider more aggressive policy options. One possibility is to take advantage of the options available under the TRIPS Agreement to issue a compulsory license. There are many complications involved in doing so, which will be discussed subsequently. Another possibility is to pursue competition law enforcement by bringing excessive pricing claims, which also involve difficulties of its own. One of the difficulties is how to define excessiveness. The imperative of securing affordable drugs in developing countries means that a substantial discrepancy between domestic prices and the prices prevailing in a number of industrialized economies should invite scrutiny from a developing country competition authority. Excessive pricing enforcement is one of the possible tools for tackling reverse price discrimination.

(b) The case for policy interventions against high drug prices in general

(1) The need to preserve innovation incentives

The arguments regarding high drug prices in general are more complicated. On the one hand, unaffordable drug prices put essential medicines out of the reach of the majority of the population in developing countries, leading to needless suffering, loss of productivity, or perhaps even death. To the extent that high drug prices are shouldered by the public coffers, high drug prices will divert precious resources from other important uses such as education and other general economic development purposes. High drug prices will indirectly reduce the development prospects of these countries. On the other hand, defenders of the pharmaceutical industry would argue that the industry needs high profit to finance its R&D. Reduced profitability due to compulsory licensing or excessive pricing enforcement will lead to the abandonment of important R&D and hence dynamic efficiency loss. We are

[123] Attaran (n 50) 163.

thus back to the question addressed in Chapter 2 regarding the extent to which patent protection and patentee reward are necessary to generate innovation.

Recall that it was argued in Chapter 2 that patent protection is not accurately calibrated to produce the appropriate amount of compensation for innovators. The Yale survey and other studies were cited for the proposition that most industries do not rely on patent protection as an appropriation mechanism. While that is true for most industries, the authors of the survey specifically find that the pharmaceutical and chemical industries are dependent on patent protection. A number of features specific to the industry mean that patents are especially important for pharmaceutical companies. The industry is characterized by poor appropriability conditions because once a drug is discovered, it is relatively easy to reverse engineer.[124] Trade secrets are hence not a viable appropriation mechanism. Some other mechanism is needed to stop imitators from replicating the technology. In the meantime, the profitability of a successful product can be very high. It is not uncommon for a blockbuster drug to earn hundreds of millions, if not billions, a year.[125] Therefore, the industry has a lot to gain by successfully defending its turf and preventing replication of its products.

The industry also invests heavily in R&D and product development such as clinical trials and is reliant on its profits to cover these expenses.[126] A number of commentators and organizations have attempted to come up with estimates for the average development costs for a drug. The figures keep rising and are plagued by a high degree of inaccuracy as only the pharmaceutical manufacturers themselves are in possession of the relevant data. Nonetheless, some estimates have been produced over the years. Back in 1990, it was estimated that it cost USD359 million and took ten to twelve years to develop a new pharmaceutical compound from scratch.[127] Another study suggests USD500 million and reports that only one out of every ten new drugs recovers its costs.[128] Another study reports a slightly higher success rate of three out of ten approved drugs recouping their R&D costs.[129] A widely cited figure puts the development costs of a drug at USD802 million.[130] A more recent study raises the estimate to around USD2.5 billion per drug.[131] This figure, however, has been widely disputed.[132]

124 Cheng (n 49) 29.

125 'The Top Selling Prescription Drugs by Revenue' (21 May 2019) <https://www.pharmaceutical-technology.com/features/top-selling-prescription-drugs/> accessed 21 September 2020.

126 Cheng (n 49) 31.

127 Michelle M Nerozzi, 'The Battle over Life-Saving Pharmaceuticals: Are Developing Countries Being TRIPped by Developed Countries' (2002) 47 Villanova Law Review 605, 620.

128 Sperbeck (n 42) 104.

129 Peggy B Sherman and Ellwood F Oakley III, 'Pandemics and Panaceas: The World Trade Organization's Efforts to Balance Pharmaceutical Patents and Access to AIDS Drugs' (2004) 41 American Business Law Journal 353, 406.

130 Ellen 't Hoen, 'TRIPS, Pharmaceutical Patents, and Access to Essential Medicines: A Long Way From Seattle to Doha' (2002) 3 Chicago Journal of International Law 27, 46.

131 Frederick M Abbott, 'Excessive Pharmaceutical Prices and Competition Law: Doctrinal Development to Protect Public Health' (2016) 6 UC Irvine Law Review 281, 307.

132 ibid.

Much of these costs are incurred to conduct the clinical trials that are needed to obtain approval from the Food & Drug Administration.[133] It has been reported that 'of every 5,000 potential new drugs tested in animals, only 5 are promising enough to be tested in humans . . . and only one of those five is eventually approved for marketing'.[134] If it is true that only one of ten new drugs recovers its costs, it means that it takes 50,000 potential new drugs tested in animals to produce one profitable drug. The pharmaceutical industry will certainly need high prices for the very few successful blockbuster drugs to make up for all the losses it sustains on the numerous failed drugs. In that case, competition authorities should proceed cautiously against excessive drug prices as doing so may threaten the pipeline of future drugs.

In the meantime, there are signs that the current high drug prices are excessive and not needed to support continual R&D. The pharmaceutical companies spend more money on marketing than R&D, which suggests that marketing is in fact more profitable.[135] Marketing costs have skyrocketed and the costs of pre-launch marketing to doctors and customers are estimated to be USD400 million per drug.[136] Close to 50 per cent of the product development costs are reported to occur post-patenting.[137] Such high marketing costs are not consistent with the thesis that a small reduction in drug prices will cause an immediate and significant loss in R&D.

This conclusion is further bolstered by the fact that the pharmaceutical industry has consistently enjoyed very high profit. Pharmaceutical companies have been some of the most profitable companies in the world for decades. Since as early as the period from the 1950s to the 1970s, pharmaceutical companies regularly outperformed companies in other industries. Between 1958 and 1975, the average rate of return for all manufacturing companies in the United States was 11 per cent while that for large pharmaceutical companies was almost twice as high at close to 20 per cent.[138] The after-tax profits for pharmaceutical companies between 1990 and 1996 were three times as high as for all other industries.[139] For the financial year ending in 2013, Pfizer, one of the largest pharmaceutical companies in the world, had a profit margin of 42 per cent.[140] The industry also does not need to finance all of its R&D with its own funds. Pharmaceutical companies receive an enormous amount of public funding to finance their R&D, including 'government grants, direct government expenditures, foundation donors, and tax incentives.

[133] Sherman and Oakley III (n 129) 404.
[134] ibid.
[135] Outterson (n 9) 221.
[136] Sherman and Oakley III (n 129) 405.
[137] Chien (n 121) 866.
[138] Pirt (n 104) 269.
[139] Outterson (n 9) 221.
[140] Mauro Nuno, 'A Fair Return Approach to Pharmaceutical Compulsory Licensing' (2016) 48 Case Western Reserve Journal of International Law 395, 404.

The industry receives substantial tax incentives, resulting in an effective US federal income tax rate of 16.2 per cent, compared with 27.3 per cent generally.'[141]

Overall, it is highly doubtful that the pharmaceutical industry must maintain its current price level to sustain current R&D and that any reduction in current price will result in a significant loss of future drugs. The imperative of sustaining the current level of R&D presumes that that level is optimal. There is, however, no conclusive evidence demonstrating the optimality of the current level of pharmaceutical R&D. The Congressional Budget Office in the United States concedes that no one knows whether the current level is optimal.[142] Given the inability of the current patent system to match patentee reward with the risk-adjusted private costs of innovation, the quest for the optimal level of R&D will probably remain elusive. Meanwhile, James Love, the Director of the Center for Consumer Project on Technology estimates that the global deadweight loss inflicted by pharmaceutical patents is over USD400 billion per year.[143]

In any case, what is contemplated is not a worldwide reduction in drug prices to reduce the profits for pharmaceutical companies. The focus of the current inquiry is limited to developing countries. Kevin Outterson and others have demonstrated that for drugs used to treat global diseases, a reduction in the returns from developing countries will not affect the innovation incentives for these drugs.[144] Reichman argues that even the issuance of compulsory licenses for these drugs in developing countries 'would have virtually no impact on incentives to innovate in rich countries'.[145]

To sum up, drug prices are unaffordable to most consumers in developing countries. Pharmaceutical companies justify their high prices in the name of maintaining their innovation incentives. Yet these companies often charge higher prices in developing countries than in the industrialized economies, which contradicts efficient pricing practices under third-degree price discrimination. The current pricing practices of these companies seem more consistent with extracting maximum profit from developing countries than facilitating the recovery of R&D costs by spreading the burden of these costs across countries based on their willingness to pay.

This gives developing countries valid grounds for regulating high domestic drug prices without the need to worry about undermining innovation incentives. This is especially so as evidence seems to suggest that prices and the profit level

[141] Outterson (n 9) 221.

[142] Congressional Budget Office, 'How Increased Competition from Generic Drugs Has Affected Prices and Returns in the Pharmaceutical Industry' (1998) 48 <https://www.cbo.gov/sites/default/files/105th-congress-1997-1998/reports/pharm.pdf> accessed 29 July 2021.

[143] James Love, 'Statement of Essential Inventions to the Commission on Intellectual Property Rights, Innovation and Public Health' 2 <https://www.who.int/intellectualproperty/news/en/eii.pdf?ua=1> accessed 20 September 2020.

[144] Reichman (n 108) 264.

[145] ibid.

for the industry exceed what is necessary to support the current R&D, which may not even be optimal. While the dynamic efficiency benefits of high drug prices are highly speculative, their short-run static efficiency harm is certain. If the global deadweight loss per year is anything close to USD400 billion, and the lack of affordable drugs is such a serious problem in developing countries, developing country authorities have very good reasons to intervene against excessive drug prices.

(2) The need to provide incentives to develop domestic innovation capacity
Another argument opposing regulatory intervention against excessive drug prices is that it will stifle growth in domestic innovation capacity. The patentee reward generated by high drug prices redounds benefit to both foreign and domestic pharmaceutical manufacturers. For the multinational manufacturers, the patentee reward will support ongoing and future R&D. For the domestic manufacturers, the patentee reward will induce them to develop their innovation capacity. It has also been argued that developing country pharmaceutical companies will be forced to invest in research for their own drugs if they can no longer copy from elsewhere.[146] Increased patent protection also benefits developing countries by attracting foreign direct investment (FDI) from multinational pharmaceutical manufacturers.[147] Although his results are not specific to the pharmaceutical industry, Maskus estimates that FDI would rise significantly in Brazil, Indonesia, Mexico, and Thailand following the coming into effect of the TRIPS Agreement.[148] The introduction of pharmaceutical patents thus should benefit developing countries by raising domestic R&D investment and attracting more FDI. According to Sherwood, when effective patent protection is introduced to developing countries:

> three things will begin to happen. Micro-firms and individual inventors will begin to be able to attract private risk capital to support development of their raw inventions for the market place. University research results will be sought by companies and developed for market application. Existing companies will begin to conduct internal research to improve their products and their process technology, and to add new products.[149]

While this argument is appealing in principle, it has not been borne out by reality. The reality is that pharmaceutical R&D is so resource- and technology-intensive that few developing countries will be able to join the ranks of the big pharma

[146] Nadia Natasha Seeratan, 'The Negative Impact of Intellectual Property Patent Rights on Developing Countries: An Examination of the Indian Pharmaceutical Industry' (2001) 3 The Scholar: St Mary's Law Review on Minority Issues 339, 381.
[147] ibid.
[148] Maskus, 'Intellectual Property Challenges for Developing Countries: An Economic Perspective' (n 65) 465.
[149] Sherwood (n 62) 89.

from the United States and Europe and produce genuinely novel drugs in the foreseeable future. The vast gap in pharmaceutical innovation capacity between developed and developing countries is evidenced by the fact the 97 per cent of the pharmaceutical patents worldwide belong to individuals and companies resident in the industrialized economies and 80 per cent of pharmaceutical patents granted in developing countries are granted to innovators based in the industrialized economies.[150]

While the precise magnitude of the estimates that were presented earlier is hotly debated, there is no denying that drug development is prohibitively expensive and is beyond the capability of most pharmaceutical companies in developing countries. Big pharmas are behemoths with huge market capitalization. The market capitalization of Pfizer at the end of 2019 was USD218 billion.[151] Its annual research budget for 2019 was USD8.65 billion,[152] which could exceed the market capitalization of many developing country pharmaceutical companies. No wonder Anna Lanoszka declares that '[i]t is virtually impossible to compete with such dominant monopolies because of the unprecedented financial resources at their disposal and their supreme research capabilities'.[153]

Successful pharmaceutical R&D also requires more than the pharmaceutical companies themselves. For example, in the United States, there is extensive collaboration between the universities and the pharmaceutical companies supported by funding from public institutions such as the National Institutes of Health, whose annual research budget are in the tens of billions.[154] An elaborate research-industrial complex is needed to generate the kind of cutting edge pharmaceutical R&D that emanates from the United States and other industrialized economies. Most developing countries simply lack such science and technology infrastructure and research capabilities in the tertiary educational institutions to support pharmaceutical research.[155]

This has led Frederick Abbott to proclaim that '[t]here is no substantial evidence to suggest that introduction of patent protection will result in a substantial increase in pharmaceutical product R & D in the developing countries'.[156] The

[150] 't Hoen (n 130) 37.

[151] Macrotrends, 'Pfizer Market Cap 2006–2020 | PFE' <https://www.macrotrends.net/stocks/charts/PFE/pfizer/market-cap> accessed 22 September 2020.

[152] Statista, 'Pfizer's Expenditure on Research and Development from 2006 to 2019' <https://www.statista.com/statistics/267810/expenditure-on-research-and-development-at-pfizer-since-2006/> accessed 21 September 2020.

[153] Anna Lanoszka, 'The Global Politics of Intellectual Property Rights and Pharmaceutical Drug Policies in Developing Countries' (2003) 24 International Political Science Review 181, 182–83.

[154] National Institutes of Health, 'Budget' <https://www.nih.gov/about-nih/what-we-do/budget> accessed 21 September 2020.

[155] Sperbeck (n 42) 102.

[156] Frederick M Abbott, 'WTO TRIPS Agreement and Its Implications for Access to Medicines in Developing Countries' (Commission for Intellectual Property Rights 2002) Background Paper 6–7.

only likely consequence of the introduction of pharmaceutical patents in developing countries is a net outflow of patent rents to multinational pharmaceutical manufacturers.[157]

This is consistent with the finding by FM Scherer and Sandy Weisburst that after Italy introduced pharmaceutical patents in 1978, there was hardly any increase in inflation-adjusted R&D expenditures in the country and no increase in the number of new drugs introduced by Italian firms.[158] Even for India, which has much more advanced capabilities in the pharmaceutical industry than most other developing countries, 'the establishment of a strict patent system is unlikely to stimulate growth or encourage research and development as industrialized countries assert. Rather, India is concerned that increased protection will have the opposite effect and actually diminish the promotion of domestic technology, research and development'.[159]

As far as the pharmaceutical industry is concerned, the vast majority of the developing countries are merely production countries. A small number of them which boast a vibrant generic sector count as technology adaptation countries. Balasubramaniam reports that of all developing countries, only Argentina, Brazil, China, India, and Mexico are capable of generic production of all new drugs and therefore constitute technology adaptation countries as far as pharmaceuticals are concerned.[160] Balasubramaniam distinguishes between advanced production capacity and basic production capacity. According to him, another seven countries have the capacity to produce active pharmaceutical ingredients from intermediate products available in the global supply chain and count as advanced production countries.[161] A further ninety countries possess the capability 'to manufacture dosage forms or finished products from raw materials available in the world market' and can be categorized as basic production countries.[162] No developing country seems to possess genuine innovation capacity in the industry to qualify as a proto-innovation country.

As for FDI, it was previously reported in Chapter 3 that FDI in the pharmaceutical industry should be sensitive to the level of patent protection and R&D of all business activities shows the highest sensitivity to the level of patent protection. However, that has not been borne out by the experience of developing countries after the introduction of pharmaceutical patents under the TRIPS Agreement. India, which should be a prime candidate for pharmaceutical FDI given its vibrant generic sector and existing manufacturing capability, has not experienced a boom

[157] Maskus, 'Intellectual Property Challenges for Developing Countries: An Economic Perspective' (n 65) 468.

[158] FM Scherer and Sandy Weisburst, 'Economic Effects of Strengthening Pharmaceutical Patent Protection in Italy' (1995) 26 International Review of Industrial Property and Copyright 1009, 1020–22.

[159] Seeratan (n 146) 368.

[160] Balasubramaniam (n 44) 5.

[161] ibid.

[162] ibid.

in FDI as predicted as will be explained subsequently. A number of studies do report an increase in FDI into the Indian pharmaceutical sector following the introduction of pharmaceutical patents.[163] The average FDI received by each recipient increased by 2.6 per cent in the four years after the introduction of pharmaceutical patents as compared to the four years prior.[164] There was also an increase in the number of FDI recipients in the industry.[165] There is, however, evidence that this boost in FDI in the industry is partly the result of a general increase in FDI in India. The sector's share of the country's overall FDI actually fell from 2.6 per cent to 0.7 per cent during the same period.[166]

George and Usha Haley proclaim that '[g]iven the size and growth of the Indian pharmaceutical market and the rate of India's economic growth, FDI in India's pharmaceutical industry may have occurred regardless of patent regime'.[167] Meanwhile, after Brazil eliminated patent protection for pharmaceuticals in 1969, there was a sixfold increase in FDI in the domestic pharmaceutical industry.[168] Even if FDI were to take place, there is no guarantee that it will benefit the local industry. After Italy introduced pharmaceutical patents in 1978, most FDI took place in the form of foreign takeover of Italian pharmaceutical companies.[169] This did not increase the R&D and manufacturing capacity of the Italian pharmaceutical industry, which eventually lost its place as the leading generic manufacturer of the world to India.

Once it is accepted that there are valid policy justifications for intervening against excessive drug prices, developing countries must contemplate the appropriate policy option. As it turns out, there are a number of possibilities. First, they can institute domestic price control like what many European countries have done. This is beyond the scope of this chapter and will not be explored further. Second, the TRIPS Agreement provides a number of options, including the issuance of a compulsory license under Article 31. The last one would be competition law enforcement against excessive pricing. What follows is an examination of the latter two options.

[163] Rajnish Kumar Rai, 'Effect of the TRIPS-Mandated Intellectual Property Rights on Foreign Direct Investment in Developing Countries: A Case Study of the Indian Pharmaceutical Industry' (2009) 11 Journal of World Intellectual Property 404; Katherine Connor Linton and Nicholas Corrado, 'A "Calibrated Approach": Pharmaceutical FDI and Evolution of the Patent Law in India' <https://papers.ssrn.com/sol3/papers.cfm?abstract_id=1031227> accessed 20 September 2020.

[164] Ishita G Tripathy, Surendra Yadav, and Seema Sharma, 'FDI Flows into the Indian Pharmaceutical Industry: An Analysis of Trends and Constraints' (2011) 16 Journal of Intellectual Property Rights 330, 331–32.

[165] ibid.

[166] ibid 331.

[167] George T Haley and Usha CV Haley, 'The Effects of Patent-Law Changes on Innovation: The Case of India's Pharmaceutical Industry' (2012) 79 Technological Forecasting & Social Change 607, 618.

[168] Sperbeck (n 42) 101.

[169] Keith Maskus, *Intellectual Property Rights in the Global Economy* (Institute for International Economics 2000) 165.

C. The TRIPS Agreement

The introduction of pharmaceutical patents under the TRIPS Agreement is at least partly to blame for the problem of unaffordable drugs in developing countries. As it turns out, the Agreement provides some possible solutions to the problem. The TRIPS Agreement provides some reprieve for developing countries. The Agreement stipulates longer transitional periods for developing countries before they need to adopt pharmaceutical patenting. It also provides a number of exceptions to patent protection under Article 30 and Article 31. These exceptions provide different extents of relief for developing countries from the adverse consequences of pharmaceutical patents. In the end, none of them provides an effective remedy for excessive drug prices in developing countries, which may compel these countries to look beyond patent law for solutions.

1. Transitional Arrangements for Developing Countries

The TRIPS Agreement gives developing countries a grace period for implementing patent protection for pharmaceuticals. The Agreement, as it was adopted in 1995, gave developing countries until 1 January 2000 and least developed countries until 1 January 2006 to meet their obligations under the Agreement.[170] Developing countries that did not provide patent protection for pharmaceuticals prior to TRIPS were given until 1 January 2005 to do so.[171] During this transitional period, these countries must provide a 'mailbox' where patent applications for drugs can be filed and safekept.[172] Upon expiration of this period, these applications would be considered. Patent protection must be granted for the remainder of the patent term counting from the date of filing for approved applications.[173] In the Doha Declaration on the TRIPS Agreement and Public Health, least developed countries (LDCs) were granted a further extension to 1 January 2016 for compliance with their TRIPS obligations as far as pharmaceutical patenting is concerned.[174] On 27 April 2002, the TRIPS Council formally adopted a decision implementing this extension, which was subsequently further extended to 1 January 2033.[175]

[170] TRIPS Agreement, arts 65 and 66; Harrison Mwakyembe and George Mpundu Kanja, 'Implications of the TRIPS Agreement on the Access to Cheaper Pharmaceutical Drugs by Developing Countries' (2002) 34 Zambia Law Journal 111, 129.
[171] ibid.
[172] ibid.
[173] ibid.
[174] ibid 130.
[175] 't Hoen (n 130) 185. Reed Beall and Randall Kuhn, 'Trends in Compulsory Licensing of Pharmaceuticals Since the Doha Declaration: A Database Analysis' [2012] Plos Medicine 2 <https://journals.plos.org/plosmedicine/article%3Fid%3D10.1371/journal.pmed.1001154> accessed 4 March 2020.

As is true of most things under TRIPS, measures that are ostensibly adopted for the benefits of developing countries often turn out to be illusory. First, despite the official grace period, many LDCs have been pressured by the industrialized economies to introduce pharmaceutical patents prior to 2033.[176] Many of them had already implemented policy measures in anticipation of the 2006 deadline when it was extended to 2016 and then 2033.[177] All but three of the LDCs in Africa had instituted pharmaceutical patents as of 2004.[178] Second, most LDCs do not manufacture drugs themselves and must rely on imports from other developing country suppliers such as India, which were no longer exempted from pharmaceutical patents after 2005.[179] This means that LDCs can no longer obtain low-cost supplies of drugs even though they are not obliged to offer patent protection to pharmaceuticals domestically. Third, prior to the expiration of the grace period, LDCs are required to safekeep patent applications. While patent applications are withheld, LDCs are required to grant exclusive marketing rights to the putative patentee for a period of five years following marketing approval of the drug.[180] For all intents and purposes, these marketing rights function as patent rights and give the pharmaceutical manufacturer the same exclusivity.[181] The veneer of benevolence created by the repeated extensions granted to LDCs is stripped away by this back-door introduction of exclusive rights for drugs. These transitional measures only provided limited relief to developing countries and the LDCs.

2. Public Health Exception

Article 27(1) of the TRIPS Agreement states that 'patents shall be available for any inventions, whether products or processes, in all fields of technology, provided that they are new, involve an inventive step and are capable of industrial application'.[182] The reference to all fields of technology suggests that patent protection must be extended to pharmaceuticals. Paragraph 3 of the Article muddies the waters by allowing members to exclude from the scope of patentability 'diagnostic, therapeutic and surgical methods for the treatment of humans or animals',[183] which could be construed to encompass pharmaceuticals as drugs are therapeutic methods of treating humans.[184] Paragraph 2 of the same Article also authorizes members to

176 Abbott (n 156) 4.

177 Reed Beall and Kuhn, 'Trends in Compulsory Licensing of Pharmaceuticals Since the Doha Declaration: A Database Analysis' (2012) 9 PLoS Medicine 2.

178 Outterson (n 9) 257.

179 Abbott (n 156) 11.

180 ibid.

181 ibid.

182 TRIPS Agreement, art 27(1).

183 ibid art 27(3).

184 Sherman and Oakley III (n 129) 368.

'exclude from patentability inventions, the prevention within their territory of the commercial exploitation of which is necessary to protect ordre public or morality, including to protect human, animal or plant life or health or to avoid serious prejudice to the environment'.[185] There is no formal definition of what constitutes public order under the TRIPS Agreement. It would not be farfetched to interpret it to cover any circumstance in which human life is implicated.[186]

Article 8 of the Agreement provides further support for this idea by empowering members to 'adopt measures necessary to protect public health and nutrition',[187] which gives rise to the possibility of adopting emergency measures to suspend or minimize patent protection of pharmaceuticals in the event of a public health crisis. Interpreting these provisions to create a general exception for patent protection for pharmaceuticals, however, would be inconsistent with the express language of Article 70(8),[188] which clearly contemplates such protection, and with the negotiation history of the Agreement, during which developing countries such as India vehemently opposed the introduction of pharmaceutical patents but eventually capitulated to US pressure.[189] There was little doubt that WTO members envisioned the TRIPS Agreement to offer patent protection to pharmaceuticals. Yet this should not preclude these provisions from being construed together as providing for a limited public health exception to pharmaceutical patents, the exact contours of which remain unspecified.[190]

3. Abuse/Anticompetitive Conduct Exception

Article 8(2) propounds the principle that members may adopt appropriate measures, provided that they are consistent with the Agreement, 'to prevent the abuse of intellectual property rights by right holders or the resort to practices which unreasonably restrain trade or adversely affect the international transfer of technology'.[191] Unreasonable restraint of trade is a term of art under US antitrust law. The inclusion of that term in Paragraph 3 can be construed as a reference to competition law. This reference to competition law regulation of patent exploitation practices is given further substance in Article 40, which concedes that '[m]embers agree that some licensing practices or conditions pertaining to intellectual property rights which restrain competition may have adverse effects on trade and may

185 TRIPS Agreement, art 27(2).
186 Sherman and Oakley III (n 129) 368.
187 TRIPS Agreement, art 8.
188 ibid art 70(8).
189 Seeratan (n 146) 352, 360.
190 Sperbeck (n 42) 28.
191 TRIPS Agreement, art 8(2).

impede the transfer and dissemination of technology'. Paragraph 2 of Article 40 proceeds to state that

> [n]othing in this Agreement shall prevent Members from specifying in their legislation licensing practices or conditions that may in particular cases constitute an abuse of intellectual property rights having an adverse effect on competition in the relevant market[192] [and empowers members to adopt] ... appropriate measures to prevent or control such practices, which may include for example exclusive grantback conditions, conditions preventing challenges to validity and coercive package licensing.[193]

Article 8 does not limit abuse to competition law violations. It also covers abuses that adversely affect the international transfer of technology. The importance of technology transfer is underscored by Article 7, which asserts that a key objective for the protection of intellectual property rights is to 'contribute to the promotion of technological innovation and to the transfer and dissemination of technology'.[194] Construed broadly, this language can encompass situations where a certain drug is sold at an excessive price which limits its availability.[195] Abuse can also be found when the supplier of the drug does not make the product available in sufficient quantity to satisfy local demand.[196] It has been further suggested that abuse may include failure to work the patent locally or 'refusal to license (trade) the patent to a willing buyer on reasonable commercial terms',[197] which has already been discussed in Chapters 5 and 6 and will not be repeated here.

Even though local working requirements have been said to be inconsistent with the TRIPS Agreement, they continue to be imposed by some developing countries.[198] Article 27(1) states that patent protection should be available without regard to whether the product is imported or manufactured locally.[199] One example of a local working requirement is Article 68 of the Brazilian intellectual property law, which requires a Brazilian patent holder to manufacture its product in Brazil or risk being subject to compulsory licensing after three years.[200] A local working requirement, if construed expansively, could impose an enormous burden on patentees as there could be a variety of legitimate business reasons why a patent owner may choose not to exploit its patent in a particular local market.

192 ibid art 40(1).
193 ibid art 40(2).
194 ibid art 7.
195 Mwakyembe and Kanja (n 170) 128.
196 ibid.
197 Cameron Hutchison, 'Over 5 Billion Not Served: The TRIPS Compulsory Licensing Export Restriction' (2008) 5 University of Ottawa Law &v Technology Journal 43, 50.
198 Mwakyembe and Kanja (n 170) 124.
199 TRIPS Agreement, art 27(1).
200 't Hoen (n 130) 32.

This requirement eventually incurred the wrath of the United States, which filed a complaint with the Dispute Settlement Body (DSB) of the WTO over this requirement in February 2001.[201] The United States subsequently came under fire from the international NGO community, which expressed serious concerns that the removal of the requirement would undermine Brazil's ability to satisfy its domestic demand for ARVs for HIV/AIDS.[202] The United States probably chose the worst time to pick a fight with Brazil over this as the saga took place at the height of the HIV/AIDS crisis. The United States eventually relented and withdrew the complaint after Brazil agreed to notify the United States in advance of any plans to impose a compulsory license under this provision.[203] Uncertainty concerning the precise scope of the exception notwithstanding, Article 8 together with Article 40 can be construed to provide an abuse exception and an anticompetitive (licensing) conduct exception from patent protection.[204]

4. Article 30

Aside from the aforementioned two exceptions whose scope is shrouded in relative uncertainty, there are two exceptions for which there is greater clarity. The first one is Article 30, which states that '[m]embers may provide limited exceptions to the exclusive rights conferred by a patent, provided that such exceptions do not unreasonably conflict with a normal exploitation of the patent and do not unreasonably prejudice the legitimate interests of the patent owner, taking account of the legitimate interests of third parties'.[205] The language of the Article suggests that it does not authorize wholesale repeal of patent rights. The exceptions created under the Article must be limited in scope. Furthermore, they must not unreasonably conflict with the normal exploitation of a patent and unreasonably prejudice a patentee's legitimate interests. These terms are obviously not self-defining and allow much flexibility in interpretation. One example of such a limited exception is the *Bolar* exception, which is named after the US case that created it.[206] Such an exception 'allows interested (generic) manufacturers to start producing test batches of a product before the patent expires, in order to collect the necessary data for submission to the registration authorities; this will reduce the delay of generic products to enter the market after the patent has expired, and thereby enhance competition'.[207]

[201] ibid.
[202] ibid 33.
[203] Sherman and Oakley III (n 129) 391.
[204] Sperbeck (n 42) 28.
[205] TRIPS Agreement, art 30.
[206] Mwakyembe and Kanja (n 170) 126.
[207] ibid.

The precise scope of this exception was further interpreted by a DSB in the *Canada—Pharmaceutical Patents* case, in which the DSB held that the stockpiling exception granted under Canadian law to generic manufacturers prior to the expiration of the patent exceeds the scope of Article 30 and cannot be justified under it.[208] The DSB panel ruled that for a measure to fall within the scope of Article 30, it should meet three requirements: (1) it should be limited; (2) it should not unreasonably conflict with a normal exploitation of the patent; and (3) it should not unreasonably prejudice the legitimate interests of the rights holder, taking into account the legitimate interests of third parties.[209] The panel asserted that a limited exception 'must connote a narrow exception' and 'makes only a small diminution of the rights in question',[210] and ultimately rejected the stockpiling exception as being insufficiently limited because there is no limit to the quantity of drugs that can be stockpiled under the exception.[211]

Both Frederick Abbott and Amit Gupta have criticized this decision as taking an excessively narrow view of the notion of a limited exception.[212] In particular, Gupta argues that 'the panel was guided purely by economic considerations and reflected a bias to protect the rights of the patent holder. The distinction drawn by the panel between the testing exception and stockpiling provision was artificial and cannot be supported by the text of the article.'[213] He further argues that the panel gave undue weight to the interests of the patent holder, which rendered it impossible for such interests to be outweighed by competing social and economic interests.[214]

Commentators have attempted to shed light on the extent to which Article 30 can be invoked to tackle excessive drug prices in developing countries. The focus of the discussion has been on whether Article 30 can justify allowing developing countries that do not possess local manufacturing capacity to import cheap generic drugs from other developing country manufacturers. This is especially important for potential developing country importers because the alternative would involve the invocation of Article 31, which imposes a host of highly restrictive conditions on the issuance of compulsory licenses.[215]

Both Abbott and Gupta have argued that such parallel trade could be permitted under Article 30 and hence there is no need to apply Article 31.[216] Article 31 does not pre-empt the application of Article 30 to parallel trade.[217] Nor does it set out exhaustively the circumstances under which compulsory licensing can be

208 WTO, *Canada—Pharmaceutical Patents* (17 March 2000) WT/DS114/R.

209 ibid para 4.30 (53).

210 ibid para 7.30

211 ibid para 7.34

212 Abbott (n 156) 33.

213 Amit Gupta, 'Patent Rights on Pharmaceutical Products and Affordable Drugs: Can TRIPS Provide a Solution' (2004) 2 Buffalo Intellectual Property Law Journal 127, 144–45.

214 ibid 145.

215 TRIPS Agreement, art 31.

216 Abbott (n 156) 24; Gupta (n 213) 141.

217 Abbott (n 156) 26.

imposed.[218] They both agree that unlike under Article 31, the decision to invoke this exception and the determination of whether its conditions are met lie with the exporting country, which must be satisfied that export of the drug without the patentee's authorization does not unreasonably prejudice the legitimate interests of the rights holder.[219]

Acknowledging that the DSB panel in the *Canada Generics* case adopted a restrictive interpretation of the normal exploitation of patent rights to mean significant diminution of the capacity to earn ordinary commercial returns, Abbott asserts that parallel export of cheaper generic drugs to low-income countries without the patentee's consent should nonetheless be consistent with such exploitation.[220] In addition, he maintains that parallel export should be consistent with the legitimate interests of the right holder as understood by the DSB panel, which espouses a social welfare notion of such interests under which the right holder's interest to earn commercial returns needs to be balanced against the social welfare interests of third parties.[221] Effect on the patent holder cannot be evaluated in a vacuum. It must be assessed in light of the public interest to obtain affordable access to medicines.[222] Ultimately, Abbott believes that the invocation of Article 30 to allow LDCs with no pharmaceutical manufacturing capacity to import drugs from other developing countries is fully justified.[223]

A definitive answer to the question of whether Article 30 can be invoked to justify parallel import of patented drugs into low-income developing countries will need to await a decision by a DSB panel. Abbott's optimism notwithstanding, it is unlikely a DSB panel will agree that the issuance of a compulsory license and direct overriding of patent rights is a limited exception to patent protection.[224] A compulsory license is a direct affront to patent rights and is unlikely to be deemed limited in nature. It is also unlikely to be considered consistent with the legitimate interests of a right holder. This is despite the fact that the imposition of a compulsory license to allow parallel export to a low-income country which cannot afford the normal prices charged by the patentee anyway probably does not affect the right holder's capacity to earn commercial returns. The patentee was never going to derive much revenue from such a country.

A further problem with relying on Article 30 is that, as Abbott and Gupta point out, the importing country is completely at the mercy of the exporting country as it is the latter that needs to invoke the exception. If the importing country constitutes a market of sufficient size, then the exporting country may have the financial

218 ibid.
219 ibid 24. Gupta (n 213) 141.
220 Abbott (n 156) 34.
221 ibid.
222 ibid 29.
223 ibid 40.
224 Sykes (n 48) 52.

incentive to invoke the exception. But if the importing country is an LDC with a negligible domestic market, the exporting country is unlikely to have the incentive to do so, unless the exception can be applied to multiple importing countries at the same time. Doing so, however, would create complications as the more importing countries are covered, the less limited will be the exception and the less likely that it will be deemed to be consistent with the legitimate interests of the right holder. An exporting country is hence in a bind.

5. Article 31

(a) An overview

Article 31 is arguably the most relevant exception under the TRIPS Agreement for developing countries to combat excessive drug prices. The Article sets out the conditions under which a WTO member can impose a compulsory license. A compulsory license 'is an authorization given by a national authority to a person, without or against the consent of the titleholder, for the exploitation of a subject matter protected by a patent or other intellectual property rights'.[225] It is 'an involuntary contract imposed upon a patent holder by a government entity; the compulsory license grants permission to the government entity or a third party to use the IPR to further some political or social objective',[226] which in this case is to provide affordable access to essential medicines to poor consumers.

As radical as compulsory licensing may sound, it in fact has a long lineage in international patent law. Compulsory licensing was recognized close to one hundred and forty years ago in the Paris Convention as a means to tackle failure to work situations.[227] It was estimated that about 100 countries had recognized compulsory licensing by the early 1990s.[228] In fact, the World Bank has endorsed the use of compulsory licenses to help secure affordable access to essential medicines.[229]

Although a compulsory license can in theory be granted without compensation, Article 31 requires the licensee to pay the patentee reasonable compensation, which, however, need not be on commercial terms. In reality, government-imposed royalty rates are likely to be substantially lower than what the patentee can obtain through bilateral private negotiations.[230] Compulsory licenses have been imposed on a variety of grounds, including a lack of or insufficient working, anticompetitive practices, national or public health emergency, and other public interest

[225] Subhasis Saha, 'Patent Law and TRIPS: Compulsory Licensing of Patents and Pharmaceuticals' (2009) 91 Journal of the Patent & Trademark Office Society 364, 366.
[226] ibid 367.
[227] Maan and Kumar (n 16) 113.
[228] Sperbeck (n 42) 29.
[229] Bass (n 79) 220.
[230] Maan and Kumar (n 16) 113.

grounds.[231] They have also been issued to satisfy unmet public demand for a patented product and to introduce price competition for an important but expensive product.[232]

Article 31 does not set out the basis upon which a compulsory license can be issued. It merely lays down the procedural and substantive requirements for such a license. Abbott argues that the Article 'permits each Member to determine in its own discretion what constitutes a national emergency or circumstances of extreme urgency', where the requirement of attempted prior negotiation with the patentee is waived under Article 31(b).[233] The fact that the prior negotiation requirement is waived in the case of national emergency or circumstances of extreme urgency suggests that Article 31 clearly contemplates other situations in which a compulsory license can be issued.

Article 31 sets out a laundry list of requirements for the issuance of a compulsory license. First, authorization of such a license shall be considered on the individual merits of each case.[234] Second, the putative licensee 'has made efforts to obtain authorization from the right holder on reasonable commercial terms and conditions and that such efforts have not been successful within a reasonable period of time'.[235] Again, this prior negotiation requirement is waived in the case of a national emergency or extreme urgency. It is also exempted when a compulsory license is imposed as a remedy for anticompetitive conduct under competition law.[236] Third, the scope and the duration of the license shall be limited to what is necessary to achieve the purpose for which it is authorized.[237] Fourth, the license shall be non-exclusive and non-assignable.[238] Fifth, the license shall be terminated if the circumstance that justifies the imposition of the license ceases to exist.[239] Sixth, the patentee shall be given adequate compensation which needs to take into account the economic value of the authorization.[240] Seventh, the decision to grant the license and the decision to determine adequate compensation shall be subject to judicial review or other independent review by a higher authority.[241]

Lastly, Article 31(f) sets out the most controversial requirement, the predominant domestic use requirement. Under this requirement, the compulsory license shall be issued predominantly for the supply of the domestic market of the member imposing the license.[242] The original impetus behind this requirement was to

[231] Carlos Correa, 'Public Health and Patent Legislation in Developing Countries' (2001) 3 Tulane Journal of Technology and Intellectual Property 1, 44.
[232] Sperbeck (n 42) 29.
[233] Abbott (n 156) 16.
[234] TRIPS Agreement, art 31(a).
[235] ibid art 31(b).
[236] ibid art 31(k).
[237] ibid art 31(c).
[238] ibid art 31(d) and (e).
[239] ibid art 31(g).
[240] ibid art 31(h).
[241] ibid art 31(i) and (j).
[242] ibid art 31(f).

ensure that the impact of a compulsory license is confined to the local market and the issuance of such a license will not give rise to significant parallel trade that may undermine the patentee's differential pricing in other countries.

It soon became apparent, however, that this requirement renders Article 31 largely meaningless for developing countries that do not possess domestic generic manufacturing capacity, which encompass a vast majority of the developing countries. This has led to reform efforts, first in the form of the Doha Declaration, then by way of an interim waiver adopted by the TRIPS Council, and finally the adoption of Article 31bis, which modified the requirement of but stopped short of repealing Article 31(f). These efforts have created a convoluted scheme that has only partially resolved the difficulties created by Article 31(f) and have led to calls for an outright repeal of Article 31(f). This will be addressed in greater detail subsequently.

(b) Compulsory licensing in developing countries

Even though compulsory licenses have been issued by quite a few developing countries, including Brazil, Egypt, India, Indonesia, Malaysia, Mozambique, Rwanda, Thailand, Zambia, and Zimbabwe,[243] the general sense is that Article 31 has been underutilized by developing countries. Initially, most of the compulsory licenses were applied to HIV/AIDS drugs. The high profile nature of the HIV/AIDS crisis in the early 2000s gave developing countries important political cover. Despite some initial efforts by the multinational pharmaceutical manufacturers and the industrialized economies such as the United States to push back, these efforts were eventually abandoned in the face of the vociferous opposition from the general public and international NGOs.

The most notable example was the saga surrounding the South African legislation that authorized the South African government to issue compulsory licenses on public health grounds and subsequent attempts by the big pharmas and the US government to challenge the legislation.[244] The US pharmaceutical manufacturers filed a lawsuit in South Africa to overturn the legislation, but eventually withdrew the suit in light of the ensuing global outcry.[245] Subsequently the attention began to shift to other chronic diseases. The Thai government threatened to issue a compulsory license for a very expensive leukaemia drug produced by Novartis.[246] The threat was ultimately aborted as Novartis reportedly agreed to donate this drug for free to a Thai public health program.[247]

While some attempts to issue compulsory licenses were successful, some developing countries backed down in the face of opposition from the industrialized

[243] Satish Saroha, Deepak Kaushik, and Arun Nanda, 'Compulsory Licensing of Drug Products in Developing Countries' (2015) 12 Journal of Generic Medicines 89, 89.

[244] Seeratan (n 146) 393–94.

[245] Nwobike (n 10) 131.

[246] Maan and Kumar (n 16) 118.

[247] ibid.

economies and the pharmaceutical manufacturers. The lack of local manufacturing capacity also created serious obstacles which necessitated the invocation of the waiver mechanism. Overall, the issuance of compulsory licenses under Article 31 has not effectively resolved the problem of unaffordable drugs for developing countries. This is especially relevant as developing countries move beyond HIV/AIDS to other chronic diseases which have garnered less public sympathy. What follows is a brief survey of the issuance of compulsory licenses by developing countries.

Most of the studies of compulsory licensing in developing countries have been anecdotal in nature. Nonetheless, there have been a few quantitative surveys of the use of compulsory licenses across the developing world which give us an overall sense of the prevalence of such licenses. Kyung-Bok Son reports that among the 199 WTO members he surveyed, 24 attempted compulsory licensing between 1995 and 2014.[248] Within this group, the number of instances of attempted compulsory licensing ranged from one to sixteen.[249] The average and median number of attempted compulsory licenses by these countries were 3.9 and 3 respectively, giving rise to a total of close to 100 instances.[250] Although Son's survey was not confined to developing countries, he notes that most of the countries that attempted compulsory licensing are in Africa, Asia, and Latin America, where most of the countries are developing countries.[251]

Reed Beall and Randall Kuhn produce another study on compulsory licenses publicly announced by WTO members between 1995 and 2011. They identify a much smaller set of compulsory licenses issued by the developing countries, only twenty-four instances of verified compulsory licenses involving forty drugs in seventeen countries.[252] They find that most instances took place between 2003 and 2005 and involved HIV/AIDS drugs.[253] Two-thirds of the twenty-four instances of compulsory licenses involved HIV/AIDS drugs.[254] Somewhat surprisingly, most of the countries that have imposed compulsory licenses were upper middle-income countries such as Brazil, Malaysia, and South Africa.[255] Thirteen out of the twenty-four instances involved an upper middle-income country and eight involved low-income countries and LDCs.[256] Three of them were imposed by high-income countries.[257] Only twelve of those twenty-four instances ended with the issuance of an actual license. In the remainder of the instances, the threat of a compulsory license was sufficient to secure substantial discounts from the manufacturer.[258] The

248 Kyung-Bok Son, 'Importance of the Intellectual Property System in Attempting Compulsory Licensing of Pharmaceuticals: A Cross-Sectional Analysis' (2019) 15 Globalization and Health 1, 4.
249 ibid.
250 ibid.
251 ibid 3.
252 Beall and Kuhn (n 177) 1.
253 ibid.
254 ibid 4.
255 ibid 1.
256 ibid 4.
257 ibid.
258 ibid 3.

authors also note that issuance of compulsory licenses became much less common after 2006.[259] Eleven out of the twenty-four instances of compulsory licensing took place between 2003 and 2005.[260] Between 2006 and 2011 there were only seven attempts contemplated by four countries, most of which were upper middle-income countries.[261]

Another survey by Ellen 't Hoen and co-authors focus on developing countries in a more recent period. Between 2001 and 2016, they find that there were one hundred instances of attempted compulsory or public non-commercial use licenses, of which eighty-one were issued and nineteen were abandoned for a variety of reasons.[262] In most instances of aborted attempts, the patentee offered a price reduction or donation or agreed to a voluntary license authorizing the purchase of generics.[263] With 140 countries classified as a developing country by the World Bank, this amounts to less than one instance of compulsory license by each developing country over a 15-year period.

Overall, it seems clear that compulsory licensing remains the exception rather than the rule for developing countries and upper middle-income countries are the most likely to impose them, which is surprising given that these countries are best able of all developing countries to afford expensive drugs. Although these studies did not specify whether the licensors relied on import or domestic production, it is possible that LDCs seldom imposed compulsory licenses for the lack of domestic manufacturing capacity.

Most of the early instances of compulsory licenses involved ARVs for HIV/AIDS. Given the prevalence of HIV in Sub-Saharan Africa, it is hardly surprising that countries in the region were some of the first to issue compulsory licenses. South Africa was perhaps one of the first countries to do that in 2001, when it issued compulsory licenses for ARVs produced by GlaxoSmithKline and Boehringer Ingelheim.[264] Mozambique, Zambia, and Zimbabwe followed suit and issued compulsory licenses on the grounds of national emergency in the face of sky-high infection rates.[265] Perhaps what is more surprising is that these countries were able to manufacture the ARVs locally and therefore managed to avoid the predominant domestic use requirement under Article 31(f).[266] Zimbabwe relied on a domestic

[259] ibid 1.
[260] ibid 4.
[261] ibid.
[262] Ellen 't Hoen and others, 'Medicine Procurement and the Use of Flexibilities in the Agreement on Trade-Related Aspects of Intellectual Property Rights, 2001–2016' (2018) 96 Bulletin of the World Health Organization 185, 186.
[263] ibid.
[264] Donald Harris, 'TRIPs after Fifteen Years: Success or Failure, as Measured by Compulsory Licensing' (2011) 18 Journal of Intellectual Property Law 367, 388–89.
[265] Saroha, Kaushik, and Nanda (n 243) 90.
[266] ibid.

manufacturer called Varichem Pharmaceuticals and Mozambique on Pharco Mogambique Lda.[267]

In 2004, Indonesia and Malaysia, which had much lower infection rates than those three Sub-Saharan countries, also issued compulsory licenses for HIV/AIDS medications on the grounds of public non-commercial use.[268] Indonesia and Malaysia became the first middle-income countries to issue compulsory licenses.[269] Malaysia relied on import from India while Indonesia turned to local production.[270] Malaysia was in fact the first WTO member to issue a compulsory license after the Doha Declaration, which had reaffirmed the right of WTO members to take appropriate measures for public health purposes.[271] The pharmaceutical companies had originally offered 30–40 per cent discount on the prices of ARVs such as didanosine, zidovudine, and the combination of zidovudine and combination.[272] But these discounts were rejected as inadequate by the Malaysian government, which then proceeded to issue a compulsory license for these drugs at a royalty rate of 4 per cent of the value of stock delivered.[273] The multinational pharmaceutical manufacturers, however, refused to accept this offer for fear of setting a dangerous precedent.[274] The use of compulsory licensing proved to be a success for the Malaysian government as it secured price reductions of more than 80 per cent for the three drugs and further price concessions from other pharmaceutical companies.[275] It also encouraged domestic generic production.[276]

In 2004, Indonesia also issued compulsory licenses for two ARVs Nevirapine and Lamivudine for public non-commercial use.[277] Indonesia turned to a domestic manufacturer Kimia Farma to produce these drugs. With the entry of cheaper locally produced generics, the price for a triple ARV regimen of lamivudine, zidovudine, and nevirapine dropped from USD600 to USD38 per sixty tablets.[278] Despite this success, it took the Indonesian government more than three years to conclude failed price negotiations with the multinational pharmaceutical manufacturers before resorting to compulsory licenses.[279]

This was followed by Eritrea and Ghana in 2005, Thailand in 2006, and Brazil in 2007.[280] Both Thailand's and Brazil's licenses concerned the HIV/AIDS drug

[267] Harris (n 264) 389.
[268] Saroha, Kaushik, and Nanda (n 243) 90.
[269] ibid.
[270] ibid.
[271] Sara Germano, 'Compulsory Licensing of Pharmaceuticals in Southeast Asia: Paving the Way for Greater Use of the TRIPS Flexibility in Low-and Middle-Income Countries' (2007) 76 UMKC Law Review 273, 286.
[272] ibid 287.
[273] ibid 288.
[274] ibid.
[275] ibid.
[276] ibid.
[277] ibid 290.
[278] ibid.
[279] ibid.
[280] Saroha, Kaushik, and Nanda (n 243) 90.

Efavirenz produced by Merck.[281] Thailand also issued a compulsory license for Abbott's HIV/AIDS drug Kaletra.[282] Five weeks after the decision was announced, the Indian generic manufacturer Ranbaxy had shipped 66,000 bottles of Kaletra to Thailand.[283] Thailand continued to rely on import until the domestic manufacturers were ready to fill domestic demand.[284] As a result, the price for Kaletra in Thailand was halved and an estimated 20,000 patients obtained access to it.[285]

Merck and Abbott reacted rather differently to the Thai government's action. Merck reduced the price for Efavirenz globally.[286] A few other pharmaceutical companies also reduced the price of their ARVs in Thailand.[287] In contrast, Abbott launched a number of retaliatory actions in reaction to this license. First, Abbott halted the production of new drugs in Thailand.[288] Second, it suspended the introduction of new drugs and announced that it would not apply for licenses for seven new products, including a heat-resistant form of an ARV and a new drug for heart disease, in Thailand.[289] The US government also joined in the action by placing Thailand on the Special 301 watch list for its failure to provide adequate intellectual property protection.[290]

The annual treatment costs for Efavirenz in Brazil had risen from USD1,336 in 2004 to USD2,500 in 2006.[291] In response, President Lula da Silva issued a compulsory license for Efavirenz on 4 May 2007.[292] The royalty was set at 1.5 per cent.[293] Before the license was issued, Merck had offered a 30 per cent discount on the drug.[294] But this offer was rejected because Brazil issued the license on the grounds of public non-commercial use under the TRIPS Agreement, which does not require prior negotiation.[295] After the license was granted, the price for the drug dropped by more than two-thirds from USD1.59 per tablet to USD0.43 per tablet.[296] This has allowed Brazil to distribute it to more than 75,000 HIV/AIDS patients.[297]

As an illustration of the difficulty with relying on compulsory licensing, even for a developing country with significant industrial capacity such as Brazil, it took

[281] ibid.
[282] Harris (n 264) 387.
[283] Germano (n 271) 292.
[284] ibid.
[285] ibid.
[286] ibid.
[287] ibid.
[288] Harris (n 264) 387.
[289] ibid 392; Maan and Kumar (n 16) 117.
[290] Harris (n 264) 387.
[291] Eric Bond and Kamal Saggi, 'Compulsory Licensing, Price Controls, and Access to Patented Foreign Products' 5.
[292] Saroha, Kaushik, and Nanda (n 243) 92.
[293] Bond and Saggi (n 291) 5.
[294] Saroha, Kaushik, and Nanda (n 243) 92.
[295] ibid.
[296] ibid 93.
[297] ibid.

the state-owned pharmaceutical company Farmanguinhos two years to acquire the know-how to produce the drug.[298] In the meantime, Brazil had to rely on import from India.[299] In 2008, Indonesia threatened multinational pharmaceutical manufacturers with further compulsory licensing and even expulsion in exchange for commitments to invest in local production.[300] Kenya and Ecuador have also taken advantage of Article 31 to issue compulsory licenses.

Over time, developing countries have begun to shift their attention to other chronic diseases such as cancer. Thailand was one of the first countries to apply compulsory licensing to a non-HIV/AIDS drug. In 2007, amid great publicity, Thailand issued a compulsory license for Plavix, a major cardiovascular medication.[301] In 2012, the Indian government imposed a compulsory license on the cancer drug Sofarenib, sold under the brand name Nexavar, produced by Bayer.[302] It was the first compulsory license issued by India for a patented drug.[303] The Indian government had tried to negotiate a voluntary license with Bayer, which had demanded a royalty payment of 15 per cent of net sales.[304] This was rejected by the Indian government, which then issued a compulsory license to Natco Pharma, a local pharmaceutical manufacturer, to produce the drug and sell it at USD176 per month, as opposed to the USD5,600 per month that Bayer had been charging.[305] The license set the royalty rate for Natco at 6 per cent of net sales.[306]

Bayer appealed the decision to the Intellectual Property Appellate Board, which rejected the appeal on the ground that only 2 per cent of the patients with kidney and liver cancer could afford the drug, which clearly showed that the drug was unaffordable to most of the Indian population.[307] The Board, however, did raise the royalty rate to 7 per cent of net sales. Bayer further appealed the Board's decision to the High Court and then the Supreme Court, which refused to accept the appeal and deferred to the Board's decision.[308]

In 2016, Colombia proposed the issuance of a compulsory license for the cancer drug imatinib, which was on the WHO's model list of essential medicines.[309] Colombia was not as lucky as Thailand and India as its attempt at a compulsory license was met with vociferous opposition from Switzerland and the US, which even threatened to withdraw financial support for the fledgling peace process.[310]

298 Bond and Saggi (n 291) 5.
299 ibid.
300 Reichman (n 108) 252.
301 ibid 251.
302 Saroha, Kaushik, and Nanda (n 243) 91.
303 ibid.
304 Nuno (n 140) 403.
305 Saroha, Kaushik, and Nanda (n 243) 91.
306 ibid.
307 ibid.
308 Nuno (n 140) 404.
309 't Hoen and others (n 262) 189.
310 ibid.

Meanwhile, Thailand did not even have to issue the license as Novartis agreed to donate the drug to the Thai government for free. This incident demonstrates the haphazard nature of the use of compulsory licenses. The use of a compulsory license for the same drug often elicits different reactions from the manufacturer and the country from which the manufacturer hails, depending on a range of somewhat random factors such as the amount of publicity the license happens to attract and whether the host country government happens to be preoccupied with other issues.

The most notorious example of an abuse of the compulsory license as a public health tool was Egypt's issuance of such a license for Viagra. Egypt had originally granted patent protection to Viagra in 2002. Two months later, under immense pressure from the domestic pharmaceutical manufacturers, the Egyptian government granted twelve manufacturers a compulsory license to produce the drug at one-twentieth the price Pfizer had charged.[311] It was reported that the chairman of a large generic manufacturer in Egypt was also the chairman of the health committee of the Upper House of Egypt's Parliament.[312] In response to the Egyptian government's egregious action, Pfizer cancelled the construction of a new production facility in the country.[313] Other pharmaceutical companies also announced the abandonment of USD300 million of investment in the country. Egypt's abuse of compulsory licensing undermined the credibility of the mechanism as a public health tool and 'encourages pharmaceutical companies to aggressively resist valid uses of compulsory licenses to prevent over-expansion of scope'.[314]

One final notable example of the invocation of compulsory licensing to obtain essential medicine was when Rwanda asked a Canadian generic manufacturer to supply it with ARV in 2007 under the interim waiver mechanism. This will be discussed in greater detail in the next section as an illustration of the limitations of the mechanism contained in the interim waiver and ultimately incorporated in Article 31bis.

This brief discussion of compulsory licensing under Article 31 illustrates the limitations of the article as a solution for unaffordable drugs. First, the various surveys show that developing countries, with the exception of a few upper middle-income countries, are generally quite reluctant to resort to compulsory licensing. This could be due to a lack of domestic manufacturing capacity, which necessitates import from other developing countries, which could run afoul of the predominant domestic use requirement. Although the WTO has implemented a number of solutions, it will be demonstrated below that none of them comprehensively addresses the obstacles posed by Article 31(f).

311 Maan and Kumar (n 16) 116.
312 Halajian (n 15) 1213.
313 Maan and Kumar (n 16) 116.
314 Halajian (n 15) 1208.

This could also be due to the occasional threats of retaliation and actual retaliation by the industrialized economies, especially the United States, and the multinational pharmaceutical manufacturers. The example of Colombia shows that a compulsory license for the same drug imposed by different countries can elicit disparate reactions and that the industrialized economies do not shy away from heavy-handed tactics to bully developing countries into submission. Part of the problem with Article 31 is that the grounds upon which compulsory licensing is imposed often only focus on the needs of developing countries. The pharmaceutical manufacturers themselves are seen to have done nothing wrong and to be merely exercising their patent rights lawfully. It is perhaps inevitable that compulsory licensing is seen as an expropriation of private properties.

Second, most instances of compulsory licensing were related to HIV/AIDS drugs. This was understandable as HIV/AIDS was the most pressing public health issue in the 2000s. The virus was spreading rapidly among the developing countries and their population was getting decimated. The attention that the HIV/AIDS crisis received across the globe has earned developing countries a lot of sympathy from the general public in the industrialized economies and the international public health community. This has helped these countries push back against the industrialized economies, which eventually were forced to back down.

While the developing world has made considerable progress in tackling the HIV/AIDS crisis, their public health problems are by no means confined to HIV/AIDS. As developing countries become wealthier, they are increasingly afflicted by the chronic illnesses that are prevalent in the industrialized economies such as cancer and cardiovascular diseases. The prices for drugs treating these diseases can be sky-high as well. The drugs for many common illnesses such as asthma can also be much more expensive in developing countries and beyond the reach of most of the developing country population. Developing countries continue to face the problem of unaffordable drugs beyond HIV/AIDS. Yet they encounter sterner resistance when they try to extend compulsory licensing to drugs for other diseases. The lack of political cover for developing countries once they move beyond HIV/AIDS means that compulsory licensing under Article 31 is unlikely to provide a comprehensive solution to the problem of unaffordable drugs.

There needs to be other tools to supplement Article 31 at the very least. This is especially the case in light of the predominant domestic use requirement under Article 31(f). In the end, Article 31 only benefits those developing countries with domestic manufacturing capacity, which are in most cases the upper middle-income countries. This perhaps explains why the majority of compulsory licenses have been imposed by these countries. LDCs, which have the most dire need for affordable medicines, are unfortunately left out by Article 31. The usefulness of Article 31 is further constrained by the political reality of possible retaliation by the industrialized economies.

These countries may find compulsory licensing imposed as a remedy for illegal conduct more palatable. It smacks less of an expropriation of private property when the compulsory license is a remedy for a wrongdoing or a lack of competition, which is often issued as a part of merger remedies. Even the US authorities themselves have regularly ordered compulsory licensing for these purposes[315] and may find it more difficult to object to developing countries doing the same. It is important, however, not to overstate the case. While countries that regulate excessive pricing under their competition law, such as the EU member states, may find compulsory licensing imposed as a remedy for excessive pricing harder to contest, the same will not be true of the United States, which does not constrain a dominant firm's pricing decisions. The United States may still find such licenses objectionable. Nonetheless, the fact that excessive pricing is regulated under EU law should provide some support for developing countries.

Excessive pricing enforcement under competition law may hence provide a promising supplement to Article 31. Compulsory licensing imposed as a remedy for a competition law violation is exempted from the predominant domestic use requirement.[316] This renders it more accessible to the LDCs and other developing countries that do not possess significant domestic manufacturing capacity. The benefit could extend well beyond the LDCs. Recall that Malaysia relied on imports when it first imposed compulsory licenses on ARVs and that it took Brazil, a proto-innovation country, two years to produce Efavirenz domestically. The availability of imports means that compulsory licensing imposed under competition law will provide a bigger boost to the access to affordable drugs in developing countries.

(c) Obstacles posed by Article 31(f)

The obstacles erected by the predominant domestic use requirement under Article 31(f) for the supply of essential medicines have been alluded to earlier. Abbott points out that Article 31(f) in fact creates difficulties on both the demand side and the supply side. On the demand side, Article 31(f) renders it very difficult for developing countries that lack domestic manufacturing capacity to rely on imports to satisfy their domestic drug needs.[317] If most developing countries must keep the predominant share of their domestic production for their own consumption, there will be little left to export to those developing countries that cannot produce the drug themselves. On the supply side, Article 31(f) limits domestic production largely to the size of the domestic market.[318] While this would not be an issue for

[315] Correa, 'Public Health and Patent Legislation in Developing Countries' (n 231) 45. Son (n 248) 6.
[316] TRIPS Agreement, art 31(k).
[317] Abbott (n 156) 17.
[318] ibid.

countries such as Brazil and India, which are blessed with a large domestic market, it would deprive manufacturers based in small countries of crucial economies of scale.[319] Economies of scale could be critical in allowing a developing country manufacturer to recover the R&D costs involved in reverse engineering the drug and acquiring the know-how to produce it. Domestic production of a compulsorily licensed drug 'often simply does not make economic sense, as the decision to sink a large investment into a generic-producing venture will only be justified if that cost can be recouped. The low retail price of generics means that expenses can often be recouped only by mass export to a great number of consumers.' Such mass exports, however, are prevented by Article 31(f).

(d) The Doha Declaration

The severe limitations imposed by Article 31(f) on compulsory licensing soon became apparent to developing countries after the TRIPS Agreement came into effect. In the meantime, there was growing momentum behind developing countries to demand greater flexibility to pursue public health policy objectives under TRIPS.[320] Things came to a head by early 2001 when the WTO could no longer ignore the mounting pressure from developing countries to provide some solutions to their public health needs.[321] At the TRIPS Council meeting in June 2001, developing countries, led by Zimbabwe, the chair of the TRIPS Council, came prepared to press their demands in the first ever Council meeting devoted to public health and access to medicine issues.[322] The meeting was a rare victory for developing countries.[323] The general consensus was that the developing countries pretty much got what they came for,[324] including a declaration that the TRIPS Agreement does not stand in the way of developing countries in the pursuit of public health policies.[325] This came to be known as the Doha Declaration.

Specifically, the Declaration clarified that compulsory licenses are not limited to national emergencies and circumstances of extreme urgency,[326] as alluded to in Article 31(b), and that, very importantly, WTO members have full discretion to determine the circumstances under which a compulsory license can be issued.[327] This was unequivocally stated in Paragraph 5 of the Declaration.[328] Proposed language

319 ibid.
320 Reichman (n 108) 249.
321 Ellen 't Hoen, 'TRIPS, Pharmaceutical Patents and Access to Essential Medicines: Seattle, Doha and Beyond' (2003) 39 <https://msfaccess.org/trips-pharmaceutical-patents-and-access-essential-medicines-seattle-doha-and-beyond> accessed 20 September 2020.
322 't Hoen (n 130) 38.
323 Sherman and Oakley III (n 129) 379.
324 Bryan Mercurio, 'TRIPS, Patents, and Access to Life-Saving Drugs in the Developing World' (2004) 8 Marquette Intellectual Property Law Review 211, 225.
325 Sherman and Oakley III (n 129) 379.
326 't Hoen (n 130) 40–41.
327 Reichman (n 108) 249.
328 Mercurio (n 324) 227.

that would have limited the discretion of WTO members to make such a determination and to limit national emergencies to specific public health crises such as HIV/AIDS was rejected.[329] There was, however, agreement that these crises would constitute national emergencies or other circumstances of extreme urgency.[330] An emergency can refer to both a short-term and a long-term crisis.[331] Paragraph 5 also expressly authorizes WTO members to adopt its own position on the issue of exhaustion of intellectual property rights and the related issue of parallel trade. The TRIPS Agreement leaves 'each member free to establish its own regime for such exhaustion without challenge'.[332] Overall, the public health community celebrated the Doha Declaration as an important triumph for developing countries.[333]

The Doha Declaration, however, has also been characterized as a pyrrhic victory. Other than a ten-year extension of the deadline for LDCs to comply with the requirements of the TRIPS Agreement, it left everything in the TRIPS Agreement untouched.[334] The Declaration clearly affirmed the validity of TRIPS.[335] It arguably left the most important issue unresolved.[336] Regarding Article 31(f), it merely stated in Paragraph 6 that

> [w]e recognize that WTO Members with insufficient or no manufacturing capacities in the pharmaceutical sector could face difficulties in making effective use of compulsory licensing under the TRIPS Agreement. We instruct the Council for TRIPS to find an expeditious solution to this problem and to report to the General Council before the end of 2002.[337]

This omission was particularly consequential because LDCs had been given a ten-year extension to comply with the requirements of the TRIPS Agreement, during which they could withhold pharmaceutical patents.[338] Most of their potential suppliers, however, were required to comply with TRIPS after 2005. These potential suppliers could no longer ignore patent protection and export patented drugs to the LDCs.

[329] 't Hoen (n 130) 40–41.

[330] Divya Murthy, 'The Future of Compulsory Licensing: Deciphering the Doha Declaration on the TRIPS Agreement and Public Health' (2002) 17 American University International Law Review 1299, 1325.

[331] Carlos Correa, 'TRIPS Agreement and Access to Drugs in Developing Countries' (2005) 3 International Journal on Human Rights 25, 27.

[332] 'WTO, Ministerial Declaration on the TRIPS Agreement and Public Health (14 November 2001) WT/MIN(01)/DEC/W/2 (WTO Ministerial Declaration)' p cl. 5(d).

[333] 't Hoen (n 130) 28.

[334] Sherman and Oakley III (n 129) 380.

[335] ibid.

[336] 't Hoen (n 130) 44; Mercurio (n 324) 229; Sherman and Oakley III (n 129) 381.

[337] WTO Ministerial Declaration, cl. 6.

[338] 't Hoen (n 130) 44.

(e) The Interim Waiver and Article 31bis

The TRIPS Council eventually picked up the issue and provided a solution to the issue of Article 31(f) in the form of a decision that constituted what has come to be known as the interim waiver. The WHO and the developing countries had originally favoured a solution based on the limited exception provided by Article 30 as being the most consistent with public health principles.[339] Meanwhile, the industrialized economies preferred a modification of Article 31(f). In the end, in exchange for developed countries relinquishing their demands for an exhaustive list of eligible WTO members, diseases, and drugs, the developing countries agreed to go along with Article 31. On 30 August 2003, the TRIPS Council laid down the interim waiver that allowed WTO members to issue a compulsory license to produce a drug to be exported to another member with insufficient domestic manufacturing capacity.[340] On 30 August 2003, the TRIPS Council announced that the interim waiver would become a permanent amendment to the TRIPS Agreement, eventually numbered as Article 31bis, once it had been approved by two-thirds of the WTO member states.[341] At the Hong Kong Ministerial Conference in 2005, the WTO formally adopted Article 31bis as an amendment to the TRIPS Agreement.[342] It would take almost twelve years, not until January 2017, for two-thirds of the WTO members to officially ratify the amendment.[343] The language of the interim waiver and the eventual Article 31bis is almost identical.[344] Hence the same analysis will apply to both.

The waiver did not impose any restrictions on the class of drugs to which a compulsory license can apply.[345] Nor did it impose any restrictions on the eligibility of an exporting country.[346] The first and only exporter of a compulsorily licensed drug under the waiver was Canada. The waiver, however, did limit the range of countries that could be an eligible importer of a compulsorily licensed drug.[347] The essence of the waiver was to 'enable any country ... to issue a compulsory license for a medicine it could not produce and then to seek help from any other country having that capacity that was willing to assist it'.[348] The practical consequence of the interim waiver was that a WTO member would be barred from initiating a complaint against another member so long as the latter complies with the terms of the

339 't Hoen (n 321) 59. Mercurio (n 324) 230.

340 Beall and Kuhn (n 177) 2.

341 ibid.

342 Hutchison (n 197) 53–54.

343 Sperbeck (n 42) 26.

344 Peter-Tobias Stoll, Jan Busche, and Katrin Arend (eds), 'Article 31bis', *WTO: Trade-Related Aspects of Intellectual Property Rights* (Martinus Nijhoff Publishers 2009) 579, 582.

345 George Tsai, 'Canada's Access to Medicines Regime: Lessons for Compulsory Licensing Schemes under the WTO Doha Declaration' (2009) 49 Virginia Journal of International Law 1063, 1071.

346 ibid.

347 ibid.

348 Reichman (n 108) 250.

waiver.[349] Article 31bis goes a step further and imposes a permanent moratorium on 'non-violation' and 'situation' complaints.[350]

The waiver imposes a host of conditions for its application. It envisions a system of bilateral compulsory licenses to be issued in both the importing and the exporting countries.[351] Under the waiver, the predominant domestic use requirement under Article 31(f) is waived.[352] Royalty will be paid by the exporting country but not the importing country to avoid double compensation.[353] Adequate compensation, which must take into account the economic value of the authorization, must be paid to the patentee.[354] An importing country

> must (1) qualify as an eligible importing member, (2) state the name and expected quantity of the drug to be imported, (3) present evidence to the TRIPS Council that it does not have manufacturing capacity to produce generic drugs, and (4) promise that the compulsory license it grants complies with Article 31 of the TRIPS Agreement.[355]

Meanwhile, the exporting country 'must (1) limit the amount they produce and export to the importing country, (2) comply with certain packaging procedures to prevent products from entering markets other than those intended, and (3) publicize the names and quantities of the medicine to be exported'.[356]

The waiver mandates a fairly complicated step-by-step process of negotiation and certification before parallel export can take place. First, the importing country must attempt to obtain a voluntary license from the patentee.[357] If that effort fails, the importing country can issue a compulsory license for the drug after determining and certifying that it possesses no local manufacturing capacity for the drug.[358] There are no objective criteria for such certification and complete discretion is reserved to the WTO member at issue.[359] LDCs are presumed to lack such capacity.[360] The importing country must then notify the WTO of its desire to trigger the waiver mechanism.[361] The notification must

[349] Correa, 'TRIPS Agreement and Access to Drugs in Developing Countries' (n 331) 31.
[350] Stoll, Busche, and Arend (n 344) 589.
[351] Reichman (n 108) 250.
[352] WTO Secretariat, 'TRIPS and Pharmaceutical Patents' 6 <https://www.wto.org/english/tratop_e/trips_e/tripsfactsheet_pharma_2006_e.pdf> accessed 20 September 2020.
[353] ibid.
[354] Tsai (n 345) 1075.
[355] Germano (n 271) 283.
[356] ibid 283–84.
[357] Correa, 'TRIPS Agreement and Access to Drugs in Developing Countries' (n 331) 33.
[358] ibid 34.
[359] Stoll, Busche, and Arend (n 344) 586.
[360] Tsai (n 345) 1075.
[361] Correa, 'TRIPS Agreement and Access to Drugs in Developing Countries' (n 331) 34.

> (i) specify[] the names and expected quantities of the pharmaceutical product(s) needed; (ii) confirm[] (unless the importing country is an LDC) that [it] has insufficient or no manufacturing capacities in the pharmaceutical sector for the product(s) in question; and (iii) confirm[] that, where a pharmaceutical product is patented in its territory, it has granted or intends to grant a compulsory license in accordance with Article 31 of the TRIPS Agreement.[362]

The importing country must identify a suitable exporter, which in the Canada–Rwanda case was the Canadian generic manufacturer Apotex, which must in turn negotiate for a voluntary license with the patentee on commercially reasonable terms.[363] In that case, it was this step that resulted in a massive delay in the process.[364] Once a voluntary license is refused, the potential exporter must obtain a compulsory license from its host country. The license will be limited to the amount necessary to satisfy the demands of the putative importing country.[365]

The potential exporter must still seek product registration and prove bioequivalence.[366] In the Canada–Rwanda case the Canadian authority was adamant that the exported drugs meet the same regulatory requirements as the domestically sold ones.[367] The exported drugs must be packaged differently and clearly identified as produced for the purpose of the waiver mechanism to prevent leakage to other markets.[368] The exporter must also post on its website information about the quantity being supplied and the specific labelling and marking.[369] This specific labelling and marking includes '(a) an alternative packaging, (b) an alternative shape of the product, and/or (c) an alternative coloring of the product than that utilized by the name-branded pharmaceutical'.[370] Such differential packaging obligation only applies to the extent it is feasible and will not substantially add to the cost of the product.[371] This process needs to be repeated for every importing country, which renders the entire mechanism extremely cumbersome.[372] In fact, it needs to be repeated even for the same importing country should the eventual need exceed what was anticipated when the compulsory license was initially issued.[373]

362 Carlos Correa, 'Will the Amendment to the TRIPS Agreement Enhance Access to Medicines?' [2019] The South Centre Policy Brief No. 57, 2 <https://www.southcentre.int/wp-content/uploads/2019/01/PB57_Will-the-Amendment-to-the-TRIPS-Agreement-Enhance-Access-to-Medicines_EN-1.pdf> accessed 29 July 2021.

363 Correa, 'TRIPS Agreement and Access to Drugs in Developing Countries' (n 331) 34.

364 Tsai (n 345) 1078.

365 Tsai 1075.

366 Correa, 'TRIPS Agreement and Access to Drugs in Developing Countries' (n 331) 34.

367 Tsai (n 345) 1082–83.

368 ibid 1075.

369 Correa, 'TRIPS Agreement and Access to Drugs in Developing Countries' (n 331) 34.

370 Sperbeck (n 42) 38.

371 Correa, 'Will the Amendment to the TRIPS Agreement Enhance Access to Medicines?' (n 362) 3.

372 Correa, 'TRIPS Agreement and Access to Drugs in Developing Countries' (n 331) 34.

373 Correa, 'Will the Amendment to the TRIPS Agreement Enhance Access to Medicines?' (n 362) 3.

Lastly, the importing country is barred from re-exporting the drug to a third country. The only exception is granted to an importing country that is a party to a regional trade agreement under which at least half of its current members are LDCs.[374] The exception applies if three conditions are met:

> (1) countries seeking to utilize economies of scale must be a member of a WTO recognized regional trade agreement ('RTA'); (2) at least half of the members of that RTA must be on the United Nations list of least-developed countries; and (3) the country seeking the compulsory license is responsible for importing the medications, but may re-export them to qualifying members of the RTA.[375]

Out of the thirty RTAs registered with the WTO, only six of them fulfil these requirements, five of which can be found in Africa and one in the Pacific Rim consisting of Fiji and Papua New Guinea, Vanuatu, and Solomon Islands.[376] This leaves out developing countries in Asia, Central and South Americas, and the Caribbean.[377] This leads Mike Gumbel to declare that the waiver mechanism erects insurmountable obstacles for the exploitation of economies of scale with its requirement on the relationship between countries and the administrative requirements.[378] He further notes that the third condition is particularly unrealistic by '[r]equiring a developing country that already has issues with infrastructure, control, corruption, and maintaining its border to be responsible for administration and re-exportation of medications to multiple countries'.[379]

The highly intricate waiver mechanism has been subject to a number of criticisms. The most obvious one is that the system is unmanageably cumbersome. It has been said that '[t]he added bureaucracy and staggered timeline of procedures also present problems for countries with fragile infrastructures and limited legal expertise'.[380] The requirement of parallel compulsory licenses to be issued in both the importing and the exporting countries adds to the unnecessary bureaucracy.[381] Apotex, the Canadian generic manufacturer that was involved in the only instance in which the waiver mechanism was used, made it clear that it would not participate in a similar process again unless the mechanism is reformed.[382]

374 Correa, 'TRIPS Agreement and Access to Drugs in Developing Countries' (n 331) 35.

375 Mike Gumbel, 'Is Article 31bis Enough—The Need to Promote Economies of Scale in the International Compulsory Licensing System' (2008) 22 Temple International and Comparative Law Journal 161, 173.

376 ibid 179.

377 ibid.

378 ibid 163.

379 ibid 182.

380 Germano (n 271) 284.

381 Brin Anderson, 'Better Access to Medicines: Why Countries Are Getting "TRIPPED" up and Not Ratifying Article 31-Bis' (2010) 1 Case Western Reserve Journal of Law, Technology & the Internet 166, 174.

382 Harris (n 264) 391.

Second, under the mechanism, there is little incentive for the patentee to grant a voluntary license or lower its prices.[383] If anything, the prior negotiation requirement means that the patentee has every incentive to drag out the negotiation to delay the issuance of the compulsory license, as was evident in the Canada–Rwanda case.[384] It has also been said that the requirement to notify the TRIPS Council serves no useful purpose apart from giving the industrialized economies and the multinational pharmaceutical manufacturers an opportunity to pile on the pressure to deter the developing country.[385]

Third, the requirement that the mechanism be triggered for each importing country exacerbates the lack of economies of scale under Article 31(f) and is unlikely 'to provide incentives to potential suppliers to make the investments necessary to develop and produce the needed drugs'[386] when the volume of production is limited by the initial application and when the exporting manufacturer needs to make substantial upfront investment for a drug that it has not produced before.[387] This investment is particularly risky because it is vulnerable to strategic behaviour by the patentee, which can effectively nullify the generic manufacturer's investment by lowering the price of the drug or even donating it to the country for free.[388]

Fourth, in many instances, amendments to national legislation are required to allow the mechanism to operate. The supply of an export market is usually not an acceptable ground for the grant of a compulsory license under most domestic legislation.[389] Canada was one of the first to undertake such an amendment. The WTO reports that as of September 2006, other than Canada, only India, Norway, and the European Union have informed the TRIPS Council that they had done so.[390] By 2011, China and Switzerland have also adopted the necessary amendments.[391] Carlos Correa expresses scepticism that many countries would go through the trouble of amending their domestic patent law for the benefit of another country.[392]

All these complexities and shortcomings of the waiver mechanism have led Médécins Sans Frontières to declare the mechanism an 'ill-researched and [un] viable plan to increase access to medicine'[393] that 'flies in the face of the practical reality of managing a health programme, where flexibility and rapidity of response to ever-changing circumstances are vital'.[394] In addition to Apotex, the Indian

[383] Correa, 'TRIPS Agreement and Access to Drugs in Developing Countries' (n 331) 36.
[384] Correa, 'Will the Amendment to the TRIPS Agreement Enhance Access to Medicines?' (n 362) 4.
[385] Anderson (n 381) 174.
[386] Correa, 'TRIPS Agreement and Access to Drugs in Developing Countries' (n 331) 36.
[387] Correa, 'Will the Amendment to the TRIPS Agreement Enhance Access to Medicines?' (n 362) 4.
[388] ibid.
[389] Correa, 'TRIPS Agreement and Access to Drugs in Developing Countries' (n 331) 32.
[390] WTO Secretariat (n 352) 6.
[391] Harris (n 264) 396.
[392] Correa, 'TRIPS Agreement and Access to Drugs in Developing Countries' (n 331) 32.
[393] Anderson (n 381) 174.
[394] MSF Canada, 'Neither Expeditious, Nor A Solution: The WTO August 30th Decision Is Unworkable' 4 <https://msfaccess.org/sites/default/files/MSF_assets/Access/Docs/ACCESS_briefing_NeitherExpeditiousNorSolution_WTO_ENG_2006.pdf> accessed 20 September 2020.

generic manufacturer Cipla has also made known that it will not make use of the mechanism as it is currently formulated.[395]

The failure of the waiver mechanism to resolve the problem of unaffordable drugs for developing countries has led Correa to suggest either the outright repeal of Article 31(f) or a declaration under Article 30 that production for export does not violate a patentee's right to exclude under Article 28.[396] He argues that an export exception should not interfere with the 'normal exploitation of the patent' or 'unreasonably prejudice the legitimate interests of the patent owner' under the language of Article 30.[397] If Article 31bis took twelve years to be ratified, the formal repeal of Article 31(f) will probably take even longer. Moreover, given that Article 31bis was only formally adopted as recent as 2017, it is difficult to imagine there being the political momentum to revisit the issue and undertake such drastic action.

The suggestion of a declaration under Article 30 is probably more feasible but it will only provide a partial solution to all the difficulties created by the waiver mechanism. It effectively only eliminates the requirement of parallel compulsory licenses in both the importing and the exporting countries. All this leads to the inevitable conclusion that the various mechanisms under TRIPS only provide limited relief to developing countries for excessive drug prices and that these countries will need to resort to other policy tools to supplement the TRIPS Agreement. This is where excessive pricing enforcement under competition law comes in.

D. Excessive Pricing Enforcement under Competition Law

The limitations of the various exceptions afforded by the TRIPS Agreement mean that developing countries must look beyond patent law for solutions to the problem of unaffordable drugs. Excessive pricing enforcement under competition law provides a promising alternative because much of the difficulty with Article 31 stems from the predominant domestic use requirement under Article 31(f) and the prior negotiation requirement under Article 31(b). Compulsory licenses imposed as a remedy for a competition law violation are exempted from both requirements. This is not to say that excessive pricing enforcement under competition law will provide the perfect antidote. The difficulty with, or perhaps even the impossibility of, coming up with an all-encompassing test for excessiveness under competition law means that there are bound to be instances of unaffordable drug prices that are beyond the remit of competition law. Excessive pricing enforcement, however,

[395] Alexandra Nightingale, 'WTO "Paragraph 6" System for Affordable Medicine: Time for Change?' *Intellectual Property Watch* (14 November 2016) <http://www.ip-watch.org/2016/11/14/wto-paragraph-6-system-affordable-medicines-time-change/> accessed 20 September 2020.

[396] Correa, 'Will the Amendment to the TRIPS Agreement Enhance Access to Medicines?' (n 362) 7.

[397] ibid.

should be able to offer assistance in some instances. Given that the implications of unaffordable drugs in developing countries are often a matter of life or death, any assistance would be highly significant from a public health perspective.

Using excessive pricing enforcement under competition law as a remedy for unaffordable drugs requires a reconciliation of the theoretical thinking behind excessive pricing and the public health needs of developing countries. This is because the benchmark for excessiveness under competition law, which is derived from such theoretical thinking, may be so stringent that competition law may end up being of limited use. The stringency of these benchmarks is largely motivated by a concern for false positives. Moreover, it is common to resort to price–cost comparison to determine the excessiveness of a price. Such a comparison, however, can be fraught with difficulty in the context of the pharmaceutical industry. It was noted earlier that there is very little transparency regarding the R&D and clinical trial costs for most drugs. This creates significant challenges for the calculation of the cost base of most drugs. Add to this the intricate issue of the allocation of the costs of failed drug R&D and cost calculation becomes practically intractable.

From a theoretical perspective, one of the greatest difficulties with excessive pricing enforcement is the inherent contradiction of the phenomenon. If we aspire to competitive markets, any price above the competitive price is supra-competitive and can be deemed to be excessive. Competition law, however, cannot outlaw all such instances of supra-competitive pricing given how common it is. Anytime the market is less than fully competitive, such as an oligopoly, the market price will exceed the competitive level. In fact, given the mantra that competition law does not prohibit a dominant position but only the abuse of such a position, the theoretical implication is that any price up to the monopoly price must be considered lawful. That is exactly how Advocate General Nils Wahl interprets the excessive pricing decision by the European Commission in *Scandlines*.[398] Given that a monopolist maximizes her profit by charging the monopolist price, a firm in theory should never charge more than the monopolist price. If a price up to the monopoly level is presumed lawful and it would defy economic rationality for a firm to raise the price beyond the monopoly level, there should never be a need to intervene against excessive pricing. This is exactly the conclusion reached by Wahl.[399] If there was to be any justification for excessive pricing enforcement, it must be that either a firm could occasionally behave irrationally or that there are policy reasons why sub-monopoly supra-competitive prices could be considered excessive under some circumstances.

In the context of developing countries, there may be reasons to suspect that when practicing reverse price discrimination, the pharmaceutical manufacturers

[398] Nils Wahl, 'Exploitative High Prices and European Competition Law—A Personal Reflection' in Konkurrensverket (ed), *The Pros and Cons of High Prices* (2007) 51.

[399] ibid 63–64.

are in fact charging above the monopoly price in developing countries if the market is taken as a whole as opposed to only certain wealthy segments. Moreover, when these manufacturers impose sudden price hikes of hundreds if not thousands of per cent, there are grounds to believe that these manufacturers may be seeking to take advantage of previously unexploited market power. Such market power could be the result of cynical attempts to exploit regulatory loopholes, as in the case of *Aspen* and *Pfizer/Flynn*, and cannot be considered the natural consequence of the normal interplay between demand and supply. If we accept that the pre-hike price ought to be profit-maximizing as well, the manufacturer must offer a valid justification for such a dramatic price increase. The mere fact that consumers have no choice but to bear the inflated price cannot be accepted as a justification. As will be argued subsequently, pharmaceutical manufacturers cannot be allowed to extract the full value of their drugs or there would be a massive windfall to them. Even if we accept Advocate General Wahl's premise that excessive pricing enforcement is rarely if ever needed in a normally functioning market, these two circumstances provide the scenario in which such enforcement can serve a useful purpose.

1. Pros and Cons of Enforcing Against Excessive Pricing

Before launching into an examination of the doctrinal approaches to excessive pricing enforcement, it will be didactic to survey some of the arguments for and against excessive pricing enforcement. These arguments are usually formulated in general terms. For our purpose, these arguments will be situated in the specific context of the regulation of excessive drug prices in developing countries. A range of arguments have been made for and against excessive pricing enforcement. Arguments in support of such enforcement include (1) excessively high prices are often viewed as unfair; (2) excessive pricing enforcement protects consumer welfare; and (3) excessive pricing enforcement under competition law avoids regulatory capture. Arguments against such enforcement include (1) high prices provide appropriate incentives for investment; (2) high prices are self-correcting; and (3) implementation difficulties. It is further argued that even if excessive pricing were to be regulated, only exclusionary excessive prices as opposed to exploitative excessive prices should be prohibited[400] and structural remedies are to be preferred to behavioural remedies such as direct price regulation.

(a) Arguments in favour of enforcement

While fairness has almost become a dirty word in the competition law community and few commentators and enforcers would advocate fairness as a benchmark for

[400] Mark Furse, 'Excessive Prices, Unfair Prices and Economic Value: The Law of Excessive Pricing under Article 82 EC and the Chapter II Prohibition' (2008) 4 European Competition Journal 59, 60–61.

the legality of competitive conduct, in the eyes of the general public, the yardstick for acceptability of business conduct is not economic efficiency or even consumer welfare, but whether particular conduct amounts to unfair exploitation of consumers. As Ariel Ezrachi and David Gilo note,

> excessive pricing by a dominant firm is one of the most noticeable and blatant forms of abuse. In many ways, it is regarded as a classic economic evil, a clear exploitation that transfers wealth from consumers to powerful undertakings and directly causes the inefficiencies that competition laws are meant to prevent.[401]

Regardless of economic orthodoxy, the general public will not comprehend the argument that competition law is concerned with economic efficiency and does not and should not regulate exploitative conduct. This is especially true of pharmaceuticals in developing countries. It would be exceedingly difficult to convince developing country consumers that the competition authority should uphold economic orthodoxy at the expense of suffering or even death of poor patients. There is no gainsaying that excessive pricing enforcement, especially with respect to a necessity such as essential medicines, carries enormous intuitive appeal with the general public. Developing country authorities ignore this at their own peril.

A related argument is that excessive pricing enforcement directly protects consumer welfare. While the orthodoxy in competition law is that competition law should protect consumer welfare by prohibiting conduct that distorts competition or the market structure, '[e]xploitative abuse is the most direct violation of the consumers' interest that antitrust policy aims to protect'.[402] Harry First hits the nail on the head when he observes that

> [w]e may argue over whether antitrust is only about consumer welfare, but it is at least about consumer welfare. These high drug prices redistribute wealth from consumers to producers, something we normally condemn. Add to this the fact that we are not just talking about abstract 'consumers,' but about sick people in need of pharmaceutical drugs, often to survive.[403]

The distinction between consumer welfare loss from direct exploitation and consumer welfare loss inflicted by anticompetitive conduct is bound to be lost on the general public. A competition authority that tells the public that it enforces the law to protect consumer welfare but takes no action against direct exploitation of

[401] Ariel Ezrachi and David Gilo, 'Are Excessive Prices Really Self-Correcting?' (2008) 5 Journal of Competition Law & Economics 249, 249.

[402] Massimo Motta and Alexandre de Streel, 'Excessive Pricing in Competition Law: Never Say Never?' in Konkurrensverket (ed), *The Pros and Cons of High Prices* (2007) 14, 20.

[403] Harry First, 'Excessive Drug Pricing as an Antitrust Violation' (2019) 82 Antitrust Law Journal 701, 736.

consumers will lose all credibility. This is an especially pertinent issue for a new authority, which is the case in many developing countries. It is very important for a new authority to establish its standing with the general public. One may even go so far as arguing that for a new developing country authority, there is no choice but to adopt excessive pricing enforcement, at least with respect to daily necessities.

Finally, relying on competition law enforcement to regulate excessive pricing helps to avoid regulatory capture.[404] Competition law is a form of sector-agnostic regulation of general applicability. A competition authority oversees all sectors in the economy. It is not a repeat player that constantly interacts with one sector, which exposes the regulator to regulatory capture. Even though the pharmaceutical industry is usually not considered a regulated sector, it is a very powerful sector, as is evident in its role in the adoption of the TRIPS Agreement.[405] A sector-specific regulator in a developing country that regularly goes up against the multinational pharmaceutical manufacturers is likely to be massively outgunned and susceptible to regulatory capture. A competition regulator is relatively free from such concerns and can be trusted to undertake its regulatory tasks relatively impartially.[406]

(b) Arguments against enforcement

Some of the strongest arguments against excessive pricing enforcement are that high prices provide investment and innovation incentives, that high prices are self-correcting, and that such enforcement faces insurmountable implementation difficulties. Many commentators have noted that high prices are needed to provide incentives for competitors to compete and invest in new technology.[407] Monopoly profits are the prize that awaits the winner of market competition. The US Supreme Court has famously made this point in the *Trinko* case.[408] Underlying this argument is the Schumpeterian assumption that monopoly profits are needed for R&D and that monopoly is more conducive to innovation. Massimo Motta and Alexandre de Streel encapsulate this argument best when they assert that 'however beneficial excessive price interventions may be *ex post*, if a competition authority pursued a policy of resorting to excessive pricing actions, this policy would have important negative effects *ex ante*, by lowering expected returns, and therefore discouraging firms' investments in all the economy'.[409] This is especially important in dynamic industries where innovation plays a critical role, such as the pharmaceutical industry.

[404] ibid 739–40.

[405] Cheng (n 49) 32.

[406] First (n 403) 739–40.

[407] Alexandr Svetlicinii and Marco Botta, 'Article 102 TFEU as a Tool for Market Regulation: "Excessive Enforcement" Against "Excessive Prices" in the New EU Member States and Candidate Countries' (2012) 8 European Competition Journal 473, 479. First (n 403) 706; Motta and de Streel (n 402) 18.

[408] *Verizon Telecommunications v. Trinko*, 540 US 398 (2004).

[409] Motta and de Streel (n 402) 18.

This argument is framed in general terms and is meant to be applicable across the board. The focus of our discussion, however, is drug prices in developing countries. We only need to be concerned with the validity of this incentive argument in this context. Previous studies have found that the pharmaceutical industry is particularly reliant on patent protection as an appropriation mechanism. They have also found that the pharmaceutical industry enjoys unusually high profit despite what they claim to be exorbitant R&D and product development costs. Most importantly, apart from tropical diseases, most of the profits for global drugs are derived from the industrialized economies. Profits from developing countries account for such a small part of the overall profits of the multinational pharmaceutical manufacturers that with the exception of populous middle-income countries with a vast domestic market such as Brazil, China, and India, it is highly unlikely that excessive pricing enforcement in developing countries will undermine the innovative incentives of the multinational pharmaceutical manufacturers.

It has been argued that high prices attract market entry and are hence self-correcting.[410] Not only do high prices reward firms for emerging victorious in market competition, they also attract new entrants to enter the market to compete away the excess profits. A number of commentators, however, have challenged this view. First characterizes the self-correction argument as weak and notes that the assumption of easy entry in general and in the pharmaceutical industry in particular has been questioned in economic scholarship.[411] Bruce Lyons argues that what matters to the new entrant is not the pre-entry monopoly price but the post-entry duopoly price.[412] If the entrant expects the incumbent to react aggressively to market entry, then even a very high pre-entry price will not induce entry.[413] This is especially the case when the entrant incurs substantial sunk investments in order to enter the market, which is true of the pharmaceutical industry.[414] Ezrachi and Gilo echo this view and elaborate further:

> High prices, in and of themselves, do not attract new entry. It is the post-entry price, and not the pre-entry price, that potential entrants consider when deciding whether to enter. Because the dominant firm can usually cut prices immediately upon entry, its excessive pre-entry prices do not affect the potential entrants' decision whether to enter, unless they somehow signal to potential entrants that entry is profitable (for example, because the dominant firm is relatively inefficient). Had the new entrant been able to secretly enter the market, without the incumbent anticipating such entry, high pre-entry prices may have been able to attract

[410] ibid.
[411] First (n 403) 737.
[412] Bruce Lyons, 'The Paradox of the Exclusion of Exploitative Abuse' in Konkurrensverket (ed), *The Pros and Cons of High Prices* (2007) 74.
[413] ibid.
[414] ibid.

> entry… Yet, in practice, such 'secret" entry is highly unlikely… The entrant, for its part, expects such competitive pricing to prevail almost immediately upon entry, and it contemplates whether to expend the costs of entry into the market given these competitive and modest post-entry profits.[415]

Like Lyons, Ezrachi and Gilo conclude that ultimately what matters is post-entry prices, and whether the incumbent can charge a lower price than does the entrant to render entry unprofitable comes down to their relative efficiency.[416] The entrant will enter the market if she perceives herself to be more efficient than the incumbent even if the pre-entry price may not be excessive.[417] The entrant will refrain from entering if she perceives the incumbent to be more efficient even if the pre-entry price was exorbitant.[418]

One further reason to doubt that excessive drug prices are self-correcting is the obvious fact that the drug is often patented. It is the existence of patent protection that prevents a generic manufacturer from replicating the drug to enter the market and allow the branded manufacturer to charge a high price. Even in the absence of patent protection, in many developing countries, there is a dearth of possible domestic supply of the drug due to the lack of domestic technological and manufacturing capacity. If it took the Brazilian state-owned pharmaceutical manufacturer Farmanguinhos two years to acquire the know-how to produce an ARV, the prospect of domestic entry that disciplines excessive prices in most developing countries is dim.

Lastly, it has also been argued that there are insurmountable implementation difficulties with excessive pricing enforcement, especially in the context of developing countries where the authority's enforcement capacity is often weak. Implementation difficulties have been set out along two dimensions. First, it is fiendishly difficult to determine the excessiveness of prices. David Evans and Jorge Padilla assert that there is no pricing rule or benchmark that can make such a determination without error.[419] They argue that price–cost comparisons are particularly problematic in dynamic industries in which the fixed costs are high and incremental costs are low, concluding that 'in these industries it is impossible to define "competitive" prices using only information on costs'.[420] The pharmaceutical industry is clearly one such industry. Nor do profit benchmarks provide a good substitute. Evans and Padilla highlight an array of issues with such benchmarks, including measurement issues and the inadequacies of accounting profits.[421] Direct

415 Ezrachi and Gilo (n 401) 255.
416 ibid 256.
417 ibid.
418 ibid.
419 David S Evans and A Jorge Padilla, 'Excessive Prices: Using Economics to Define Adminsitrable Legal Rules' (2005) 1 Journal of Competition Law & Economics 97, 99.
420 ibid 101.
421 ibid 102.

price comparisons are plagued by the obvious challenge of identifying the appropriate comparator.[422]

The second implementation difficulty relates to remedies. A determination of excessive pricing necessarily implies mandating the defendant to lower its prices, which in turn requires the regulator or the court to first determine an acceptable price level.[423] A pricing remedy would also require the regulator or the court to monitor the firm for compliance on an ongoing basis and perhaps adjust the pricing remedy as market conditions change.[424] This would impose an enormous burden on the enforcement capacity of the regulator or the court. The US authorities declare in their submission to the OECD that 'antitrust agencies have found that determining the reasonableness of prices charged by a lawful monopolist goes beyond their competence'.[425] Pinar Akman and Luke Garrod have asserted that structural remedies, which obviate the need for ongoing monitoring, are to be preferred where possible.[426]

These would be formidable obstacles in an ordinary excessive pricing case where the remedy entails the determination of a non-excessive price and continuous monitoring. The situation, however, is different in the pharmaceutical context. The most likely remedy in an excessive drug price case would be compulsory licensing, which fundamentally changes the market structure. In other words, it is a structural remedy that should not require continuous monitoring apart from ensuring compliance with the compulsory license. The monitoring can cease once the technology has been successfully transferred to the compulsory licensee. This remedy also obviates the need for the determination of an acceptable price level. The entry of a new generic competitor will necessarily result in a substantial price reduction. The incumbent will be forced to lower her price to stay competitive with the new entrant. The competition agency need not tell the incumbent what price to charge. This still leaves the first implementation difficulty of the determination of excessiveness. This is no doubt a serious challenge and will be addressed subsequently.

Regarding the argument that excessive pricing enforcement should be limited to when the effects of high prices are exclusionary, such an argument has limited applicability to the context of drug prices in developing countries. Most developing countries do not have domestic pharmaceutical manufacturers to compete with the multinational ones. There are no competitors to be excluded. In any case, these multinational manufacturers have no need for exclusionary conduct. Their patents have already done their job for them. It is of course the essence of patents

422 ibid 110.
423 Motta and de Streel (n 402) 19.
424 ibid.
425 OECD, 'Excessive Pricing in Pharmaceutical Markets - Note by the United States' (2018) 4 <www.oecd.org/daf/competition/excessive-pricing-in-pharmaceuticals.htm> accessed 20 September 2020.
426 Pinar Akman and Luke Garrod, 'When Are Excessive Prices Unfair?' (2011) 7 Journal of Competition Law & Economics 403, 426.

to exclude. The argument here is not to question whether the patentee's right to exclude is justified. It is simply that given patent protection, there are few incentives for the patentee to undertake further exclusionary conduct.

2. Theoretical Discussion

Commentators have proposed a number of frameworks for excessive pricing enforcement. Some of these frameworks are crafted with a view to minimizing false positives of enforcement and focus on articulating pre-conditions for excessive pricing enforcement. These frameworks are intentionally stringent to minimize instances of enforcement. They, however, do not reach the crux of the issue of the determination of excessiveness. When reviewing these frameworks, it is important to bear in mind whether developing countries should share the same preoccupation with minimizing false positives when enforcing against excessive drug prices. Attention will then turn to the critical issue of determination of the excessiveness of prices.

(a) Enforcement preconditions

Evans and Padilla put forward three preconditions for the application of excessive pricing claims. They propound that such claims should not be allowed unless

> (a) the firm enjoys a (near) monopoly position in the market, which is not the result of past investments or innovations, and which is protected by insurmountable legal barriers to entry; (b) the prices charged by the firm widely exceed its average total costs; and (c) there is a risk that those prices may prevent the emergence of new goods and services in adjacent markets.[427]

These conditions are cumulative and there can be no successful excessive pricing claims if one of them is not met.[428]

Motta and de Streel propose a four-part test for when excessive pricing claims can be appropriately brought. The four factors are: '(1) high and non-transitory barriers to entry leading to a monopoly or near monopoly; (2) this (near) monopoly being due to current or past exclusive or special rights; (3) no effective means to eliminate the entry barriers; and (4) no sector regulator being competent to regulate the excessive prices'.[429] They explain that there should be a higher threshold for the requisite market power that justifies excessive pricing enforcement. What is

[427] Evans and Padilla (n 419) 119.
[428] ibid.
[429] Motta and de Streel (n 402) 14.

required should be more than a normal dominant position and closer to a super-dominant position where the firm's market share is very high.[430]

They further stipulate that the dominant position must be 'due to current or past exclusive or special rights or un-condemned past exclusionary anticompetitive practices' and not the result of past investments and innovation.[431] They specifically note that excessive pricing enforcement is unsuitable against goods or services protected by intellectual property rights due to the risks of false positives.[432] They further argue that these two conditions are most likely to apply in regulated industries, and where there is a sectoral regulator, the competition authority should defer to this regulator unless that regulator's decision is manifestly wrong.[433] In terms of the test for excessiveness, Motta and de Streel opt for a profitability analysis that can be complemented by price comparisons.[434]

There is quite a bit of overlap between Evans and Padilla's test and Motta and de Streel's test. The first condition in Evans and Padilla's test is an amalgamation of the first three conditions in Motta and de Streel's test. In terms of the test for excessiveness, while Evans and Padilla prefer a price–cost comparison, Motta and de Streel favour a profitability analysis or direct price comparisons. Both tests are principally concerned with minimizing false positives and therefore their main contributions are in the articulation of pre-conditions for applying excessive pricing claims. In addition to these conditions that focus on market structure, both tests have one additional factor that perhaps reflects their authors' particular pre-occupations. Motta and de Streel pay special attention to institutional competence and want the competition authority to defer to the sectoral regulators. Evans and Padilla express greater solicitude for consumer welfare and would only permit excessive pricing claims where there is concrete consumer harm in the form of denial of a new product or service. It is this last requirement that leads Motta and de Streel to characterize Evans and Padilla's framework as 'the strictest test', arguing that 'this condition would be extremely difficult to implement and its restrictive role is not justified'.[435]

There are three other tests put forward by Lars-Hendrik Röller, Damien Géradin, and Amelia Fletcher and Alina Jardine that harp on similar themes. All of these tests are similarly preoccupied with minimizing false positives. Röller lists out the following five conditions for intervention: '(1) there are significant entry barriers, (2) the market is unlikely to self-correct, (3) the dominant position was due to exclusionary abuse or government actions, (4) there is no regulator or there

[430] ibid 23.
[431] ibid 24.
[432] ibid 26.
[433] ibid 29.
[434] Claudio Calcagno and Mike Walker, 'Excessive Pricing: Towards Clarity and Economic Coherence' (2010) 6 Journal of Competition Law & Economics 891, 896.
[435] Motta and de Streel (n 402) 29.

is a regulatory failure, and (5) no (structural) remedy is available'.[436] Géradin focuses instead on '(i) significant and long-lasting barriers to entry and expansion, (ii) extreme difficulty or impossibility to remove those barriers, and (iii) limited investment and innovation'.[437] Fletcher and Jardine emphasize the lack of possible market entry within a reasonable time as a precondition for enforcement and counsel against excessive pricing enforcement during the patent term.[438] They call for particular attention to how *ex-post* intervention will affect *ex-ante* investment incentives.[439] They also express a preference for structural remedies to price regulation.[440]

We can combine these various tests into a list of essential prerequisites for the application of excessive pricing claims and see whether enforcement against excessive drug prices in developing countries meets these requirements. Most of these commentators emphasize that the firm must possess a very high degree of market power protected by significant and non-transitory barriers to entry. The importance of these structural requirements is that there is little possibility for the market to self-correct. A number of commentators further stipulate that the market power is undeserved, resulting from either the grant of special rights by the government or past unredressed anticompetitive conduct. Market power that was the product of investment and innovation would exempt the firm from excessive pricing enforcement. Both Motta and de Streel and Röller emphasize the importance of deference to sectoral regulators. Both Röller and Fletcher and Jardine express a preference for structural remedies to pricing remedies. Lastly, Evans and Padilla are unique in focusing on the preclusion of new goods or services in adjacent markets.

What is the relevance of these factors to the enforcement against excessive drug prices in developing countries? First, it is conceded that excessive pricing enforcement regarding drug prices should be confined to markets in which there is super dominance. The kind of market power and entry barriers required by most commentators for the application of excessive pricing claims are usually found in the pharmaceutical markets where there are no therapeutic substitutes for the drug concerned. For example, there are unlikely to be therapeutic substitutes for the anti-cancer drugs in India that cost tens of thousands of US dollars a year. Excessive pricing enforcement should be limited to such markets to minimize false positives.

[436] Lars-Hendrik Roller, 'Exploitative Abuses' (2007) 6 <https://www.eui.eu/Documents/RSCAS/Research/Competition/2007ws/200709-COMPed-Roeller.pdf> accessed 20 September 2020.

[437] Damien Geradin, 'The Necessary Limits to the Control of "Excessive" Prices by Competition Authorities—A View from Europe' (2007) 2007–32 44 <https://papers.ssrn.com/sol3/papers.cfm?abstract_id=1022678> accessed 20 September 2020.

[438] Amelia Fletcher and Alina Jardine, 'Towards an Appropriate Policy for Excessive Pricing' (2007) 2, 9 <https://www.eui.eu/Documents/RSCAS/Research/Competition/2007ws/200709-COMPed-Fletcher-Jardine.pdf> accessed 20 September 2020.

[439] ibid 12.

[440] ibid.

Second, there is a clear desire among these commentators to avoid undermining investment and innovation incentives through excessive pricing enforcement. These are no doubt important and valid sentiments in the general context. Once it is established that profits derived from most developing countries have negligible impact on the investment decisions of multinational pharmaceutical manufacturers, however, protection of investment incentives fades in importance. It is largely for this same reason that Motta and de Streel caution against applying excessive pricing to products protected by intellectual property rights and their advice can be similarly disregarded.

Third, deference to sectoral regulators has little relevance in the context of drug prices, at least in most developing countries. There is price control for drugs in many European countries, but not in most developing countries.[441] Lastly, this author agrees with Röller and Fletcher and Jardine that structural remedies are to be preferred where feasible. Compulsory licensing takes precedence over direct price regulation. This is exactly what is being proposed here.

(b) Determination of excessiveness

A number of tests have been proposed to determine the excessiveness of prices. These tests have all been discussed in detail in the case law. These include price–cost comparison, comparison of prices charged by the same firm in comparable markets (which mostly illustrates the existence of price discrimination), comparison of prices charged by the same firm across time (which is particularly relevant for sudden and dramatic price hikes), and comparison with a competitor's prices in the same or a similar market. The formulation of every test must tackle two issues. The first is that of appropriate comparators. It seems that there are two possible types of comparison. The first one is a direct price comparison between the price at issue and some other reference price. The second type of comparison is one between the market price and some measure of cost to ascertain the profit margin. This kind of price–cost comparison measures profitability. The second is a benchmark for excessiveness. In other words, how much is too much. If the firm's price is found to exceed a comparator price, how significant does the margin have to be for the price to be deemed excessive? Or if the comparison is a price–cost comparison, how big does a profit margin have to be?

(c) The appropriate comparator

There are many possible comparators for the firm's prices. These include the firm's past prices in the same market, the firm's current prices in a different geographic market or with a different customer group, and a competitor's prices in the same market or a similar market. The firm's prices can also be compared against some

[441] Nerozzi (n 127) 628.

measure of costs. Each of these comparators has its own strengths and weaknesses, which have led the European courts to suggest the concurrent use of multiple tests. While such a suggestion may be sensible in the context of a sophisticated and mature jurisdiction such as the European Union, it would put an unreasonable strain on the enforcement capacity of most developing country competition authorities. It would be enormously cumbersome for a developing country authority to be required to demonstrate the excessiveness of prices under three or four tests in one single case. Imposing such a hefty burden would only discourage developing countries from excessive pricing enforcement. A more sensible approach would be to require the authority to demonstrate excessiveness under one test, after which the burden shifts to the defendant to rebut the presumption of excessiveness with countervailing evidence.

In the context of excessive drug prices in developing countries, the two most relevant comparators are arguably the firm's past prices in the same market and the firm's current prices in a different geographic market, especially in the industrialized economies or a wealthier developing country. The first comparator that can be dismissed is costs. While a price–cost comparison would be most appropriate if the rationale of excessive pricing enforcement was to ensure fair profit, it is fraught with the difficulties that have been mentioned earlier. There are myriad problems with cost accounting, including the apportionment of joint and shared costs, the amortization of goodwill, the valuation of assets based on historical acquisition costs versus replacement costs, and the incorporation of opportunity costs, among others. There is the added complication that reliance on a price–cost comparison would give the firm significant incentives to be wasteful in order to inflate costs.[442] It takes away the firm's motivation to improve its cost efficiency. This leads to the question of whether the reference cost measure should refer to the firm's costs as they are or to the costs of a hypothetical efficient firm.[443]

As mentioned earlier, in the context of the pharmaceutical industry, a price–cost comparison faces the further challenge that the cost measure needs to take into account failed R&D and that cost data are almost entirely in the possession of the pharmaceutical companies themselves. If even the United States, including the US Congress, faced significant difficulties in obtaining accurate data on the R&D costs of the industry,[444] a developing country competition authority would face even more daunting hurdles. Even if such data are obtained, they are likely to be voluminous and beyond the capacity of most developing country authorities to process. Therefore, price–cost comparison or profitability analysis are ill-suited for excessive pricing enforcement in developing countries.

[442] Thomas Kauper, 'Article 86, Excessive Prices, and Refusals to Deal' (1991) 59 Antitrust Law Journal 441, 447.
[443] Akman and Garrod (n 426) 414.
[444] Abbott (n 131) 288.

Comparison with a competitor's prices in the same or a similar market is likewise not likely to be useful. There are many markets in which there are close therapeutic substitutes for a drug which can be used for price comparisons. In such a market, comparisons with a competitor's prices would be feasible and useful for determining excessiveness of prices. These markets, however, are unlikely to suffer from excessive pricing. The existence of close therapeutic substitutes would constrain the pricing power of the incumbent firm and prevent the firm from raising prices so high that excessive pricing concerns arise. In markets in which excessive pricing is probable, the firm holds a highly dominant position or perhaps offers the only treatment for a disease or condition. There will be no competitor's drugs with which to undertake a price comparison. If excessive pricing is to be limited to markets where there is super dominance, as was previously argued, comparison with a competitor's prices is unlikely to be relevant.

Meanwhile, comparison with the firm's prices in other geographical markets is highly pertinent as it sheds light on reverse price discrimination. While such discrimination may be a rational pricing strategy from these manufacturers' perspective by allowing them to extract the maximum surplus from the wealthiest consumers in the poorest countries, this strategy puts essential medicines further beyond the reach of most developing country patients. By adopting such a pricing strategy, these pharmaceutical manufacturers implicitly give up on a large segment of the general population in these countries and effectively deny them any realistic chance of access to these drugs. These manufacturers should not be allowed to do that.

The obvious counter-argument is that most of the general population could never afford these drugs anyway and therefore these manufacturers' policy makes no difference. While these patients may not be able to afford these drugs out of pocket, the public healthcare system in these countries may provide access at heavily subsidized prices. Grossly inflated prices that target the richest customers will significantly increase the financial burden on the public healthcare system in these countries. Reverse price discrimination hence should not be tolerated and should be an enforcement priority for developing countries. Proof of such discrimination should only require a straightforward price comparison between developing countries and the industrialized economies or between lower- and higher-income developing countries.

Recall that even the staunchest defenders of the pricing discretion of the pharmaceutical manufacturers concede that developing countries should have lower prices for the same drug than the industrialized economies. Therefore, any kind of price excess in developing countries as compared to the industrialized economies would constitute sufficient evidence of reverse price discrimination. Such a strict stance, however, may not be practical in reality. The test may require the authority to demonstrate that the price of a drug in the country exceeds its price in a number of, say, five to ten, industrialized economies or wealthier countries by a not insubstantial margin, say 20 per cent over a non-transitory period of time, say a year. The defendant is then given a chance to rebut the presumption of excessiveness with legitimate reasons that are consistent with the public health objective of providing affordable access to essential medicines to the consumers in these countries. A desire on the part of the pharmaceutical manufacturer to maximize profits should not constitute a legitimate reason.

The firm's past prices would be another appropriate comparator. Akman and Garrod assert that 'the comparator that has the greatest potential to overcome such problems and to provide the most informative comparison is a past price charged by the dominant firm in the investigated market'. One reason for the superiority of past prices as a comparator is its availability.[445] Apart from new products, there is always going to be a past price that can be used for comparison.[446] In contrast, other possible comparators may not always be available. Price comparison with a competitor in the same market may not be feasible if such a competitor does not exist.[447] Price comparison with the firm's prices in other markets can be misleading due to different demand and supply conditions.[448]

Another reason that a firm's past prices is a good comparator is because it means that the focus is on price increases, especially sudden, large, and unexplained price hikes. Once a sudden and substantial price increase has been shown, the analysis shifts to whether there are plausible explanations for such a price hike. Given that the prices in comparison are found in the same market, the focus of the analysis can be on what has changed in the market to justify such a price increase. Market conditions that have not been explicitly specified as different can be presumed to be the same or similar enough that they should not lead to significant changes in prices. This is different from a comparison with prices in different markets or with a competitor's prices, where such a presumption cannot be taken for granted.

In sum, for the purpose of enforcement against excessive drug prices in developing countries, the most appropriate comparators are the firm's past prices and the firm's current prices in the industrialized economies or other wealthier developing countries. A competitor's prices in the same market are either unavailable because no competitors of a sufficient size exist in the relevant market or irrelevant because the existence of sufficient competition means that prices cannot be excessive. Price–cost comparisons are likely to be fraught with difficulty in the form of arriving at an accurate estimate of costs or obtaining the pertinent information from the defendant.

[445] Akman and Garrod (n 426) 419.
[446] ibid.
[447] ibid.
[448] ibid 420.

(d) Benchmark for excessiveness

Another implementation difficulty with a test for excessiveness is the need for a benchmark for excessiveness. It is probably impossible to come up with a bright-line rule for when how much is too much. Such a benchmark is likely to be circumstance-specific. Thankfully, at least for one of the comparators that has been identified as suitable—the firm's prices in other geographic markets—a benchmark is less critical. If the concern is reverse price discrimination, any price excess in a poor developing country would be problematic. An astute reader at this point may ask if the concern is reverse price discrimination, why should we stop at enforcing against price excesses in developing countries? By the same logic, an insufficient discount in developing countries vis-à-vis the industrialized economies should be a matter of enforcement concern.

While that would be a logically consistent position, it would turn the notion of excessive pricing on its head. Excessive pricing after all should require the price to exceed some comparator. The only sense in which this can be true in the case of insufficient discount is if the comparator is some sort of hypothetical price that the manufacturer should charge in light of the demand and supply conditions in the country. Such a hypothetical price would be very difficult to calculate even for an advanced competition authority, let alone a developing country one. It would introduce significant uncertainty and implementation difficulties in excessive pricing enforcement. Developing countries should resist this temptation.

The remaining question is what is the requisite magnitude for a sudden and unexplained price hike to be considered excessive? Over the last few years, there have been a number of excessive pricing cases in Europe, such as *Aspen* and *Pfizer/Flynn*, that were premised on a sudden and dramatic price increase. The price hikes in these cases were often in the hundreds or thousands per cent. Therefore, it was not difficult to establish that the price increase was excessive. It is probably very challenging for the defendant to justify a price increase of over 1000 per cent overnight. Anything short of such a massive price increase will entail a judgment call. The significance of the benchmark can be alleviated by the creation of a presumption of excessiveness. A presumption of excessiveness obtains once a threshold percentage of price increase is found. The defendant is then given an opportunity to justify the price hike. The precise magnitude of the threshold is less consequential if it only creates a rebuttable presumption instead of directly resulting in liability. A desire to maximize profit or take advantage of short-term shortage or surge in demand should not be accepted as a justification.

That still would not obviate the need for some sort of threshold for excessiveness that would trigger the presumption. It is probably impossible to adopt a bright-line rule such that a 100 per cent price increase would be deemed excessive while a 99 per cent price increase would not. One obvious factor to take into account in the determination of the threshold is whether the industry has a history of price stability. A higher threshold for excessiveness would be justified if the industry is prone to sharp swings in prices. It is probably helpful that the pharmaceutical industry rarely suffers from a sudden surge in input prices, as most of the ingredients are chemicals as opposed to input that is subject to the vagaries of weather and other unpredictable factors. There are seldom supply-side factors that justify dramatic price hikes.

E. Case Law on Excessive Pricing

1. The United States

The US Courts have repeatedly asserted that it is perfectly lawful for a monopolist to charge whatever price that the market can bear. As early as 1979, the Court of Appeals for the Second Circuit declared in *Berkey Photo, Inc. v. Eastman Kodak Co.* that '[s]etting a high price may be a use of monopoly power, but it is not in itself anticompetitive ... Judicial oversight of pricing policies would place the courts in a role akin to that of a public regulatory commission'.[449] The Court of Appeals for the Seventh Circuit echoed this sentiment in *Blue Cross v. Marshfield* when it stated that

> [a] natural monopolist that acquired and maintained its monopoly without excluding competitors by improper means is not guilty of 'monopolizing' in violation of the Sherman Act ... and can therefore charge any price that it wants ... for the antitrust laws are not a price-control statute or a public-utility or common-carrier rate-regulation statute.[450]

In *Trinko*, Justice Scalia, writing for the majority, went one step further and proclaimed the virtue of monopoly prices, asserting that

> [t]he mere possession of monopoly power, and the concomitant charging of monopoly prices, is not only not unlawful; it is an important element of the free-market system. The opportunity to charge monopoly prices-at least for a short period-is what attracts 'business acumen' in the first place; it induces risk taking that produces innovation and economic growth.[451]

US commentators have made similar observations about excessive prices. Thomas Kauper notes that US antitrust law has 'assumed that normal market forces will cause the erosion of monopoly power except in cases where such power

[449] *Berkey Photo, Inc. v. Eastman Kodak Co.*, 603 F.2d 263, 294 (2d Cir. 1979).
[450] *Blue Cross & Blue Shield v. Marshfield Clinic*, 65 F.3d 1406, 1413 (7th Cir. 1995).
[451] *Trinko*, 540 US at 407.

is the result of greater efficiency (which the law ought not condemn), government protection, or predatory conduct'.[452] Despite protestations by Harry First to the contrary,[453] the weight of scholarly opinion and judicial pronouncements is firmly in favour of the view that excessive pricing is beyond the ambit of US antitrust law. Thus the focus of our discussion will be on EU jurisprudence on excessive pricing.

2. The European Union

Article 102(a) of the Treaty on the Functioning of the European Union (TFEU) expressly prohibits 'directly or indirectly imposing unfair purchase or selling prices or other unfair trading conditions'.[454] Even though the language of Article 102 is clear that excessive pricing is subject to the purview of EU competition law, excessive pricing enforcement has been restrained. Alison Jones and Christopher Stothers observe that under EU law, 'a cautionary approach [to excessive pricing] is adopted; prosecutorial discretion is frequently exercised not to take excessive pricing cases and instead resources are focused on exclusionary conduct which damages the structure of competition on the market'.[455] James Killick and Assimakis Komninos refer to 'a broad consensus among competition authorities that excessive pricing cases should be pursued very rarely, if at all, and that decisions of companies to increase their prices would usually have long-term procompetitive effects by creating incentives for new players to enter markets'.[456] The European courts have never condemned 'a particular pricing practice, in a free and unregulated market, as amounting to unfairly high and exploitative prices'.[457] The Commission itself has adopted only six formal decisions on excessive pricing.[458]

EU officials and commentators have tried to downplay the importance of excessive pricing enforcement. Emil Paulis, a former Director for Policy and Strategic Support at the Directorate General of Competition (DG COMP), considers the implementation difficulties of excessive pricing so overwhelming and the risks of false positives so high that 'enforcement actions against exploitative conduct [] should only be taken as a last resort'.[459] Mark Furse has likewise been highly critical of the

[452] Kauper (n 442) 444.

[453] First (n 403) 712–16.

[454] Consolidated Version of the Treaty on European Union [2008] OJ C115/13, art. 102(a).

[455] Alison Jones and Christopher Stothers, 'Establishing Unfairly High Prices: The Implications of the CAT's Judgment in Flynn and Pfizer v Competition and Markets Authority' (2018) 17 Bio-Science Law Review 19, 720.

[456] James Killick and Assimakis Komninos, 'Excessive Pricing in the Pharmaceutical Market—How the CAT Shot Down the CMA's Pfizer/Flynn Case' (2018) 9 Journal of European Competition Law & Practice 530, 530.

[457] Wahl (n 398) 62.

[458] Motta and de Streel (n 402) 30.

[459] Emil Paulis, 'Article 82 EC and Exploitative Conduct' (2020) 3 <https://www.eui.eu/Documents/RSCAS/Research/Competition/2007ws/200709-COMPed-Paulis.pdf> accessed 20 September 2020.

EU's enforcement record against excessive pricing and suggested that enforcement action should be limited to exclusionary excessive pricing.[460] This consensus on restraint, however, has loosened in recent years with a renewed interest in excessive pricing enforcement, especially in the pharmaceutical industry. Notable examples include the *Aspen* case in Italy and the *Pfizer/Flynn* case in the United Kingdom. Commissioner Margrethe Vestager has reaffirmed the Commission's enforcement focus on excessive pricing in the industry.[461] It is particularly relevant to developing countries that the European Union has chosen to focus on the pharmaceutical industry in its excessive pricing enforcement. Its enforcement record will offer some useful lessons for developing countries.

(a) *General Motors*

This was the Commission's first decision on excessive pricing. The case concerned the issuance of certificates of conformity for vehicles that were imported into Belgium. A much higher price was charged for these certificates for vehicles produced in the United States than for those produced in Europe in order to discourage parallel imports from the United States to Belgium.[462] On appeal, the Court of Justice propounded the concept of economic value of a product, noting that

> such an abuse might lie, inter alia, in the imposition of a price which is excessive in relation to the economic value of the service provided and which has the effect of curbing parallel imports by neutralizing the possibly more favourable level of prices applying in other sales areas in the Community.[463]

The Court, however, did not elaborate on the meaning of the concept as there was no doubt that the charges by General Motors was excessive.[464] The legacy of this relatively obscure case is the concept of economic value, which has continued to befuddle the courts and commentators ever since. It is a concept that seems to be clear at first glance but either leads to absurd results when pushed to its logical limits or is so vacuous as to be meaningless. It will be elaborated subsequently.

460 Furse (n 400) 60–62.

461 Margrethe Vestager, 'Protecting Consumers from Exploitation' (Chillin' Competition Conference, Brussels, 21 November 2016) <https://wayback.archive-it.org/12090/20191129221154/https://ec.europa.eu/commission/commissioners/2014-2019/vestager/announcements/protecting-consumers-exploitation_en> accessed 20 September 2020.

462 Cases 26/75, *General Motors Continental NV. v. Commission* [1975] ECR 1367, 1369.

463 ibid para. 12.

464 MAH Schrijen, 'Excessive Prices in the Pharmaceutical Sector: Is Competition Law the Best Remedy?' Master Thesis European Law (Utrecht University 29 June 2018) 28 <https://mededingingscongres.nl/wp-content/uploads/2021/03/Thesis-Maureen-Schrijen.pdf> accessed 29 July 2021.

(b) *United Brands*

The facts of this case are familiar to most competition lawyers versed in EU competition law. The case concerned United Brands, a banana supplier, which was accused by the European Commission of engaging in excessive pricing in a number of member states. The Commission relied mainly on a price comparison across the member states to establish its case. It was alleged that the prices in a number of member states such as Belgium, Denmark, Germany, Luxembourg, and the Netherlands, were at least twice as high as those in Ireland.[465] There seems to have been evidence that United Brands was profitable in Ireland, which means that it must have covered its costs, including the delivery costs of bananas first to Rotterdam and then to Ireland.[466] The Commission concluded that United's prices outside of Ireland were excessive by 15 per cent without much analysis or evidence.[467] It did not attempt to determine United's production costs.[468] The bulk of the Commission's case seems to have been built on cross-country price comparisons.

The European Court of Justice nullified the Commission's decision with respect to excessive pricing. The Court found a number of deficiencies in the Commission's analysis. First, there was no analysis of United's cost structure.[469] Second, there were some doubts as to the validity of Ireland as a comparator, and this doubt must benefit United.[470] Third, the prices for bananas have stayed level in real terms for nearly twenty years.[471] Fourth, United's prices were only 7 per cent above those of the competitors, which casts doubt on claims of excessiveness.[472] The Court clarified that the key question is whether 'the dominant undertaking has made use of the opportunities arising out of its dominant position in such a way as to reap trading benefits which it would not have reaped had there been normal and sufficiently effective competition'.[473] This seems to contrast with assertions by commentators such as Motta and de Streel that excessive pricing should require an extraordinary amount of market power of super-dominance. The Court seems to suggest that charging prices afforded by a dominant position would be sufficient. This would amount to penalizing the possession of a dominant position instead of the abuse of such a position.

The Court proceeded to lay down the authoritative formulation of an excessive pricing claim:

[465] Case 27/76, *United Brands v. Commission* [1978] ECR 207, para 239.
[466] ibid para 238.
[467] ibid para 241.
[468] ibid para 238.
[469] ibid para 256.
[470] ibid para 265.
[471] ibid.
[472] ibid para 266.
[473] ibid para 249.

> In this case charging a price which is excessive because it has no reasonable relation to the economic value of the product supplied would be such an abuse.
>
> This excess could, inter alia, be determined objectively if it were possible for it to be calculated by making a comparison between the selling price of the product in question and its cost of production, which would disclose the amount of the profit margin; however, the Commission has not done this since it has not analysed [United Brands'] cost structure.
>
> The questions therefore to be determined are whether the difference between the costs actually incurred and the price actually charged is excessive, and, if the answer to this question is in the affirmative, whether a price has been charged which is either unfair in itself or when compared to competing products.[474]

This language has been interpreted to establish a two-part test for excessive pricing. First, there needs to be a price–cost comparison to show that the prevailing price does exceed costs by a substantial margin and is therefore excessive. Second, it needs to be shown that the price is unfair in itself or by comparison to other competitors' products. The Court held that the Commission's decision failed this test because there was no price–cost comparison and the difference between United's and competitors' prices was negligible.

The Court's formulation of the test for excessively pricing has been roundly criticized on a number of grounds. First, and most obviously, is the lack of clarity in the formulation and the lack of guidance on its application. There is no benchmark for delineating excessiveness and no explanation of what unfairness in itself means and how the comparison should be made with other products.[475] The Commission has attempted to provide some clarity by stating that in the assessment of costs, regard must be had 'not only to the cost of capital but also to the investment risks involved in the industry concerned',[476] and that in the determination of unfairness, one of the relevant factors would be whether a high profit margin is due to the exercise of market power or superior efficiency.[477] These clarifications, however, do not get at the crux of the problem as they still do not address how much of a margin above costs would be deemed excessive. It only addresses the calculation of costs. The second clarification resurrects the difficulty posed by the Court's pronouncement in *United Brands* in that it seems to suggest that excessive pricing encompasses full exploitation of market power to charge a price that the market can bear. Moreover,

[474] ibid paras 250–52.

[475] Margherita Colangelo and Claudia Desogus, 'Antitrust Scrutiny of Excessive Prices in the Pharmaceutical Sector: A Comparative Study of the Italian and UK Experiences' (2018) 41 World Competition 225, 228.

[476] OECD, 'European Union: Article 102 and Excessive Prices' (2012) 318 <https://www.oecd.org/competition/abuse/49604207.pdf> accessed 21 September 2020.

[477] OECD (n 425) 318.

in reality, the source of the profit margin for a dominant firm is likely to be a mix of market power and superior efficiency. It is very difficult to disentangle them.

Evans and Padilla argue that the first limb of the test is both ambiguous and beyond the expertise of most competition authorities as it involves complex cost accounting issues.[478] They criticize the second limb for its subjectivity as the determination of unfairness necessarily entails value judgment.[479] There is no objective and reliable method for determining a competitive profit margin in most industries.[480] One possible way to reduce the ambiguity in the test is to eliminate the second limb,[481] which in many ways can be regarded as superfluous. That, however, as Akman and Garrod point out, would go against the case law.[482] The ambiguity extends to the Court's definition of an excessive price as well. A price that bears 'no reasonable relation to the economic value of the product' is far from a model of clarity. Reasonableness and economic value are both undefined in the case law.[483]

(c) *British Leyland*

The facts in *British Leylands* closely parallel those in *General Motors*. It was the only judgment by the European courts confirming a finding of excessive pricing by the Commission.[484] At issue was also discriminatory fees that had the ostensible purpose of retarding parallel imports. British Leylands was in charge of issuing certificates of conformity for parallel-imported cars.[485] It charged GBP150 for a certificate for left-hand-drive cars and GBP25 for a certificate for right-hand-drive ones.[486] This was seemingly done to reduce competition for domestically produced left-hand-drive cars. This case was in many ways a very straightforward one because issuance of a certificate of conformity is a mere administrative procedure that cannot entail significant costs.[487] The existence of lower fees for right-hand-drive cars was highly suggestive that the fees for left-hand-drive cars were excessive as there was no reason why it would cost six times as much to issue a certificate for left-hand-drive cars as it was for right-hand-drive ones. Despite it being the only case by the Court of Justice affirming a finding of excessive pricing, the precedential value of the case has been cast in doubt. Advocate General Wahl argues that the case should be viewed through the lens of single market integration as British Leylands' pricing scheme was clearly intended to deter parallel imports

[478] Evans and Padilla (n 419) 108–09.
[479] ibid 109.
[480] ibid 108.
[481] Akman and Garrod (n 426) 405.
[482] ibid 406.
[483] ibid 409.
[484] ibid 422.
[485] Case 226/84, *British Leyland v. Commission* [1986] ECR 3263, para 4.
[486] ibid para 25.
[487] Akman and Garrod (n 426) 422.

and that the case 'may not be taken as proof that the Court has interfered in a free market where the dominant actor charges excessively high prices'.[488]

(d) *Scandlines*

Scandlines was one of the most important excessive pricing cases since *United Brands*.[489] The case concerned the pricing by the port authority in Helsingborg for ferry traffic. The complainant's chief argument was that the charges by the port authority were neither cost-based nor transparent.[490] The Commission applied the two-part test from *United Brands* to the excessive pricing claim.[491] The Commission was not entirely explicit about whether the price in that case substantially exceeded costs.[492] It did, however, determine that HHAB, the port authority in the case, was able to cover the losses from other operations at the port with the profits from the ferry operations, suggesting that its revenues were in excess of the costs.[493]

Where the complaint failed was at the second limb of the test. The Commission concluded that it could not establish that the charges imposed by HHAB were unfair. The Commission noted that unfairness needs to be established through comparison with the prices charged for other services at the port and the prices charged to ferry operators at other ports and in light of the economic value of the service.[494] The Commission declared that:

> [i]n the present case, the economic value of the product/service cannot simply be determined by adding to the approximate costs incurred in the provision of this product/service as assessed by the Commission, a profit margin which would be a pre-determined percentage of the production costs. The economic value must be determined with regards to the particular circumstances of the case and take into account also non-cost related factors such as the demand for the product/service.[495]

The Commission proceeded to conclude that the prices were not unfair because the economic value of the service includes the high sunk costs of the port, the opportunity costs of the land on which the port facilities were situated, and the ideal location of the port, which was highly valuable to ferry passengers.[496] In other

[488] Wahl (n 398) 53–54.
[489] Furse (n 400) 67.
[490] COMP/36568, *Scandlines Sverige v. Port of Helsingborg* 23 July 2004 and COMP/36570, *Sundbusserne v. Port of Helsingborg* 23 July 2004 (*Scandlines*), para 19.
[491] ibid para 101.
[492] Akman and Garrod (n 426) 425.
[493] Furse (n 400) 69.
[494] *Scandlines*, para 225.
[495] ibid para 232.
[496] ibid para 234.

words, the price for the port services was not excessive because consumers value the port's location and were ready to pay higher prices for access to the port.

The Commission's analysis exposes the limitation of the concept of economic value as a tool for determining excessiveness of prices. First, as Akman and Garrod point out, the Commission conflated the definition of the abuse of excessive pricing with one of the analytical steps in the two-part test from *United Brands*.[497] Second, and more importantly, allowing the incorporation of demand-side factors in the analysis effectively nullifies excessive pricing as an abuse. Advocate General Wahl argues that:

> if the reasoning of the Commission is correct it would seem practically impossible to strike down on a price which is not higher than the monopoly price. The monopoly price, i.e. the highest price that a dominant company would be able to charge without loosing [sic] sales in excess of revenues generated by the high price, would seem to reflect the prevailing attitude of the customers, thus being a good indication of the value which customers attribute to the service or product.[498]

Given that there would be no economically rational reasons for a firm to ever charge a price higher than the monopoly price, there will be no occasion for excessive pricing enforcement. Akman and Garrod go one step further and observe that 'if demand-side factors contribute to the economic value of the product, then in all cases, it could be argued that any price must reflect its economic value to a buyer, since, otherwise, there would be no sale'.[499] The Commission's argument essentially means that if there are consumers willing to pay the price, the price must reflect the economic value of the good or service because no consumers will pay a price that exceeds the value they attach to the good or service. No market price can ever be excessive.

The flaws in the Commission's reasoning notwithstanding, the Commission's decision reaffirms that the two steps in the *United Brands* test are distinct and must be satisfied separately. The excessiveness prong may be met through a price–cost comparison while the unfairness prong cannot. The unfairness prong can be met through comparisons with appropriate comparators or demonstrated by pointing to the inherent unfairness of the price. The implication seems to be that a price–cost comparison on its own will not suffice to satisfy the *United Brands* two-part test.

[497] Akman and Garrod (n 426) 425.
[498] Wahl (n 398) 61–62.
[499] Akman and Garrod (n 426) 426.

(e) *AKKA/LAA*

The *AKKA/LAA* case is the most recent decision by the Court of Justice of the European Union (CJEU) on excessive pricing. The case concerned a Latvian copyright management organization that issues licenses for the performance of musical works on behalf of its members. The Latvian Competition Council had found that the copyright society charged excessive rates for its licenses mostly on the grounds that its rates were higher than the equivalent rates in the neighbouring countries of Lithuania and Estonia.[500] The decision was then appealed to the Latvian courts, which made a preliminary reference to the CJEU. The case is notable for both the Court's decision and the opinion by Advocate General Wahl.

The CJEU reaffirmed the two-part test from *United Brands*, noting that the first prong consists of a determination of excessiveness based on a comparison with a benchmark and the second prong an assessment of unfairness dependent on whether the excessive price is unfair in itself or when compared to other comparable products.[501] The Court clarified that there is no single method of determination under the first prong.[502] One method is a price–cost comparison. Another method is a comparison with the dominant undertaking's prices in other comparable markets. It is not clear whether this overlaps with the comparative analysis for unfairness under the second prong. The two tests, however, are not treated by the Court to be on equal footing. A price–cost comparison seems to require to be complemented by the consideration of non-cost factors whereas cross-market price comparisons seem to suffice on their own.[503] Margherita Colangelo and Claudia Desogus explain this different treatment 'by the fact that the comparative methods already embody the consideration of non-cost related factors, whereas the price–cost test allegedly does not'.[504]

The Latvian Competition Council had only compared the rates of AKKA/LAA with those in two other countries. The Court affirmed that 'there can be no minimum number of markets to compare'[505] so long as 'the reference Member States are selected in accordance with objective, appropriate and verifiable criteria, which may include consumption habits and other economic and sociocultural factors, such as gross domestic product per capita and cultural and historical heritage'.[506] The Court further reiterated that there is no minimum threshold for excessiveness and that the benchmark varies according to the facts of the case.[507] The price difference, however, must be 'significant' and 'persistent' and must constitute important

500 *AKKA/LAA*, para 9.
501 ibid para 36.
502 ibid para 49.
503 Colangelo and Desogus (n 475) 242.
504 ibid.
505 *AKKA/LAA*, para. 41.
506 ibid para 42.
507 ibid para 55.

deviations and not just any price difference.[508] The dominant undertaking bears the burden to justify the excessive price in the second prong of the test.[509]

Advocate General Wahl's opinion provides further elucidations on the analysis of excessive pricing. He agreed that there is no single methodology for determining excessiveness. Possibilities include comparisons with prices of similar products, comparisons with prices charged by the company at different points in time, and comparisons with prices charged for the same product in other countries.[510] It is crucial for an authority to combine multiple methods to minimize false positives.[511] In situations where only one methodology is available, Wahl observed that it is 'of the utmost importance that the authority consider other indicators which may corroborate or, conversely, cast doubt on the result of that method'.[512] On the selection of comparator markets, Wahl cautions that the reviewing national court should ensure that the authority did not strategically omit suitable countries because the comparison would yield unfavourable results and undermine its own case.[513]

On the threshold for excessiveness, Wahl concedes that there cannot be a precise threshold laid down in advance and every case depends on its facts.[514] He warns that an authority should intervene 'only when it feels sure that, regardless of the limitations and uncertainties surrounding the calculation of the benchmark price, the difference between that price and the actual price is of such a magnitude that almost no doubt remains as to the latter's abusive nature'.[515] The authority can act with greater confidence 'the more significant the difference between the benchmark price and the actual price, and the longer the period in which that high price is applied'.[516] Wahl also clarifies the meaning of unfairness in and of itself, stating that inherent unfairness should only be found under exceptional circumstances, such as where the customers receive nothing of value in return or where the dominant firm sets an excessive price because it is ultimately not interested in making a sale but has other ulterior, anticompetitive motives.[517]

The Court's judgment and the Advocate General opinion provide a number of important insights into the analysis of excessive pricing. The call for the deployment of multiple methodologies may be appropriate for well-resourced authorities found in most EU member states, but would exceed the capacity of most developing country authorities and should hence be rejected. The importance of the

[508] ibid para 55.
[509] ibid para 57.
[510] *AKKA/LAA AG Opinion*, paras 37–41.
[511] ibid para 43.
[512] ibid para 46.
[513] ibid para 65.
[514] ibid para 111.
[515] ibid para 112.
[516] ibid.
[517] ibid paras 122–23.

avoidance of arbitrary exclusion of an appropriate comparator applies to both EU member states and developing countries. Arguably the most important insight from the case is that excessiveness should be understood as a difference between the firm's price and the comparator so substantial that there can be no doubt about exploitation of consumers.

(f) *Napp*

Napp was a case decided by the Office of Fair Trading (OFT), the predecessor of the Competition and Markets Authority (CMA), the current UK competition regulator. Napp was a UK-based pharmaceutical company and was the first to introduce a sustained-release morphine product in 1980 and held a patent on the product until 1992.[518] The OFT found that there were two relevant customer segments for the drug: the hospital segment and the community/general practitioner segment.[519] Napp's market share in both segments was in excess of 90 per cent.[520] Napp allegedly charged a very low price in the hospital segment, which was found to be predatory, and a very high price in the community segment, which was found to be excessive.[521]

To show that prices in the community segment were excessive, the OFT suggested that two elements must be proven: first, 'prices are higher than would be expected in a competitive market',[522] and second, 'there is no effective competitive pressure to bring them down to competitive levels, nor is there likely to be'.[523] The OFT used a comparative approach, comparing Napp's profit margins on the sustained-release morphine product with those on Napp's other products and those of Napp's competitors.[524] Napp's profit margins on the morphine product were found to be excessive. Napp earned a 40–60 per cent margin in the hospital segment and a margin in excess of 80 per cent in the community segment.[525] Napp's prices in the community segment were 33–67 per cent higher than its competitors' in 2000.[526] Napp's prices also did not change for ten years after its patent had expired.[527] It was also found that Napp's prices in the community segment were at least ten times higher than those offered to the hospitals.[528]

The OFT went beyond the price–cost comparison that was mandated by *United Brands* and employed a variety of comparative tools to establish excessiveness, foreshadowing the view of Advocate General Wahl in *AKKA/LAA*. These price

518 *Napp Pharmaceutical Holdings Ltd. v. Director General of Fair Trading* [2002] CAT 1, paras 13–14.
519 ibid paras 17, 19.
520 ibid paras 17, 20.
521 ibid para 32.
522 ibid para 390.
523 ibid.
524 ibid paras 65–69.
525 ibid para 65.
526 ibid para 60.
527 ibid para 62.
528 ibid para. 63.

comparisons undertaken by the OFT were criticized by Evans and Padilla. First, they argue that prices in the hospital segment could not be a valid comparator because they were deemed to be predatory by the OFT.[529] Second, competitors' prices may not shed relevant light on excessiveness either because Napp was the longstanding product in the market which enjoyed brand recognition and consumer trust.[530] Yet the OFT arbitrarily decided that Napp's brand recognition was not worth a 40 per cent premium.[531] Evans and Padilla's criticisms illustrate the difficulty with a valid price comparison. Given that no two markets and no two firms are the same, it is always possible to find some relevant difference to undermine the validity of the comparison.

Napp put forward a number of justifications for the high prices, which were all rejected by the OFT. These include the need to cover its R&D costs, including failed R&D projects, and the need to protect its brand value. The OFT rejected the R&D recoupment argument on the ground that the patent on the drug had already expired and Napp was expected to have recouped its R&D costs during the patent term.[532] The OFT accepted that Napp could charge a higher premium for its product in the community segment due to brand recognition, but not to the tune of a 40 per cent premium.[533] The OFT and subsequently the Competition Appeal Tribunal (CAT) incorporated an additional requirement that an excessive pricing claim would be defeated if it was shown that entry 'within a reasonable period of time' would erode the high prices.[534] The OFT fined Napp GBP3.21 million for the infringement and ordered Napp to raise its prices in the hospital segment so that they cover the average total costs of the drug and to lower its prices in the community segment by 15 per cent.[535] Napp appealed the OFT's decision to the CAT, which upheld the OFT's analysis but reduced the fine to GBP2.2 million.[536]

From a developing country perspective, the most pertinent lesson from the *Napp* case is the need to scrutinize innovation incentives arguments closely. In the case, the OFT rejected the argument on the grounds that Napp should have recouped its R&D costs during the patent term. In the developing country context, even if the patent has not expired, unless the country is a middle-income one with a large domestic market such as Brazil and Mexico, profits from the country are unlikely to matter significantly to the innovator's recoupment of R&D costs. There is no need to accord much weight to the innovation incentives argument.

529 Evans and Padilla (n 419) 109–10.
530 ibid 110.
531 ibid.
532 *Napp*, para 358.
533 ibid para 366.
534 ibid paras 56, 397.
535 ibid para 485.
536 ibid para 538.

(g) *Aspen*

Aspen and *Flynn* are two very recent excessive pricing cases in the pharmaceutical industry. The two cases had very similar facts.[537] In both cases, the drugs at issue, for one reason or another, had no therapeutic substitutes and therefore were not constrained by competition, but were essential and life-saving.[538] Both cases also featured a glitch in the regulatory regime that was exploited by the pharmaceutical manufacturers to maximize their market and bargaining power.[539] The flaw in the UK regime in *Flynn* was eventually rectified by legislation.[540]

Aspen took place in Italy and concerned a sudden price hike of hundreds of per cent. Aspen, a South African pharmaceutical company, purchased the marketing rights for the anti-cancer drugs Alkeran (melphalan), Leukeran (chlorambucil), Purinethol (mercaptopurine), and Tioguanine (thioguanine), collectively known as the Cosmos drugs, from GlaxoSmithKline (GSK) in 2009.[541] What Aspen did was consistent with 'a business strategy that pharmaceutical companies have been employing in recent times in relation to old drugs that are used to treat diseases that have a low incidence in the population, Aspen "converted" the Cosmos drugs into 'specialty' drugs for which it demanded very high prices'.[542] Having purchased the marketing rights, it raised prices between 300 per cent and 1,500 per cent and proceeded to adopt very aggressive negotiation positions vis-à-vis the Italian Medicines Agency (AIFA).[543] Aspen put pressure on AIFA to delist the drugs so that they would no longer be subject to the national reimbursement scheme and their prices could be set freely by Aspen and directly borne by the patients.[544] When Aspen's request was rejected, it nonetheless persisted in its aggressive negotiation and pushed for substantial price increases under the national reimbursement scheme.[545] Aspen went so far as threatening to cut Italy off from the supply of the drug.[546] It eventually managed to extract a 300 per cent to 1500 per cent price increase for the drugs.

On 29 September 2016, the Italian Competition Authority (ICA) fined Aspen more than EUR5 million for charging unfair prices for these essential drugs.[547] The ICA found that Aspen had a dominant position in the relevant market, being the sole holder of marketing rights for drugs based on the active pharmaceutical

[537] Colangelo and Desogus (n 475) 11.
[538] ibid.
[539] ibid.
[540] Jones and Stothers (n 455) 23.
[541] Italian Competition Authority, 'A480-Price Increase of Aspen Drugs Measure No. 26185' para 23 <https://en.agcm.it/dotcmsDOC/pressrelease/A480_eng.pdf> accessed 21 September 2020. [*Aspen Decision*]
[542] Colangelo and Desogus (n 475) 11.
[543] *Aspen Decision*, paras 91–110.
[544] ibid paras 91–95.
[545] ibid paras 96–106.
[546] ibid para 103.
[547] ibid 58.

ingredients (API) of the Cosmos drugs.[548] It was important to note that Aspen did not bear any R&D costs or marketing costs for the drugs; it was only responsible for distributing them.[549] The ICA concluded that the AIFA's countervailing buyer power was insufficient to counterbalance Aspen's market power as the AIFA eventually capitulated to Aspen's demands.[550] The ICA undertook a price–cost comparison and demonstrated that prices exceeded Aspen's costs by 100 per cent to 300 per cent.[551] The ICA, however, excluded the costs incurred by Aspen in acquiring the marketing rights from GSK because these costs 'were not indispensable for the production and/or distribution of the goods and that were, rather, caused by erroneous business decisions taken by the company, thereby representing potential sources of inefficiencies'.[552] The ICA thus concluded that the price increases were excessive.

Aspen attempted to justify the price increases on the grounds that they were necessary to deter parallel imports into other EU member states and to compensate for the costs related to pharmacovigilance.[553] These arguments were rejected.[554] The ICA established that the price increases were unfair because there was no reasonable justification for them. The ICA referred to the absence of economic justifications for the sudden price increases, the inelastic demand for the drugs due to their life-saving nature, the lack of any qualitative improvement to the drugs, and the fact that Aspen did not bear any of the R&D costs for the drugs as Aspen was a generic manufacturer and the drugs had been in the market for decades.[555] The ICA also noted that Aspen's business model was speculative in nature, acquiring the marketing rights for drugs that lack substitutes to raise their prices exponentially,[556] and attached significant weight to the impact of the price increases on the public health budget.[557] Aspen's price increases quintupled public expenditure on these drugs.[558]

The ICA did not undertake a price comparison with competitors or in other markets in the case and relied exclusively on a price–cost comparison to establish the excessiveness of the price increases.[559] Competitors' prices were shunned because they were not considered valid alternatives.[560] Prices in other member states were also not taken into account because of different market conditions and the

548 ibid paras 292–306.
549 ibid para 269.
550 ibid para 305.
551 ibid para 320.
552 Colangelo and Desogus (n 475) 14.
553 ibid para 338.
554 ibid para 338.
555 ibid para 339.
556 ibid para 349.
557 ibid para 350.
558 ibid.
559 ibid paras 315–28.
560 ibid para 347.

fact that high prices in other member states may be the consequence of similar strategies by Aspen.[561] The lack of appropriate comparators was also an issue in *Pfizer/Flynn*.[562] The CMA, however, took a different approach. The ICA eschewed cross-country comparisons completely, while the CMA chose five countries which had not been subject to price increases for comparison.[563] Aspen appealed the ICA's decision to the Regional Administrative Court of Lazio, which upheld the ICA's decision.[564] About a year later, Aspen reached an agreement with the AIFA on new prices for the Cosmos drugs, cutting their prices by 30–82 per cent, to be applied retroactively to 2014.[565]

(h) *Pfizer/Flynn*

Pfizer/Flynn basically shared the same plot as Aspen's. In September 2012, Pfizer sold the distribution rights for its anti-epilepsy drug Epanutin, which consists of phenytoin sodium capsules, to Flynn Pharma in the United Kingdom.[566] After the transaction, Pfizer stopped selling the drug in the United Kingdom except for Flynn.[567] Flynn debranded the drug, which took it out of the UK regulatory regime and allowed it to raise the price of the drug by at least 2000 per cent overnight.[568] All branded drugs are subject to price regulation, under which their profits are capped and any price increase must be approved by the Department of Health.[569] Generics, however, are exempt from this scheme. Permissible reimbursement for generics is determined by the average price of a basket of generics.[570] The rationale for this exemption was that competition among generics would keep their prices low and thus price regulation was unnecessary.[571]

The drug was already off-patent.[572] But because of the special characteristics of the drug, clinical guidance advised doctors to keep patients on the same drug even in the presence of substitutes.[573] The CMA noted that 'patients who are stabilized on Pfizer-manufactured phenytoin sodium capsules are effectively captive customers'.[574] Patients' reluctance to switch suppliers made it difficult for new entrants

[561] Schrijen (n 464) 44.
[562] Colangelo and Desogus (n 475) 13.
[563] ibid.
[564] Behrang Kianzad and Timo Minssen, 'How Much Is Too Much? Defining the Metes and Bounds of Excessive Pricing in the Pharmaceutical Sector' (2018) 2 European Pharmaceutical Law Review 15, 20–21.
[565] ibid 21.
[566] Case CE/9742-13, *Decision of the Competition and Markets Authority: Unfair Pricing in Respect of the Supply of Phenytoin Sodium Capsules in the UK* (7 Dec 2016), <https://assets.publishing.service.gov.uk/media/594240cfe5274a5e4e00024e/phenytoin-full-non-confidential-decision.pdf> accessed 2 September 2020, paras 1.9, 1.12.
[567] ibid para 1.14.
[568] ibid paras 1.13, 1.18.
[569] ibid paras 3.130–3.138.
[570] ibid para 3.126.
[571] ibid para 3.143.
[572] ibid para 1.9.
[573] ibid para 3.30.
[574] ibid para 5.391.

to enter the market.[575] There was evidence that one of the main reasons for the transaction was to introduce an intermediary to shield Pfizer from the reputational damage from a sudden and dramatic price hike.[576]

The Department of Health complained about the price hikes with the CMA, which opened a formal investigation in May 2013 and imposed on the two companies a fine in 2016 that was its largest since its establishment in 2013.[577] One complication in the case was that the inflated price for the capsule form of the drug was still 25 per cent below the price for the tablet form, a price that the National Health Service (NHS), the public health care provider in the United Kingdom, had been paying for years.[578]

The CMA found that Pfizer/Flynn were dominant in the relevant market for a variety of reasons. The CMA inferred from the continuity of supply principle and the patients' reluctance to switch suppliers that rival generic products were in a different relevant market.[579] The finding of dominance was corroborated by the high market shares, high entry barriers, and lack of countervailing power on the part of the NHS and the Department of Health.[580] The CMA applied the two-part test from *United Brands* to establish the excessiveness of Flynn's prices.[581] Under the first prong, the CMA undertook a price–cost comparison applying a rate of return of 6 per cent.[582] The CMA argued that this rate of return was reasonable in light of the non-innovative nature of the product.[583] The CMA acknowledged that the identification of an appropriate rate of return required judgment and a balance between the competing interests of consumer welfare and the generation of innovation incentives.[584]

Contrary to the European Commission's position in *Scandlines*, the CMA held that there were no non-cost-related factors to take into account when determining the economic value of the drug.[585] Consumers' willingness to pay is hence meaningless. The CMA's analysis found that Pfizer's prices exceeded its costs plus the reasonable rate of return by 29–705 per cent and Flynn's prices exceeded these costs by 31–133 per cent.[586] Such a margin was sufficient to substantiate a finding of excessiveness under the existing case law of CAT.[587]

575 ibid paras 1.24–1.25.
576 ibid para 1.15.
577 ibid para 2.43, Tables 7.1 and 7.2.
578 ibid paras 1.46–1.47.
579 ibid paras 4.53–4.56.
580 ibid paras 4.269–4.324.
581 ibid paras 5.8–5.9.
582 ibid para 5.86.
583 ibid para 5.91.
584 ibid para 5.92.
585 ibid paras 5.253–5.254.
586 ibid paras 5.125, 5.218.
587 ibid para 5.222.

Under the second prong, the CMA concluded that Flynn's prices were unfair in and of themselves and also on a comparative basis. The prices were inherently unfair because of the substantial disparity between the price and the economic value of the product.[588] The CMA further substantiated its finding of unfairness on the grounds that (1) Pfizer and Flynn were able to sustain excessive prices because they were shielded from competition and that was unlikely to change in the near future;[589] (2) the prices charged by Pfizer and Flynn were significantly higher than the previous prices and the prices in other European countries;[590] (3) Flynn benefited from such dramatic price increases despite performing a negligible role in the supply chain, incurring little commercial risks, and delivering few benefits to patients;[591] and (4) the drug 'has long been off-patent and has been genericised, [] it has not been subject to any recent innovation, and [] the arrangement between Pfizer and Flynn has not produced any benefits for patients'.[592] After concluding that the prices were inherently unfair, the CMA noted that it could not establish unfairness through price comparisons due to the lack sufficiently similar product to allow for a meaningful comparison.[593]

The CMA rejected a number of counter-arguments by Pfizer and Flynn. They had argued that the price increase was necessary to return the drug to profitability, as the drug had been loss-making. The CMA noted that the price increase went way beyond what was necessary to restore profitability of the drug; the losses were offset in two months.[594] The CMA also rejected their argument that the price–cost comparison should take into account Pfizer's overall R&D costs.[595] The patent for the drug had long expired and any relevant R&D costs should have been recouped long ago.[596]

Pfizer and Flynn appealed the CMA's decision to the CAT, which partially overturned the CMA's decision. The CAT found that the CMA had committed legal errors in the following respects: (1) conclusions on Pfizer and Flynn's dominance in the relevant market; (2) the legal test for the unfairness of the prices; (3) determination of the economic value of the product; and (4) the omission of comparison with other comparable products, especially the phenytoin sodium tablets.

The CAT concluded that the CMA had been wrong to rely exclusively on price–cost comparisons to establish the excessiveness of the prices when there were alternative methods simply because price–cost comparisons yielded the most

588 ibid para 5.350.
589 ibid para 1.43.
590 ibid.
591 ibid.
592 ibid para 1.44.
593 ibid para 1.45.
594 ibid para 1.43.
595 ibid Annex L, L.6.
596 ibid.

favourable results.[597] The CJEU's judgment in *United Brands* and Advocate General Wahl's opinion in the recent *AKKA/LAA* case did not support such reliance.[598] It also questioned the CMA's use of the 6 per cent rate of return, suggesting that the CMA should have considered the rates of return on other products.[599] It rejected the CMA's approach to the determination of the economic value of the drug by excluding non-cost related factors such as patient benefits.[600] The CAT further faulted the CMA for shunning the comparative approach, especially a comparison with the phenytoin sodium tablets, to determine unfairness of the prices.[601] The fact that Pfizer and Flynn had taken advantage of a regulatory loophole to raise prices on its own was not sufficient to establish unfairness.[602]

According to the CAT, the CMA did not have complete discretion in choosing between the inherent unfairness and the comparative approaches and must consider the latter when there was sufficient evidence to assess whether a prima facie case of unfairness can be made.[603] The CAT also cautioned against the weight that the CMA had attached to the dramatic price hikes, stating that 'a large price rise, sustained over a considerable period, may be indicative of an abuse of a dominant position that needs to be examined ... it should not be confused with the test for unfair pricing itself'.[604]

The CMA further appealed the CAT judgment to the Court of Appeal. One of the main points of contention was whether a comparative approach is necessary to determine the unfairness of the price. The Court of Appeal held that while the CMA should be free to choose between alternative approaches to demonstrate unfairness, the authority cannot ignore exculpatory evidence even if it has not chosen that particular approach.[605] The Court emphasized that the ultimate issue is what is the economic value of the product at issue, and there are many ways to ascertain that.[606] The implication is thus that the two approaches are not strictly alternative approaches and may need to be considered together under some instances. The Court held that by failing to give due regard to countervailing evidence presented by Pfizer and Flynn, the CMA had failed its duty of good administration and failed to discharge its burden of proof.[607] The Court cautioned that the authority cannot

[597] *Flynn Pharma Ltd. v. Competition and Markets Authority and Pfizer Inc. v. Competition and Markets Authority* [2018] CAT 11, para. 52.
[598] ibid paras 291–294.
[599] ibid paras 318–325.
[600] ibid paras 411–412.
[601] ibid paras 379–386.
[602] ibid para 404.
[603] ibid para 345.
[604] ibid para 439.
[605] *Competition and Markets Authority v. Flynn Pharma Ltd. and Another* [2020] EWCA Civ 339, para 202.
[606] ibid para 253.
[607] ibid para 260.

bury its head in the sand and ignore countervailing evidence that suggested that the price was fair.[608]

Green LJ specifically referred to the CJEU's judgment in *Intel v. Commission* for the notion that 'if an undertaking adduces evidence of a type unlike that which the competition authority relies upon to establish an abuse then the authority is under a duty to consider that evidence'.[609] Mindful of the possible implications of the judgments, which may require the CMA to consider every possible counter-argument and every possible piece of countervailing evidence, Vos LJ asserted that

> [t]he CMA does not have any duty actively to investigate in every case, in the sense of obtaining evidence about, any comparators put forward by the undertakings... it has a considerable margin of manoeuvre and it may decide how it wishes to deal with comparators put forward by an undertaking. If it rejects comparators wrongly or without giving appropriate reasons, its infringement decision will be more vulnerable, if and when the matter comes before the CAT on appeal.[610]

Another important clarification by the Court of Appeal was that the CAT was wrong in suggesting that the CMA should have considered other hypothetical benchmarks for excessiveness than the 6 per cent rate of return. The Court of Appeal reiterated that the CMA had a 'margin of manoeuvre' in deciding how to construct its case and it can choose among a variety of methods to demonstrate excessiveness. The Court, however, endorsed the CAT's criticism of the CMA's decision that the CMA had failed to consider alternative means of assessing the economic value of the drug beyond the reasonable rate of return approach and had failed to give due regard to patient benefits in determining such value.[611]

While the Court of Appeal's decision fell short of a resounding victory for the CMA, it at least clarified some important issues and affirmed that the CMA need not consider every possible approach to establish excessiveness and unfairness. By requiring such a comprehensive and exhaustive analysis of both prongs under the *United Brands* two-part test, the CAT's approach would have effectively eliminated excessive pricing as an enforcement option. Faced with such an exacting standard of proof, one cannot imagine any authority venturing down the route of bringing an excessive pricing case. The CAT's approach would have effectively required the CMA to prove excessiveness using both a price–cost test and ascertaining the economic value of the drug with reference to some non-cost related factors such as patient benefits, and to prove unfairness applying both the inherent unfairness test and a comparative approach. One cannot help but think that the

[608] ibid para 116.
[609] ibid para 89.
[610] ibid para 270.
[611] ibid para 172.

CAT was motivated by an ideological aversion to excessive pricing enforcement and price regulation in general to erect practically insurmountable hurdles to an excessive pricing claim. As the former Director General of DG Competition Johannes Laitenberger observed, the standard laid down by the CAT went much further than what was required in the case law.[612]

In no other kind of competition law claim is the authority required to present multiple theories, or perhaps every possible theory, of harm and successfully demonstrate harm under each of them in order to prevail. There is no reason why excessive pricing should be singled out for such a stringent standard, at least not in the context of excessive drug prices in developing countries. While the industrialized economies may be concerned about the deterrent effect on investment due to excessive pricing enforcement and may prefer to make proof of an excessive pricing claim as difficult as possible, most developing countries apart from the middle-income ones with a large domestic market need not share such a concern. By affirming the authority's right to choose the appropriate analytical approach, the Court of Appeal has laid down a framework that is much more realistic for developing country authorities.

There is, however, some ambiguity still in the Court of Appeal's approach. While the Court was right in ruling that the authority has a duty to consider countervailing evidence, the burden to rebut countervailing evidence should fall short of full satisfaction of an alternative test. It is one thing to expect the CMA to show that the phenytoin sodium tablets are not equivalent to the capsules, it is quite another to require it to demonstrate unfairness under a full comparative analysis. The Court of Appeal was careful to limit its admonition of the CMA to failure to address countervailing evidence. The CMA should be obliged to go no further than that.

The Court of Appeal indicates that the inquiry about excessiveness is ultimately about the economic value of the product. While this may be a valid observation in theory, it is practically impossible to determine the inherent economic value of a product. The economic value of a product is what consumers are willing to pay for it. Jones and Stothers observe in the context of the *Pfizer/Flynn* case that

> [o]ne complication with this obligation is that, arguably, if the economic value of the product is simply what the buyer is willing to pay for it, then pushed to its logical conclusion a finding of excessive pricing seems difficult to make in any case where the buyer has actually bought the product (it might define excessive prices under competition law out of existence).[613]

[612] Johannes Laitenberger, 'Competition Assessments and Abuse of Dominance: Remarks on the Two Themes of the EUI Competition Workshop' (2018) <http://ec.europa.eu/competition/speeches/text/ sp201 8_1 en.pdf> accessed 28 August 2018.

[613] Jones and Stothers (n 455) 25.

There are no scientific and reliable ways to determine the economic value of a product aside from the consumers' willingness to pay. It is time for the authorities and the courts to stop insisting on a proof of such a value as part of the excessiveness test.

Furthermore, the concept of economic value is an especially dangerous one when applied in the context of pharmaceuticals, as it necessarily implicates the value of good health or even human life. One must wonder whether it is right to allow the pharmaceutical manufacturers to extract the full value that patients place on their good health or their lives. An affirmative answer to this question would mean that these manufacturers should be allowed to charge hundreds of thousands if not millions for life-saving drugs such as ARVs for HIV/AIDS and anti-cancer drugs. Based on the assumptions that the value of statistical life year is USD100,000 and the ARVs have benefited 1.5 million patients, the total economic value of ARVs would be in the vicinity of USD750 billion.[614] This value would exceed USD1 trillion once future patients are taken into account.[615]

In contrast, the lifetime profits for ARVs were estimated to be about USD56 billion, or 5 per cent of their overall economic value.[616] If the ARV manufacturers had been allowed to capture the full economic value of their drugs, they could have raised the prices of their drugs by twenty times without falling foul of a prohibition of excessive pricing. If the current price of a particular ARV is USD10,000 a year, the manufacturer would be allowed to charge USD200,000 for this drug annually. Allowing pharmaceutical manufacturers to capture the full economic value of their drugs technically would mean that consumers would be indifferent between paying for the drug and live and forgoing the drug and die. Not even the most ardent defenders for the pharmaceutical industry would countenance such a position.

Pfizer/Flynn should have been a straightforward case. The case involved a deliberate scheme to exploit a regulatory loophole to raise prices by more than 2000 per cent. A 2000 per cent price increase would surpass any reasonable threshold for excessiveness. No additional showing should have been required of the CMA. The burden should have shifted to Pfizer and Flynn to justify their price increases. Developing countries may want to reconsider whether they want to emulate the EU approach and require a showing of unfairness in an excessive pricing claim. The language of Article 102(a) may necessitate such a requirement. But developing countries need not follow that. In any case, if there was ever a textbook definition of unfairness, the blatant exploitation of a regulatory loophole by way of a phony transaction to take advantage of consumers to the tunes of a 2000 per cent price

[614] JP Sevilla, 'On the Potential Impact of Value Pricing by Developing Countries on Allocative and Dynamic Efficiency in the Global Pharmaceutical Industry' (2016) 12 Journal of Law, Economics & Policy 147, 169.

[615] ibid.

[616] ibid.

increase should come close to it. A twenty-five-fold increase in annual expenditure by the NHS should seal the case. While an impressionistic survey seems to suggest that cases involving such dramatic price hikes tend to concentrate in the industrialized economies, developing country authorities should adopt a hard line against them if they are ever found in developing countries. Excessive pricing does not come more blatant and exploitative than this.

3. Developing Countries

One notable excessive pricing case from a developing country is the Mittal-Harmony case from South Africa. Mittal, a steel producer, was accused of excessive pricing by imposing import parity prices on its domestic customers, which means that Mittal would sell steel products to its domestic customers charging international shipment costs even though domestically produced steel products incur no such costs.[617]

Section 8(a) of the South African Competition Act, which governs excessive pricing claims, was clearly inspired by *United Brands*.[618] It states that '[i]t is prohibited for a dominant firm to (a) charge an excessive price to the detriment of consumers',[619] where an excessive price is defined as 'a price for a good or service which, (aa) bears no reasonable relation to the economic value of that good or service; and (bb) is higher than the value referred to in subparagraph (aa)'.[620] Claudio Calcagno and Mike Walker explain the market in which Mittal operates as follows:

> Mittal faced a kinked demand curve, with the kink at the price of imports. Above IPPs [import parity prices], Mittal faced highly elastic demand, as domestic consumers could substitute imports for purchasing from Mittal. Below IPPs, domestic consumers had a choice only of domestic production from either Mittal or Mittal's sole domestic rival, Highveld Steel and Vanadium Corporation. The limited choice for steel inputs priced below IPPs made the demand curve facing Mittal below IPPs less elastic than demand above IPPs.[621]

In light of these facts, Calcagno and Walker express scepticism about the plaintiff's claims. They assert that 'the ability to price above the marginal cost for domestic sales does not mean that the firm has market power in a sense that is relevant to antitrust analysis. It certainly does not say anything about whether prices are excessive or not.'[622]

[617] Calcagno and Walker (n 434) 893.
[618] ibid.
[619] Competition Act 1998 (SA), s 8(a).
[620] ibid s 1(1)(vii).
[621] Calcagno and Walker (n 434) 897–98.
[622] ibid 899–900.

The Competition Tribunal upheld the excessive pricing claim. The Tribunal rejected profitability analysis and international price comparisons as regulatory approaches and deemed them not suitable for a competition authority.[623] Instead, the Tribunal opted for a structural approach.[624] Rather than trying to determine directly whether a price is excessive in relation to costs or some comparator prices, the Tribunal chose to rely on structural indicators that suggest that the defendant has the power to impose an excessive price. The Tribunal observed that Mittal was super-dominant in the South African market, with over 80 per cent market share.[625] The domestic steel market was protected by such high barriers to entry that there was no prospect of market entry even in response to excessive pricing.[626] The Tribunal describes the structural approach as follows:

> the judgement then that we are required to make is not of the price level itself but rather of the market conditions that generated the price level. In other words, we must ask ourselves whether the relevant market in question is capable of functioning in a manner that is likely to produce a reasonable relationship of price to economic value, or rather, whether the structure of the market and, conceivably, ancillary conduct that depends on that anti-competitive structure, forestalls the effective functioning of the market... thus generating a price, the level of which, is unrelated to, is not influenced by, any cognizable competition considerations.[627]

The Tribunal concluded that Mittal's prices were not influenced by 'cognisable competition considerations' and could be considered excessive in light of its super-dominant position and high entry barriers to the market.[628]

The Competition Appeal Court (CAC) rejected the Tribunal's structural approach. The CAC insisted that the Tribunal must follow the statutory language and determine whether the price bears no reasonable relation to the economic value of the good.[629] The CAC acknowledged that there are different approaches for determining the excessiveness of prices, but profitability analysis is the standard approach.[630] The CAC argued that having established the economic value of the product, it was still necessary to determine whether the actual price bore a reasonable relation to the value.[631]

[623] *Harmony Gold Mining Company Ltd. & Another and Mittal Steel South Africa Ltd. and Another* [2007] ZACT 21 (SA 2007), para 89.
[624] ibid.
[625] ibid paras 109–110.
[626] ibid para 121.
[627] ibid para 142.
[628] ibid para 147.
[629] *Mittal Steel South Africa Limited and Others v. Harmony Gold Mining Company Limited and Another* [2009] ZACAC 1 (SA 2009), para 49.
[630] ibid paras 50–51.
[631] ibid para 77.

Calcagno and Walker criticize the Tribunal's decision on a number of grounds. First, they observe that the Tribunal's reasoning leads to the absurd situation where Mittal's prices are more likely to be deemed excessive as they become lower, as lower prices would increase its market share.[632] Second, they fault the Tribunal's structural approach as circular logic because the essence of market power is the ability to price above competitive level. Having used an indirect structural approach to determine market dominance, the Tribunal then used the same structural factors to conclude that pricing must be excessive.[633] Third, they argue that what Mittal practiced was price discrimination, which can be pro-competitive and certainly does not constitute evidence of market power.[634]

The Tribunal was correct to observe that excessive pricing would only be possible if the defendant had a great deal of market power, which the Tribunal called super dominance. It is, however, probably not correct to assume that every super-dominant firm charges excessive prices. Super dominance is a necessary but probably insufficient condition for establishing excessive pricing. The lack of super dominance can refute excessive pricing, but the presence of super dominance cannot be equated to such pricing. Although one can argue that it is only economically rational for every super-dominant firm to charge the maximum price that the market can bear, which for such a firm may be an excessive price, given the gravity of a competition law violation, it cannot be established based on an assumption of economic rationality alone. Super dominance should probably only be used as a screen to eliminate implausible cases from consideration.

A number of complaints have been lodged with the South African Competition Commission (SACC) in the early 2000s over alleged anticompetitive conduct concerning ARVs. One such complaint that did not lead to full proceedings but nonetheless to a satisfactory outcome was that by Treatment Action Campaign (TAC) against GlaxoSmithKline (GSK) and Boehringer Ingelheim (BI) in 2002. In September 2002, TAC, a South African NGO focusing on affordable access to medicine in developing countries, filed a complaint with the SACC against GSK and BI over their business conduct.

In October 2003, the SACC issued a press release announcing that it had decided to refer the matter to the Competition Tribunal.[635] In particular, the SACC concluded that the two firms had engaged in denial of access to an essential facility to a competitor, excessive pricing, and an exclusionary act 'that [has] an anticompetitive effect that outweighs technological, efficiency or other pro-competitive gains'.[636] Commissioner Menzi Simelane observed that '[o]ur investigation

[632] Calcagno and Walker (n 434) 904–05.
[633] ibid 905.
[634] ibid.
[635] South African Competition Commission, 'Competition Commission Finds Pharmaceutical Firms in Contravention of the Competition Act' <http://www.cptech.org/ip/health/sa/cc10162003.html> accessed 23 April 2021.
[636] ibid.

revealed that each of the firms has refused to license their patents to generic manufacturers in return for a reasonable royalty. We believe that this is feasible and that consumers will benefit from cheaper generic versions of the drugs concerned.'[637]

Settlement negotiations had begun prior to the Commission announcement. By December 2003, both GSK and BI had settled the complainant with the SACC, agreeing to allow multiple non-exclusive and low-royalty licences for the production, importation, and sale of the ARVs by generic companies in South Africa.[638] While this was a welcome development for patients in South Africa, an opportunity was missed for the Competition Tribunal to develop its jurisprudence on excessive pricing and the essential facilities doctrine in the context of pharmaceuticals.

The Competition Commission of India (CCI) is another developing country competition authority to have been confronted with an excessive pricing claim. Both cases have arisen in the pharmaceutical sector and the CCI seems to be ambivalent about excessive pricing claims thus far. In *Biocon Limited v. F. Hoffmann-La Roche AG*, the CCI rejected an allegation of excessive pricing of the anti-cancer drug Trastuzumab on the grounds that the price increase was justified by the huge R&D costs incurred by the developer of the drug.[639]

In *In Re Vivek Sharma v. Becton Dickinson India (P) Ltd.*, the CCI was much more receptive to the claim. The complainant alleged that Max Super Speciality Hospital overcharged him for disposable syringes.[640] The hospital's price was almost twice as high as the open market price.[641] In a 2015 order directing the Director General (DG) of the CCI to open an investigation, the CCI was persuaded that the complainant was charged a higher price than in the open market and that this high price was the result of the hospital's patients being captive customers upon admission to the hospital.[642] The CCI was convinced that the syringes sold at the hospital were of the same quality and design as the ones sold in the open market.[643]

In a 2018 judgment directing the DG to conduct further investigation, the CCI noted that the hospital made a profit between 277 per cent and 527 per cent in the financial year 2015–16 from the sale of syringes.[644] Furthermore, the CCI suggested that the excessive pricing claim be investigated as an aftermarket abuse. The

[637] ibid.

[638] South African Competition Commission, 'Competition Commission Concludes an Agreement with Pharmaceutical Firms' <http://www.cptech.org/ip/health/sa/cc12102003.html> accessed 23 April 2021.

[639] Anshuman Sakle, 'Excessive Pricing: A Neglected Antitrust Concept?' (*Competition Law: A Cyril Amarchand Mangaldas Blog*, 6 December 2017) <https://competition.cyrilamarchandblogs.com/2017/12/excessive-pricing-neglected-antitrust-concept/> accessed 21 April 2021.

[640] Case No 77 of 2015, *Vivek Sharma v. Becton Dickinson India (P) Ltd. & Max Super Speciality Hospital* CCI Order 17 November 2015, para 4.

[641] ibid para 11.

[642] ibid.

[643] ibid.

[644] Case No 77 of 2015, *Vivek Sharma v. Becton Dickinson India (P) Ltd. & Max Super Speciality Hospital* CCI Judgment 31 August 2018, para 7.

CCI alluded to 'a locked-in effect for a patient which may enable [the hospital] to exercise its dominance over its in patients',[645] which is exacerbated by the hospital's requirement that its patients can only purchase medical supplies from its in-house pharmacy. The CCI noted that lock-in means that 'patients do not hold any countervailing buying power and they are completely dependent on OP-2 [the hospital]. Such a conduct may be considered as an aftermarket abuse even if OP-2 is found to be not dominant in the primary market for the provision of healthcare services in Delhi.'[646] The excessive pricing claim has arguably morphed into a tying claim. The parallel between the CCI's theory of harm and the reasoning of the US Supreme Court in the *Kodak* case is unmistakable.

The DG had relied on the hospital's profit margins on the syringes to establish an abuse of excessive pricing. The CCI deemed the scope of the evidence too narrow and directed the DG to look into the hospital's absolute total profits from 'the after-market products which are not required on an urgent basis for any medical procedure or which do not involve any high degree of quality issue from the medical procedure point of view'[647] such as medicines and surgical tools. The CCI suggested that it may constitute an abuse of dominance for a hospital to charge its locked-in in-patients supra-competitive prices for consumable medical supplies and observed that '[i]t is common knowledge that this practice of exploitative pricing from the locked-in patients is followed with impunity by most of the hospitals'.[648] If these two cases are any indication of CCI's attitude toward excessive pricing, it seems that the CCI is more sympathetic toward exploitation of locked-in customers than customers in an open market for primary products.

F. A Proposed Framework for Developing Countries

1. The Case for Intervention Against Excessive Drug Prices in Developing Countries

Despite admonitions by commentators against excessive pricing enforcement, there is probably no other industry where the case for intervention is stronger than in the pharmaceutical industry. The public health implications of excessive drug prices are enormous. The denial of affordable drugs could cost thousands if not millions of lives. At the very least, it results in significantly lower quality of life and reduced capacity to learn, which could have serious implications for lifelong earning potential. The problem of unaffordable drugs was extensively documented

[645] ibid para 8.
[646] ibid para 8.
[647] ibid para 9.
[648] ibid para 10.

in section B1. It is a serious problem afflicting many developing countries. While it is true that excessive pricing enforcement would not resolve the problem completely—there is some truth to Attaran's assertion that the ultimate culprit is poverty—it does not mean that the problem cannot be alleviated, however so slightly, by reduced drug prices. Given that developing country public health authorities only have a limited budget, reduced drug prices will increase the supply of essential drugs to the public. Competition law enforcement is not the panacea. But together with other policy interventions such as more effective drug price control and measures adopted under the various exemptions provided by the TRIPS Agreement, excessive pricing enforcement can make some useful contribution to the problem. The consequences of inaction are too great for competition law to stand idly by.

A number of objections have been raised against excessive pricing enforcement, some specifically in relation to the pharmaceutical industry. First and foremost, it is argued that excessive pricing enforcement will reduce the patentee reward and hence the financial incentives available to potential innovators. It was illustrated earlier that the multinational pharmaceutical manufacturers derive the vast majority of their profits from the industrialized economies and perhaps a handful of middle-income countries with large domestic markets. For most small developing countries, their contribution to the global innovation incentive calculus of these manufacturers will be negligible. It is difficult to imagine that the R&D effort for a major innovative drug would collapse because the manufacturer is deprived of the profits from a small sub-Saharan or Andean country. As Dina Halajian observes, '[b]ecause the majority of sales occur in developed countries, lower prices in developing countries will not be a significant burden on profits. Such reduced profits should be considered as "additional" profits that otherwise would not exist, instead of being negatively viewed as "reduced" profits.'[649] In contrast, middle-income countries with a large domestic market may need to proceed more cautiously with excessive pricing enforcement.

Second, it is contended that excessive pricing enforcement is a distortion of the free market, which should be kept to a minimum, especially in many developing countries where the free market is nowhere near as entrenched as in the industrialized economies. This may be true in many industries which are not subject to any distortions and market forces are allowed a free rein. As Abbott asserts, however,

> no market is 'less free' than the pharmaceutical market. It is regulated every step of the way, except in the United States with respect to prices. It is somewhat odd to argue that patent owners protected by legislative monopolies are pricing in a freely competitive market. It is obvious that they are not.

[649] Halajian (n 15) 1227.

Arguably, the truly free market devoid of government distortions would be one in which there is no patent protection but no price regulation of any kind. The conventional wisdom, however, is that the pharmaceutical industry would collapse in such a market.

Having benefited from government-created market power, the pharmaceutical manufacturers cannot be heard to complain about distortion of the free market. Advocate General Wahl concurs, asserting that 'unfair prices under Article 102 TFEU can only exist in regulated markets, where the public authorities exert some form of control over the forces of supply and, consequently, the scope for free and open competition is reduced'.[650] Patent protection certainly constitutes some form of control over the forces of supply. The existence of patent protection provides an additional reason for excessive pricing enforcement.

Third, one further counter-argument against excessive pricing enforcement is that competition law intervention should only be a last resort and that other policy measures such as direct price regulation by the public health authority or solutions internal to patent law should be preferred. The cases of *Napp*, *Aspen*, and *Pfizer/Flynn* firmly suggest that it is unrealistic to expect a regulatory regime to anticipate and forestall all sorts of excessive pricing problems. In all three cases, the existence of price regulation did not prevent the pharmaceutical manufacturers from exploiting a loophole in the regulatory regime to raise prices to an astronomical level. Every regulatory regime has its limits and the pharmaceutical companies have proven themselves very adept at exploiting these loopholes, as evidenced by the slew of cases across the Atlantic involving reverse payments,[651] the cases in the US involving citizen petitions and REMS,[652] and the excessive pricing cases in the European Union mentioned above.

As Commissioner Vestager said in 2016,

> there can be times when prices get so high that they just can't be justified... The best answer is often to adjust regulation, or to give the health systems that buy those medicines better bargaining power. But as the recent action by the British and Italian competition authorities shows, there can be times when competition rules need to do their bit to deal with excessive prices.[653]

This is especially true for developing countries, which generally have lower regulatory capacity than the industrialized economies. If the United Kingdom and

[650] *AKKA/LAA AG Opinion*, para 48.

[651] *Federal Trade Commission v. Actavis, Inc.*, 570 US 136 (2013). Case T-472/13, *H. Lundbeck A/S and Lundbeck Ltd. v. European Commission* [2016] EU:T:2016:449.

[652] Michael A Carrier, 'Five Actions to Stop Citizen Petition Abuse' (2018) 118 Columbia Law Review Online 81; Tyler A Garrett, 'Anticompetitive Manipulation of REMS: A New Exception to Antitrust Refusal-to-Deal Doctrine' (2018) 60 William & Mary Law Review 655.

[653] Vestager (n 461).

Italy cannot put in place a fool-proof price regulatory regime for drugs, there is little hope for countries such as Mozambique and Zimbabwe.

Lastly, implementation difficulties are often mentioned as an insurmountable hurdle for excessive pricing enforcement, especially for the low-enforcement capacity authorities in developing countries. Many commentators have noted the difficulty with a determination of excessiveness and the imperative to minimize false positives. Advocate General Wahl went so far as proposing the use of multiple tests for excessiveness. There is no question that a definitive proof of excessiveness is challenging, no less because the theoretically sound definition of excessiveness is unquantifiable and unimplementable in reality and other means to demonstrate excessiveness all suffer from their own infirmities. The competitive price for a product is essentially unmeasurable and the economic value of a product is whatever price consumers are willing to pay and producers are willing to sell at. In other words, it is the prevailing market price. Any kind of comparative analysis is susceptible to challenges concerning the suitability of the comparator. Given that no two firms and no two markets are identical, it is always possible to identify some differences that may undermine the validity of the comparison.

Here it is again important not to let the best be the enemy of the good. There is no reason to abandon efforts that may provide valuable help to poor patients in developing countries simply because the competition authority may get it wrong sometimes. False positives are costly if they have a severe impact on innovation incentives. They are less consequential, however, if the benefits of lower drug prices are overwhelming and their impact on innovation incentives is minimal, which would be the case if the patentee reward generated in most developing countries is treated as additional profits that otherwise would not exist, as Halajian asserts. There are hence no good reasons for a developing country authority to insist on multiple tests to establish excessiveness. One test, when administered properly, should suffice. The burden should then shift to the defendant to justify its high prices or price increases.

Detailed formulation of the test will be left to the next section. The main message here is that implementation difficulties can be effectively managed taking into account the development needs of developing countries and the enforcement capacity of their competition authorities. The only exception is middle-income countries with large domestic markets. These countries may have a genuine impact on the innovation incentives of the multinational pharmaceutical manufacturers. While that does not necessarily mean that these countries need to adopt multiple tests for excessiveness or reinstitute a requirement of unfairness, they may need to proceed with extra care. They may want to opt for a higher threshold for excessiveness or be more amenable to justifications for excessive prices.

2. Test for Excessiveness

Given that the European Union has a long line of jurisprudence on excessive pricing, its case law serves as a good starting point for developing countries to construct their approach to excessive pricing. This, however, does not mean that developing countries should copy the EU approach wholesale. There are two features in the EU approach that should be jettisoned. The first is the notion of economic value. Although the case law has not been entirely clear on the proper role or function of this concept—the concept has appeared in both prongs of the *United Brands* two-part test—it creeps in whenever the courts perceive the need to provide greater clarity in the analysis. The result is invariably counter-productive as it is close to impossible to give any concrete meaning to the term apart from the price determined by the interplay of demand and supply. As a number of commentators have noted, when pushed to its logical conclusion, the application of the concept simply means the evisceration of excessive pricing enforcement. This, together with its inability to elucidate the analysis, means that this concept should have no place in a well-constructed framework for analysing excessive pricing.

The second is the bifurcated analytical structure in the two-part test. *United Brands* holds that it is necessary to establish both the excessiveness and the unfairness of a price. As mentioned earlier, this is due to the language of Article 102(a), which does not directly prohibit excessive pricing but only proscribes unfair pricing. But as Motta and de Streel argue, the second prong of the two-part test adds nothing but confusion to the analysis. After decades of application, there is still no consensus on the precise content of the notion of inherent unfairness. And the comparative approach arguably conflates the issue of excessiveness with unfairness. The fact that a price exceeds the price of comparable products should be more relevant to the question of excessiveness than to unfairness. Akman and Garrod defend the retention of the second prong, but only on the grounds that it is required by the case law.

Developing countries are obviously not bound by the EU case law, and therefore should not slavishly copy the two-part test. If the prohibition is against excessive pricing, a showing of excessiveness should suffice. An illustration of unfairness, whatever that is supposed to mean, adds nothing to the analysis, unless it is meant to provide defendants with an opportunity to justify the high price or price increase. But if the purpose is to invite justifications, subsuming it under the heading of unfairness only obfuscates the inquiry. A better approach would be to create a second step in the analysis that expressly calls for justifications.

The crux of the analysis in an excessive pricing claim is understandably a determination of excessiveness. Many approaches have been proposed for this purpose, including a price–cost comparison, a comparison with the firm's own prices in the past, thereby implicitly focusing on sudden price hikes, a cross-country comparison with the same product, and a comparison with a competitor's product in the same or a similar market. As argued earlier, two of them, price–cost comparison and comparison with a competitor's prices, can be readily disposed. A price–cost comparison suffers from practically insurmountable difficulties in the context of the pharmaceutical industry, given the general unavailability of data on R&D costs and the need to account for the R&D costs of failed projects. There is no principled way to apportion the costs of these failed projects to successful products. Any allocation of such costs will be necessarily arbitrary and will be surely subject to challenge in court. If the reviewing courts apply a level of scrutiny anywhere near that applied by the CAT in *Pfizer/Flynn*, there is a very significant chance that such a challenge will torpedo the entire excessive pricing claim.

A comparison with a competitor's prices is feasible theoretically. The reason for abandoning it is because developing countries should only seek to enforce excessive pricing against drugs for which there are no effective therapeutic substitutes. In other words, the defendant should hold a super-dominant position in the market. This is both a concession to those commentators who have laid down stringent preconditions for excessive pricing enforcement, and a recognition that a simplified test for excessiveness requires mitigation of risks of false positives. These risks can be best minimized by requiring super-dominance on the part of the defendant. The discussion of the South African Competition Tribunal's structural approach in the *Mittal-Harmony* case indicates that while super dominance should not replace a test for excessiveness, it can certainly be used to supplement such a test to screen out false positive cases. If the insight is that only super-dominant firms can impose excessive prices, excessive pricing claims should only be brought against these firms. Such claims should be barred in the absence of super dominance. While it is erroneous to assume that super-dominant firms must charge excessive prices, having screened out firms that are incapable of imposing such prices, we are in a position to adopt slightly less stringent tests for excessiveness.

The remaining two tests of excessiveness focus the attention on sudden price hikes and reverse price discrimination. Intervention against these two subcategories of excessive prices is both easier to implement and more justified as a matter of policy. A comparison with the firm's own prices has the advantage that most market conditions can be presumed to have remained the same. The comparison will be less susceptible to challenges based on differences between the two comparators. Any identified difference will not immediately undermine the validity of the comparison. It will instead shed light on reasons for the price increase. Once the authority can demonstrate a sudden price increase beyond a certain threshold, the burden should shift to the defendant to point to any sudden and substantial changes in market conditions that would justify such a price hike. This position is supported by commentators. Harry First has argued that sudden price hikes are a prime target for intervention.[654] Akman and Garrod have suggested

[654] First (n 403) 738–39.

that scrutiny of sudden price increases is most consistent with their principle of dual entitlement.[655]

A cross-country price comparison will help to verify the existence of reverse price discrimination. As was previously argued, there are no reasons for developing countries to condone such discrimination, as it both defies economic logic and has serious public health implications. And if the purpose is to demonstrate the existence of such discrimination, the magnitude of the difference between the two prices becomes less important. Any kind of price difference in favour of industrialized economy consumers is problematic from a developing country's perspective and justifies intervention. This does not mean that an excessive pricing claim based on reverse price discrimination can be established by a showing that the drug is cheaper in one industrialized economy than the developing country at issue. What needs to be shown is that the drug is cheaper in a significant number of industrialized economy by a non-trivial amount for a non-transitory period of time.

The precise number of countries where this needs to be shown would vary with the facts of the case. One would imagine that five to ten countries should suffice in most instances. The larger are the industrialized economies in the sample, probably the smaller number of them is needed. It was previously suggested that an excess of over 20 per cent for a year would suffice. It is important, however, to ensure that the cheaper prices in the industrialized economies chosen are not due to price regulation. The pharmaceutical manufacturer cannot be faulted for reverse price discrimination if the more favourable prices in the industrialized economies are due to government compulsion. Under both tests for excessiveness, the threshold for excessiveness will need to be heightened in middle-income countries with large domestic markets to minimize the risks of false positives.

Once the test for excessiveness is satisfied, the burden shifts to the defendant to justify the sudden price hike or the higher prices charged in a particular developing country. Possible justifications run the gamut, from a sudden increase in production costs to higher tariffs or distribution costs in the country. It is impossible to list all of them here. The competition authority will need to exercise its judgment to scrutinize the proffered justifications. If the proffered justification adequately explains the excessive price, the claim should be dismissed. Otherwise, the claim should be upheld.

One of the arguments against excessive pricing enforcement is the difficulty in fashioning an appropriate remedy. Direct price regulation would require the competition authority to set a price for the product, which most competition authorities are understandably reluctant to do. This implementation problem, however, need not concern us because the recommended remedy for excessive pricing of pharmaceuticals is compulsory licensing. This effectively allows the authority to sidestep

[655] Akman and Garrod (n 426) 412–13.

the challenges of direct price regulation. If there is domestic manufacturing capacity, the license should be issued to domestic manufacturers. If such capacity is absent, it will have to be issued to allow import of the drug concerned. The issue of a compulsory license under these circumstances will still need to comply with the various requirements of Article 31 of the TRIPS Agreement. Where these requirements are too onerous to provide an effective remedy for a developing country, direct price regulation may be necessary.

G. Conclusion

This chapter introduces the dire situation facing developing countries in terms of access to affordable drugs. It concludes that patent protection for pharmaceuticals is partly to blame for the unaffordable prices of many essential medicines. It also highlights the phenomenon of reverse price discrimination, under which developing country consumers often pay much higher prices for the same drug than industrialized economy patients. Both high drug prices in general and reverse price discrimination in particular call for policy intervention by developing countries. It then surveys the various possible mechanisms under the TRIPS Agreement for intervention and concludes that none of them provides a comprehensive and effective solution. It suggests that developing countries should turn to excessive pricing enforcement to target at least two types of situation, sudden and massive price hikes and reverse price discrimination. While it acknowledges that excessive pricing enforcement is unlikely to be the panacea for drug affordability in developing countries, it can nonetheless provide limited but valuable assistance. Developing country competition authorities should give it some serious consideration.

9
Reverse Payment Settlements

A. Introduction

Excessive pricing by pharmaceutical companies is not the only concern for developing country competition authorities keen on ensuring affordable drug prices for their domestic consumers. Another type of conduct that has captured the attention of competition authorities in established jurisdictions in recent years is reverse payment settlements between manufacturers of branded drugs and generic manufacturers to secure the latter's agreement to stay out of the market.

B. An Overview of Reverse Payment Settlements

Reverse payment settlements began to emerge in the United States in the early 2000s and soon became an enforcement focus of the US Federal Trade Commission (FTC). The FTC, however, was not initially successful in its effort, suffering a string of defeats at the appellate level, culminating in the *Schering-Plough* case, where the US Court of Appeals for the Eleventh Circuit held that a patent settlement is legal so long as it is within the scope of the patentee's rights.[1] This means that a settlement agreement that does not extend beyond the patent term is effectively *per se* legal. Soon after this loss the FTC began to roll back its enforcement against reverse payment settlements, which then quickly proliferated.[2] The FTC's fortune did not turn until the *Actavis* case in 2013, in which the US Supreme Court overturned the permissive approach adopted by the Eleventh Circuit and promulgated a Rule of Reason for reverse payment settlements under US antitrust law.

For a while, reverse payment settlements seemed to be a phenomenon unique to the United States. Commentators argue that reverse payments are the consequence of the peculiar regulatory design of the Hatch–Waxman Act, which enacts a complex scheme to facilitate generic entry while striking a delicate balance between the commercial interests of branded manufacturers and generics.[3] It turns out

[1] *Schering-Plough Corp. v. Federal Trade Commission*, 420 F.3d 1056 (11th Cir. 2005).

[2] Michael A Carrier, 'Unsettling Drug Patent Settlements: A Framework for Presumptive Illegality' (2009) 108 Michigan Law Review 37, 51.

[3] Michael A Carrier, 'A Response to Chief Justice Roberts: Why Antitrust Must Play a Role in the Analysis of Drug Patent Settlements' (2014) 15 Minnesota Journal of Law, Science & Technology 31, 38–39; Thomas F Cotter, 'Antitrust Implications of Patent Settlements Involving Reverse Payments: Defending a Rebuttable Presumption of Illegality in Light of Some Recent Scholarship'

The Patent–Competition Interface in Developing Countries. Thomas K. Cheng, Oxford University Press. © Thomas K. Cheng 2021. DOI: 10.1093/oso/9780192857354.003.0009

that this allegation of American exceptionalism was unfound. By the early 2010s, the European Commission began to turn its attention to them, first by issuing a sectoral study of the pharmaceutical industry and subsequently by bringing enforcement action. The first decision against the Danish branded pharmaceutical manufacturer Lundbeck was adopted in June 2013.[4] A year later in July 2014, the Commission issued another decision against the French branded manufacturer Servier and five other generic producers for entering into anticompetitive settlement agreements to forestall generic entry into the market for Servier's bestselling hypertension medication.[5] Appeal against the Commission's decisions is still making its way through the European courts.

The General Court thus far has sided with the Commission. In early 2020, the Court of Justice of the European Union (CJEU) issued a decision in a preliminary ruling from the UK Competition Appeal Tribunal which took a fairly hard line against reverse payment settlements.[6] If the *Generics (UK)* case is any indication, the approach to reverse payments under EU competition law is unlikely to be more lenient than under US antitrust law. This seems to have been affirmed by the recent dismissal by the CJEU of all appeals against the General Court's judgment in *Lundbeck*.[7] In more recent years, reverse payment settlements have also received attention in other jurisdictions such as Australia.[8]

Developing country competition authorities need to fashion an appropriate approach for reverse payment settlements in the pharmaceutical industry. Do these settlements inflict significant consumer harm with a sufficient degree of likelihood that a hard-line approach such as presumptive or even *per se* illegality is called for, or are there mitigating circumstances and sufficient uncertainty regarding the competitive effects of these settlements that a more circumspect attitude is needed? The choice of legal standard must also be made in light of the enforcement capacity of developing country authorities and courts. One of the

(2004) 71 Antitrust Law Journal 1069, 1076–80; Scott Hemphill, 'Paying for Delay: Pharmaceutical Patent Settlement as a Regulatory Design Problem' (2006) 81 New York University Law Review 1553, 1560; Herbert J Hovenkamp, 'Anticompetitive Patent Settlements and the Supreme Court's Actavis Decision' (2014) 15 Minnesota Journal of Law, Science & Technology 3, 14, 16.

4 Damien Geradin, Douglas Ginsburg, and Graham Safty, 'Reverse Payment Patent Settlements in the European Union and the United States' (George Mason University 2015) 15–38 20 <ssrn.com/abstract=2662575> accessed 20 June 2021.

5 ibid 22.

6 Tommi Lahtinen, 'Reverse Payment Settlements in the European Union after the Generics (UK) Judgment—Perplexing Legal Uncertainty' (*Lexxion Competition Blogs*, 5 March 2020) <https://www.lexxion.eu/en/coreblogpost/reverse-payment-settlements-in-the-european-union-after-the-generics-uk-judgment-perplexing-legal-uncertainty/> accessed 14 March 2021.

7 Case C-591/16 P, *H. Lundbeck A/S and Lundbeck Ltd. v. European Commission* EU:C:2021:243.

8 Christopher Kew, 'Patently Uncertain: Developments in Pay-For-Delay Agreements in Australia' (*King & Wood Mallesons In Competition*, 11 June 2020) <https://incompetition.com.au/2020/06/patently-uncertain-developments-in-pay-for-delay-agreements-in-australia/> accessed 14 March 2021.

long-running disagreements regarding the legal treatment of reverse payment settlements is the relevance of patent validity. If the legality of these settlements can only be determined after patent validity is adjudicated, developing country authorities and courts would be saddled with a very onerous burden and may rightfully shun reverse payments as being beyond their enforcement capacity. If, however, an assessment of patent validity is unnecessary, developing country authorities would be in a better position to police against anticompetitive reverse payment settlements.

C. Competitive Concerns of Reverse Payment Settlements

Patent settlements can often be pro-competitive.[9] This is especially the case when two parties possess complementary or even blocking patents neither of which can be practised without a license to the other. Such settlements may not involve cash payments; cross-licenses suffice. Reverse payment settlements are different because a large cash payment is involved. The reason these payments are labelled as reverse is because the direction of payment is not what one would expect. In normal patent infringement litigation, the alleged infringer pays the patentee to settle the dispute. In contrast, in a reverse payment settlement, it is the patentee branded manufacturer that pays the generic to stay out of the market.

Some commentators have insisted that there is nothing unusual about this direction of payment.[10] The reason that the alleged infringer does not pay is because at least in the context of a patent infringement dispute under the Hatch–Waxman Act in the United States, the generic has not commenced production and the patentee hence has not suffered any actual damages.[11] The act of infringement is the Paragraph IV certification filed by the generic under the Act.[12] This, however, has not necessarily swayed other commentators, many of whom are persuaded by the highly intuitive anticompetitive account of reverse payments.

[9] Carl Shapiro, 'Antitrust Limits to Patent Settlements' (2003) 34 RAND Journal of Economics 392, 394.

[10] Daniel A Crane, 'Exit Payments in Settlement of Patent Infringement Lawsuits: Antitrust Rules and Economic Implications' (2002) 54 Florida Law Review 747, 767–68, 774–76; Daniel A Crane, 'Actavis, the Reverse Payment Fallacy, and the Continuing Need for Regulatory Solutions' (2014) 15 Minnesota Journal of Law, Science & Technology 51, 55–58; Marc G Schildkraut, 'Patent-Splitting Settlements and the Reverse Payment Fallacy' (2004) 71 Antitrust Law Journal 1033, 1033–35, 1058–60; Cotter (n 3) 1083, 1085.

[11] Schildkraut (n 10) 1036.

[12] Hemphill (n 3) 1566.

1. Economic Incentives

The story goes as follows. If the branded manufacturer's patent was valid, it would be well within its right to exclude the generic from the market. That is the essence of the patent right to exclude. If the branded manufacturer was confident of the validity of its patent, there would be scant reasons for it to offer payments to the generic to stay out of the market. If the patent was in fact invalid or not infringed, or highly likely to be so, the branded manufacturer would be earning a monopoly profit to which it should be not entitled. The branded manufacturer would not be able to stop generics from entering the market and eroding its monopoly profit with an invalid or uninfringed patent. Given that monopoly profit is always greater than duopoly profit between two competing firms, the branded manufacturer would be able to pay the generic entrant a sufficient sum out of its monopoly profit to stay out of the market and still earn more than its share of the duopoly profit if the generic had entered the market.[13] Scott Hemphill calls this the gain-from-trade condition.[14]

The generic would only accept the settlement offer if the payment exceeds its expected profit from market entry.[15] The branded manufacturer can well afford such an offer.[16] The generic manufacturer would be better off accepting the reverse payment from the branded manufacturer than entering the market itself.[17] In fact, this would be the case even if the generic is completely certain about the patent's invalidity[18] or if the generic wins the patent validity challenge.[19] The branded manufacturer would be better off paying the generic than letting the latter enter the market if there is a nonnegligible degree of uncertainty about the patent's validity.[20] By paying the generic, the patentee can delay generic market entry and extend her period of exclusivity beyond what would be justified by the expected odds of litigation.[21] It is only when the branded manufacturer is practically certain about the patent's validity that it will be willing to pay no more than its expected litigation costs to ward off the nuisance of litigation.[22]

That is the reason why many tests proposed by scholars for determining the legality of reverse payments compare the size of the payment with the expected litigation costs.[23] It is recognized that it would be economically rational for the

[13] Cotter (n 3) 1080.
[14] Hemphill (n 3) 1580.
[15] Hovenkamp (n 3) 13.
[16] ibid 8.
[17] ibid.
[18] ibid 13.
[19] Hemphill (n 3) 1581.
[20] Hovenkamp (n 3) 13.
[21] Carrier (n 3) 36.
[22] Hovenkamp (n 3) 13.
[23] Einer Elhauge and Alex Krueger, 'Solving the Patent Settlement Puzzle' (2012) 91 Texas Law Review 283, 305–306. Cotter (n 3) 1082. Hovenkamp (n 3) 5.

patentee to make a settlement offer commensurate with its expected litigation costs even absent any nefarious motives. However, so long as the branded manufacturer is short of being almost certain about the patent's validity, a reverse payment in excess of litigation costs would be economically rational and mutually beneficial.[24]

Einer Elhauge and Alan Krueger underscore the importance of antitrust intervention against reverse payment settlements by noting that

> unless constrained by the risk of antitrust liability, settling parties would (no matter how weak the patent) always have incentives to set the settlement entry date at the end of the patent term because that maximizes joint profits (by precluding competition for as long as possible), and they can use the reverse payment to split those joint profits in a way that leaves both better off.[25]

Murat Mungan concurs on the importance of antitrust intervention to deter anticompetitive reverse payment settlements.[26] Where payments are the only mode of compensation between the branded and the generic manufacturers, the latter would have no incentive to enter the market unless it expects a reverse payment.[27]

Michael Carrier best encapsulates the dynamics of reverse payment settlements when he states that

> [b]y delaying generic entry, the brand firm can increase its monopoly profits. It can then use a portion of these profits to pay the generic more than it would have received by entering the market. From an antitrust perspective, these payments for delay threaten to divide markets, a particularly egregious offense eliminating competition between rivals.[28]

The doubtful validity of the patent and probable non-infringement means that the branded manufacturer is effectively paying the generic manufacturer to stay out of the market when it would be within the latter's legal right to enter.[29] A reverse payment settlement amounts to nothing more than a market allocation agreement between a branded and a generic manufacturer under the veneer of a patent infringement suit. These manufacturers gain while consumers lose as it is consumers who will continue to pay monopoly prices for the drug.[30] Their loss of consumer surplus is what funds the reverse payment by the branded manufacturer and is

[24] Carrier (n 3) 36.
[25] Elhauge and Krueger (n 23) 285.
[26] Murat C Mungan, 'Reverse Payments, Perverse Incentives' (2013) 27 Harvard Journal of Law & Technology 1, 34.
[27] ibid 33.
[28] Carrier (n 2) 39–40.
[29] Cotter (n 3) 1080.
[30] ibid 1075; Hovenkamp (n 3) 11.

likely to outweigh the gains to the branded and generic manufacturers.[31] Total social welfare is harmed by these settlements.

2. Consumer Harm

There seems to be an overwhelming consensus that reverse payment settlements lead to higher prices for consumers and a loss of consumer welfare. Scott Hemphill sums up the welfare effects of such settlements as follows: 'The effect of such pay-for-delay agreements is to remove the possibility of early competition in the drug, and to deny consumers the allocative benefit of low prices, which would have followed with some probability had the litigation proceeded to conclusion.'[32]

Both formal economic models and empirical evidence show that these settlements lower consumer welfare.[33] One model indicates that 92 per cent of reverse payment settlements were likely to harm consumers and that less than 0.5 per cent of efficient settlements were consummated due to reverse payments.[34] A US FTC study finds that on average consumers save 77 per cent on drug costs after generics are established in the market.[35] The introduction of generics for four drugs, Prozac, Platinol, Taxol, and Zantac, saved consumers almost USD10 billion.[36] The first generic is usually 39 per cent cheaper than the branded drug.[37] The second generic entrant pushes the price to 54 per cent below the brand price.[38] The market price for a drug with six or more generic entrants can be as low as 5 per cent of the brand price.[39] While one would expect branded manufacturers to lower prices to fend off such competition, the reality is that these manufacturers often rather counterintuitively raise prices after generic entry.[40] What these manufacturers do is to cede the price-sensitive patients to the generics and focus on the price-insensitive ones who are willing to pay even higher prices for the branded drugs. No longer constrained

[31] Cotter (n 3) 1075.

[32] Hemphill (n 3) 1557.

[33] Shapiro (n 9) 407–08.

[34] Cristofer Leffler and Keith Leffler, 'Settling the Controversy Over Patent Settlements: Payments by the Patent Holder Should Be Per Se Illegal' in John B Kirkwood (ed), *Antitrust Law and Economics*, vol 21 (Emerald Publishing Limited 2004) 484.

[35] Federal Trade Commission, 'Pay-For-Delay: How Drug Company Pay-Offs Cost Consumers Billions' (Federal Trade Commission 2010) FTC Staff Study 8 <https://www.ftc.gov/sites/default/files/documents/reports/pay-delay-how-drug-company-pay-offs-cost-consumers-billions-federal-trade-commission-staff-study/100112payfordelayrpt.pdf> accessed 14 March 2021.

[36] Kathleen D Jaeger, Statement at Hearing before the Committee on Commerce, Science, and Transportation of the US Senate (23 April 2002) Generic Pharmaceuticals: Marketplace Access and Consumer Issues 56 61.

[37] Ryan Conrad and Randall Lutter, 'Generic Competition and Drug Prices: New Evidence Linking Greater Generic Competition and Lower Generic Drug Prices' (Food and Drug Administration 2019) 2 <https://www.fda.gov/media/133509/download> accessed 14 March 2021.

[38] ibid.

[39] ibid 3.

[40] Hovenkamp (n 3) 9.

by the need to serve the price-sensitive patients, the branded manufacturers can raise prices following generic entry.

Such low prices result in massive market share losses for the branded drug. One study finds that generics take over three-quarters of the market after two months.[41] Not only does generic entry have significant impact on drug prices, it has also become a widespread phenomenon. By the late 2000s, almost 100 per cent of popular drugs with an expired patent face generic competition.[42] Such prevalence of generics also means that they account for an increasing share of overall prescriptions. By 2008, 65 per cent of all prescriptions were for generics.[43]

In light of these statistics, it is not surprising that reverse payment settlements, which prevent generic entry, inflict huge losses on consumers. The same FTC study estimates such loss to be USD3.5 billion per year.[44] The magnitude of the estimated consumer welfare loss is hardly surprising in light of the evidence that patented drugs frequently face validity challenges and generics often prevail in these challenges. In 2000, nine of the ten bestselling drugs were subject to such challenges.[45] One study reports that of the fifty-nine drugs which were subject to validity challenges that were neither pending nor settled, generics prevailed in twenty-two of them, and the branded manufacturer refrained from suing for infringement in twenty-nine of them.[46] Carrier reports that generics won nearly 75 per cent of their validity challenges against patented drugs in the 1990s.[47]

The significance of reverse payment settlements for drug prices further needs to be viewed in light of the massive pharmaceutical inflation in the last two decades. The average price for the 100 most frequently dispensed drugs rose by almost 25 per cent between 2000 and 2004. Branded drugs accounted for much of this price inflation as the prices for these drugs rose three times faster than generic prices.[48] Between 2007 and 2018, list prices for branded pharmaceutical products increased by 159 per cent, or 9.1 per cent per year, while net prices increased by 60 per cent, or 4.5 per cent per year.[49] Between 2012 and 2017, drugs that exceeded USD500 million in US sales or USD1 billion in worldwide sales experienced massive price

[41] Carrier (n 2) 49.

[42] Congressional Budget Office, 'How Increased Competition from Generic Drugs Has Affected Prices and Returns in the Pharmaceutical Industry' (1998) 37 <https://www.cbo.gov/sites/default/files/105th-congress-1997-1998/reports/pharm.pdf> accessed 29 July 2021.

[43] Carrier (n 2) 49.

[44] Federal Trade Commission (n 35) 8.

[45] Hemphill (n 3) 1567.

[46] Federal Trade Commission, 'Generic Entry Prior to Patent Expiration: An FTC Study' (Federal Trade Commission 2002) 15 <https://www.ftc.gov/sites/default/files/documents/reports/generic-drug-entry-prior-patent-expiration-ftc-study/genericdrugstudy_0.pdf> accessed 14 March 2021.

[47] Carrier (n 2) 39.

[48] United States Government Accountability Office, 'Prescription Drugs: Price Trends for Frequently Used Brand and Generic Drugs from 2000 through 2004' (2005) 10 <https://www.gao.gov/assets/gao-05-779.pdf> accessed 14 March 2021.

[49] Inmaculada Hernandez and others, 'Changes in List Prices, Net Prices, and Discounts for Branded Drugs in the US, 2007–2018' (2020) 323 Journal of the American Medical Association 854, 856.

increases of a median of 76 per cent.[50] Of the thirty-six drugs that have been available since 2012, twenty-eight have witnessed an increase in insurer and out-of-pocket costs by more than 50 per cent and sixteen have more than doubled in price.[51] The proportion of drugs supplied by one to three manufacturers that doubled in price within a year was 3.6 times higher in the period 2012–2015 than in 2005–2009.[52] Even more worrying is that prices no longer seem to be disciplined by market competition. Prior to 2010, a higher number of suppliers for a particular drug meant lower prices.[53] This changed after 2010, after which drugs supplied by four to seven manufacturers showed increases similar to or higher than those supplied by one to three manufacturers.[54]

3. Effects on Innovation Incentives and Generics' Incentive to Challenge

(a) Innovation incentives

Harm to consumer welfare is never the only relevant consideration in determining the legality of a patent exploitation practice. There is the additional factor of innovation incentives. Any patent exploitation practice which increases patentee profit can be potentially justified on innovation incentive grounds. Based on this simplistic view of innovation incentives, any boost to patentee reward is beneficial to innovation. Such a simplistic view, of course, has been debunked by Louis Kaplow, who proposes the ratio test and argues that every patent exploitation practice must be evaluated in light of its efficiency in generating patentee reward.[55] This efficiency is to be ascertained by the ratio between the additional patentee reward it redounds against the monopoly deadweight loss it inflicts.[56] Kaplow suggests that the default way to boost patentee reward is by lengthening the patent term, and that the ratio of every patent exploitation practice must be measured against this benchmark ratio.[57]

As Hemphill observes, reverse payment settlements are not an efficient way to raise patentee reward as any increase in profit must be shared with the generic challenger and the 'payment reduces its profits and hence the incremental innovation incentive gained by arranging for the extension. This deficit in innovation

[50] Nathan E Wineinger, Yunyue Zhang, and Eric J Topol, 'Trends in Prices of Popular Brand-Name Prescription Drugs in the United States' (2019) 2 JAMA Network Open 1, 4.

[51] ibid.

[52] Inmaculada Hernandez and others, 'Number of Manufacturers and Generic Drug Pricing From 2005 to 2017' (2019) 25 The American Journal of Managed Care 348, 350.

[53] ibid 349.

[54] ibid.

[55] Louis Kaplow, 'The Patent-Antitrust Intersection: A Reappraisal' [1984] Harvard Law Review 1831–32.

[56] ibid 1831.

[57] ibid 1832.

efficiency makes the agreements more difficult to justify as a reasonable effectuation of'[58] patent policy. Assuming that 30 per cent of the monopoly profit is shared with the generic through a reverse payment, reverse payment settlements would be 30 per cent less efficient than a comparable patent exploitation practice in generating patentee reward.

This lack of efficiency is only one of the drawbacks of reverse payment settlements. The denominator of Kaplow's ratio is monopoly loss. A complete analysis under the ratio test must also consider the monopoly loss inflicted by the patent exploitation practice. Reverse payment settlements tend to generate an enormous amount of such loss. Most patent exploitation practices such as package licensing, patent tying, and various licensing restrictions make marginal contribution to the patent's market power. The prohibition of the practice will not result in a wholesale loss of the patentee's market position. Reverse payment settlements are different. Assuming that the underlying patent is likely to be invalid, allowing reverse payments would allow the patentee to extend artificially its patent exclusivity to which the patentee should not be entitled. The patentee would be able to extract monopoly rent during this artificially extended patent term.

In contrast, the patentee would be subject to full-fledged competition from the generics if she was barred from paying them off, hence only earning a competitive return. The difference is between a monopolized market and a competitive market. As mentioned in the previous section, the difference in prices can be upward of 75 per cent. The monopoly loss is enormous. Reverse payment settlements are hence a patent exploitation practice that inflicts an enormous amount of deadweight loss at a low level of innovation generating efficiency. These settlements are likely to fail Kaplow's ratio test.

Mungan bolsters the case for prohibiting reverse payment settlements by demonstrating that such prohibition boosts incentives to invest in strong patents and lessens incentives to invest in weak patents, which is obviously beneficial to social welfare. He observes that a reverse payment settlement 'generates a surplus equal to the difference between monopoly profits and duopoly profits plus litigation costs'.[59] Prohibition of these settlements reduces the incentives of generics to bring patent validity challenges.[60] This is because when such settlements are allowed, generics can expect to extract some payment from the patentee so long as there is a non-negligible degree of uncertainty regarding patent validity. In contrast, when reverse payment settlements are illegal, there are only three possible outcomes for generics in a patent validity challenge: a win, a loss, or an abandonment of the suit. Generics can only gain from the suit if they prevail. There is no longer the intermediate option of a partial victory in the form of a reverse payment.

[58] Hemphill (n 3) 1613.
[59] Mungan (n 26) 5.
[60] ibid 7.

Therefore, generics will only sue when it is reasonably confident of its case, that is, when the patent is weak and likely to be invalidated or not infringed.[61] Generics will refrain from challenging when the patent is reasonably strong or likely to be infringed.[62]

This means that returns to relatively strong patents are enhanced by a prohibition of reverse payment settlements while returns to relatively weak patents are unaffected by a prohibition. This should skew investment toward relatively strong patents.[63] A shift from prohibition to *per se* legality for reverse payment settlements reduces returns to relatively strong patents as compared to relatively weak patents.[64] From a social welfare perspective, investments should be directed to relatively strong patents, which represent more novel and less obvious inventions, instead of relatively weak patents.[65] A strict rule against reverse payment settlements thus promotes social welfare.

Not every commentator shares the same pessimistic view of the detrimental effects of reverse payment settlements on innovation incentives. Thomas Cotter argues that 'restricting the range of settlements in this fashion would decrease the value of some patents, because otherwise the patentee would have voluntarily licensed the defendant; and that reducing the value of patents in this manner may reduce patent owners' incentives to invent, disclose, and innovate'.[66] The critical assumption of this argument is that the patentee would license her patent to the generic entrant if reverse payments were allowed, and that prohibition of such payments hence results in a loss of licensing revenue, reducing the value of the patent to the patentee. In other words, reverse payments enhance the value of the patent. There are two problems with this assumption. First, if reverse payments were to enhance the value of a patent, it is not by facilitating licensing activities. Reverse payment settlements result in the generic entrant staying out of the market instead of entering the market under a license from the patentee. Second, as argued by Mungan earlier, permitting reverse payments enhances the value of weak patents relative to that of strong patents. It is not socially desirable to incur considerable consumer welfare loss to bolster weak patents.

Daniel Crane has made a number of other arguments in support of a more lenient attitude toward reverse payments. First, he contends that a strict rule against reverse payment settlements 'could force patent litigants—often horizontal competitors—into licensing relationships that may impose greater social costs than exit payments'.[67] While this concern may be plausible in other contexts, it is

[61] ibid.
[62] ibid.
[63] ibid 44.
[64] ibid.
[65] ibid 25.
[66] Cotter (n 3) 1087.
[67] Crane, 'Exit Payments in Settlement of Patent Infringement Lawsuits: Antitrust Rules and Economic Implications' (n 10) 749.

difficult to imagine how any kind of licensing relationship in the pharmaceutical industry can be more detrimental than reverse payments and hence the maintenance of a questionable monopoly of a patented drug. The worst that can be happen with a license is that market output level remains at the monopoly level and the patentee and the licensee divide this output between them. This is no worse than the outcome that obtains following a reverse payment.

Second, Crane argues that prohibition of reverse payment settlements will aggravate the problem of risk aversion and deter risk-averse investors from making the optimal level of investment in pharmaceutical research and development (R&D).[68] Risk aversion is a favourite argument of those opposing legal intervention against corporate conduct. The reasoning is that by introducing a legal rule prohibiting certain business practices, it may deter businesses from undertaking legitimate activities that may be difficult to distinguish from the prohibited conduct due to risk aversion. To what extent is risk aversion relevant to a publicly held corporation is open to question.[69] In any case, risk aversion is likely to be a more serious issue with weak patents than with strong patents. Risk aversion is unlikely to sway a patentee to settle with a validity challenger if the patentee is reasonably confident of the patent's validity.

Third, Crane argues that prohibiting reverse payments deters inventing around by the alleged infringer.[70] His reasoning is that a licensee paying royalty to the patentee under a licensing agreement is unlikely to invest to circumvent the patent. A potential infringer receiving a reverse payment from the patentee to stay out of the market would retain the incentive to invent around the patent. This reasoning is premised on the patentee's oversight in allowing the infringer to enter the market with another drug after receiving a reverse payment. Given that reasonable substitutes for a drug are generally not difficult to identify or delineate in advance—substitutes include all the therapeutic equivalents of the drug at issue—such an oversight would stretch credulity. Moreover, this reasoning ignores the reality of the pharmaceutical industry and assumes that the settling generic engages in R&D and is capable of inventing around the patent. Generics by definition do not engage in R&D to invent new drugs and only replicate off-patent drugs. An argument premised on inventing around simply has no application to generics.

Fourth, while acknowledging that prohibiting reverse payment settlements is social welfare enhancing from an *ex post* perspective, Crane argues that this ignores the *ex ante* incentive effects of the patent system. Mungan has effectively addressed this objection. If prohibiting reverse payments deters R&D investments,

[68] ibid 760, 762.

[69] Elhauge and Krueger (n 23) 312.

[70] Crane, 'Exit Payments in Settlement of Patent Infringement Lawsuits: Antitrust Rules and Economic Implications' (n 10) 768.

the deterrent impact will be mostly confined to relatively weak patents. Investments in relatively strong patents are encouraged in comparison.

In sum, none of the defences of reverse payment settlement on innovation incentive grounds is convincing and prohibiting reverse payment settlements is unlikely to deter worthwhile innovation. Even if one ignores the salutary effect of a prohibition of reverse payment settlements on innovation as articulated by Mungan, one can at least assume that the innovation incentive effect is no better than neutral. The analysis can thus focus on harm on consumer welfare, which, as argued earlier, is overwhelmingly negative.

(b) Generics' incentives to bring validity challenges

Prohibition of reverse payment settlements may also affect the incentives of generic entrants to bring patent validity challenges. While this is generally not the main focus of the patent–competition interface, to the extent that such challenges help to remove invalid patents and lead to lower drug prices for consumers, a reduction of such incentives can be detrimental to consumers.

As mentioned earlier, prohibition of reverse payment settlements limits the range of settlement options for generic challengers. This can have a range of possible effects. It may encourage the patentee and the challenger to litigate the case to the end,[71] which may be welfare-enhancing to the extent that it helps to remove invalid patents which otherwise would have been allowed to stand. It would result in a waste of litigation resources in cases in which the patent is upheld. But unless the vast majority of cases falls within the latter category, there are reasons to believe that the consumer welfare gains from the elimination of invalid patents should far outweigh wasted litigation expenses from a social welfare perspective. There is no reason to expect that every challenger will litigate its case to conclusion once reverse payments are banned. The generic challenger can simply abandon the challenge and walk away. As Hemphill observes, a ban on reverse payments will 'lower the value of the generic firm's abandonment option',[72] which should reduce the number of validity challenges brought by generics. This would be socially undesirable.

Whether a ban on reverse payments is socially beneficial overall would depend on the proportion of cases in which the generic challenger is induced to litigate the case to conclusion and eventually prevails when it otherwise would have settled and cases in which validity challenges are deterred by the reduction of the value of the abandonment option to the challenger. Hemphill believes that the latter effect should be small because there are already significant incentives for generics to bring validity challenges under the Hatch–Waxman Act.[73] This means that the

[71] Schildkraut (n 10) 1049.
[72] Hemphill (n 3) 1615.
[73] ibid 1579.

main impact of a ban on reverse payments will be to incentivize parties to litigate validity challenges to conclusion, which should be a welcome development for consumers. Therefore, a prohibition of reverse payment settlements is justified on account of the impact on both the patentee's innovation incentives and the generics' incentive to bring validity challenges.

D. Doctrinal Approaches

There is a wide spectrum of views among commentators on the appropriate legal rule for reverse payment settlements, ranging from *per se* illegality to presumptive illegality to the Rule of Reason, with a majority of the leading commentators favouring a presumptive illegality approach.

1. *Per Se* Illegality

Jeremy Bulow is one of the few commentators to have advocated *per se* illegality for reverse payment settlements.[74] He argues that the *per se* rule should apply because 'you don't get to pay your competitor to stay out of the market'.[75] He would, however, allow settlements that involve no value transfers from the patentee to the generic challenger.[76] He casts doubts on the efficiency justifications for these settlements and cautions against settlements that involve complex side deals because the parties would have an 'overwhelming incentive … to game the system' to achieve a value transfer to the generic.[77] This rule is premised on the simple yet appealing logic that reverse payment settlements constitute an agreement between two competitors to divide up the market and split monopoly profits. The appeal of this logic explains the hostility of most commentators toward reverse payments. While a *per se* rule can be commended for its simplicity, it probably goes too far. Most commentators would at least allow a payment by the patentee up to the value of expected litigation expenses, which even a patentee with no intention to buy off a competitor would rationally be willing to offer.

[74] Jeremy Bulow, 'The Gaming of Pharmaceutical Patents' in Adam B Jaffe, Josh Lerner, and Scott Stern (eds), *Innovation Policy and the Economy*, vol 4 (2004) 145, 180 <https://www.nber.org/system/files/chapters/c10802/c10802.pdf> accessed 14 March 2021.

[75] ibid 166.

[76] ibid 180.

[77] ibid.

2. Presumptive Illegality

A host of commentators, including Herbert Hovenkamp, Michael Carrier, Scott Hemphill, Thomas Cotter, Einer Elhauge, and Alan Krueger, advocate a presumptive legality approach to reverse payment settlements.

(a) Thomas Cotter

Cotter acknowledges that a presumptive illegality approach may be over- and under-inclusive.[78] He argues that such an approach, however, is justified in light of his belief

> that outside of Hatch-Waxman, reverse-payment settlements are uncommon, and that while they can be consistent with a high probability of success on the merits of the patent owner's suit, they are more likely than other settlements to reflect a lack of confidence in the probability of success and thus to be more consistent with a scheme to divide the market.[79]

A harsh rule against reverse payment settlements is sound so long as his hypothesis remains defensible.[80]

He is careful to distinguish his suggested presumptive illegality approach from a *per se* rule. A reverse payment in excess of such a threshold only raises a presumption of illegality, which can be rebutted upon a showing that (1) the generic is cash-strapped, and therefore willing to accept cash payments in exchange for deferred entry; or (2) the patentee has successfully obtained an injunction against the generic entrant; or (3) the generic entrant has agreed to waive the 180-day exclusivity provided by the Hatch–Waxman Act, which significantly lowers the anticompetitive potential of the settlement; or (4) the patent at issue has withstood other validity challenges.[81]

(b) Michael Carrier

Carrier shares Cotter's assumption that a patentee would normally have no reason to pay the alleged infringer anything more than its litigation costs unless it is trying to delay generic entry.[82] He justifies a presumptive illegality approach for reverse payment settlements on five grounds: '(1) The existence of Hatch–Waxman's regulatory structure; (2) The regime's ineffectiveness in promoting patent challenges; (3) The severe anticompetitive harm of market allocation; (4) The uniquely

[78] Cotter (n 3) 1091.
[79] ibid.
[80] ibid.
[81] Thomas F Cotter, 'FTC v. Actavis, Inc.: When Is the Rule of Reason Not the Rule of Reason' (2014) 15 Minnesota Journal of Law, Science & Technology 41, 42.
[82] Carrier (n 2) 76.

concerning nature of reverse payments; and (5) A rebuttal for reverse payments reflecting reasonable assessments of patent validity.'[83] He explains that in light of the first four premises, a Rule of Reason approach is inappropriate because reverse payment settlements are generally not pro-competitive.[84] At the same time, 'because some agreements could conceivably be justified if the reverse payments reflected the parties' reasonable assessments of patent validity', Carrier believes that a *per se* rule against such settlements as proposed by Bulow would be a step too far.

He concludes that the default position should be one of presumptive illegality. The burden to rebut the presumption should rest on the settling parties because settlement agreements have become increasingly complicated, with the value transfer disguised as licenses, raw material supply agreements, and co-promotion agreements.[85] The complexity of these agreements means that it will be more difficult for the plaintiff to demonstrate the unreasonableness of the payment. Given that the settling parties have better access to relevant information and a more intimate understanding of the industry, the burden to rebut the presumption of unreasonableness should rest with them.

Similar to Cotter, Carrier believes that a patentee generally would have few incentives to settle with a generic entrant with a payment that exceeds its litigation costs unless it results in a delayed entry by the generic.[86] This raises a presumption of illegality of such payments, which can be rebutted if the patentee can demonstrate the payment's reasonableness. Reasonableness can be demonstrated under any of the following four conditions holds: (1) the payment does not exceed litigation costs; (2) the generic is cash-strapped; (3) there is asymmetric information between the parties; or (4) other explanations justifying the reasonableness of the payment.[87] The first two justifications have been explained previously. Under the third justification, the patentee and the generic may disagree on the patent's value, with the generic underestimating the value.[88] In that case, the generic may undervalue an offer which incorporates an earlier entry date. The generic may underestimate the value of accelerated entry by one year, for example. To circumvent this difficulty, the patentee may instead offer the generic a cash payment and an entry date that is consistent with the patent's expected value.[89] The fourth justification represents a more general defence, under which the patentee can demonstrate the reasonableness of a reverse payment with reference to '(1) sales projections, (2) market analyses, (3) payments for similar products, and (4) the brand's interest in the product and due diligence'.[90]

83 ibid 67.
84 ibid.
85 ibid 78.
86 ibid 76.
87 ibid.
88 ibid 77.
89 ibid.
90 ibid.

(c) Herbert Hovenkamp, Mark Janis, and Mark Lemley

Hovenkamp, Janis, and Lemley offer a slightly different justification for limiting reverse payments to the patentee's expected litigation costs. They argue that in a world of zero transaction costs, a patentee that is certain about the validity of its patent and infringement would have no incentive to pay another firm to stay out of the market.[91] The inclusion of transaction costs, however, changes the calculus. If it costs USD15 million to bring and win an infringement suit to obtain an injunction, as suggested by Cotter, the patentee might be willing to offer the generic up to that amount because the patentee would be able to achieve the same outcome as an injunction at a lower cost.[92] They further argue that the existence of a large reverse payment suggests that the patentee harbours some doubt about the validity of the patent.

A Rule of Reason analysis, however, is not the appropriate vehicle for resolving this uncertainty concerning patent validity. The Rule of Reason is meant to balance anticompetitive effects against pro-competitive justifications.[93] It is not intended to be used to engage in the policy trade-off between consumer welfare and innovation incentives that underpins the patent system.[94] It is not necessary to resolve the uncertainty regarding patent validity because '[t]he very fact of that uncertainty suggests that exclusion payments are anticompetitive-that on average such agreements exclude at least some generics that in fact had a legal right to compete'.[95]

This fact justifies a presumptive illegality approach for reverse payments. Hovenkamp and co-authors offer a narrow range of possible justifications for the reverse payment. They would allow the settling parties to justify the payment 'by showing both (1) that the *ex ante* likelihood of prevailing in its infringement lawsuit is significant, and (2) that the size of the payment is no more than the expected value of litigation and collateral costs attending the lawsuit'.[96]

(d) Einer Elhauge and Alan Krueger

Elhauge and Krueger offer a more complex proof that reaches the same conclusion. They assert that their proof 'showed that reverse patent settlements necessarily harm consumer welfare when: (a) The reverse payment exceeds the payor's anticipated future litigation costs; [and] (b) The size of this reverse payment exceeds the payor's anticipated future litigation costs even after subtracting the value of any goods or services the payor received in return'.[97] These premises establish a

[91] Herbert Hovenkamp, Mark D Janis, and Mark A Lemley, 'Anticompetitive Settlement of Intellectual Property Disputes' (2003) 87 Minnesota Law Review 1719, 1750–51.

[92] ibid 1751.

[93] ibid 1729.

[94] ibid.

[95] ibid 1758.

[96] ibid 1759.

[97] Alexander Krueger, 'Implementing Actavis: Three Tips for Future Courts Assessing Reverse Patent Settlements under Rule of Reason Analysis' (2014) 15 Minnesota Journal of Law, Science & Technology 115, 115.

rule of presumptive illegality so long as the reverse payment exceeds the patentee's anticipated litigation costs. They categorically assert that 'a reverse payment that exceeds the patent holder's anticipated litigation costs is never necessary to secure a desirable settlement. Instead, a reverse payment of this size can be necessary to reach settlement only when both the patent holder and entrant know the settlement is anticompetitive'.[98] A reverse payment would be presumptively illegal if it exceeds 'the upper bound of litigation costs from similar cases'.[99] Economic literature indicates that such an upper bound should be around USD15 million in most pharmaceutical cases.[100]

The presumption can be rebutted 'by proving either: (a) the entrant would have entered at risk and is judgment proof to a sufficient extent to indicate the settlement exclusion period could or would be within the optimal patent exclusion period or (b) that some other procompetitive justification exists that offsets the anticompetitive effects'.[101] When (a) holds true, the generic's entry decision would no longer be determined by its own objective assessment of patent validity. It would enter even if it believed that the patent had a high likelihood of validity. In a way, this judgment proof entrant is similar to the cash-strapped entrant hypothesized by Cotter and Carrier. Both postulate an entrant whose entry decision is no longer determined by its objective assessment of patent validity. Elhauge and Krueger note that the settling parties can maximize their joint profits by agreeing on an entry date at the end of the patent term.[102] They will have an overwhelming incentive to do just that absent antitrust liability. It is on the basis of this incentive that Elhauge and Krueger argue against the highly permissive scope of the patent test espoused by the Eleventh Circuit in the *Schering-Plough* case.[103]

An important implication of their argument is that their conclusion of the anticompetitive effects of a reverse payment settlement where the payment exceeds the patentee's anticipated litigation costs holds true regardless of the perceived validity of the patent by the patentee and the generic entrant.[104] Nor would risk aversion alter their conclusion.[105] Another important implication is that the defendants should not be permitted to argue the lack of market power on the part of the patentee as a defence because their analysis shows that the patentee would never offer a reverse payment that exceeds the patentee's anticipated litigation costs unless it wielded the requisite market power.[106] Justice Breyer would subsequently endorse this position in *Actavis*. They also emphasize that the relevant benchmark is not

[98] Elhauge and Krueger (n 23) 303.
[99] ibid 306.
[100] ibid 307.
[101] ibid 291.
[102] ibid 285.
[103] ibid 289.
[104] ibid 291.
[105] ibid 311.
[106] ibid 291–92.

all litigation costs, but 'only the patent holder's future anticipated litigation costs at the time of settlement'.[107] Past litigation expenses are sunk costs and should not affect the patentee's willingness to settle.[108] Elhauge and Krueger concur with the USD15 million benchmark proposed by Cotter. They report that the largest publicly known amount of litigation expense in a patent infringement litigation in the pharmaceutical industry was USD15 million.[109]

3. Rule of Reason

(a) Dan Crane

What Crane suggests is not a Rule of Reason analysis in the classic sense of a balancing of anticompetitive effects and pro-competitive justifications. Instead, he suggests disparate treatment for reverse payment settlements depending on the likelihood of success of the patentee's infringement claim.[110] Crane argues that '[t]he higher the likelihood that the patentee's infringement claim is valid, the more likely it is that the costs of a rule prohibiting exit settlement payments outweigh the costs of permitting the exit payment, and vice versa'.[111] Therefore, some assessment of patent validity is necessary for the determination of the legality of a reverse payment. In general, he concludes that reverse payments should be permitted when the patentee's likelihood of success in its infringement suit is high and should be prohibited when the patentee's likelihood of success is low.[112]

He proposes a structured approach under which reverse payments should be presumed lawful once the district court grants a preliminary injunction against the alleged infringer.[113] This establishes a bright-line safe harbour. An examination of the merits would be required if a request for a preliminary injunction has not been adjudged. Under this 'quick look' review, the reverse payment should be upheld if the court determines that the patentee is likely to prevail.[114] If the review reveals serious doubts about the validity of the patent, then 'a full trial on the merits of the infringement claim'[115] would be required. Crane's approach stands out because commentators have warned against exactly this kind of examination of the merits of the infringement claim.[116]

[107] ibid 293.
[108] ibid 305.
[109] ibid 307.
[110] Crane, 'Exit Payments in Settlement of Patent Infringement Lawsuits: Antitrust Rules and Economic Implications' (n 10) 780.
[111] ibid.
[112] ibid 782.
[113] ibid 783.
[114] ibid 785.
[115] ibid 787.
[116] Cotter (n 3) 1082; Hovenkamp (n 3) 21.

He further suggests an alternative to this kind of full-fledged inquiry into patent validity. As opposed to the likelihood of success of the infringement claim, he urges courts to focus on the percentage of monopoly rent that the patentee is willing to share with the generic.[117] A high percentage of rent shared indicates a low probability of patent validity or actual infringement by the generic and supports a finding against the reverse payment.[118] Crane's approach encounters the obvious problem that legality is contingent on validity of the patent and the infringement claim. It requires courts to examine the merits of the patent and the infringement claim, which would significantly complicate the proceedings.

In addition, Hovenkamp, Janis, and Lemley have heavily criticized the basic premise of Crane's argument that proscribing reverse payments will render generic entry more difficult and markets less competitive. It is in light of this premise that Crane argues for a permissive approach to reverse payment settlements. They reject Crane's assertion that prohibiting reverse payments would prolong patent litigation and freeze inventive activity for years.[119] They point out that the very settlements which Crane defends freezes generic entry for the rest of the patent term.[120] They dismiss Crane's contention that requiring generics to litigate to conclusion raises barriers to entry on the grounds that reverse payment settlements raise even higher entry barriers.[121] These settlements bar entry by both the first generic entrant and subsequent entrants.[122] Finally, they find unconvincing Crane's argument that a prohibition of reverse payments would force patentees to enter into licensing agreements with generic entrants, which may allow the patentee to impose licensing restrictions on price, quantity, or other sales conditions.[123] They maintain that 'a settlement with a license is almost certainly better for competition than the alternative of an exclusion payment, which prevents any generic from entering the market at all'.[124]

(b) Murat Mungan

Mungan's espousal of a Rule of Reason approach is somewhat surprising in light of his conclusion that 'absent "probably rare" circumstances, restricting RPSs [reverse payment settlements] leads to static benefits without increasing expected litigation costs and dynamic benefits in the form of increased R&D for relatively stronger inventions'.[125] He observes that the standard assumptions upon which he derives

[117] Crane, 'Exit Payments in Settlement of Patent Infringement Lawsuits: Antitrust Rules and Economic Implications' (n 10) 788.
[118] ibid.
[119] Herbert Hovenkamp, Mark D Janis, and Mark A Lemley, 'Balancing Ease and Accuracy in Assessing Pharmaceutical Exclusion Payments' (2004) 88 Minnesota Law Review 712, 714.
[120] ibid 716.
[121] ibid.
[122] ibid 717.
[123] ibid.
[124] ibid 718.
[125] Mungan (n 26) 8.

his results may not hold true in some instances which may render reverse payment settlements pro-competitive. He gives a liquidity-constrained generic entrant as an example. This is consistent with what other commentators have suggested as a possible justification for a reverse payment. But other commentators are able to accommodate this exception to the general rule of anticompetitive effects of reverse payments under a presumptive illegality approach while Mungan resorts to a Rule of Reason. This is despite his admission that '[a]bsent such deviations from standard assumptions, RPSs ought to be prevented'.[126]

His formulation of Rule of Reason—'applying the rule of reason to allow RPSs only when there is clear indication that the settlement would further pro-competitive goals'[127]—is probably more akin to a presumptive illegality approach proposed by other commentators. This conclusion is bolstered by his observation that courts should lean toward prohibiting reverse payments if it is decided that incentivizing strong inventions in favour of weak inventions is socially beneficial,[128] which would most certainly be true. In short, what Mungan has in mind is probably more of a presumptive illegality approach, which leaves Crane as one of the few commentators to have advocated for a Rule of Reason for reverse payments.

The weight of the scholarly opinion is firmly in favour of a presumptive illegality approach for reverse payments, the decisions adopted by the appellate courts prior to *Actavis* notwithstanding. This is unsurprising in light of the preponderance of anticompetitive effects of reverse payment settlements and the ease with which exceptions to the general rule can be accommodated under a rule of presumptive illegality. As Hovenkamp, Janis, and Lemley have illustrated, arguments in support of a Rule of Reason approach are unconvincing and precious litigation and judicial resources would be wasted if such an approach were applied to reverse payment settlements.

E. Case Law on Reverse Payment Settlements

The United States has had a relatively longer history of tackling reverse payment settlements. Cases involving such settlements began to emerge in the early 2000s. Most of the enforcement action was spearheaded by the US FTC and did not meet with much success. The appellate courts were by and large sceptical of the FTC's claims that such settlements were anticompetitive. Many of the courts such as the Eleventh Circuit adopted the scope of the patent test, under which a settlement will be deemed lawful so long as it stays within the scope of the patentee's rights. Because settling a patent infringement claim is clearly within a patentee's rights

[126] ibid.
[127] ibid.
[128] ibid 45–46.

in a formalistic sense, the scope of the patent test is tantamount to a rule of *per se* legality for reverse payment settlements. Understandably, this ruling led to a proliferation of reverse payment settlements. This trend did not reverse until the *Actavis* case, in which the US Supreme Court adopted a Rule of Reason approach for reverse payment settlements.

The European Union (EU) got off to a relatively late start with reverse payment settlements. European Commission enforcement against these settlements did not begin in earnest until the Commission adopted the *Lundbeck* decision in June 2013.[129] Other decisions such as *Servier* have followed.[130] With the exception of a minor setback in one part of the *Servier* case,[131] the General Court has largely endorsed the Commission's hard-line approach against reverse payment settlements. The CJEU has upheld the General Court's judgment in *Lundbeck*. It also endorsed a similar approach in a preliminary ruling in the *Generics (UK)* case.[132]

1. The United States

(a) Early cases

Among the early cases decided by the various Courts of Appeals on the legality of reverse payment settlements, the US Court of Appeals for the Sixth Circuit was a relative outlier in adopting a hard-line approach against these settlements. In *In re Cardizem CD Antitrust Litigation*, the Sixth Circuit held that reverse payment settlements are illegal *per se*.[133] The Court concluded that the agreement would exclude Hoechst's only potential competitor from the market and emphasized that reverse payments are inherently suspicious due to the counterintuitive directional flow of the payment.[134]

Most other appellate courts have adopted highly permissive analytical frameworks for reverse payment settlements. In *Schering-Plough Corp. v. FTC*, the Eleventh Circuit asserted that anticompetitive effects of these settlements need to be treated with more circumspection because patents '[b]y their nature ... create an environment of exclusion and ... cripple competition'.[135] The Court instead propounded the scope of the patent test, which focuses on '(1) the scope of the exclusionary potential of the patent; (2) the extent to which the agreements exceed that scope; and (3) the resulting anticompetitive effects'.[136] The Court noted that the patent gave Schering the right to exclude generic entrants until the generics

[129] Geradin 20.
[130] COMP/39226, *Lundbeck* [2015] OJ C80.
[131] COMP/39612, *Perindopril (Servier)* [2016] OJ C393.
[132] Case 307/18, *Generics (UK) and Others v. Competition and Markets Authority* EU:C:2020:52.
[133] *In re Cardizem CD Antitrust Litigation*, 332 F.3d 896 (6th Cir. 2003).
[134] ibid 907, 908.
[135] *Schering-Plough Corp. v. Federal Trade Commission*, 402 F.3d 1056, 1065 (11th Cir. 2005).
[136] ibid 1066.

managed to prove that the patent was invalid or not infringed[137] and that the settlement agreements did not restrict competition beyond the scope of the patent.[138] The settlement terms were 'within the patent's exclusionary power'[139] and a patentee 'should not be in a worse position'[140] than other parties in settling a lawsuit. Finally, the Court concluded that any restrictions on competition were ancillary to the settlement agreement and necessary for achieving the settlement.[141] Unlike the Sixth Circuit, the Eleventh Circuit was not perturbed by the directional flow of the payment, declaring that reverse payments were 'a natural by-product of the Hatch–Waxman process'.[142] Although the Court stopped short of so declaring, the scope of the patent test amounted to *per se* legality.

In *In re Tamoxifen Citrate Antitrust Litigation*, the US Court of Appeals for the Second Circuit adopted a similar line of reasoning, holding that so long as a settlement is not a sham or otherwise baseless and is within the scope of patent rights, a patentee is entitled to enter into a settlement 'to protect that to which it is presumably entitled: a lawful monopoly over the manufacture and distribution of the patented product'.[143] The Second Circuit rejected the *per se* rule adopted by the Sixth Circuit in *In re Cardizem CD Antitrust Litigation*, asserting that competitive concerns about reverse payment settlements were lessened by the presumption of patent validity, under which a patent settlement was 'merely an extension of the valid patent monopoly'.[144] As noted by the dissent in that case, the majority seemed to harbour greater concerns for the innovation-retarding effects of regulating reverse payment settlements than the possible consumer harm that may arise from such settlements.[145]

In *In re Ciprofloxacin Hydrochloride Antitrust Litigation*, the United States Court of Appeals for the Federal Circuit adopted a similar approach. It asserted that the 'essence of the inquiry'[146] was 'whether the agreements restrict competition beyond the exclusionary zone of the patent'.[147] It concluded that in the absence of fraud on the Patent and Trademark Office (PTO) or sham litigation, the Court 'need not consider the validity of the patent'.[148] The Court offered three arguments in support of its conclusion. First, the settlement agreement did not go beyond the scope of the patent rights in excluding competitors.[149] Second, the presumption of

[137] ibid 1066–67.
[138] ibid 1071.
[139] ibid 1072.
[140] ibid 1072.
[141] ibid 1072–73.
[142] ibid 1074.
[143] *In re Tamoxifen Citrate Antitrust Litigation*, 466 F.3d 187, 208–09 (2d Cir. 2006).
[144] ibid 211.
[145] ibid 227–28.
[146] *In re Ciprofloxacin Hydrochloride Antitrust Litigation*, 544 F.3d 1323, 1336 (Fed Cir. 2008).
[147] ibid 1336.
[148] ibid.
[149] ibid 1333.

patent validity means that it is perfectly within the patentee's right to exclude others from practicing the claimed invention.[150] Third, there is a long-standing policy in favour of settlements and it is common for patent settlements to require the alleged infringer to refrain from challenging the validity of the patent.[151]

The US Court of Appeals for the Third Circuit was one of the few appellate courts to have sided with the Sixth Circuit. In *In re K-Dur Antitrust Litigation*, the Third Circuit rejected the scope of the patent test on the grounds that the 'test improperly restricts the application of antitrust law and is contrary to the policies underlying the Hatch–Waxman Act and a long line of Supreme Court precedent on patent litigation and competition'.[152] The Court perceptively noted that the scope of the patent test creates an 'almost unrebuttable presumption of patent validity'.[153] Instead, the Court adopted a quick look approach, under which a reverse payment settlement is presumptively illegal unless the defendant can show that 'the payment (1) was for a purpose other than delayed entry or (2) offers some pro-competitive benefit'.[154]

It emphasized that the presumption of illegality cannot be rebutted by proof of the merits of the infringement suit because the existence of a reverse payment is highly suggestive of a purpose to delay generic entry.[155] To show a purpose other than to delay entry, the patentee must demonstrate that it has received sufficient separate consideration in exchange for the reverse payment.[156] Otherwise, the settling parties must prove some pro-competitive benefit that could not have been achieved without the reverse payment.[157] The Court justified its approach by arguing that 'the only settlements subject to antitrust scrutiny are those involving a reverse payment from the name brand manufacturer to the generic challenger. Data analyzed by the FTC suggest that this will leave the vast majority of pharmaceutical patent settlements unaffected.'[158]

Overall, a majority of the appellate courts prior to *Actavis* showed much leniency toward reverse payment settlements, resorting to similar arguments along the lines of settlements being within the scope of patent rights and the exclusionary potential of a settlement not going beyond that of the patent itself. There was, however, a clear circuit split between the Second, the Eleventh, and the Federal Circuits on the one hand, which have adopted variations of the scope of the patent test, and the Third and Sixth Circuits on the other, which have taken a much harsher stance

[150] ibid.
[151] ibid.
[152] *In re K-Dur Antitrust Litigation*, 686 F.3d 197, 214 (3d Cir. 2012).
[153] ibid.
[154] ibid 218.
[155] ibid.
[156] ibid.
[157] ibid.
[158] ibid.

against reverse payment settlements. This circuit split would eventually lead the US Supreme Court to take up the issue in the *Actavis* case.

(b) *Federal Trade Commission v. Actavis*

In *Federal Trade Commission v. Actavis*,[159] Justice Stephen Breyer, writing for the majority, rejected the scope of the patent test as being overly permissive. The Court acknowledged that a valid patent carries with it the right to settle.[160] It qualified this right by observing that 'an *invalidated* patent carries with it no such right'[161] and that 'even a valid patent confers no right to exclude products or processes that do not actually infringe'.[162] It asserted that in light of the anticompetitive potential of reverse payment settlements,

> it would be incongruous to determine antitrust legality by measuring the settlement's anticompetitive effects solely against patent law policy, rather than by measuring them against procompetitive antitrust policies as well... this Court has indicated that patent and antitrust policies are both relevant in determining the 'scope of the patent monopoly'—and consequently antitrust law immunity—that is conferred by a patent.[163]

As opposed to the scope of the patent test, which seems to suggest that the legality of reverse payment settlements is solely a patent law question, the US Supreme Court believed that it posed an antitrust question which should be answered 'by considering traditional antitrust factors such as likely anticompetitive effects, redeeming virtues, market power, and potentially offsetting legal considerations present in the circumstances'.[164]

What explains the divergent attitudes of the US Supreme Court and the appellate courts that have adopted the scope of the patent test is perhaps the former's recognition of 'the patent-related policy of eliminating unwarranted patent grants so the public will not "continually be required to pay tribute to would-be monopolists without need or justification"'.[165] Those appellate courts seemed disinclined to entertain the possibility that a patentee's rights may be undeserved in the case of an invalid or uninfringed patent, while the Supreme Court recognized that consumers have the right to insist that supra-competitive prices are only paid to owners of valid patents.

159 Federal Trade Commission v. Actavis, 570 US 136 (2013).
160 ibid 141.
161 ibid 147.
162 ibid.
163 ibid 148.
164 ibid 149.
165 ibid 151.

Moreover, unlike these appellate courts, the Supreme Court did not indulge in the pretence that there is nothing unusual about the alleged infringer receiving large sums in a settlement. It noted that '[i]n reverse payment settlements, in contrast, a party with no claim for damages (something that is usually true of a paragraph IV litigation defendant) walks away with money simply so it will stay away from the patentee's market. That, we think, is something quite different.'[166] The Court recognized that reverse payments can be used to split the monopoly profits between the patentee and the generic entrant, whereby '[t]he patentee and the challenger gain; the consumer loses'.[167] The Court further observed that 'patentees sometimes pay a generic challenger a sum even larger than what the generic would gain in profits if it won the paragraph IV litigation and entered the market'.[168] It underscored the anticompetitive potential of these settlements by noting that '[t]he payment may instead provide strong evidence that the patentee seeks to induce the generic challenger to abandon its claim with a share of its monopoly profits that would otherwise be lost in the competitive market'.[169]

Despite the Court's recognition of the anticompetitive potential of reverse payment settlements, it stopped short of endorsing the quick look or presumptive illegality approach advocated by the FTC. It noted that

> the likelihood of a reverse payment bringing about anticompetitive effects depends upon its size, its scale in relation to the payor's anticipated future litigation costs, its independence from other services for which it might represent payment, and the lack of any other convincing justification. The existence and degree of any anticompetitive consequence may also vary as among industries.[170]

The Court left it to the lower courts to fashion a structured Rule of Reason approach to reverse payment settlements. It did, however, leave some guidance to the lower courts. In terms of possible justifications for a reverse payment, in line with what commentators have argued, the Court indicated that a payment that amounts to 'a rough approximation of the litigation expenses saved through the settlement'[171] would be justified. So would a payment for services that are genuinely provided by the generic to the patentee.[172]

The Court also made two important observations. The first one is that 'it is normally not necessary to litigate patent validity to answer the antitrust question'.[173] This is in line with what some commentators have argued. The second one is that

[166] ibid 152.
[167] ibid 154.
[168] ibid.
[169] ibid.
[170] ibid 159.
[171] ibid 156.
[172] ibid 156.
[173] ibid 157.

the existence of an unusually large sum of payment to the generic is a strong indicator of market power.[174] This is what Elhauge and Krueger have suggested. The Court deduced that it is unlikely for a firm without market power to pay large sums to a competitor to induce the latter to stay out of its market.[175] This has by and large obviated the need to prove the existence of market power in a reverse payment case, which is consequential because plaintiffs often founder at this stage in a Rule of Reason case.

It is in part because of this qualification by the Court that has led Cotter to conclude that the Rule of Reason analysis adopted by the Court is tantamount to a presumptive illegality approach. Cotter argues that there are seven analytical steps in a typical Rule of Reason case: (1) proof of the existence of an agreement in restraint of trade; (2) showing of anticompetitive effects; (3) showing of plausible pro-competitive benefits; (4) proof of the defendant's market power; (5) showing of actual pro-competitive benefits; (6) existence of less restrictive means to achieve the benefit; (7) a balance of anticompetitive effects against pro-competitive benefits.[176] According to Cotter, the practical implications of the majority opinion in *Actavis* is that the plaintiff can skip the first four steps and start at the fifth one.[177]

Given that the burden of persuasion usually rests with the defendant at the fifth step, 'it is a little hard to see how that framework differs in any functional manner from presumptive illegality'.[178] This is particularly true because under the proposed approach, 'the plaintiff is not going to have to prove, except inferentially by reference to the amount of the payment, that the probability of patent invalidity was high'.[179] A requirement to demonstrate patent invalidity would be highly onerous for the plaintiff. Hovenkamp concurs that the plaintiff bears a low burden in terms of proof of market power and anticompetitive effects.[180] These are largely presumed under the analytical framework in *Actavis*.

2. The European Union

Unlike the US courts, the European Commission and the European courts have consistently exhibited a hostile attitude toward reverse payment settlements. Although the General Court did annul the Commission's decision in part of the *Servier* case, it was largely over assessment of facts. The General Court and the

174 ibid.
175 ibid.
176 Cotter (n 81) 44.
177 ibid 46.
178 ibid.
179 ibid 47.
180 Hovenkamp (n 3) 24.

CJEU have largely upheld the Commission's legal approach to reverse payment settlements.

(a) *Lundbeck*

In June 2013, the Commission issued its decision against Lundbeck, the manufacturer of a bestselling antidepressant citalopram, and several generic manufacturers, fining Lundbeck €93.8 million and the generic manufacturers €52.2 million for entering into settlement agreements between them.[181] Citalopram was a very important product for Lundbeck; it accounted for 85 per cent of Lundbeck's turnover.[182] At the time of the agreements, Lundbeck's product patent over citalopram had already expired; what remained was the patent over the manufacturing process.[183] Under the agreements, Lundbeck agreed to purchase the generic manufacturers' stock of the drug, which was then to be destroyed, and to offer the generics guaranteed profits in a distribution agreement.[184] In return, the generics undertook not to enter the market with a generic version of citalopram, regardless of whether the manufacturing process was covered by Lundbeck's process patent.[185] The Commission found that the payments made by Lundbeck to the generics far exceeded the sales value of the purchased stock and were benchmarked against the generics' anticipated profits upon market entry.[186]

The Commission held that a settlement agreement would amount to restriction of competition by object where the parties to the agreement were '(i) at least potential competitors, (ii) the generic undertaking committed itself in the agreement to restrict its entry and (iii) the agreement was related to a value transfer from the originator to the generic undertaking which substantially reduced the incentives of the generic undertaking to enter the market'.[187] The Commission considered that a company would be a potential competitor if it had a 'real and concrete possibility' to enter the market, which could be achieved even absent market authorization so long as the generics were pursuing efforts to obtain regulatory approvals.

The Commission was satisfied that the generics were Lundbeck's potential competitors for a variety of reasons. First, Lundbeck itself had considered that there was a 60 per cent chance that a court would invalidate its process patent and the generics thought the process covered by the patent was nothing more than high school chemistry.[188] Second, both Lundbeck and the generics believed that there were alternative processes which the generics could use to produce Citalopram.[189]

[181] *Lundbeck (Commission)*, Decision art 2.
[182] ibid para 623.
[183] ibid para 3.
[184] ibid paras 307, 477, 547.
[185] ibid para 6.
[186] ibid paras 208, 526, 942.
[187] ibid para 661.
[188] ibid para 627.
[189] ibid paras 634–35.

This implies that generics are more likely to be considered potential competitors of the branded manufacturer if the patent at issue covers a process as opposed to a product. As far as the value transfer is concerned, just like the US courts, the Commission recognized that a payment can be made to cover the costs of litigation.[190] If, however, the payment is tied to the generic's anticipated profits upon market entry, it is likely to raise competitive concerns. The Commission concluded that the payments by Lundbeck to the generics played a critical role in securing the generics' commitment to abstain from the market.[191]

The parties appealed the Commission decision to the General Court, which upheld the Commission's decision. The General Court made a number of important findings. First, it held that '[w]hilst patents are indeed presumed valid until they are expressly revoked or invalidated by a competent authority or court, that presumption of validity cannot be equated with a presumption of illegality of generic products validly placed on the market which the patent holder deems to be infringing the patent'.[192] The Court endorsed the Commission's conclusion that the generics in the case were Lundbeck's potential competitors because they had a real concrete possibility of entering the market.[193] The Court was satisfied that the generics could have entered 'at risk' by defending against Lundbeck's infringement suit or by challenging the validity of Lundbeck's patents.[194] Significantly, the Court was convinced that Lundbeck would not have offered such substantial payments to the generics if the possibility of their market entry had been purely theoretical.[195]

Second, the Court emphasized that a reverse payment would not raise competitive concerns

> when (i) that payment is linked to the strength of the patent, as perceived by each of the parties, (ii) it is necessary in order to find an acceptable and legitimate solution in the eyes of the two parties and (iii) it is not accompanied by restrictions intended to delay the market entry of generics.[196]

However, in that case, the Court found that the payments made by Lundbeck were benchmarked against the generics' expected profits upon market entry and hence the settlements constituted agreements to share Lundbeck's monopoly profits with the generics to delay market entry.[197] The Court concluded that the generics accepted the restrictions on market entry not due to the strength of Lundbeck's

[190] ibid paras 1221–23.
[191] ibid paras 802, 869, 957, 1008, 1082, 1169.
[192] Case T-472/13, *H. Lundbeck A/S and Lundbeck Ltd. v. European Commission* EU:T:2016:449, para 121.
[193] ibid paras 115–330.
[194] ibid para 122.
[195] ibid paras 352–53.
[196] ibid paras 350.
[197] ibid paras 366, 377, 388.

process patent but due to the financial inducements offered by Lundbeck.[198] The size of the payment is thus a relevant factor for determining whether a reverse payment settlement is a restriction of competition by object. Most importantly, the Court held that the Commission need not establish the anticompetitive effects of a reverse payment settlement agreement in order to find that it restricts competition.[199] In short, the General Court upheld the Commission's by object approach.

The parties appealed the General Court's decision to the CJEU. Advocate General Kokott has advised the Court of Justice to uphold the General Court's judgment. First and foremost, AG Kokott endorsed the by object approach adopted by the General Court.[200] An agreement constitutes a restriction of competition by object if a branded manufacturer offers money or other value transfer to induce the generic to refrain from entering the market. AG Kokott also agreed with the General Court's conclusion that the generics were Lundbeck's potential competitors. He asserted that potential competition exists if an undertaking has 'a firm intention and an inherent ability to enter the market'[201] and faces no insurmountable barriers to entry.[202] In practice, a potential competitive relationship arises when a generic undertakes concrete steps in preparation for market entry.[203] AG Kokott goes one step further than the General Court in finding a potential competitive relationship between Lundbeck and the generics. While the General Court seemed to rely on the fact that process patents can be circumvented through an alternative production process not covered by the patent, AG Kokott believed that a potential competitive relationship can arise even with a product patent because such a patent can be challenged and invalidated in legal proceedings.[204]

The CJEU has largely endorsed AG Kokott's position and has upheld the General Court's judgment on the definition of potential competition and the circumstances under which a reverse payment settlement amounts to a restriction of competition by object.[205] The CJEU reiterated that whether a generic manufacturer constitutes a potential competitor depends on whether there are 'real and concrete possibilities'[206] of the generic entering the market. This in turn depends on whether the generic has 'a firm intention and an inherent ability to enter the market'.[207] Assessment of intention and ability requires establishing that the generic 'does not meet barriers to entry that are insurmountable' and has taken 'sufficient preparatory steps' for market entry.[208] Following AG Kokott's lead the CJEU asserted that

198 ibid paras 366.
199 ibid paras 436.
200 Case C-591/16, *Lundbeck v. Commission* EU:C:2020:428, para 158.
201 ibid para 78.
202 ibid para 64.
203 ibid para 47.
204 ibid para 49.
205 Case C-591/16 P, *Lundbeck v. Commission* EU:C:2021:243.
206 ibid para 54.
207 ibid para 56.
208 ibid para 57.

the existence of a process patent protecting the manufacturing process of an active pharmaceutical ingredient that is already in the public domain does not represent an insurmountable entry barrier.[209]

The CJEU proclaimed that whether a reverse payment settlement amounts to restriction of competition by object needs to be determined on a case-by-case basis and can only be established 'when it is plain ... that the transfers of value ... cannot have any explanation other than the commercial interest of both the holder of the patent at issue and the party allegedly infringing the patent not to engage in competition on the merits'.[210] The Court, however, clarified that there is no requirement that the value transfers 'should necessarily be greater than the profits which that manufacturer of generic medicines would have made if it had been successful in the patent proceedings'.[211] The Court eventually upheld the General Court's characterization of the agreement as a restriction of competition by object on the grounds that it was 'principally the size of the reverse payments to the manufacturers of generic medicines which had induced them to accept the limitations governing their behaviour'.[212]

(b) *Servier*

A year after the Lundbeck decision, the Commission imposed fines of €427.7 million on Servier and five generic manufacturers for a series of settlement agreements aimed at forestalling generic entry into the market for Servier's best-selling hypertensive, perindopril. Similar to *Lundbeck*, the product patent for the perindopril molecule had expired in most member states between 2003 and 2005.[213] There remained a number of secondary patents covering production processes and form.[214] Servier acquired alternative enabling technologies which would have allowed for generic entry, thereby strengthening the protection of Servier against generic entry.[215] It subsequently came to Servier's attention that five generic manufacturers were preparing to enter the market and had filed opposition procedures against Servier's patents in front of the European Patent Office.[216] Servier eventually settled with the generic challengers, offering them large sums of payment in exchange for their agreement to withdraw challenges to Servier's patents and not to enter the market with generics manufactured by processes covered by Servier's process patents.[217] The agreements stated that the payments were made to compensate for the generics' litigation costs and production and development costs.

209 ibid para 58.
210 ibid para 114.
211 ibid para 115.
212 ibid para 117.
213 *Servier*, para 95.
214 ibid paras 113–23.
215 ibid paras 139–44.
216 ibid paras 153–58.
217 ibid para 1149.

The Commission found that these settlement agreements constituted a restriction of competition by object. The agreements were not legitimate agreements to settle ongoing litigation but agreements to share monopoly profits in order to buy off generic entry. The generic manufacturers had abstained from market entry in exchange for large cash payments by Servier.[218] However, the Commission went beyond its analysis in *Lundbeck* by showing that the settlement agreements also amounted a restriction of competition by effect and abuse of dominance by Servier. The Commission concluded that the settlement agreements 'had also a distinct unilateral aspect, based on the fact that Servier used its market power in order to induce a number of closed generic threats to withdraw from competition with Servier with their respective generic products'.[219]

The parties appealed the Commission's decision to the General Court, which by and large upheld the Commission's decision. The Court upheld the Commission's finding of restriction of competition by object with respect to Servier's settlements with four of the five generics. It, however, annulled the Commission's decision with respect to the settlement with Krka on the grounds that the Commission was unable to show that Krka would have entered the market absent the settlement agreement.[220] Krka had recognized the validity of Servier's patent and therefore it was unlikely that it would have entered the market at risk.[221] The Court also annulled the Commission's finding of an abuse of dominance on the grounds that the Commission had adopted an erroneous market definition.[222]

The Court made a number of important observations. First, the fact that there is a value transfer from the patentee to the generic is insufficient to support a finding of restriction of competition by object.[223] It is only when there is evidence that the generic is induced by the reverse payment, and not the patent's strength, to withdraw from the market that such a finding is justified.[224] This is consistent with the position eventually adopted by the CJEU in *Lundbeck*.

Second, the Court again endorsed the Commission's three-part test for determining whether a reverse payment settlement restricts competition by object: (1) whether the parties are potential competitors; (2) whether the settlement agreement requires the generic to refrain from market entry; and (3) whether the generic's agreement is the result of the branded manufacturer's financial inducement rather than the patent's strength.[225] Where the generic's agreement is the result of the brand's financial inducement, the settlement agreement amounts to market exclusion.[226]

218 ibid para 1150.
219 ibid para 2931.
220 Case T-691/12, *Servier and Ors v. European Commission* EU:T:2018:922, paras 943–1032.
221 ibid para 947.
222 ibid paras 1611-22.
223 ibid para 527.
224 ibid.
225 ibid para 308.
226 ibid para 527.

Third, the Court again conceded that a value transfer that covered litigation costs would have been legitimate and would not have raised competitive concerns.[227] However, the payments by Servier in the case went beyond litigation costs and were hence unjustified.[228] Fourth, the Court reiterated that the existence of a patent does not constitute an insurmountable barrier to entry given the possibility of a patent validity challenge and a finding of non-infringement.[229] Even a valid patent does not preclude potential competition by a generic so long as there remains a possibility for the generic to contest the patent's validity and infringement.[230] This is again consistent with the position taken by the CJEU in *Lundbeck*. Finally, there was some discussion about the side deals in the case and how they were related to the anticompetitive potential of the settlement agreements.[231]

(c) *Generics (UK)*

In early 2020, the CJEU delivered a judgment in a preliminary ruling sought by the UK Competition Appeal Tribunal (CAT) concerning settlement agreements between a branded manufacturer and generic suppliers of an antidepressant. As in *Lundbeck* and *Servier*, the patent covering the chemical compound had expired but there remained a patent governing the manufacturing process for the product at issue.[232] The question presented by CAT to the CJEU was whether a patent settlement agreement between an originator and a generic manufacturer could be considered as restriction of competition by object when the generic agreed:

> (i) not to enter the market, and not to manufacture and/or import the generic medicines manufactured under the patent at issue, and not to persist in their litigation against that patent, (ii) to the conclusion of a distribution agreement enabling them to enter the market with a limited quantity of the relevant generic medicine produced by the originator, and (iii) to receive payments from the originator which were significantly higher than the costs of litigation avoided and which do not constitute payment for goods or services supplied by the generics to the originator.[233]

The CJEU's judgment is largely in line with the approach adopted by the General Court in *Lundbeck* and *Servier*. The CJEU held that the threshold inquiry in the application of Article 101 to reverse payment settlements is whether the parties to the agreement are potential competitors. The parties are potential competitors if

[227] ibid paras 529–30.
[228] ibid para 532.
[229] ibid para 364.
[230] ibid para 368.
[231] *Generics (UK)*, para 9.
[232] ibid.
[233] ibid para 75.

there are 'real and concrete possibilities of the [generic manufacturer] joining the market'.[234] To ascertain such possibilities, the court must examine the 'structure of the market and the economic and legal context'.[235] In particular, the court must be satisfied that the generic manufacturer 'has in fact a firm intention and an inherent ability to enter the market, and that market entry does not meet barriers to entry that are insurmountable'.[236] The CJEU would repeat similar language in *Lundbeck*.

Regarding the former criterion, the relevant factors to consider would be action taken by the generic manufacturer to obtain administrative authorizations and the generic's ability to produce or source the product. Regarding the latter criterion, the CJEU appears to go even further than the General Court in downplaying the importance of patents. It asserted that even if the originator has successfully obtained an injunction against the generic manufacturer, which had happened in the case, this 'in no way prejudge[s] the merits of an infringement action'[237] and does not establish that the patent constitutes an insurmountable barrier to entry. In this regard, the Court did not seem to draw a clear distinction between different types of patents. Therefore, the same reasoning could apply to the stronger product patents.

The Court further held that a designation of restriction of competition by object is justified where there is no other explanation for the value transfer than to induce the generic manufacturer to withdraw from competition.[238] The test is whether the value transfer is 'sufficiently beneficial to encourage the manufacturer of generic medicines to refrain from entering the market concerned and not to compete on the merits with the manufacturer of originator medicines'.[239] Where the value transfer is made to compensate for litigation costs and disruptions caused by the litigation or to remunerate the generic manufacturer for services rendered to the originator, the settlement agreement will not be deemed to a restriction of competition by object.[240] Uncertainty regarding the outcome of the patent validity dispute is not sufficient to justify the value transfer.[241]

The Court further elaborated on the test, explaining that a value transfer would constitute a restriction of competition by object where the value transfer 'can have no other explanation than the commercial interest of the parties to the agreement not to engage in competition on the merit'[242] unless there are 'proven pro-competitive effects capable of giving rise to a reasonable doubt that it causes a sufficient degree of harm to competition'.[243] In determining the absence of an

[234] ibid para 36.
[235] ibid para 39.
[236] ibid para 58.
[237] ibid para 53.
[238] ibid para 87.
[239] ibid para 94.
[240] ibid para 86.
[241] ibid para 101.
[242] ibid para 87.
[243] ibid para 111.

alternative explanation for the value transfer, the court must take into account (1) all transfers of value between the parties (pecuniary and non-pecuniary), (2) whether the net gain of the value transfer may be justified by legitimate and proven quid pro quo or waivers, and (3) whether the net gain is a sufficiently large incentive for the generics to refrain from entering the market.[244]

The burden is on the settling parties to demonstrate the existence of a legitimate, non-anticompetitive explanation for the value transfer.[245] Consistent with its position in *Lundbeck*, the Court asserted that 'there is no requirement that the transfers of value should necessarily be greater than the profits which the manufacturer of generic medicines would have received from a successful outcome by following through with the patent proceedings'.[246] Finally, the CJEU also affirmed that a dominant originator would be abusing its dominant position by entering into reverse payment settlements to keep potential competitors out of the market.[247]

The European Union ostensibly seems to have adopted a stricter approach to reverse payment settlements than did the US Supreme Court in *Actavis*. The Supreme Court applied the Rule of Reason whereas the European courts have consistently upheld the designation of restriction of competition by object. A closer scrutiny, however, would reveal that the difference in approach is not as great as it initially seems. As Cotter argued, the Supreme Court adopted a presumptive illegality approach in *Actavis* in all but name. Meanwhile, it is possible to justify a value transfer under the EU approach if it is made to cover litigation expenses, which is one of the justifications recognized by the *Actavis* court.

One aspect in which the US approach would seem to be preferable is the omission of the detailed analysis of potential competition. While such an element may be required by EU jurisprudence, it adds little to our understanding of the potential anticompetitive effects of the settlement agreement. The fact is that the branded manufacturer or the originator would have no incentive to offer large payments to a generic manufacturer if it did not deem market entry by the latter to be imminent and probable. It is unclear why courts should expend so much effort on this issue when the party best positioned to judge the situation, the branded manufacturer or the originator, has already made its determination and underlined this determination with hefty sums. Overall, the general similarity in analytical frameworks adopted by the United States and the European Union simplifies the decision for developing country authorities as it obviates the need to choose between wildly divergent approaches.

[244] ibid paras 90, 92, and 93.
[245] ibid paras 96–98.
[246] ibid para 94.
[247] ibid para 151.

F. A Proposed Framework for Developing Countries

Given the importance of the affordability of drugs to developing country consumers, any business practice that may help to inflate drug prices artificially deserves the attention of developing country competition authorities. There is convincing evidence that reverse payment settlements delay generic entry and help to prop up drug prices. Therefore, these settlements should be an enforcement priority for developing country authorities.

1. Determination of Legality

The first question that needs to be answered is what kind of legal rule should be applied to reverse payment settlements by developing country authorities and courts. The choice is between a presumptive illegality or by object restriction approach, and a Rule of Reason framework or a full-fledged effects-based analysis which the European Commission furnished alongside a by object rule in *Servier*. As mentioned earlier, the European Courts have consistently endorsed a by objects approach so long as three conditions are met: (1) the parties to the agreement are potential competitors; (2) the settlement agreement requires the generic to refrain from market entry; and (3) the generic's acquiescence to stay out of the market is the result of the financial inducement offered by the originator.

Even though the US Supreme Court ostensibly adopted the Rule of Reason in *Actavis*, the framework laid down in the case amounts to a rule of presumptive illegality. The anticompetitive effects of a settlement agreement under which the reverse payment exceeds the branded manufacturer's litigation costs are assumed. What is left for the defendant to do is to provide alternative pro-competitive justifications for the settlement agreement, such as the payment being an approximation of the patentee's litigation costs or compensation for services offered by the generic for the branded manufacturer.

The weight of the scholarly opinion is that a presumptive illegality approach is preferable. There is a consensus that a reverse payment in excess of the patentee's anticipated litigation costs is presumptively anticompetitive and would require a justification. The highest courts on both sides of the Atlantic have both effectively embraced a presumptive illegality rule. The two justifications for a reverse payment enumerated by Justice Breyer in *Actavis* are widely accepted by commentators. The European courts have also accepted these two justifications as possible defences for a reverse payment settlement. Beyond these, it would take a rather persuasive justification to save a reverse payment settlement.

It would thus seem that an appropriate rule for developing country authorities and courts to apply to reverse payment settlements would be one under which a reverse payment in excess of the patentee's anticipated litigation costs would be presumed illegal unless the parties can show that the payment is made as compensation for services rendered by the generics or other justifications, which, as Cotter has argued, may include the fact that the generic is cash-strapped and hence in need of money, or that there are other reliable indications of patent validity, such as that the patent has withstood other validity challenges or that the patentee has successfully obtained an injunction against the generic.

One issue remains to be addressed. That is whether developing country authorities and courts should adopt the three conditions applied by the European courts before applying the by object condemnation under Article 101. Condition (2), that the generic is required to refrain from market entry, is the *sine qua non* of every reverse payment settlement and does not present a meaningful requirement. Conditions (1) and (3), that the parties to the agreement are potential competitors and that the generic's acquiescence to stay out of the market is the result of the financial inducement offered by the originator, are more problematic. As evident from the *Lundbeck* and *Servier* judgments, the European courts have devoted much attention to the potential competitor issue and to the extent to which the existence of a valid patent constitutes an insurmountable barrier to entry for the generic.

While the European courts may be compelled by precedents to apply this requirement, it is largely superfluous from the perspective of developing country enforcement against reverse payment settlements. As suggested earlier, the best judge of whether a generic entrant presents a serious competitive threat must be the branded manufacturer itself. There is no reason why a branded manufacturer would offer to pay huge sums to a generic entrant if generic entry was not imminent. The branded manufacturer may think that its patent may be invalidated, held to be not infringed, or the generic entrant may enter the market at risk. Whatever the circumstance, what matters is that the branded manufacturer has determined that the competitive threat is real enough that it is worth paying off the generic to forestall market entry.

Once it is determined that the reverse payment exceeds anticipated litigation costs or is not justified as compensation for services rendered by the generic, the presumption must be that the branded manufacturer is paying the generic to stay out of the market. Any *ex-post* evaluation of the competitive relationship between the branded manufacturer and the generic and the likelihood of generic entry despite the various legal or economic barriers adds nothing to our understanding of the anticompetitive effects and needlessly complicates the analysis. The potential competition condition under EU law should be eschewed by developing country authorities and courts. One may perhaps argue that by downplaying the significance of an injunction against the generic as a barrier to entry in *Generics (UK)*, the CJEU has so watered down the potential competition condition that it ceases to be a meaningful requirement.

Condition (3), that the generic agreed to stay out of the market due to the financial inducement of the reverse payment, in a way can be tied to justification for the payment. The best way to approach this condition is to say that once it is shown that the payment exceeds the anticipated litigation costs and does not constitute compensation for services rendered by the generic, the presumption is that the excess payment is made to induce the generic to stay out of the market. That would be the most obvious logical conclusion to draw based on the objective facts. The inquiry should end there. Any attempt to delve into the generic's subjective state of mind would again needlessly complicate the analysis. In short, developing country authorities and courts need not adopt the three conditions imposed by the European courts for the application of the by object approach or presumptive illegality rule to reverse payment settlements.

2. Appropriate Remedy

There is a host of possible remedies for an anticompetitive reverse payment settlement. It is of course possible to impose fines. But if the main motivation behind prosecution against such kind of settlement in developing countries is to help bring down drug prices, fines will probably be of limited utility. What is needed is a remedy that will help to bring about price reduction. One possible remedy is compulsory licensing. The branded manufacturer or the originator can be required to license its patented drug for production by generic entrants. If it is determined that a reverse payment settlement has forestalled generic entry into the market which would have happened otherwise, the obvious solution would be to require the branded manufacturer to allow generic entry through a compulsory license.

The thorny issue, however, is the appropriate level of royalty required for the generic compulsory licensee. This is difficult because the appropriate royalty would be zero if the patent was deemed invalid or not infringed but would be a positive figure if there was a non-insignificant chance that the patent is valid and infringed. Royalty would need to be weighted by the probability that the patent is valid and infringed. Determination of the appropriate royalty level would hence require assessment of patent validity and the patentee's infringement claim, which is what courts have assiduously avoided in reverse payment settlement cases. It would be immensely counterproductive for courts to avoid these two issues in the liability phase of the case, just to be forced to resurrect them in the remedy stage.

There is probably no satisfactory solution to the dilemma here absent a full patent validity and infringement trial, which most commentators except for Crane have suggested that we avoid. The logic of the legality of a reverse payment that does not exceed a patentee's anticipated litigation costs is that it is within the patentee's legal right to avoid litigation costs if litigation will result in a confirmation of patent validity and infringement. Once the patent is deemed valid and infringed, the generic will not be able to enter the market without the patentee's blessing, in which case a reverse payment settlement does not alter the market outcome. Regardless of whether the settlement is upheld or not, there is no generic entry.

A reverse payment that exceeds the anticipated litigation costs must indicate that there is a non-negligible probability that the patent will be deemed invalid or not infringed. By considering such a payment presumptively illegal, a judgment has been made that a patentee should not be allowed to pay a generic to ward off such a non-negligible probability. The implication is that if there is any doubt about patent validity and infringement, it should be resolved against the patentee's interest and in favour of competition. The same logic would dictate that if there is any doubt concerning patent validity and infringement in the imposition of a compulsory license, it should be resolved in favour of competition and against the patentee. This would lend support for a royalty-free compulsory license.

Lastly, there may also be complications with the imposition of compulsory licensing under the Agreement on Trade-Related Aspects of Intellectual Property Rights (TRIPS Agreement), which has been discussed in Chapter 8 and will not be repeated here.

3. Implementation Issues

There could be particular implementation issues when a developing country authority enforces against reverse payment settlements. These issues arise from the fact that the branded manufacturer or originator and the generics are most likely to be located elsewhere. Almost all branded manufacturers of pharmaceuticals and many generic manufacturers hail from the industrialized economies. They may have no domestic operations in a developing country and only export their drugs through an authorized distributor. There is a risk that a drug company may simply abandon the domestic market of a developing country once its settlement agreement has been condemned. Developing country competition authorities hence may encounter difficulty exercising jurisdiction, conducting investigation, and imposing effective remedies on these foreign firms.

These problems do not lend themselves to an obvious solution. One solution that may help to deter the strategy of market abandonment is for developing country authorities to band together and undertake enforcement as a group. There are numerous regional groupings in Africa, Latin America, and South East Asia, such as Mercosur, the Caribbean Community (CARICOM), the Economic Community of West African States (ECOWAS), and the Association of South east Asian Nations (ASEAN) that have different degrees of competition law enforcement capabilities.

To the extent that enforcement can be undertaken on a regional level, it may make it less likely for a pharmaceutical company to resort to market abandonment as a strategy. A much larger market will need to be foregone if it is a regional bloc pursuing an investigation.

Another solution, which is less about market abandonment and more concerned with the difficulty in exercising jurisdiction and carrying out effective investigation, is for developing country authorities to import the decision of an established jurisdiction and impose remedies on the basis of that decision. Michal Gal has advocated this concept previously in the context of international cartels.[248] This suggestion is particularly well-suited for reverse payment settlements because it is often the same underlying agreement that inflicts consumer harm in different jurisdictions. This would be true if the same settlement applies to multiple jurisdictions and prevents generic entry in these jurisdictions. Once the authority in an established jurisdiction has analysed and condemned it, there is no good reason for a developing country authority to reinvent the wheel, especially given the complexity of these cases and the amount of enforcement and judicial resources necessary to tackle one case.

It would be advisable for a developing country authority to incorporate the liability findings from an established jurisdiction and focus on fashioning an appropriate remedy. This not only helps to economize on enforcement resources, it also helps to minimize possible obstacles in conducting an effective investigation. The lack of a local operation in a developing country may mean that a pharmaceutical company may have little incentive to cooperate with an investigation by turning over relevant documents and making executives available for interviews.

G. Conclusion

Like excessive pricing enforcement in pharmaceuticals, enforcement against reverse payment settlements will not be easy for developing country competition authorities. The difficulty does not chiefly stem from legal analysis. If developing countries adopt the rule of presumptive illegality suggested above, the condemnation of reverse payment settlements should be relatively straightforward. Most reverse payment settlements entail payments that far exceed the patentee's anticipated litigation costs. While the proliferation of more complex settlement agreements featuring licensing, co-promotion, and other agreements to disguise the value transfer may render the analysis less straightforward, this can be alleviated by shifting the burden to demonstrate the legitimacy of the payment to the defendants. The difficulty arises in exercising jurisdiction over foreign pharmaceutical

[248] Michal S Gal, 'Free Movement of Judgments: Increasing Deterrence of International Cartels Through Jurisdictional Reliance' (2010) 51 Virginia Journal of International Law 57.

companies and in crafting and imposing effective remedies. Despite these challenges, securing affordable drugs for their consumers is too important a duty for developing country competition authorities to shirk. It would be a worthwhile endeavour even if these authorities are largely confined to piggy-backing on the enforcement effort of the established jurisdictions.

10
Restrictive Licensing Practices

A. Introduction

Thus far this book has focused on patent exploitation practices that are pertinent to most developing countries regardless of their technological capacity. Unilateral refusal to deal, tying, excessive pricing, and reverse payment settlements affect most developing countries. There exists a category of patent exploitation practices— restrictive licensing practices —that only matter to jurisdictions in which licensing takes place. For countries that are not recipients of technology licensing—the production countries—perhaps because domestic production activities are not sufficiently technologically advanced to absorb patented technologies, restrictive licensing practices should attract little attention from them. These practices, however, are highly salient to beneficiaries of foreign technology licensing, the technology adaptation countries and proto-innovation countries. Given that technology licensing is one of the three modes of technology transfer and redounds the greatest direct benefits to the host country, competition authorities in these countries must approach restrictive licensing practices in a thoughtful manner.

The potential impact of patent-competition rules on licensing has already been discussed in Chapter 3. It may be helpful to recall a number of insights from that discussion. First, it was asserted that the relationship between patent–competition rules and technology transfer is more nuanced than that between those rules and innovation. While patentee reward and revenue from other appropriation mechanisms largely dictate the amount of innovation incentives, a much larger basket of factors influence a firm's decision to undertake technology transfer. These include size of the market, domestic manufacturing and technological capacity, proximity to major markets, and many other factors that have been captured in Dunning's OLI paradigm. Legal rules are only one part of the puzzle.

Second, the impact of legal rules may be more pronounced on the decision between foreign direct investment (FDI) and licensing, which Dunning refers to as internalization advantages. Rules on licensing practices, including competition regulation of licensing restrictions, can steer the decision from FDI to licensing and vice versa. More permissive licensing rules allow the patentee to impose restrictions to protect her technology and to extract greater licensing revenue, which render licensing a more attractive option than FDI. Given that licensing is generally

The Patent–Competition Interface in Developing Countries. Thomas K. Cheng, Oxford University Press. © Thomas K. Cheng 2021. DOI: 10.1093/oso/9780192857354.003.0010

more beneficial than FDI—it results in a genuine transfer of technology ownership to a developing country—developing country competition authorities may need to take that into account when enforcing against restrictive licensing practices.

Third, patent–competition rules can be classified into three categories as far as their impact on technology transfer is concerned. The first category includes rules that directly adjust the scope of patent rights outside of the licensing context, such as those that regulate patent tying and retail price maintenance (RPM) for a patented product. The second category includes rules that implicate the robustness of patent protection, such as those pertaining to no challenge clauses, reverse payments, and unilateral refusal to license. These rules call for special attention because economic studies have shown that the robustness of patent protection can have a significant and direct impact on technology transfer. The third category encompasses rules governing restrictive licensing practices. These rules determine the profitability of technology licensing and alter the attractiveness of licensing vis-à-vis other modes of technology transfer.

This category can be further divided into two sub-categories. There are licensing practices that do not enhance or extend the patentee's market power and those that do. Licensing practices that generate greater licensing revenue without strengthening the patentee's market power can be viewed as potentially exploitative practices that allow the patentee to extract more consumer surplus. The trade-off underlying regulation of these practices is between the patentee's incentives to license and consumer welfare. This trade-off is relatively more straightforward. It is consequently easier for developing country competition authorities to regulate these practices. In contrast, licensing practices that do enhance or extend the patentee's market power present more complications and need to be handled with greater care.

Fourth, economic studies have produced a number of insights into the relationship between the degree of patent protection, which by analogy also applies to the patent–competition rules, and licensing. With the exception of one study, the thrust of these studies seems to be that among the three modes of technology transfer, licensing faces the greatest imitation risk and therefore relies most heavily on patent protection. These studies find that heightened patent protection generally leads to a shift to licensing. The reliance of licensing on patent protection suggests that restrictive licensing practices that implicate the robustness of this protection will be particularly important to a patentee's licensing decision.

While patent protection prevents unauthorized imitation, a successful patent validity challenge will permit legal replication of the technology. A licensing restriction that prevents the most probable validity challenges offers the patentee the same kind of protection as effective patent enforcement. No challenge clauses can perform precisely this function. In fact, one can argue that forestalling validity challenges is more critical to the security of patent ownership than rooting out unauthorized copying. Once a patent has been invalidated, it will open a floodgate to legal imitators. The impact of the legal ruling is not confined to the challenger. No challenge clauses thus deserve special attention.

B. No Challenge Clauses

1. An Overview

A patentee may insert a no challenge clause[1] into a licensing agreement to prevent the licensee from launching a challenge to the validity of the licensed patent.[2] According to Inger Orstavik, '[t]he object of a no-challenge clause is to fortify a position granted by law'. It 'weaken[s] the ability and motivation of licensees to challenge invalid patents'.[3] The obligation not to challenge usually lasts for the duration of the licensing agreement, although some no challenge clauses impose an obligation that spans the entire patent term. These clauses do not provide patentees absolute protection from validity challenges. Unrelated third parties remain free to launch challenges.[4] Moreover, to the extent that courts do not enforce these clauses with an injunction, a patentee may only receive damages for a breach of contract while her patent risks being invalidated.[5]

No challenge clauses can be classified into two types. The first type imposes an outright prohibition of validity challenges. Alan Miller and Michal Gal call these no contest clauses.[6] The second type does not expressly prohibit challenges but exacts penalties of various kinds in the event of a challenge. Miller and Gal have called these challenge penalty clauses.[7] The difference between the first and the second types is by no means categorical. One can easily imagine the penalty imposed to be so onerous that the clause effectively functions as an outright ban.[8]

Miller and Gal have identified five kinds of challenge penalty clauses. The first is termination-upon-challenge clauses.[9] These clauses terminate the licensing agreement either automatically or at the licensor's discretion in the event of a licensee's validity challenge. The licensee loses her rights under the agreement upon

[1] The following section is partly based on Thomas K Cheng, 'Antitrust Treatment of No Challenge Clause' (2016) 5 New York University Journal of Intellectual Property and Entertainment Law 437.

[2] Inger B Orstavik, 'Technology Transfer Agreements: Grantbacks and No Challenge Clauses in the New EC Technology Transfer Regulation' (2005) 36 International Review of Intellectual Property and Competition Law 83, 87.

[3] Michal S Gal and Alan D Miller, 'Patent Challenge Clauses: A New Antitrust Offense' (2017) 102 Iowa Law Review 1477, 1483.

[4] ibid.

[5] Cheng (n 1) 441.

[6] Alan D Miller and Michal S Gal, 'Licensee Patent Challenges' (2015) 32 Yale Journal on Regulation 122, 127.

[7] ibid 131.

[8] *Rates Technology, Inc. v. Speakeasy, Inc.*, 685 F.3d 163 (2d Cir. 2012).

[9] Gal and Miller (n 3) 1482.

termination. Continual implementation of the licensed technology will constitute infringement, perhaps even wilful infringement, which results in trebled damages under US patent law.[10] The second type are elevated royalty clauses. These stipulate a higher royalty in the event of a challenge, or in some cases, in the event of an unsuccessful challenge.[11] The third type penalizes a challenging licensee by curtailing the technology to be transferred, which can be unrelated to the licensing agreement at issue.[12] The fourth type erects procedural impediments to validity challenges, for example by mandating arbitration or imposing a fee shifting obligation.[13] The final type imposes an implicit penalty by rewarding the licensee with a bonus for refraining from a challenge.[14] A challenge would result in a financial loss to the licensee under this clause just as it would under a more conventional challenge penalty clause.

2. Arguments for and Against No Challenge Clauses

The arguments for and against no challenge clauses are fairly straightforward. The competitive harm of these clauses turns on the validity and the market power of the underlying patent. A no challenge clause allows a patentee to extract consumer surplus despite the invalidity of her patent.[15] It allows the patentee to continue to impose supra-competitive prices when the invention deserves no patent protection and should face full competition. In contrast, a no challenge clause inflicts no consumer harm if the underlying patent is valid.[16] All it does is to pre-empt unsuccessful validity challenges, something which has been argued to avoid a waste of litigation resources. Imposition of supra-competitive prices is premised on market power. A patent unaccompanied by market power will not allow the patentee to extract monopoly profit from consumers. Consumer harm will only arise when a no challenge clause protects an invalid patent that possesses market power.

There are two possible justifications for no challenge clauses. The most obvious one is that they help to preserve the incentives of technology owners to license their technology. Because it is often said that licensees are the best positioned and most incentivized to launch a validity challenge,[17] no challenge clauses give patentees greater confidence to license their technology. This is especially true because licensing may expose the patentee to more validity challenges.[18] A patentee will have

[10] Patent Act 2011 (US) s 284.
[11] Cheng (n 1) 442.
[12] Gal and Miller (n 3) 1482.
[13] ibid.
[14] ibid.
[15] Cheng (n 1) 477.
[16] ibid.
[17] *Lear Inc. v. Adkins*, 395 US 653, 670 (1969).
[18] Cheng (n 1) 479.

to disclose proprietary information about her technology during the licensing process. This information may cast doubt on the novelty or the non-obviousness of her invention and attract validity challenges. A patentee may not be willing to contemplate such disclosure unless she is assured that the disclosed information will not be used against her.

The second justification can be thought of as an extension of the first. Prohibition of no challenge clauses hampers licensing activities. A more limited scope for licensing reduces the ability of patentees to monetize their inventions. This would be especially detrimental to independent inventors who are not backed by significant commercialization capacity. Foreclosure of the licensing option may deprive these inventors of the most effective, if not the only, means to profit from their inventions. It may cause these inventors to forsake inventive activities altogether.

These are the pros and cons of no challenge clauses in the industrialized economy context. As mentioned earlier, the loss of licensing incentives takes on extra significance in the technology adaptation countries. Technology transfer is the main avenue for technology upgrade. These countries cannot rely on their own innovation due to the lack of domestic innovation capacity. Because licensing is the most beneficial to the host country, developing country competition authorities need to craft a cautious approach to enforcement against no challenge clauses. A loss of licensing incentives on the part of foreign technology owners can severely affect a technology adaptation country.

(a) Consumer harm

The consumer harm of no challenge clauses is contingent on the validity of the underlying patent. If the patent turns out to be invalid, no challenge clauses inflict harm on consumers by forcing them to continue to pay supra-competitive prices when such prices are unjustified. They artificially and unjustifiably extend the patentee's market power. If the patent is valid, however, these clauses are arguably beneficial as they save needless litigation expenses.

The incidence of consumer harm of no challenge clauses thus depends on the likelihood of patent invalidation. If invalidation is rare, these clauses do not raise serious concerns. If, in contrast, patents are regularly nullified, consumer harm can be widespread. One fundamental difference between intellectual property (IP) and real property is that while real property rights are relatively certain, patent rights are probabilistic in nature. Carl Shapiro famously asserts that patents do not provide a right to exclude but only the right to try to exclude.[19] Patents are often erroneously granted due to the dearth of time and resources on the part of patent examination bodies to devote to patent examination. Until recent reforms,

[19] Carl Shapiro, 'Antitrust Limits to Patent Settlements' (2003) 34 RAND Journal of Economics 392, 395.

examiners at the US Patent and Trademark Office (USPTO) are said to spend no more than eighteen hours on each patent application.[20]

As a consequence, patents are frequently invalidated in litigation. John Allison and Mark Lemley find that 46 per cent of patents that were litigated to judgment were found to be invalid.[21] A later study found a higher invalidation rate of approximately 70 per cent.[22] This is despite the fact that, under the Patent Act in the United States, a patent is entitled to a presumption of validity and a challenger must show by clear and convincing evidence that the patent is invalid.[23] The invalidation rate is even higher for patent assertion entities, otherwise known as 'patent trolls'. According to one study, patent trolls win only 8 per cent of the cases in which patent validity is litigated to judgment.[24]

This state of affairs means that patent validity cannot be presumed or taken for granted. It also means that determination of the legality of no challenge clauses may require an evaluation of patent validity. This is a highly controversial proposition. In the context of reverse payment settlements, which share many similarities with no challenge clauses,[25] commentators have warned against considering patent validity.[26] The US Supreme Court has declared such consideration to be unnecessary in a reverse payment case.[27] Miller and Gal similarly warn against assessing patent validity in a no challenge clause case.[28] Their main justifications are that determination of patent validity would introduce needless complexity to the proceedings and that there are scant pro-competitive justifications for these clauses.[29] The lack of pro-competitive justifications means that a presumptive illegality approach, which they advocate and which would not require determination of patent validity, would be suitable.

The analogy between no challenge clauses and reverse payment settlements, however, is incomplete and the argument against considering patent validity in a reverse payment case is not fully applicable to a no challenge clause case. The crucial difference between no challenge clauses and reverse payment settlements is that with the latter, there is a readily available a proxy indicator for the parties' own assessment of patent validity and likely consumer harm. That indicator is the size

[20] Mark A Lemley, 'Rational Ignorance at the Patent Office' (2001) 95 Northwestern University Law Review 1495, 1496.

[21] John R Allison and Mark A Lemley, 'Empirical Evidence on the Validity of Litigated Patents' (1998) 26 American Intellectual Property Law Association Quarterly Journal 185, 205.

[22] Paul M Janicke and LiLan Ren, 'Who Wins Patent Infringement Cases?' (2006) 34 American Intellectual Property Law Association Quarterly Journal 1, 20–22.

[23] Patent Act 2011 (US) s 282.

[24] John R Allison, Mark A Lemley, and Joshua Walker, 'Patent Quality and Settlement Among Repeat Patent Litigants' (2011) 99 Georgetown Law Journal 677, 694.

[25] Cheng (n 1) 470–75.

[26] Einer Elhauge and Alex Krueger, 'Solving the Patent Settlement Puzzle' (2012) 91 Texas Law Review 283, 289.

[27] *Federal Trade Commission v. Actavis*, 570 US 136, 158 (2013).

[28] Gal and Miller (n 3) 1529.

[29] ibid.

of the reverse payment. The US Supreme Court has acknowledged that there is no reason for a patentee to make a large payment to the alleged infringer if she is confident about the validity of her own patent.[30] An unusually large payment by the patentee thus can serve as evidence of the likely infirmity of the underlying patent.

Such a proxy indicator is missing in no challenge clause cases. Under a normal licensing agreement, the direction of payment is what one would expect. The licensee pays royalty to the patentee and not the other way round. It is possible that the patentee makes an implicit payment to the licensee by offering a royalty discount to induce the latter to accept a no challenge clause. The ascertainment of the magnitude of such a discount, however, would be well-nigh impossible, especially when no challenge clauses are incorporated in all licensing agreements of a patentee and hence a comparative analysis will not be informative. Therefore, there is no convenient proxy for patent validity in a no challenge clause case.

Miller and Gal also justify their presumptive illegality approach in light of the lack of pro-competitive justifications. While that may be true in the industrialized economies, the importance of licensing as a means of technology transfer means that a diminution of licensing incentives needs to be taken more seriously in developing countries. The potentially deleterious impact of no challenge clauses on licensing incentives cannot be dismissed out of hand. If the existence of consumer harm and hence the legality of no challenge clauses is contingent on patent validity, there seems to be no way to sidestep assessing patent validity in a no challenge clause case. Miller and Gal are certainly right to say that it will introduce considerable complexity to the proceedings. The question is whether this complexity can be rendered more manageable. This will be addressed in section 4(b).

No challenge clauses inflict harm on consumers by forcing them to continue to pay supra-competitive prices for the patented product. A patent, however, does not necessarily allow a patentee to charge supra-competitive prices. A patentee also needs market power in order to do that. There was a time when a patent was presumed to confer market power under US antitrust law. That presumption, however, was overturned in *Illinois Tool Works v. Independent Ink, Inc.*[31] This decision stemmed from a realization that where there are reasonable substitutes for the patented product, the patent does not wield market power and the patentee will not be able to charge supra-competitive prices.[32] Market power thus needs to be independently proved. Absent market power, the incorporation of a no challenge clause in the licensing agreement makes scant difference to consumers. Market power is a prerequisite for competition law intervention against no challenge clauses.[33]

[30] *Actavis*, 570 US at 154-55.
[31] *Illinois Tool Works, Inc. v. Independent Ink, Inc.*, 547 US 28, 31 (2006).
[32] Cheng (n 1) 489.
[33] Elhauge and Krueger (n 26) 323.

In sum, no challenge clauses only create consumer harm when the underlying patent is invalid and yet possesses market power, allowing the patentee to charge supra-competitive prices for products incorporating the patented technology. Nonetheless, it is unrealistic to expect a developing country competition authority or court to conduct a mini patent validity trial in the midst of a competition proceeding. Alternative ways to address the issue of patent validity are needed. As for market power, one possible approach is to apply a presumption of legality when a no challenge clause is attached to a patent with no market power. This will be discussed in greater detail in section 4(d).

(b) Impact on incentives to license

One of the most obvious drawbacks of prohibiting no challenge clauses is that it will lead to a reduction in licensing incentives. This is particularly problematic for technology adaptation countries that rely on foreign technology transfer for technology upgrade. If there is no way to mitigate the incentive reduction effects, there will be an inevitable trade-off between consumer harm and licensing incentives.

Miller and Gal have argued that even if a prohibition of no challenge clauses leads to a loss in licensing activities, the foregone licensing activities redound few social benefits and may even inflict social harm.[34] They posit three scenarios—where the patentee has a comparative advantage in production over all competitors,[35] where one producer who is not the patentee possesses a significant comparative advantage over all rivals,[36] and where the most efficient producer, who is not the patentee, does not enjoy a significant comparative advantage over rivals[37]—and conclude that in none of the three scenarios would a loss of licensing bring about a substantial reduction in social welfare. While this conclusion may be true where licensing takes place in the domestic context, the welfare considerations would be entirely different when licensing represents a technology transfer to a developing country. It can no longer be safely assumed that prohibition of no challenge clauses will not reduce social welfare in the recipient country, especially when the technology is sufficient novel and valuable.

The more convincing response to the concern about reduction in licensing incentives is that prohibition of no challenge clauses will have greater impact on the licensing of weaker patents than that of stronger patents.[38] This stems from the fact that the owner of a stronger patent has less to be concerned about validity challenges. In contrast, validity challenges matter more to the owner of a weaker patent, who may be more deterred from licensing when she cannot use no challenge clauses to forestall these challenges. In a regime where no challenge clauses are

[34] Gal and Miller (n 3) 1509.
[35] ibid.
[36] ibid.
[37] ibid 1510.
[38] Cheng (n 1) 499.

illegal, the patentee will examine its patent closely and assess how strong it is before deciding to license her invention. If she is assured of the strength of the patent, she would pay little heed to validity challenges. If she harbours concerns about her patent, however, she will have to decide whether she wants to take the risk and proceed with licensing, especially when licensing will give the licensees more information about the technology and put them in a better position to challenge.

Patentees are uniquely placed to evaluate their own patents as they have access to proprietary information pertaining to patent validity.[39] They should be able to make this choice in an informed manner. If we allow the owner of a weak patent to impose a no challenge clause, the patentee will be able to enjoy the double benefit of profiting from a patent of questionable validity and doing so in the most cost-effective manner by deploying the most efficient downstream producers without regard to the likelihood of validity challenges. And more pertinently from a developing country's perspective, a loss in licensing incentives raises few concerns if it only affects weaker patents that cover less valuable technologies. The impact on a developing country's ability to acquire valuable technology will be limited.

Prohibition of no challenge clauses may still deter risk averse owners of stronger patents to license their technologies. Given the substantial loss to a patentee in the event of an invalidation, a risk averse technology owner may refrain from licensing rather than putting her patent at risk. The extent to which a developing country needs to be concerned about the deterrent effect on licensing activities thus depends on the proportion of foreign technology owners that are risk averse. Einer Elhauge and Alan Krueger cast doubt on the prevalence of risk aversion on the part of corporations.[40] Yet it probably cannot be categorically ruled out, especially when the technology is licensed to a developing country. The deterrent effect of banning no challenge clauses on licensing activities is likely to be smaller than initially feared but cannot be dismissed completely.

(c) Impact on innovation incentives

It has been argued that prohibiting no challenge clauses and allowing licensees to mount indiscriminate challenges would bring uncertainty to patentee reward and undermine innovation incentives.[41] For the quid pro quo underlying the patent system to function properly, 'inventors need to be confident that their rights will be secure. Such confidence is fundamental to providing this incentive to innovate.'[42]

[39] Rochelle Cooper Dreyfuss and Lawrence S Pope, 'Dethroning Lear? Incentives to Innovate After MedImmune' (2009) 24 Berkeley Technology Law Journal 971, 1001. For example, only the patentee is likely to know the true date of invention and the identity of the inventor.

[40] Elhauge and Krueger (n 26) 312.

[41] Crane similarly argued that prohibiting reverse payments would undermine innovation incentives. Daniel A Crane, 'Exit Payments in Settlement of Patent Infringement Lawsuits: Antitrust Rules and Economic Implications' (2002) 54 Florida Law Review 747, 751.

[42] Nicholas Roper, 'Limiting Unfettered Challenges to Patent Validity, Upholding No-Challenge Clauses in Pre-Litigation Patent Settlements Between Preexisting Parties to a License' (2014) 35 Cardozo Law Review 1649, 1662.

This line of argument is addressed by the notion of probabilistic patents. Patentees should only be entitled to risk-adjusted reward for their invention.[43] So long as they receive such a reward, innovation incentives will be properly maintained. To put it slightly differently, it has been argued that 'profits that accrue to patent holders incentivize innovation when, and only when, the patent is properly awarded. In other words, the patent holder should not receive any profits that he would not have received had the PTO done its job properly.'[44] If all patentees, regardless of the strength of their patents, receive a risk-free reward, there will be over-compensation for weak patents.[45] The very nature of a probabilistic patent means that patentee reward should be weighted by the probability of invalidation. No challenge clauses artificially lower the risk of invalidation and hence render return to a patented invention essentially risk-free.

The artificial inflation of the returns to a patented invention can have distortionary effects on innovation incentives. When a firm makes a research and development (R&D) investment decision, the size of its investment is dependent on the level of technical advancement it wants to pursue. Generally, a more technically advanced invention will be more costly to create and more deserving of patent protection. Stronger patents, which cover more novel and valuable inventions, hence cost more to procure and deserve greater compensation from society. Weaker patents, which involve inventions that are less novel and less technically meritorious, can be obtained more cheaply and should be less generously rewarded. If no challenge clauses cause inventions of varying merits to receive the same reward, potential inventors will rationally gravitate toward inventions of more questionable merit to save costs. As Miller and Gal observe, '[a]n increase in the prize given to unwarranted patents does not strengthen incentives to develop patentable ideas. It merely strengthens incentives to patent non-innovative ideas, a form of undesirable rent-seeking.'[46]

The levelling effect of no challenge clauses on patentee returns is not necessarily complete. A patentee may need to offer some financial enticements in order to induce licensees to accept a no challenge clause for a relatively weak invention. A patentee may hence receive a lower financial reward for a weak invention than for a strong invention. Whatever enticements the patentee offers to the licensees, however, are unlikely to be commensurate with the usual adjustments to patentee reward due to the risk of invalidation when patents are not protected by no challenge clauses.

[43] Shapiro (n 19) 395.
[44] Gal and Miller (n 3) 1516.
[45] Elhauge and Krueger (n 26) 294.
[46] Gal and Miller (n 3) 1516.

Overall, instead of reducing innovation incentives, a prohibition on no challenge clauses helps to align patentee reward with the technical merit of the invention and generate incentives to pursue stronger patents. It helps to ensure that the patent system functions as intended. In contrast, prohibiting no challenge clauses will reduce the variations in patentee reward that tend to reflect the technical merits of the invention and skew innovation incentives toward weaker patents. The concern that the prohibition of no challenge clauses will hamper innovation incentives is hence unfounded.

(d) Avoidance of wasteful litigation costs

One further justification for no challenge clauses is that they help to avoid needless litigation over patent validity and reduce the transaction costs of the patent system. Costs for patent litigation could be substantial. It can cost up to USD32 million for one party to litigate a patent infringement suit in the United States.[47] Double those costs for two parties and add in the costs associated with the disruption to the business operation of the two parties and the overall costs could be substantial.

It would be indeed beneficial to minimize the significant costs involved in patent litigation. Litigation costs, however, are not the only relevant consideration. Whether litigation expenses are wasteful crucially depends on the validity of the underlying patent. If the challenged patent turns out to be valid, litigation costs would have been better avoided. If the patent is invalidated, however, litigation costs are well spent as the suit saves consumers significant surplus that would have been extracted by the patentee and the deadweight loss that would have resulted from the supra-competitive pricing. The wastefulness of litigation costs can only be confirmed *ex post* after the validity of the patent has been adjudicated. It cannot be established *ex ante*.

The *ex ante* optimal amount of patent validity challenges can be ascertained by balancing litigation costs weighted by the probability of patent validity against total welfare loss (consumer welfare loss plus deadweight loss) weighted by the probability of invalidity. Assuming that the probability of invalidation is 50 per cent, which is toward the low end of the range estimated by commentators, litigation would be socially optimal so long as the total welfare loss inflicted by an invalid patent outweighs litigation costs. If the technology at issue is at all valuable—and most patents subject to a validity challenge cover a valuable technology—the total welfare loss would be likely to far outweigh the avoided litigation costs. This would imply that patent validity challenges are socially optimal *ex ante* and litigation costs are not wasteful. No challenge clauses do not avoid wasteful litigation expenses.

[47] Elhauge and Krueger (n 26) 306.

3. Case Law on No Challenge Clauses

(a) The United States

The United States has handled no challenge clauses mostly as an issue of enforceability under its patent law. No US court seems to have ruled on the legality of these clauses under antitrust law.[48] In a way, deeming no challenge clauses unenforceable under patent law has similar effects as enjoining the enforcement of these clauses under antitrust law. If no challenge clauses are challenged in a government civil enforcement action where the remedy is limited to injunctive relief, an antitrust determination of illegality is tantamount to a finding of unenforceability under patent law. The consequences would be entirely different, however, if no challenge clauses were pursued in a private damages action.

Any discussion of the treatment of no challenge clauses under US law must begin with *Lear, Inc. v. Adkins*. The doctrine of licensee estoppel, which had originated in the 1856 US Supreme Court decision in *Kinsman v. Parkhurst*,[49] held that once a licensee assents to a licensing agreement, she is deemed to have accepted the validity of the patent being licensed and is estopped from challenging its validity subsequently. In *Lear*, the Supreme Court changed course and ruled that the doctrine of licensee estoppel no longer prevents a licensee from pleading patent invalidity in an infringement suit. It declared that the public policy of clearing invalid patents overrides the equitable considerations favouring the patentee:

> Surely the equities of the licensor do not weigh very heavily when they are balanced against the important public interest in permitting full and free competition in the use of ideas which are in reality a part of the public domain. Licensees may often be the only individuals with enough economic incentive to challenge the patentability of an inventor's discovery. If they are muzzled, the public may continually be required to pay tribute to would-be monopolists without need or justification. We think it plain that the technical requirements of contract doctrine must give way before the demands of the public interest in the typical situation involving the negotiation of a license after a patent has issued.[50]

Appellate courts have proceeded to apply *Lear's* holdings to no challenge clauses in the ensuing decades.[51] The result of this application, however, is far from uniform. The US Court of Appeals for the Federal Circuit, unsurprisingly, has taken a pro-patentee approach and allowed these clauses to be enforced under various

[48] Cheng (n 1) 447.

[49] *Kinsman v. Parkhurst*, 59 US 289 (1855).

[50] Lear, 395 US at 670–71.

[51] Christian Chadd Taylor, 'No-Challenge Termination Clauses: Incorporating Innovation Policy and Risk Allocation into Patent Licensing Law' (1993) 69 Indiana Law Journal 215, 235–41.

circumstances.[52] The other circuits have tended to take a more hostile attitude.[53] However, most cases from these latter courts tend to be of an older vintage and may not be indicative of the latest judicial thinking.

US courts tend to attach a great deal of significance to the agreement in which the no challenge clause is embodied when determining its enforceability. Most appellate courts that have ruled on the issue have refused to enforce no challenge clauses found in a licensing agreement.[54] The only exception is the Federal Circuit.[55] In a relatively recent case, the US Court of Appeals for the Second Circuit struck down a no challenge clause in a settlement agreement entered into by the parties prior to the initiation of litigation.[56] While acknowledging that 'the important policy interests favoring the settlement of litigation *may* support a different rule with respect to no-challenge clauses in settlements entered into after the initiation of litigation',[57] the court held that 'enforcing no-challenge clauses in pre-litigation settlements would significantly undermine the "public interest in discovering invalid patents"'.[58] Despite its reference to the initiation of litigation, the court set the boundary of enforceability at the conduct of discovery. Believing that discovery would give the parties a more informed basis to make a decision about settlement and would tend to indicate the existence of a genuine dispute over patent validity, the court noted that it would enforce a no challenge clause in a settlement agreement entered into after discovery, but not one entered into prior to discovery.[59]

While this stance has been endorsed by a number of other appellate courts,[60] this consensus is not universal. One case held, or at least proclaimed, that a no challenge clause is unenforceable regardless of the type of agreement at issue.[61] One court refused to enforce a no challenge clause, or at least something similar to it, incorporated in a settlement agreement entered into after discovery.[62] There was also one court willing to enforce a no challenge clause in a settlement agreement entered into prior to discovery.[63]

In sum, the US approach to no challenge clauses focuses on somewhat arbitrary and tangential considerations such as the timing of the agreement vis-à-vis discovery and neglects factors that go directly to the issue of consumer harm such as

[52] *Baseload Energy, Inc. v. Roberts*, 619 F.3d 1357 (Fed Cir. 2010); *Flex-Foot v. CRP*, 238 F.3d 1362 (Fed Cir. 2001).

[53] *Bendix Corp. v. Balax, Inc.*, 421 F.2d 809 (7th Cir. 1970); *Massillon-Cleveland-Akron Sign Co. v. Golden State Advertising Co.*, 444 F.2d 425 (9th Cir. 1971); *Warner-Jenkinson Co. v. Allied Chemical Corp.*, 567 F.2d 184 (2d Cir. 1977).

[54] *Bendix*, 421 F.2d 809; *Massillon-Cleveland-Akron*, 444 F.2d 425; *Speakeasy*, 685 F.3d 163.

[55] *Baseload Energy*, 619 F.3d 1357.

[56] *Speakeasy*, 685 F.3d 163.

[57] ibid 172.

[58] ibid.

[59] ibid.

[60] *Aro Corp. v. Allied Witan Co.*, 531 F.2d 1368 (6th Cir. 1976); Flex-Foot, 238 F.3d 1362.

[61] *Massillon-Cleveland-Akron*, 444 F.2d at 427.

[62] *Warner-Jenkinson*, 567 F.2d at 188.

[63] *Baseload Energy*, 619 F.3d 1357.

the patentee's market power and the validity of the patent. One may question why courts should pay attention to how informed the parties are when they generally do not delve into the parties' subjective state of mind in determining the enforceability of a contract. The only exception is when there are vitiating factors such as mistake or duress. Developing countries have little guidance from the United States on the appropriate approach to no challenge clauses under competition law and will need to turn to other jurisdictions such as the European Union for assistance.

(b) European Union

Unlike the United States, the European Union has analysed no challenge clauses under competition law and has generally taken a tough stance toward them. The Court of Justice of the European Union (CJEU) first encountered a no challenge clause in *Windsurfing International v. Commission*.[64] While the Court stopped short of designating such clauses as restrictive of competition by object, it condemned the clause at issue without examining its competitive effects. The Court justified its approach on public interest grounds, declaring that 'the public interest in ensuring an essentially free system of competition and therefore in the removal of a monopoly perhaps wrongly granted to the licensor must prevail over any other considerations'.[65]

The CJEU softened its approach to no challenge clauses in a subsequent case. In *Bayer v. Süllhöfer*, the Court rejected the Commission's suggestion that these clauses be, in principle, considered a restriction of competition under Article 101(1) and proclaimed that 'the legal and economic context' must be taken into account when assessing their legality.[66] The Court also rejected the Commission's contention that no challenge clauses in a settlement agreement should be treated more leniently and held that, as a matter of law, the type of agreement in which a no challenge clause is found makes no difference to the question of legality.[67] The court proceeded to enumerate two circumstances under which no challenge clauses would be permissible: (1) when the license is royalty-free, which means that the licensee suffers no competitive disadvantage from having to make royalty payments, and (2) 'when the licence relates to a technically outdated process which the licensee undertaking did not use'.[68]

In the more recent *Huawei Technologies v. ZTE Corp.* case, the CJEU had another opportunity to discuss the importance of the right of a licensee to challenge the validity of the licensed patent.[69] Advocate General Wathelet stated in his opinion that:

[64] Case 193/83, *Windsurfing International, Inc. v. Commission* [1986] ECR 611.
[65] ibid 664.
[66] Case 65/86, *Bayer AG v. Süllhöfer* [1988] ECR 5249, 5286.
[67] ibid.
[68] ibid.
[69] Case C-170/13, *Huawei Technologies Co. v. ZTE Corp.* EU:C:2015:477.

> it is in the public interest for an alleged infringer to have the opportunity, after concluding a licensing agreement, to challenge the validity of an SEP (as ZTE did). As the Commission has pointed out, the wrongful issue of a patent may constitute an obstacle to the legitimate pursuit of an economic activity. Moreover, if undertakings supplying standard-compliant products and services cannot call into question the validity of a patent declared to be essential to that standard, it could prove effectively impossible to verify the validity of that patent because other undertakings would have no interest in bringing proceedings in that regard.[70]

The European Commission's enforcement policy is arguably as important as the case law for understanding the EU position on no challenge clauses. In 2014, the Commission issued the most recent set of Technology Transfer Block Exemption Regulation (TTBER) and the accompanying guidelines. No challenge clauses continue to be an excluded restriction, which means that they are excluded from the block exemption and must be assessed individually for their compatibility with Article 101(1). The TTBER Guidelines supplement that no challenge clauses are likely to fall afoul of Article 101(1) and unlikely to benefit from Article 101(3) when the technology is valuable and thereby bestows a competitive advantage upon the licensee.[71] This aligns the Commission's position with that adopted by the CJEU in *Windsurfing*. The Guidelines proceeded to endorse the two exemptions propounded by the CJEU in *Bayer v. Süllhöfer*.

The 2014 TTBER saw the Commission change its position on termination-upon-challenge clauses, which are now classified as an excluded restriction as well unless they are incorporated in an exclusive license and the market share thresholds provided in Article 3 of the TTBER are met.[72] The Commission explained this shift by saying that: '[s]uch a termination right can have the same effect as a non-challenge clause, in particular where switching away from the licensor's technology would result in a significant loss to the licensee ... or where the licensor's technology is a necessary input for the licensee's production'.[73] The Commission also amended its position on no challenge clauses in a settlement agreement, acknowledging that these clauses could be restrictive of competition under some circumstances.[74] This is consistent with the Commission's approach in the *Motorola Mobility* case, in which the Commission struck down a termination-upon-challenge clause imposed in a settlement agreement by Motorola on Apple on the grounds that the clause discourages Apple and other licensees from launching validity challenges

[70] Case C-170/13, *Huawei Technologies Co. v. ZTE Corp.* EU:C:2014:2391, para 95.

[71] Guidelines on the Application of Article 101 of the Treaty on the Functioning of the European Union to Technology Transfer Agreements (TTBER Guidelines), 2015 OJ C89/3, para 134.

[72] Commission Regulation (EU) 316/2014 of Mar. 21, 2014, The Application of Article 101(3) of the Treaty on the Functioning of the European Union to Categories of Technology Transfer Agreements, OJ L93/17, art 5(1)(b).

[73] TTBER Guidelines, para 136.

[74] ibid para 243.

against Motorola's standard-essential patents.[75] This could potentially raise the licensees' production costs, which could be passed on to consumers.[76]

(c) Developing countries

Not many developing countries have taken enforcement action against no challenge clauses. China is one exception. In February 2015, the National Development and Reform Commission (NDRC), one of the former enforcement authorities of the Anti-Monopoly Law (AML), adopted a decision against the American technological giant Qualcomm over a range of licensing practices.[77] One of the condemned licensing conditions is that Qualcomm will terminate supply of baseband chips if a licensee initiates a validity challenge against Qualcomm's patents.[78] Even though the clause is ostensibly a challenge penalty clause, the NDRC deems it as an outright prohibition as the cessation of chip supply is sufficient to deter any licensee from launching a validity challenge.[79] The NDRC condemned the clause on the grounds that it deprives licensees of their legal right to challenge the validity of Qualcomm's patents and that it restricts competition by excluding potential licensees that reject the no challenge clause from the market.[80] With little elaboration, the NDRC also rejected Qualcomm's justifications for the clause.

The reasons given by the NDRC to nullify the no challenge clause supports the inference of a *per se* rule against no challenge clauses, especially when possible justifications are accepted sparingly. These reasons would apply to every no challenge clause as it is in the very nature of no challenge clauses to forestall validity challenges. Furthermore, the NDRC's understanding of the notion of restriction of competition is highly problematic. It implies that Qualcomm restricts competition if it offers licensing terms that are unacceptable to a licensee. This means that Qualcomm would be expected to accept whatever terms proposed by a licensee. Qualcomm would be effectively compelled to accept whatever royalty a licensee is willing to pay, which cannot be the purpose of competition law enforcement.

The State Administration for Market Regulation (SAMR), the current AML enforcement authority, issued the long-awaited Intellectual Property Guidelines under the AML in November 2020. The IP-Competition Guidelines seem to reaffirm the NDRC's tough stance on no challenge clauses. Article 10 of the Guidelines prohibits licensing conditions that prevent a licensee from challenging

[75] COMP/39985, *Motorola-Enforcement of GPRS Standard-Essential Patents* [2014] OJ C344/6, para 336.

[76] ibid 67–68.

[77] National Development and Reform Commission Administrative Penalty Decision [2015] No 1, 9 Feb. 2015 [NDRC Qualcomm Decision].

[78] ibid.

[79] ibid.

[80] ibid.

the validity of the licensor's intellectual property absent a valid justification.[81] The Guidelines do not elaborate on what constitutes such a justification. Depending on the SAMR's readiness to accept justifications, this could amount to a presumptive illegality approach if not outright *per se* illegality for no challenge clauses in mainland China.

4. A Proposed Framework for Developing Countries

(a) Basic considerations

Setting aside the United States, which has chosen to address no challenge clauses under patent law, both the European Union and China have taken a fairly hard line against these clauses. Although both jurisdictions have stopped short of applying the *per se* rule, their approaches amount to a rule of presumptive illegality. The two exceptions admitted by the CJEU and the European Commission—where the license is royalty-free and where the licensed technology is obsolete—are so narrow that they are likely to be of little help to defendants. It is also unclear what kind of justification would be accepted by SAMR. If no challenge clauses are condemned because they restrict the licensees' legal right to launch validity challenges, it is difficult to imagine what kind of justifications could save them. It is contended that the EU and Chinese approach to no challenge clauses is unsuitable for developing countries that rely on licensing for technological upgrade in light of the possible deterrent effect on licensing activities.

The formulation of a suitable approach to no challenge clauses for developing countries depends on the trade-off between a number of considerations. Consumer harm is premised on the existence of market power. A no challenge clause attached to an insignificant technology for which there exists plenty of reasonable substitutes raises no competitive concerns. The patentee will not be able to charge supracompetitive prices for the technology regardless of the no challenge clause. The requirement of market power for consumer harm would seem to call for a Rule of Reason, as this author has advocated elsewhere in the context of the United States. A full effects-based approach, however, would greatly complicate the analysis and may put enforcement against no challenge clauses beyond the capability of developing country enforcement authorities and courts. This is especially likely to be the case for authorities with low enforcement capacity.

Fortunately, no challenge clauses are likely to be confined to developing countries with a more advanced technological capacity. Countries bereft of a technology adaptation capacity, many of which are the least developed countries where

[81] PRC State Administration for Market Regulation Guidelines on Prohibition of Abuses of Intellectual Property Rights (3 Nov. 2020), art 10, < http://gkml.samr.gov.cn/nsjg/fgs/202011/t20201103_322857.html> accessed 27 March 2020 [SAMR IP-Competition Guidelines].

competition law enforcement capacity is most lacking, are unlikely to confront no challenge clauses on a regular basis, if at all. These are the production countries alluded to earlier. Countries that have to tackle these clauses are middle-income developing countries where competition law enforcement capacity is higher. These are likely to be the technology adaptation and the proto-innovation countries. Enforcement capacity should not be an important consideration when fashioning the appropriate legal rule for no challenge clauses.

(b) Patent validity

It was argued earlier that consideration of patent validity is inevitable when determining the legality of no challenge clauses. No challenge clauses only inflict consumer harm when the underlying patent is invalid. This still leaves one important question unaddressed: the time frame at which patent validity is to be considered. There are two possibilities. Patent validity can be considered either *ex ante*, when the clause was adopted, or *ex post*, when the legality of the clause is litigated in courts. Commentators have argued that patent validity should be assessed from an *ex ante* perspective in the context of reverse payment settlements. *Ex ante* assessment is superior *ex post* evaluation because a patentee who in good faith believed her patent to be valid when the no challenge clause was initially agreed could end up facing massive liability if the court arrives at a different conclusion with the benefit of hindsight.

Adopting the *ex ante* perspective means that patent validity is not determined by the court's own evaluation in trial and is evaluated on a different basis. There are again two possibilities. Reference can be made to either the patentee's subjective perception or some objective assessment of what a reasonable patentee would believe in light of the information available to her at the time. A subjective test is probably easier to administer as it focuses on what the patentee herself thought at the time. It is simply a matter of evidentiary proof. It is, however, open to manipulation. Patentees would have every incentive to make self-serving statements about patent validity to satisfy the subjective test.[82]

An objective test sidesteps this problem and instead focuses on a reasonable belief about validity in light of the information at the patentee's disposal. For example, if the patent turns out to be invalid because of anticipation by prior art which the patentee could not have discovered after reasonable search effort at the time the no challenge clause was agreed, but the patent otherwise looks valid, the patentee's *ex ante* belief in patent validity would be reasonable. This approach would probably entail some inquiry into the objective merits of the patent that Elhauge and Krueger warn against.[83] It should, however, avoid a full-fledged trial on patent validity that can be extremely costly and cumbersome.[84]

[82] Elhauge and Krueger (n 26) 289.
[83] ibid.
[84] ibid 288.

Given the high percentage of patents that are invalidated in courts in advanced jurisdictions such as the United States, developing country competition authorities would be justified in adopting a sceptical attitude toward patent validity. If it is true that a majority of patents are erroneously granted, the burden should rest on the defendant to demonstrate patent validity rather than on the plaintiff to negate it. A sound approach would be to adopt a presumption of patent invalidity which can be rebutted by evidence tending to support a reasonable *ex ante* belief in patent validity. Patent validity can be treated as a defence in a general framework under which a no challenge clause covering a patent that enjoys market power is presumed to be anticompetitive.

From a theoretical perspective, patent validity is an indispensable element in the determination of the legality of no challenge clauses. The practical reality, however, is that even in the simplified form suggested above, an evaluation of patent validity is no easy task and developing country competition authorities are justifiably apprehensive about it. Developing countries leery of their enforcement capacity may consider sidestepping patent invalidity and focusing on other issues such as market power instead. This would be tantamount to adopting an irrebuttable presumption of patent invalidity, under which consumer harm is established once market power is proven. Such a presumption is defensible in light of patent invalidation rates of 70 per cent or higher. Ultimately, whether to adopt such a presumption is a question about enforcement capacity which needs to be answered by each developing country.

(c) Justifications for no challenge clauses

The chief justifications for no challenge clauses are deterrence of licensing activities, detrimental effect on innovation, and avoidance of wasteful litigation costs. The latter two justifications have been rejected. It was contended earlier that prohibition of no challenge clauses does not undermine innovation incentives. In fact, no challenge clauses artificially remove the element of risk from patentee returns and steer inventors to target investments in weaker patents covering less meritorious invention.

It was further argued that litigation is only redundant if the patent turns out to be valid and there is no way to determine whether litigation costs will be wasted *ex ante*. If the patent invalidation rate is anywhere near as high as that in the United States—and there is no reason to expect developing country patent examination authorities to do a better job of reviewing patent applications than does the USPTO—savings in the welfare loss from the invalidation of unworthy patents will dwarf avoided litigation expenses. This is especially true for developing countries, where patent litigation costs are likely to pale in comparison to the USD32 million that has been quoted for the United States. Avoidance of wasteful litigation costs should not be an important consideration for developing countries.

Deterrence of licensing activities is a different matter. The importance of licensing as a means of technology transfer to developing countries has been emphasized on more than one occasion. If prohibition of no challenge clauses ends up putting off foreign licensors, the consequence for developing countries could be grave. It was suggested earlier that prohibition of no challenge clauses should have a larger deterrent effect on the licensing of weaker patents than of stronger patents unless the patentee is risk averse. It was also pointed out that commentators have doubted the extent of risk aversion among corporate actors. The picture, however, could be more complicated for developing countries. Foreign licensors may have less confidence in the patent system in developing countries and may prefer to avoid entanglement in patent lawsuits by deploying a no challenge clause. The lack of trust in developing country legal systems may exacerbate the extent of risk aversion on the part of foreign licensors and cause a prohibition of no challenge clauses to have a material impact on licensing activities.

(d) Trade-off between consumer harm and deterrence for licensing activities

Adjudicating the legality of no challenge clauses in developing countries ultimately comes down to a trade-off between consumer harm and a possible loss of licensing activities, which may necessitate a balancing exercise under the Rule of Reason. Genuine balancing between two such incongruent qualities is fraught with difficulty but can be alleviated by some simple rules of thumb. These rules delineate the circumstances under which either of these two considerations can be de-emphasized.

Some developing countries may decide to prioritize the dynamic efficiency benefits of technology transfer over consumer welfare. A developing country keen on maximizing technology transfer may want to avoid loss of licensing activities to the extent possible. Such a country may gravitate toward presumptive or even *per se* legality. To the extent that potential licensors would be deterred by the uncertain status of no challenge clauses under competition law, even a case-by-case analysis under the Rule of Reason could hamper licensing activities. The only way to minimize such a deterrent effect would be to resort to presumptive or *per se* legality.

Per se legality probably should only be contemplated if a developing country is satisfied that it has the requisite domestic technological capacity to benefit from foreign technology licensing or perhaps a demonstrated track record of attracting foreign licensors. Even when the country at issue has not chosen to prioritize technology transfer across the board, a more lenient stance toward no challenge clauses can be justified on an industry-specific basis. This could be the case when there is convincing evidence that prohibiting the no challenge clause at issue will have significant deterrent effect on licensing activities, such as when a no challenge clause is found in an industry where domestic firms are recipients of a substantial amount of foreign technology licensing. An adverse ruling on the no challenge clause may have a deleterious effect on foreign technology licensing and a presumptive legality approach may be preferred.

Alternatively, there could be instances where it is possible to conclude that consumer harm is unlikely, in which case a presumptive legality approach may be appropriate. This could be because the technology clearly lacks market power or because the no challenge clause applies to portfolio licensing, where the invalidation of a handful of patents is unlikely to make a difference to the patentee's overall market power.[85] These are industry- or market-specific factors and cannot be translated into a blanket rule of presumptive or *per se* legality for an entire industry or even country as was discussed immediately above. This case-specific presumption of legality can be rebutted if the enforcement authority can somehow still demonstrate consumer harm despite initial indications of the improbability of such harm. This could be the case when the market power of a patent portfolio mainly stems from a few key patents that are of questionable validity and the invalidation of these patents would largely nullify the portfolio's market power.

There could also be instances where the developing country at issue has valid reasons for disregarding consumer harm. This could be because the technology at issue is not consumed domestically, which means that whatever harm there is will be borne by foreign consumers. While some may question whether developing country competition authorities should draw a distinction between domestic and foreign consumers, given the imperative of securing technology transfer for these countries, it would be difficult to justify asking developing countries to jeopardize their own technological upgrade in order to protect foreign consumers.

Where none of these simple rules of thumb apply and the patentee is shown to possess market power, what may be required is a comprehensive analysis of the relationship between the patentee and the licensees and the market structure at the licensee level. These are relevant for determining what kind of economic incentives are present, which determines the probability of a licensee challenge. Economic incentives shed light on the likelihood that a challenge is being blocked, which in turn indicates how much harm is being done by the no challenge clause. The more likely is a licensee challenge, the greater is the harm wrought by a no challenge clause. If the assessment shows that the market structure is such that licensees have substantial incentives to challenge, the no challenge clause will be blocking a probable challenge and is more likely to inflict consumer harm. It should be struck down.

One may consider whether a licensee enjoys technical, cost, or commercial advantages over other licensees such that she has strong incentives to bring a challenge. If such a licensee exists, a no challenge clause will be more damaging as this licensee will have significant incentives to challenge a patent and will be unperturbed by competition in the post-invalidation market. Conversely, if the licensees

[85] Cheng (n 1) 490.

are similarly situated as third party non-licensees in terms of technical expertise and cost structure, none of the licensees will have the incentive to launch a validity challenge as doing so will only invite more competition by opening the market to non-licensees. In that case, validity challenges are unlikely to be forthcoming regardless of the inclusion of a no challenge clause. One final aspect of the market structure to consider is whether competition is keen at the licensee level. If it is, the licensees would have limited ability to pass on the royalty payment to the final consumers, in which case consumers will suffer little harm even if the patent turns out to be invalid.

C. Other Licensing Practices

Unlike no challenge clauses, there are myriad other restrictive practices arising in the licensing context that do not implicate the robustness of patent protection. These licensing practices run the gamut, ranging from package licensing, which is a form of tying that was not dealt with in Chapter 7, to grantbacks, from royalty-related provisions such as post-expiration royalty to vertical distribution restraints such as resale price maintenance and vertical non-price restraints. The range of restrictive licensing practices is so extensive that it is impossible to cover them all in the remaining space of this chapter. Instead, these practices can be roughly classified into two categories, those that do not enhance or extend the patentee's market power and those that do. These two categories of practices may have different policy implications for developing countries.

A patentee engages in practices in the former category mainly to extract more licensing revenue. To the extent that licensees pass on the elevated royalty to the end consumers, these practices present a trade-off between consumer welfare and patentee reward. Aside from innovation incentives, licensing revenue may also implicate licensing incentives, which may affect the prospect of developing countries attracting technology licensing. A determination of the appropriate legal rule for these practices in the developing country context entails a resolution of this trade-off between consumer welfare and innovation and licensing incentives. It comes down to whether the welfare of domestic consumers, often those mired in poverty, should be sacrificed in order to generate licensing incentives.

The treatment of the latter category of licensing practices presents a more complex calculus. The patentee may be able to extend its market power and/or exclude rivals in the primary or adjacent market through licensing restrictions. When the excluded rival is a domestic firm that plays an important role in the country's technological upgrade, exclusion may have dynamic efficiency implications for a developing country. The design of an appropriate legal rule for an exclusionary licensing practice may require the delicate balancing between the need to protect licensing incentives and the need to ensure that domestic firms are not unfairly foreclosed from opportunities for technological upgrade.

1. Licensing Practices That Do Not Enhance the Patentee's Market Power

There is a range of restrictive licensing practices whose main effect is to allow the patentee to extract more licensing revenue without extending the patent's market power or excluding rivals. These include royalty-related practices such as imposition of post-expiration royalties and in some circumstances, vertical distribution restraints such as RPM and vertical non-price restraints. On the one hand, these types of practices may harm consumer welfare to the extent that the increased royalty burden is passed on to consumers. On the other hand, they may boost incentives to engage in licensing activities by augmenting licensing revenue. Licensing revenue ultimately contributes to patentee reward which, depending on the relative importance of the various appropriation mechanisms, may boost innovation incentives. The policy trade-off is thus between consumer welfare on the one hand and licensing incentives and possibly innovation incentives on the other.

Given the variety of restrictive licensing practices in this category, it is impossible to examine each of them in detail. The ensuing discussion will focus on one particular practice: imposition of post-expiration royalty. The competitive harm and justifications for this practice are relatively straightforward. The extent of consumer harm crucially depends on whether the practice allows the licensor to extract additional royalty or, to put it slightly differently, whether the practice only alters the timing of royalty payments or also the amount of aggregate royalty payments. If the impact is only limited to the timing of payment, consumers do not end up paying more and suffer no additional harm. Conversely, if the practice allows the patentee to charge more royalty over time, consumers will be harmed by the practice.

There are divergent views on the validity of these two contrasting accounts of the practice. Adherents to the Chicago School argue that a patent only entitles the patentee to a fixed amount of monopoly profit.[86] The patentee can extract the entire amount with an upfront payment or spread the royalty payments over time. The length of time can fall short of the patent term, coincide with it, or even exceed it. But regardless of the chosen time period, the aggregate royalty payments remain the same. No restrictive practice would allow the patentee to extract greater

[86] Hershey Kelley, 'Note, Scheiber v. Dolby Laboratories, Inc.' (2003) 18 Berkeley Technology Law Journal 159, 173; A Douglas Melamed and Ali M Stoeppelwerth, 'The CSU Case: Facts, Formalism and the Intersection of Antitrust and Intellectual Property Law' (2002) 10 George Mason Law Review 407, 418.

monopoly profit than to what she is otherwise entitled. As the US Court of Appeals for the Seventh Circuit asserted in *Scheiber v. Dolby Laboratories*, 'charging royalties beyond the term of the patent does not lengthen the patentee's monopoly; it merely alters the timing of royalty payments'.[87] Post-expiration royalty is merely the result of negotiations between the licensor and the licensee on the optimal scheduling of the fixed amount of royalty payments which the patent entitles the licensor to receive.

This is but a variation of the single monopoly profit theorem espoused by Chicago School scholars to justify tying.[88] They argue that tying does not earn the dominant firm extra monopoly profit. The choice facing a dominant firm is to charge all the monopoly profit from the tying product, all the monopoly profit from the tied product, or to spread it between the two products.[89] The overall amount of monopoly profit extracted by the dominant firm remains the same whichever option is chosen. Others disagree and assert that post-expiration royalty allows the patentee to charge more royalty. The US Supreme Court in *Bruoltte v. Thys* condemned post-expiration royalty under a leverage theory by analogizing it to tying, whereby post-expiration royalty is tied to pre-expiration royalty.[90] To the extent that part of the burden of increased royalty is shifted to consumers, charging of post-expiration royalty harms consumers.

If the Chicago School scholars are correct, consumers do not pay additional royalties and the patentee does not receive extra licensing revenue. There is no trade-off between consumer welfare and licensing and innovation incentives. Competition law should be agnostic about the practice, which is the position taken in the United States where post-expiration royalty is not regulated under antitrust law at all but is dealt with as a patent misuse. If, in contrast, the practice does augment aggregate royalty payments, it may give rise to consumer harm, which may provide the basis for competition law intervention.

If post-expiration royalty is revenue-neutral, there must be other reasons why the licensor chooses a longer payment term. There are two possibilities: either the licensor has a preference for cash flow to be spread over a longer period of time or the licensor is for some reason constrained from extracting its full royalty entitlement during the patent term. While it is not the role of competition law to frustrate the licensor's attempt to structure her cash flow, the same objective can also be easily achieved through other means. The licensor can take the royalty revenue and invest it in some financial instrument which gives her a long-term pay-off that mirrors the cash flow of post-expiration royalty. Post-expiration royalty seems

87 *Scheiber v. Dolby Laboratories, Inc.*, 293 F.3d 1014, 1018 (2002).

88 Robert H Bork, *The Antitrust Paradox: A Policy at War with Itself* (The Free Press 1978) 372–75, 80–81; Ward S Bowman, Jr, 'Tying Arrangements and the Leverage Problem' (1957) 67 Yale Law Journal 19, 20–23.

89 Christina Bohannan, 'IP Misuse as Foreclosure' (2011) 96 Iowa Law Review 475, 517.

90 *Brulotte v. Thys Co.*, 379 US 29, 33 (1964).

superfluous. A preference for post-expiration royalty must be due to other reasons, such as where the technology requires a very long investment time frame and will not produce the bulk of its revenue until after the patent term. A technology with such a long investment horizon, however, is unlikely to be commonplace, unless the licensing takes place toward the end of the patent term.

Constraints on the licensor's ability to extract her full royalty entitlement may emanate from market conditions or the licensee's inability to afford the full royalty. The licensor may believe that there is a threshold level of royalty beyond which the licensee or competing inventors will be incentivized to invest to circumvent the licensor's patent. This could be because a potential substitute technology entails a certain level of fixed cost investment that can only be recouped at a given royalty level. So long as the licensor maintains the royalty below this level, licensees would be happy to continue to pay the royalty and would refrain from pursuing an alternative technology. The emergence of a competing technology would not concern the licensor so long as the licensing agreement is not terminable at will and royalty payments are due regardless of actual use of the licensed technology. If these conditions do not apply, however, the licensor would have the incentives to stymie competing technologies. This is a version of limit pricing in the patent royalty context. Outside of the patent context, there is no limit on how long the dominant firm can charge supra-competitive prices so long as no substitutes emerge. If the product or the technology is patented, supra-competitive prices lapse once the patent expires regardless of the existence of substitutes.

There are two objections, one theoretical and one practical, to such limit pricing. The theoretical objection is that it leads to a loss in dynamic efficiency. Given that the paramount policy objective of the patent system is to spur innovation, any patent exploitation practice that may deter innovation raises concerns. The practical objection is that there seem to be other less restrictive alternatives than post-expiration royalty that may allow the licensor to achieve the same purpose. For example, the licensing agreement may stipulate royalty payment on total sales regardless of actual use of the licensed technology. This guarantees the licensor a fixed licensing income regardless of the state of technological competition.

A licensor may also be constrained to extend royalty payment beyond the patent term due to the licensee's inability to afford the full royalty before the patent expires. The licensee could also prefer delayed royalty payments for other reasons. Post-expiration royalty could be a concession to the licensee.[91] This seems to be exactly what happened in the *Scheiber* case, where the post-expiration royalty was requested by the licensee Dolby.[92] The concession may be necessary because the

[91] Comment, 'Validity of Patent License Provisions Requiring Payment of Post-Expiration Royalties' (1965) 65 Columbia Law Review 1256, 1269.

[92] Herbert Hovenkamp and others, *IP and Antitrust: An Analysis of Antitrust Principles Applied to Intellectual Property Law* (2nd edn, Aspen Publishers 2011) s 23.2.

licensee is cash-strapped and is unable to afford the full amount of the royalty payment during the patent term. It may be needed because implementing the licensed technology requires a considerable upfront investment and the licensee needs some room to recoup her investment first.[93] Post-expiration royalty can in fact be pro-competitive by facilitating and boosting licensing activities.

This justification is consistent with both the revenue-neutral and the revenue-augmenting account of post-expiration royalty. The licensor may have accommodated the licensee without demanding greater aggregate royalty, in which case the practice would result in no additional consumer harm, or the patentee may have required larger royalty payments over time for the privilege of deferred payments. This assessment will need to be done on a net present value (NPV) basis as the patentee may have asked for larger payments further down the road simply to reflect the time value of money.[94] Post-expiration royalty may still be justified even if it results in larger aggregate payments on an NPV basis. The licensor may insist on extra compensation for the privilege of deferred payments.

The validity of this justification depends on whether the licensee would have foregone the licensing arrangement without the deferral option. This, however, can be difficult to ascertain. If it is the licensee who challenges the post-expiration royalty, as is most likely the case, the licensee could be expected to furnish plenty of *ex post* self-serving statements suggesting that deferral was unnecessary. Contemporaneous evidence would be more probative and deserves greater weight. Another way to ascertain the validity of the justification is by focusing on the origin of the request for deferral. If the post-expiration royalty was put in place to accommodate the licensee, one would expect that the request would emanate from the licensee or that there be evidence from the negotiation process indicating the licensee's concern about its ability to pay. If the post-expiration royalty was resisted by the licensee, it is much less likely that it was instituted as an accommodation to her and the applicability of this justification would be doubtful.

There are no grounds for competition law intervention if post-expiration royalty has no impact on aggregate royalty payments. Consumers suffer no additional harm. In that case, competition law has no business telling licensors how to structure their royalty payments. Even if it can be confidently established that the licensor enlarges the aggregate royalty payments through post-expiration royalty, it still does not necessarily justify competition law intervention. Competition law intervention would make no difference if prohibition of post-expiration royalty only squeezes the same amount of royalty payments into a shorter period of time. If anything, it would make matters worse from both a licensee affordability and a social welfare perspective. It would be preferable to spread the same amount of

[93] Roger M Milgrim and Eric E Bensen, *Milgrim on Licensing*, vol 4 (Lexis-Nexis 2021) s18.05.

[94] Martin Hopkinson, *Net Present Value and Risk Modelling for Projects* (Taylor & Francis Ltd. 2017).

market power and hence supra-competitive pricing over more markets (or longer time period) to help lower the aggregate welfare loss.[95]

There is one further reason for caution. The foregoing discussion implicitly assumes that the higher royalty burden will be fully passed on to end consumers. If the market at the licensee level is competitive and the demand for the licensed product is elastic, licensees will be forced to absorb a considerable part of the increased royalty. Consumer impact would be even more attenuated if the final product incorporates hundreds or even thousands of patents, in which case increased royalty for one license should have limited impact on the price of the final product. It is only when there is strong evidence of consumer harm and passing on that competition law intervention may be justified.

It has even been argued that post-expiration royalty could be pro-competitive. Assume that the patentee sells a machine, as in the case of *Brulotte*, the original US Supreme Court case on post-expiration royalty, and charges an annual royalty for the use of the machine beyond the patent term. Once the patent expires, rivals would be free to copy the previously patented technology and produce the exact same machine.[96] If the patentee continues to charge royalty, rivals could enter the market with the same product without the royalty charge and would instantly have a pricing advantage over the patentee.[97] If the licensee is free to terminate the licensing agreement, she would have significant financial incentives to do so and switch to a rival's product.[98] Post-expiration royalty would help to spur market entry.

This ostensibly compelling story relies on a number of critical assumptions. First, it largely only works when a physical product is involved. Market entry will not happen in a pure technology licensing context. The pro-competitive account is premised on the possibility of a rival replicating the previously patented technology to produce a competing physical product. A rival can only enter a technology licensing market by licensing a competing technology. If this technology is novel and valuable enough, it will be patented and entails a royalty payment. The rival technology may not have a pricing advantage over the original patentee's technology, especially when post-expiration royalty is usually lower than pre-expiration royalty.[99] Even if the new technology does not meet the requirements for patentability, it may still be licensed as a trade secret. In a technology licensing market, a rival entrant will need to charge royalty to make money, which means

[95] Ian Ayres and Paul Klemperer, 'Limiting Patentees' Market Power Without Reducing Innovation Incentives: The Perverse Benefits of Uncertainty and Non-Injunctive Remedies' (1999) 97 Michigan Law Review 985, 1026–27.

[96] Hovenkamp and others (n 92) s 23.2a.

[97] ibid.

[98] ibid.

[99] ibid.

that the post-expiration royalty may not necessarily put the original patentee at a competitive disadvantage.

Even if a physical product is involved, this pro-competitive account would only be valid if two further assumptions hold. The first one is that the machine or the physical product is nearing the end of its useful life, or at least the savings in royalty payments outweigh the loss of use of the existing machine. This is more likely to be the case if the machine is close to obsolescence. A licensee will not give up a machine that still has ten, twenty years of use left in order to save royalty payments, unless such payments are hefty. The second one is that the licensee is free to terminate the licensing agreement. If the licensee must continue to pay royalty regardless of use of the machine, post-expiration royalty will not attract market entry. The same royalty will need to be paid either way. One may argue that the post-expiration royalty may not affect the licensee's choice of machine because it is a fixed cost.[100] But the post-expiration royalty will not spur market entry, as was argued earlier. Overall, this pro-competitive account of post-expiration royalty is of highly limited applicability.

There are two other pro-competitive justifications for post-expiration royalty. First, spreading of the aggregate royalty over a longer period of time reduces per-period royalty and allows the licensee to charge more competitive prices.[101] Lower per-period royalty reduces the deadweight loss associated with supra-competitive prices. It will also help to attract consumers from competing technologies to the extent they exist. Licensees, however, will only have the incentive to lower their prices if they are under competitive pressure to do so. Second, lower per-period royalty will render the license more affordable, which could increase competition at the licensee level in the pre-expiration market.[102]

2. Licensing Practices That May Enhance the Patentee's Market Power

There are restrictive licensing practices that not only allow the licensor to extract more consumer surplus but also enhance or extend the licensor's market power, either in the primary or adjacent markets. The trade-off presented by these practices is no longer a straightforward one between consumer welfare and innovation incentives. Condoning them may lead to further distortions of competition or other harmful effects down the road. For instance, it may lead to foreclosure of competitors that may retard technological progress in a developing country. It is necessary

[100] ibid.
[101] Kelley (n 86) 171.
[102] ibid.

to take these effects into account when determining the appropriate approach to these practices.

One example of such practice is package licensing. When patents are licensed as a package, the licensor may either refuse to license the patents individually or price individual licenses so unattractively that such licenses are not an economically viable option. There would be no competitive concern if individual licenses remain available at attractive enough prices. Therefore, the first element of a potentially anticompetitive package license is coercion, which can be found either

> when the licensor refuses to license its intellectual property rights except in bundles or packages, or when the licensor's royalty structure is such that the price of licensing the bundle or package is significantly lower than the price of separate licensing and the difference cannot be justified by the lower cost of package licensing.[103]

A discount on a package license, even a substantial one, does not automatically result in condemnation. Package licensing enables many cost savings, which the licensor is fully entitled to pass on to the licensees through discounts. There could be substantial transaction cost savings when multiple patents are licensed as a package. Negotiation costs are saved when the licensor avoids multiple individual licensing negotiations and instead licenses tens if not hundreds of patents through one agreement. Monitoring costs are minimized when a package license obviates the need to police against unauthorized use of patents. The *Automatic Radio* case in the United States aptly illustrates this point. The patents at issue in the case were closely related and their boundaries were difficult to delineate in the circuitry of the radio products.[104] Close inspection would be required to determine which of the hundreds of patents in the licensor's portfolio were implemented in a particular radio equipment.[105] For a licensee that produces numerous products, multiple detailed inspections would be needed to determine the appropriate licensee fee. A package license that covers the licensor's entire portfolio would obviate the need for such inspections.

In fact, cost savings can be so substantial that the package license can be deemed a single product. This will be the case 'when (1) two items can be produced or marketed more cheaply together than separately; but (2) much of the advantage of joint provision would be lost if the seller were obligated to offer the products separately to a subset of customers'.[106] This would seem to apply to the transaction cost savings mentioned in the previous paragraph. If package licensing were to be a

103 Hovenkamp and others (n 92) s 23.2a.
104 ibid s 23.3b2.
105 ibid.
106 ibid.

competition law violation it would be as an illegal tie, which is premised on a tying product and a tied product. If the package license constituted a single product due to economies of joint provision, there would not be an illegal tie between two separate products.

The demarcation of product boundary is slightly more complicated in the package license context than with physical products. With physical products, there is usually little doubt as to which product the consumers truly want. When the sale of a printer is tied to the sale of its replacement ink cartridges, consumers are forced to purchase the ink cartridges in order to gain access to the printer. With patent licenses, it is not always clear which licenses are wanted and which are unwanted. It may vary from licensee to licensee depending on their technical needs and technical capability. Thus the question should be approached from the buyer's perspective.[107] The tying product would be those licenses that a particular licensee wants while the tied product are those licenses which a licensee is forced to take in order to obtain her desired licenses.[108] Sometimes, especially in the context of standard-essential patents (SEPs), there may be a small group of patents within a package that lack reasonable substitutes and are particularly valuable while the rest of the patents are more fungible.[109] In that case, the valuable patents would be the tying product and the rest of the package the tied product.

Under standard tying analysis, a tie would only be capable of inflicting competitive harm if the licensor possesses market power in the tying product market of wanted patents. There was a time when patents were presumed to possess market power for the purpose of tying analysis under US antitrust law. That changed after the *Illinois Tool Works* case in 2006.[110] Market power now depends on whether there are reasonable substitutes for the tying patents, as is the case when physical products are involved. SEPs are more likely to possess market power than other patents given that they are essential to the implementation of an industry-wide technical standard.

The first and foremost anticompetitive effect of package licensing is foreclosure of rivals in the tied product market of unwanted patents. Foreclosure would result if the licensee would have preferred to use another patent but was forced to accept the tied patent from the tying licensor due to package licensing. Herbert Hovenkamp and co-authors describe foreclosure as follows:

> Suppose one patentee holds *patents A* and *B*, which relate to the same product or use. A second patentee holds *patent B"*, covering a competitive alternative to *patent B*. The licensee prefers to employ patents *A* and *B"* in its own process, but the

[107] ibid s 22.3b.
[108] ibid.
[109] ibid.
[110] *Illinois Tool Works v. Independent Ink*, 547 US 28 (2006).

> first patentee's package licensing provision requires the licensee to license both *A* and *B*. The *B*" patentee is thus foreclosed from the licensee's business.[111]

The fact that the licensee has a license for *B* does not stop her from obtaining another license for *B*". The problem is that with the package license, the incremental cost of using *B* would be zero while the incremental cost of using *B*" would be the license fee that the second licensor charges.[112] The playing field is no longer level between *B* and *B*" and the benefits of *B*" over *B* would need to be substantial enough to justify the additional incremental cost.

There would be no foreclosure if the licensee does not want the tied patent at all. The licensee would not obtain a substitute patent from a rival licensor if the tie was forbidden. The licensee's chief grievance in that case is that she is forced to take an unwanted patent.[113] To the extent that the licensor charges royalty for the unwanted patent, the licensee's complaint amounts to one about excessive royalty, in which courts are loathe to get involved.[114] Intervention would require courts to adopt 'a rule that required licensors of multiple patents to offer subsets at reduced royalties [which] would place the court in the indefensible position of royalty rate regulator. Further, regulating licensing rates is particularly difficult because short run costs are so low.'[115] If the unwanted patent is offered for free, which is how the US Court of Appeals for the Federal Circuit characterized the tied patents in *US Philips Corp. v. International Trade Commission*, there would be no foreclosure at all. In that case, the Federal Circuit argued that the arrangement is tantamount to Philips declaring unilaterally that it will not enforce those tied patents.[116]

3. Case Law on Restrictive Licensing Practices

(a) Imposition of post-expiration royalty

Similar to no challenge clauses, post-expiration royalty has been dealt with under patent law rather than antitrust law in the United States. Ever since *Brulotte* in the 1960s, the US Supreme Court has held that post-expiration royalty constitutes patent misuse. The Court held that 'a patentee's use of a royalty agreement that projects beyond the expiration date of the patent is unlawful *per se*. If that device were available to patentees, the free market visualized for the post-expiration period would be subject to monopoly influences that have no proper place there.'[117] In an

[111] Hovenkamp and others (n 92) s 22.4a2.
[112] ibid s 22.3d.
[113] ibid.
[114] ibid.
[115] ibid.
[116] *US Philips Corp. v. International Trade Commission*, 424 F.3d 1179, 1192.
[117] Brulotte, 379 US at 32–33.

apparent acknowledgement of the aforementioned argument that post-expiration royalty is not harmful so long as aggregate royalty payments remain unchanged, the Court drew a distinction between post-expiration royalty and the deferral of pre-expiration royalty, holding that only the former constituted patent misuse.[118] To the Court, imposition of post-expiration royalty is tantamount to impermissible enlargement of the patent monopoly such as patent tying, which at the time of the case was practically *per se* illegal under US antitrust law.

Brulotte has been roundly criticized by commentators and the lower courts who have long advocated that the case be overturned.[119] The criticisms have focused on a few grounds. First, there is no principled basis upon which to distinguish pre-expiration and post-expiration royalty. A ban on the latter can be easily circumvented through a royalty restructuring that would make no difference in economic substance. As Thomas Cotter argues, it is 'hard to see what policy, other than an empty formalism, could possibly justify the Brulotte rule of per se illegality'.[120] Second, the fixed patent term only caps the maximum size of the patentee reward but not the period over which this reward can be collected.[121] Post-expiration royalty often amounts to nothing more than the amortization of pre-expiration royalty. Whether patent monopoly has been impermissibly extended does not depend on 'when payment occurs, but [on] whether the discounted present value of the aggregate royalty payments exceeds the value of accessing the patent during its (remaining) term'.[122] The argument is perhaps not so much that post-expiration royalty can never cause consumer harm but rather that it should not be condemned across the board under a *per se* rule.[123]

The Supreme Court was presented an opportunity to overturn *Brulotte* in *Kimble v. Marvel Entertainment*, but ultimately declined to do so. The Court acknowledged that there may be valid reasons for parties to agree to post-expiration royalty, such as accommodation of a cash-strapped licensee or better allocation of the risks of and returns to the commercialization of an invention.[124] The Court further acknowledged the wide economic consensus that post-expiration royalty is most likely not anticompetitive.[125] Nonetheless, the Court insisted that *Brulotte* be upheld in light of *stare decisis* and the simplicity of its rule.[126] Statutory *stare decisis*,

[118] ibid 31.

[119] Brief for Petitioners at 13, Kimble v. Marvel Entertainment, 576 US 446 (2015) (No. 13-720).

[120] Thomas F Cotter, 'Comparative Patent Remedies' (*Postexpiration Patent Royalties, Comparative Patent Remedies*, 5 November 2014) <http:// comparativepatentremedies.blogspot.com/2014/11/ postexpiration-patent-royalties.html>.

[121] Vincent Chiappetta, 'Living with Patents: Insights from Patent Misuse' (2011) 15 Marquette Intellectual Property Law Review 1, 41.

[122] ibid 42.

[123] Kelley (n 86) 172.

[124] *Kimble v. Marvel Entertainment*, LLC, 576 US 446, 453 (2015).

[125] ibid 461.

[126] ibid 459.

under which the courts interpret and Congress retains the prerogative to amend, prevails in patent law because unlike the antitrust law, 'the patent laws do not turn over exceptional law-shaping authority to the courts'.[127]

The Court dismissed the economic arguments against *Brulotte* on the grounds that it was a patent misuse case and not an antitrust case. The *Kimble* court pointed out that *Brulotte* was not premised on the economic harm of post-expiration royalty.[128] The infirmity of the decision from an economic perspective hence does not justify its overrule. Moreover, as a patent law issue, 'Congress is the right entity to fix it' if *Brulotte* turns out to be erroneous.[129] Finally, the Court noted that *Brulotte* admits of exceptions such as the deferral of pre-expiration royalty. Under *Brulotte*, a 'licensee could agree, for example, to pay the licensor a sum equal to 10% of sales during the 20–year patent term, but to amortize that amount over 40 years'.[130] Therefore, the licensor still retains some flexibility to structure royalty payments.

The EU courts have analysed post-expiration royalty as a competition law issue but has consistently taken a permissive view. In *Kai Ottung v. Klee & Weilbach*, which seems to be the first case where the CJEU encountered the issue, the Court upheld such a royalty provision so long as the licensee is free to terminate the licensing agreement. Free termination suggests that the continual payment of royalty post-expiration is voluntary. The Court asserted that

> [a]n obligation to continue to pay royalty after the expiry of a patent can result only from a licensing agreement which either does not grant the licensee the right to terminate the agreement by giving reasonable notice or seeks to restrict the licensee's freedom of action after termination... Where, however, the licensee may freely terminate the agreement by giving reasonable notice, an obligation to pay royalty throughout the validity of the agreement cannot come within the scope of the prohibition contained in Article 85(1).[131]

In 2016, the CJEU reiterated the position it had taken in *Kai Ottung* on post-expiration royalty in *Genentech v. Hoechst*.[132] *Genentech* itself did not concern post-expiration royalty. Instead, the issue in the case was whether a licensee is still under an obligation to pay royalty accrued prior to the termination of a licensing agreement when a court subsequently held that there was no infringement in the first place. The Court summarized the ruling in *Kai Ottung* as follows:

[127] ibid 462.
[128] ibid.
[129] ibid.
[130] ibid 454.
[131] Case 320/87, *Kai Ottung v. Klee & Weilbach A/S and Thomas Schmidt A/S.* [1989] EU:C:1989:195.
[132] Case C-567/14, *Genentech Inc. v. Hoechst GmbH and Sanofi-Aventis Deutschland GmbH* [2016] EU:C:2016:526.

> Article 101(1) TFEU does not prohibit the imposition of a contractual requirement providing for payment of a royalty for the exclusive use of a technology that is no longer covered by a patent, on condition that the licensee is free to terminate the contract... As long as the licence agreement at issue is still valid and can be freely terminated by the licensee, the royalty payment is due, even if the industrial-property rights derived from patents which are granted exclusively cannot be used against the licensee due to the fact that the period of their validity has expired... the contention may be rejected that the payment of a royalty undermines competition by restricting the freedom of action of the licensee or by causing market foreclosure effects.[133]

The European Commission shares the same view as the CJEU that post-expiration royalty has limited anticompetitive effects. In the TTBER Guidelines, the Commission noted that:

> the parties can normally agree to extend royalty obligations beyond the period of validity of the licensed intellectual property rights without falling foul of Article 101(1) of the Treaty. Once these rights expire, third parties can legally exploit the technology in question and compete with the parties to the agreement. Such actual and potential competition will normally be sufficient to ensure that the obligation in question does not have appreciable anti-competitive effects.[134]

The European courts stopped short of an unequivocal endorsement of post-expiration royalty. There are two conditions for its legality. The first one is that the licensee is free to terminate the licensing agreement at any time. The second one, which the Court in *Genentech* mentioned when describing the ruling in *Kai Ottung*, is that the licensing agreement is exclusive. It is unclear what exactly is the relevance of the exclusivity of the licensing agreement. One possible, and perhaps not very convincing, argument is that the grantor of an exclusive license should be given greater right to insist on royalty payment given that the license is her only source of revenue. But if this argument was accepted, exclusivity can be used to justify all sorts of licensing restrictions. Thankfully, upon closer reading of the judgment in *Kai Ottung*, it seems that the Court's reference in *Genentech* to the exclusivity of the licensing agreement was largely fortuitous. The *Kai Ottung* court attached no significance to the exclusivity of the agreement at all. In fact, exclusivity was not even mentioned once in the judgment. It is unlikely that the *Genentech* court intended to limit the ruling of *Kai Ottung* to exclusive licenses.

That leaves the condition of the licensee having the right to terminate the licensing agreement at will. This condition indicates that the licensee was not coerced

[133] ibid para 40.
[134] TTBER Guidelines, para 187.

into accepting the post-expiration royalty and that the arrangement was likely to be an accommodation to the licensee. This condition, however, opens the door to licensee *ex post* opportunism. Having acceded to the licensee's request for deferral of payments, the licensor would be at the licensee's mercy if the latter chooses to walk away from the licensing agreement. With an unconditional right to terminate the agreement, it is difficult to imagine why any licensee would keep making royalty payments beyond the patent term, after which the technology would be free for all to use. The only check on licensee *ex post* opportunism would be reputational risks. A licensee that is a repeat player in technology licensing may hesitate to engage in post-expiration opportunistic behaviour for fear of acquiring a bad reputation. There are good reasons to question the soundness of this condition.

Again, China is one of the developing country jurisdictions to have confronted the legality of post-expiration royalty. The NDRC ruled that Qualcomm violated the AML by charging licensees the same royalty even though some of the patents covered by its package license had expired and new patents were added to the package.[135] Although the NDRC did not explicitly characterize Qualcomm's conduct, one way to look at Qualcomm's licensing practice is that it charged royalty for expired patents.[136] Without offering a detailed explanation, the NDRC held that Qualcomm's package licensing practice and refusal to allow licensees to verify the content of the package infringed the AML. The NDRC's strict position on post-expiration royalty seems to be confirmed by SAMR's IP-Competition Guidelines. Article 18(4) of the Guidelines states that assertion of IP rights after expiration of those rights would constitute an abuse of dominance under the AML.[137]

There is hence a variety of approaches to post-expiration royalty among the surveyed jurisdictions. The United States does not scrutinize the practice under antitrust law at all and instead considers it a misuse under patent law. The European Union adopts a permissive stance under competition law so long as the licensee is free to terminate the licensing agreement. China takes the most hard-line approach of all and deems the practice to be an abuse of dominance with no apparent regard to competitive effects and accepting no justification such as accommodation of a cash-strapped licensee. Again, as in the case of no challenge clauses, if a violation is only met with injunctive relief and is not subject to fines, there is probably not much of a difference between the US treatment of the practice as a patent misuse and China's designation of the practice as an abuse of dominance. The NDRC Qualcomm case, however, shows that the Chinese competition authority does not shy away from imposing fines for the practice.

[135] NDRC Qualcomm Decision.

[136] Thomas K Cheng, 'The PRC NDRC Case against Qualcomm: A Misguided Venture or Justified Enforcement of Competition Law?' (2017) 5 Journal of Antitrust Enforcement 76, 85.

[137] SAMR IP-Competition Guidelines, art 18(4).

(b) Package licensing

Package licensing is dealt with both as a misuse under patent law and under antitrust law in the United States. The ensuing discussion will focus on package licensing as a possible antitrust violation. It seems that the US Supreme Court first encountered package licensing in *Automatic Radio Manufacturing v. Hazeltine Research*.[138] The issue of the legality of a package license was not directly in front of the Court. Nonetheless, the Court made a number of approving statements about the practice. The Court noted that the licensee was not coerced to accept the package license. It characterized the arrangement as 'the privilege to use any or all of the patents and developments as it desired to use them. If it chooses to use none of them, it has nevertheless contracted to pay for the privilege of using existing patents plus any developments resulting from respondent's continuous research.'[139]

The importance of the lack of coercion in upholding a package license was further underscored by the Court in *Zenith Radio Corp. v. Hazeltine Research*, in which the Court struck down a license under which the licensee was required to pay royalty over its total sales regardless of whether the patents were implemented in the licensee's products.[140] The *Zenith* court emphasized the lack of coercion in *Automatic Radio* when distinguishing the two cases.[141] The Court further noted that the package license in *Automatic Radio* had the advantage of obviating the need for constant monitoring.[142]

In *Philips*, the US Court of Appeals for the Federal Circuit upheld the package license at issue under both the *per se* rule and the Rule of Reason. Contrasting the package license with the earlier Supreme Court cases on block booking of film distribution rights, the Federal Circuit observed that none of the licensees were coerced to use any of the licensed patents contained in the package.[143] The Federal Circuit asserted that:

> [a] package license is in effect a promise by the patentee not to sue his customer for infringing any patents on whatever technology the customer employs in making commercial use of the licensed patent. That surrender of rights might mean that the customer will choose not to license the alternative technology offered by the patentee's competition, but it does not compel the customer to use the patentee's technology. The package license is thus not anticompetitive in the way that a compelled purchase of a tied product would be.[144]

138 *Automatic Radio Manufacturing v. Hazeltine Research*, 339 US 827 (1950).
139 ibid 834.
140 Zenith Radio Corp. v. Hazeltine Research, 395 US 100 (1969).
141 ibid 138–39.
142 ibid 138.
143 Philips Corp., 424 F.3d at 1189.
144 ibid 1190.

The Federal Circuit further concluded that there was no evidence that the licensing fee would have been lower if the unwanted patents had been excluded from the package license or if individual licenses had been offered. The Court argued that the overall package largely derived its value from the essential patents in it.[145] The non-essential patents could be effectively valueless if they could be replaced by alternative technologies that are available for free.[146] The Court, however, seemed to be of two minds about whether to treat the non-essential patents as free.[147] Finally, the Court rejected the application of the *per se* rule in light of the efficiencies of package licensing, which include reduction of transaction costs, minimization of litigation risks, and ease of pricing of royalty.[148]

Package licensing is ultimately a form of tying and therefore the general law on tying remains applicable. After *Jefferson Parish v. Hyde*, the *per se* rule for tying would not apply unless the defendant possesses at least a 30 per cent market share in the tying product market.[149] Where the *per se* rule does not apply a tie would be analysed under the Rule of Reason. Under tying law, there would be no illegal tie if the licensee was not coerced to accept the tie. Therefore, coercion remains a critical element in the analysis of package licensing under US antitrust law.

There seem to be no EU cases on package licensing. The TTBER Guidelines mention package licensing in a number of instances, even though some of the discussions are in the specific context of patent pool, where the market power of the tying patents is generally undisputed. The Guidelines acknowledge the potential anticompetitive effects and pro-competitive benefits of package licensing. They specifically refer to foreclosure of rival technologies as a potential competitive harm.[150] They explain that when the royalty for a package license already covers a substitute technology, there is very little incentive for licensees to seek out alternative technologies.[151]

A concern about foreclosure is further evident in the discussion about the safe harbour for patent pools, under which one of the considerations is whether the pool offers distinct licensing packages for different applications.[152] The rationale is that licensees should not be forced to accept overly broad licensing packages containing patents that are unnecessary for their desired applications. A further consideration is 'whether licensees have the possibility of obtaining a licence for only part of the package with a corresponding reduction of royalties',[153] which may

145 ibid 1191.
146 ibid.
147 ibid 1191–92.
148 ibid 1192–93.
149 Herbert Hovenkamp, *Federal Antitrust Policy: The Law of Competition and Its Practice* (4th edn, West Publishing Co 2011) s 10.3a.
150 TTBER Guidelines, para 172.
151 ibid para 262.
152 ibid para 264(c).
153 ibid para 264(d).

reduce the deterrent effect on licensees to pursue alternative technologies. Finally, the Guidelines also allude to savings in transaction costs where multiple licensors put together a technology package to be licensed to third parties, obviating the need for multiple licenses.[154]

Some developing country jurisdictions have also issued decisions on package licensing. In the NDRC Qualcomm decision, Qualcomm was found to have violated the AML by tying licenses for wireless SEPs to licenses for non-wireless SEPs.[155] Wireless SEPs are those that are needed to deploy wireless 2G, 3G, and 4G technologies. Non-wireless SEPs relate to other technologies in a smartphone, including the touchscreen, the camera, etc. Wireless SEPs are what licensees truly value in Qualcomm's portfolio. Qualcomm allegedly required licensees to take out licenses to non-wireless SEPs if they wanted access to the wireless SEPs.

The NDRC found Qualcomm's package licensing practice to have violated the AML after rejecting Qualcomm's three defences.[156] First, Qualcomm insisted that it had actually offered licensees the option to license wireless and non-wireless SEPs separately but none of the licensees took up the offer. This was contradicted by the factual record. Second, Qualcomm asserted that it was difficult to distinguish wireless SEPs from non-wireless SEPs and that licensees would be exposed to unnecessary litigation risks if they eschewed licenses to the non-wireless SEPs. It would seem highly implausible that a patent for wireless technology is difficult to differentiate from a patent for the touchscreen. Third, Qualcomm argued that the tie did not foreclose alternative technologies and licensees were free to access them despite the package license. The obvious answer to this argument is that alternative technologies can still be foreclosed even if licensees are not required to use the tied patents because, as mentioned earlier, the package license artificially inflated the incremental cost of using an alternative technology.

Article 17 of SAMR's IP-Competition Guidelines states that package licensing may violate the AML if a dominant licensor restricts competition through tying practices without valid justifications.[157] The Guidelines do not provide much guidance on how restriction of competition is to be ascertained apart from listing six factors to be considered: (1) whether the tie is imposed against the will of the transaction counterparty; (2) whether the tie is consistent with transactional norms and consumer habits; (3) whether the tie ignores the differences and the relationship between the intellectual properties or products at issue; (4) whether the tie is reasonable or necessary in light of technological compatibility, product safety, and product functions; (5) whether the tie excludes or forecloses other business operators from transactional opportunities; and (6) whether the tie restricts consumer

154 ibid para 176.
155 NDRC Qualcomm Decision.
156 NDRC Qualcomm Decision.
157 SAMR IP-Competition Guidelines, art 17.

choice.[158] Some of these factors are consistent with those that would be considered under US antitrust law such as (1), which refers to the existence of coercion of the licensee. Some of the factors are somewhat peculiar. For example, a tie by definition restricts consumer choice unless consumers are completely indifferent about whether they obtain the tied product together with the tying product or separately. It would be difficult to find a tie that does not restrict consumer choice.

In a case that seems to follow the same rationale as the NDRC *Qualcomm* decision, CADE in Brazil approved a patent pool for Blu-ray Disc technology formed by Sony, Philips, Panasonic, Hitachi, Samsung, and Cyberlink on the condition that only essential patents were incorporated in the pool and non-essential patents were excluded.[159] CADE was concerned that the inclusion of non-essential patents would result in a tie-in situation where licensees were forced to accept licenses for non-essential patents in order to obtain access to essential patents. This concern is similar to that evinced by the NDRC over Qualcomm's tie of wireless SEPs with non-wireless SEPs.

4. A Proposed Framework for Developing Countries

(a) Imposition of post-expiration royalty

It was said that a more permissive attitude toward restrictive licensing practices will increase returns to licensing activities and boost licensing incentives. Given that licensing provides the greatest boost to the technological capacity of developing countries, developing countries that possess technological absorption capacity will need to approach restrictive licensing practices with caution.

Whether regulation of post-expiration royalty affects licensing incentives depends crucially on whether such royalty allows the licensor to charge more. If the answer is in the negative, there is no trade-off between licensor financial incentives on the one hand and licensee interests and consumer welfare on the other. Licensees do not end up paying more royalty and consumers do not pay higher prices for access to the technology. Allowing the practice will give licensors greater flexibility and will help to boost licensing incentives at no cost to the licensees and the consumers. And if permitting post-expiration royalty helps to accommodate cash-strapped licensees, it may even be a boon to local licensees and help boost the local technological capacity.

Even if post-expiration royalty results in larger aggregate royalty payments, harm to developing countries is still not conclusive. Recall the two pro-competitive

[158] ibid.

[159] CADE, 'Contribution to Round Table on: "Examining the Interface between the Objectives of Competition Policy and Intellectual Property", Intergovernmental Group of Experts on Competition Law and Policy' (19–21 October 2016) s 2.5 <https://unctad.org/system/files/non-official-document/ciclp2016c02_ccBrazil_en.pdf> accessed 29 July 2021.

accounts of post-expiration royalty. Even if aggregate royalty payments are higher, if the lower per-period royalty attracts more licensees to enter the market and compete, the increased overall royalty may be offset by the heightened competition at the licensee level. Consumers may not be worse off overall. Lower per-period royalty will also allow more licensees to afford the license, which may help to boost the country's technological capacity. It is important, however, not to overestimate this benefit. If no domestic licensees can afford the license absent post-expiration royalty, the boost to the country's technological capacity is tangible. Otherwise, the extra licensee may merely represent a duplication of technological capacity and the benefit to the developing country may be small.

Competition law enforcement against post-expiration royalty needs to be sensitive to the development stage of the country at issue. Post-expiration royalty is unlikely to be an enforcement concern in the production countries where technology licensing is rare. Even in the rare cases in which the issue does arise in these countries, considerations about licensing incentives would be largely redundant. These countries are bereft of the technological capacity to implement licensed technologies from the industrialized economies. Post-expiration royalty matters more in the technological adaptation countries and the proto-innovation countries. These countries harbour technology adaptation capacity and thus impact on licensing incentives will be a relevant consideration. Consideration of licensing incentives should take into account of the capacity of a particular industry. They can be accorded little weight in an industry that is devoid of technological adaptation capacity.

First and foremost, it is clear that revenue-neutral post-expiration royalty raises no competition concerns and should not be subject to competition law intervention. The scholarly consensus seems to take revenue neutrality for granted, which implies that post-expiration royalty should never be regulated. This author is slightly more sceptical about the notion of single monopoly profit and believes that it must be proven and not facilely assumed. The challenge lies in establishing revenue neutrality, which may require a counterfactual comparison that would be fraught with difficulty. One scenario in which this can be relatively easily proven is when post-expiration royalty is nothing more than the amortization of pre-expiration royalty. This is one of the exceptions recognized in *Kimble* to the general rule in *Brulotte*.[160] This exception, however, also opens the door for exploitation through clever drafting. Beyond this, the burden should be on the licensor to provide cogent evidence that establishes revenue neutrality.

A more readily available indicia of lack of competitive harm is whether the request for royalty deferral emanated from the licensee or the licensor. If the request was made to accommodate a cash-strapped licensee, it should lead to wider

[160] Kimble, 576 US at 453–54.

adoption of the licensed technology, which in turn suggests a lower likelihood of consumer harm due to heightened competition at the licensee level. And if the licensor acceded to the request, it should be beneficial to both the licensor and the licensee. There will be no deterrent effect on licensing activities while adoption of the licensed technology will be promoted. If the institution of post-expiration royalty leads to a significant increase in the number of licensees or the inclusion of a particularly low-cost licensee, consumers will be highly unlikely to suffer harm. It may hence be justified to adopt a rule of presumptive legality under which post-expiration royalty that is put in place at the behest of the licensee is presumed legal unless rebutted by clear and convincing evidence of consumer harm.

Where the deferral of royalty is imposed by the licensor and its revenue neutrality cannot be proven, more nuanced analysis is in order. In the unlikely cases involving post-expiration royalty in the production countries, licensing incentives carry little weight and the policy trade-off is between the licensor's innovation incentives and consumer welfare. If the product that utilizes the licensed technology is not widely used by domestic consumers, then the trade-off mainly concerns foreign innovators and foreign consumers. In that case, the competition authority may be better off adopting a rule of *per se* legality and defer the matter to the competition authorities in industrialized economies where these innovators and consumers are located.

For countries that possess the requisite technological adaptation capacity at least in some industries, an industry-specific approach is required. In industries where technological adaptation capacity is weak or entirely absent, licensing is likely to be rare and post-expiration royalty is unlikely to be a regular occurrence. If it does arise, the approach suggested for the production countries can be adopted. In industries that possess such a capacity, it becomes necessary to take into account licensing considerations, which include both the impact on licensing incentives and licensee interests.

The question of revenue neutrality becomes critical. If the licensor's overall royalty intake would remain the same, there would be no impact on licensing incentives whatever the legal position is on post-expiration royalty. Licensors should be indifferent between pre- and post-expiration royalties. The legality of post-expiration royalty matters, however, if a licensor is able to extract more royalty through post-expiration royalty. A ban on post-expiration royalty may conceivably reduce licensing incentives and cause a licensor to abstain from licensing to firms in a particular developing country. A ban, however, will also help to protect licensees from possible licensor exploitation such as perpetual royalty.[161] Ideally, developing countries would prefer to a rule under which licensor incentives are preserved while licensees are afforded adequate protection. The reality is that there is probably no legal rule that will reach such a Goldilocks situation.

161 Cassandra E Havens, 'Saving Patent Law from Competition Policy and Economic Theories: Kimble v. Marvel Entertainment, LLC' (2016) 31 Berkeley Technology Law Journal 371, 387.

From the perspective of a developing country in need of technology transfer, it is probably advisable to permit post-expiration royalty. There are a number of reasons for this. First, there is a risk that depressing licensing revenue will deter licensing activities. Even a minor risk may be too much to bear if the country prioritizes technology transfer. Second, regardless of whether the royalty deferral was requested by the licensee, it most likely will result in a reduction of per-period royalty and a greater affordability of the licensed technology, at least over the short term. It should boost technology transfer. Third, given the uncertainty regarding the revenue neutrality of post-expiration royalty, it is probably best to adopt a rule that would suit both scenarios.

The only exception is if there is clear and convincing evidence of consumer harm. It is possible that post-expiration royalty raises the overall royalty burden on licensees, which pass on the heavier royalty burden to consumers because competition is weak at the licensee level and the increased affordability of the license fails to spur competition among the licensees. Consumer harm would particularly deserve the attention of developing country competition authorities if the affected consumers are mostly domestic. These authorities need to be particularly vigilant about protecting their consumers, many of whom are poor.

In sum, where the deferral of royalty payments is requested by the licensee, post-expiration royalty should be presumptively legal. Where the deferral is imposed by the licensor, a development stage-specific approach is required. The production countries may want to defer to the competition authorities of the industrialized economies, especially when domestic consumers are relatively unaffected. Licensing incentives are unlikely to concern these countries. Enforcement resources can be better spent elsewhere where domestic welfare is more at stake. A rule of presumptive legality or even *per se* legality may be appropriate. In any case, these countries are unlikely to confront post-expiration royalty on a regular basis given the dearth of licensing activities.

For the technological adaptation and the proto-innovation countries, the enforcement approach should be industry-specific. For industries bereft of technological adaptation capacity, post-expiration royalty is again unlikely to feature prominently. If it does come up, the same approach as that for the production countries may apply. For industries that are capable of technological adaptation from the industrialized economies, it becomes a balance between protecting domestic licensee interests and maintaining the incentives of licensors to transfer technology. The balance tilts in favour of condoning post-expiration royalty for a variety of reasons explained earlier. Overall, a rule of presumptive legality subject to a rebuttal of clear and convincing evidence of consumer harm may be best suited for the needs of developing countries.

The position on post-expiration royalty under the PRC's AML is thus unsuitable for most developing countries. It is unjustifiable to prohibit post-expiration royalty across the board. The EU approach of leniency is probably closer to the mark.

The United States does not deal with post-expiration royalty under antitrust law. The practice is only treated as a misuse under patent law. The US Supreme Court conceded that as a matter of economic theory, the rule in *Brulotte* was probably unsound.[162] The Court in *Kimble* clarified that it was upholding *Brulotte* in light of patent policy and the principle of *stare decisis*, which has no pertinence for developing countries.[163] Therefore, the US approach to post-expiration royalty provides little guidance to developing countries.

(b) Package licensing

For package licensing, the analysis is in a way more straightforward. Unlike post-expiration royalty, package licensing does not pose a direct conflict between licensor interests and consumer welfare, especially if it is assumed that the licensor can charge more royalty through post-expiration royalty. The main competitive harm of package licensing is foreclosure of rival technologies, which is unlikely to result directly in higher prices for consumers in the short term. It could also cause the licensee to pay more royalty than necessary if the licensee does not require a tied patent that cannot be regarded as free under the logic of *Philips*. It was said in the context of the developed jurisdictions that intervening in such a case would be ill-advised as doing so would turn the competition authority into a price regulator.

Contrary to most restrictive licensing practices, it cannot be assumed that prohibiting package licensing will reduce licensing revenue and hence impair licensing incentives. Prohibiting package licensing may not have a material impact on licensing revenue. This is especially true if one subscribes to the single monopoly profit theorem, under which the legality of package licensing would not affect the patentee's ability to extract profit. The patentee can extract the entire monopoly profit from the monopolistic patent alone if package licensing is banned. Alternatively, the package license makes no difference whatsoever to the patentee's profit if the tied patent is offered for free. The royalty would remain the same irrespective of the package license.

This greatly simplifies the policy trade-off for developing countries. Consumer harm deserves less attention due to the relatively remote impact of the practice on consumer welfare. Licensing incentives likewise need not concern us because the licensor presumably can extract the same revenue without resorting to package licensing. Foreclosure of rival technologies may boost the licensor's profit. Yet the opportunity to foreclose rivals is unlikely to be determinative in the licensor's decision. Therefore, the only remaining considerations for the competition authority are foreclosure of rival technologies (without regard to its impact on licensor profit) and possible concerns about overpaying by licensees.

[162] Kimble, 576 US at 455.
[163] ibid 461–62.

Package licensing is likely to be rare in production countries. To the extent it arises, foreclosure of rival technologies is irrelevant for these countries because they presumably are incapable of generating technologies that can challenge a patented technology from an industrialized economy. Overpaying by licensees does not deserve much weight either as these countries do not have many potential licensees. In contrast, the technological adaptation and the proto-innovation countries are capable of producing potential licensees while the latter may also generate rival technologies to those licensed from the industrialized economies. Therefore, package licensing deserves closer attention from these countries.

Foreclosure of rival technologies is a serious concern for the proto-innovation countries because the innovators in these countries may be particularly susceptible to foreclosure by their industrialized economy rivals. These innovators may not be as well-resourced as their industrialized economy counterparts and their technologies may be less advanced and hence more fungible. A slight increase in the incremental costs of using these technologies may be sufficient to deter potential licensees from considering them. Recall that a package license is capable of tilting the playing field against rival technologies by raising the relative incremental costs of deploying these technologies. Therefore, competition authorities in the proto-innovation countries need to take foreclosure seriously, which may imply a relatively strict approach to package licensing.

Coercion is a necessary element for establishing an illegal package license under US antitrust law and should likewise be required by developing countries. There can be no tie without coercion. Market power in the tying product market is another necessary element. The US approach under *Jefferson Parish* where a market share above 30 per cent may suffice to show market power may be suitable for developing countries that wish to adopt a strict approach. The Federal Circuit in *Philips* suggested that the tied patents may be offered for free. Obviously there can be no foreclosure if that is true. The problem is it is often very difficult to verify whether particular patents in a package are offered for free. Developing countries that are keen to offer maximum protection to its innovators may choose to err on the side of over-inclusion and assume that patents are not offered for free absent clear and convincing evidence to the contrary. In sum, foreclosure should be presumed once the plaintiff demonstrates coercion and a market share in excess of 30 per cent in the tying product market.

The technological capacity of these countries may vary by industry and there may not be the requisite capacity in certain industries. Foreclosure will not be a relevant concern in these industries and package licensing will raise few competitive issues. The aforementioned analytical approach applies in industries in which foreclosure is pertinent.

A concern about foreclosure turns into one about excessive royalty when the licensee does not want the tied patent. In the context of the industrialized economies, it was argued that the competition authority should not get involved lest it risks being turned into a price regulator. In the context of developing countries, the strongest reason against intervention is perhaps the possible impact on licensing incentives. In theory, if the single monopoly profit theorem holds, removal of the competitive tied patents from a package license will have no impact on the licensor's profitability. The reality is likely to be more complicated because patents may have varying degrees of market power. As mentioned earlier, different licensees may need different patents, which means that the designation of tying and tied patents may vary across licensees. If one licensee succeeds in unbundling the package, other licensees may demand the same and that may cause the licensor to lose licensing revenue. It is conceivable that a licensor would rather forego one licensing market than to risk unravelling the whole packaging licensing scheme across multiple markets. This may complicate the picture and suggest that prohibiting package licensing is not as innocuous for licensing incentives as was originally suggested.

Possible impairment of licensing incentives may be a price worth paying when foreclosure is at stake. Foreclosure of a domestic innovator may deprive a developing country an important opportunity for technological upgrade. It may not be worth jeopardizing licensing incentives when the concern is overpayment by licensees. This is especially true because foreign technology transfer is the only avenue for technological upgrade for the technological adaptation countries. Even for proto-innovation countries, technology transfer probably remains more important than domestic innovation for technological upgrade. Therefore, the suggestion would be for developing countries to refrain from intervention when foreclosure is absent.

D. Conclusion

The policy trade-off underlying regulation of restrictive licensing practices is more intricate as there could be impact on the incentives of licensors to license their technologies to developing countries. Given that licensing is the most beneficial form of technology transfer for developing countries, developing country competition authorities need to be mindful about possible deterrent effect on licensing incentives. The wide variety of restrictive licensing practices precludes an exhaustive survey of them in this chapter. Instead, it focuses on no challenge clauses, imposition of post-expiration royalty, and package licensing. It puts forward a development stage-specific approach to analysing these practices under which developing countries adopt rules for regulating these practices that reflect their technological capacity.

Licensing activities are likely to be extremely rare in production countries, which means that restrictive licensing practices should be a low enforcement priority for these countries. For the technological adaptation and the proto-innovation countries, the extent to which these restrictive licensing practices should be regulated would depend on the emphasis on attracting technology transfer. Countries that wish to prioritize technology licensing may want to adopt a rule of presumptive legality or even *per se* legality for no challenge clauses. There are other rules of thumb such as where consumer harm is unlikely or where consumer harm is concentrated among foreign consumers which may simplify the analysis. Where none of these simple rules of thumb apply and the patentee is shown to possess market power, a comprehensive analysis of the relationship between the patentee and the licensees and the market structure at the licensee level may be needed to settle the legality of no challenge clauses. A rule of presumptively legality subject to a rebuttal of clear and convincing evidence of consumer harm may be the appropriate rule for post-expiration royalty for most developing countries. Lastly, developing countries in general should adopt a strict rule against package licensing where foreclosure of rival technologies from a domestic firm is likely.

11
Conclusion

This book has proposed a development stage-specific approach to the patent–competition interface that takes into account an individual country's technological capacity. It argues that innovation incentives matter less for most developing countries for a variety of reasons. These include the tendency of the patent system to overcompensate innovators, the availability of other appropriation mechanisms such as lead time that allow the innovator to monetize her innovation, and the lack of potential innovators with the appropriate technological capacity in most developing countries to take advantage of the incentives generated by the patent system. The patent system in these countries of course is not only geared toward domestic innovators. Foreign innovators such as multinational corporations may take into account the patentee reward generated by the patent system in developing countries. This, however, is mostly only true for developing countries with a large domestic market. For the numerous developing countries that only possess a small domestic market, it is highly unlikely that the patentee reward provided by their patent system will feature prominently in foreign innovators' investment decisions. These countries can by and large ignore the innovation incentive externalities generated by their domestic patent systems. The conclusion is thus that for most developing countries, innovation incentives should carry little weight in calibrating an appropriate approach for the patent–competition interface. This conclusion may well lead to increased intervention and possible negative externalities on the innovation incentives of foreign innovators, yet it may be justifiable from the perspective of a developing country jurisdiction seeking to protect the welfare of its downtrodden consumers.

Developing countries differ in their technological capacities and can be roughly classified into production countries, technology adaptation countries, and proto-innovation countries. The production countries are only capable of production and implementation of basic technology. The technology adaptation countries are in a position to adapt and implement sophisticated imported technology or perhaps to imitate or reverse engineer such technology. Proto-innovation countries, of which there are only a few, possess the capacity to innovate in at least some industries. For the vast majority of developing countries bereft of genuine innovation capacity, the main vehicle for technological progress is technology transfer from foreign innovators. Therefore, for these countries, dynamic efficiency considerations are concerned with incentives of foreign innovators to transfer technology and not innovation incentives as such. Technology transfer can be divided into voluntary and

The Patent–Competition Interface in Developing Countries. Thomas K. Cheng, Oxford University Press. © Thomas K. Cheng 2021. DOI: 10.1093/oso/9780192857354.003.0011

involuntary technology transfer. Voluntary technology transfer can be undertaken in three mains ways: importation of technological goods, foreign direct investment (FDI), and licensing. Involuntary technology transfer consists of outright copying and reverse engineering.

Competition law regulation of patent exploitation practices interacts with the three means of technology transfer in varied and complex ways. Impact on the three means of voluntary technology transfer also varies depending on the type of patent exploitation practice at issue. For practices that implicate the robustness of patent protection, a permissive attitude toward these practices may increase the country's attractiveness as a destination of technology transfer and may skew the mode of technology transfer to FDI and licensing, which tend to produce greater benefits in terms of enhancement of technological capacity. This is especially true for licensing. The relationship between competition law regulation of patent exploitation practices and FDI tends to be industry- and activity-specific. The positive impact seems to be much more pronounced in countries that are otherwise viable FDI destinations. The impact also tends to be stronger for research-related activities as opposed to non-research-related ones such as sales and marketing. The actual amount of technology transfer through FDI is dependent on the bargaining power of the host country at issue. It is possible for FDI to take place without significant technology transfer. Host countries often need to put pressure on the foreign investor to undertake meaningful technology transfer.

Under the development stage-specific approach to the patent–competition interface, for production countries without meaningful innovation capacity, the primary consideration when approaching the patent–competition interface would be static efficiency and consumer welfare. The technology adaptation countries will need to take into account how their approach to the patent–competition interface affects the incentives of foreign technology owners to transfer their technology. This means that patent exploitation practices that implicate robustness of patent protection, such as unilateral refusal to license, deserve special attention. Relaxed regulation of licensing restrictions may steer potential licensors toward licensing. Proto-innovation countries will require an industry-specific approach to the patent–competition interface as their technological capacity varies across industries.

The proposed approach to the patent–competition interface is then applied to a variety of patent exploitation practices. The unilateral refusal to deal doctrine and the related essential facilities doctrine could provide potent tools for facilitating technology transfer to developing countries. The former is mainly applicable to refusal to supply a patented product while the latter is more pertinent to refusal to license technology. First and foremost, the most often-invoked criticism against compulsory licensing—undermining of innovation incentives—is dismissed. Both on a theoretical and an empirical level, it is not immediately clear that compulsory licensing necessarily undermines innovation incentives. Once one takes into account the impact of compulsory licensing on cumulative innovation, the argument becomes even less convincing. It is argued that the existing case law in the United States and the European Union under these two doctrines generally lack a coherent theory of harm. Developing countries should avoid this pitfall by insisting on a coherent theory of harm when invoking either doctrine. It is also argued that a number of theoretical approaches put forward in the case law or the literature, including *per se* legality, the scope of the patent test, the monopoly leveraging test, the intent/pretext test, and the no business justification rule, all suffer from their infirmities and are unsuitable for developing countries.

An approach to unilateral refusal to deal built on the surveyed theories of harm is proposed for developing countries, under which it is suggested that only mere authorization licenses should be available in technology adaptation and proto-innovation countries. Such licenses do not compel the patentee to provide assistance to the compulsory licensee and only require the patentee to acquiesce to the licensee's implementation of the technology. Active assistance licenses, under which the patentee is expected to transfer know-how and help the licensee implement the technology, should only be granted by production countries. In the end, it is argued that developing countries need to be careful in invoking the unilateral refusal to deal doctrine or the essential facilities doctrine to compel technology transfer due to possible retaliation by the industrialized economies.

Patent tying involves the tied sale of a patented product with an unpatented product. It is probably one of the most common patent exploitation practices. Patent tying is often justified on the grounds that it helps to boost innovation incentives. It is demonstrated that patent tying does not boost innovation incentives, especially in the tied product market. There are additionally a number of other reasons that it would be counterproductive to rely on patent tying to generate innovation incentives. For example, relying on patent tying to generate innovation incentives would skew innovation toward technologies for which tying is possible. Innovation incentive considerations do not call for a more lenient treatment of patent tying. If anything, the balance of the argument seems to point in the opposite direction. Other procompetitive justifications for tying are likewise found to be wanting.

Meanwhile, it is established that tying allows extraction of consumer surplus and foreclosure in the form of offensive leveraging in the tied product market and defensive leveraging in the tying product market. Various kinds of foreclosure may retard technological upgrade by developing country firms and have different degrees of relevance to developing countries depending on their technological capacity. Offensive leveraging is of particular concern because developing country firms are more likely to be engaged in innovation in the tied product market, which is generally less technologically intensive than innovation in the tying product market. In light of the various anticompetitive effects of patent tying, a relatively strict rule against patent tying is suggested for developing countries. Developing countries are urged to adopt a rule of presumptive illegality under which a patent tie is presumed illegal once a defendant is shown to possess market power in the tying product market and fails to provide evidence of pro-competitive benefits. Rules of different levels of complexity are proposed based on the enforcement capacity of the competition authority in question.

Excessive drug prices are a scourge in developing countries. Unaffordable drugs could mean untold human suffering and can even be a matter of life or death. The causes for high drug prices in developing countries are myriad and complex and cannot be entirely attributed to patent protection or the lack of competition, but the complex causes do not lessen the urgency for developing countries to tackle the problem. The Agreement on Trade-Related Aspects of Intellectual Property Rights (TRIPS) provides a number of potential mechanisms for addressing high drug prices, including Articles 30 and 31. None of these mechanisms, however, are satisfactory due to their various shortcomings. It is argued that competition law has a limited but important role to play in combatting exorbitant drug prices in developing countries. Competition law intervention is especially justified in cases of a sudden but sharp price hike and of reverse price discrimination against developing countries. It is further argued that while developing countries should draw reference from the EU experience with excessive pricing regulation, the existing EU approach is needlessly complicated. It is suggested that the second prong of unfairness under *United Brands* should be dropped and that a simple price comparison with past prices in the same market in the case of sharp price hikes and a cross-country price comparison in the case of reverse price discrimination should suffice to demonstrate excessiveness. Once excessiveness is established, the burden shifts to the defendant to justify the price increase or price difference.

One of the most controversial issues in competition law over the last two decades is the treatment of reverse payment settlements. Until the issue was finally settled by the US Supreme Court in *Actavis*, lower courts and commentators in the United States have furnished a wide variety of approaches to such settlements, ranging from tests that amount to per se legality to rules that border on *per se* illegality. Meanwhile, there is mounting evidence that reverse payment settlements result in higher drug prices for consumers. While reverse payment settlements seemingly present great theoretical complexity and pose enormous enforcement difficulty for developing country competition authorities, the potential impact on domestic drug prices renders them too important to be overlooked by these authorities. While the *Actavis* court ostensibly adopted a rule of reason, commentators have argued that the truncated rule of reason adopted by the Court amounts to a rule of presumptive illegality. The EU courts, including the very recent decision by the Court of Justice of the European Union (CJEU) in *Lundbeck*, have consistently taken a hardline approach toward these settlements. It is suggested that developing countries could do well to follow the lead of the United States and the European Union in taking a presumptive illegality approach to reverse payment settlements to prevent pharmaceutical companies from colluding to raise prices on hapless patients. There is no need for developing countries to engage in needless theoretical hair-splitting when the consumer harm of the practice is so apparent.

The policy trade-off underlying regulation of restrictive licensing practices is more intricate as there could be impacts on the incentives of licensors to license their technologies to developing countries. Given that licensing is the most beneficial form of technology transfer for developing countries, developing country competition authorities need to be mindful about possible deterrent effects on licensing incentives. A development stage-specific approach to restrictive licensing practices is proposed to take into account the fact that licensing activities may have varying degrees of relevance to developing countries depending on their technological capacity. The approach is illustrated with the examples of no challenge clauses, post-expiration royalty, and package licensing. Licensing activities are likely to be extremely rare in production countries, which means that restrictive licensing practices should be a low enforcement priority for these countries. For the technological adaptation and the proto-innovation countries, the extent to which these restrictive licensing practices should be regulated would depend on the emphasis on attracting technology transfer. Countries that wish to prioritize technology licensing may want to adopt a rule of presumptive legality or even *per se* legality for no challenge clauses. A rule of presumptive legality subject to a rebuttal of clear and convincing evidence of consumer harm may be the appropriate rule for post-expiration royalty for most developing countries. Developing countries should adopt a strict rule against package licensing where foreclosure of rival technologies from a domestic firm is likely.

Underlying this book is the belief that one size does not fit all in competition law. The approaches developed in the leading jurisdictions of the United States and European Union, which are continental-sized industrialized economies, could be ill-suited for developing countries, especially those with a small economy. Developing countries face policy considerations that have lesser or little relevance for industrialized economies, such as the need to prioritize economic growth, the need to alleviate abject poverty, and the need to promote technology transfer. By putting forward a development stage-specific approach to the patent–competition interface, this book implicitly challenges the drive for convergence that has dominated the global competition law community over the last two decades and puts forward a case for informed divergence. The drive for convergence may serve the interests of the industrialized economies but neglect the different policy considerations facing developing nations. The international mainstream approach to the patent–competition interface may only reflect the policy choices of the leading jurisdictions with scant regard for the development needs and market realities of the developing countries. There is a risk that the drive for convergence will repeat the debacle for developing countries that was inflicted upon them by the TRIPS Agreement in the realm of intellectual property. It is hoped that this book has presented a cogent case for that.

Bibliography

Abbott FM, 'WTO TRIPS Agreement and Its Implications for Access to Medicines in Developing Countries' (Commission for Intellectual Property Rights 2002) Background Paper

Abbott FM, 'Excessive Pharmaceutical Prices and Competition Law: Doctrinal Development to Protect Public Health' (2016) 6 University of California Irvine Law Review 281

Abramson B, 'Intellectual Property and the Alleged Collapsing of Aftermarkets' (2007) 38 Rutgers Law Journal 399

'Agreement on Trade-Related Aspects of Intellectual Property Rights (Adopted 15 April 1994, Entered into Force 1 January 1995) 1869 UNTS 299 (TRIPS Agreement)'

Ahlborn C, Evans DS, and Padilla AJ, 'The Antitrust Economics of Tying: A Farewell to Per Se Illegality' (2004) 49 Antitrust Bulletin 287

Akman P and Garrod L, 'When Are Excessive Prices Unfair?' (2011) 7 Journal of Competition Law & Economics 403

Allinder SM and Fleischman J, 'The World's Largest HIV Epidemic in Crisis: HIV in South Africa' *Center for Strategic & International Studies* (2 April 2019) <https://www.csis.org/analysis/worlds-largest-hiv-epidemic-crisis-hiv-south-africa> accessed 21 September 2020

Allison JR and Lemley MA, 'Empirical Evidence on the Validity of Litigated Patents' (1998) 26 American Intellectual Property Law Association Quarterly Journal 185

Allison JR, Lemley MA and Walker J, 'Patent Quality and Settlement Among Repeat Patent Litigants' (2011) 99 Georgetown Law Journal 677

Allred B and Park W, 'The Influence of Patent Protection on Firm Innovation Investment in Manufacturing Industries' (2007) 13 Journal of International Management 91

Allred BB and Park WG, 'Patent Rights and Innovative Activity: Evidence from National and Firm-Level Data' (2007) 38 Journal of International Business Studies 878

Altenburg T and Lütkenhorst W, *Industrial Policy in Developing Countries: Failing Markets, Weak States* (Edward Elgar Publishing Ltd 2015)

Amsden A, *Escape from Empire: The Developing World's Journey through Heaven and Hell* (The MIT Press 2007)

Ancori B, Bureth A, and Cohendet P, 'The Economics of Knowledge: The Debate about Codification and Tacit Knowledge' (2000) 9 Industrial and Corporate Change 255

Anderson B, 'Better Access to Medicines: Why Countries Are Getting 'TRIPPED' up and Not Ratifying Article 31-Bis' (2010) 1 Case Western Reserve Journal of Law, Technology & the Internet 166

Apostolopoulos H, 'Refusal-to-Deal Cases of IP Rights in the Aftermarket of US and EU Law: Convergence of Both Law Systems through Speaking the Same Language of Law and Economics' (2007) 5 DePaul Business and Commercial Law Journal 237

Armstrong M and Vickers J, 'Price Discrimination, Competition and Regulation' (1993) 41 Journal of Industrial Economics 335

Arrow K, 'Economic Welfare and the Allocation of Resources for Invention' (National Bureau of Economic Research, Inc 1962) NBER Chapters <https://econpapers.repec.org/bookchap/nbrnberch/2144.htm> accessed 31 March 2019

Arundel A, 'The Relative Effectiveness of Patents and Secrecy for Appropriation' (2001) 30 Research Policy 611

Atik J and Lidgard H, 'Embracing Price Discrimination: TRIPS and the Suppression of Parallel Trade in Pharmaceuticals' (2006) 27 University of Pennsylvania Journal of International Law 1043

Attaran A, 'How Do Patents and Economic Policies Affect Access to Essential Medicines in Developing Countries?' (2004) 23 Health Affairs 155

Avenali A, D'Annunzio A, and Reverberi P, 'Bundling, Competition and Quality Investment: A Welfare Analysis' (2013) 43 Review of Industrial Organization 221

Ayres I and Klemperer P, '"Limiting Patentees" Market Power Without Reducing Innovation Incentives: The Perverse Benefits of Uncertainty and Non-Injunctive Remedies' (1999) 97 Michigan Law Review 985

Babar Z-U-D and others, 'The Availability, Pricing and Affordability of Three Essential Asthma Medicines in 52 Low- and Middle-Income Countries' (2013) 31 PhamacoEconomics 1063

Babar Z-U-D and others, 'The Availability, Pricing, and Affordability of Essential Diabetes Medicines in 17 Low-, Middle-, and High-Income Countries' (2019) 10 Frontiers in Pharmacology 1375

Baker J, 'Promoting Innovation Competition through the Aspen/Kodak Rule' (1999) 7 George Mason Law Review 495

Baker J, 'Beyond Schumpeter vs. Arrow: How Antitrust Fosters Innovation' (2007) 74 Antitrust Law Journal 575

Balasubramaniam K, 'Equitable Pricing, Affordability and Access to Essential Drugs in Developing Countries: Consumers Perspective', Paper delivered at WHO/WTO Secretariat Workshop on Differential Pricing and Financing of Essential Drugs (8–11 April 2001)

Bardhan P and Udry C, *Development Microeconomics* (Oxford University Press 1999)

Barton JH, 'Patents and Antitrust: A Rethinking in Light of Patent Breadth and Sequential Innovation' (1997) 65 Antitrust Law Journal 449

Basheer S and Primi A, 'The WIPO Development Agenda: Factoring in the 'Technologically Proficient' Developing Countries' in Jeremy DeBeer (ed), *Implementing WIPO's Development Agenda* 100 (Wilfred Laurier University Press 2008)

Bass NA, 'Implications of the TRIPS Agreement for Developing Countries: Pharmaceutical Patent Laws in Brazil and South Africa in the 21st Century' (2002) 34 George Washington University International Law Review 191

Bauer JP, 'Refusals to Deal with Competitors by Owners of Patents and Copyrights: Reflections on the Image Technical and Xerox Decisions' (2006) 55 DePaul Law Review 1211

Baumol W, *The Free-Market Innovation Machine: Analyzing the Growth Miracle of Capitalism* (Princeton University Press 2004)

Beall R and Kuhn, 'Trends in Compulsory Licensing of Pharmaceuticals Since the Doha Declaration: A Database Analysis' (2012) 9 PLoS Medicine

Beall R and Kuhn R, 'Trends in Compulsory Licensing of Pharmaceuticals Since the Doha Declaration: A Database Analysis' [2012] PLoS Medicine <https://journals.plos.org/plosmedicine/article%3Fid%3D10.1371/journal.pmed.1001154> accessed 4 March 2020

Benoliel D, *Patent Intensity and Economic Growth* (Cambridge University Press 2017)

Bernstein J, 'The Structure of Canadian Inter-Industry R&D Spillovers, and the Rates of Return to R&D' (1989) 37 Journal of Industrial Economics 315

Besen SM, 'Why Royalties for Standard Essential Patents Should Not Be Set by the Courts' (2015) 15 Chicago-Kent Journal of Intellectual Property 19

Bessen J and Meurer M, *Patent Failure: How Judges, Bureaucrats, and Lawyers Put Innovators at Risk* (Princeton University Press 2009)

Blair RD and Kaserman DL, 'Vertical Integration, Tying, and Antitrust Policy' (1978) 68 The American Economic Review 397

Bogaisky J, 'Boeing's Vertical Leap: Where Will It Squeeze Suppliers Next?' (*Forbes*, 6 June 2018) <https://www.forbes.com/sites/jeremybogaisky/2018/06/06/boeings-vertical-leap-where-will-it-squeeze-suppliers-next/#5a175a5f248a> accessed 4 March 2020

Bohannan C, 'IP Misuse as Foreclosure' (2011) 96 Iowa Law Review 475

Boldrin M and Levine DK, *Against Intellectual Monopoly* (Cambridge University Press 2008)

Boldrin M and Levine DK, 'The Case Against Patents' (2013) 27 Journal of Economic Perspectives 3

Bond E and Saggi K, 'Compulsory Licensing, Price Controls, and Access to Patented Foreign Products' <https://www.wipo.int/edocs/mdocs/mdocs/en/wipo_ip_econ_ge_4_12/wipo_ip_econ_ge_4_12_ref_saggi.pdf> accessed 29 July 2021

Borenstein S, Mackie-Mason JK, and Netz JS, 'Antitrust Policy in Aftermarkets' (1995) 63 Antitrust Law Journal 455

Bork RH, *The Antitrust Paradox: A Policy at War with Itself* (The Free Press 1978)

Bowman, Jr WS, 'Tying Arrangements and the Leverage Problem' (1957) 67 Yale Law Journal 19

Boyle PM, Lister PM, and Everett Jr JC, 'Antitrust Law at the Federal Circuit: Red Light or Green Light at the IP-Antitrust Intersection' (2001) 69 Antitrust Law Journal 739

Branstetter L, Fisman R, and Foley CF, 'Do Stronger Intellectual Property Rights Increase International Technology Transfer? Empirical Evidence from US Firm-Level Panel Data' (2006) 121 Quarterly Journal of Economics 321

Branstetter L and Saggi K, 'Intellectual Property Rights, Foreign Direct Investment and Industrial Development' (2011) 121 The Economic Journal 1161

Bresnahan T, 'Measuring the Spillovers from Technical Advance: Mainframe Computers in Financial Services' (1986) 76 The American Economic Review 742

Briggs K, 'Does Patent Harmonization Impact the Decision and Volume of High Technology Trade?' (2013) 25 International Review of Economics & Finance 35

Bulow J, 'The Gaming of Pharmaceutical Patents' in Adam B Jaffe, Josh Lerner, and Scott Stern (eds), *Innovation Policy and the Economy*, vol 4 (2004) 145 <https://www.nber.org/system/files/chapters/c10802/c10802.pdf> accessed 14 March 2021

Burk DL and Lemley MA, 'Policy Levers in Patent Law' (2003) 89 Virginia Law Review 1575

Burstein ML, 'The Economics of Tie–In Sales' (1960) 42 Review of Economics and Statistics 68

CADE, 'Contribution to Round Table on: "Examining the Interface between the Objectives of Competition Policy and Intellectual Property", Intergovernmental Group of Experts on Competition Law and Policy' (19–21 October 2016) <https://unctad.org/system/files/non-official-document/ciclp2016c02_ccBrazil_en.pdf> accessed 29 July 2021

Cairns JW, 'Watson, Walton, and the History of Legal Transplants' (2013) 41 Georgia Journal of International and Comparative Law 637

Calcagno C and Walker M, 'Excessive Pricing: Towards Clarity and Economic Coherence' (2010) 6 Journal of Competition Law & Economics 891

Caldera A and Zarnic Z, 'Affordability of Pharmaceutical Drugs in Developing Countries' (Kiel Institute for World Economics 2015) No 419

Cameron A and others, 'Medicine Prices, Availability, and Affordability in 36 Developing and Middle-Income Countries: A Secondary Analysis' (2009) 373 Lancet 240

Carlton DW, 'A General Analysis of Exclusionary Conduct and Refusal to Deal: Why Aspen and Kodak Are Misguided' (National Bureau of Economic Research 2001) Working Paper 8105

Carlton DW and Waldman M, 'The Strategic Use of Tying to Preserve and Create Market Power in Evolving Industries' (2002) 33 RAND Journal of Economics 194

Carlton DW and Waldman M, 'How Economics Can Improve Antitrust Doctrine towards Tie-In Sales: Comment on Jean Tirole's "The Analysis of Tying Cases: A Primer"' (2005) 1 Competition Policy International 27

Carlton DW and Waldman M, 'Tying, Upgrades, and Switching Costs in Durable Goods Market' (2005) <http://economics.mit.edu/files/4057> accessed 29 July 2021

Carlton DW and Waldman M, 'Theories of Tying and Implications for Antitrust' (Cornell University The Johnson School (2005) #24-06 <https://papers.ssrn.com/sol3/papers.cfm?abstract_id=809304> accessed 29 July 2021

Carlton DW and Waldman M, 'Robert Bork's Contributions to Antitrust Perspectives on Tying Behavior' (2014) 57 Journal of Law & Economics S121

Carrier MA, 'Unsettling Drug Patent Settlements: A Framework for Presumptive Illegality' (2009) 108 Michigan Law Review 37

Carrier MA, 'A Response to Chief Justice Roberts: Why Antitrust Must Play a Role in the Analysis of Drug Patent Settlements' (2014) 15 Minnesota Journal of Law, Science & Technology 31

Carrier MA, 'Five Actions to Stop Citizen Petition Abuse' (2018) 118 Columbia Law Review Online 81

Carter SL, 'Does It Matter Whether Intellectual Property Is Property' (1992) 68 Chicago-Kent Law Review 715

Center for Global Development, 'New Study Finds Some Poor Countries Paying 20 to 30 Times More for Basic Medicines Than Others' (17 June 2019) <https://www.cgdev.org/article/new-study-finds-some-poor-countries-paying-20-30-times-more-basic-medicines-others> accessed 20 September 2020

Chalkidou K, 'More Health for the Money through Better Purchasing Decisions: The Case of Ghana' (21 November 2017) <https://www.cgdev.org/blog/more-health-money-through-better-purchasing-decisions-case-ghana> accessed 20 September 2020

Chan SM and Tang TC, 'Foreign Direct Investment Inflows and Intellectual Property Rights: Empirical Evidence from Different Income Groups' (2017) 46 Global Economic Review 372

Chang HF, 'Patent Scope, Antitrust Policy and Cumulative Innovation' (1995) 26 The RAND Journal of Economics 34

Chaudhuri S, 'Are Medicine Prices High and Unaffordable after TRIPS? Evidence from Pharmaceutical Industry in India' (Centre for Development Studies 2019)

Che J, Qiu L and Zhou W, 'Entry, Reputation and Intellectual Property Rights Enforcement' (2014) 47 The Canadian Journal of Economics 1256

Chen Y, 'Refusal to Deal, Intellectual Property Rights, and Antitrust' (2013) 30 Journal of Law, Economics & Organization 533

Cheng TK, 'A Developmental Approach to the Patent-Antitrust Interface' (2012) 33 Northwestern Journal of International Law & Business 1

Cheng TK, 'Antitrust Treatment of No Challenge Clause' (2016) 5 New York University Journal of Intellectual Property and Entertainment Law 437

Cheng TK, 'The PRC NDRC Case against Qualcomm: A Misguided Venture or Justified Enforcement of Competition Law?' (2017) 5 Journal of Antitrust Enforcement 76

Chiappetta V, 'Living with Patents: Insights from Patent Misuse' (2011) 15 Marquette Intellectual Property Law Review 1

Chien CV, 'Cheap Drugs at What Price to Innovation: Does the Compulsory Licensing of Pharmaceuticals Hurt Innovation' (2003) 18 Berkeley Technology Law Journal 853

Chien CV, 'Holding Up and Holding Out' (2014) 21 Michigan Telecommunications & Technology Law Review 1

Choi JP, 'Preemptive R&D, Rent Dissipation, and the "Leverage Theory"' (1996) 111 Quarterly Journal of Economics 1153

Choi JP, 'Tying and Innovation: A Dynamic Analysis of Tying Arrangements' (2004) 114 The Economic Journal 83

Choi JP and Stefanadis C, 'Tying, Investment, and the Dynamic Leverage Theory' (2001) 32 RAND Journal of Economics 52

Ciongaru E, 'Negative Effects of Incorrect Legal Transplantation of European Union Legislation' (2013) 92 Procedia—Social and Behavioral Sciences 186

Co CY, 'Do Patent Rights Regimes Matter?' (2004) 12 Review of International Economics 359

Coco R, 'Antitrust Liability for Refusal to License Intellectual Property: A Comparative Analysis and the International Setting' (2008) 12 Marquette Intellectual Property Law Review 1

Coe D and Helpman E, 'International R&D Spillovers' (1995) 39 European Economic Review 859

Cohen WM and others, 'R&D Spillovers, Patents and the Incentives to Innovate in Japan and the United States' (2002) 31 Research Policy 1349

Cohen WM, Nelson R, and Walsh JP, 'Protecting Their Intellectual Assets: Appropriability Conditions and Why US Manufacturing Firms Patent (or Not)' (National Bureau of Economic Research, Inc 2000) NBER Working Paper 7552 <https://econpapers.repec.org/paper/nbrnberwo/7552.htm> accessed 5 April 2019

Colangelo M and Desogus C, 'Antitrust Scrutiny of Excessive Prices in the Pharmaceutical Sector: A Comparative Study of the Italian and UK Experiences' (2018) 41 World Competition 225

Comment, 'Validity of Patent License Provisions Requiring Payment of Post-Expiration Royalties' (1965) 65 Columbia Law Review 1256

Commission on Intellectual Property Rights, 'Integrating Intellectual Property Rights and Development Policy' (2002) <www.iprcommission.org/papers/pdfs/final_report/CIPRfullfinal.pdf> accessed 5 April 2019

Congressional Budget Office, 'How Increased Competition from Generic Drugs Has Affected Prices and Returns in the Pharmaceutical Industry' (1998) <https://www.cbo.gov/sites/default/files/105th-congress-1997-1998/reports/pharm.pdf> accessed 29 July 2021

Conrad R and Lutter R, 'Generic Competition and Drug Prices: New Evidence Linking Greater Generic Competition and Lower Generic Drug Prices' (Food and Drug Administration 2019) <https://www.fda.gov/media/133509/download> accessed 14 March 2021

Cornell University, INSEAD, and World Intellectual Property Organization, 'Global Innovation Index 2020—Who Will Finance Innovation?' (World Intellectual Property Organization 2020)

Correa C, *Intellectual Property Rights, the WTO and Developing Countries: The TRIPS Agreement and Policy Options* (Zed Books–Third World Network 2000)

Correa C, 'Public Health and Patent Legislation in Developing Countries' (2001) 3 Tulane Journal of Technology and Intellectual Property 1

Correa C, 'TRIPS Agreement and Access to Drugs in Developing Countries' (2005) 3 International Journal on Human Rights 25

Correa C, 'Will the Amendment to the TRIPS Agreement Enhance Access to Medicines?' (2019) The South Centre Policy Brief No 57 <https://www.southcentre.int/wp-content/uploads/2019/01/PB57_Will-the-Amendment-to-the-TRIPS-Agreement-Enhance-Access-to-Medicines_EN-1.pdf> accessed 29 July 2021

Cotter TF, 'Intellectual Property and the Essential Facilities Doctrine' (1999) 1999 The Antitrust Bulletin 211

Cotter TF, 'Antitrust Implications of Patent Settlements Involving Reverse Payments: Defending a Rebuttable Presumption of Illegality in Light of Some Recent Scholarship' (2004) 71 Antitrust Law Journal 1069

Cotter TF, 'Four Principles for Calculating Reasonable Royalties in Patent Infringement Litigation' (2011) 27 Santa Clara Computer & High Technology Law Journal 725

Cotter TF, 'FTC v. Actavis, Inc.: When Is the Rule of Reason Not the Rule of Reason' (2014) 15 Minnesota Journal of Law, Science & Technology 41

Cotter TF, 'Comparative Patent Remedies' (*Postexpiration Patent Royalties, Comparative Patent Remedies*, 5 November 2014) <http:// comparativepatentremedies.blogspot.com/2014/11/postexpiration-patent-royalties.html>

Crane DA, 'Exit Payments in Settlement of Patent Infringement Lawsuits: Antitrust Rules and Economic Implications' (2002) 54 Florida Law Review 747

Crane DA, 'Intellectual Liability' (2009) 88 Texas Law Review 253

Crane DA, 'Actavis, the Reverse Payment Fallacy, and the Continuing Need for Regulatory Solutions' (2014) 15 Minnesota Journal of Law, Science & Technology 51

da Costa PN, 'A Lack of Education Can Literally Be Deadly' (*World Economic Forum*, 13 February 2018) <https://www.weforum.org/agenda/2018/02/this-startling-imf-chart-shows-how-poverty-and-lack-of-access-to-education-are-literally-deadly> accessed 4 March 2020

Dasgupta P and Stiglitz J, 'Industrial Structure and the Nature of Innovative Activity' (1980) 90 Economic Journal 266

David PA, 'Intellectual Property Institutions and the Panda's Thumb: Patents, Copyrights, and Trade Secrets in Economic Theory and History' in MB Wallerstein, ME Mogee, and RA Schoen (eds), *Global Dimensions of Intellectual Property Rights in Science and Technology* (National Academic Press 1992) 33

de Lima L and others, 'Potent Analgesics Are More Expensive for Patients in Developing Countries' (2009) 18 Journal of Pain & Palliative Care Pharmacotherapy 59

Deardorff AV, 'Welfare Effects of Global Patent Protection' (1992) 59 Economica 35

Delrahim M, 'Forcing Firms to Share the Sandbox: Compulsory Licensing of Intellectual Property Rights and Antitrust' (2004) 2004 European Business Law Review 1059

Delrahim M, 'The "New Madison" Approach to Antitrust and Intellectual Property Law' (University of Pennsylvania Law School, Philadelphia, 16 March 2018) <https://www.justice.gov/opa/speech/file/1044316/download> accessed 29 July 2021

Derclaye E, 'Abuses of Dominant Position and Intellectual Property Rights: A Suggestion to Reconcile Community Courts Case Law' (2003) 26 World Competition 685

Devlin A, 'A Neo-Chicago Perspective on the Law of Product Tying' (2007) 44 American Business Law Journal 521

Devlin A and Jacobs M, 'Antitrust Divergence and the Limits of Economics' (2010) 104 Northwestern University Law Review 253

Devlin A, Jacobs M, and Peixoto B, 'Success, Dominance, and Interoperability' (2009) 84 Indiana Law Journal 1157

Dhar B and Joseph R, 'The Rise of the South and New Paths of Development in the 21st Century' (UNCTAD 2012) No 6

Di Maio M, 'Industrial Policies in Developing Countries: History and Perspectives' in Mario Cimoli, Giovanni Dosi, and Joseph Stiglitz (eds), *Industrial Policy and Development: The Political Economy of Capabilities Accumulation* (Oxford University Press 2009) 107

Diamantis ME, 'Corporate Criminal Minds' (2016) 91 Notre Dame Law Review 2049

DiMatteo LA, 'Terminology Matters: Dangers of Superficial Transplantation' (2019) 37 Boston University International Law Journal 35

Dinopoulos E and Segerstrom P, 'Intellectual Property Rights, Multinational Firms and Economic Growth' (2010) 92 Journal of Development Economics 13

Drahos P, 'The Regulation of Public Goods' (2004) 7 Journal of International Economic Law 321

Drake KM, Starr MA, and McGuire T, 'Do "Reverse Payment" Settlements of Brand-Generic Patent Disputes in Pharmaceutical Industry Constitute an Anticompetitive Pay for Delay?' (National Bureau of Economic Research 2014) 20292

Dreyfuss RC and Pope LS, 'Dethroning Lear? Incentives to Innovate After MedImmune' (2009) 24 Berkeley Technology Law Journal 971

Duggan M, Garthwaite C, and Goyal A, 'The Market Impacts of Pharmaceutical Product Patents in Developing Countries: Evidence from India' (2016) 106 The American Economic Review 99

Dumont B and Holmes P, 'The Scope of Intellectual Property Rights and Their Interface with Competition Law and Policy: Divergent Paths to the Same Goal?' (2002) 11 Economics of Innovation and New Technology 149

Dunning JH and Lundan SM, *Multinational Enterprises and the Global Economy* (2nd edn, Edward Elgar Publishing Ltd 2008)

Eaton J and Kortum S, 'Trade in Ideas Patenting and Productivity in the OECD' (1996) 40 Journal of International Economics 251

Economides N, 'Tying, Bundling, and Loyalty/Requirement Rebates' in Einer Elhauge (ed), *Research Handbook of the Economics of Antitrust Law* (Edward Elgar Publishing Ltd 2012) 121

Economides N, 'Bundling and Tying' (NYU Stern School of Business 2014) #14-22

Economides N and Hebert WN, 'Patents and Antitrust: Application to Adjacent Markets' (2008) 6 Journal of Telecommunications and High Technology Law 455

Economides N and Lianos I, 'Elusive Antitrust Standard on Bundling in Europe and in the United States in the Aftermath of the Microsoft Case' (2009) 76 Antitrust Law Journal 483

Economides N, Lianos I, and Rubini L, 'The Quest for Appropriate Remedies in the EC Microsoft Cases: A Comparative Appraisal' in Rubini L (ed), *Microsoft on Trial: Legal and Economic Analysis of a Transatlantic Antitrust Case* (Edward Elgar 2010) 393

Elberfeld W and Wolfstetter E, 'A Dynamic Model of Bertrand Competition with Entry' (1999) 17 International Journal of Industrial Organization 513

Elhauge E, 'Tying, Bundled Discounts, and the Death of the Single Monopoly Profit Theory' (2009) 123 Harvard Law Review 397

Elhauge E and Krueger A, 'Solving the Patent Settlement Puzzle' (2012) 91 Texas Law Review 283

Epstein RA and Noroozi KB, 'Why Incentives for "Patent Holdout" Threaten to Dismantle FRAND, and Why It Matters' (2017) 32 Berkeley Technology Law Journal 1381

European Commission, 'Patent Costs and Impact on Innovation' (European Commission 2014) <https://ec.europa.eu/jrc/communities/sites/jrccties/files/patent_costs_and_impact_on_innovation.pdf> accessed 23 June 2021

European Patent Office, 'Patents, Trade and Foreign Direct Investment in the European Union' (2017) <http://www.iprhelpdesk.eu/news/epo-study-patents-trade-and-foreign-direct-investment-european-union> accessed 9 April 2019

Evans DS, 'Tying: The Poster Child for Antitrust Modernization' in Robert W Hahn (ed), *Antitrust Policy and Vertical Restraints* (Brookings Institution 2006) 65

Evans DS and Padilla AJ, 'Excessive Prices: Using Economics to Define Administrable Legal Rules' (2005) 1 Journal of Competition Law & Economics 97

Ezrachi A and Gilo D, 'Are Excessive Prices Really Self-Correcting?' (2008) 5 Journal of Competition Law & Economics 249

Farrell J and others, 'Standard Setting, Patents, and Hold-Up' (2007) 74 Antitrust Law Journal 603

Farrell J and Katz, ML, 'Innovation, Rent Extraction, and Integration in Systems Markets' (2000) 48 The Journal of Industrial Economics 413

Federal Trade Commission, 'Generic Entry Prior to Patent Expiration: An FTC Study' (Federal Trade Commission 2002) <https://www.ftc.gov/sites/default/files/documents/reports/generic-drug-entry-prior-patent-expiration-ftc-study/genericdrugstudy_0.pdf> accessed 14 March 2021

Federal Trade Commission, 'Pay-For-Delay: How Drug Company Pay-Offs Cost Consumers Billions' (Federal Trade Commission 2010) FTC Staff Study <https://www.ftc.gov/sites/default/files/documents/reports/pay-delay-how-drug-company-pay-offs-cost-consumers-billions-federal-trade-commission-staff-study/100112payfordelayrpt.pdf> accessed 14 March 2021

Feldman RC, 'The Insufficiency of Antitrust Analysis for Patent Misuse' (2003) 55 Hastings Law Journal 399

Ferran E, 'Corporate Attribution and the Directing Mind and Will' (2011) 127 Law Quarterly Review 239

First H, 'Excessive Drug Pricing as an Antitrust Violation' (2019) 82 Antitrust Law Journal 701

Fletcher A and Jardine A, 'Towards an Appropriate Policy for Excessive Pricing' (2007) <https://www.eui.eu/Documents/RSCAS/Research/Competition/2007ws/200709-COMPed-Fletcher-Jardine.pdf> accessed 20 September 2020

Fortune A and Mitchell W, 'Unpacking Firm Exit at the Firm and Industry Levels: The Adaptation and Selection of Firm Capabilities' (2012) 33 Strategic Management Journal 794

Friedman G, 'The Sanctity of Property Rights in American History' (University of Massachusetts Amherst 2001) No 14 <https://scholarworks.umass.edu/cgi/viewcontent.cgi?article=1008&context=peri_workingpapers> accessed 29 July 2021

Frischmann B and Waller SW, 'Revitalizing Essential Facilities' (2008) 75 Antitrust Law Journal 1

Fromer JC, 'Patent Disclosure' (2008) 94 Iowa Law Review 539

Furse M, 'Excessive Prices, Unfair Prices and Economic Value: The Law of Excessive Pricing under Article 82 EC and the Chapter II Prohibition' (2008) 4 European Competition Journal 59

Gal M, 'The Ecology of Antitrust Preconditions for Competition Law Enforcement in Developing Countries' in Brusick P, Alvarez AM, Cernat L, and Holmes P (eds), *Competition, Competitiveness and Development* (UNCTAD 2004) 21

Gal, Michal S., 'Free Movement of Judgments: Increasing Deterrence of International Cartels Through Jurisdictional Reliance' (2010) 51 Virginia Journal of International Law 57

Gal MS and Miller AD, 'Patent Challenge Clauses: A New Antitrust Offense' (2017) 102 Iowa Law Review 1477

Gallini N and Scotchmer S, 'Intellectual Property: When Is It the Best Incentive System?' in Lerner J and Stern S (eds), *Innovation Policy and the Economy* (MIT Press 2002)

Gallus N, 'The Mystery of Pharmaceutical Parallel Trade and Developing Countries' (2004) 7 Journal of World Intellectual Property 169

Ganslandt M, 'Intellectual Property Rights and Competition Policy' in Maskus KE (ed), *Intellectual Property, Growth and Trade* (Emerald Insight 2015)

Garcia CT, 'Realities of Patent Pools in the Telecommunication Sector', in Proceedings of 7th International Conference on Standardization and Innovation in Information Technology, SIIT (IEEE 28–30 September 2011)

Garrett TA, 'Anticompetitive Manipulation of REMS: A New Exception to Antitrust Refusal-to-Deal Doctrine' (2018) 60 William & Mary Law Review 655

Gathii JT, 'How Necessity May Preclude State Responsibility for Compulsory Licensing under the TRIPS Agreement' (2006) 31 North Carolina Journal of International Law and Commercial Regulation 943

Genevaz S, 'Against Immunity for Unilateral Refusals to Deal in Intellectual Property: Why Antitrust Law Should Not Distinguish between IP and Other Property Rights' (2004) 19 Berkeley Technology Law Journal 742

Geradin D, 'The Necessary Limits to the Control of 'Excessive' Prices by Competition Authorities—A View from Europe' (2007) 2007–32 <https://papers.ssrn.com/sol3/papers.cfm?abstract_id=1022678> accessed 20 September 2020

Geradin D, Ginsburg D, and Safty G, 'Reverse Payment Patent Settlements in the European Union and the United States' (George Mason University 2015) 15–38 <ssrn.com/abstract=2662575>

Germano S, 'Compulsory Licensing of Pharmaceuticals in Southeast Asia: Paving the Way for Greater Use of the TRIPS Flexibility in Low-and Middle-Income Countries' (2007) 76 UMKC Law Review 273

Gilbert R and Shapiro C, 'Optimal Patent Length and Breadth' (1990) 21 RAND Journal of Economics 106

Gilbert RJ and Shapiro C, 'An Economic Analysis of Unilateral Refusals to License Intellectual Property' (1996) 93 Proceedings of National Academy of Sciences 12749

Gilbert RJ and Sunshine SC, 'The Use of Innovation Markets: A Reply to Hay, Rapp, and Hoerner' (1995) 64 Antitrust Law Journal 75

Goldstein DA and others, 'A Global Comparison of the Cost of Patented Cancer Drugs in Relation to Global Differences in Wealth' (2017) 8 Oncotarget 71548

Gollier C and Bruno J, 'National Champions under Credit Rationing' in Oliver Falck, Christian Gollier, and Ludger Woessmann (eds), *Industrial Policy and National Champions* (The MIT Press 2011) 135

Graham SJ and others, 'High Technology Entrepreneurs and the Patent System: Results of the 2008 Berkeley Patent Survey' (2009) 24 Berkeley Technology Law Journal 1255

Granstrand O, 'Innovation and Intellectual Property Rights' in Fagerberg J, Mowery D, and Nelson R (eds), *The Oxford Handbook of Innovation* (Oxford University Press 2006) 266

Griliches Z, Pakes A, and Hall BH, 'The Value of Patents as Indicators of Inventive Activity' (National Bureau of Economic Research 1986) Working Paper 2083 <http://www.nber.org/papers/w2083> accessed 4 April 2019

Grimes W, 'The Antitrust Tying Law Schism: A Critique of Microsoft III and a Response to Hylton and Salinger' (2002) 70 Antitrust Law Journal 199

Gumbel M, 'Is Article 31bis Enough—The Need to Promote Economies of Scale in the International Compulsory Licensing System' (2008) 22 Temple International and Comparative Law Journal 161

Gupta A, 'Patent Rights on Pharmaceutical Products and Affordable Drugs: Can TRIPS Provide a Solution' (2004) 2 Buffalo Intellectual Property Law Journal 127

Halajian D, 'Inadequacy of TRIPS & the Compulsory License: Why Broad Compulsory Licensing Is Not a Viable Solution to the Access Medicine Problem' (2013) 38 Brooklyn Journal of International Law 1191

Haley GT and Haley UCV, 'The Effects of Patent-Law Changes on Innovation: The Case of India's Pharmaceutical Industry' (2012) 79 Technological Forecasting & Social Change 607

Hall BH and others, 'The Importance (or Not) of Patents to UK Firms' (2013) Working Paper 19089 <https://www.nber.org/system/files/working_papers/w19089/w19089.pdf> accessed 29 July 2021

Hall BH, Jaffe AB, and Trajtenberg M, 'Market Value and Patent Citations' (2005) 36 RAND Journal of Economics 16

Hardy Q, 'Search 500,000 Documents, Review 160,000 Pages In 20 Hours, And Then Do It All Over Again' (*Forbes*, 24 June 2002) <https://www.forbes.com/asap/2002/0624/050.html> accessed 4 March 2020

Harris D, 'TRIPs after Fifteen Years: Success or Failure, as Measured by Compulsory Licensing' (2011) 18 Journal of Intellectual Property Law 367

Hausman JA and Mackie-Mason JK, 'Price Discrimination and Patent Policy' (1988) 19 RAND Journal of Economics 253

Havens CE, 'Saving Patent Law from Competition Policy and Economic Theories: Kimble v. Marvel Entertainment, LLC' (2016) 31 Berkeley Technology Law Journal 371

Heiden B and Petit N, 'Patent "Trespass" and the Royalty Gap: Exploring the Nature and Impact of Patent Holdout' (2017) 34 Santa Clara High Technology Law Journal 179

Heller MA and Eisenberg RS, 'Can Patents Deter Innovation? The Anticommons in Biomedical Research' (1998) 280 Science 698

Helpman E, 'Innovation, Imitation, and Intellectual Property Rights' (1993) 61 Econometrica 1247

Helpman E, *The Mystery of Economic Growth* (Harvard University Press 2004)

Hemphill S, 'Paying for Delay: Pharmaceutical Patent Settlement as a Regulatory Design Problem' (2006) 81 New York University Law Review 1553

Hernandez I and others, 'Number of Manufacturers and Generic Drug Pricing From 2005 to 2017' (2019) 25 The American Journal of Managed Care 348

Hernandez I and others, 'Changes in List Prices, Net Prices, and Discounts for Branded Drugs in the US, 2007–2018' (2020) 323 Journal of the American Medical Association 854

Herndon JB, 'Intellectual Property, Antitrust, and the Economics of Aftermarkets' (2002) Summer–FallThe Antitrust Bulletin 309

Herrera H and Schroth E, 'Profitable Innovation Without Patent Protection: The Case of Derivatives' (2003) Discussion Paper 03-02 <https://ftp.itam.mx/pub/academico/inves/herrera/03-02.pdf> accessed 29 July 2021

Hjelmfelt DC and Strother, Jr CD, 'Antitrust Damages for Consumer Welfare Loss' (1991) 39 Cleveland State Law Review 505

Hoekman BM, Maskus KE, and Saggi K, 'Transfer of Technology to Developing Countries: Unilateral and Multilateral Policy Options' (World Bank 2004) No 3332 <http://documents.worldbank.org/curated/en/737591468762912473/pdf/wps3332.pdf> accessed 4 March 2020

Holgersson M and Wallin MW, 'The Patent Management Trichotomy: Patenting, Publishing, and Secrecy' (2017) 55 Management Decision 1087

Hopkinson M, *Net Present Value and Risk Modelling for Projects* (Taylor & Francis Ltd 2017)

Hovenkamp E and Hovenkamp HJ, 'Tying Arrangements and Antitrust Harm' (2010) 52 Arizona Law Review 925

Hovenkamp H, 'United States Antitrust Policy in an Age of IP Expansion' (Social Science Research Network 2004) SSRN Scholarly Paper ID 634224 <https://papers.ssrn.com/abstract=634224> accessed 31 March 2019

Hovenkamp H, *Federal Antitrust Policy: The Law of Competition and Its Practice* (4th edn, West Publishing Co 2011)

Hovenkamp H, *IP and Antitrust: An Analysis of Antitrust Principles Applied to Intellectual Property Law* (2nd edn, Aspen Publishers 2011)

Hovenkamp H, Janis MD, and Lemley MA, 'Anticompetitive Settlement of Intellectual Property Disputes' (2003) 87 Minnesota Law Review 1719

Hovenkamp H, Janis MD, and Lemley MA, 'Balancing Ease and Accuracy in Assessing Pharmaceutical Exclusion Payments' (2004) 88 Minnesota Law Review 712

Hovenkamp HJ, 'IP and Antitrust Policy: A Brief Historical Overview' (University of Iowa 2005) No 05-31

Hovenkamp HJ, 'Anticompetitive Patent Settlements and the Supreme Court's Actavis Decision' (2014) 15 Minnesota Journal of Law, Science & Technology 3

Hovenkamp HJ, Janis MD, and Lemley MA, 'Unilateral Refusals to License in the US' [2005] Faculty Scholarship at Penn Law 13 <https://scholarship.law.upenn.edu/faculty_scholarship/1920> accessed 29 July 2021

Hovenkamp HJ, Janis MD, and Lemley MA, 'Unilateral Refusals to License' (2006) 2 Journal of Competition Law & Economics 1

Hurwitz MA, 'Bundling Patented Drugs and Medical Services: An Antitrust Analysis' (1991) 91 Columbia Law Review 1188

Hutchison C, 'Over 5 Billion Not Served: The TRIPS Compulsory Licensing Export Restriction' (2008) 5 University of Ottawa Law & Technology Journal 43

Huttunen K, Møen J, and Salvanes KG, 'How Destructive Is Creative Destruction? The Costs of Worker Displacement' (2006) EconPapers <https://econpapers.repec.org/paper/izaizadps/dp2316.htm> accessed 24 June 2021

Hylton KN and Salinger M, 'Tying Law and Policy: A Decision-Theoretic Approach' (2001) 69 Antitrust Law Journal 469

Hylton KN and Salinger M, 'Reply to Grimes: Illusory Distinctions and Schisms in Tying Law' (2002) 70 Antitrust Law Journal 231

Italian Competition Authority, 'A480-Price Increase of Aspen Drugs Measure No. 26185' (2016) <https://en.agcm.it/dotcmsDOC/pressrelease/A480_eng.pdf> accessed 21 September 2020

Ivus O, 'Do Stronger Patent Rights Raise High-Tech Exports to the Developing World?' (2010) 81 Journal of International Economics 38

Ivus O, 'Trade-Related Intellectual Property Rights: Industry Variation and Technology Diffusion' (2011) 44 The Canadian Journal of Economics 201

Kathleen D Jaeger, Statement at Hearing before the Committee on Commerce, Science, and Transportation of the US Senate (23 April 2002) Generic Pharmaceuticals: Marketplace Access and Consumer Issues 56

Jaffe AB and Lerner J, *Innovation and Its Discontents: How Our Broken Patent System Is Endangering Innovation and Progress, and What to Do About It* (Princeton University Press 2004)

Janicke PM and Ren L, 'Who Wins Patent Infringement Cases?' (2006) 34 American Intellectual Property Law Association Quarterly Journal 1

'Japan Rail Pass (JR Pass)' <https://www.japan-guide.com/e/e2361.html> accessed 8 May 2020

Javorcik BS, 'The Composition of Foreign Direct Investment and Protection of Intellectual Property Rights: Evidence from Transition Economies' (2004) 48 European Economic Review 39

Jewell C, 'Giving Innovation Wings: How Boeing Uses Its IP' (*World Intellectual Property Organization*, February 2014) <https://www.wipo.int/wipo_magazine/en/2014/01/article_0004.html> accessed 4 March 2020

Jones A and Stothers C, 'Establishing Unfairly High Prices: The Implications of the CAT's Judgment in Flynn and Pfizer v Competition and Markets Authority' (2018) 17 Bio-Science Law Review 19

Jones A and Sufrin B, *EU Competition Law: Text, Cases, and Materials* (5th edn, Oxford University Press 2014)

Kanwar S, 'Intellectual Property Protection and Technology Licensing: The Case of Developing Countries' (2012) 55 The Journal of Law and Economics 539

Kaplow L, 'The Patent-Antitrust Intersection: A Reappraisal' (1984) 97 Harvard Law Review 1813

Katsoulacos YS, 'Optimal Legal Standards for Refusals to License Intellectual Property: A Welfare-Based Analysis' (2009) 5 Journal of Competition Law & Economics 269

Kaufer E, *The Economics of the Patent System* (Harwood Academic Publishers 1989)

Kauper T, 'Article 86, Excessive Prices, and Refusals to Deal' (1991) 59 Antitrust Law Journal 441

Keller W, 'International Technology Diffusion' (2004) 42 Journal of Economic Literature 752

Kelley H, 'Note, Scheiber v. Dolby Laboratories, Inc.' (2003) 18 Berkeley Technology Law Journal 159

Kew C, 'Patently Uncertain: Developments in Pay-For-Delay Agreements in Australia' (*King & Wood Mallesons In Competition*, 11 June 2020) <https://incompetition.com.au/2020/06/patently-uncertain-developments-in-pay-for-delay-agreements-in-australia/> accessed 14 March 2021

Kianzad B and Minssen T, 'How Much Is Too Much? Defining the Metes and Bounds of Excessive Pricing in the Pharmaceutical Sector' (2018) 2 European Pharmaceutical Law Review 15

Killick J and Komninos A, 'Excessive Pricing in the Pharmaceutical Market—How the CAT Shot Down the CMA's Pfizer/Flynn Case' (2018) 9 Journal of European Competition Law & Practice 530

Kinda T, 'Investment Climate and FDI in Developing Countries: Firm-Level Evidence' (2010) 38 World Development 498

Kitch E, 'The Nature and Function of the Patent System' (1977) 20 Journal of Law & Economics 265

Klemperer P, 'How Broad Should the Scope of Patent Protection Be?' (1990) 21 RAND Journal of Economics 113

Kobayashi BH, 'Does Economics Provide a Reliable Guide to Regulating Commodity Bundling by Firms? A Survey of the Economic Literature' (2005) 1 Journal of Competition Law & Economics 707

Krasteva S, 'Imperfect Patent Protection and Innovation' (2014) 62 Journal of Industrial Economics 682

Krueger A, 'Implementing Actavis: Three Tips for Future Courts Assessing Reverse Patent Settlements under Rule of Reason Analysis' (2014) 15 Minnesota Journal of Law, Science & Technology 115

Kumar V, Kumar U, and Persaud A, 'Building Technological Capability Through Importing Technology: The Case of Indonesian Manufacturing Industry' (1999) 24 Journal of Technology Transfer 81

Lahtinen T, 'Reverse Payment Settlements in the European Union after the Generics (UK) Judgment—Perplexing Legal Uncertainty' (*Lexxion Competition Blogs*, 5 March 2020) <https://www.lexxion.eu/en/coreblogpost/reverse-payment-settlements-in-the-european-union-after-the-generics-uk-judgment-perplexing-legal-uncertainty/> accessed 14 March 2021

Lai E, 'International Intellectual Property Rights Protection and the Rate of Product Innovation' (1998) 55 Journal of Development Economics 133

Laitenberger J, 'Competition Assessments and Abuse of Dominance: Remarks on the Two Themes of the EUI Competition Workshop' (2018) <http://ec.europa.eu/competition/speeches/text/sp201 8_1 en.pdf> accessed 28 August 2018

Lamping M, 'Refusal to Licence as an Abuse of Market Dominance: From Commercial Solvents to Microsoft' in Reto M Hilty and KC Liu (eds), *Compulsory Licensing: Practical Experiences and Way Forward* (Springer-Verlag 2015) 121

Landes W and Posner R, *The Economic Structure of Intellectual Property Law* (Harvard University Press 2003)

Langenfeld J, 'Intellectual Property and Antitrust: Steps Toward Striking a Balance' (2001) 52 Case Western Reserve Law Review 91

Lanjouw JO, 'A Patent Policy Proposal for Global Diseases' (2001) <https://www.brookings.edu/research/a-patent-policy-proposal-for-global-diseases-2/> accessed 8 April 2019

Lanjouw JO and Schankerman M, 'Patent Quality and Research Productivity' (2004) 114 Economic Journal 441

Lanoszka A, 'The Global Politics of Intellectual Property Rights and Pharmaceutical Drug Policies in Developing Countries' (2003) 24 International Political Science Review 181

Lao M, 'Unilateral Refusals to Sell or License Intellectual Property and the Antitrust Duty to Deal' (1999) 9 Cornell Journal of Law and Public Policy 193

Lee J-Y and Mansfield E, 'Intellectual Property Protection and US Foreign Direct Investment' (1996) 78 The Review of Economics and Statistics 181

Leffler C and Leffler K, 'Settling the Controversy Over Patent Settlements: Payments by the Patent Holder Should Be Per Se Illegal' in John B Kirkwood (ed), *Antitrust Law and Economics*, vol 21 (Emerald Publishing Limited 2004) 475

Lemley M, 'A New Balance Between IP and Antitrust' (2007) 13 Southwestern Journal of Law and Trade in the Americas 237

Lemley MA, 'Economics of Improvement in Intellectual Property Law' (1996) 75 Texas Law Review 989

Lemley MA, 'Rational Ignorance at the Patent Office' (2001) 95 Northwestern University Law Review 1495

Lemley MA, 'Property, Intellectual Property, and Free Riding' (2005) 83 Texas Law Review 1031

Lemley MA, 'Industry-Specific Antitrust Policy for Innovation' (Social Science Research Network 2010) SSRN Scholarly Paper ID 1670197 <https://papers.ssrn.com/abstract=1670197> accessed 29 March 2019

Lemley MA and Shapiro C, 'Patent Holdup and Royalty Stacking' (2007) 85 Texas Law Review 1991

Lerner J, 'Patent Protection and Innovation Over 150 Years' (National Bureau of Economic Research 2002) Working Paper 8977 <http://www.nber.org/papers/w8977> accessed 6 April 2019

Leslie CR, 'Patent Tying, Price Discrimination, and Innovation' (2011) 88 Antitrust Law Journal 811

Levin R and others, 'Appropriating the Returns from Industrial Research and Development' (1987) 3 Brookings Papers on Economic Activity 783

Lim E, 'A Critique of Corporate Attribution: "Directing Mind and Will" and Corporate Objectives' [2013] Journal of Business Law 333

Linsu K, 'Technology Transfer & Intellectual Property Rights: The Korean Experience' (UNCTAD 2002) Issue Paper No 2

Linton KC and Corrado N, 'A "Calibrated Approach": Pharmaceutical FDI and Evolution of the Patent Law in India' <https://papers.ssrn.com/sol3/papers.cfm?abstract_id=1031227> accessed 20 September 2020

Lipsky Jr AB and Sidak JG, 'Essential Facilities' (1999) 51 Stanford Law Review 1187

Lopatka JE and Page WH, 'Monopolization, Innovation, and Consumer Welfare' (2001) 69 George Washington University Law Review 368

Love BJ, 'Interring the Pioneer Invention Doctrine' (2011) 90 North Carolina Law Review 379

Love J, 'Statement of Essential Inventions to the Commission on Intellectual Property Rights, Innovation and Public Health' <https://www.who.int/intellectualproperty/news/en/eii.pdf?ua=1> accessed 20 September 2020

Lyons B, 'The Paradox of the Exclusion of Exploitative Abuse' in Konkurrensverket (ed), The Pros and Cons of High Prices (2007) 65

Maan J and Kumar D, 'Product Patent in Pharmaceuticals and Compulsory Licensing' in Jatinder Maan and Dinesh Kumar (eds), *Product Patent in Pharmaceuticals and Compulsory Licensing* (IGI Global 2019) 108

Mackie-Mason JK, 'What to Do about Unilateral Refusals to License?', Testimony for the Federal Trade Commission and Department of Justice Hearing on Competition and Intellectual Property Law and Policy in the Knowledge-Based Economy (1 May 2002)

Macrotrends, 'Pfizer Market Cap 2006–2020 | PFE' <https://www.macrotrends.net/stocks/charts/PFE/pfizer/market-cap> accessed 22 September 2020

Mansfield E, 'Patents and Innovation: An Empirical Study' (1986) 32 Management Science 173

Mansfield E, 'Intellectual Property Protection, Foreign Direct Investment, and Technology Transfer' (International Finance Corporation 1994) No 19

Mansfield E, Schwartz M and Wagner S, 'Imitation Costs and Patents: An Empirical Study' (1981) 91 The Economic Journal 907

Market Research Reports, 'World's Top 10 Pharmaceutical Companies by Revenue' (*Market Research Reports*, 7 March 2019) <https://www.marketresearchreports.com/blog/2019/01/30/world%E2%80%99s-top-10-pharmaceutical-companies-revenue> accessed 4 March 2020

Marty F and Pillot J, 'Intellectual Property Rights, Interoperability and Compulsory Licensing: Merits and Limits of the European Approach' (2012) 2012 Journal of Innovation Economics and Management 35

Maskus K, *Intellectual Property Rights in the Global Economy* (Institute for International Economics 2000)

Maskus K, *Private Rights and Public Problems: The Global Economics of Intellectual Property in the 21st Century* (Peterson Institute for International Economics 2012)

Maskus K, 'Intellectual Property Rights and Economic Development in China' in M Cimoli and others (eds), *Intellectual Property and Development* (Oxford University Press 2005) 298

Maskus KE, 'Intellectual Property Challenges for Developing Countries: An Economic Perspective' (2001) 2001 University of Illinois Law Review 457

Maskus KE, 'Parallel Imports in Pharmaceuticals: Implications for Competition and Prices in Developing Countries' (World Intellectual Property Organization 2001) <https://www.wipo.int/export/sites/www/about-ip/en/studies/pdf/ssa_maskus_pi.pdf> accessed 20 September 2020

Maskus KE, 'The Role of Intellectual Property Rights in Encouraging Foreign Direct Investment and Technology Transfer' in Fink C and Maskus KE (eds), *Intellectual Property and Development: Lessons from Recent Economic Research* (Oxford University Press 2005) 41

Matutes C, Regibeau P, and Rockett K, 'Optimal Patent Design and Diffusion of Innovations' [1996] 27 The RAND Journal of Economics 60

Maziarz A, 'Tying and Bundling: Applying EU Competition Rules for Best Practices' (2013) 3 International Journal of Public Law and Policy 263

McGowan D, 'Networks and Intention in Antitrust and Intellectual Property' (1999) 24 Journal of Corporation Law 485

McTaggart D, Findlay C, and Parkin M, *Economics* (7th edn, Pearson Australia 2015)

Melamed AD and Stoeppelwerth AM, 'The CSU Case: Facts, Formalism and the Intersection of Antitrust and Intellectual Property Law' (2002) 10 George Mason Law Review 407

Mendis Shanti and others, 'The Availability and Affordability of Selected Essential Medicines for Chronic Diseases in Six Low- and Middle-Income Countries' (2007) 85 Bulletin of the World Health Organization 279

Mercurio B, 'TRIPS, Patents, and Access to Life-Saving Drugs in the Developing World' (2004) 8 Marquette Intellectual Property Law Review 211

Merges R and Nelson R, 'On the Complex Economics of Patent Scope' [1990] Columbia Law Review 839

Milgrim RM and Bensen EE, *Milgrim on Licensing*, vol 4 (Lexis-Nexis 2021)

Miller AD and Gal MS, 'Licensee Patent Challenges' (2015) 32 Yale Journal on Regulation 122

Mokyr J, 'The Industrial Revolution and the New Economic History' in Joel Mokyr (ed), *The Economics of the Industrial Revolution* (Routledge 2012) 1

Morel CM, McGuire A, and Mossialos E, 'The Level Of Income Appears To Have No Consistent Bearing On Pharmaceutical Prices Across Countries' (2011) 30 Global Pharmaceutical Pricing 1545

Moser P, 'How Do Patent Laws Influence Innovation? Evidence from Nineteenth-Century World's Fairs' (2005) 95 The American Economic Review 1214

Moser P, 'Innovation without Patents: Evidence from World's Fairs' (2012) 55 Journal of Law & Economics 43

Moser P, 'Patents and Innovation: Evidence from Economic History' (2013) 27 Journal of Economic Perspectives 23

Motta M and de Streel A, 'Excessive Pricing in Competition Law: Never Say Never?' in Konkurrensverket (ed), *The Pros and Cons of High Prices* (2007) 14

MSF Canada, 'Neither Expeditious, Nor A Solution: The WTO August 30th Decision Is Unworkable' (2006) <https://msfaccess.org/sites/default/files/MSF_assets/Access/Docs/ACCESS_briefing_NeitherExpeditiousNorSolution_WTO_ENG_2006.pdf> accessed 20 September 2020

Mungan MC, 'Reverse Payments, Perverse Incentives' (2013) 27 Harvard Journal of Law & Technology 1

Murthy D, 'The Future of Compulsory Licensing: Deciphering the Doha Declaration on the TRIPS Agreement and Public Health' (2002) 17 American University International Law Review 1299

Mwakyembe H and Kanja GM, 'Implications of the TRIPS Agreement on the Access to Cheaper Pharmaceutical Drugs by Developing Countries' (2002) 34 Zambia Law Journal 111

Nair-Reichert U and Duncan R, 'Patent Regimes, Host Country Policies, and the Nature of MNE Activities' (2008) 16 Review of International Economics 783

Nalebuff B, 'Bundling as an Entry Barrier' (2004) 119 The Quarterly Journal of Economics 159

National Institutes of Health, 'Budget' <https://www.nih.gov/about-nih/what-we-do/budget> accessed 21 September 2020

Nerozzi MM, 'The Battle over Life-Saving Pharmaceuticals: Are Developing Countries Being TRIPped by Developed Countries' (2002) 47 Villanova Law Review 605

Nguyen AT and others, 'Medicine Prices, Availability, and Affordability in Vietnam' (2009) 2 Southern Med Review 2

Nicholson M, 'The Impact of Industry Characteristics and IPR Policy on Foreign Direct Investment' (2007) 143 Review of World Economics 27

Niens LM and others, 'Quantifying the Impoverishing Effects of Purchasing Medicines: A Cross-Country Comparison of the Affordability of Medicines in the Developing World' (2010) 7 PLoS Medicine 1

Nightingale A, 'WTO "Paragraph 6" System For Affordable Medicine: Time For Change?' *Intellectual Property Watch* (14 November 2016) <http://www.ip-watch.org/2016/11/14/wto-paragraph-6-system-affordable-medicines-time-change/> accessed 20 September 2020

Nunnenkamp P and Spatz J, 'Intellectual Property Rights and Foreign Direct Investment: A Disaggregated Analysis' (2004) 140 Review of World Economics 393

Nuno M, 'A Fair Return Approach to Pharmaceutical Compulsory Licensing' (2016) 48 Case Western Reserve Journal of International Law 395

Nuvolari A, 'Collective Invention during the British Industrial Revolution: The Case of the Cornish Pumping Engine', Paper prepared for the DRUID Winter Conference, Copenhagen (18–20 January 2001) <https://silo.tips/download/collective-invention-during-the-british-industrial-revolution-the-case-of-the-co> accessed 29 July 2021

Nwobike JC, 'Pharmaceutical Corporations and Access to Drugs in Developing Countries: The Way Forward' (2006) 4 International Journal on Human Rights 127

OECD, 'Oslo Manual: Guidelines for Collecting and Interpreting Innovation Data' (2005) <https://www.oecd-ilibrary.org/docserver/9789264013100-en.pdf?expires=1619714349&id=id&accname=guest&checksum=8CF7080707935F70C826812901A98516> accessed 29 April 2021

OECD, 'European Union: Article 102 and Excessive Prices' (2012) <https://www.oecd.org/competition/abuse/49604207.pdf> accessed 21 September 2020

OECD, 'Excessive Pricing in Pharmaceutical Markets—Note by the United States' (2018) <www.oecd.org/daf/competition/excessive-pricing-in-pharmaceuticals.htm> accessed 20 September 2020

Orstavik IB, 'Technology Transfer Agreements: Grantbacks and No Challenge Clauses in the New EC Technology Transfer Regulation' (2005) 36 International Review of Intellectual Property and Competition Law 83

Outterson K, 'Pharmaceutical Arbitrage: Balancing Access and Innovation in International Prescription Drug Markets' (2005) 5 Yale Journal of Health Policy, Law & Ethics 193

Parello CP, 'A North-South Model of Intellectual Property Rights Protection and Skill Accumulation' (2008) 85 Journal of Development Economics 253

Park W and Lippoldt D, 'International Licensing and the Strengthening of Intellectual Property Rights in Developing Countries During the 1990s' (2005) 40 OECD Economic Studies 7

Pate RH, 'Refusals to Deal and Intellectual Property Rights' (2002) 10 George Mason Law Review 429

Patel M, 'Drug Costs in Developing Countries and Policies To Reduce Them' (1983) 11 World Development 195

Paulis E, 'Article 82 EC and Exploitative Conduct' (2020) <https://www.eui.eu/Documents/RSCAS/Research/Competition/2007ws/200709-COMPed-Paulis.pdf> accessed 20 September 2020

Petroski H, *Invention by Design; How Engineers Get from Thought to Thing* (Harvard University Press 1996)

Pharmaceutical Technology, 'The World's Biggest Generic Pharmaceutical Companies in 2018' (*Pharmaceutical Technology*, 3 April 2019) <https://www.pharmaceutical-technology.com/features/biggest-generic-pharmaceutical-companies-2018/> accessed 4 March 2020

Pirt NE, 'Regulation of the Export of Pharmaceuticals to Developing Countries' (1987) 25 Duquesne Law Review 255

Pitofsky R, 'Antitrust and Intellectual Property: Unresolved Issues at the Heart of the New Economy' (2001) 16 Berkeley Technology Law Journal 535

Pitofsky R, 'Challenges of the New Economy: Issues at the Intersection of Antitrust and Intellectual Property' (2001) 68 Antitrust Law Journal 913

Pitofsky R, Patterson D, and Hooks J, 'The Essential Facilities Doctrine Under United States Antitrust Law' (2002) 70 Antitrust Law Journal 443

Pittman R, 'Consumer Surplus as the Appropriate Standard for Antitrust Enforcement' (2007) 3 Competition Policy International 210

Pressman L and others, 'Pre-Production Investment and Jobs Induced by MIT Exclusive Patent Licenses: A Preliminary Model to Measure the Economic Impact of University Licensing' (1995) 7 Journal of the Association of University Technology Managers 28

Pretorius W, 'TRIPS and Developing Countries: How Level Is the Playing Field?' in Peter Drahos and Ruth Mayne (eds), *Global Intellectual Property Rights: Knowledge, Access and Development* (2002) 183

Primo Braga C and Fink C, 'The Relationship Between Intellectual Property Rights and Foreign Direct Investment' (1998) 9 Duke Journal of Comparative & International Law 163

Qian Y, 'Do National Patent Laws Stimulate Domestic Innovation in a Global Patenting Environment? A Cross-Country Analysis of Pharmaceutical Patent Protection, 1978–2002' (2007) 89 The Review of Economics and Statistics 436

Rai RK, 'Effect of the TRIPS-Mandated Intellectual Property Rights on Foreign Direct Investment in Developing Countries: A Case Study of the Indian Pharmaceutical Industry' (2009) 11 Journal of World Intellectual Property 404

Reichman JH, 'Compulsory Licensing of Patented Pharmaceutical Inventions: Evaluating the Options' (2009) 37 Journal of Law, Medicine & Ethics 247

Reinganum JF, 'A Dynamic Game of R and D: Patent Protection and Competitive Behavior' (1982) 50 Econometrica 671

Ritter C, 'Refusal to Deal and "Essential Facilities": Does Intellectual Property Require Special Deference Compared to Tangible Property?' (2005) 28 World Competition 281

Roller L-H, 'Exploitative Abuses' (2007) <https://www.eui.eu/Documents/RSCAS/Research/Competition/2007ws/200709-COMPed-Roeller.pdf> accessed 20 September 2020

Romer PM, 'Increasing Returns and Long-Run Growth' (1986) 94 Journal of Political Economy 1002

Romer PM, 'Endogenous Technological Change' (1990) 98 Journal of Political Economy S71

Roper N, 'Limiting Unfettered Challenges to Patent Validity, Upholding No-Challenge Clauses in Pre-Litigation Patent Settlements Between Preexisting Parties to a License' (2014) 35 Cardozo Law Review 1649

Rozek RP and Berkowitz R, 'The Effects of Patent Protection on the Prices of Pharmaceutical Products: Is Intellectual Property Protection Raising the Drug Bill in Developing Countries' (1998) 1 Journal of World Intellectual Property 179

Sachs J, 'The Global Innovation Divide' in Adam Jaffe, Josh Lerner, and Scott Stern (eds), *Innovation Policy and the Economy*, vol 3 (National Bureau of Economic Research 2003) 131

Saha S, 'Patent Law and TRIPS: Compulsory Licensing of Patents and Pharmaceuticals' (2009) 91 Journal of the Patent & Trademark Office Society 364

Sakakibara M and Branstetter L, 'Do Stronger Patents Induce More Innovation? Evidence from the 1988 Japanese Patent Law Reforms' (2001) 32 The RAND Journal of Economics 77

Sakle A, 'Excessive Pricing: A Neglected Antitrust Concept?' (*Competition Law: A Cyril Amarchand Mangaldas Blog*, 6 December 2017) <https://competition.cyrilamarchandblogs.com/2017/12/excessive-pricing-neglected-antitrust-concept/> accessed 21 April 2021

Saroha S, Kaushik D, and Nanda A, 'Compulsory Licensing of Drug Products in Developing Countries' (2015) 12 Journal of Generic Medicines 89

Schankerman M, 'How Valuable Is Patent Protection? Estimates by Technology Field' (1998) 29 RAND Journal of Economics 77

Scherer FM, *Industrial Market Structure and Economic Performance* (Houghton Mifflin 1980)

Scherer FM, 'Antitrust, Efficiency, and Progress' (1987) 62 New York University Law Review 998

Scherer FM, 'A Note on Global Welfare in Pharmaceutical Patenting' (2004) 27 World Economy 1127

Scherer FM, 'Technological Innovation and Monopolization' (2005) No 05-07 <https://www.antitrustinstitute.org/work-product/aai-working-paper-no-05-07-technological-innovation-and-monopolization/> accessed 31 March 2019

Scherer FM and Watal J, 'Post-TRIPS Options for Access to Patented Medicines in Developing Nations' (2002) 5 Journal of International Economic Law 913

Scherer FM and Weisburst S, 'Economic Effects of Strengthening Pharmaceutical Patent Protection in Italy' (1995) 26 International Review of Industrial Property and Copyright 1009

Schildkraut MG, 'Patent-Splitting Settlements and the Reverse Payment Fallacy' (2004) 71 Antitrust Law Journal 1033

Schmalensee R, 'Commodity Bundling by Single Product Monopolies' (1982) 25 Journal of Law & Economics 67

Schmalensee R, 'Sunk Costs and Antitrust Barriers to Entry' (2004) 94 The American Economic Review 471

Schneider PH, 'International Trade, Economic Growth and Intellectual Property Rights: A Panel Data Study of Developed and Developing Countries' (2005) 78 Journal of Development Economics 529

Schrijen MAH, 'Excessive Prices in the Pharmaceutical Sector: Is Competition Law the Best Remedy?' Master Thesis European Law(Utrecht University 29 June 2018) <https://mededingingscongres.nl/wp-content/uploads/2021/03/Thesis-Maureen-Schrijen.pdf> accessed 29 July 2021

Schumpeter JA, *Capitalism, Socialism, and Democracy* (3rd edn, Harper Perennial Modern Classics 2008)

Scotchmer S, 'Standing on the Shoulders of Giants: Cumulative Research and the Patent Law' (1991) 5 Journal of Economic Perspectives 29

Scotchmer S, 'Incentives to Innovate' in Peter Newman (ed), *New Palgrave Dictionary of Economics and the Law* (MacMillan 1998) 273

Scotchmer S, *Innovation and Incentives* (MIT Press 2004)

Seeratan NN, 'The Negative Impact of Intellectual Property Patent Rights on Developing Countries: An Examination of the Indian Pharmaceutical Industry' (2001) 3 The Scholar: St Mary's Law Review on Minority Issues 339

Sevilla JP, 'On the Potential Impact of Value Pricing by Developing Countries on Allocative and Dynamic Efficiency in the Global Pharmaceutical Industry' (2016) 12 Journal of Law, Economics & Policy 147

Shapiro C, 'Patent Licensing and R&D Rivalry' (1985) 75 The American Economic Review 25

Shapiro C, 'Antitrust Limits to Patent Settlements' (2003) 34 RAND Journal of Economics 392

Shelanski HA, 'Unilateral Refusals to Deal in Intellectual and Other Property' (2009) 76 Antitrust Law Journal 369

Sherman PB and Oakley III EF, 'Pandemics and Panaceas: The World Trade Organization's Efforts to Balance Pharmaceutical Patents and Access to AIDS Drugs' (2004) 41 American Business Law Journal 353

Sherwood RM, 'A Larger Context for Considering Pharmaceutical Patents in Developing Countries' (1999) 1999 World Bulletin 76

Smith P, 'Are Weak Patent Rights A Barrier to US Exports?' (1999) 48 Journal of International Economics 151

Smith P, 'How Do Foreign Patent Rights Affect US Exports, Affiliate Sales, and Licenses?' (2001) 55 Journal of International Economics 411

Son K-B, 'Importance of the Intellectual Property System in Attempting Compulsory Licensing of Pharmaceuticals: A Cross-Sectional Analysis' (2019) 15 Globalization and Health 1

South African Competition Commission, 'Competition Commission Finds Pharmaceutical Firms in Contravention of the Competition Act' (2003) <http://www.cptech.org/ip/health/sa/cc10162003.html> accessed 23 April 2021

South African Competition Commission, 'Competition Commission Concludes an Agreement with Pharmaceutical Firms' (2003) <http://www.cptech.org/ip/health/sa/cc12102003.html> accessed 23 April 2021

Sperbeck AE, 'A Mathematical Solution to the Sine of Madness That Is Pharmaceutical Compulsory Licensing Under the TRIPS Agreement and the Doha Declaration' (2019) 23 Marquette Intellectual Property Law Review 21

Squitieri M, 'Refusals to License Under European Union Competition Law After Microsoft' (2014) 11 Journal of International Business and Law 65

Statista, 'Pfizer's Expenditure on Research and Development from 2006 to 2019' (2021) <https://www.statista.com/statistics/267810/expenditure-on-research-and-development-at-pfizer-since-2006/> accessed 21 September 2020

Stedman JC, 'Patents and Antitrust—The Impact of Varying Legal Doctrines' (1973) Utah Law Review 588

Stigler GJ, 'United States v. Loew's Inc.: A Note on Block-Booking' (1963) 1963 The Supreme Court Review 152

Stoll P-T, Busche J, and Arend K (eds), 'Article 31bis', *WTO: Trade-Related Aspects of Intellectual Property Rights* (Martinus Nijhoff Publishers 2009) 579

Subramanian A, 'Trade-Related Intellectual Property Rights and Asian Developing Countries: An Analytical View' in Arvind Panagariya, Muhammad Ghulam Quibria, and Narhari Rao (eds), *The Global Trading System and Developing Asia* (Cambridge University Press 1997) 305

Sun Y and others, 'subcontracting and Supplier Innovativeness in a Developing Economy: Evidence from China's Information and Communication Technology Industry' (2013) 47 Regional Studies 1766

Svetlicinii A and Botta M, 'Article 102 TFEU as a Tool for Market Regulation: "Excessive Enforcement" Against "Excessive Prices" in the New EU Member States and Candidate Countries' (2012) 8 European Competition Journal 473

Swanson DG and Baumol WJ, 'Reasonable and Nondiscriminatory (RAND) Royalties, Standards Selection, and Control of Market Power' (2005) 73 Antitrust Law Journal 1

Sykes AO, 'TRIPS, Pharmaceuticals, Developing Countries, and the Doha "Solution"' (2002) 3 Chicago Journal of International Law 47

't Hoen E, 'TRIPS, Pharmaceutical Patents, and Access to Essential Medicines: A Long Way From Seattle to Doha' (2002) 3 Chicago Journal of International Law 27

't Hoen E, 'TRIPS, Pharmaceutical Patents and Access to Essential Medicines: Seattle, Doha and Beyond' (2003) <https://msfaccess.org/trips-pharmaceutical-patents-and-access-essential-medicines-seattle-doha-and-beyond> accessed 20 September 2020

't Hoen E, 'Medicine Procurement and the Use of Flexibilities in the Agreement on Trade-Related Aspects of Intellectual Property Rights, 2001–2016' (2018) 96 Bulletin of the World Health Organization 185

Tanaka H and Iwaisako T, 'Intellectual Property Rights and Foreign Direct Investment: A Welfare Analysis' (2014) 67 European Economic Review 107

Tandon P, 'Rivalry and the Excessive Allocation of Resources to Research' (1983) 14 Bell Journal of Economics 152

Taylor CC, 'No-Challenge Termination Clauses: Incorporating Innovation Policy and Risk Allocation into Patent Licensing Law' (1993) 69 Indiana Law Journal 215

'The Top Selling Prescription Drugs by Revenue' (21 May 2019) <https://www.pharmaceutical-technology.com/features/top-selling-prescription-drugs/> accessed 21 September 2020

Tirole J, 'The Analysis of Tying Cases: A Primer' (2005) 1 Competition Policy International 1

Torti V, *Intellectual Property Rights and Competition in Standard Setting: Objectives and Tensions* (Routledge 2016)

Tripathy IG, Yadav S, and Sharma S, 'FDI Flows into the Indian Pharmaceutical Industry: An Analysis of Trends and Constraints' (2011) 16 Journal of Intellectual Property Rights 330

Tsai G, 'Canada's Access to Medicines Regime: Lessons for Compulsory Licensing Schemes under the WTO Doha Declaration' (2009) 49 Virginia Journal of International Law 1063

Turner D, 'Basic Principles in Formulating Antitrust and Misuse Constraints on the Exploitation of Intellectual Property Rights' [1984] Antitrust Law Journal 485

UNCTAD, 'Transfer of Technology and Knowledge Sharing for Development: Science, Technology and Innovation Issues for Developing Countries' (UNCTAD 2014) No 8 <https://unctad.org/system/files/official-document/dtlstict2013d8_en.pdf> accessed 4 March 2020

United Nations, 'sustainable Development Goals Kick off with Start of New Year' (2015) <https://www.un.org/sustainabledevelopment/blog/2015/12/sustainable-development-goals-kick-off-with-start-of-new-year/> accessed 4 March 2020

United Nations Conference on Trade and Development, 'World Investment Report 2019' (United Nations Conference on Trade and Development 2019) <https://unctad.org/system/files/official-document/wir2019_en.pdf> accessed 29 April 2021

United States Government Accountability Office, 'Prescription Drugs: Price Trends for Frequently Used Brand and Generic Drugs from 2000 through 2004' (2005) <https://www.gao.gov/assets/gao-05-779.pdf> accessed 14 March 2021

US Department of Justice and Federal Trade Commission, 'Antitrust Guidelines for the Licensing of Intellectual Property' (2017) <https://www.justice.gov/atr/IPguidelines/download> accessed 29 July 2021

Väisänen TA, *Enforcement of FRAND Commitments under Article 102 TFEU: The Nature of FRAND Defence in Patent Litigation* (Nomos Verlagsgesellschaft mbH 2011)

van Mourik MSM and others, 'Availability, Price and Affordability of Cardiovascular Medicines: A Comparison Across 36 Countries Using WHO/HAI Data' (2010) 10 BMC Cardiovascular Disorders 1

Vandenbussche J, Aghion P, and Meghir C, 'Growth, Distance to Frontier and Composition of Human Capital' (2006) 11 Journal of Economic Growth 97

Varian HR, *Intermediate Microeconomics with Calculus: A Modern Approach* (W W Norton & Company 2014)

Vermont S, 'Independent Invention as a Defense to Patent Infringement' (2006) 105 Michigan Law Review 475

Vermont S, 'Independent Invention as a Defense to Patent Infringement' (2006) 105 Michigan Law Review 475

Vestager M, 'Protecting Consumers from Exploitation' (Chillin' Competition Conference, Brussels, 21 November 2016) <https://wayback.archive-it.org/12090/20191129221154/https://ec.europa.eu/commission/commissioners/2014-2019/vestager/announcements/protecting-consumers-exploitation_en> accessed 20 September 2020

Vickers J, 'Competition Policy and Property Rights' (2010) 120 The Economic Journal 375

Villasenor J, 'The Comprehensive Patent Reform of 2011: Navigating the Leahy-Smith America Invents Act' (Brookings Institution 2011) Policy Brief No. 184 <https://www.brookings.edu/research/the-comprehensive-patent-reform-of-2011-navigating-the-leahy-smith-america-invents-act/>

Wahl N, 'Exploitative High Prices and European Competition Law—A Personal Reflection' in Konkurrensverket (ed), *The Pros and Cons of High Prices* (2007) 47

Wakasugi R and Ito B, 'The Effects of Stronger Intellectual Property Rights on Technology Transfer: Evidence from Japanese Firm-Level Data' (2009) 34 Journal of Technology Transfer 145

Walker SP and others, 'Child Development: Risk Factors for Adverse Outcomes in Developing Countries' (2007) 369 The Lancet 145

Waller SW, 'Areeda, Epithets, and Essential Facilities' (2008) 2008 Wisconsin Law Review 359

Wenders JT, 'Entry and Monopoly Pricing' (1967) 75 Journal of Political Economy 755

Werden GJ, 'The Law and Economics of the Essential Facility Doctrine' (1987) 32 St. Louis University Law Journal 433

Whinston MD, 'Tying, Foreclosure, and Exclusion' (1990) 80 The American Economic Review 837

Wineinger NE, Zhang Y, and Topol EJ, 'Trends in Prices of Popular Brand-Name Prescription Drugs in the United States' (2019) 2 JAMA Network Open 1

Winter S, 'Appropriating the Gains from Innovation', in George Day and Paul Schoemaker (eds), *Wharton on Managing Emerging Technologies* (Wiley 2000) 242

World Bank, 'World Bank Country and Lending Groups—World Bank Data Help Desk' <https://datahelpdesk.worldbank.org/knowledgebase/articles/906519-world-bank-country-and-lending-groups> accessed 6 April 2019

World Health Organization, 'WHO Medicines Strategy: Framework for Action in Essential Drugs and Medicines Policy 2000–2003' (World Health Organization 2000) <https://apps.who.int/iris/bitstream/handle/10665/66503/WHO_EDM_2000.1.pdf;jsessionid=BF71C740AA4CB0FB07832BDA2F3CDF50?sequence=1> accessed 20 September 2020

World Health Organization, 'Economic Costs of Malaria' <https://www.malariaconsortium.org/userfiles/file/Malaria%20resources/RBM%20Economic%20costs%20of%20malaria.pdf> accessed 4 March 2020

World Intellectual Property Organization, *World Intellectual Property Indicators 2018* (World Intellectual Property Organization 2018)

World Intellectual Property Organization, 'World Intellectual Property Indicators 2018' (World Intellectual Property Organization 2018)

World Intellectual Property Organization, 'Filings for Patents, Trademarks, Industrial Designs Reach New Records in 2017' <https://www.wipo.int/pressroom/en/articles/2018/article_0012.html> accessed 6 April 2019

WTO, Ministerial Declaration on the TRIPS Agreement and Public Health (14 November 2001) WT/MIN(01)/DEC/W/2 (WTO Ministerial Declaration)'

WTO Secretariat, 'TRIPS and Pharmaceutical Patents' <https://www.wto.org/english/tratop_e/trips_e/tripsfactsheet_pharma_2006_e.pdf> accessed 20 September 2020

WTO, 'Compulsory Licensing of Pharmaceuticals and TRIPS' (*World Trade Organization TRIPS and Health: Frequently Asked Questions*, March 2018) <https://www.wto.org/english/tratop_e/trips_e/public_health_faq_e.htm> accessed 4 March 2020

Yang G and Maskus K, 'Intellectual Property Rights and Licensing: An Econometric Investigation' (2001) 137 Review of World Economics 58

Yang G and Maskus K, 'Intellectual Property Rights, Licensing, and Innovation in an Endogenous Product-Cycle Model' (2001) 53 Journal of International Economics 169

Yang L and Maskus K, 'Intellectual Property Rights, Technology Transfer and Exports in Developing Countries' (2009) 90 Journal of Development Economics 231

Zaby A, *The Decision to Patent* (Springer 2010) <https://www.springer.com/us/book/9783790826111> accessed 4 April 2019

Index

For the benefit of digital users, indexed terms that span two pages (e.g., 52–53) may, on occasion, appear on only one of those pages.